THE NEW YORK TIMES MENU COOK BOOK

HARPER & ROW, PUBLISHERS NEW YORK | EVANSTON LONDON

The New York Times
MENU
COOK
BOOK

BY CRAIG CLAIBORNE

DRAWINGS BY BILL GOLDSMITH

For Pierre Franey,
good friend and great chef,
and Mrs. Jean Hewitt,
The New York Times home economist.
With gratitude and affection.

CONTENTS

. . . .

PREFACE   *11*

PART I: MENUS

    Breakfast and Brunch   *15*
    Luncheon   *16*
    Picnic and Barbecue   *20*
    Dinner   *22*
    Supper   *42*
    Menus for Entertaining   *44*
    Holiday Menus   *48*
    International Menus   *52*

PART II: RECIPES

1. APPETIZERS   *59*

2. SOUPS   *99*

3. FISH AND SHELLFISH   *121*
    Fish   *123*
    Shellfish   *151*

4. MEATS   *173*
    Beef   *175*
    Veal   *204*
    Pork   *217*
    Ham   *229*
    Lamb   *235*
    Specialty Meats   *251*
    Game   *259*

CONTENTS

5. POULTRY   *265*
    Chicken   *267*
    Turkey   *294*
    Duck and Goose   *299*
    Game Birds   *306*
    Poultry Stuffings   *312*

6. EGGS, CHEESE, RICE AND PASTA   *319*
    Egg Dishes   *321*
    Cheese Dishes   *329*
    Rice and Other Grains   *334*
    Pasta Dishes   *346*

7. VEGETABLES   *365*

8. SALADS AND SALAD DRESSINGS   *439*
    Salads   *441*
    Salad Dressings   *464*

9. SAUCES AND GARNISHES   *471*
    Stocks and Aspic Garnishes   *473*
    Sauces   *477*
    Marinades and Basting Sauces   *495*
    Composed Butters and Bread Garnishes   *498*
    Relishes   *501*

10. SANDWICHES   *507*

11. BREADS   *517*
    Yeast Breads   *519*
    Quick Breads   *529*
    Pancakes and Dumplings   *535*

12. DESSERTS   *543*
    Fruit Desserts   *545*
    Mousses, Frozen Desserts and Meringues   *555*
    Creams, Custards, Puddings and Soufflés   *567*
    Cookies   *593*
    Cakes   *608*
    Pies and Pastries   *636*
    Fillings, Frostings and Glazes   *676*
    Dessert Sauces   *683*

13. BEVERAGES   *691*

    INDEX   *699*

PREFACE

. . . .

A menu is a fascinating thing. In the proper perspective it deals with har-
monies and values that are totally absorbing, and there are, perhaps, more
dimensions to it than the casual diner is ever aware of. In its simplest form
the considerations of a well-planned menu are three—texture, flavor and color.
Repetition of either in the course of one meal is anathema to the whole
concept.

It is a commonplace that if a custard pie of a savory sort is served in the
course of a meal, it would not logically be followed by a custard or pie of any
sort. If the soup that begins the meal is watercress, the green should be
eschewed in the salad.

In a similar sense, if cheese is a prominent ingredient in the meal's main
course, the service of cheese should be avoided later. If the meal has been
altogether heavy along the lines of a hearty stew and several courses, it would
be best to select an ice or sherbet in preference to ice cream or a heavier
dessert to end the meal.

Contrasts in color within the course of a meal are wholly desirable, although time was at the end of World War I when monochromatic meals were
fashionable in certain European circles. One such meal, contrived to be mono-
chromatically red, began with smoked salmon, followed by a cold rose-tinted
cherry soup, rare roast beef with a hot purée of beets (blended with mashed
potatoes), sliced tomato salad, a centerpiece of radishes and, finally, raspberry
sherbet topped with red ripe strawberries. The whole meal was served on
red china on red tablecloths in a red room, and it sounds absolutely awful.
There is a certain humor in the fact that during a green meal in the same
period Roquefort cheese appeared with the salad.

Perhaps the most interesting menus ever conceived are those that appeared during the siege of Paris. Almost anything that walked or crawled was
considered edible, and the zoo is said to have been a prime and protean source

for food. Thus a menu served on Christmas Day, in 1870, at the Café Voisin, rue Saint Honoré, included stuffed donkey's head, elephant consommé, roast camel and jugged kangaroo.

It is fervently hoped that the menus in this book will be of value to the reader. There are more than four hundred of them in the menu section, and they embrace special dinners, international meals, simple suppers and menus for everyday dining.

But this is far more than a book of menus. It is a companion volume to *The New York Times Cook Book,* published in 1961. That edition contained nearly fifteen hundred recipes that had appeared in *The New York Times* during the decade 1950–1960. This menu cook book contains more than twelve hundred recipes culled from the thousands printed in the newspaper from 1960 to 1966. These are the best of the lot. Asterisks in the menu section indicate those dishes for which recipes may be found elsewhere in the book.

Like the recipes in *The New York Times Cook Book,* the recipes herein are derived from endless sources. Some are from international books on food, others from friends and many created in my own home and in *The New York Times* test kitchen. In several of the finest French recipes found here the hand of Pierre Franey, former chef at New York's famed Le Pavillon restaurant and now a vice president of Howard Johnson, can be discerned. I have spent countless pleasant hours working and discussing food with him in the kitchen of my East Hampton home.

The work of Jean Hewitt, *The New York Times* home economist, has been beyond measure in testing and polishing the vast majority of the recipes in this volume. She is tireless, inspired and dedicated.

Miss Inez Krech did the honors of assembling, analyzing, putting together, pasting up, deleting and editing the material that follows, and for her burdensome, painstaking labor I have nothing but awe and gratitude.

Credits for the photographs go to *The Times* studio photographers, Bill Aller, Gene Maggio and Al Wegener, for whom I have the keenest personal and professional admiration. The drawings are those of Bill Goldsmith, an eminently talented illustrator and artist.

To Mrs. Velma Cannon of the food news staff, my heartfelt thanks for her invaluable aid and inspiration through the years in seeing to it that *The Times* recipes were put into proper order.

CRAIG CLAIBORNE
The New York Times

PART I

· · · · · · · · · · · · · · · · · · · ·

MENUS

BREAKFAST AND BRUNCH

Fresh Orange Juice
Thick Bacon
Fried Green Tomatoes*
Southern Corn Bread*
Coffee   Tea

Cantaloupe with Honeydew Balls*
Creamed Chipped Beef with
Nutmeg*
Toast Points
Coffee   Tea

Fresh Grapefruit Juice
Herbed Kidney Ragout*
Fennel Oatmeal Bread*
Coffee   Tea

Anise Coddled Apples*
Eggs Mornay*
Toast
Coffee   Tea

Vanilla Poached Pears*
Fried Chicken
Fresh-Corn Pancakes*
Coffee

Prunes with Cream
Corned-Beef Hash Chez Soi*
Cheese Muffins*
Coffee   Tea

Stewed Apricots
Eggs Mollet*
Banana Walnut Bread*
Coffee   Tea

Peaches and Plums
Fresh-Herb Omelet*
Whole-Wheat Bacon Biscuits*
Coffee   Tea

Melon Delight*
French Toast with Maple Syrup
Grilled Bacon
Grape and Green-Tomato Chutney*
Coffee   Tea

Tomato Juice
Broiled Chicken Livers*
Bacon
Cheese-Herb Bread*
Coffee   Tea

Fresh Figs
Rosemary Sausage*
Fresh-Corn Spoon Bread*
Coffee   Tea

Fresh Papaya with Lime Juice
Broiled Haddock with Lemon Sauce*
Orange Oatmeal Bread*
Coffee   Tea

Fruit-Filled Honeydew*
Whole-Wheat Pancakes*
Grilled Sausages
Coffee   Tea

SUNDAY OR HOLIDAY BRUNCH

Bloody Mary Cocktails
Fresh Fruits
Lamburger Mixed Grill*
Corn in Cream*
Cranberry-Nut Bread*
Butter and Jam
Coffee   Tea

Grilled Kippered Herring
Scrambled Eggs
Grilled Tomato Halves
Pickled Walnuts*
Cheese Brioche*
Butter and Bitter Orange Marmalade
Brut Champagne
Caffe Espresso

LUNCHEON

Mustard Baked Eggs*
Grilled Tomatoes
Watercress Salad
Brazil-Nut Tartlets*

Brazilian Stuffed Green Peppers*
Buttered Noodles
Grapefruit and Greens Tossed Salad*

Caraway Macaroni Rabbit*
Lettuce and Tomato Salad
Orange Sherbet
Crisp Citron Cookies*

Black and Green Olives
Carrot and Celery Strips
Hot Crab Salad*
Mushroom-Stuffed Tomatoes*
Hot Biscuits
Peaches in White Wine*

A WINTER LUNCHEON

Salmon Chowder*
Toasted English Muffins
Winter Salad*
Bread-and-Butter Pudding*

Poached Red Snapper*
Green Mayonnaise*
Rice and Peas Salad*
Lemon Sherbet
Cookies

Cymlings Stuffed with Veal*
Cauliflower Salad Napolitana*
Bread Sticks
No-Cook Peach Ice Cream*

Ham and Pepper Omelet*
Caesar Salad
Vanilla Ice Cream
Raisin Nut Sauce*

A SPRING LUNCHEON

Shrimp and Cheese Spaghetti*
Escarole with Pine Nuts*
Cucumbers with Oil and
    Lemon Dressing
Oranges

Grilled Shad Roe and Asparagus*
Hot Toast
Spring Potato Salad*
Strawberries with Rum Cream*

Shrimp Quiche*
Baked Onions*
Watercress and Endive Salad
Lemon Dressing
Nutmeg Sand Tarts*

Stuffed Cucumbers*
Field Salad and Belgian Endive
Cheese and Vegetable Salad Dressing*
Raspberry Bavarian*

Chicken Livers Hongroise*
Rice
Cucumbers with Romaine Lettuce
Fruit Mélange*

Venetian Fish Soup*
Italian Bread
Broccoli Salad*
Italian Cottage-Cheese Pie*

Clams Mexicaine*
Mexican Avocado Salad*
Bread Sticks

Ham and Cheese Hero*
Mustard Butter*
Sliced Tomatoes
Apples

AN ELEGANT
SPRING LUNCHEON

Cold Curried Avocado Soup*
Chive Shrimp in Shells*
Asparagus Salad*
Hot Biscuits
Red Currant Jelly
Crème Celeste*
Strawberries

Creamed Eggs with Olives*
Toast
Purée of Lima Beans*
Romaine Lettuce with Diced Fruits
Orange French Dressing*

Fruit Curry Soup*
Sliced Cold Roast Lamb
Spinach Casserole*
Lemon Rice*

Cock-a-Leekie*
Toast
Mixed Salad Greens with Sliced Beets
Shortbread*

Salmon Custard Pie*
Green Beans with Dill*
Muffins
Fresh or Stewed Plums

Cream of Lima-Bean Soup*
Open-Faced Tomato Sandwich*
Watercress
Apple Dumplings*

Eggplant and Chicken-Liver
Casserole*
Tomatoes Vinaigrette*
Ice Cream
Florentines*

Stuffed Avocado Andean*
Boston Lettuce
Sliced Tomatoes, Stuffed Olives,
Radish Roses
Brazil-Nut Cake*

Potato and Leek Soup with Yoghurt*
Shrimp Salad Sandwich*
Watercress
Cookies

Shrimp Rabbit*
Hot Toast
Salade Forestière*
Cranberry Bars*

AN ELEGANT LUNCHEON

Seafood with Tarragon*
Bean Sprouts Vinaigrette*
Bibb Lettuce
Hot Biscuits
Pears in Port Wine*
Poundcake*

Swiss Mushrooms*
Artichokes with Foie Gras*
Buttered Toast
Fruit Compote
Fruited Almond Cookies*

A SUMMER LUNCHEON

Lobster-Stuffed Tomatoes*
Bibb Lettuce
Thin Slices of Whole-Wheat Bread
Cantaloupe Royal*
Raspberries

Burgundy Burgers*
Caraway Potatoes*
Sliced Tomatoes and
Watercress Sprigs
Dutch Apple Pie*

Oyster Noodle Casserole*
Vegetable Salad
Blue-Cheese Dressing
Double Fudge Brownies*

Club Sandwich*
Celery and Fennel Sticks
Green and Black Olives
Maple Custard*

Cucumber Velouté*
Chef Salad à l'Adam*
Honey Pecan Pie*

Cracked-Wheat Soup*
Sabra Salad*
Black Olives
Feta Cheese
Sesame-Seed Crackers

A COUNTRY LUNCHEON

Palaver Sauce (spinach stew)*
Steamed Rice
Curly Endive with Bacon Dressing*
Cheese and Crackers

Celery Liptauer*
Salted Nuts
Mushroom Crêpes*
Creole Salad*
Olive-Oil and Wine-Vinegar Dressing
Ice Cream and Cookies

PICNIC AND BARBECUE

Egg and Tomato Hero*
Cauliflower Salad Napolitana*
Romaine Lettuce
Bread Sticks
Gorgonzola Cheese
Italian Red Wine

Lahmajoon*
Hard-Cooked Eggs
Eggplant Relish*
Radishes, Cucumbers, Watercress
Fresh Apricots
Almonds

A WINTER PICNIC

Sesame Beef Strips*
Peanut Dip*
Cold Rice Salad
Red Plum Tomatoes
Lemon Nut Wafers*

Onion Soup with Vermouth*
(in an insulated container)
Raclette*
New Potatoes
Pickled Onions and Sour Gherkins
Dry White Wine   Beer

Cold Sliced Tongue
Rye Bread*
Olive-Vegetable Relish*
Cherry Tomatoes Stuffed with
                    Blue Cheese
Watermelon

Cold Chili Fried Chicken*
Chick-Pea Salad*
Garden Lettuce
French Bread
Peaches and Plums
Red Rioja Wine

Sandwiches of Duck Pâté*
on
Individual Loaves of French Bread
French Black Olives
Pickled Mushrooms*
Chilled Cooked New Potatoes
                    in Jackets
Greengage Plums
Rosé Wine

Cream-Cheese Pastry Turnovers*
with
Spinach Filling*
Spit-Roasted Leg of Lamb
Basting Sauce*
Cold Rice
Cold Zucchini and Cucumbers
                    in Sour Cream*
Persian Melon Wedges

Grilled Frankfurters
Corn Roasted in the Husks
Ensalada de Cebolla Burriana
(onion salad, Burriana style)*
Sesame-Cheese Roll*
Crackers
Beer

Marinated Cube Steaks*
French Bread
Chilled Green Beans*
Cold Boiled New Potatoes
Curried Mayonnaise*
Apples
Cheddar-Cheese Cubes

Chilled Potage Saint-Germain*
(in an insulated container)
Dilled Beef Kebabs*
Hard Rolls
Red-Onion Rings
Green-Pepper Rings
Belgian-Endive Leaves
Fruit-Filled Cantaloupe*

Roquefort Hamburgers*
Toasted Buns
New England Baked Beans*
Shredded Green and Red Cabbage
Caraway-Seed and Cottage-Cheese
Dressing*
Chewy Coconut Bars*

Cheese-Stuffed French Bread*
Cold Sliced Ham
Dijon Mustard
Mixed Salad Greens
Pecan Bars*

Scallop Blankets*
Toasted Rolls
Tomatoes Antiboise*
Celery and Fennel Strips
Cranberry Apple Tarts*

Grilled Swordfish Steaks
Green-Pepper Barbecue Sauce*
Foil-Baked Potatoes
Sabra Salad*
Oranges
Nutmeg Hermits*

James Beard's Pâté for Picnics*
Assorted Breads
Mustard Butter*   Dill Butter*
Slices of Bermuda Onion,
Tomatoes, Cucumbers
Cheddar Cheese
Dry Red Wine

A PARTY PICNIC

Salty Russian Cocktails*
Caviar and Egg Sandwiches*
Cold Roast Chicken*
Potato Salad with Anchovies*
Beans and Tuna Vinaigrette*
Watercress
Pears
Iced Tea, Cold Beer, Dry White Wine

Cheese-Garlic Spread*
Crackers
Meat-on-a-Stick*
Foil-Baked Corn on the Cob
Whole Tomatoes
Mixed Green Salad*
Fresh Peaches and Blueberries
Sour Cream and Brown Sugar

Lahm Mashwi (lamb on skewers)*
Toasted Long Rolls
Rice and Peas Salad*
Tomato and Spinach Salad*
Fresh Pineapple Grilled in Foil
Almond Thins*

Charcoal-Grilled Spareribs
Barbecue Sauce for Spareribs*
Seeded Hard Rolls
Bean and Mushroom Salad*
Apple Orange Nut Loaf*
Cream Cheese

Lobster Roll*
Toasted Hamburger Buns
Celery with Garlic Cheese*
Mushroom-Stuffed Eggs*
Cookies

Barbecued Chicken*
Potato Salad*
Romaine Lettuce
Whole Tomatoes
Cantaloupes

Savory Eggplant Spread*
Bread Sticks
Rice and Ham Vinaigrette*
Salad Greens
Mangoes

CHEFS' PICNIC

One day in August, 1965, five chefs assembled on Gardiners Island for a picnic. They were René Verdon, Pierre Franey, Jean Vergnes, Roger Fessaguet and Jacques Pepin. Each chef prepared specialties of his own and thirty guests enjoyed a truly elegant party picnic.

Mussels Ravigote*
Pâté
Bluefish au Vin Blanc*
Beef Salad
Seviche*
Poached Striped Bass*
with
Sauce Rouille*
Grilled Squab
Cold Stuffed Lobster*
Mélange of Fruits
Assorted Cheeses
French Bread
Chablis   Beaujolais Supérieur

. . . .
DINNER
. . . .

Caraway Meat Balls*
Noodles
Spinach and Roquefort*
Chicory and Tomato Salad
Raisin-Rhubarb Pie*

London Broil
Barley and Mushroom Casserole*
Batter-Fried Onion Rings*
Mixed Green Salad*
Frozen Lime Foam*

Souffléed Frogs' Legs*
Watercress
Shoestring Potatoes
Snap Beans in Casserole*
Rice Pudding*

Tongue with Almonds and Grapes*
Rice with Peas*
Salad of Diced Fruits
White-Wine Dressing
Chocolate Cheesecake*

Scampi*
Pink Rice*
Italian Eggplant*
Escarole Salad
Ricotta Pie*

Broiled Steak
Tabasco Roquefort Steak Spread*
German Fried Potatoes*
Steamed Cauliflower
Green-Bean Salad
Baked Custard
Apricot Sauce*

Spaghetti alla Carbonara*
Cauliflower Salad Napolitana*
Banana Slices, Orange Sections
and Strawberries

Beef with Chick-Peas*
Squash and Onion Casserole*
Boston Lettuce Salad
Bananas in Sherry*

Andalusian Lamb Stew*
Ensalada de Cebolla Burriana (onion salad, Burriana style)*
French Bread Stuffed with Garlic Butter and Chopped Parsley
Fresh Fruits with Cheese

A FISHERMAN'S DINNER

Clam Broth*
Cheese Straws*
Trout with Bay Leaf*
Buttered Boiled Potatoes with Parsley
Asparagus, Milanese Style*
Fresh Pineapple

Roast Crown of Pork Florida Style*
Rice
Steamed Green and Yellow
Snap Beans
Tossed Salad
Puerto Rican Pudding*
Clove Whipped Cream*

Italian-Style Squid with Tomatoes*
Rice
Steamed Zucchini
Romaine Lettuce with Ripe Olives
Fresh Fruits with Cheese

Appetizer Eggs*
Veal Chateaubriand*
Noodles
Alvina Mattes's Onion Scallop*
Brown-Sugar Pie*

23

Pork, Apples and Sauerkraut*
Sweet Potatoes Mousseline*
Cold Diced Cooked Vegetables
Mustard French Dressing*
Coffee Bread-and-Butter Pudding*

Green Peppers with Meat Balls*
Macaroni Shells
Romaine Lettuce Salad
Sliced Peaches
Jamaica Rum and Coconut Sauce*

Sliced Turkey
Potato Chips
Lentils à l'Indienne*
Molded Roquefort Salad
with Vegetables*
Mayonnaise*
Lemon Sour-Cream Pie*

Eggplant Relish*
Melba Toast
Braised Lamb Chops*
Steamed Rice
Asparagus Cheese Pudding*
Vanilla Ice Cream
Chocolate Marmalade Sauce*

Breaded Chicken Breasts*
Shaker Green Corn Pudding*
Spinach and Bacon Salad*
Ambrosia*

Breaded Sea Squabs*
Potato Puffs*
Broiled Tomatoes
Boston Lettuce Salad
Frozen Lime Foam*
Cookies

A SATURDAY NIGHT DINNER

Tomato and Anchovy Appetizer*
Chicken Bake*
Noodles
Broccoli Salad*
Orange Meringue Pie*

Shepherd's Pie*
Bean and Mushroom Salad*
Anise Fruit Compote*
Vanilla Wafers

Fumet of Celery*
Venison Chops with Mushrooms*
Rissolé Potatoes
Brussels Sprouts à la Crème*
Watercress
Strawberry Angel Pie*

Sweetbreads with Madeira*
Wild Rice
Green Beans with Slivered Almonds
Mixed Salad Greens
Herbed French Dressing*
Almond Tart*

Beef Slices with Caper Sauce*
Devonshire Potato-Mushroom Pie*
Beet Salad*
Apple Turnovers

Broccoli and Lobster Mornay*
Tomatoes Vinaigrette*
French Bread
Walnut Chiffon Pie*

Camarones Estilo Barbarchano Ponce
(pickled shrimp)*
Cornmeal Beef Casserole*
Spinach and Endive Salad*
Pears in Port Wine*

Broiled Cheese on Toast Fingers
Ham and Vegetable Casserole*
Escarole Salad
Fruit Sherbet
Black-Pepper Chocolate Cookies*

Stuffed Leg of Lamb*
Rice
Steamed Jerusalem Artichokes
Lemon Sauce*
Tomatoes and Zucchini Vinaigrette
Athenian Tea Cakes*

Veal Chops with Sauce Soubise*
Browned Potatoes
Brussels Sprouts Polonaise*
Cucumber Salad
Gingerbread with Applesauce
Topping

Brown Chicken Fricassee*
Herb Dumplings*
Parsleyed White Onions*
Watercress Salad
Dorothy Stanford's Lemon Curd*

Scallops and Rice au Gratin*
French-Fried Eggplant Sticks*
Mixed Green Salad*
Stewed Fresh Fruit

A HEARTY MAN'S DINNER

Boiled Beef
Herb Sauce for Boiled Beef*
Boiled Potatoes
Buttered Leeks
Hearts of Lettuce
Curried Mayonnaise*
Apple Sour-Cream Pie*

Rosemary Broiled Chickens*
Celery Knob Parmigiana*
Buttered Green and Yellow
Snap Beans
Watercress and Plum Tomatoes
Fresh Pears
Honey-Chocolate Bars*

Pork Chops Bermudiana*
Oven-Browned Potatoes
Creamed Spinach*
Tomato and Avocado Salad
Chocolate Pudding I*

Barbecued Lamb Ribs*
Scalloped Potatoes
Spinach and Roquefort*
Watercress and Tomato Salad
Fresh Pineapple

Tripe à la Creole*
Baked Rice*
Cauliflower Salad Napolitana*
Vanilla Poached Pears*

Lamb Stew with Zucchini*
Noodles
Romaine Lettuce Salad
Butterscotch Meringue Pie*

A SUMMER DINNER

Sweetbreads in Individual Casseroles*
Filet Mignon
Sauce Périgueux*
Wild Rice
Braised Endive*
Brittany Crêpes with Filbert Butter*

Baked Chicken Summer Style*
Steamed Brown Rice
Broccoli Ring*
Cheese Sauce*
Fruit-Filled Cantaloupe*

Tuna-Parmesan Canapés*
Green Olives
Braised Round Roast of Beef*
Mashed Potatoes
Buttered Green Beans
Cranberry Cake*

Braised Veal Shanks*
Rice
Buttered Spinach
Salade Provençale*
Lemon Chiffon Cake*
Fresh Strawberries

Scallop Blankets*
Northwest Style Halibut*
Cracked-Wheat Pilaff*
Salad of Mixed Cooked Vegetables
Grape and Apple Pie*

Oxtail Ragout*
Parsleyed Noodles*
Stewed Red Cabbage*
Endive Salad
Apple Dumplings*

Hamburgers with Marrow*
Steamed Potatoes
Asparagus with Tomato Sauce
and Sour Cream*
Lettuce, Scallion and Radish Salad
Strawberry Compote
Almond Squares*

Guacamole in Celery Stalks
Lamb Chops Maria*
Parsleyed Potatoes
Spinach Mold*
Beet and Onion Salad*
Normandy Applesauce Pie*

Turkey Pie with Sage Cornmeal
Pastry*
Cranberry Jelly*
Corn Salad, Mexican Style*
Pumpkin Pudding

Shrimp with Tarragon*
Straw Potatoes
Sautéed Escarole*
Cherry Tomatoes
Grape and Melon Mousse*

Chicken in Sour Cream*
Potato Balls
Mushroom-Stuffed Tomatoes*
Blueberry Torte*

Pot Roast Jardinière*
Noodles with Fresh Mushrooms*
Escarole Salad
Peach and Ginger Pie*

A COUNTRY DINNER

Country Pork Chops*
Baked Potatoes
Corn and Mushroom Sauté*
Hot Biscuits
Dilled Tomato and Cucumber Slices
Blueberries and Watermelon Balls
Clove Whipped Cream*

Duck in Savory Sauce*
Brown Rice
Peas in Lettuce*
Mushroom and Celery Pickles*
Lemon Sherbet
Cookies Anisette*

Fillets of Flounder in Wine Sauce*
Noodle Soufflé*
Spinach with Sautéed Mushrooms*
Watercress Sprigs and
Tomato Wedges
Lemon Cake Pie*

Coquilles Aloyse*
Roast Chicken
Sweet-Potato Soufflé*
Sautéed Mushrooms with Dill
Hearts of Palm Salad
Cheesecake de Luxe*

Steak Fromage*
Baked Potatoes
Steamed Asparagus
Lemon Sauce*
Tomato Salad
Butterscotch Meringue Pie*

Stuffed Spareribs*
Rice
Confetti Cauliflower*
Endive with Onion and
Green-Pepper Rings
Raspberry Custard Pie*

A SEPTEMBER DINNER

Bay Scallops with White Wine*
Buttered Noodles
Steamed Zucchini and
Summer Squash
Pears Baked with Grapes and Wine*

Rosemary Beef Rolls*
Buttered Buckwheat Groats
Baked Tomatoes
Romaine Lettuce Salad
Frozen Eggnog*

Chicken Consommé
Matzoh Balls*
Stuffed Squabs*
Israeli Rice*
Fresh Asparagus Tips
Tomato Salad Vinaigrette
Carrot Torte*

Cantaloupe
Minted Lamb Patties with
Fresh Pineapple*
Boiled New Potatoes
Buttered Green Peas
Carrot and Celery Salad
Lemon Soufflé*

Antipasto Mushrooms*
Veal and Tuna Loaf*
Tomato Sauce III*
Barley Pilaff
Buttered Broccoli
Fresh Pears with Blue Cheese

Oven-Breaded Fish*
Baked Potatoes
Stewed Tomatoes
Spinach Mimosa*
Rum Custard*
Vanilla Wafers

Sliced Cold Roast Chicken
Asparagus and Eggplant Mornay*
Shoestring Potatoes
Watercress
Pineapple Upside-Down Cake*

Gingered Beef Pot Roast*
Browned Potatoes
Orange-Glazed Carrots*
Tomato and Watercress Salad
Cranberry Cheesecake*

Oriental Hamburgers*
Rice
Buttered Spinach
Grenadine-Cashew Pie*

Macaroni and Meat Puff*
Broiled Tomatoes
Escarole with Caper Dressing
Lemon Cake Pie*

AN AUGUST DINNER

Celery-Stuffed Flounder*
Grilled Tomatoes
Zucchini with Herbs*
Cucumbers and Minced Scallions
with Garden Lettuce
Poundcake*
Sliced Fresh Peaches

Raw Vegetables and Avocado Dip
Kidney Trifolati*
Pilaff*
Steamed Green Beans
Sesame Bread Sticks
Strawberry Parfait*

Corn and Watercress Soup*
Red Snapper with Lemon Butter*
Browned Potatoes
Brussels Sprouts Creole*
Fresh Fruits
Cheese

Grilled Hamburgers
Sautéed Potatoes
Cauliflower with Caper Sauce*
Bread and Butter Pickles
Cherry Tomatoes
Coffee Charlotte*

Esau's Lamb*
Buttered Carrots
Watercress Salad
Anise Fruit Compote*
Spongecake*

Shrimp à la Turque*
Steamed Rice
Artichokes with Butter Sauce*
Sliced Tomatoes
Pears Baked with Mincemeat*

Roast Veal with Lemon-Rice Stuffing*
Baked Acorn Squash*
Endive and Beet Salad
Banana Sour-Cream Pie*

Mushroom Consommé
Braised Steak*
Mashed Potatoes
Buttered Green Beans
Raspberry Macaroon Mousse*

Marinated Artichoke Hearts
Scallop Casserole*
Baked Potatoes
Peas in Lettuce*
Tomato and Spinach Salad*
Lemon Pudding*

Lemon Chicken Sauté*
Gratin Savoyard*
Asparagus Salad*
Apricot Rice Pudding*

Baked Sea Bass in White-Wine Sauce*
Rice
Creole Fresh Broccoli*
Watercress Salad
Danish Apple Cake*

Ham Loaf*
Orange Ham Glaze*
Candied Sweet Potatoes*
Buttered Spinach
Watercress and Boston Lettuce
Coffee Cream Chantilly*

A SUNDAY DINNER

Citrus Herring in Wine Sauce*
Braised Leg of Veal*
Pilaff*
Glazed Carrots*
Watercress and Tomato Salad
Fresh Fruits with Kirsch
Spiced Pecanettes*

Steak au Poivre with Red-Wine
Sauce*
Potato Croquettes
Confetti Cauliflower*
Beet and Onion Salad*
Baked Apples
Nutmeg Date Bars*

Beef Brazilien*
Buttered Potato Balls
Puréed Green Peas
Escarole Salad
Brazil Banana Cake*

Cheese Straws*
Black Olives Marinated in Red Wine
Lamb Pilau*
Mango Chutney
Toasted Slivered Almonds
Herbed Tomato Salad*
Boston Lettuce
Frozen Mocha Mousse*

Crisp Raw Vegetables and
Cheese Log*
Flounder Baked in Sour Cream*
Green Noodles
Melon-Ball Salad
Grapefruit French Dressing*
Lemon Cream*

Chicken Puff*
Baked Acorn Squash*
Buttered Green Beans
Orange and Onion Salad
Custard Ice Cream*

Lamb and Spinach Stew*
Buttered Noodles
Eggplant with Sour Cream*
Cantaloupe with Honeydew Balls*

Sea Squab Provençale*
Rice with Peas*
Tomato and Spinach Salad*
Cottage Cheesecake*

Pork Chops Piquante*
Noodles
Zucchini with Herbs*
Chicory Salad
Almond Fritters*

Grilled Steak
Spanish Corn Casserole*
Romaine and Avocado Salad
Lemon Ice Cream
Nutmeg Pressed Cookies*

Sole Amandine*
Tomato Soufflé*
Buttered Spinach
Field Salad and Endive
Lemon Sherbet
Orange Butter Cookies*

Veal Loaf with Anchovies*
Parsleyed Noodles*
Buttered Artichoke Hearts
Dandelion Greens with
Slivered Pimientos
Coffee Cream Cake*

Beef and Vodka Casserole*
Riced Potatoes
Buttered Lima Beans
Shredded Lettuce and Carrot Salad
Baked Vanilla Custard
Peach Sauce*

Pulpetas (stuffed veal steaks)*
Buttered Noodles
Broiled Tomato Halves
Escarole Salad
Lemon-Orange Pudding*
Sabayon Sauce*

Baked Red Snapper, Southern Style*
Saffron Rice*
Buttered Spinach
Romaine Lettuce Salad
Sesame-Seed Butter Cake*

Mushroom Appetizer*
Deviled Stuffed Pork Chops*
Rice and Olive Casserole*
Green Beans Vinaigrette*
Fresh Peaches

Beef Goulash*
Noodles with Spinach*
Tomato Salad
Caraway-Seed and Cottage-Cheese
Dressing*
Plum Dumplings

Roast Chicken
Wild-Rice Stuffing*
Butternut Squash Hawaiienne*
Watercress Salad
Cherry Tart*

Herbed Meat Fritters*
Swedish Potato Cakes*
Tomato Sauce II*
Buttered Spinach
Endive Salad
Grapefruit and Orange Sections
with Kirsch

Poached Bluefish*
Sauce Rouille*
Puréed Celery Knob
Herbed Green Beans*
Sliced Cucumbers and Tomatoes
Vanilla Ice Cream
Chocolate Rum Sauce*

Sautéed Cube Steaks
Zucchini Cheese Custard*
Mexican Avocado Salad*
Strawberries
Poundcake*

Beef and Cheese Roll*
Tomato Sauce I*
Baked Leeks with Rice
Zucchini and Onion Salad
Lemon Fromage with Blueberries*

A SATURDAY NIGHT DINNER

Salmon and Mushrooms Royale*
Laurel Rice*
Sautéed Escarole*
Lemon Cake*

Circassian Chicken*
Cracked-Wheat Pilaff*
Braised Leeks
Endive and Carrot Salad
Sesame-Seed Butter Cake*

Rolled Flank Steak with
Celery Stuffing*
Boiled Potatoes
Polish Beets*
Watercress Salad
Cherry-Walnut Pudding*

Onion Soup with Cheese*
Braised Lamb Shanks*
Poppy-Seed Noodles
Beets in Orange-Butter Sauce*
Broccoli Salad*
Molasses Walnut Pie*

Chicken and Kidney-Bean Casserole*
Very Thin Noodles
Shredded Cabbage and Radishes
Coffee Charlotte*

Haddock with Herbed Crumbs*
Steamed Rice
Baked Zucchini and Tomatoes*
Watercress and Radish Salad*
Fruit Compote

Minted Honeydew-Melon Balls
Tropical Steak*
Curried Rice*
Sautéed Eggplant
Romaine Lettuce Salad
Molded Coconut Cream*

Celery with Garlic Cheese*
Green Olives
Beef Birds*
Parsleyed Potatoes
Creole Fresh Broccoli*
Baked Apples

31

Cheeseburger Pie*
Spinach Soufflé
Broiled Tomato Halves
Avocado and Grapefruit Salad*
Brazil-Nut Tartlets*

Chicken in Saffron Cream Sauce*
Noodles
Sautéed Cucumbers
Mexican Avocado Salad*
Orange Chiffon Cake*

A JANUARY DINNER

Curry of Beef*
Rice
Chutney   Golden Raisins
Chopped Peanuts
Puréed Lentils
Diced Tomatoes, Cucumbers
and Green Peppers
Cantaloupe Royal*

Artichoke Hearts and Shrimp*
Roast Lamb with Herb Sauce*
Barley and Mushroom Casserole*
Tiny Peas and Onions
Belgian Endive Salad
Chocolate Custard*

Baked Red Snapper with
Shrimp Stuffing*
Stuffed Potatoes Aïoli*
Green Beans with Toasted Almonds
Watercress Salad
Orange Meringue Pie*

Pork Chops with Caper Sauce*
Wild Rice
Eggplant Slices with Parmesan*
Dandelion Greens and Field Salad
Vanilla Ice Cream
Jam Sauce*

Swordfish in Tomato Sauce*
Steamed Rice
Herbed Green Beans*
Romaine Lettuce Salad
Coffee Charlotte*

Shrimp Cocktail à la Française*
Chicken with Artichokes*
Buttered Noodles
Watercress and Orange Salad*
Lime-Pistachio Chiffon Pie*

Chipped Beef and Cheese*
Winter Salad*
Raisin-Rhubarb Pie*

London Broil on Toast
Sauce Bercy*
Corn Creole*
Spinach Salad
Watermelon

Swedish Meat and Onion Casserole*
Boiled Potatoes
Beets à la Crème*
Boston Lettuce Salad with Fresh Dill
Swedish Pancakes*
Lingonberries

Avocado Appetizer*
Beef-Marjoram Loaf* with
Puréed Green Peas
Mushroom Sauce*
Bibb Lettuce with Lemon Dressing
Chilled Melon

Stuffed Mussels*
Chicken alla Romana*
Italian Rice
Buttered Zucchini
Romaine Lettuce Salad
Italian Cottage-Cheese Pie*

Swordfish with Capers*
Buttered Barley
Cucumber-Stuffed Tomatoes*
Escarole with Green Peppers and
Marinated Mushrooms
Lime Meringue Pie*

Clam and Tomato Juice
Halibut Steaks with Mushrooms*
Parsleyed Potatoes
Cauliflower with Caper Sauce*
Lemon Cheese Pie*

Roast Duck with Grapes*
Steamed Rice
Brussels Sprouts with Chestnuts*
Watercress Salad
Pineapple Refrigerator Pudding*

Armenian Beef Loaf*
Tomato Sauce II*
Baked Marinated Eggplant*
Walnut Chiffon Pie*

Shrimp Marengo*
Steamed Rice
Broccoli Salad*
Banana Pudding, Italian Style*

A SUMMER DINNER

Avocado Balls Marinated in
Lemon Juice
Baked Salmon*
Boiled Tiny Potatoes with
Chopped Fresh Dill
Cucumber Salad
Norwegian Mocha Cake*

Chicken-Almond Croquettes*
Onion-Pimiento Sauce*
Allumette Potatoes
Snap Beans in Casserole*
Stewed Pears
Sour-Cream Orange Sauce*

Cold Borscht with Cucumbers*
Marinated Cube Steaks*
Swedish Potato Cakes*
Vegetable Medley*
Honeydew Melon with Lime Wedges

Andalusian Beef Roll*
Saffron Rice*
Steamed Spinach
Red-Onion and Green-Pepper Rings
Flan (Spanish caramel custard)*

Lamb à la Suède*
Buttered Boiled Potatoes
Steamed Baby Beets and Greens
Cucumber Salad
Swedish Fruitcake*
Hard Sauce*

Curried Chicken*
Chutney and Kumquats
Nut Pilaff*
Fried Green Peppers*
Watercress and Radish Salad*
Coconut Blancmange*

33

Barbecued Pork Chops*
Mashed Potatoes
Buttered Lima Beans
Eggplant and Sesame Salad*
Orange Sherbet
Almond Ginger Cookies*

Chile con Carne*
Mexican Avocado Salad*
Tabasco Croûtes*
Baked Apples

Spinach Soup Modenese*
Broiled Whiting with Lemon-Mustard
Sauce*
Parsleyed Noodles*
Broiled Tomato Halves
Watercress and Orange Salad*
Pineapple Refrigerator Cheesecake*

Chicken Livers Madeira*
Pink Rice*
Buttered Zucchini Rounds
Chicory Salad
Poundcake*
Fresh Berries

Herring in Sour Cream
Spicy Meat Balls in Wine Sauce*
Green Noodles
Glazed Carrots*
Tossed Salad
Danish Apple Cake*

Turkey Stew*
Herb Dumplings*
Crusty French Bread
Shredded Lettuce with
Diced Tomatoes
Apple Compote*

Chicken Breasts Véronique*
Rice Croquettes
Steamed Asparagus
Cherry-Tomato and Sour-Cream
Salad*
Orange Queen Pie*

Lemon-Barbecued Spareribs*
Browned Potato Balls
Asparagus with Brown Butter Sauce*
Escarole Salad
Spiced Rhubarb Pie*

Ginger-Cheese Almond Spread*
Melba Toast
Paupiettes of Sole* with
Mushroom Sauce*
Green Noodles
Steamed Onions
Beet and Endive Salad
Citrus Rum Chiffon Cream*

James Beard's Braised Shoulder
of Lamb*
Risotto Ring*
Buttered Cabbage
Tomato and Mushroom Salad
Chocolate Nut Torte*

A FALL DINNER

Braised Beef Pot Roast
Rutabaga Pudding*
Steamed Green Beans and Onions
Romaine Lettuce Salad
Pears Baked with Grapes and Wine*

Pepper Steak*
Rice
Steamed Summer Squash with Onions
Tomato and Watercress Salad
Sponge Roll*
Fresh Strawberries

A HUNTER'S DINNER

Cream of Pumpkin Soup*
Individual Meat Loaves*
Rosemary Potatoes with Cheese*
Parsleyed Steamed Leeks
Green-Bean Salad
Fresh Pears

Spicy Mushrooms*
Wild Ducks with Madeira*
Wild Rice
Glazed Carrots*
Chess Pie*

Chicken Hollandaise*
Spinach with Orégano*
Tomato and Mushroom Salad
Brazil Banana Cake*

Cheese and Cornmeal Casserole*
Baked Onions*
Tossed Salad
Pears Baked in Grenadine*

Corned-Beef Casserole*
Fried Green Tomatoes*
Watercress Salad
Vanilla Ice Cream
Orange Pecan Shortbread*

Marinated Pork Chops*
Glazed Pumpkin*
Swiss Chard
Lettuce and Tomato Salad
Black Bottom Parfait*

Savory Short Ribs with Olives*
Braised Potatoes
Mixed Vegetable Salad
Caraway-Seed and Cottage-Cheese
Dressing*
Stewed Fruit
Cookies

Pheasant Smitane*
Braised Carrots and Potatoes
Artichoke Bottoms with
Puréed Mushrooms
Watercress Salad
Jacqueline Cardelli's Mousse
au Chocolat*

Mushrooms Stuffed with Pâté
Sliced Roast Veal
Turnips with Poulette Sauce*
Rice and Peas Salad*
Pears Baked with Mincemeat*

Broiled Marinated Shrimp*
Potato Puffs*
Scalloped Tomatoes
Boston Lettuce Salad
Frozen Citron Mousse*

Curried Mushroom Rolls*
Stuffed Beef Birds*
Scalloped Potatoes
Beet and Onion Salad*
Fresh Pineapple

Bitocks à la Russe*
Mashed Potatoes and Yellow Turnips
Buttered Steamed Mushrooms
Cucumber Salad
Lime Meringue Pie*

Tarragon Chicken*
Paprika Rice*
Peas in Lettuce*
Hearts of Palm, Black Olives and
Cherry Tomatoes
French Dressing*
Frangipane Tart*

A SPRING DINNER

Roast Leg of Spring Lamb*
Baked Potatoes with Sour Cream
and Scallions*
Grilled Tomatoes
Escarole Salad
Rhubarb Custard Pie*

Braised Tongue*
Cumberland Sauce*
Baked Potatoes
Buttered Spinach
Cherry-Grapefruit Port-Wine
Gelatin*

Chicken-Liver Omelet*
Buttered New Potatoes
Romaine Lettuce
Sea Goddess Dressing*
Blueberry Betty*
Vanilla Ice Cream

Avocado Appetizer*
Salmon with Fresh Lemon Sauce*
Braised Leeks
Cranberry Cheesecake*

Ham Steaks with Cranberry Stuffing*
Whipped Potatoes
Buttered Green Beans and Scallions
Lemon Soufflé Pie*

Pot Roast with Wine*
Parsleyed Rice
Deep-Fried Zucchini Strips
Watercress Salad
Coffee Ice Cream
Cookies Anisette*

Baked Sea Bass in Lemon-Mushroom
Sauce*
Boiled Potatoes
Artichokes with Butter Sauce*
Chicory and Watercress Salad
Meringues Glacées*

Moroccan-Style Chicken*
Steamed Cracked Wheat
Fennel au Gratin*
Cherry Tomatoes Provençale*
Flamri de Semoule*
Purée of Fresh Fruit

Chick-Peas Rémoulade*
Spaghetti with Bacon and
Mushroom Sauce*
Garlic Bread
Spinach and Anchovy Salad
Spumoni

Crabmeat Dewey*
Rice
Herb-Baked Cucumbers*
Tomato and Scallion Salad
Peach and Ginger Pie*

Quail Smitane*
Riced Potatoes
Asparagus Polonaise
Watercress and Orange Salad*
Frozen Mocha Mousse*

Fanny Todd Mitchell's Beet Soup*
Broiled Chicken
Vegetable Medley*
Boston Lettuce Salad
Pecan Pie*

Gingered Veal Steaks*
Chutney
Noodles with Fresh Mushrooms*
Steamed Leeks
Fresh Pineapple Mousse*

Calf's Liver with Parsley Sauce*
Buttered Barley
Broiled Tomato Halves
Hot Cabbage Slaw*
Orange-Custard Pie*

Braised Boned Veal*
Baked Potatoes
Leeks with Red Wine*
Mixed Green Salad*
Pears Baked in Grenadine*

Panamanian Stew*
Grapefruit and Greens Tossed Salad*
Molded Coconut Cream*

Almond and Macaroni Casserole*
Mixed Green Salad*
Grape and Melon Mousse*

AN ELEGANT DINNER

Stuffed Snails*
Broiled Steak
Sauce Bordelaise*
Sautéed Potatoes
Buttered Tiny Peas and Pearl Onions
Mixed Green Salad*
Beignets Soufflés*
Strawberry Sauce*

Poached Striped Bass*
Parsley Sauce*
Buttered New Potatoes
Spinach with Sesame Seeds*
Endive and Beet Salad
Lemon Sherbet
Cookies

Oeufs Aptos*
Buttered Hominy
Cucumbers au Gratin*
Orange Pecan Shortbread*

Sliced Cold Pot Roast
Scalloped Potatoes with Sour Cream*
Summer Squash with Orégano*
Maple Custard*

New Potato Lamb Fricassee*
Zucchini and Corn Casserole*
Carrot and Fennel Strips
Green Olives
Rhubarb Meringue Pie*

Ninette Lyon's Poulet Flambé*
Thin Noodles
Artichoke Hearts
Salade Forestière*
Chocolate-Orange Mousse*

Tomato and Anchovy Appetizer*
Calf's Liver with Avocado*
Shoestring Potatoes
Brussels Sprouts with
Water Chestnuts*
Apple Pie and Cheese

Chinese Roast Duck*
Fried Rice*
Chilled Green Beans* with
Water Chestnuts
Vinaigrette Sauce I*
Fresh Pineapple and Strawberries

Beef with Dumplings*
Baked Carrots
Asparagus Salad*
Lemon Cake*

Ham and Noodle Casserole*
Green Beans with Mushrooms
Spinach and Onion Salad
Citrus Chiffon Pie*

Crab Pilaff*
Steamed Rice
Peas with Mushrooms
Watercress and Tomato Salad
Apple-Oatmeal Crisp*

Curried Shrimp with Grapes*
Chutney
Saffron Rice*
Grapefruit and Greens Tossed Salad*
Pistachio Ice Cream

Ham and Celery Loaf*
Horseradish Sauce*
Scalloped Potatoes
Steamed Broccoli
Tomato and Green-Pepper Salad
Alice Petersen's Danish Cream Cake*

Veal Chops with Mushroom Stuffing*
Mashed Potatoes
Celery Braised in White Wine*
Sliced Tomatoes and
Bermuda Onions
Lemon Cream Pie*

A DO-IT-YOURSELF DINNER

Cheese and Parsley Pie*
Fondue Orientale*
Steamed Rice
Baked Apples
Lemon-Nutmeg Sauce*

Boeuf en Daube*
Noodles
Parsleyed White Turnips
Tomatoes Vinaigrette*
Jacqueline Cardelli's Mousse
au Chocolat*

Steak and Kidney Pie*
Peas in Lettuce*
Baked Tomatoes
Cucumbers with Scallions
Lemon Ambrosia*

Lamb and Eggplant Balls*
Pilaff*
Spinach-Stuffed Tomatoes
Apple Sour-Cream Pie*

Anise Duck and Rice Casserole*
Brussels Sprouts
Herbed Caper Butter*
Romaine Lettuce Salad
Chocolate Pudding II*
Mocha Cream Sauce*

Turkey-Filbert Casserole*
Spiced Crabapples
Broccoli with Lemon Butter
Tossed Green Salad
Dutch Apple Pie*
Cheese

Mexican Chicken*
Rice
Parsleyed Carrots
Avocado and Grapefruit Salad*
Melon

Flounder Duglère with Noodles*
Steamed Asparagus
Crusty French Bread
Mixed Green Salad*
Strawberry Parfait*

A SPRING DINNER

Minestrone
Stuffed Manicotti*
French-Fried Eggplant Sticks*
Crusty Italian Bread
Chicory and Cauliflower Salad
Tortoni

Rognons de Veau en Casserole*
Braised New Potatoes and Carrots
with Dill*
Buttered Asparagus
Fresh Pineapple Mousse*

Stuffed Clams*
Cheese Soufflé*
French Bread
Mixed Green Salad*
Peaches in White Wine*

Korean Rice with Beef*
Tomatoes Stuffed with Tongue*
Deep-Fried Zucchini
Boston Lettuce Salad
Coffee Mousse

Cocktail Croquettes*
Braised Liver*
Hashed Brown Potatoes
Tomatoes Stuffed with Vegetables*
Pear Tart

Tagliarini (beef and macaroni
casserole)*
Red and Green Peppers with
Lemon Dressing
Coconut Pudding*

Roast Chicken
Noodle Stuffing*
Broccoli with Anchovy-Cheese Sauce*
Boston Lettuce Salad
Raspberry Sherbet
Almond Thins*

Cold Spinach Soup Smitane*
Ham and Pepper Omelet*
Sautéed Potatoes
Sliced Tomatoes with Chives,
Oil and Vinegar
Citrus Chiffon Pie*

Roast Pork with Grenadine Glaze*
Wild Rice
Creamed Onions
Escarole Salad
Frozen Macaroon Cream*

Ground-Beef and Tomato
Custard Pie*
Vegetable Medley*
Hot Muffins
Fresh Peaches

Ruth Ellen Church's Shrimp
Rémoulade*
Roast Duck*
Browned Potatoes
Braised Red Cabbage*
Watercress
Fruit Mélange*

Esther Cory's Baked Whole Fish*
Baked Potatoes
Herb-Baked Cucumbers*
Spinach and Endive Salad*
Sliced Bananas and Peeled Orange
Sections

Golden Buck*
Winter Salad*
Cardamom Apple Pie*

Anchovy and Pimiento Salad*
Noodle Casserole*
Spinach Salad with Lemon Dressing
Oranges

Jeanne Owen's Squab Pie*
Brown Rice with Mushrooms
Steamed Whole Cauliflower
Sesame-Seed and Lemon Butter*
Coffee Mousse

Sliced Cold Roast Lamb
Potato and Tomato Pie*
Kidney Beans Vinaigrette*
Vanilla Ice Cream
Apricot Sour-Cream Sauce*

AN ELEGANT DINNER

June Platt's Roast Loin of Pork*
Baked Sweet Potatoes
Buttered Spinach
Tomato and Hearts of Palm Salad
Tarragon French Dressing*
Vanilla Ice Cream
Chocolate Squares*

Crab-Stuffed Avocados*
Stuffed Breast of Chicken Molière*
Wild Rice
Buttered Green Beans
Field Salad with Lemon Dressing
Croquembouche*

Broiled Breaded Oysters*
Sautéed Potatoes
Green Beans, Italian Style*
Escarole Salad
Anise Coddled Apples*

Veal Chops with Mustard Sauce*
Steamed Rice
Purée of Lima Beans*
Cucumber and Beet Salad
Baked Bananas à l'Orange*

Eggs Mollet with Spinach Purée*
Baked Potatoes
Creole Salad*
Vanilla Poached Pears*

Mexican Rabbit*
Tortillas de Maíz (corn tortillas)*
Escarole with Red-Onion Rings
Melon

Broiled Marinated Shad*
Asparagus Pudding*
Spring Potato Salad*
Ice Cream
Anise Fork Cookies*

Chicken-Liver Timbales*
Sauce Poulette*
Carrots with Artichoke Hearts*
Sliced Tomatoes in Basil Dressing
Cranberry Dumplings*

A SUNDAY DINNER

Standing Rib Roast*
Individual Yorkshire Puddings*
Roast Potatoes
Brussels Sprouts with Sautéed Mushrooms*
Watercress and Radish Salad*
Apple Soufflé with Lemon-Nutmeg Sauce*

DINNER FOR ONE

Although man's nature is essentially gregarious, there comes a time when a meal in solitude can be a comfort. As for the man or woman who by necessity dines alone, in this day it is not necessary to be at the mercy of the corner drugstore or the TV dinner; dining alone can be a pleasure. Delicious meals and a well-balanced diet are possible with today's equipment and storage facilities.

Broiled Chicken*
Watercress
Boiled Rice for One*
Mushrooms au Gratin*
Vanilla Ice Cream
Strawberry-Rhubarb Sauce*

Tomato Consommé
Brennan's Eggs Sardou*
Stuffed Potato for One*
Fresh Pear
Cookies

Wienerschnitzel for One*
Risotto for One*
Puréed Spinach
Tomato and Cucumber Salad
Apple Strudel

Chicken Supreme*
Baked Potato for One*
Artichoke with Butter Sauce*
Salad for One*
Baked Apple

SUPPER

Spaghetti with Meat Balls*
Spinach and Mushroom Salad*
Bread Sticks
Spumoni Ice Cream

Pork Loaf*
Mushroom Sauce*
Spinach Mimosa*
Raspberry Ice

Sliced Cold Roast Meats
Corn on the Cob with Pepper Butter*
Cherry-Tomato and Sour-Cream
                    Salad*
Cottage Cheesecake*

Olive-Stuffed Eggs*
Maria's Lentils*
Sliced Tomatoes
Spongecake*
Orange Sherbet

Seafood Chowder*
Toasted English Muffins
Fresh Lime Cream*

Beef and Beans Casserole*
Tomato and Onion Salad*
Diced Fresh Fruits with Sherbet

Cheese and Rice Avocados*
French Bread
Buttered Onions and Mushrooms
Cranberry Pear Pie*

Euell Gibbons's Periwinkle Omelet*
Summer Squash with Orégano*
Black-Pepper Crackling Bread*
Apples and Walnuts

Polenta with Mushrooms*
Baked Onions with Pork
            and Scallions*
Belgian Endive Salad
Oranges

Rice-Stuffed Green Peppers*
Spinach and Bacon Salad*
Red and Yellow Apples
Camembert Cheese

AN AUGUST SUPPER

Corn and Potato Chowder*
Sliced Cold Meats
Assorted Breads
Scallions, Carrot Sticks,
Green-Pepper Rings
Blackberry and Apple Pie*

Anchovy and Pimiento Salad*
Spaghetti with Crabmeat*
Mixed Salad Greens
Mustard French Dressing*
Lemon Sherbet

Chicken Livers with Belgian Endive*
Beet and Onion Salad*
Frozen Mocha Mousse*

Caraway Noodle Ring with Tuna*
Buttered Green Peas
Apple Compote*

Corn and Cheese Pudding*
Sautéed Mushrooms
Salad Greens
Tarragon French Dressing*
Chocolate Skillet Cake*

Spanish Fish Chowder*
Garlic French Bread
Watercress and Chicory Salad
with Black Olives
Lemon Custard Pudding*

Chicken and Oyster Pie*
Spinach and Endive Salad*
Fresh Fruits
Cookies

Linguine with White Clam Sauce*
Tomatoes Stuffed with Vegetables*
Mixed Salad Greens
Almond Blancmange*

Seafood-Okra Gumbo*
Boiled Rice
Celery Sticks, Carrot Curls
Stuffed Green Olives
Chocolate Pecan Pie*

Nargisi Kebabs*
Chutney
Laurel Rice*
Watercress Salad
Lime Sherbet

Scallop and Mushroom Casserole*
Baked Tomatoes
Mimosa Salad*
Pecan Pie*

Spinach and Cheese Hamburgers*
Toasted Hamburger Buns
Herbed Tomato Salad*
Melon Wedges

Stuffed Eggs au Gratin*
Toast
Watercress and Orange Salad*
Fresh Pears and Blue Cheese

Salmon Bake Italiano*
Spinach with Orégano*
Cherry Tomatoes
Italian Macaroons*

Kooftah Curry*
Steamed Rice
Cucumber Yoghurt Relish*
Belgian Salad*

Mexican Macaroni Casserole*
Chilled Cooked Vegetables
Herbed French Dressing*
Blueberry Pie*

Grilled Frankfurters
Assorted Mustards
Potato and Avocado Salad*
Boston Lettuce
Cardamom Apple Pie*

Veal Croquettes*
Mustard Hollandaise Sauce*
Green Noodles
Escarole Salad
Cream Cheese and Bar-le-Duc

Chicken-Liver and Mushroom
Spaghetti*
Romaine Lettuce with
Tomato Wedges
Garlic Bread
Baked Bananas à l'Orange*

Sliced Cold Roast Beef
Devonshire Potato-Mushroom Pie*
Mixed Salad Greens
Cheese and Vegetable Salad Dressing*
Stewed Red and White Cherries

Chicken and Noodles Casserole*
Chicory Salad
Orange Foam*
Ladyfingers

Salmon Neptune*
Buttered Green Beans
Clove Cakes*

Sausage Cream Pie*
Fresh-Corn Muffins*
Diced Cucumbers, Green Peppers
and Tomatoes
Peaches

Hamburger Pie*
Beets in Orange-Butter Sauce*
Dandelion Salad
Baked Apples
Cookies Anisette*

Lentil and Macaroni Soup*
Green Salad with Diced Apples
and Pears
Grapefruit French Dressing*
French Bread
Brie Cheese

Artichokes Stuffed with Veal
and Peppers*
Thin Bread Sticks
Romaine Lettuce with Anchovies
French Dressing*
Grape and Sherbet Cup*

MENUS FOR ENTERTAINING

A SMALL TEA

Cinnamon Toast
Buttered Thin Slices of Swiss-Cheese
Loaf*
Butter-Sugar Cookies*
Marble Cake*
Jasmine Tea
Lapsang Souchang Tea

A SMALL COCKTAIL PARTY

Camembert Amandine*
Cucumber Spread*
Crackers and Toast Rounds
Cocktail Croquettes*
Mushroom Cocktail Strudels*

A LARGE TEA

Watercress Sandwiches
Cucumber Sandwiches
Almond Squares*
Pepparkakor*
Whole Fresh Strawberries
Holiday Fruit Bread*
Norwegian Mocha Cake*
Clove-Studded Lemon and
                    Orange Slices
Darjeeling Tea
Formosa Oolong Tea

A LARGE COCKTAIL PARTY

Buttered Nuts*
Chicken-Liver Pâté*
Toast Rounds and Crackers
Mushroom-Stuffed Eggs*
Tuna-Stuffed Eggs*
Cheese Straws and Twists*
Wild-Rice Pancakes*
Cream-Cheese Pastry Turnovers*
Meat Filling*
Cherry Tomatoes
Green and Ripe Olives

A WINTER BUFFET

Cold Beef Wellington*
Artichokes Clamart*
Mounds of Duchesse Potatoes
Tomatoes Stuffed with Spinach and
                    Mushrooms
Cucumber Aspic
Endive and Watercress with
                    Hearts of Palm
Rice Maltaise*

A SPRING BUFFET

Roquefort-Stuffed Mushrooms*
Salmon Verte*
Noodles with Cream Cheese*
Asparagus Vinaigrette
Cauliflower Vinaigrette
Allemande Torte*

A SUMMER BUFFET

Cold Chicken in Aspic*
Tuna-Stuffed Eggs*
Potato Salad with Anchovies*
Cucumber Salad
Cherry Tomatoes
Dry White Wine
Grenadine Iced Soufflé*
Macaroons*

AN AUTUMN BUFFET

Salmon Mousse*
Green Mayonnaise*
Curried Turkey and Ham*
Risotto Ring*
Squash and Onion Casserole*
Broccoli Vinaigrette
Lemon Fromage with Blueberries*

LUNCH FOR A
FOOTBALL GAME

Bean and Olive Soup*
(in an insulated container)
Ham and Cheese Hero*
Mustard Butter*
Egg and Tomato Hero*
Carrot and Fennel Sticks
Apples
Nutmeg Date Bars*
Beer   Coffee

A GRADUATION LUNCHEON

Fruit Punch*
Buttered Nuts*
Olive-Stuffed Eggs*
Salmon Eggs Montauk*
Chicken and Rice Casserole*
Spinach with Sesame Seeds*
Strawberries
Custard Sauce*
Lemon Chiffon Cake*

A WINTER DINNER PARTY

Cucumber Velouté*
Sole Turbans with Crab Stuffing*
Potted Squabs*
Wild Rice
Buttered Tiny Peas with Mushrooms
and Onions
Bibb Lettuce with Mandarin Oranges
Dacquoise*
Cognac

A CHILDREN'S PARTY

Carrot Sticks
Grilled Frankfurters on Toasted Rolls
Raggedy Ann Salad
Chocolate Cake*
Frozen Fruit Chunks*
Watermelon Punch*

A RECEPTION AFTER A BAR MITZVAH

Challah
Sweet Wines

Cocktail Frankfurters
Barbecued Chicken Wings
Tiny Egg Rolls
Liver Knishes

Chopped Liver
Gefillte Fish
Sturgeon
Caviar

Cold Roast Turkey*
Cold Glazed Corned Beef*
Stuffed Cabbage Leaves
Eggplant and Sesame Salad*
Fresh Fruits in Salad
Carrot Torte*
Bar Mitzvah Cake
Tea

A SUPPER
AFTER A SKATING PARTY

Hot Buttered Rum
Old-Fashioned Vegetable Soup*
Crusty French Bread
Mixed Green Salad*
Cranberry Cheese Cupcakes*

DINNER BEFORE THE
THEATER

Antoine's Eggs à la Russe*
Sliced Prosciutto
Gratin Dauphinois*
Molded Cantaloupe Salad*
Coffee

AN AFTER-THEATER SUPPER

Shrimp Quiche*
Tomato and Onion Salad*
Brown-Sugar Pie*
Caffe Espresso

A SUMMER LUNCHEON PARTY

Bicyclette Cocktails*
Crabmeat Soufflé*
Sherried Mushrooms*
Cucumber-Stuffed Tomatoes*
Watercress
Frozen Macaroon Cream*

A SUMMER DINNER PARTY

Cold Borscht with Cucumber*
Seafood with Tarragon*
Shredded Lettuce
Veal Chops au Vin Blanc*
New Potatoes, French Style*
Broccoli Ring*
Pears Carmelite*

LUNCH ON THE BOAT

Black-Bean Soup*
(in an insulated container)
Sandwiches of Game Pâté*
Tuna and Peperoni Hero*
Salmon Eggs Montauk*
Spring Potato Salad*
Cucumbers
Peaches and Plums
Beer

A BUFFET DINNER
IN A SMALL APARTMENT

Tomato and Anchovy Appetizer*
Cucumber Spread*
Buttered Toast Rounds
Braciolette Ripiene (stuffed veal rolls)*
Mushroom Pilaff*
Marinated Artichokes*
Grape Cream Tarts*

A BIRTHDAY SUPPER PARTY

Tomatoes Stuffed with Chicken
Livers*
Potato-Cheese Charlotte*
Avocado and Grapefruit Salad*
Dry White Wine
Custard Ice Cream*
Birthday Butter Cake*

AN ENGAGEMENT PARTY

Pink Champagne
Chicken-Liver Tartlets*
Sliced Cold Ham
Cherry Tomatoes Provençale*
Gratin Savoyard*
Watercress and Radish Salad*
Raspberry Macaroon Mousse*
Valentine Cake*

A SMALL WEDDING LUNCHEON

Vintage Punch*
Liver Pâté with Pistachios*
Curried Lobster Salad*
Tomatoes and Green Beans
à la Française*
Finger Rolls
Strawberries al Asti*
Wedding Cake
Coffee

A WEDDING BUFFET FOR ONE HUNDRED

Champagne Punch*
Turkey Salad*
Seafood Casserole*
Buttered Asparagus
Parsley Butter Sandwiches*
Wedding Cake
Coffee   Tea

. . . .

HOLIDAY MENUS

. . . .

A DINNER FOR NEW YEAR'S DAY

1. Cantaloupe with Honeydew Balls*
Stuffed Squabs*
Wild Rice
Brussels Sprouts with Celery Knob*
Chicory with Mandarin Oranges
Chestnut Pie*

2. Consommé Julienne
Beef Wellington*
Sauce Madère*
Rissolé Potatoes
Spinach with Sautéed Mushrooms*
Grand Marnier Pudding*

A LUNCHEON FOR ST. VALENTINE'S DAY

Eggs Forestière*
Belgian Salad*
Whole-Wheat Toast
Valentine Cake*
Frozen Whole Strawberries with
Confectioners' Sugar

A DINNER FOR WASHINGTON'S BIRTHDAY

Oysters on the Half Shell
Breast of Chicken Virginienne*
Sweet-Potato Soufflé*
Buttered Onions with Chopped
Peanuts
Green Beans Vinaigrette*
Cherry Tart*

A DINNER FOR
ST. PATRICK'S DAY

Watercress Soup
Roast Loin of Pork*
Colcannon with Kale*
Buttered Baby Beets
Green-Pepper Rings on Shredded
Lettuce
Bishop's Bread*
Irish Coffee

A DINNER FOR
PATRIOTS' DAY

Clam Broth*
Pan-Fried Scallops*
Corn and Tomato Casserole*
Boston Brown Bread*
Vanilla Ice Cream
Indian Pudding*

A DINNER FOR EASTER DAY

Fumet of Celery*
Roast Lamb with Cherries*
Roast Potatoes
Carrots with Artichoke Hearts*
Mousse of Green Peas*
Boston Lettuce
Lemon Easter Pie*

A DINNER FOR EASTER DAY

Appetizer Eggs*
Glazed Baked Ham*
Grenadine Ham Glaze*
Sweet Potatoes Mousseline*
Asparagus with Brown Butter Sauce*
Cantaloupe Flower Salad*
Orange French Dressing*
Apple Tart*

A LUNCHEON FOR MAY DAY

Dry Sherry
Chicken and Cucumber Soup*
Indian Melon Salad*
Cheese Brioche*
Crème Beau Rivage*
Demitasse

A PICNIC FOR MEMORIAL DAY

Crab-Stuffed Shrimp*
Chicken Salad with Almonds*
Tomatoes and Green Beans
à la Française*
Cucumber Sandwiches
Fresh Cherries
Iced Tea   Dry White Wine

A BUFFET FOR JULY FOURTH

Salmon in Aspic*
Green Mayonnaise*
Stuffed Hard-Cooked Eggs
Rice and Peas Salad*
Romaine and Boston Lettuce
Corn Bread*
Molasses Walnut Pie*
Iced Tea   Beer   Champagne

A DINNER FOR JULY FOURTH

Chilled Salmon Bisque*
Cucumber Spread*
Toast Rounds
Chicken Loaf Niveraise*
New Potatoes with Parsley
Asparagus Vinaigrette
Peaches Romanoff*

49

A COOKOUT FOR LABOR DAY

Chilled Potage Saint-Germain*
(in an insulated container)
Grilled Lobsters with Tarragon*
Baked Zucchini and Tomatoes*
Toasted Cheese-Herb Bread*
Plums, Peaches, Pears
Dry White Wine   Coffee

A DINNER FOR ROSH HA-SHANAH

Baked Carp or Pike*
Chicken in a Bag*
Israeli Rice*
Carrot Tzimmes*
Sabra Salad*
Challah
Apples Baked with Honey
Spongecake*
Red Wine

A COOKOUT FOR COLUMBUS DAY

Salmon Eggs Montauk*
Planked Split Whole Fish
Whole Onions Baked in Foil
Chick-Peas Rémoulade*
Tomatoes
Italian Bread
Roasted Apples Rolled in Brown Sugar
Macaroons*
Coffee with Rum

A SUPPER FOR HALLOWE'EN

Witches' Brew
(Hot Buttered Rum with Cinnamon Sticks)
Shrimp Toast*
Buttered Nuts*
Eleanor Hempstead's Scalloped Oysters*
Mushrooms Florentine*
Orange Bavarian Cream*
Chocolate Pudding I*

A DINNER FOR THANKSGIVING DAY

1. Chilled Celery and Olives
Cream of Mushroom Soup*
Roast Turkey with Pork Stuffing*
Glazed Sweet Potatoes with Walnuts*
Creamed Onions
Buttered Broccoli
Gingered Cranberry Sauce*
Pumpkin and Mincemeat Pies

2. Roquefort-Stuffed Mushrooms*
Roast Turkey
Brazil-Nut Stuffing*
Puréed Celery Knob and Potatoes
Sweet Potatoes à la Ann Seranne*
Brussels Sprouts with Water
Chestnuts*
Cranberry-Orange Relish
Rum Pumpkin Cream Pie*

A SUPPER FOR CHRISTMAS EVE

Mulled Wine   Mulled Cider
Shrimp Pâté de Luxe*
Cheese Log*
Assorted Breads and Crackers
Cold Ham
Potato Boats*
Salade Provençale*
Frozen Eggnog*

A BUFFET FOR CHRISTMAS DAY

Champagne Punch*
Smoked Turkey
Parsley Butter Sandwiches*
Curried Mushroom Rolls*
Cream-Cheese Pastry Slices*
Chicken-Liver Filling*
Molded Cantaloupe Salad*
Whipped-Cream Dressing
Frozen Chestnut Pudding*
Chocolate Roll*

A DINNER FOR CHRISTMAS DAY

1. Consommé Chiffonade
Roast Goose with Chestnut Stuffing*
Carrots and Potatoes Mousseline*
Brussels Sprouts with Sautéed
Mushrooms*
Watercress and Belgian Endive
Steamed Sponge Pudding*
Custard Sauce*

2. Caviar Roulade*
Standing Rib Roast*
Potatoes-in-the-Shell Soufflé*
Cauliflower with Mustard Sauce*
Buttered Green Beans
Frozen Fruitcake*

A DINNER FOR HOGMANAY
(Scottish New Year's Eve)

Scotch Broth*
Grilled Smoked Haddock
Buttered Leeks
Black Bun*
Shortbread*
Het Pint

A BUFFET SUPPER FOR NEW YEAR'S EVE

Punch Charentaise*
Anchovy-Egg Boats*
Chicken-Liver Pâté*
Sesame-Cheese Roll*
Thin Slices of Dark Bread
Cold Glazed Corned Beef*
Cauliflower Pickle
Mixed Salad Greens
Mustard French Dressing*
Cranberry Sponge Roll*
Bisque Tortoni

INTERNATIONAL MENUS

A FRENCH DINNER

Tarte à l'Oignon*
Poitrine de Veau Farcie aux Olives*
New Potatoes, French Style*
Haricots Verts
Salade Forestière*
Perles de Cantaloupe au Rhum*
Café Filtre

A GREEK FEAST

Artichokes à la Grecque
Crown of Lamb with Okra*
Moussaka à la Grecque
Chicken in Greek Pastry*
Greek Nut Roll à la Aphrodite
Lianides*
Greek Coffee
Retsina Wine

AN ITALIAN DINNER

ANTIPASTO:
Antipasto Mushrooms*
Roasted Peppers*
Salami
Stuffed Mussels*

Chicken Cannelloni*
Mixed Green Salad*
Italian Ices
Macaroons*
Soave
Caffe Espresso

A SWEDISH SUPPER

Swedish Beef Balls*
Boiled Potatoes
Swedish Cucumbers*
St. Lucia's Cardamom Buns*
Stewed Prunes

A SPANISH SUPPER

Caldo Gallego*
Omelet
Mixed Salad Greens
Anchovy Dressing
Bananas in Sherry*

A HUNGARIAN DINNER

Celery Liptauer*
Veal Goulash*
Galuska (Hungarian dumplings)*
Steamed Cabbage
Mushrooms in Sour Cream on Toast*
Stewed Plums

AN ALSATIAN DINNER

Pâté de Foie Gras
Riesling
Pierre Franey's Choucroute Garnie*
Tomatoes and Green Beans
à la Française*
Kugelhopf
Mirabelle

SMØRREBRØD (DANISH LUNCHEON)

Shrimp Sandwich*
Smoked-Eel Sandwich*
Matjes-Herring Sandwich*
Danish-Cheese Sandwich*
Lumpfish-Caviar Sandwich*
Roast-Chicken Sandwich*
Frikadeller Sandwich*
Smoked-Salmon Sandwich*
Liver-Pâté Sandwich*
Ham and Egg Sandwich*
Fresh-Pork Sandwich*
Roast-Duck Sandwich*
Bismarck-Herring Sandwich*
Tongue Sandwich*
Sardine Sandwich*
Tartare Steak Sandwich*
Egg and Tomato Sandwich*
Akvavit
Danish Beer

A VIENNESE DINNER

Caviar Roulade*
Cream of Spinach Soup*
Roast Squabs with Madeira Sauce*
Paprika Rice*
Artichokes Clamart*
Filbert Torte*
Grinzinger Spätlese
Viennese Coffee

A NORWEGIAN DINNER

Multerberry Soup*
Steamed Fresh Codfish
Melted Butter
Horseradish Sauce*
Boiled Potatoes
Carrots with Dill
Pickled Red Cabbage
Fyrstekake (royal cake)*

A GREEK FEAST

Salata Melitzanes (eggplant salad)*
Stuffed Squid Greek Style*
Ghourounaki Psito
(roast stuffed suckling pig)*
Rice
Diples (honey rolls)*
Greek Coffee
Retsina Wine

AN IRANIAN MIDDAY DINNER

Dook*
Chello Kebab*
Chello (Persian rice)*
Baked Small Eggplants
Cucumbers with Mint
Stewed Raisins and Pine Nuts

AN ITALIAN DINNER

ANTIPASTO:
Anchovy and Pimiento Salad*
Savory Eggplant Spread*
Mushroom and Celery Pickles*

Crusty Italian Bread
Linguine with Butter and
Parmesan Cheese
Veal Scaloppine Camillo*
Sautéed Zucchini Rounds
Escarole and Chicory Salad
Ricotta Pie*

A MEXICAN DINNER

Seviche*
Guacamole
Barbecued Stuffed Flank Steak*
Salsa Fria*
Frijoles Refritos (crisp fried beans)*
Buñuelos (Mexican fritters)*
Cinnamon Pumpkin Flan*
Beer
Warm Tortillas with Butter

A CHINESE DINNER

Hot and Sour Soup*
Batter-Fried Shrimp*
Barbecued Spareribs*
Steamed Chinese Dumplings*
Fried Rice*
Kumquats
Litchi Nuts
Tea

A FRENCH COUNTRY DINNER

Poule au Pot*
Sauce Gribiche*
Tossed Salad with Garlic Dressing
Crusty French Bread
Coeur à la Crème
Wild Strawberries
Dry White Wine

AN INDONESIAN DINNER

Atjar Ketimum
(sweet and sour relish)*
Sates*
Nasi Goreng*
Nasi (Indonesian boiled rice)*
Sambelans (side dishes)*
Fresh Fruits
Beer

A COSTA RICAN
CHRISTMAS FEAST

Roast Suckling Pig
Frijoles Fritos (fried black beans)*
Tamales à la Anita Kniberg*
Heart of Palm and Avocado Salad*
Flan (Spanish caramel custard)*
Vin Rosé

A JAPANESE DINNER

Teriyaki
Chicken Soup with Mushrooms*
Chawanmushi*
Japanese Rice*
Shioyaki (salmon with salt)*
Steamed Vegetables
Rice Cakes
Green Tea   Sake

A NORWEGIAN SUPPER

Norwegian Fish Pudding*
Sour-Cream and Dill Sauce*
Steamed Cauliflower
Lettuce with Sliced Beets
Blotkake (Norwegian Spongecake)*

A FRENCH LUNCHEON

Eggs with Herb Mayonnaise*
Sliced Cold Veal
Rice Salad à la Française*
Bibb Lettuce
Chocolate-Orange Mousse*

AN ITALIAN SUPPER

Salami and Mortadella
Seeded Bread Sticks
Italian Eggplant*
Tomato and Spinach Salad*
Fresh Fruits
Bel Paese Cheese

A NORTH AFRICAN DINNER

Tunisian Couscous*
Sauce Piquante*
Loubia (savory white beans)*
Couscous with Fruits and Nuts*
Mint Tea

A DANISH COLD TABLE

Assorted Herring
Anchovy Sprats
Thin Slices of Smoked Salmon
Radishes
Cold Shrimp with Mayonnaise and Dill
Crabmeat Salad
Lobster Salad
Cold Boiled Salmon
Cucumber Mayonnaise*
Boiled Potatoes with Dill
Pickled Beets*
Green Salad
Potato Salad*
Stuffed Eggs
Liver Pâté
Sliced Ham and Tongue
Sliced Headcheese
Salami Cornucopias
Frikadeller (Danish meat balls)*
Baked Brown Beans
Stewed Red Cabbage*
Roast Duck or Goose with Prunes
Platter of Assorted Cheeses
Small Pancakes with Lingonberries

. . . .

PART II

RECIPES

CHAPTER ONE

· · · · · · · · · · · · · · · · · ·

APPETIZERS

Whether it is an olive from a Mediterranean grove or a morsel of robust Cheddar, the appetizer is firmly entrenched in the American social scene. Almost any tasty tidbit seems welcome as the preface to a meal.

Many appetizers seem particularly well suited to summer and spring entertaining. They are adaptable to an open-air buffet on a terrace or lawn; or, when presented in larger portions, they may well constitute an entire meal of an informal nature.

TUNA-PARMESAN CANAPÉS   *About 1½ cups spread*

½ cup grated Parmesan cheese
7 ounces canned Italian tuna in olive oil
2 to 3 tablespoons milk
Toast triangles
3 tablespoons chopped parsley

1. Place the grated cheese and fish with its oil in a mortar and pound it until well mashed. Add more cheese if desired. Press through a sieve into a bowl.

2. Blend in the milk, a little at a time, until the pâté is of spreading consistency.

3. Spread on triangles of unbuttered warm toast. Sprinkle lightly with chopped parsley.

SHRIMP TOAST   *24 hot canapés*

½ pound raw shrimp, shelled and de-veined
4 water chestnuts, chopped
1 teaspoon salt
1 teaspoon sugar
1 tablespoon cornstarch
1 egg, lightly beaten
6 slices of bread, at least two days old
2 cups peanut oil

1. Mince the shrimp and mix with water chestnuts, salt, sugar, cornstarch and egg.

2. Trim the crusts off the bread slices and cut each slice into four triangles. Spread each triangle with one teaspoon of the shrimp mixture.

3. Heat the oil to 375° F. on a frying thermometer. Gently lower bread into the oil with shrimp side down. After one minute turn over and fry for a few more seconds, until golden. Fry only a few at a time. Drain.

CAMEMBERT AMANDINE   *1 cheese round or about 32 balls*

1 round Camembert cheese
(8 ounces)
Dry white wine

½ cup butter
1 tablespoon cognac
½ cup chopped toasted almonds

1. Place the cheese in a dish and add wine to cover. Store the cheese in the refrigerator overnight.

2. Remove the cheese from the wine and gently scrape off the rind. Blend the cheese with the butter, beating with a wooden spoon. Beat in the cognac. Chill the mixture.

3. Shape the mixture into the original form of the cheese, or roll it into bite-size balls. Roll the balls in the chopped almonds, or sprinkle almonds over the entire outside of the large round.

CHEESE-GARLIC SPREAD   *About 2 cups*

1 cup soft butter
¼ cup olive oil
3 garlic cloves, finely minced
1 tablespoon Worcestershire sauce
3 tablespoons finely chopped chives

1 tablespoon finely chopped parsley
1 teaspoon freshly ground black pepper
1 cup freshly grated Parmesan cheese

Mix all the ingredients together and blend thoroughly. Allow to stand at room temperature for at least two hours; then chill in the refrigerator until ready to use. This makes enough to spread two long loaves of French bread.

GINGER-CHEESE-ALMOND SPREAD   *About 2 cups*

1 pound cream cheese
½ cup drained preserved ginger-root, finely chopped

1½ teaspoons lemon juice
1 cup toasted blanched almonds, chopped

Beat the cheese with the gingerroot and lemon juice until thoroughly combined, or blend in an electric blender. Stir in the almonds.

CHEESE LOG   *About 2 cups*

½ pound sharp American cheese, shredded (2 cups)
⅓ cup crumbled Roquefort cheese
½ garlic clove, very finely minced

¼ cup sour cream, approximately
⅛ teaspoon Tabasco
¼ cup finely chopped ripe olives
½ cup finely minced parsley

Combine the cheeses, garlic and enough sour cream to bind them together. Add the Tabasco and olives. Chill until firm enough to form into a long roll. Roll in parsley. Wrap in clear plastic wrap and store in the refrigerator.

SESAME-CHEESE ROLL   *36 to 48 thin slices*

½ cup sesame seeds
½ pound blue cheese
½ pound cream cheese
1 cup butter
¾ cup chopped green olives

1 tablespoon finely chopped chives
1 tablespoon finely chopped parsley
1 garlic clove, finely minced
2 tablespoons cognac or sherry

1. Preheat oven to moderate (350° F.).
2. Spread the sesame seeds in a large baking dish and bake for twenty to twenty-two minutes, or until golden brown. Remove from the oven and let cool. Turn off the oven.
3. Cream together the blue cheese, cream cheese and butter. Add the olives, chives, parsley, garlic and cognac. Beat with a wooden spoon until well blended.
4. Divide the mixture into quarters and shape each quarter into a small roll. Place each roll on a piece of wax paper and sprinkle generously with toasted sesame seeds. Roll each roll tightly in the wax paper and store in the freezer until ready to use. When ready to use, let rolls stand until they reach room temperature. Cut into slices one-quarter inch thick and serve on toast or crackers.

CELERY WITH GARLIC CHEESE   *6 to 12 servings*

8 ounces cream cheese
1 tablespoon milk or light cream
1/16 teaspoon salt
1/16 teaspoon ground white pepper

¼ teaspoon crushed fresh garlic
24 celery ribs, each 3 inches long, crisped (see note, page 64)
1 can (2 ounces) anchovy fillets

Blend the cream cheese with milk until fluffy and smooth. Add the salt, pepper and garlic. Mix well. Stuff into celery ribs. Garnish as desired with anchovy fillets.

CELERY LIPTAUER   *6 to 12 servings*

½ cup creamy cottage cheese
½ cup soft butter
1½ teaspoons dry mustard
1½ teaspoons caraway seeds
1½ teaspoons chopped chives or fresh onion

1½ teaspoons capers
2 teaspoons minced anchovies
24 celery ribs, each 3 inches long, crisped (see note)
Paprika and chopped fresh parsley

Mix the cottage cheese with the butter. Add the mustard, caraway seeds, chives, capers and anchovies. Mix well. Stuff into celery ribs. Garnish with paprika and parsley.

Note: To crisp celery ribs, separate the ribs of celery and wash well, removing any blemishes. Remove all coarse leaves, but leave on the young tender inside leaves if desired. Put the ribs in ice water and let stand in the refrigerator for about three hours. Drain and dry thoroughly.

CUCUMBER SPREAD *About 1 cup*

8 ounces cottage cheese
1 cucumber, peeled, seeded and diced
1 tablespoon chopped chives
   Mayonnaise

Salt and freshly ground black pepper
Lemon juice
Dash of cayenne pepper

1. Combine the cottage cheese with the diced cucumber and chives. Add enough mayonnaise to bind the mixture.

2. Season with salt, black pepper, lemon juice and cayenne to taste. Serve as a spread for toast rounds or triangles.

SAVORY EGGPLANT SPREAD *About 4 cups*

2 medium eggplants
3 tablespoons peanut oil
1 small green pepper, cored, seeded and chopped
3 celery ribs with leaves
2 cups finely chopped onions
1 garlic clove, finely minced
   Salt and freshly ground black pepper

$\frac{1}{4}$ teaspoon grated nutmeg, or more
$\frac{1}{4}$ teaspoon curry powder, or more
$\frac{1}{4}$ teaspoon dried orégano
$\frac{1}{2}$ teaspoon monosodium glutamate
1 teaspoon Worcestershire sauce
2 tablespoons tomato paste, or more
   Toasted sesame seeds

1. Trim off the ends of the eggplants. Do not peel the eggplants, but cut them into one-inch cubes.

2. Heat the oil and cook the eggplants, green pepper, celery, onions and garlic with salt and pepper to taste, the nutmeg, curry powder and orégano until the vegetables are tender.

3. Stir in monosodium glutamate, Worcestershire sauce and tomato paste. While still hot, blend in a blender or put the mixture through a food mill.

4. Spread on toast or crackers and serve sprinkled with toasted sesame seeds.

Note: This dish is also good when spread on toast, sprinkled with Parmesan cheese, and broiled.

BUTTERED NUTS   *About 2 cups*

1 pound shelled nuts (pecans, walnuts   2 tablespoons melted butter
  or almonds)

    1. Preheat oven to slow (250° F.).

    2. Place the nuts on a baking sheet and pour the butter over them. Toss the nuts or otherwise shift them around in the butter to coat well.

    3. Bake for ten to fifteen minutes, until nuts are crisp and golden brown. Shake the pan occasionally or stir with a spoon to achieve even browning. When the nuts are cool, taste them; if desired, sprinkle with salt.

CHEESE STRAWS AND TWISTS

    Line up leftover scraps of flaky pastry, pressing them together to make one layer of dough. Roll out into a rectangle one-eighth inch thick. Sprinkle with a thin layer of grated sharp Cheddar cheese, keeping one-quarter inch from all edges. Fold one half of the pastry over the other half and seal the edges. Roll into a rectangle one-quarter inch thick.

    To make cheese twists, cut strips four inches long and one-half inch wide. Twist each strip before placing on a cookie sheet. Brush lightly with beaten egg and bake in a hot even (425° F.) for ten to fifteen minutes, until golden brown. Cool.

    To make straws, cut strips four inches long and one-eighth inch wide. Place on a cookie sheet. Make rings of pastry two inches in diameter and three-quarters inch wide, using cookie cutters. Place the rings on the cookie sheet. Brush lightly with beaten egg and bake in a hot oven (425° F.) for ten to fifteen minutes, until golden brown. Cool. Place six straws through each ring.

OLIVE-STUFFED EGGS   *6 servings*

6 hard-cooked eggs
½ teaspoon dry mustard
3 tablespoons butter, at room temperature
2 tablespoons finely chopped olives
Salt and freshly ground black pepper
2 to 3 tablespoons mayonnaise
6 small stuffed green olives, halved

    1. Peel the eggs and halve them lengthwise. Remove yolks and press them through a fine sieve into a mixing bowl. Reserve whites.

    2. Add to the egg yolks the mustard, butter, chopped olives, salt and pepper to taste and just enough mayonnaise to bind the mixture. The mixture should be fairly firm.

    3. Using a spoon or pastry tube, fill the reserved egg-white halves with the mixture. Top each with an olive half.

EGGS WITH HERB MAYONNAISE   *3 to 6 servings*

1 tablespoon chopped fresh tarragon   Fresh tarragon leaves for garnish
½ cup mayonnaise
3 hard-cooked eggs, halved lengthwise

Mix the chopped tarragon with the mayonnaise and spread in a shallow dish. Place eggs on top and garnish with tarragon leaves.

MUSHROOM-STUFFED EGGS   *6 servings*

6 medium mushrooms   1 tablespoon finely chopped fresh
   Juice of ½ lemon   dill or 1 teaspoon dried dill
¼ cup butter   Salt and freshly ground black
6 hard-cooked eggs   pepper

1. Mince mushrooms finely. Sprinkle with lemon juice.
2. Heat one tablespoon of the butter and cook mushrooms in it, stirring, until they give up their liquid. Continue to cook until almost all liquid evaporates. Cool.
3. Peel and halve the eggs. Mash the yolks in a bowl. Add the remaining butter, the mushroom mixture, dill, and salt and pepper to taste. Stuff the whites with the mixture.

SALMON EGGS MONTAUK   *6 servings*

6 hard-cooked eggs   ¼ cup mayonnaise
¼ cup flaked boned salmon   1 tablespoon lemon juice
1 teaspoon minced onion   1 teaspoon salt
1 pimiento, chopped   ¼ teaspoon cayenne pepper

1. Peel the eggs, slice them into halves, and remove the yolks.
2. Mash the yolks and mix in the salmon, onion, pimiento, mayonnaise, lemon juice, salt and cayenne.
3. Fill the egg whites with the salmon filling. Garnish the serving dish with lemon wedges.

TUNA-STUFFED EGGS   *6 servings*

6 hard-cooked eggs   ½ garlic clove, finely minced
¼ cup flaked tuna fish   1 tablespoon mayonnaise
1 teaspoon prepared mustard (pref-   Lemon juice and Tabasco or
   erably Dijon or Düsseldorf)   cayenne
2 tablespoons butter, at room tem-   Salt and freshly ground black
   perature   pepper
1 tablespoon minced parsley   Capers

1. Peel the eggs and cut them into halves. Force the yolks through a fine sieve into a mixing bowl; reserve whites.

2. Add tuna, mustard, butter, parsley, garlic and mayonnaise to the yolks and mix well to make a paste. Add lemon juice, Tabasco, and salt and pepper to taste.

3. Use the mixture to stuff the egg whites. Arrange the eggs neatly on a platter and garnish each with a caper.

APPETIZER EGGS   *16 servings*

8 hard-cooked eggs
¾ cup mayonnaise
   Salt and freshly ground black pepper
16 toast rounds (2 inches across), buttered

16 rounds of smoked salmon
½ cup sour cream
2 ounces caviar
1 tablespoon lemon juice
   Watercress sprigs

1. Peel the eggs and cut them into halves crosswise. Remove yolks and sieve. Add one-quarter cup of the mayonnaise to the yolks and season with salt and pepper to taste. Fill egg whites with the mixture.

2. Top each toast round with a round of salmon. Place an egg half, cut side down, on each salmon round.

3. Mix remaining mayonnaise with the sour cream, caviar and lemon juice. Spoon the sauce over the eggs to coat them completely. Garnish with watercress.

ROQUEFORT-STUFFED MUSHROOMS   *6 servings*

12 large raw mushroom caps
½ cup butter
½ cup Roquefort cheese

½ teaspoon dry mustard
2 tablespoons chopped chives
1 tablespoon chopped parsley

1. Wipe the mushroom caps, but peel them only if discolored.

2. Blend together the butter and cheese and mix in the mustard.

3. Stuff the mushroom caps with the cheese mixture and sprinkle with the chives mixed with the parsley.

ANTOINE'S EGGS À LA RUSSE   *4 servings*

4 teaspoons caviar
4 cooked artichoke bottoms
4 poached eggs

   Sauce Hollandaise (page 485)
4 truffle slices

1. Spoon one teaspoon caviar into each cooked artichoke bottom. Heat briefly in the oven.

2. Place one poached egg on each artichoke bottom and cover with hollandaise sauce. Garnish each with a truffle slice.

EGGS AND ARTICHOKES FORESTIÈRE:

Put three tablespoons butter in a skillet. Add one cup finely chopped mushrooms and cook until reduced to a paste. Follow directions for Eggs à la Russe, but substitute mushroom mixture for the caviar.

MUSHROOM APPETIZER   *6 to 8 servings*

24 medium to large mushroom caps
   or 40 tiny caps
¼ cup olive oil
 1 can (2 ounces) flat anchovy fillets
 1 garlic clove, finely minced

 1 teaspoon lemon juice
¾ cup soft fresh bread crumbs
¼ cup chopped parsley
   Freshly ground black pepper

1. Preheat oven to moderate (350° F.).

2. Remove the stems from the mushroom caps. Chop the stems and sauté them in three tablespoons of the oil for two or three minutes.

3. Chop the anchovies with the garlic. Add the lemon juice, bread crumbs and parsley, then the sautéed mushroom stems; mix. Season with pepper to taste.

4. Fill the caps with the mixture, drizzle remaining oil over them, and bake for fifteen minutes, or until hot.

ANTIPASTO MUSHROOMS   *6 servings*

¼ cup finely minced prosciutto
⅓ cup finely chopped parsley
½ cup soft fresh bread crumbs
¼ cup freshly grated Parmesan
   cheese

   Olive oil
18 medium mushroom caps
 3 cups Marinara Sauce (page 493)

1. Preheat oven to moderate (350° F.).

2. Mix the prosciutto with the parsley, bread crumbs and cheese. Add enough olive oil to bind the mixture. Spoon a little of the filling into each of the mushroom caps.

3. Spoon three-quarters of the marinara sauce over the bottom of a baking dish and arrange the mushrooms over it. Spoon the remaining sauce over the stuffed mushrooms. Bake for thirty minutes. Serve hot or cold as antipasto.

ROASTED PEPPERS   *6 to 8 servings*

6 large sweet green or red peppers
⅓ cup Italian olive oil
2 large garlic cloves, coarsely chopped
½ cup finely chopped Italian parsley

1 teaspoon finely chopped fresh mint
Salt and freshly ground black pepper

1. Spear the stem ends of the peppers with a large fork and roast them over a gas flame until the skin is black and blistered, turning the peppers as they roast. Peel off the skin and remove the core and seeds. Do not wash the peppers. Cut them into slices.

2. Place the peppers in a mixing bowl and add the remaining ingredients and seasoning to taste. Refrigerate until ready to serve.

CHICK-PEAS RÉMOULADE   *6 servings*

2 cups dried chick-peas
2 anchovy fillets
1 garlic clove, finely minced
1 tablespoon capers, chopped
1 teaspoon finely chopped shallot or green onion

2 tablespoons finely chopped parsley
¼ to ½ cup mayonnaise
Salt and freshly ground black pepper
Lemon juice
Parsley sprigs for garnish

1. Cover the chick-peas with water, bring to a boil, and drain. Add fresh water to cover and salt to taste. Bring to a boil again.

2. Simmer the peas for two to two and one-half hours, until they are tender. Let cool in the cooking liquid; drain.

3. Chop the anchovy fillets and garlic together and blend with the capers, shallot, and parsley. Use just enough mayonnaise to bind the mixture. Add seasonings and lemon juice to taste. Fold in the drained chick-peas and chill. Garnish with parsley sprigs.

ANCHOVY AND PIMIENTO SALAD   *4 to 6 servings*

2 hard-cooked eggs
3 pimientos
2 cans (2 ounces each) flat anchovy fillets
Romaine lettuce leaves
2 tablespoons lemon juice

1 small onion, minced
⅛ teaspoon freshly ground black pepper
⅛ teaspoon dried orégano
1 tablespoon minced parsley

1. Chop the egg whites fine. Push the yolks through a sieve. Cut the pimientos into strips the same size as the anchovies.

2. Drain off the oil from the anchovies and reserve. Separate the anchovy

fillets and place them in a row on the lettuce leaves. Lay the pimiento strips across the fillets to form a lattice pattern.

3. Combine the anchovy oil with the lemon juice, onion and pepper, and pour the mixture over the anchovies. Sprinkle with the orégano, chopped egg whites, sieved yolks, and parsley.

TOMATO AND ANCHOVY APPETIZER   *6 servings*

6 small or 3 large ripe tomatoes
Boston lettuce leaves
1 can (2 ounces) flat anchovy fillets
1 tablespoon fresh lemon juice

¼ teaspoon dried orégano
1 tablespoon capers
Freshly ground black pepper
12 ripe olives, preferably Greek style

1. Wash and core the tomatoes. Slice them and arrange on lettuce leaves.
2. Drain the oil from the anchovies and combine it with lemon juice, orégano, capers and pepper to taste. Arrange the anchovy fillets on the sliced tomatoes and pour the oil mixture over all. Garnish with the olives and serve as a first course with buttered toast.

TOMATOES ANTIBOISE   *6 servings*

6 ripe medium tomatoes
Salt
1 can (7 ounces) tuna
2 hard-cooked eggs, chopped
2 tablespoons capers
1 tablespoon finely chopped parsley

1 tablespoon finely chopped chives or green onion
2 tablespoons mayonnaise
1 teaspoon anchovy paste or chopped anchovy

1. Cut out the core of each tomato and use a small sharp knife or scoop to cut out most of the seeds. Sprinkle the interiors of the tomatoes with salt and invert them on a rack to drain.
2. Mash the tuna and blend it well with the chopped eggs, capers, parsley, chives, mayonnaise and anchovy paste. Season with salt to taste.
3. Use the tuna mixture to stuff the tomatoes, piling it high in a dome shape. Serve with toast or heated French bread.

ARTICHOKE HEARTS AND SHRIMP   *6 servings*

1 package (9 ounces) frozen artichoke hearts
24 medium shrimp
1 egg yolk
½ cup olive oil
½ cup peanut oil

¼ cup wine vinegar
2 tablespoons prepared mustard, preferably Dijon or Düsseldorf
2 tablespoons minced parsley
2 tablespoons minced chives
1 tablespoon minced shallots

1. Cook the artichoke hearts according to package directions. Drain and chill.

2. Cook the shrimp in boiling salted water to cover for three to five minutes. Peel and devein.

3. Place the egg yolk in a mixing bowl and add the oils, vinegar and mustard. Beat well. Add the remaining ingredients, then the artichoke hearts and shrimp. Marinate in the refrigerator for at least two hours, turning the artichokes and shrimp occasionally. Serve as a first course with buttered toast.

The fruit known as avocado is a gastronomic chameleon. Its rich nutlike taste is an admirable foil for other flavors. It complements crabmeat and other seafood, and has a natural affinity for tomato and onion.

Select ripe avocados for perfect flavor and smooth texture. Press the shells gently with the fingers to test them.

When an avocado is cut, the exposed surface tends to darken rather quickly. To prevent this, coat all cut surfaces lightly with a little lemon or lime juice.

The simplest way to serve an avocado is in its own half shell with only vinegar and oil, salt and pepper, but it may be used in many other ways.

AVOCADO APPETIZER   *6 servings*

6 small thin-skinned potatoes
1 large ripe avocado
  Juice of ½ lemon
1 large firm ripe tomato
3 anchovy fillets, cut into small pieces
2 tablespoons capers
2 tablespoons chopped parsley

4 hard-cooked eggs, peeled and quartered
1 tablespoon wine vinegar
1 tablespoon dry mustard
½ to 1 cup mayonnaise
  Cayenne pepper, freshly ground black pepper, and salt
  Buttered toast

1. Cook the potatoes in boiling salted water to cover until tender. Drain and chill. Peel the potatoes and cut them into one-quarter-inch slices.

2. Peel and halve the avocado, discarding the pit. Cut avocado into rough pieces. Sprinkle with lemon juice to prevent discoloration.

3. Spear the stem end of the tomato with a two-pronged fork. Dip into boiling water for exactly ten seconds. Peel and section the tomato, discarding core and seeds. Cube flesh.

4. Combine avocado, potatoes, tomato, anchovies, capers, parsley and eight egg sections in a mixing bowl.

5. Combine vinegar and mustard. Let stand for ten minutes. Blend with mayonnaise. If mixture is too thick, thin it with a little water.

6. Add mayonnaise and seasonings to avocado mixture. Toss carefully. Spoon the mixture into a serving bowl and garnish with remaining egg wedges. Chill well. Serve with toast.

Note: This dish, accompanied by a crusty loaf of bread, may be served for luncheon.

CRAB-STUFFED AVOCADOS   *6 servings*

4 large ripe avocados
⅓ cup lime juice
1 cup mayonnaise
3 tablespoons chopped chives
½ teaspoon salt
¼ teaspoon freshly ground black pepper

1 pound fresh or frozen lump crab-meat
Boston lettuce leaves
3 tablespoons capers
Stuffed green olives

1. Peel and halve the avocados, discarding pits. Dip all surfaces of the avocados into lime juice to prevent discoloration. Cut two avocado halves into small cubes.

2. Combine the lime juice with mayonnaise, chives, salt and pepper. Pick over crabmeat to remove pieces of shell, taking care not to break up the crabmeat too much. Add crabmeat and avocado cubes to mayonnaise. Mix gently.

3. Place lettuce leaves on a serving platter. Arrange the remaining avocado halves on lettuce. Pile crabmeat mixture into the halves. Garnish with capers and olives.

STUFFED CLAMS   *4 servings*

2 dozen cherrystone clams
¼ cup water
4 slices of toast with crusts removed, broken into rough pieces
1 tablespoon finely chopped shallots

½ garlic clove, finely minced
2 tablespoons butter
1 tablespoon cognac
1½ tablespoons chopped chives
Quick Aspic for Fish (page 476), chopped

1. Wash the clams well in cold running water and place them in a kettle. Add the water, cover, and bring to a boil. Steam until the clams open, for six to fourteen minutes, depending on the size of the clams. Remove from the heat.

2. Scrape the meat of each cooked clam into the container of an electric blender. Add one-quarter cup of the clam liquor, reserving the rest to be used in the aspic. Reserve sixteen half shells.

3. Add the toast to the blender container and blend briefly on low speed until a paste forms, stopping the motor and stirring the mixture down with a rubber spatula as necessary.

4. Cook the shallots and garlic in the butter until translucent and add them to the blended mixture. Add the cognac and blend briefly. Stir in the chives without blending.

5. Spread the mixture into the reserved shells. Chill. At serving time garnish each clam with about one teaspoon of the chopped aspic.

CITRUS HERRING IN WINE SAUCE   *6 to 8 servings*

2 jars (8 ounces each) herring in wine sauce
1 lemon
1 seedless orange
2 tablespoons wine vinegar
1 large onion, sliced as thin as possible
1 cup sour cream

1. Drain the herring and discard the liquid. Remove and discard the onion and spices.
2. Cut the lemon and orange into halves. Cut half of the lemon and half of the orange into the thinnest slices possible. Combine the slices with the herring. Squeeze the juice from the unsliced halves over the herring.
3. Add the vinegar, onion and sour cream and stir until blended. Let stand overnight in the refrigerator. Serve with dark bread and butter.

STEAMED MUSSELS   *4 to 6 servings*

2 pounds mussels
½ cup dry white wine or water
½ teaspoon dried thyme
1 small onion, quartered
1 bay leaf

Scrub the mussels and remove the beards. Rinse in several waters. Put them in a kettle with all the other ingredients. Cover. Bring to a boil and simmer for about ten minutes, until the mussels open. Discard any mussels that have not opened. Let the mussels chill and remove them from the shells. Chill until ready to use.

STUFFED MUSSELS   *6 servings*

2 pounds mussels
1 cup soft fresh bread crumbs
½ cup grated Parmesan cheese
½ cup finely chopped Italian parsley
1 to 2 garlic cloves, finely minced
1 teaspoon finely chopped sweet basil or ½ teaspoon dried basil
⅓ cup Italian olive oil

1. Preheat oven to hot (400° F.).
2. Scrub the mussels and steam them (see above). Open the mussels and discard the top shells. Place the mussels on a baking sheet.
3. Combine the remaining ingredients to make a stuffing and blend well. Place a generous amount of stuffing on top of each mussel. Bake for five to ten minutes, until crumbs are golden brown. Serve hot on an antipasto tray.
Note: The stuffed mussels may be kept in the refrigerator for an hour or so before baking.

MUSSELS RAVIGOTE   *6 servings*

2 pounds mussels
2 shallots, coarsely chopped
2 small onions, quartered
2 parsley sprigs
Salt and freshly ground black pepper

Pinch of cayenne pepper
1 cup dry white wine
2 tablespoons butter
½ bay leaf
½ teaspoon dried thyme
Sauce Ravigote (see below)

1. Scrub the mussels well to remove all exterior sand and dirt. Place them in a large kettle with the shallots, onions, parsley, salt and pepper to taste, cayenne, wine, butter, bay leaf and thyme. Cover and bring to a boil. Simmer for five to ten minutes, or until the mussels have opened.

2. Lift mussels from the broth and discard any that have not opened. Strain the broth through a cloth-lined sieve and reserve one cup for the sauce.

3. Take the mussels out of the shells and spoon into a serving dish. Cover with sauce ravigote.

SAUCE RAVIGOTE: *About 1½ cups*

3 tablespoons shallots
⅓ cup chopped capers
1 tablespoon chopped fresh tarragon
2 tablespoons chopped fresh parsley
1 cup broth in which mussels cooked

½ cup mayonnaise
3 tablespoons mustard, preferably Dijon or Düsseldorf
¼ teaspoon Tabasco
Freshly ground black pepper

1. Combine the shallots and capers in a mixing bowl. Add the tarragon and parsley.

2. Reduce the mussel broth by half by boiling over high heat.

3. Add the mayonnaise to the bowl and, using a wire whisk, beat in the hot liquid. Add the mustard, Tabasco, and pepper to taste. Let the sauce cool to room temperature. Pour over shelled mussels and serve.

SEVICHE   *6 to 8 servings*

2 cups ½-inch cubes of fish fillets (weakfish, bluefish, sea squab, flounder, red snapper, bass, etc.)
½ cup coarsely chopped onion
2 small hot green peppers, finely chopped, or dashes of Tabasco
⅓ cup fresh lime juice
½ cup tomato juice
⅓ cup olive oil
1 large tomato, peeled and chopped

1½ garlic cloves, finely minced
½ teaspoon dried thyme or 2 fresh thyme sprigs, finely chopped
Salt and freshly ground black pepper
1 tablespoon finely chopped parsley
1 tablespoon finely chopped fresh coriander leaves (optional)
¼ cup finely chopped sweet red peppers (optional)

The essential thing in making this dish is that the fish be as fresh as possible, since the only "cooking" is the action of the lime juice on the raw fish. To make it, combine all ingredients and let stand in the refrigerator overnight.

SHRIMP COCKTAIL À LA FRANÇAISE   *6 servings*

½ cup mayonnaise
½ cup sour cream
2 teaspoons cognac
1 tablespoon tomato catchup
36 shrimp, cooked, shelled and deveined

Combine the mayonnaise, sour cream, cognac and catchup. Blend well and chill. Arrange the shrimp on six individual serving dishes and serve with the sauce spooned over them.

RUTH ELLEN CHURCH'S SHRIMP RÉMOULADE
4 to 6 servings

¾ cup olive oil
¼ cup prepared mustard
¼ cup vinegar
1 teaspoon salt
½ teaspoon paprika
1 hard-cooked egg, chopped
½ cup minced celery
1 tablespoon grated onion
2 tablespoons minced parsley
½ tablespoon minced green pepper
2 pounds shrimp, cooked and cleaned

Whip the oil, mustard, vinegar, salt and paprika thoroughly. Fold in the egg, celery, onion, parsley and green pepper. Add the shrimp and chill for several hours until ready to serve.

CAMARONES ESTILO BARBACHANO PONCE (pickled shrimp)
6 to 10 servings

4 pounds raw shrimp
1 carrot, scraped and cut into thin strips
1 celery rib with leaves
1 bay leaf
1 small dried hot red pepper
12 peppercorns
1 teaspoon salt, or more
½ cup thinly sliced onion (the slices should be almost transparent)
2 cups salad oil
1 cup vinegar
2 garlic cloves, finely minced
3 medium tomatoes, peeled, seeded and chopped
Freshly ground black pepper
Chopped parsley
1 ripe avocado, peeled, seeded and cubed

1. Using a pair of kitchen shears, cut the shell of each shrimp along the back. Remove the shell and rinse the shrimp under water to remove the black vein along back.

2. Put enough water to cover the shrimp in a saucepan and add the carrot, celery, bay leaf, hot pepper, peppercorns and salt. Bring to a boil and simmer for ten minutes.

3. Add the shrimp and cook for five minutes after the liquid returns to a boil. Let the shrimp cool in the cooking liquid.

4. Combine the onion slices, oil, vinegar, garlic, tomatoes and additional salt to taste. Drain the shrimp and dry them. Add them to the sauce and chill for twelve hours.

5. Just before serving, sprinkle the shrimp with black pepper and parsley. Garnish with avocado cubes and serve with slices of French bread.

BATTER-FRIED SHRIMP   *4 servings*

1 pound jumbo shrimp	¼ teaspoon monosodium glutamate
¾ cup all-purpose flour	¾ cup cold water
1½ teaspoons baking powder	Vegetable oil
¾ teaspoon salt	

SAUCE:

2 teaspoons Hoisin sauce	¼ cup catchup
2 tablespoons chili sauce	

1. Shell the shrimp, leaving on the tail section; devein. Wash and dry the shrimp.

2. Combine the flour, baking powder, salt and monosodium glutamate. Gradually blend in the water to make a smooth batter.

3. Heat the oil to 375° F. on a frying thermometer. Holding the shrimp by the tail, coat with the batter, except for the tail section, and drop into the hot oil, a few at a time. Cook for three to four minutes, or until browned on all sides. Drain on paper towels. Serve with the sauce for dipping.

STUFFED SNAILS   *4 to 6 servings*

¼ teaspoon finely minced garlic	¾ cup soft fresh bread crumbs
5 tablespoons butter	1 can (6½ ounces) French snails
2 tablespoons chopped parsley	24 snail shells
½ teaspoon salt	
Dash of freshly ground black pepper	

1. Preheat oven to hot (450° F.).
2. Sauté the garlic in three tablespoons of the butter for about four minutes, until limp and transparent. Remove from heat. Add the parsley, half of the salt, the pepper and bread crumbs. Mix lightly.
3. Melt the remaining butter and combine it with the remaining salt. Dip each snail into this mixture and place it in a shell. Fill the rest of the shell with the bread-crumb mixture, using about one-half teaspoon for each.
4. Place the snails in snail holders and bake for five to eight minutes.

SCALLOP BLANKETS *4 to 6 servings*

½ pound scallops, cut into ½-inch cubes
2 tablespoons sherry
½ teaspoon sugar
½ teaspoon salt
6 slices of bacon, halved
6 water chestnuts, sliced
1 scallion, cut into 1-inch pieces

1. Marinate the scallops in the sherry and sugar for thirty minutes. Sprinkle salt on the scallops.
2. Preheat broiler.
3. Wrap a piece of bacon around a piece of scallop, a slice of water chestnut and a piece of scallion. Secure with a food pick.
4. Broil for ten minutes, turn over, and broil for five minutes longer.

COCKTAIL CROQUETTES *About 30 croquettes*

¼ cup butter
¾ cup all-purpose flour
1 cup milk
2 cups chopped seafood (shrimp, crab, lobster)
Salt and freshly ground black pepper
¼ teaspoon grated nutmeg
1 egg yolk
2 eggs, beaten
¾ cup fine dry bread crumbs
Fat for deep frying

1. Melt the butter and stir in one-quarter cup of the flour with a wire whisk. Add the heated milk all at once, stirring vigorously with the whisk. When mixture is thickened and smooth, remove it from the heat. Let cool slightly.
2. Stir in the seafood, seasonings and egg yolk. Shape into bite-size croquettes. Roll croquettes in the remaining flour and then in egg and bread crumbs.
3. Heat fat to 380° F. on a frying thermometer. Drop the croquettes into the fat, a few at a time, and fry until brown. Drain. Serve on food picks.

SESAME BEEF STRIPS   *4 appetizer servings*

½ pound boneless beef sirloin or eye round
¼ cup imported soy sauce
¼ cup sherry
½ cup sesame or peanut oil
1 garlic clove, finely minced

1 tablespoon finely chopped onion
1 tablespoon finely chopped fresh gingerroot
¼ cup toasted sesame seeds
Peanut Dip (below)

1. Cut the beef into strips (⅛ × 1 × 3 inches).
2. Combine the soy sauce, sherry, oil, garlic, onion and gingerroot and marinate the beef in the mixture for at least two hours.
3. Thread the beef, as though sewing, onto individual skewers. Dip into the sesame seeds and broil over charcoal or under the broiler for about three minutes, or until cooked to the desired degree of doneness. Turn once. Serve with peanut dip.

PEANUT DIP: *About ½ cup*

2 tablespoons peanut butter
2 tablespoons soy sauce
1 tablespoon lemon juice

¼ teaspoon crushed red pepper, or more
¼ cup heavy cream

Mix all ingredients together and heat gently.

SATES   *4 to 6 servings*

½ onion, finely minced
1 garlic clove, finely minced
6 Kemiri nuts, ground (Macadamia nuts may be substituted)
⅛ teaspoon *sambal ulek* (hot chili paste)
½ teaspoon *trassi udang* (Java-processed shrimp), optional

1 tablespoon *bumbu sesate* (spice mixture)
¼ cup *ketjap bentang* (sweet Java soy sauce)
½ cup water
18 to 24 cubes or pieces (1 inch) of shrimp, chicken breast or leg of lamb

1. Combine the onion, garlic, nuts, *sambal ulek, trassi udang, bumbu sesate, ketjap bentang* and water in a bowl.
2. Add the cubed meat or shrimp pieces and marinate in the refrigerator overnight.
3. Thread the pieces on small bamboo skewers and broil over charcoal until lightly browned, basting frequently with the marinade.
Note: Sates may be served with *gado gado* sauce for dipping made by mixing one-half cup purchased *gado gado* (spiced peanut paste) with enough hot water to make a thick sauce. Serve warm.

CHEESE-STUFFED FRENCH BREAD   *About 6 servings*

1 loaf of French bread
1 cup grated Gruyère or Cheddar cheese
½ cup chopped onion
1 garlic clove, finely minced
3 tablespoons oil
1 tablespoon vinegar
¼ teaspoon dried orégano
¼ cup chopped capers

1. Preheat oven to moderate (350° F.).
2. Cut a slice from the top of the bread and scoop out some of the soft crumb. Combine the remaining ingredients and stuff the bread with the mixture. Replace the top of the bread and wrap the loaf with aluminum foil.
3. Bake the loaf for about twenty minutes, until well heated. Cut into slices to serve.

CURRIED MUSHROOM ROLLS   *12 to 14 rolls*

12 to 14 thin slices of white bread
Softened butter
½ pound fresh mushrooms, finely chopped
2 tablespoons melted butter
½ teaspoon curry powder
1 tablespoon lemon juice
½ teaspoon salt
Dash of freshly ground black pepper
Dash of cayenne pepper
Additional melted butter

1. Preheat oven to hot (425° F.).
2. Remove the crusts from the bread slices and roll each slice to one-eighth-inch thickness with a rolling pin. Spread the surface of each slice thinly with softened butter and set it aside.
3. Sauté the mushrooms until tender in two tablespoons melted butter with the curry powder and lemon juice. Add the salt, pepper and cayenne.
4. Spread about one tablespoon of this mixture over each slice of buttered bread. Roll like a jelly roll and fasten the ends with food picks. Brush each roll with a little melted butter. Heat in the oven for about ten minutes, until brown. Serve hot as a first course.

MUSHROOM COCKTAIL STRUDELS   *15 to 20 appetizers*

6 tablespoons butter, at room temperature
1 pound mushrooms, finely chopped
2 tablespoons finely chopped shallots or scallions
Salt and freshly ground black pepper
2 tablespoons Madeira
½ teaspoon dried tarragon
½ cup sour cream
2 to 4 sheets of phyllo pastry (strudel leaves)
Melted butter, about ½ cup
1 cup fine dry bread crumbs

1. Preheat oven to moderate (375° F.).

2. Melt the butter and add the mushrooms, shallots, salt and pepper to taste, wine and tarragon. Cook, stirring occasionally, until most of the liquid has evaporated and the mixture is mushy. Let cool slightly. Stir in the sour cream.

3. Spread one strudel leaf on a cloth that has been moistened with cold water and wrung out. Keep the other leaves covered with a damp cloth. Brush the opened strudel leaf generously with melted butter and sprinkle with dry bread crumbs. Using a spoon, form half of the mushroom mixture into a sausage shape along the bottom of the strudel leaf from left to right. Fold over the bottom rim of the strudel to enclose the filling lightly. Lift the towel gently so that the strudel envelops the filling over and over like a jelly roll. Brush top generously with melted butter. Continue filling leaves until all filling is used. Freeze any remaining leaves for future use.

4. Roll the strudel onto a buttered baking sheet or transfer it carefully with the fingers. Using a sharp knife, cut the strudel into individual servings measuring about one and one-half inches. Bake for fifteen to twenty minutes, or until strudel is crisp and well browned.

CAVIAR ROULADE   *10 to 12 servings*

¼ cup butter
½ cup sifted all-purpose flour
2 cups milk
4 eggs, separated

3 ounces cream cheese
1 cup sour cream
4 ounces gray or black caviar

1. Preheat oven to moderate (325° F.) and place the rack near the bottom of the oven. Grease a jelly-roll pan (10 × 15 inches); line pan with wax paper greased and sprinkled with flour.

2. Melt the butter, blend in the flour with a wire whisk, add the milk, and cook, stirring, until mixture boils. Simmer, stirring, for one minute.

3. Add a little hot sauce to the beaten egg yolks, then blend yolks with the hot sauce. Beat egg whites until stiff and fold into the mixture.

4. Spread the batter in the prepared pan and bake for about forty minutes. Meanwhile, prepare filling. Remove cake when it rebounds to the touch and top is a deep golden brown. Turn out on wax paper.

5. While roll is baking, mix the cream cheese and three tablespoons of the sour cream. Add half of the caviar and mix gently. Spread lightly on turned-out cake. Roll the cake like a jelly roll.

6. Make a sauce by blending remaining sour cream and caviar. Additional caviar may be added to the sauce if desired, and additional caviar also may be stirred into the filling before it is spread on the cake.

7. To serve, cut the cake into thin slices and top each slice with a spoonful of the sauce.

LAHMAJOON   *12 pastries*

Lahmajoon is an Armenian pastry topped with a mint-flavored meat mixture. It is presented here as an appetizer, but it also makes a good picnic specialty.

½ package active dry yeast
½ cup lukewarm water, approximately
2 cups sifted all-purpose flour

½ teaspoon salt
½ teaspoon sugar
¼ cup butter, melted and cooled
Lamb and Mint Filling (below)

1. Soften the yeast in the water. Add the flour, salt, sugar and butter. Mix, adding more water if needed to make a moderately stiff dough. Knead on a lightly floured surface for ten to fifteen minutes, or until very smooth and elastic.

2. Place in a lightly greased bowl, turn over to grease the top, cover, and let the dough rise in a warm place for about one hour, until doubled in bulk. While the dough is rising, prepare the meat mixture.

3. Preheat oven to hot (450° F.).

4. Divide the raised dough into twelve portions. Shape it into balls and let stand for ten minutes.

5. Roll or press each ball into a six-inch round. Place the rounds on a greased baking sheet. Spread each round to the edge with some of the prepared filling.

6. Bake the pastries for about fifteen minutes, until crust is golden. Serve immediately, or cool on a rack and reheat before serving.

LAMB AND MINT FILLING:

1 pound lean lamb, ground
2 cups finely chopped onions
¼ cup finely chopped parsley
½ small green pepper, chopped
2 teaspoons minced fresh mint leaves
½ garlic clove, minced

½ teaspoon ground hot pepper
⅓ cup tomato paste
1 cup solid part of canned tomatoes, chopped
Salt and freshly ground black pepper

Mix all ingredients thoroughly.

LAHM-EL-GINE   *24 pastries*

½ teaspoon active dry yeast
⅓ cup warm water
½ teaspoon sugar
1½ teaspoons salt
¼ cup corn oil
1 cup sifted all-purpose flour
½ pound ground beef

2 onions, finely minced
2 tablespoons Worcestershire sauce
2 tablespoons tomato sauce
¼ teaspoon ground cinnamon
¼ teaspoon ground allspice
6 dozen pine nuts

1. Dissolve the yeast in the water. Add the sugar, one-half teaspoon salt and the oil to softened yeast. Gradually add the flour, kneading in the last portion if it is too difficult to stir in with a spoon.

2. Place the dough in a bowl, cover, and let it rise in a warm place free from draft for about three hours, until doubled in bulk.

3. Combine the beef, onions, Worcestershire, tomato sauce, cinnamon, allspice and remaining salt.

4. Preheat oven to hot (400° F.).

5. Roll out the raised dough on a lightly floured board to a rectangle one-sixteenth inch thick. Cut circles from the dough with a glass or cookie cutter two and one-half inches in diameter. Repeat process until all dough is used.

6. Place one tablespoon filling on each dough round and spread evenly over the surface. Garnish with three pine nuts. Bake for fifteen to twenty minutes, or until golden. Serve hot.

Note: These appetizers can be frozen after they are baked, and reheated before serving.

YERBRA   *About 30 stuffed vine leaves*

1 jar (1 pound) vine leaves	1 teaspoon salt
½ pound ground beef	15 dried apricots, halved
2 onions, finely minced	1 teaspoon sugar
¼ cup uncooked white rice	1 teaspoon chopped fresh or dried
2 tablespoons Worcestershire sauce	mint
¼ teaspoon ground cinnamon	2 tablespoons lemon juice
½ teaspoon ground allspice	½ cup cold water

1. Drain vine leaves. Store half of the leaves in the refrigerator for use at another time. Place the other leaves in a bowl, wash thoroughly under running water, and let soak for five hours.

2. Combine the ground beef, onions, rice, Worcestershire, cinnamon, allspice and salt.

3. Place one vine leaf on a plate with stem end toward you. Place one teaspoon beef filling on the base of leaf. Fold sides over filling. Starting from stem end, roll leaf up. Place the stuffed leaf, seam side down, in a large shallow heatproof casserole or serving dish. Stuff the remaining leaves and place them all in the casserole in a single layer. Tuck the apricot halves among the filled vine leaves.

4. Combine the sugar, mint, lemon juice and water. Pour the liquid over vine leaves and cover. Simmer over low heat for one hour. Remove from heat and cool. Refrigerate or freeze until twenty minutes before serving time.

5. Preheat oven to moderate (375° F.).

6. Bake the casserole for twenty minutes. Serve immediately.

A well-spiced pâté is a delicious and convenient dish for a casual summer meal, whether on patio, porch or lawn. Pâtés may be made with almost any meat, poultry or seafood. The pâté may be served out of a crock as a spread, or it may be sliced and garnished, or it may be molded into an attractive shape for use in a buffet meal.

CHICKEN-LIVER PÂTÉ   *5 cups*

2 cups butter
2 pounds chicken livers
2 medium onions, quartered
1 teaspoon curry powder
1 teaspoon paprika
¼ teaspoon salt

¼ teaspoon freshly ground black pepper
2 tablespoons cognac
1¼ cups pimiento-stuffed olives, sliced

1. Melt one-half cup of the butter in a saucepan. Add the chicken livers, onions, curry powder, paprika, salt and pepper. Cover and cook over low heat for eight minutes.

2. Blend the mixture in an electric blender until smooth. Add the cognac and remaining butter and blend in. Chill until firm.

3. Mold the mixture into the shape of a pineapple and completely cover with the sliced olives. Cap with a fresh pineapple top, if desired.

PÂTÉ EN CROÛTE   *8 to 10 servings*

Unbaked Pie Pastry, 2-crust (page 637)
1 pound veal shoulder, diced
1 pound lean fresh pork shoulder, diced
1 pound pork fat, diced
4 raw eggs, lightly beaten
1 tablespoon salt
½ teaspoon freshly ground black pepper

¼ teaspoon ground allspice
2 tablespoons cognac
½ pound lean smoked ham, cut into ½-inch strips
2 truffles (optional), cut into ½-inch strips
2 hard-cooked eggs
1 tablespoon water
1 envelope unflavored gelatin
2 cups Chicken Stock (page 475)

1. Preheat oven to moderate (350° F.).

2. Reserve one quarter of the pastry for the pie cover. Roll the remainder to one-eighth-inch thickness and use it to line a loaf pan (9 × 5 × 3 inches) or large oblong pâté form. Take care not to stretch the pastry or to have overlapping folds at the corners.

3. Combine the veal, pork, pork fat, three of the raw eggs, the salt, pepper, allspice and cognac.

4. Place a layer of the meat mixture in the bottom of the pastry-lined pan and arrange some of the ham and truffle strips lengthwise on top.

5. Cover with more of the meat mixture. Place the hard-cooked eggs in the middle and pack more meat mixture over and around them. Arrange another layer of ham and truffle strips and finish with the remaining meat mixture.

6. Roll out the reserved pastry for a cover. Moisten the pastry edges and seal the cover onto the sides. Decorate the edges.

7. Make a hole in the center of the cover to allow the steam to escape. Cut pastry leaves from the scraps, moisten the undersides of the leaves, and place them around the steam hole. Cut an oblong of pastry four inches long and one-half inch wide. Roll up lengthwise and pinch one end to make a rosette. Place a metal or Pyrex funnel in the hole to prevent liquid from bubbling over pastry during baking.

8. Combine the remaining raw egg with the water and brush over the surface of the pie and rosette. Place both on a baking dish and bake for two hours. Cool. Chill.

9. Soften the gelatin in one-quarter cup of the stock. Heat the remaining stock, add to the gelatin mixture, and stir to dissolve. Cool and chill until partially set.

10. Pour the jellied stock through the hole into the chilled pie until it will hold no more. Chill. Remove from the pan and cover the hole with the rosette.

PÂTÉ DE FOIE EN TERRINE   *About 3 cups*

1 pound choice fresh chicken livers
½ cup dry sherry
⅜ teaspoon ground allspice
1 truffle
½ cup ground bacon

1 cup ground smoked ham
2 egg yolks
  Salt and freshly ground black pepper
4 slices of fat bacon

1. Add the livers to the sherry to which one-quarter teaspoon allspice and the truffle have been added. Soak for two hours, then drain, reserving livers and truffle. Discard the marinade.

2. Preheat oven to slow (300° F.).

3. Trim the livers, cutting off and discarding stringy pieces and skins. Cut off and reserve irregular and small pieces and edges of the lobes; grind all these little bits. Reserve rounded whole pieces of livers for the center of the pâté.

4. Using a mortar and pestle, make a paste of the ground bacon, ham, ground liver trimmings, and any trimmings from truffle, ground. Add egg yolks, salt and pepper to taste and one-eighth teaspoon allspice.

5. Line the bottom of a small greased terrine with half of the paste. Arrange the whole pieces of liver carefully over the bed of paste and place wedge-shaped pieces of the truffle in the spaces between.

6. Cover with the remaining paste, pressing down gently to fill in all spaces. Cover entire surface with the bacon slices. Cover the terrine and seal the edges of the cover with a paste of flour and water.

7. Set the terrine in a pan containing water one inch deep. Bake for about two hours. Cool, and remove the top bacon slices. Store pâté in refrigerator. Serve from the terrine.

DUCK PÂTÉ   *24 servings*

1 duck (4 to 5 pounds)
2 pounds lean pork
1 tablespoon salt
1/2 teaspoon coarsely ground black pepper
1 onion, finely chopped
1/4 cup butter
1/2 pound chicken or pork liver

2 eggs
2 tablespoons cognac
1/2 cup dry white wine
1/2 pound fresh pork fat back, diced fine
6 julienne strips of smoked ham
6 slices of bacon

1. Preheat oven to moderate (350° F.).

2. Cut the raw duck meat from the bones and finely grind it. Finely grind the pork. Combine the duck, pork, salt and pepper in a large bowl. Beat well.

3. Sauté the onion in the butter until soft but not browned. Add the liver. Increase the heat and cook the liver for two or three minutes. Finely chop or grind the liver and add it to the other meats.

4. Add the eggs, cognac, wine and pork fat and mix everything well. Pack half of the mixture into a three-quart terrine or into two loaf pans (9 × 5 × 3 inches). Arrange the strips of ham lengthwise over the top.

5. Pack remaining meat mixture over the ham strips and top with the bacon strips. Cover the pan tightly with a cover or foil. Set it in a pan with boiling water extending two-thirds of the way up the pan. Bake for about two hours, depending on the depth of the terrine, or until the internal temperature has reached 185° F.

6. Place weights on top of the cooked meat mixture. Cool and then chill. Unmold onto a platter and garnish.

SHRIMP PÂTÉ DE LUXE   *2½ cups*

3 or 4 tablespoons Pernod
Juice of 1/2 lemon
1 pound cooked shrimp, shelled and deveined
1/2 teaspoon ground mace

Dash of Tabasco
1 teaspoon Dijon mustard
1/2 cup butter, softened
Salt and freshly ground black pepper

1. Put the Pernod, lemon juice, shrimp and seasonings into the container of an electric blender. Blend by turning the blender on and off and stirring with a spatula until the mixture is coarsely chopped.

2. Stir the blended mixture into the softened butter and add salt and pepper to taste. Place in a mold or bowl and chill.

Note: If desired, dry sherry may be substituted for the Pernod. If sherry is used, add one-half teaspoon dried tarragon to the seasonings.

Rillettes de Tours, a French meat spread, makes an excellent cold-weather dish served with sour gherkins and pickled onions.

RILLETTES DE TOURS   *3 to 4 cups*

1½ pounds lean fresh pork	1 bay leaf
2 pounds pork fat back	1 shallot
Salt and freshly ground black pepper	1 thyme sprig
	2 cloves
¼ teaspoon ground cinnamon	1 cup boiling water
¼ teaspoon grated nutmeg	

1. Dice the pork and fat. Put into a heavy pot with two teaspoons salt, pepper to taste, the cinnamon and nutmeg. Tie the bay leaf, shallot, thyme and cloves in a cheesecloth bag and add the herb bag to the pork.

2. Add the water; cover and cook slowly for two to three hours, stirring occasionally. If fat begins to burn, add more water.

3. Brown the meat slightly toward the end of the cooking time. Remove herb bag and drain the meat, reserving the fat.

4. Grind meat and cracklings through a food chopper. Season with additional salt and pepper if needed.

5. Heat the fat and mix all but one cup with the meat. Pack the mixture into small crocks and coat the top of each crock with some of the reserved fat. Store in a cold place. Serve at room temperature.

JAMES BEARD'S PÂTÉ FOR PICNICS   *About 24 servings*

¼ cup butter
1 pound chicken livers
2 eggs
6 garlic cloves
1 medium onion, peeled
1⅓ cups cognac, approximately
2 pounds veal, ground
2 pounds pork, ground
2 tablespoons salt
1 teaspoon freshly ground pepper

1 teaspoon dried thyme
½ teaspoon dried summer savory
Pinch of grated nutmeg
Pinch of ground cloves
12 slices of bacon, approximately
2 pounds cold boiled tongue, cut into long strips about ⅜ inch thick
1 pound fresh pork fat, cut into thin strips about ¼ inch thick

1. Preheat oven to moderate (325° F.).

2. Purée the livers in an electric blender with the eggs, garlic, onion and one-half cup of cognac. Or chop the livers, garlic and onion exceedingly fine and blend well with eggs and cognac.

3. Place the mixture in a large bowl and add the veal, pork, salt and pepper. Blend well with the hands. Add two-thirds cup cognac, the thyme, savory, nutmeg and cloves. Blend thoroughly.

4. Line a shallow baking dish with eight slices of bacon and place a third of the pâté mixture on the strips in an oval shape. Add half of the strips of tongue and pork fat. Add another third of the mixture in an oval shape, the remaining tongue and pork fat, and finally a top layer of the pâté mixture. Shape all into a loaf and top with additional slices of bacon.

5. Bake the pâté for three to three and one-half hours. Let cool. Remove to a carving board or platter and slice thin. The pâté will keep under refrigeration for a week if wrapped in foil and kept moist.

LIVER PÂTÉ WITH PISTACHIOS   *About 2 quarts*

1½ pounds chicken or calf's liver
¼ cup cognac
1 set calf's brains (optional)
½ garlic clove
1 shallot or ½ small onion, chopped
2 eggs
1 cup heavy cream
2 teaspoons salt

Freshly ground white pepper
½ teaspoon ground allspice
1 truffle, chopped (optional)
¼ cup peeled pistachios, chopped
Fat back, cut into wafer-thin slices
Quick Aspic for Chicken (page 476)

1. Marinate the chicken livers in the cognac for two hours or more.
2. Preheat oven to moderate (325° F.).
3. Place the chicken livers in their marinade in the container of an electric blender. Add the brains, garlic, shallot, eggs, cream, salt, pepper to taste and the allspice. Blend until all ingredients are puréed. Fold in the truffle and pistachios.
4. Line a two-quart casserole or terrine with fat back and pour in half of the liver mixture. Cover with a layer of fat back and add the remaining liver mixture. Cover.
5. Bake the pâté for one and one-half hours. Cool and chill. When chilled, cover with cool but still liquid aspic. Chill again until the aspic sets.

Pirogi and their smaller versions, piroshki, are savory hot Russian turnovers traditionally served at luncheon with a clear borscht or a meat broth. They are either rectangular or shaped like a slice of flattened jelly roll. The turnovers may be made with either raised dough or pastry, which is then filled with a meat or vegetable mixture. Pats of butter to slip between crust and filling can be served with each portion.

For variation, a combination pirog can be made by filling half of the roll with meat filling, the other half with cabbage-carrot filling. In serving, small slices from each end are offered.

PIROG   *1 pirog, about 12 servings*

1 envelope active dry yeast	2 teaspoons sugar
¼ cup lukewarm water	4½ to 5 cups sifted all-purpose flour
½ cup butter	3 eggs, lightly beaten
1 cup milk, scalded	Filling (pages 89 and 90)
1 teaspoon salt	1 egg yolk, lightly beaten

1. Dissolve the yeast in the lukewarm water in a large bowl. Melt the butter in the milk. Add the salt and sugar to the milk and cool to lukewarm. Add the milk mixture to the yeast mixture.
2. Beat in one cup of the flour. Beat in the eggs and then gradually beat in enough more flour to make a soft dough. Turn the dough out on a lightly floured board and knead until soft and elastic.
3. Place in a lightly greased bowl and turn to grease the top. Cover with a clean cloth and place in a warm place for about two hours, until the dough has doubled in bulk.
4. Preheat oven to hot (400° F.).

5. Roll out the dough on a lightly floured pastry cloth into a rectangle (18 × 14 inches).

6. Place the filling in a meat-loaf shape in the center of the dough, leaving at least four inches clear all around.

7. Draw the long edges of the dough together over the filling and pinch to seal. Cut off a triangle from each corner, then fold remaining triangular ends like envelope flaps over the covered filling and seal.

8. Place a lightly greased and floured baking sheet face down on the sealed edges. Holding the pastry cloth firmly, turn the cloth, filled roll, and pan over, all together, so that the smooth dough is uppermost and the seam side down.

9. Brush pirog with the egg yolk mixed with two tablespoons of water. Make three or more steam holes in the top. Bake the pirog for fifteen minutes, or until browned. Reduce the heat to moderate (350° F.) and cook for fifteen minutes longer, or until bottom dough is cooked.

CABBAGE-CARROT FILLING FOR PIROG:

5 cups chopped tender white cabbage
2 tablespoons salt
2 onions, chopped
1/3 cup butter

6 carrots, finely cubed
2 tablespoons chopped parsley
4 hard-cooked eggs, chopped
  Salt and freshly ground black
  pepper

1. Mix the cabbage with the salt; let stand for fifteen minutes. Squeeze out water. Blanch the cabbage in a colander over steam for six minutes; drain.

2. Sauté the onions in the butter. Add cabbage and carrots and cook slowly for thirty minutes. Add the parsley and eggs and season with salt and pepper to taste. Cool before using.

SALMON FILLING FOR PIROG:

4 fresh salmon steaks, about 1 inch
  thick
1/2 cup finely chopped shallots
1 garlic clove, finely minced
1/3 cup butter
3/4 pound mushrooms, sliced
2 tablespoons snipped fresh dill
1/2 cup Fish Stock (page 475)

1 teaspoon salt
1/4 teaspoon freshly ground black
  pepper
  Dash of grated nutmeg
4 cups cold cooked rice
6 hard-cooked eggs, chopped
  Salt and freshly ground black
  pepper

1. Cook the salmon and cool it. Remove skin and bones and cut the fish into large pieces.

2. Sauté the shallots and garlic in the butter until tender. Add the mushrooms and dill and cook for three to five minutes.

3. Add the stock, salt, pepper and nutmeg and bring the mixture to a boil. Consistency should be mushy. If there is excess liquid, evaporate it; if the mixture is dry, add a little more fish stock.

4. Mix the mushroom mixture with the salmon chunks and cool to room temperature.

5. Spread two cups of the rice in the middle of the prepared dough. Spread half of the salmon mixture on top of the rice, cover with the chopped eggs, and season with salt and pepper to taste. Pile the remaining salmon and then the remaining rice on top of the eggs, making a meat-loaf shape.

MEAT FILLING FOR PIROG:

½ cup butter
2 large onions, finely chopped
1 garlic clove, finely minced
2 pounds beef chuck, ground
1 pound veal, ground
2 teaspoons salt
½ teaspoon freshly ground black pepper

3 tablespoons all-purpose flour
⅓ cup Beef Stock (page 473)
¼ cup finely chopped parsley
4 cups cold cooked rice
4 hard-cooked eggs, chopped
Salt and freshly ground black pepper

1. Melt the butter in a large heavy skillet and sauté the onions and garlic in it until tender but not browned.

2. Add the beef and veal and cook, stirring occasionally, until the meat loses all pink color.

3. Sprinkle the salt, pepper and flour over the surface and cook, stirring, until the flour disappears. Stir in the stock and parsley and heat until the mixture thickens slightly. Cool to room temperature.

4. Spread two cups of the rice in the middle of the prepared dough. Spread half of the meat mixture on top of the rice, cover with the chopped eggs, and season with salt and pepper to taste. Pile the remaining meat and then the remaining rice on top of the eggs, making a meat-loaf shape.

PIROSHKI *36 piroshki*

Make the raised dough for pirog (page 88). Prepare any filling for turnovers or pirog. When the dough is ready, roll it out to one-quarter-inch thickness. Cut it into three-inch rounds or rectangles (3 × 2 inches). Place about one teaspoon filling in the center of each round or rectangle, moisten the edges, and pinch together to seal. The rectangles will make a pillow shape.

FRIED PIROSHKI:

Place the filled piroshki on a flour-sprinkled cloth and cover with another cloth. Let the piroshki rise for about twenty minutes.

Heat deep fat to 375° F. on a frying thermometer. Using a wire basket, gently lower a layer of piroshki into the fat. Fry for about four minutes, until golden brown, turning often with a slotted spoon. Drain on paper towels.

BAKED PIROSHKI:

Place the filled piroshki on a greased baking sheet, cover, and let stand for about twenty minutes, until dough is light. Preheat oven to hot (425° F.). Bake the piroshki for fifteen minutes. Lower the temperature to 400° F. and bake for about fifteen minutes longer, until piroshki are golden.

TARTE À L'OIGNON   *4 to 6 servings*

Unbaked Pie Pastry, 1-crust (page 637)
2 tablespoons butter
1½ pounds onions, thinly sliced
¼ pound bacon, diced
  Salt and freshly ground white pepper
1 tablespoon flour
1 cup heavy cream
4 eggs, lightly beaten
  Pinch of grated nutmeg

1. Preheat oven to hot (400° F.).
2. Line a nine-inch pie plate with the pastry and flute the edges.
3. Heat the butter in a saucepan. Add the onions and bacon and cook over low heat, stirring occasionally, until the onions are slightly golden. Add salt and pepper to taste.
4. Stir in the flour. Add the cream and continue to cook over low heat for five minutes, stirring constantly with a wooden spoon.
5. Remove from the heat and add the eggs and nutmeg. Mix well and pour into the pastry-lined pie pan.
6. Bake for about thirty minutes, until the top is golden brown. Serve hot.

SHRIMP QUICHE   *6 servings*

Unbaked Pie Pastry, 1-crust (page 637)
1 pound raw shrimp, shelled and deveined
¼ pound fresh mushrooms, sliced
1 large onion, thinly sliced
3 tablespoons salad oil
1 can (4 ounces) pimientos, drained
5 eggs, lightly beaten
1 cup milk
1 cup heavy cream
1 teaspoon salt
⅛ teaspoon freshly ground black pepper
  Dash of cayenne pepper
  Dash of grated nutmeg
1 cup grated Swiss cheese
¼ cup sour cream

1. Preheat oven to hot (400° F.).

2. Line a nine-inch pie pan with the pastry. Trim the pastry and flute the edges. Chill the pastry.

3. Sauté the shrimp, mushrooms and onion in the oil for five to eight minutes, until shrimp turn pink. Spread the mixture in the bottom of the pastry-lined pie pan and arrange the pimientos on top.

4. Beat the eggs with the milk, cream, salt, pepper, cayenne and nutmeg; pour the mixture over the shrimp. Bake for ten minutes, then reduce oven heat to moderate (325° F.) and continue to bake for about thirty minutes, until custard sets.

5. Combine the cheese with the sour cream and spread over the top of the quiche. Place under a broiler for one to two minutes, or until lightly browned.

CHICKEN-LIVER TARTLETS   *4 dozen 2-bite-size tartlets*

PASTRY:

2 cups sifted all-purpose flour
½ cup butter
2 tablespoons shortening

½ teaspoon salt
5 to 6 tablespoons ice water

FILLING:

5½ tablespoons butter
1 tablespoon all-purpose flour
⅔ cup light cream
¼ teaspoon salt
⅛ teaspoon freshly ground black pepper
⅛ teaspoon grated nutmeg
 Cayenne pepper
¼ cup grated Parmesan cheese

1 egg yolk, lightly beaten
4 shallots, finely chopped
1 garlic clove, finely minced
8 medium mushroom caps, chopped
12 chicken livers (about ¾ pound)
2 tablespoons cognac
2 tablespoons chopped parsley
 Salt and freshly ground black pepper

1. Place the flour in a bowl with the butter, shortening and salt, and with the finger tips or a pastry blender blend together.

2. Mix to a dough with the water. Roll out half of the dough on a lightly floured pastry cloth or board to one-eighth inch thickness. Use the pastry to line one-and-one-half-inch muffin cups or barquette tins. Chill well or freeze.

3. Meanwhile, melt one and one-half teaspoons of the butter in a small pan. Blend in the flour, gradually stir in the cream, and add the salt, black pepper, nutmeg, and cayenne. Bring to a boil, stirring. Stir in the cheese.

4. Add a small quantity of the hot sauce to the egg yolk and return all to the pan.

5. Melt the remaining butter in a small skillet and sauté the shallots and garlic until tender. Add the mushrooms and cook for two minutes.

6. Increase the heat, add the chicken livers, and cook quickly until brown on all sides. Turn the mixture out onto a chopping board and chop until fine. Add the cognac and parsley and season with salt and pepper to taste. Add to the sauce.

7. Preheat oven to hot (400° F.).

8. Place foil over each pastry-lined muffin tin, or barquette tin, pushing it down into the hollows. Fill each cup with rice or beans. Bake for seven minutes, remove foil and beans, and bake for two minutes longer.

9. Fill the partly baked shells with the liver mixture. Bake for eight to ten minutes longer, or until the pastry is cooked. Serve warm or cold as appetizers.

ANCHOVY-EGG BOATS   *About 12 boats*

Unbaked Pie Pastry, 2-crust (page 637), well chilled
2 hard-cooked eggs, mashed
1/4 teaspoon salt
1/8 teaspoon freshly ground black pepper
2 tablespoons mayonnaise
1/2 teaspoon prepared mustard
1 teaspoon sweet relish
1 can (2 ounces) flat anchovy fillets
8 ounces cream cheese
Heavy cream

1. Preheat oven to hot (425° F.).

2. Roll out the chilled pastry as thin as possible and cut into rectangles approximately 2 1/2 × 5 inches. Carefully line boat-shaped tins with the pastry; do not stretch. Trim, and prick all over with a fork.

3. Bake for ten to fifteen minutes, until lightly browned. During baking it may be necessary to push down the centers of the boats as they rise. Allow to cool on a rack.

4. Mix together the eggs, salt, pepper, mayonnaise, mustard and relish. Fill the cooled boats with the egg mixture. Place an anchovy fillet atop the egg mixture.

5. Add enough heavy cream to the cream cheese to make it of spreading consistency. Using a pastry bag and decorating tube, decorate the tarts with the cream cheese.

CREAM-CHEESE PASTRY
Enough for 2-crust 9-inch pie, or for 4 to 5 dozen tiny pastries

8 ounces cream cheese, at room temperature
1 cup butter, at room temperature
2 1/4 cups sifted all-purpose flour
1 teaspoon salt

1. Beat the cream cheese and the butter in an electric mixer, or by hand, until very smooth and creamy.

2. Gradually mix in the flour and salt with the mixer at low speed, or use

Cream-Cheese Pastry may be shaped into appetizer slices or turnovers with a variety of fillings.

a spatula or a fork to mix in the flour and salt. Knead the dough only until it just clings together.

3. Wrap the dough in wax paper and refrigerate for three to four hours or overnight.

4. If the dough has been in the refrigerator ovenight, let it stand at room temperature for at least thirty minutes before trying to roll it. Roll out the chilled pastry, one quarter at a time, on a lightly floured pastry cloth or between two sheets of wax paper according to one of the instructions given below.

SLICES:

Roll out one quarter of the dough into a rectangle (20 × 4 inches). The dough will be about one-eighth inch thick. Place one cup of one of the fillings (chicken filling and chicken-liver filling take especially well to this method of shaping) down the center of the strip in a sausage shape slightly flattened on top.

Draw one of the edges over the filling and press slightly. Moisten the other edge with egg white and draw up to seal the filling in. Roll the filled pastry onto a cookie sheet with the seam side down. Chill for at least one hour. Cut the roll slantwise into one-inch slices and separate slightly. Brush with lightly beaten egg mixed with one tablespoon of water and bake in a preheated moderate oven (325° F.) for twenty-five to thirty minutes, or until lightly browned. Alternatively, the slices may be frozen and then baked, while still frozen, for thirty minutes, until browned and heated through.

TURNOVERS:

Roll out one quarter of the pastry until it is about one-eighth inch thick. Cut into three-inch rounds or squares. Place one-half teaspoon of one of the fillings in the middle of each round or square and fold over to make half-moons or triangles, sealing the edges with egg white or water. Pinch or flute the edges. Place the turnovers on an ungreased baking sheet and chill or freeze before baking. Brush the surface with lightly beaten egg and make a pinpoint hole to allow steam to escape. Bake in a preheated moderate oven (325° F.) for about thirty minutes, or until lightly browned.

Each quarter of the dough will make about a dozen pieces. Smaller rounds (two inches) can be stacked atop each other with the filling in between to give round shapes.

CHICKEN-LIVER FILLING: *About 2 cups*

½ cup butter
2 onions, finely chopped
1 garlic clove, finely minced
1 pound chicken livers
2 hard-cooked eggs

2 tablespoons cognac
¼ cup finely chopped parsley
   Salt and freshly ground black pepper

1. Melt the butter in a heavy skillet. Sauté the onions and garlic until tender but not browned.

2. Increase the heat, add the chicken livers, and cook quickly, stirring to brown all sides, for about three minutes.

3. Turn the livers onto a chopping board and chop with the eggs until very fine. Mix in the cognac and parsley and add salt and pepper to taste. Cool before using.

CHICKEN FILLING: *About 2 cups*

1 small onion, finely chopped
¼ cup butter
2 cups very finely chopped cooked chicken
½ cup finely chopped parsley
2 tablespoons finely chopped or minced celery

1 egg, lightly beaten
½ teaspoon salt
⅛ teaspoon freshly ground black pepper

Sauté the onion in the butter until tender but not browned. Add remaining ingredients and mix well. Cool before using.

SPINACH FILLING: *About 2 cups*

4 slices of bacon
2 garlic cloves, finely minced
2 small onions, finely chopped
1 pound fresh spinach leaves, washed, or 1 package (10 ounces) frozen chopped spinach, partially thawed

1 cup pot cheese
Salt and freshly ground black pepper
⅛ teaspoon grated nutmeg

1. Dice the bacon and sauté it until crisp. Remove the bacon pieces and reserve.

2. Sauté the garlic and onions until tender but not browned. Add the spinach, cover, and cook until the spinach is tender. If fresh spinach is used, drain excess liquid and chop after cooking.

3. Stir in the pot cheese, seasonings to taste and reserved bacon. Cool before using.

MEAT FILLING: *About 2 cups*

1 large onion, finely chopped
½ cup butter
2 tablespoons chopped chives
2 cups firmly packed cooked ground beef

2 eggs, lightly beaten
½ cup chopped parsley
Salt and freshly ground black pepper

1. Sauté the onion in the butter until tender but not browned. Add the chives and meat and mix well.

2. Beat in the eggs, stir in the parsley, and season with salt and pepper to taste.

3. The consistency of the filling should be like mashed potatoes; if it is too dry, add another egg. Cool before using.

CHAPTER TWO

SOUPS

Old-fashioned vegetable soup

ONION SOUP WITH CHEESE   *10 to 12 servings*

The onion is prized today in kitchens around the world, particularly in onion soup. It is the best of soups for cold weather. In France onion soup may be made with stock or with water; it may be enriched with dry white wine or a bit of dry red wine.

½ cup butter
2 pounds sweet onions, thinly sliced
1 tablespoon flour
2 quarts Chicken or Beef Stock (pages 475 and 473)
Salt and freshly ground white pepper

1 loaf of French bread, sliced
2 cups dry white wine
¼ pound Swiss cheese, coarsely grated
¼ pound Swiss cheese, sliced

1. Melt half of the butter in a saucepan. Cook the onions in it until they are transparent and golden. Add the flour and stir. Cook for three minutes longer. Add the stock and simmer for at least thirty minutes. Add salt and pepper to taste.

2. Toast the bread slices and butter the toast with the remaining butter.

3. Preheat oven to moderate (375° F.).

4. Pour the soup into a large earthenware casserole. Add the wine and half of the grated cheese. Cover the surface with the pieces of buttered toast. Sprinkle all with the remaining grated cheese and add the slices of cheese. The object is to cover the liquid completely with toast and cheese.

5. Place the casserole, uncovered, in the oven for about fifteen minutes, until the cheese and bread are brown and crusty.

VARIATIONS:

Serve the soup without the toast and cheese; just before serving, stir in two to four tablespoons cognac.

Serve the soup without the toast and cheese; instead beat two eggs, blend with a little hot soup, and stir into the boiling soup before serving.

Omit the wine; instead stir in one-half cup dry vermouth along with the stock.

POTATO AND LEEK SOUP WITH YOGHURT   *6 servings*

1½ cups diced uncooked potatoes
 ⅓ cup finely chopped celery
 ½ cup finely chopped leeks (about 2 leeks)
  1 cup boiling salted water
  3 cups milk

1 cup whipped yoghurt
1 teaspoon salt
¼ teaspoon celery salt
⅛ teaspoon freshly ground white pepper
Chopped chives

1. Cook the potatoes, celery and leeks in the water in a tightly covered saucepan. Press through a sieve.

2. Combine the sieved vegetables with the milk and yoghurt in the top part of a double boiler. Stir in the salt, celery salt and pepper. Heat over boiling water for fifteen minutes, stirring occasionally. Sprinkle each serving with chives.

Note: To serve this soup cold, omit the yoghurt when adding the milk. When the soup is done, pour it into a bowl and chill thoroughly. When ready to serve, stir in the yoghurt and sprinkle each serving with chives.

CORN AND POTATO CHOWDER   *6 servings*

  3 slices of bacon
 ½ cup chopped onion
 ½ cup diced celery
  2 cups boiling water
  2 cups diced uncooked potatoes
  4 cups milk

2 cups fresh corn, cut off the cobs
2 teaspoons salt
½ teaspoon freshly ground black pepper
¾ teaspoon fresh lemon juice

1. Fry the bacon until crisp. Remove bacon from fat and reserve. Add the onion and celery to bacon fat and sauté until onion is limp and transparent.

2. Add the water and potatoes. Cook, covered, for twenty minutes, or until potatoes are tender.

3. Add the milk, corn, salt and pepper. Cook for five to six minutes, until corn is just tender. Add the lemon juice.

4. Ladle the soup into individual serving dishes. Crumble some of the reserved cooked bacon over the top of each serving.

SPINACH SOUP MODENESE   *6 servings*

1½ pounds fresh spinach
  3 tablespoons butter
    Salt and freshly ground black pepper
    Grated nutmeg
  3 egg yolks, beaten

3 tablespoons grated Parmesan cheese
4½ cups boiling Beef or Chicken Stock (pages 473 and 475)
Sautéed croutons

1. Wash the spinach well and cook it in the water that clings to the leaves until barely soft. Drain and chop it finely or force it through a sieve or food mill.

2. Melt the butter, add the spinach, and cook for two or three minutes. Add salt, pepper and nutmeg to taste. Add the egg yolks and the cheese and mix.

3. Add the stock and reheat to boiling. The egg yolks will curdle, but they are intended to. Serve hot with croutons.

CUCUMBER VELOUTÉ   *4 to 6 servings*

2 medium cucumbers
¼ cup butter
¼ cup all-purpose flour
2 cups Chicken Stock (page 475), approximately

½ teaspoon salt
¼ teaspoon freshly ground white pepper
Croutons

1. Peel the cucumbers, cut them lengthwise into halves, and remove the seeds. Place the cucumber halves in boiling salted water to cover and simmer for three minutes. Drain and then chop.

2. Melt the butter and blend in the flour; stir in two cups stock. Bring the mixture to a boil and add the chopped cucumbers, salt and pepper. Continue to simmer for about twenty minutes, until the cucumbers are tender.

3. Force the mixture through a fine sieve or purée in an electric blender. Correct the consistency by adding more stock, if needed, and adjust the seasoning. Reheat the soup and serve garnished with croutons.

CREAM OF MUSHROOM SOUP   *4 servings*

3 tablespoons butter
½ pound fresh mushrooms, chopped
1 medium onion, sliced
1 celery rib, coarsely chopped
1 teaspoon salt

1 cup milk
Freshly ground white pepper
½ cup heavy cream
¼ cup dry sherry

1. Melt the butter and cook the mushrooms in it, stirring, until the mushroom liquid evaporates. Add the onion and celery and cook until the vegetables are wilted.

2. Put the mixture into the container of an electric blender. Add the salt, milk and pepper to taste and blend for thirty seconds. Remove the cover of blender and, with motor on, add the cream.

3. Return the mixture to the saucepan and heat for five minutes. Add the sherry just before serving.

CREAM OF SPINACH SOUP   *6 servings*

¼ cup butter
½ cup chopped Bermuda onion
1 pound fresh spinach or 1 package (10 ounces) frozen chopped spinach
3 tablespoons all-purpose flour
6 cups Chicken or Veal Stock (pages 475 and 474)

Salt and freshly ground black pepper
2 egg yolks
½ cup heavy cream
Grated nutmeg

1. Melt three tablespoons of the butter in a saucepan and cook the onion in it until it is translucent. Do not brown.

2. Pick over the spinach and wash it well; tear off the tough stems and shred the leaves with a knife. Dry on paper towels. Add the spinach to the saucepan. Cook over low heat, stirring with a two-pronged fork, just until the leaves are wilted.

3. Sprinkle with the flour. Pour in the stock and, stirring constantly, bring to a boil.

4. Put the soup through a food mill or purée it in a blender. Return it to the saucepan and add salt and pepper to taste.

5. In a small mixing bowl combine egg yolks and cream. Beat slightly, then add a little of the hot soup. When blended, pour the egg mixture into the saucepan, stirring rapidly.

6. Heat thoroughly, but do not boil or the soup will curdle. Add a little nutmeg and stir in remaining butter. Serve immediately in very hot soup plates.

CREAM OF LIMA-BEAN SOUP   *6 servings*

2 tablespoons butter
1 package (10 ounces) frozen baby lima beans
⅓ cup sliced scallions
¼ teaspoon salt
⅛ teaspoon freshly ground black pepper

½ teaspoon dried marjoram
4 parsley sprigs, chopped
½ cup light cream or milk
2 cups Chicken Stock (page 475)
Chopped chives or parsley for garnish

1. Melt the butter in a saucepan. Add the lima beans and scallions and cook until the beans are tender.

2. Empty the mixture into the container of an electric blender. Add the salt, pepper, marjoram and parsley; cover and blend on high speed for twenty seconds.

3. Remove the blender cover and, with the motor on, gradually add the cream or milk. Turn off the motor as soon as all the cream is added.

4. Pour the mixture into a saucepan and add the stock. Heat over simmering water. Garnish with chopped chives or parsley.

CREAM OF PUMPKIN SOUP   *6 servings*

2 cups cubed peeled pumpkin
2 cups milk
½ bay leaf
2 thin slices of onion
2 parsley sprigs

½ teaspoon sugar
Grated nutmeg
2 tablespoons quick-cooking tapioca
1 cup Chicken Stock (page 475)
1 cup heavy cream, scalded

1. Cook the pumpkin in water barely to cover for about fifteen minutes, until pumpkin is tender. Purée the pumpkin in a food mill or blender.
2. Combine the milk, bay leaf, onion and parsley and bring to a boil. Strain the seasoned milk into the pumpkin mixture and add the sugar and nutmeg to taste.
3. Cook the tapioca in the stock until tender. Add the mixture to the soup. Add cream, bring to a boil, and serve.

FANNY TODD MITCHELL'S BEET SOUP   *6 to 8 servings*

6 medium beets
2 tablespoons butter, at room temperature
2 tablespoons all-purpose flour
4 cups milk

1 cup heavy cream
½ teaspoon dried thyme
1 teaspoon celery salt
Salt

1. Cook the beets until they are soft. Remove the skins. Chop the beets, then put them through a ricer or food mill.
2. With the fingers, blend the butter and flour.
3. Bring the milk and cream to a boil and add the puréed beets, the thyme, celery salt, and salt to taste. Stir in the butter-flour mixture bit by bit and let the soup simmer for five minutes before serving.

CORN AND WATERCRESS SOUP   *6 servings*

1 garlic clove, minced
⅓ cup small onion rings
¼ cup butter
1½ cups fresh corn, cut off the cobs (3 or 4 ears)
1½ teaspoons salt

½ teaspoon sugar
1 cup water
1½ cups milk
1 cup chopped watercress
2 egg yolks, beaten
½ cup heavy cream

1. Sauté the garlic and onion rings in the butter in a saucepan for about three minutes, until transparent and limp. Add the corn, salt, sugar and water, and bring to a boil. Cover and cook for fifteen minutes.

2. Add the milk and chopped watercress. Cover and cook for five minutes longer, but do not boil.

3. Remove the mixture from the heat and put a small amount at a time through an electric blender or a coarse sieve, then blend in the egg yolks and cream. Return the mixture to the stove and heat only until hot. Serve garnished with additional watercress.

FUMET OF CELERY   *6 servings*

6 cups Chicken Stock (page 475)
1 cup julienne strips of celery

¼ teaspoon freshly ground black pepper

Put the stock in a kettle and add the celery strips. Bring to a boil and simmer, covered, for fifteen to twenty minutes. Add the pepper. Strain the soup, reheat, and serve.

Note: Other vegetables and mushrooms may be cooked in stock in the same way. The stock may be clarified to make an absolutely clear soup. Also, it may be garnished with cooked slivers of the vegetable.

CHICKEN AND CUCUMBER SOUP   *4 or 5 servings*

1 large cucumber
1 uncooked chicken breast

4 cups Chicken Stock (page 475)
2 to 4 tablespoons sherry

1. Peel the cucumber, cut it crosswise into halves, and remove the seeds. Slice it into thin rings.

2. Remove the skin and bones from the chicken breast and cut the meat into thin bite-size slices.

3. Heat the stock to boiling. Add the cucumber and chicken and boil for two minutes. Add the sherry.

CHICKEN SOUP WITH MUSHROOMS   *12 to 16 servings*

3 pounds chicken wings
3 quarts water
3 scallions, trimmed
1 celery rib with leaves
3 parsley sprigs

1 tablespoon salt
1 piece of fresh gingerroot, crushed (optional)
½ teaspoon monosodium glutamate
Mushrooms, sliced thin

1. Simmer chicken, water, scallions, celery, parsley, salt and gingerroot in a large kettle for one to one and one-half hours. Strain the broth and discard wings and vegetables.

2. Boil broth to concentrate flavor. Add monosodium glutamate to broth.

3. Serve hot in hot cups or soup bowls. Float two mushroom slices on each serving.

Note: Leftover broth can be frozen for later use.

HOT AND SOUR SOUP   *6 to 8 servings*

2 tablespoons (4 or 5) dried Chinese fungi (tree ears)
3 or 4 medium-size dried Chinese mushrooms
8 dried tiger-lily buds
4 cups Chicken Stock (page 475)
⅓ cup shredded bamboo shoots
⅓ cup lean boneless pork shreds
½ cake fresh bean curd, cut into slices (¼ × ¼ × 1 inch)
1 teaspoon imported soy sauce
½ teaspoon sugar
1 teaspoon salt
¼ teaspoon freshly ground black pepper
2 tablespoons wine vinegar
¼ teaspoon monosodium glutamate
2 tablespoons cornstarch
3 tablespoons water
1 egg, lightly beaten
1 teaspoon sesame oil

1. Soak the fungi, mushrooms and tiger-lily buds in warm water for twenty minutes. Cut the fungi and mushrooms into slices.
2. Place the fungi, mushrooms, tiger-lily buds, stock, bamboo shoots, pork shreds and bean curd in a saucepan. Bring to a boil and simmer for ten minutes.
3. Add the soy sauce, sugar, salt, pepper, vinegar and monosodium glutamate. Combine the cornstarch with the water.
4. Add a little of the hot soup to the cornstarch, return all to the pan, and heat to boiling, stirring. Cook for one to two minutes.
5. Just before serving, turn off the heat, add the egg, and stir a few times. Add the oil.

Soups made with dried beans have a particular appeal in cold weather. They are hearty and filling. Dried beans have a splendid pantry life; properly stored, they will keep for a year or two. Note, however, that the longer the beans stand, the longer cooking time they require because water penetrates them more slowly.

BLACK-BEAN SOUP   *10 to 12 servings*

2 cups dried black beans
¼ cup butter
2 celery ribs, chopped
2 medium onions, chopped
1 tablespoon all-purpose flour
¼ cup chopped parsley
Rind and bone from a smoked ham
2 bay leaves
1½ teaspoons salt
¼ teaspoon freshly ground black pepper
½ cup dry Madeira
2 tablespoons vinegar
Chopped hard-cooked egg whites

1. Pick over and wash the beans. Cover them with water and soak overnight. Drain the beans, add eight cups of cold water, cover, and simmer for one and one-half hours.

2. Melt the butter in a heavy kettle. Add the celery and onions and sauté until tender but not browned. Blend in the flour and cook the mixture, stirring, for one minute.

3. Add the parsley, the beans and cooking liquid, the ham rind and bone, bay leaves, salt and pepper. Cover and simmer for three hours.

4. Discard the ham bone and rind, but keep any bits of meat. Put the soup through a sieve or purée in an electric blender. Add the wine and vinegar. Reheat the soup and serve topped with chopped egg whites.

LENTIL AND MACARONI SOUP   *4 to 6 servings*

1 pound dried lentils
¼ cup olive oil
½ cup diced celery
½ cup chopped onion
1 cup crushed tomatoes

2 cups macaroni or other pasta, broken into 1-inch pieces
Salt and freshly ground black pepper

1. Wash the lentils thoroughly. Place them in a large saucepan with cold water to cover and cook over medium heat for about one and one-half hours, until tender.

2. In a separate saucepan, heat the oil. Add the celery and onion and sauté until golden brown. Add the tomatoes and simmer for ten minutes. Add to the lentils.

3. Bring two quarts of salted water to a boil in a kettle. Add the macaroni and cook for ten minutes. Drain.

4. Add the macaroni to the lentils, season with salt and pepper to taste, and simmer slowly until the pasta is tender. Serve accompanied by a tossed green salad and a favorite cheese.

BEAN AND OLIVE SOUP   *6 servings*

1 cup dried white beans
5 whole cloves
5 peppercorns
5 allspice berries
1 ham hock

1 large onion, chopped
1 garlic clove, finely minced
1 teaspoon salt
½ cup ripe olives, cut into wedges
2 tablespoons chopped parsley

1. Cover the beans with water and soak overnight.

2. Drain the beans and place them in a kettle. And one and one-half quarts water. Tie the cloves, peppercorns and allspice berries in a muslin bag and add to the kettle. Add the ham hock, onion, garlic and salt. Bring to a boil, cover, and simmer for about one and one-half hours, until the beans are tender.

3. Discard the muslin bag of spices. Remove the ham and cut the meat from the bone. Dice the meat and return it to the kettle with the olives. Re-

heat. Mash a few of the beans to give body to the soup. Adjust the consistency by adding more water, if necessary. Sprinkle with parsley.

CALDO GALLEGO   *About 12 servings*

½ pound dried chick-peas
¼ pound lean salt pork, diced
¼ cup diced cooked smoked ham
¼ pound chorizos (Spanish sausages), sliced
2 tomatoes, peeled and chopped
2 garlic cloves, finely minced
1 ham bone

2 quarts water
1½ teaspoons cuminseeds, crushed
Salt and freshly ground black pepper
4 small potatoes, peeled and diced
½ pound dandelion greens, spinach or romaine lettuce, washed and cut into large pieces

1. Cover the chick-peas with water, bring to a boil, drain, and discard the water.
2. Sauté the salt pork until lightly browned. Add the ham and sausages and cook until all the meats are lightly browned.
3. Put the chick-peas, tomatoes, garlic, ham bone, water, cuminseeds, and salt and pepper to taste in a large kettle. Add the browned meats. Cover, bring to a boil, and simmer for about two and one-half hours, until chick-peas are tender.
4. Add the potatoes and cook for twenty-five minutes. Add the greens and cook for five minutes longer. Remove the ham bone. Season soup with salt and pepper.

CLAM BROTH   *8 to 10 servings*

24 cherrystone or steamer clams, scrubbed
1 tablespoon olive oil
6 cups water

3 shallots, coarsely chopped
4 parsley sprigs
½ cup heavy cream, whipped
Freshly chopped parsley

1. Place the clams in a large kettle and sprinkle with olive oil. Add the water, shallots and parsley; cover. Steam for ten to fifteen minutes, until the clams open. Discard the shells and reserve the clams for another use.
2. Strain the broth through a flannel-lined sieve or through several layers of cheesecloth.
3. Serve the broth piping hot in bouillon cups. Spoon whipped cream over each serving and sprinkle with chopped parsley.
Note: Clam broth can be used instead of fish stock in recipes.

MANHATTAN CLAM CHOWDER   *10 to 12 servings*

¼ pound salt pork, diced
2 onions, finely chopped
4 potatoes, peeled and diced
3 cups Clam Broth (page 109)
3 cups tomato juice
1 teaspoon salt

¼ teaspoon freshly ground black pepper
2 dozen fresh cherrystone clams or 3 cups drained canned chopped clams
½ teaspoon dried thyme

1. Sauté the salt pork until it is crisp and lightly browned. Add the onions and sauté until they are translucent but not browned.

2. Add the potatoes, clam broth, tomato juice, salt and pepper. Bring to a boil, cover, and simmer for about fifteen minutes, until potatoes are barely tender.

3. Meanwhile, open the fresh clams, drain them, remove the meats, and chop finely or put through a food grinder using a medium knife.

4. Add the thyme and chopped clams to the potatoes. Cover and cook for five minutes longer.

SPANISH FISH CHOWDER   *6 to 8 servings*

¼ cup olive oil
1 tablespoon paprika
2 large onions, sliced
2 garlic cloves, finely minced
1 medium green pepper, cut into strips
1 pound tomatoes, sliced
¼ cup chopped parsley
1 cup flaked cooked lobster or 1 can (6½ ounces) lobster, drained

1 pound shrimp, shelled and deveined
½ cup chopped pimiento-stuffed green olives
2 cups water
2 cups tomato juice
Salt and freshly ground black pepper
1 pint shucked oysters

1. Heat the olive oil, add the paprika, and blend. Add the onions and garlic and cook until tender. Add the green pepper, tomatoes and parsley. Cook for thirty minutes, stirring occasionally.

2. Add the lobster, shrimp, olives, water, tomato juice, and salt and pepper to taste. Cover and cook over low heat for thirty minutes, stirring occasionally. Add the oysters and mix well. Cook until the edges of the oysters curl.

SALMON CHOWDER   *6 servings*

¼ cup butter
⅓ cup finely chopped onion
⅓ cup finely chopped green pepper
½ cup finely chopped celery
3 tablespoons all-purpose flour
1 teaspoon salt

⅛ teaspoon freshly ground black pepper
4 cups milk
1 can (7¾ ounces) salmon, drained
2 tablespoons chopped pimiento

1. Melt the butter in a saucepan. Sauté the onion, green pepper and celery in it until lightly browned. Add flour, salt and pepper, mixing to a smooth paste. Cook over medium heat for about one minute.

2. Remove from heat and add half of the milk, stirring until blended. Return to heat and stir constantly until mixture begins to thicken.

3. Add remaining milk. Heat to simmering point; cook for about five minutes. Add the salmon, broken into chunks, and the pimiento. Heat to serving temperature.

SEAFOOD CHOWDER *6 servings*

2 slices of bacon, diced
2 tablespoons finely minced onion
2 tablespoons butter
¼ pound mushrooms, sliced
3 cups milk
1 cup heavy cream
1½ teaspoons grated lemon rind
½ teaspoon salt
¼ teaspoon ground mace
⅛ teaspoon freshly ground black pepper

⅛ teaspoon ground basil
1 pint shucked oysters or 2 cups (two 8-ounce cans) frozen oysters
½ pound raw shrimp, shelled and deveined
1 can (7 to 8 ounces) crabmeat, picked over and flaked
1 egg yolk
2 teaspoons chopped parsley
2 tablespoons dry sherry

1. Sauté the bacon and onion together until the onion is tender. Add the butter and mushrooms and cook for two minutes. Stir in the milk, all but two tablespoons of the cream, the lemon rind, salt, mace, pepper and basil.

2. Bring the mixture slowly to a boil. Add the oysters, shrimp and crabmeat. Heat for about five minutes, until the shrimp turn pink.

3. Beat the remaining cream with the egg yolk. Beat the mixture into the soup with a wire whisk. Heat the soup, stirring, until very hot, but do not boil. Add the parsley and sherry. Serve immediately.

VENETIAN FISH SOUP *5 or 6 servings*

3 pounds cleaned fish with heads
3 cups water
Salt and freshly ground black pepper
1 small onion
2 bay leaves
2 parsley sprigs

½ teaspoon dried thyme
2 garlic cloves
½ cup olive oil
½ cup dry white wine
1 cup canned tomatoes
½ teaspoon ground saffron

1. Trim the fish and cut it into half-inch slices. Boil the trimmings with the water, salt and pepper to taste, the onion, one bay leaf, the parsley and half of the thyme for forty minutes. Strain the stock and reserve it.

2. Brown the fish slices with the garlic and remaining bay leaf in the olive oil in a large saucepan or a kettle. Add the fish stock and remaining ingredients. Simmer for fifteen minutes.

One sublime formula for a cold winter's day includes a roaring fire on the hearth, a kettle of freshly made soup and convivial friends. Hearty soups are among the easiest of dishes to prepare; also they abound in nourishment and have superb flavor. They make excellent luncheon dishes served with a crusty loaf and butter, a green salad and some cheese.

OLD-FASHIONED VEGETABLE SOUP   *About 10 servings*

3½ pounds shin of beef
  1 beef knuckle bone, cracked
  4 quarts water
2½ cups (one 20-ounce can) tomatoes
  2 garlic cloves, minced (optional)
  1 tablespoon salt
  ¼ teaspoon peppercorns
  1 dried Spanish hot red pepper
  1 bay leaf
  ½ teaspoon dried thyme
  4 parsley sprigs
  2 cups chopped onions
  2 cups diced celery
  2 cups chopped cabbage
  2 cups diced carrots
  ½ cup diced turnip
  ½ cup diced parsnip
  1 medium potato, diced
  1 package (10 ounces) frozen cut green beans
  ½ package (10-ounce package) frozen baby lima beans
  ½ package (10-ounce package) frozen whole-kernel corn

1. Place the shin and knuckle bone in a large kettle. Add the water, tomatoes, garlic and salt and bring to a boil. Tie the peppercorns, red pepper, bay leaf, thyme and parsley loosely in cheesecloth. Add to the meat. When the mixture is again boiling, lower the heat, cover, and let simmer for three hours or longer, until the meat falls from the bones.
2. Remove the shin, knuckle bone and cheesecloth bag of herbs.
3. Return the broth to boiling and add all the vegetables. Simmer gently, covered, for about forty minutes, until all the vegetables are tender.
4. Skim off excess fat. If desired, add the meat from the shin. Reheat and serve piping hot.

SCOTCH BROTH   *6 servings*

1½ pounds neck of lamb, bone in
  6 cups cold water
  3 carrots, diced
  3 leeks, sliced
  2 small turnips, diced
  2 celery ribs, diced
  1 teaspoon salt
  ¼ teaspoon freshly ground black pepper
  2 tablespoons pearl barley
  1 tablespoon chopped parsley

1. Wipe the meat with a damp cloth and place in a soup kettle with the water, one carrot, one leek, one turnip and one celery rib. Add the salt and pepper. Bring to a boil, cover, and simmer for one and one-half hours.

2. Strain the soup. Place the broth in a clean kettle and remove as much surface fat as possible. Remove the meat from the bones, dice, and add to the broth. Add the barley, cover, and let the soup simmer for thirty minutes.

3. Add the remaining vegetables and cook for thirty minutes longer, or until vegetables and barley are tender. Sprinkle with the parsley before serving.

CRACKED-WHEAT SOUP   *4 to 6 servings*

1 pound stewing beef
1 large marrowbone
1 onion
1 celery rib with leaves
1 parsley sprig
2 garlic cloves, unpeeled
Pinch of dried thyme
1 bay leaf
1 carrot, quartered

10 peppercorns
2½ quarts water
Salt and freshly ground black pepper
½ cup cracked wheat
2 potatoes, peeled and cut into cubes
1 cup fresh or frozen peas

1. In a large kettle combine the beef, marrowbone, onion, celery, parsley, garlic, thyme, bay leaf, carrot, peppercorns and water. Bring to a boil and skim the surface. Simmer for one and one-half hours, or until the beef is almost tender.

2. Transfer the beef to another kettle and strain the liquid over it. Season with salt and pepper to taste; add the cracked wheat. Cook for thirty minutes longer. Add the potatoes and peas and cook for about twenty minutes, until the potatoes are tender. Cut the meat into small pieces and serve in the soup.

COCK-A-LEEKIE   *6 servings*

1 frying chicken (3½ pounds), cut up
3 quarts water
3 onions, sliced
4 parsley sprigs, tied together
1 bay leaf

1 teaspoon poultry seasoning
1 tablespoon salt
½ teaspoon peppercorns
8 to 12 leeks
6 medium potatoes, peeled and cubed, or ½ cup uncooked rice

1. Simmer the chicken, covered, in the water with the onions, parsley, bay leaf, poultry seasoning, salt and peppercorns for about one hour, until tender. Remove the chicken and cool.

2. Split the leeks lengthwise and wash thoroughly. Cut into one-inch lengths, using both the white and green portions. Add to the chicken stock.

Add the potatoes or rice and boil for about twenty minutes, until tender. Remove the parsley and bay leaf.

3. Meanwhile, remove the skin and bones of the chicken and cut the meat into large bite-size pieces. Add to the soup, adjust seasonings, and reheat.

COLD YOGHURT SOUP   *4 or 5 servings*

½ cup raisins
2 to 3 cups yoghurt
½ cup light cream
1 hard-cooked egg, chopped
6 ice cubes
1 cucumber, chopped
¼ cup chopped green onions

2 teaspoons salt
½ teaspoon freshly ground white pepper
1 tablespoon chopped parsley
1 tablespoon chopped fresh dill or 1 teaspoon dried dill

1. Soak the raisins in cold water for five minutes.
2. Place the yoghurt in a large mixing bowl and add the cream, egg, ice cubes, cucumber, green onions, salt and pepper. Drain the raisins and add them to the yoghurt mixture.
3. Add one cup of cold water and mix well. Let stand in the refrigerator for two or three hours. Serve garnished with parsley and dill.

COLD BORSCHT WITH CUCUMBER   *6 to 8 servings*

2 small bunches of fresh beets
6 cups Beef Stock (page 473)
2 teaspoons sugar, or more
3 teaspoons lemon juice

1 cucumber
Salt
1 cup sour cream
Chopped fresh dill

1. Wash, trim, and scrape the beets. Dice them into a saucepan and add the stock. Bring to a boil and simmer, covered, for about forty-five minutes.
2. Strain the liquid and discard the beets. Stir in the sugar and lemon juice. Chill.
3. Peel the cucumber, halve it lengthwise, and remove the seeds. Cut the cucumber into fine dice or into very thin strips. Add to the soup. Add salt to taste. Ladle the soup into cups, top with sour cream, and sprinkle with dill.

CHILLED POTAGE SAINT-GERMAIN   *About 6 servings*

1 cup finely chopped onions
2 tablespoons butter
2 cups diced uncooked potatoes
2 cups Chicken Stock (page 475)
1½ cups shelled fresh peas or 1 package (10 ounces) frozen peas

1 cup light or heavy cream
½ cup very dry sherry
Tabasco (optional)

1. Cook the onions in the butter in a small kettle. Add the potatoes and stock and simmer for about fifteen minutes, until potatoes are barely tender.

2. If fresh peas are used, cook them in a little boiling salted water until nearly tender. Add them to the potatoes so they will finish cooking with the potatoes. If frozen peas are used, add them to the potatoes five minutes before the end of cooking time.

3. When done, pour the mixture into the container of an electric blender. Blend on high speed until puréed. Pour into a mixing bowl and stir in the cream. Chill thoroughly. Add the sherry and Tabasco to taste and serve very cold.

COLD CURRIED AVOCADO SOUP   *4 servings*

1 large or 2 small ripe avocados
2¼ cups Chicken Stock (page 475)
1 teaspoon curry powder
¾ teaspoon salt
⅛ teaspoon freshly ground white pepper

½ cup heavy cream
4 thin slices of avocado
2 tablespoons lemon juice

1. Peel and halve the avocado, discarding the pit. Cut avocado into rough pieces. Place the avocado and one cup of the stock in the container of an electric blender. Add the curry powder, salt and pepper. Blend at high speed for thirty seconds.

2. Pour mixture into an enamelware saucepan. Add remaining stock and heat, stirring, to boiling. Cool. Stir in cream and chill.

3. Serve in chilled soup cups. Garnish each serving with an avocado slice dipped into lemon juice to prevent discoloration.

COLD SPINACH SOUP SMITANE   *4 to 6 servings*

2 pounds fresh spinach
1 egg yolk
3 scallion tops, chopped
Juice of 1 lemon

Salt and freshly ground black pepper
1 cup sour cream
Finely chopped chives

1. Pick over the spinach, remove and discard any tough stems, and wash the leaves in several changes of water. Drain the spinach. Put it in a saucepan with a tight-fitting lid. Do not add more water. Do not add salt. Cook the spinach over low heat for three to five minutes, until it is thoroughly wilted and tender.

2. Drain the spinach and reserve three-quarters cup of the cooking liquid. Place the spinach and the juice in the container of an electric blender and blend, stirring down if necessary with a rubber spatula. Pour the mixture into a saucepan.

3. Bring to a boil and then cool slightly. Beat in the egg yolk. Add the scallions, lemon juice, and salt and pepper to taste. Chill thoroughly. When ready to serve, stir in the sour cream and serve in chilled soup plates. Garnish with a sprinkling of finely chopped chives.

CHILLED SALMON BISQUE   *4 servings*

½ garlic clove
1 small onion, sliced
½ green pepper, chopped
1 tablespoon butter
1 can (7¾ ounces) salmon
1½ cups milk
¼ cup chopped fresh dill

¼ teaspoon Tabasco
1 teaspoon salt
¼ teaspoon freshly ground black pepper
½ cup heavy cream
2 tablespoons dry sherry

1. Sauté the garlic, onion and pepper in the butter.
2. Put the sautéed vegetables, the salmon, milk, dill and seasonings in the container of an electric blender. Cover and blend on high speed for fifteen seconds. Or mix the ingredients thoroughly and force through a strainer.
3. Pour in the cream and chill the soup. Just before serving, stir in the sherry.

GAZPACHO À LA FRANÇAISE   *6 servings*

1 garlic clove, finely minced
5 tablespoons olive oil
3 chili peppers, coarsely chopped
3 green peppers, seeded and coarsely chopped
2 onions, coarsely chopped
4 ripe tomatoes, peeled and coarsely chopped
2 cucumbers, peeled and coarsely chopped

1½ teaspoons paprika
4 cups Beef Stock (page 473)
1 cup tomato juice
¼ cup wine vinegar
6 tablespoons white wine
Salt and freshly ground black pepper

1. Lightly sauté the garlic in the oil in a large saucepan. Add the chopped vegetables and paprika and sauté for five minutes. Add the stock, tomato juice, vinegar and wine. Boil for one hour.
2. Purée the mixture through a fine sieve or in a blender. Add seasonings to taste. Chill.
3. Serve in chilled bowls and surround with small bowls of garnishes (croutons and diced vegetables).

Cherry Soup, chilled and served with sweet or sour cream, is well suited as first course for a summer dinner.

On a hot summer day, a fruit soup, ice cold, tart and tangy, can be tremendously refreshing.

Spices such as nutmeg, cinnamon and cloves, or lemon peel or, occasionally, bay leaf or celery, may be used to heighten the flavor of fruit soups. Both red and white wines, preferably dry, may be used.

Fruit soups may be used either as a first course or as a dessert. When used at the beginning of a meal, the tart smoothness of sour cream admirably complements the soups. For dessert, a spoon of whipped cream, slightly sweetened and dusted with cinnamon or nutmeg, is preferable.

CHERRY SOUP   *4 to 6 servings*

1 cup pitted cherries	2 tablespoons sugar, or more
1 slice of lemon	Pinch of salt
1 cinnamon stick (2 inches)	1 tablespoon cornstarch
2 cups water	¼ cup heavy cream

1. Boil the cherries, lemon and cinnamon in the water for about ten minutes, until the cherries are very soft. Add the sugar and salt.

2. Mix the cornstarch with a small amount of water, add it to the boiling mixture, and cook, stirring, for one minute. Remove the cinnamon.

3. Purée the mixture through a sieve or in an electric blender, add the cream, mix, and chill. Garnish each serving with additional cherries.

Note: To make berry soup, substitute one cup blueberries for the cherries.

PLUM SOUP   *6 to 8 servings*

1 pound ripe plums, pitted	½ cup dry red wine (optional)
4 cups water	½ cup sugar, or more
Juice of 1 lemon	2 tablespoons cognac (optional)
3 whole cloves	1 cup sour cream
Pinch of salt	

1. Boil the plums in the water with the lemon juice, cloves and salt until the plums are very tender. Remove the cloves and purée the plum mixture through a sieve or in an electric blender.

2. Add the wine and the sugar, and chill. Just before serving stir in the cognac and sour cream. Garnish each serving with an additional dollop of sour cream.

MULTERBERRY SOUP   *6 to 8 servings*

2 tablespoons arrowroot or potato starch	1½ cups canned or frozen multerberries (cloudberries)
¼ cup cold water	½ cup heavy cream, whipped
4 cups hot water	

1. Mix the arrowroot with the cold water. Slowly add the hot water while stirring. Simmer the mixture over low heat, stirring constantly, for one minute after it reaches the boiling point.

2. Add the multerberries and pour the mixture into the container of an electric blender. Blend for twenty seconds. Strain to remove the seeds. Chill.

3. Stir the whipped cream into the chilled soup and serve.

FRUIT CURRY SOUP   *12 servings*

1½ tablespoons curry powder	1 slice of watermelon
2 tablespoons all-purpose flour	4 apricots
3 tablespoons butter	4 peaches
4 cups Chicken Stock (page 475)	½ teaspoon salt
4 plums	6 tablespoons lemon juice
¼ cantaloupe	1 cup light cream

1. Bring the curry powder, flour, butter and stock to a boil and cook for about ten minutes, until the mixture thickens. Cool.

2. Remove the rinds and pits from the fruits and purée them through a sieve or in an electric blender. Add the purée to the cooled soup stock.

3. Stir well. Add the salt and lemon juice and mix in the cream. Chill.

CHAPTER THREE

FISH AND SHELLFISH

A variety of fish

There are as many good ways of dishing fish as there are creative cooks and there is almost no method of cookery that is not adaptable to the creatures that, as humorist Wallace Irwin once put it, "swim or swish." They may be poached and curried, baked and fried. Broiled fish is one of the most delectable of dishes and sautéed fish, whether amandine *or* belle meunière, *is admired the world around.*

There was a time within recent memory when fish for America's middle country was limited almost entirely to the fresh-water varieties, but with freezing, ice pack and modern transportation the piscatorial vistas have broadened considerably. That is not to say, however, that anything surpasses fish freshly caught from ocean, lake or mountain stream.

. . . .

FISH

. . . .

BAKED SEA BASS IN LEMON-MUSHROOM SAUCE   *6 servings*

2 pounds sea-bass fillets	¼ cup finely chopped shallots
2 tablespoons butter	1½ cups milk
2 tablespoons all-purpose flour	1 teaspoon grated lemon rind
1 tablespoon chopped parsley	2 tablespoons lemon juice
1 teaspoon salt	¼ pound mushrooms, sliced
⅛ teaspoon white pepper	Lemon wedges

1. Preheat oven to moderate (350°F.).
2. Arrange the fish in a shallow two-quart baking dish.
3. Melt the butter in a small pan. Add the flour, parsley, salt, pepper and shallots and stir to blend. Gradually stir in the milk and bring to a boil, stirring.
4. Add the lemon rind, lemon juice and mushrooms. Pour the sauce over the fish, cover, and bake for twenty to thirty minutes, or until the fish flakes easily when tested with a fork. Serve garnished with lemon wedges.

BAKED SEA BASS IN WHITE-WINE SAUCE   *6 to 8 servings*

½ cup plus 1 tablespoon butter
1 sea bass (4 to 5 pounds)
  Salt and freshly ground black
  pepper
3 shallots, chopped

1 small onion, chopped
3 tablespoons finely chopped parsley
1 garlic clove, minced
3 large mushrooms, thinly sliced
2 cups dry white wine

1. Preheat oven to moderate (350° F.).
2. Butter an oven dish. Dry the fish and season it well inside and outside with salt and pepper. Place it in the buttered dish and spread with the shallots, onion, parsley, garlic and mushrooms. Dot the fish well with remaining butter except for the one tablespoon and pour the wine over it.
3. Bake for forty to forty-five minutes, basting frequently. Remove the fish to a heated platter.
4. Add the one tablespoon cold butter to the sauce in the baking dish to bind it. Do not heat. Pour the sauce over the fish without straining. Decorate, if desired, with lemon slices and additional chopped parsley.

PIERRE FRANEY'S STUFFED STRIPED BASS   *6 to 8 servings*

This is one of the most delectable dishes ever created. The preparation takes considerable time since it necessitates boning the fish and making the stuffing and the white-wine sauce, but the result makes the effort well worth it.

2 striped bass (2½ pounds) or 1
  bass (5 pounds)
  Salt and freshly ground black
  pepper
¾ cup butter
½ pound mushrooms, finely
  chopped
½ lemon
¼ cup finely chopped onion
½ teaspoon minced garlic
¼ teaspoon ground thyme

½ teaspoon ground sage
¼ teaspoon finely chopped bay leaf
¼ cup finely chopped shallots or
  green onions
1 cup dry white wine
1½ cups soft fresh bread crumbs
1 egg yolk
2 tablespoons finely chopped
  parsley
  White-Wine Sauce (page 125)

1. Preheat oven to moderate (350° F.).
2. Bone the fish or have it boned, but without splitting fish in two. To do this, carefully trim around rib bones and back bones to, but not through, the back section. Pull out remaining bones with tweezers. Reserve the bones for sauce recipe (below). Sprinkle inside of fish with salt and pepper.
3. Melt half of the butter in a skillet. Add mushrooms to the butter and immediately sprinkle with lemon juice. Cook until mushrooms are

wilted. Add the onion, garlic, thyme, sage, bay leaf, half of the shallots, and salt and pepper to taste.

4. Stuff fish with mushroom and herb mixture. Cover the opening with a neat length of aluminum foil and tie with string.

5. Rub a baking dish with two tablespoons butter and sprinkle with salt, pepper and the remaining shallots. Place the stuffed fish in the baking dish and dot it with remaining butter. Pour the wine over the fish and cover with aluminum foil.

6. If small fish are used, bake for forty minutes; if large fish is used, bake for one hour. In any event, bake until fish flakes easily when tested with a fork.

7. Transfer fish to a warm serving platter and remove foil and string. Use pan liquid as indicated in sauce recipe (below). Serve the fish with the white-wine sauce and with boiled whole small potatoes buttered and sprinkled with parsley.

WHITE-WINE SAUCE: *About 2 cups*

Bones from fish
⅓ cup dry white wine
2 cups water
1 garlic clove, peeled
2 parsley sprigs
1 small white onion, peeled
Salt
10 peppercorns

¼ cup butter
3 tablespoons all-purpose flour
Pan liquid from baking fish (see above)
¼ teaspoon cayenne pepper
¾ cup heavy cream
1 teaspoon lemon juice

1. Place the fish bones in a small saucepan and add the wine, water, garlic, parsley, onion, salt to taste and peppercorns. Bring to a boil and simmer for twenty minutes to make stock.

2. Melt half of the butter in a saucepan and stir in the flour, using a wire whisk. Add one and one-half cups of the stock, stirring vigorously until the mixture is thickened and smooth. Simmer for thirty minutes over very low heat, stirring occasionally.

3. When fish is cooked, add the pan liquid from the baking dish. Stir in the cayenne pepper. Put the sauce through a sieve.

4. Reheat the strained sauce. Stir in the cream, the remaining butter and the lemon juice. Stir briefly and serve immediately with the fish.

POACHED STRIPED BASS   *6 servings*

1 striped bass (4 pounds) or other fresh fish
4 quarts cold water (about)
1 carrot, scraped and cut into ½-inch lengths

1 celery rib, cut into 1-inch lengths
4 teaspoons salt, or more
12 peppercorns
Pinch of ground thyme
1 bay leaf

1. Leave the fish whole and keep it cold until ready to cook. It must be thoroughly cleaned and scaled. Rinse in cold water and pat dry with a towel. Wrap the fish loosely in aluminum foil. Do not seal the foil because the water must penetrate the flesh.

2. Place the foil-wrapped fish in the cold water and add remaining ingredients. Bring to a boil and reduce the heat. Cook the fish for exactly twelve minutes. Let stand in the cooking liquid until ready to serve. Serve with Parsley Sauce (page 488).

BAKED FISH WITH ALMOND STUFFING   *6 generous servings*

½ cup plus 2 tablespoons butter
¼ cup chopped onion
3 cups soft fresh bread crumbs
½ cup chopped celery
½ cup chopped green pepper
2 tablespoons chopped parsley
3 eggs, lightly beaten

1 teaspoon salt
Freshly ground black pepper
1 teaspoon dried tarragon or thyme
½ cup chopped toasted almonds
1 striped bass, sea bass or red snapper (5 to 7 pounds), cleaned, washed and dried well

1. Preheat oven to hot (400° F.).

2. Melt two tablespoons of the butter and cook the onion until tender but not browned. Add the bread crumbs, celery, green pepper, parsley, eggs, salt, pepper to taste, tarragon and almonds. Mix well and use the mixture to stuff the fish. Sew up the cavity.

3. Melt the remaining butter. Line a large baking dish with aluminum foil and pour a little of the butter over the foil. Lay the fish on the foil and sprinkle with additional salt and pepper.

4. Bake the fish for about one hour and fifteen minutes, basting frequently with the remaining melted butter. The fish is done when it flakes easily when tested with a fork.

POACHED BLUEFISH   *8 or more servings*

2 leeks, trimmed, split and cut into 1-inch pieces
2 onions, coarsely chopped
3 carrots, scraped and coarsely chopped
4 bay leaves
2 fresh thyme sprigs or 1 teaspoon dried thyme

2 tablespoons peppercorns
3 garlic cloves, peeled
4 fresh tarragon sprigs or 1 teaspoon dried tarragon
4 quarts water
3 cups dry white wine
Salt
1 bluefish (6 pounds), cleaned

1. In a fish cooker or other utensil large enough to hold the fish, put all ingredients except the fish. Bring this court bouillon to a boil and simmer for ten minutes.

2. Place the fish on the rack of the fish cooker or put it in a cheesecloth sling. Lower the fish into the court bouillon and simmer for twenty minutes. Let the fish stand in the liquid until ready to serve.

3. When ready to serve, gently transfer the fish to a board. Discard the thyme and tarragon sprigs and the garlic; use the remaining vegetables for garnish. Serve with Sauce Rouille (page 492).

BLUEFISH AU VIN BLANC   *6 servings*

2 cups thinly sliced onions
1 tablespoon peanut oil
3 garlic cloves
2 fresh thyme sprigs or 1 teaspoon dried thyme
2 parsley sprigs
2 bay leaves
Tabasco

⅓ cup white vinegar
3 cups dry white wine
Salt and freshly ground black pepper
6 bluefish or mackerel fillets
2 lemons, thinly sliced
1 carrot, scraped and thinly sliced

1. Preheat oven to moderate (350° F.).

2. Cook the onions in the oil in a skillet until barely wilted. Do not brown. Add the garlic, thyme, parsley, bay leaves, Tabasco to taste, vinegar and white wine. Season with salt and pepper. Simmer for fifteen minutes.

3. Oil a shallow baking dish large enough to accommodate the fish fillets without overlapping. Arrange the fillets on the dish and spoon the hot sauce over. Sprinkle with additional salt and pepper. Arrange the lemon slices and carrots neatly over the fish. Bring to a boil.

4. Cover the dish with aluminum foil and place it in the oven. Bake for twenty to twenty-five minutes, depending on the size of the fish. Remove from the oven and chill.

ESTHER CORY'S BAKED WHOLE FISH   *4 servings*

1 whole bluefish, mackerel, porgy or flounder (2 pounds)
3 tablespoons olive oil
½ teaspoon salt
¼ teaspoon freshly ground black pepper

3 tablespoons chopped parsley
2 tablespoons finely chopped onion
2 tablespoons butter
1 tablespoon lemon juice

1. Preheat oven to moderate (350° F.).

2. Wash and dry the fish. Coat with the oil and season with the salt and pepper. Place in a buttered shallow pan and bake for fifteen minutes, or until the fish flakes easily when tested with a fork.

3. Combine the parsley, onion, butter and lemon juice and spread over the cooked fish.

4. Place the fish under the broiler and cook until lightly browned.

BAKED CARP OR PIKE   *4 servings*

1 whole carp or pike (2 pounds), cleaned, washed and dried	Salt and freshly ground black pepper
2 tablespoons olive oil	1 or 2 lemons, halved and sliced
¼ cup lemon juice	Parsley

1. Preheat oven to moderate (325° F.).

2. Brush the entire surface of the fish with the olive oil and sprinkle both inside and outside with the lemon juice and salt and pepper. Place in a shallow baking pan.

3. Bake the fish for fifteen to twenty minutes, or until the flesh flakes easily when tested with a fork. Serve the fish whole and garnish with the lemon slices and parsley.

MARINER'S STEW   *8 servings*

2 cups canned tomatoes	¼ teaspoon dry mustard
1 tablespoon all-purpose flour	¼ teaspoon whole allspice
1½ cups onion rings	1 small piece of gingerroot
2 teaspoons salt	2 pounds codfish steak, diced
½ teaspoon freshly ground black pepper	2 tablespoons butter
	2 eggs, lightly beaten
2 tablespoons chopped parsley	2 tablespoons lime or lemon juice
⅓ teaspoon dried orégano	

1. In a large skillet break up the tomatoes with a fork. Add the flour and stir until all the lumps disappear. Add the onion rings, salt, pepper, parsley, orégano and mustard. Tie the allspice and gingerroot in a cheesecloth bag and add to the skillet. Cook, covered, for fifteen minutes.

2. Add the fish and cook for five to ten minutes, until flaky. Remove from the heat and discard spice bag. Stir in the beaten eggs and lime or lemon juice. Return to heat and cook for two or three minutes, until slightly thickened. Serve hot.

FLOUNDER BAKED IN SOUR CREAM   *6 servings*

2 pounds flounder fillets	¼ cup grated Parmesan cheese
All-purpose flour	1 cup sour cream
Salt and freshly ground pepper	Fine dry bread crumbs
¼ cup butter	Lemon slices
1 to 2 tablespoons paprika, or more (optional)	

1. Preheat oven to hot (400° F.).

2. Roll the fillets in flour seasoned with salt and pepper. Shake off excess flour.

3. Heat the butter in a skillet and sauté the fish until golden. Arrange the fillets in a shallow baking dish and sprinkle with paprika.

4. Stir the grated cheese into the sour cream and pour over the fish. Top with bread crumbs and dot with butter. Bake, uncovered, for about ten minutes, until the fish flakes easily when tested with a fork. Serve with lemon slices.

Salt cod is a staple food all around the Mediterranean. Some salt-cod dishes have become classics, especially brandade de morue, *a purée of codfish made with milk and olive oil, and the Provençal Christmas Eve dish of cod cooked in a sauce or stew made of vegetables, herbs and olive oil. But there are many other ways to serve this salty dried fish; when properly prepared, it is delicious.*

POACHED SALT COD   *About 4 servings*

Soak one and one-half pounds salt cod for several hours, changing the water three times. Drain and cut into three-inch squares. Place in a skillet and cover with fresh water. Bring to a boil and simmer gently for not longer than eight minutes. Remove the skin and bones. Flake the fish or leave it whole, as desired. Serve warm with buttered potatoes and Aïoli sauce (page 492). The cod also may be served with lemon juice, chopped parsley and brown butter, or it may be creamed. It also may be served hot in a curry or creole sauce.

SALT COD, PORTUGUESE STYLE   *6 servings*

1½ pounds salt cod or fresh cod fillets, boned
2 tablespoons butter
1 cup chopped onions
2 garlic cloves, finely minced
1 green pepper, cored, seeded and chopped
¼ teaspoon ground thyme
1 bay leaf
2 cups (one 1-pound can) Italian plum tomatoes
Salt and freshly ground black pepper
1 large eggplant
¼ cup olive oil
1 cup rice, cooked according to package directions
½ teaspoon cuminseeds, crushed, or ¼ teaspoon ground cuminseed
3 tablespoons capers
Butter

1. If salt cod is used, soak it for several hours in water to cover, changing the water three times. Drain the cod and cut it into three-inch squares. Place the salt-cod squares or the fresh fillets in a skillet and cover with fresh

water. Bring to a boil and simmer for not more than eight minutes. Drain; remove bones and skin.

2. Meanwhile, melt the butter and cook the onions, garlic, green pepper, thyme and bay leaf until the vegetables are tender. Add the tomatoes and simmer for thirty minutes, or until the mixture has thickened somewhat. Season to taste with salt and pepper.

3. Preheat oven to hot (400° F.).

4. Peel the eggplant and cut it into half-inch slices. Place the slices on a greased baking sheet and brush with oil. Bake for about twelve minutes, until the eggplant is tender, turning once. Brush with more oil as necessary.

5. When the eggplant is tender, line the bottom of a baking dish with the slices. Cover with the poached salt cod or the fresh cod fillets.

6. Combine the cooked rice with the cuminseed and capers. Spoon it over the fish. Add the tomato sauce and dot with butter. Cover and bake for thirty minutes. Uncover and continue to bake for ten to fifteen minutes longer. Serve from the baking dish.

FLOUNDER DUGLÈRE WITH NOODLES   *4 servings*

4 large flounder fillets	½ cup dry white wine
Salt and freshly ground black pepper	1 cup canned tomatoes, drained
	2 tablespoons finely chopped shallots
2 tablespoons lemon juice	2 tablespoons finely chopped parsley
2 tablespoons butter	8 ounces noodles, cooked and
¼ cup Fish Stock (page 475)	drained

1. Season the fillets with the salt and pepper and sprinkle with the lemon juice. Roll up and tie loosely.

2. Place the rolled fillets in a skillet and add the butter, stock, wine, tomatoes, shallots and parsley. Bring to a boil, cover, and simmer very gently for ten to twelve minutes, or until fish flakes easily when tested with a fork. Turn the rolls once.

3. Remove strings from rolls and arrange the fillets atop the noodles in a warm serving dish. Cook the sauce for two to five minutes, until it reaches the desired consistency. Season with salt and pepper to taste and pour over the fish.

CELERY-STUFFED FLOUNDER   *6 servings*

2 pounds flounder fillets	¼ cup butter
1½ teaspoons salt	2 cups soft fresh bread crumbs
½ teaspoon freshly ground black pepper	¼ teaspoon crumbled dried rosemary
4 teaspoons lemon juice	Fresh lemon slices and parsley for garnish
¼ cup finely chopped onion	
1½ cups finely chopped celery	

1. Preheat oven to moderate (350° F.).

2. Wipe the fish with a damp cloth. Mix together one teaspoon of the salt, one-quarter teaspoon of the pepper and three teaspoons of the lemon juice. Rub over both sides of the fish. Let stand for twenty minutes.

3. Meanwhile, sauté the onion and celery in three tablespoons of the butter. Stir in the bread crumbs, remaining salt and pepper, the rosemary and remaining lemon juice; mix well.

4. Grease a one-and-one-half-quart long shallow baking dish. Place half of the fish fillets in the dish. Cover with the bread-crumb mixture. Top with the remaining fish. Melt the remaining butter and brush over the top. Cover and bake for thirty to forty minutes.

5. Remove the cover and place under the broiler to brown. Garnish with lemon slices and parsley.

FILLETS OF FLOUNDER IN WINE SAUCE   *6 servings*

1 cup clam juice	6 flounder fillets (4 to 6 ounces each)
3 onion slices	Salt and freshly ground black
1 teaspoon lemon juice	pepper
2 parsley sprigs	¼ pound mushrooms, sliced
1 bay leaf	½ cup butter
4 peppercorns	⅓ cup dry white wine
⅛ teaspoon ground thyme	5 egg yolks
12 raw shrimp, shelled and deveined	

1. Preheat oven to moderate (325° F.).

2. Combine the clam juice, onion slices, lemon juice, parsley, bay leaf, peppercorns and thyme in a small pan. Bring mixture to a boil, add the shrimp, and cook them for three to five minutes. Drain shrimp, reserving both liquid and shrimp.

3. Place the flounder fillets in a double layer in a two-inch-deep baking dish, seasoning between the layers with salt and pepper. Strain the reserved liquid over the fillets. Cover and bake for fifteen to twenty minutes, or until the fish flakes easily when tested with a fork.

4. Meanwhile, sauté the mushrooms in two tablespoons of the butter.

5. Drain the liquid from the fish into a small skillet and boil rapidly until it is reduced to about one-third cup. Add the remaining butter.

6. Mix the wine with the egg yolks until well blended. Add to the reduced liquid. Heat, stirring, until the mixture thickens, but do not allow to boil. Season to taste with salt and pepper.

7. Sprinkle the mushrooms over the fillets and pour the sauce over all. Garnish with the reserved shrimp. Place under the broiler until lightly browned and bubbly hot.

BROILED HADDOCK WITH LEMON SAUCE *6 servings*

2 pounds haddock fillets
3 tablespoons lemon juice
Salt and freshly ground black pepper

2 tablespoons butter
½ cup olive oil
½ teaspoon dry mustard
1½ teaspoons water .

1. Preheat broiler.

2. Cut the fish into serving pieces and place on an oiled broiler pan. Brush with one tablespoon of the lemon juice and season with salt and pepper. Dot with the butter.

3. Broil for about seven minutes, or until the fish flakes easily when tested with a fork.

4. Combine the oil, mustard, water, additional salt to taste, and the remaining lemon juice. Beat and heat. Pour over the fish.

HADDOCK WITH HERBED CRUMBS *4 to 6 servings*

2 pounds haddock fillets (or other fish fillets)
Salt
⅔ cup butter, melted
3 cups soft fresh bread crumbs

¼ teaspoon freshly ground black pepper
½ teaspoon crumbled dried orégano
½ teaspoon crumbled dried marjoram

1. Preheat oven to moderate (350° F.).

2. Cut the fish into four to six serving pieces. Arrange the pieces in a buttered baking pan. Sprinkle with salt and pour half of the melted butter over the fish.

3. Blend all the remaining ingredients and sprinkle the mixture over the fish. Bake for twenty-five to thirty minutes, or until fish flakes easily when tested with a fork.

HALIBUT STEAK AU BEURRE BLANC *6 servings*

Salt
1 tablespoon crab boil (available on grocery spice shelf)

1 halibut steak, 1½ inches thick (about 3 pounds)
Beurre Blanc (page 498)

1. Pour water into a fish cooker to a depth of two inches. There should be enough water to cover the halibut steak when it is added later. Add salt to taste and the crab boil. If crab boil is not available, add one teaspoon dried thyme and one bay leaf to the poaching liquid. Cover and bring to a boil. Simmer for fifteen minutes.

2. Add the halibut steak to the poaching liquid. Return to the boil, partially cover the kettle, and simmer the fish for twenty to thirty minutes, until it flakes easily when tested with a fork. Do not overcook. Drain the fish well and serve immediately with beurre blanc.

NORTHWEST STYLE HALIBUT   *6 servings*

2 pounds halibut steaks
¼ cup all-purpose flour
1 teaspoon salt
¼ teaspoon freshly ground pepper
⅛ teaspoon grated nutmeg
¼ cup melted butter
1½ cups milk

⅓ cup grated Parmesan cheese
½ teaspoon Worcestershire sauce
1 package (10 ounces) frozen
  chopped spinach, cooked and
  drained
Paprika

1. Preheat oven to moderate (350° F.).
2. Remove the skin and bones from the fish and cut the fish into serving pieces.
3. Blend the flour, salt, pepper, nutmeg and butter together in a small pan. Gradually stir in the milk and bring to a boil, stirring. Add the cheese and Worcestershire.
4. Combine the spinach with half of the sauce and spread in the bottom of a well-greased shallow baking dish.
5. Arrange the fish over the top of the spinach. Pour remaining sauce over the fish. Sprinkle with paprika and bake for about twenty-five minutes, or until the fish flakes easily when tested with a fork.

HALIBUT STEAKS WITH MUSHROOMS   *4 servings*

5 tablespoons butter
4 halibut steaks, 1 inch thick
  Salt and freshly ground black
  pepper
1 tablespoon minced shallots

½ pound mushrooms, chopped
3 tablespoons dry white wine
1 tablespoon lemon juice
1 tablespoon chopped parsley

1. Preheat oven to hot (400° F.).
2. Lightly grease the center of four pieces of heavy-duty aluminum foil with one tablespoon of the butter. Place a steak on each piece of foil. Season with salt and pepper.
3. Sauté the shallots in the remaining butter until translucent. Add the mushrooms. Cook for five minutes.
4. Add the wine, lemon juice and parsley and continue to cook until most of the liquid has evaporated. Spoon the mixture over the fish. Season with salt and pepper to taste.
5. Draw the edges of the foil together and seal the packages. Bake for twenty minutes, or until fish flakes easily when tested with a fork. Serve in the foil.

BAKED STUFFED MACKEREL   *4 or 5 servings*

1 mackerel (3 pounds)
¼ cup butter
½ chopped onion
¼ cup chopped celery
2 cups crumbs of day-old bread, lightly toasted
3 tablespoons finely chopped parsley
½ teaspoon crumbled dried thyme
¼ cup toasted sesame seeds
2 teaspoons salt
½ teaspoon freshly ground black pepper
2 slices of bacon, cut into halves
Lemon slices and parsley sprigs for garnish

1. Have fish cleaned but leave tail and head intact. Wash the fish well and pat it dry with paper towels.

2. Preheat oven to moderate (350° F.).

3. Heat the butter and in it cook the onion until it is wilted. Combine with the celery, bread crumbs, parsley, thyme, sesame seeds, half of the salt and half of the pepper.

4. Sprinkle the inside of the fish with the remaining salt and pepper. Spoon the filling into the cavity of the fish and skewer the opening. Place the fish in a baking dish and cover with the bacon slices.

5. Bake for forty-five minutes to one hour, or until fish flakes easily when tested with a fork. Garnish the fish with lemon slices and parsley, and serve.

SALMON WITH FRESH LEMON SAUCE   *6 servings*

1 onion, sliced
Salt
1 teaspoon freshly ground black pepper
1 bay leaf
2 tablespoons dillseeds
4 cups boiling water
2 tablespoons white vinegar
6 slices of fresh salmon
Fresh Lemon Sauce (see below)
Paprika for garnish

1. Combine onion, two teaspoons salt, the pepper, bay leaf, dillseeds, boiling water and vinegar in a deep nine- or ten-inch skillet or saucepan and bring to the boiling point.

2. Place the salmon on a plate or pie pan and tie in a cheesecloth to keep the fish from breaking apart. Immerse in the boiling mixture, cover, and cook for ten to fifteen minutes, until the fish flakes easily when tested with a fork. Remove from cooking liquid. Strain the liquid and reserve one and one-quarter cups.

3. Unwrap the fish and place it on a serving dish; keep warm. Sprinkle fish with salt to taste and serve with fresh lemon sauce. Garnish with paprika.

FRESH LEMON SAUCE: *About 2 cups*

3 tablespoons butter
3 tablespoons all-purpose flour
1¼ cups reserved cooking liquid
½ cup heavy cream
1 teaspoon salt
¼ teaspoon freshly ground black pepper
3 tablespoons fresh lemon juice

Melt the butter in a saucepan and blend in the flour. Add the cooking liquid and heavy cream gradually. Cook, stirring constantly, until the mixture is smooth and medium thick. Add remaining ingredients.

BAKED SALMON   *4 servings*

1 whole small salmon (5 pounds)
Salt and freshly ground black pepper
4 slices of bacon, finely chopped
3 small white onions, peeled and thinly sliced
½ green pepper, seeded and chopped
4 celery ribs, chopped
2 tablespoons butter
1 teaspoon finely chopped parsley
1 cup dry white wine

1. Have the fish dealer clean the salmon and split it without detaching the halves. Open it, wipe it clean, and season with salt and pepper. Arrange the opened fish in a shallow ovenproof dish.

2. Preheat oven to moderate (375° F.).

3. Cook the bacon slowly. When there is some fat in the skillet, add the onions, green pepper and celery. Continue cooking slowly; when the vegetables are soft, add one tablespoon of the butter and the parsley. When the parsley is wilted, season the mixture with pepper to taste.

4. Spoon the vegetable mixture on half of the opened fish. Fold over the other half. Pour the wine over the fish and dot the surface with the remaining butter.

5. Bake for forty-five to fifty minutes, or until the fish flakes easily when tested with a fork. Serve hot, with the pan juices.

SALMON IN ASPIC   *7 to 12 servings*

1 whole salmon (5 to 8 pounds)
1 teaspoon dried thyme
1 bay leaf, crumbled
1 onion, thinly sliced
Salt and freshly ground black pepper
¾ cup dry white wine
2½ cups Mayonnaise Aspic (page 468)
Cucumber slices, pimiento rounds, parsley sprigs and lemon wedges
Mayonnaise

1. Preheat oven to moderate (375° F.).

2. Rinse salmon inside and outside and dry with paper towels. Measure fish and oven. If fish is too long, remove head.

3. Place fish lengthwise on a long double-fold sheet of heavy-duty aluminum foil. Sprinkle inside of fish with thyme, bay leaf and onion. Sprinkle both inside and outside with salt and pepper. Bring up edges of foil and pour wine over fish. Completely enclose fish with foil, sealing edges tightly.

4. Place fish on a large baking sheet with edges. Bake for twelve to fifteen minutes a pound. To test for doneness, open foil and insert a fork into fish. If fish flakes easily, it is done. If not done, reclose foil and continue baking.

5. Open the foil, leaving fish in it. Chill.

6. Carefully remove fish to a large platter. Peel away skin from upper side. Spoon mayonnaise aspic over skinned surface. Rechill fish. Continue coating and chilling fish until all aspic is used.

7. Garnish fish with cucumber, pimiento, parsley and lemon. Serve with mayonnaise.

SALMON VERTE   *6 servings*

⅓ cup dry white wine
1 tablespoon lemon juice
¼ cup water
¼ teaspoon peppercorns
½ bay leaf
1 teaspoon salt
3 salmon steaks (8 ounces each), fresh or frozen, about 1 inch thick

1 cup mayonnaise
2 tablespoons finely chopped chives
2 tablespoons finely chopped parsley
2 tablespoons finely chopped cooked spinach
Cucumber and tomato slices (optional)

1. In a large skillet bring to a boil the wine, lemon juice, water, peppercorns, bay leaf and salt. Add the salmon steaks, cover, and poach for fifteen minutes, or until the salmon flakes easily when tested with a fork. Cool. Drain the salmon and arrange it on a serving dish.

2. Combine the mayonnaise, chives, parsley and spinach and mask the salmon with this mixture. Chill. Garnish with cucumber and tomato slices if desired.

SALMON AND MUSHROOMS ROYALE   *2 servings*

1 cup thinly sliced mushrooms
1 tablespoon finely chopped onion
¼ cup butter
1 can (7¾ ounces) salmon
¾ cup milk, approximately
2 tablespoons all-purpose flour
¼ teaspoon salt

Freshly ground black pepper
¼ teaspoon cayenne pepper (optional)
1 egg yolk, beaten
1 tablespoon finely chopped parsley
1 tablespoon dry sherry

1. Cook the mushrooms and onion in half of the butter, stirring. When mushrooms are wilted and most of the liquid has evaporated, remove them from the heat.

2. Drain the liquid from the salmon and combine the liquid with enough milk to make one cup. Melt the remaining butter and stir in the flour, using a wire whisk. Add the liquid, stirring rapidly with the whisk. When the mixture is thickened and smooth, add the mushroom mixture, salt, pepper to taste and cayenne. Cover and simmer for ten minutes.

3. Mix a little of the hot sauce with the egg yolk and then return all to the pan. Heat thoroughly. Stir in the salmon, parsley and sherry. Cook for about three minutes, or until thoroughly hot.

SALMON BAKE ITALIANO   *6 servings*

2 tablespoons butter
2 tablespoons all-purpose flour
1½ cups milk
2 cups grated Cheddar cheese
¼ teaspoon dry mustard
1 teaspoon salt
¼ teaspoon freshly ground black pepper

8 ounces elbow macaroni, cooked according to package directions
1 zucchini, sliced
1 can (1 pound) salmon, drained, boned and flaked
½ cup toasted bread crumbs

1. Preheat oven to moderate (350° F.).
2. In a saucepan melt the butter and blend in the flour. Add the milk gradually and cook over low heat, stirring constantly, until thickened. Stir in the cheese, seasonings, macaroni, zucchini and salmon.
3. Pour into a two-quart casserole and sprinkle bread crumbs around the edge. Bake for thirty minutes.

SALMON NEPTUNE   *6 servings*

1 can (1 pound) salmon, drained, boned and flaked
2 cups soft fresh bread crumbs
⅓ cup sliced pitted ripe olives
1 cup grated sharp Cheddar cheese
½ cup finely chopped parsley
1 cup milk
3 eggs

¼ cup minced onion
1 teaspoon salt
¼ teaspoon freshly ground black pepper
¼ cup lemon juice
Additional sliced pitted ripe olives for garnish

1. Preheat oven to moderate (375° F.).
2. In a large mixing bowl combine the flaked salmon with the bread crumbs, olives, cheese and parsley.
3. In a small mixing bowl mix lightly with a fork the milk, eggs, onion, salt and pepper.
4. Add the milk mixture and the lemon juice to the salmon and bread-crumb mixture and mix thoroughly.
5. Pack into a well-greased one-and-one-half-quart mold or a loaf pan (9 × 4 × 2 inches).
6. Set the mold or loaf pan in a larger pan containing water one inch deep. Bake for about one hour, until set.
7. Let the mold stand for five minutes. Then turn it out onto a serving dish and serve garnished with additional olives.

SHIOYAKI   (salmon with salt)   *2 servings*

1 teaspoon salt
2 small salmon steaks
1½ teaspoons fresh lime or lemon
   juice

2 lime or lemon wedges (optional)

1. Sprinkle half of the salt over the steaks and allow to stand for about thirty minutes.

2. Sprinkle the remaining salt over steaks. Broil six inches from source of heat for about four minutes on one side. Turn and broil on the other side for about six minutes, or until fish flakes easily when tested with a fork. If the steaks are to be broiled over charcoal, they may be skewered with two or three slender skewers to facilitate turning.

3. To serve, sprinkle with lime or lemon juice. If desired, garnish each steak with a lime or lemon wedge.

Salmon Mousse is an elegant first-course or light luncheon dish. Here are two methods for making such a dish. One uses a sieve or food mill, the other an electric blender.

SALMON MOUSSE   *6 servings*

1 envelope unflavored gelatin
¼ cup cold water or the liquid from
   canned salmon
½ cup boiling water
1 can (1 pound) salmon

1 tablespoon grated fresh horseradish
1 teaspoon lemon juice
1 cup heavy cream, whipped

1. Soften the gelatin in the cold water. Add the boiling water and stir until gelatin is completely dissolved.

2. Flake the salmon into a mixing bowl. Add horseradish and lemon juice. Gradually beat in the gelatin. Press through a fine sieve or food mill.

3. Fold the whipped cream into the mixture. Pour into a four-cup timbale mold and chill until set.

4. To serve, garnish with cucumber slices and parsley or watercress, or with Aspic Shells (page 477) placed on top and sides.

SALMON MOUSSE   *(blender method)*   *6 servings*

1 envelope unflavored gelatin
2 tablespoons lemon juice
1 small slice of onion
½ cup boiling water
½ cup mayonnaise

¼ teaspoon paprika
1 teaspoon dried dill
1 can (1 pound) salmon, drained
1 cup heavy cream

1. Empty the envelope of gelatin into container of an electric blender. Add the lemon juice, onion slice and boiling water.

Fish dishes with a different and delicate taste include Norwegian Fish Pudding and fish soufflé. Lobster Sauce and Egg Sauce go well with these.

2. Place blender cover on the container. Turn the motor to high speed and blend ingredients for forty seconds.

3. Turn the motor off. Add the mayonnaise, paprika, dill and salmon. Cover and blend at high speed.

4. Remove the cover and add the cream, one third at a time, blending for a few seconds after each addition. Blend for thirty seconds longer. Pour into a four-cup mold. Chill.

BREADED SEA SQUABS   *6 servings*

18 sea squabs (blowfish), cleaned
2 eggs, lightly beaten
1 tablespoon water

2 cups soft fresh bread crumbs
½ cup butter

1. Dip the sea squabs into a mixture of the eggs and water, then roll them in the bread crumbs.

2. Heat the butter and cook the fish on all sides until golden brown.

SEA SQUAB PROVENÇALE   *6 servings*

18 sea squabs (blowfish), cleaned
Milk
Seasoned all-purpose flour
Peanut oil

3 tablespoons butter
1 garlic clove, finely minced
Lemon juice
Finely chopped parsley

1. Dip the sea squabs into milk, then dredge them with seasoned flour.

2. Pour peanut oil into a skillet to a depth of one-quarter inch; heat. When hot, cook the sea squabs on all sides for six to eight minutes, until they are just cooked through.

3. Transfer the sea squabs to a hot platter. Pour off and discard the oil from the skillet. Add the butter to the skillet and cook to a golden brown. Quickly add the garlic, then pour the butter over the fish. Sprinkle with lemon juice and chopped parsley and serve immediately.

BROILED SHAD   *2 servings*

1 shad fillet
Salt and freshly ground black
pepper

Melted butter
Lemon wedges

1. Preheat oven to moderate (375° F.).

2. Place the shad in a heatproof baking dish and sprinkle with salt and pepper. Brush the fish generously with butter and place it under the broiler for about three minutes, until it is lightly browned.

3. Brush the fish with additional butter and bake for twelve to fifteen minutes, until the fish flakes easily when tested with a fork. Serve with lemon wedges and boiled potatoes.

BROILED MARINATED SHAD   *4 servings*

2 tablespoons lemon juice
1 bay leaf, crushed
⅛ teaspoon ground thyme
¼ cup salad oil
¼ teaspoon salt

Freshly ground black pepper
2 pounds boneless shad fillets
3 tablespoons melted butter
1 lemon, thinly sliced

1. Combine the lemon juice, bay leaf, thyme, oil, salt and pepper to taste in a shallow pan. Add the fish and marinate for thirty minutes, turning once. Drain.
2. Preheat broiler.
3. Place the fish on the broiler rack and broil for ten to fifteen minutes, or until fish flakes easily when tested with a fork. Turn once as it broils. Transfer fish to a hot platter. Sprinkle with melted butter and garnish with lemon slices.

GRILLED SHAD ROE WITH ASPARAGUS   *3 to 6 servings*

3 pairs of shad roe
1 teaspoon salt
⅛ teaspoon freshly ground black
  pepper
⅓ cup butter

¾ teaspoon lemon juice
⅓ cup chopped parsley
Lemon wedges
2 pounds fresh asparagus, steamed
  and buttered

1. Wipe the shad roe with a damp cloth and sprinkle them with salt and pepper.
2. Melt the butter in a heavy nine-inch skillet and add the shad roe. Cook over low heat for ten to fifteen minutes, until delicately browned, turning once. Remove the roe to a warm platter.
3. Add the lemon juice to the pan drippings and pour over the roe. Sprinkle with chopped parsley and serve with lemon wedges. Serve with buttered steamed asparagus.

SHAD ROE SOUFFLÉ   *3 or 4 servings*

2 pairs of shad roe
½ teaspoon salt
1 tablespoon lemon juice
6 tablespoons melted butter
¼ cup all-purpose flour
¾ cup milk

Salt and freshly ground white
  pepper
1 tablespoon chopped chives
4 eggs yolks, lightly beaten
6 egg whites, stiffly beaten

1. Preheat oven to moderate (375° F.).
2. Place the shad roe in a shallow pan, cover with water, and simmer for ten minutes.

3. Remove the roe from the water and cool, reserving two tablespoons of the cooking water. Break the roe into small pieces and add the salt, lemon juice and two tablespoons of the melted butter.

4. Blend the flour into the remaining butter in a saucepan. Slowly add the reserved cooking liquid and the milk, stirring. Bring to a boil, stirring, and simmer for one minute. Season with salt and pepper to taste; add the chives.

5. Add the egg yolks and shad roe to the sauce. Fold in the beaten egg whites.

6. Pour the mixture into a buttered two-quart soufflé dish and bake for thirty to forty minutes, until puffed and brown. Serve at once.

POACHED RED SNAPPER   *6 to 8 servings*

1 red snapper (4 pounds)	1 bay leaf
2 teaspoons salt, or more	1 teaspoon dried thyme
2 celery ribs	10 peppercorns
4 parsley sprigs	

1. Have the red snapper thoroughly cleaned and scaled but leave the head and tail intact. Wrap the fish in cheesecloth to facilitate removing it from the pan when cooked.

2. Place the fish in a large oval baking pan or fish cooker. Add enough water to cover and the remaining ingredients.

3. Bring to a boil and simmer for about forty-five minutes, until the fish flakes easily when tested with a fork. Very carefully remove the fish from the cooking liquid, using two flat spatulas or pancake turners. Place the first on a long oval platter and remove the cheesecloth carefully.

4. Chill the fish and serve as a first-course or luncheon dish with Green Mayonnaise (page 468).

BAKED RED SNAPPER, SOUTHERN STYLE   *6 to 8 servings*

1 red snapper (6 pounds)	½ cup chopped parsley
Butter	½ cup butter
Salt and freshly ground black pepper	1 onion, thinly sliced
	2 garlic cloves, finely minced
Pinch of ground thyme	¼ cup all-purpose flour
1 bay leaf	4 cups canned tomatoes, preferably
¾ cup chopped celery	Italian style with basil
1 cup chopped green peppers	

1. Preheat oven to moderate (325° F.).

2. Have the red snapper thoroughly cleaned and scaled but leave the head and tail intact.

3. Rub the fish with butter and sprinkle both inside and outside with salt and pepper. Place the fish in a pan lined with heavy-duty aluminum foil.

4. Sprinkle the fish with thyme, bay leaf, celery, green peppers and parsley.

5. Heat the butter and sauté the onion and garlic in it until golden but not brown. Stir in the flour; when it is blended, stir in the tomatoes. When the mixture comes to a boil and is slightly thickened, season with salt and pepper.

6. Pour the sauce over the fish and place pan in the oven. Bake, basting frequently, for about one hour, until the fish flakes easily when tested with a fork. Serve with steamed potatoes or rice.

RED SNAPPER WITH LEMON BUTTER   *4 to 6 servings*

3 pounds red-snapper fillets
All-purpose flour
Salt and freshly ground black pepper
¼ cup vegetable oil

¾ cup butter
2 tablespoons lemon juice
4 slices of lemon
2 tablespoons chopped parsley

1. Dredge the fish lightly on both sides with flour, salt and pepper.

2. Heat the oil in a skillet and cook the fish until golden brown on both sides, three to five minutes to a side. Do not overcook. The fish is done when the flesh flakes easily when tested with a fork.

3. Meanwhile, melt the butter and add lemon juice. Simmer briefly. Transfer the fish to a hot platter, pour the butter over it, and garnish with lemon slices and parsley.

BAKED RED SNAPPER WITH SHRIMP STUFFING
6 to 8 servings

1 red snapper (4 to 6 pounds), cleaned
Salt and freshly ground black pepper
½ cup butter
3 tablespoons minced onion
1 tablespoon all-purpose flour
½ teaspoon crumbled dried basil

1 tablespoon minced parsley
½ cup milk
½ pound shrimp, cooked and chopped (about 1 cup)
1 cup cooked rice
3 tablespoons lemon juice
Lemon slices and watercress for garnish

1. Wipe the fish with damp paper towels. Sprinkle inside generously with salt and pepper.

2. Melt half of the butter in a skillet. Add the onion and cook until transparent. Stir in the flour, basil and parsley. Season with salt and pepper.

Gradually add milk, stirring to form a thick sauce. Add shrimp, rice and lemon juice. Stir until blended. Remove stuffing from heat.

3. Preheat oven to hot (400° F.).

4. Place the fish in a foil-lined pan. Place skewers through both edges of body cavity and fill cavity with stuffing. Lace closed with string. Cover tail with foil to prevent burning.

5. Melt remaining butter and pour over fish. Bake for fifty to seventy minutes, or until fish flakes easily when tested with a fork. Baste occasionally with pan drippings, or with more butter if needed. Serve garnished with lemon slices and watercress.

SOLE AMANDINE   *4 servings*

4 sole fillets	¼ cup peanut oil, approximately
Milk	½ cup butter
All-purpose flour	Toasted slivered almonds
Salt and freshly ground white pepper	

1. Place the fillets in a dish and add milk barely to cover. Let stand for one hour.

2. Drain the fish, wipe lightly, and dredge with flour seasoned with salt and pepper.

3. Cook the fish in hot oil until golden brown on both sides, turning once. Remove the fish to a warm platter.

4. Quickly wipe out the skillet and add the butter. When the butter is hot and foamy, add the almonds. Pour butter and almonds over the fish.

SOLE BELLE AURORE   *6 servings*

3 tablespoons butter	1 tablespoon minced shallots or onion
2 tablespoons all-purpose flour	
1 cup milk or half milk and half light cream	2 egg yolks, beaten
6 sole fillets	¼ cup minced parsley
½ cup clam juice or Fish Stock (page 475)	

1. Melt two tablespoons of the butter in a saucepan. Stir in the flour. Gradually stir in the milk and cook, stirring, until the sauce is very thick. Cook sauce over low heat, stirring occasionally, while preparing and cooking fillets.

2. Roll the fillets and tie them at both ends with coarse thread or secure with food picks. Heat the remaining butter in a skillet and arrange the fillets

in it. Add the clam juice and shallots, bring the liquid to a boil, and cook fillets over very low heat for ten to twelve minutes.

3. Place fillets on a hot serving dish and discard the threads. Gradually stir the liquid from the fillets into the egg yolks, then stir egg-yolk mixture into the hot sauce. Cook the sauce, stirring, for two minutes. Stir in the parsley and pour sauce over the fish.

MOUSSE OF SOLE   *4 servings*

1½ pounds fillet of sole
2 egg whites
2 cups heavy cream
¾ teaspoon salt
¼ teaspoon freshly ground black pepper
Dash of cayenne pepper
¼ teaspoon grated nutmeg

1. Grind the sole four times, using a fine grinding wheel, or blend in an electric blender on high speed. If using the blender, work on only a little of the fish at a time, blending until the fish is very finely shredded. Then pound it with a wooden spoon.

2. Place the sole in a mixing bowl and place the bowl over cracked ice. Gradually beat in the egg whites, using a whisk or wooden spoon.

3. Stir in the cream, a little at a time, making certain it is absorbed after each addition.

4. Season with the salt, pepper, cayenne and nutmeg. Allow the mixture to stand in the bowl over ice for one hour.

5. Preheat oven to moderate (350° F.).

6. Stir the mousse and pour it into a buttered fish mold. Cover with wax paper or buttered brown paper and set the mold in a pan containing one inch of hot water.

7. Bake for about twenty-five minutes, until firm. Unmold the mousse and serve it hot with Lobster Sauce (page 482) or Shrimp Sauce (page 482).

Note: Any extra mousse mixture that will not fit into the fish mold may be poured into individual custard cups, set in a pan containing a little hot water, and baked until firm.

PAUPIETTES OF SOLE WITH MUSHROOM SAUCE   *6 servings*

1 can (7¾ ounces) salmon, drained, boned and flaked
2 tablespoons minced parsley
2 tablespoons chopped chives
½ teaspoon dried tarragon
½ teaspoon paprika
1 tablespoon lemon juice
6 sole fillets
1 tablespoon melted butter
Mushroom Sauce (page 480)

1. Preheat oven to moderate (350° F.).
2. Mix the salmon, parsley, chives, tarragon, paprika and lemon juice.

3. Spread some of the salmon filling on each piece of sole to within one-quarter inch of the edge. Roll up the sole in jelly-roll fashion, starting with the tail end. Secure with food picks.

4. Place the sole in a buttered shallow baking dish. Brush the sole with melted butter and bake for twenty-five minutes, or until the fish flakes easily when tested with a fork. Drain sole and remove food picks. Arrange on a serving dish and top with mushroom sauce.

SOLE TURBANS WITH CRAB STUFFING   *6 servings*

6 sole fillets
Salt and freshly ground black pepper
½ pound crabmeat, fresh, frozen or canned
1 tablespoon minced onion

1 tablespoon chopped parsley
1 tablespoon chopped celery
6 tablespoons melted butter
½ cup cracker crumbs
1 egg

1. Preheat oven to moderate (375° F.).

2. Sprinkle fish with salt and pepper. Coil each fillet inside a buttered muffin tin or six-ounce custard cup. If necessary, trim top of each fillet to make it even. Drain crabmeat, remove fibers, and flake.

3. Sauté onion, parsley and celery in two tablespoons of the butter until tender. Remove from heat. Add crumbs, crabmeat and egg. Mix well and season with salt and pepper.

4. Spoon crabmeat mixture into center of fillets. Brush with remaining butter. Bake for fifteen minutes, or until fish flakes easily when tested with fork. Remove fillets carefully with two spoons.

FISH CURRY   *8 servings*

1 cup yoghurt
2 teaspoons lemon juice
½ teaspoon ground turmeric
1 teaspoon ground coriander
1 teaspoon cayenne pepper
1 teaspoon ground ginger
1 garlic clove, minced

¼ teaspoon curry powder
1 teaspoon dried orégano
¼ cup chopped onion
4 fish fillets (sole or pike)
½ cup olive or vegetable oil
⅛ teaspoon cuminseeds

1. Preheat oven to moderate (350° F.).

2. Put all ingredients except the fish fillets, oil and cuminseeds through a food mill, or blend in an electric blender at high speed for two minutes.

3. Cut the fish fillets into halves. Roll each half and arrange in a shallow baking dish.

4. Combine the oil and cuminseeds in a skillet and heat until dark brown. Add the blended ingredients and brown, stirring constantly. Pour the mixture over the fish and bake for thirty minutes.

TURBAN OF SOLE WITH MOUSSE   *6 to 8 servings*

½ cup Fish Stock (page 475)
½ cup water
¼ cup butter
  Salt
1 cup sifted all-purpose flour
2 large whole eggs
2 egg whites
½ pound skinless and boneless sole, flounder or whiting fillets, put through the finest blade of a food grinder (about 1 cup)

White pepper and grated nutmeg
⅓ cup chilled heavy cream
6 skinless and boneless sole, flounder or whiting fillets
  Sauce Aurore (page 482)

1. Bring the fish stock, water, butter and one teaspoon salt to a boil in a saucepan. As soon as butter has melted, remove the mixture from the heat and add the flour all at once. Beat vigorously with a wooden spoon to blend. Return saucepan to heat and continue beating over moderate heat until mixture leaves the sides of the saucepan and begins to film the bottom. Remove from the heat. Make a well in the center, break in one egg, and beat vigorously until thoroughly blended. Repeat with second egg and one egg white. Finally beat in last egg white. This mixture is called a panade.

2. Measure the one cup of ground fish into a mixing bowl. Add exactly one cup of the panade. Beat vigorously and add salt, pepper and nutmeg to taste. Beat in the cream by spoonfuls, beating well after each addition so that mixture retains its body.

3. Butter generously a six-cup ring mold. Score the fish fillets lightly and arrange them, scored side up, at right angles to the circumference of the mold, like the spokes of a wheel. Pack the mousse mixture into the lined mold. Fill fillets to within one-quarter inch of the top. (Extra mousse may be baked separately.) Cover mold with buttered foil and refrigerate until ready to bake.

4. Preheat oven to moderate (375° F.).

5. Set the mold in a pan of boiling water and place in the bottom third of the oven. Bake for forty-five minutes, or until mousse has swelled over top of mold and a knife plunged into the center comes out clean.

6. Unmold onto a hot buttered platter. Center of mousse may be filled with creamed shellfish or mushrooms. Spoon a little sauce aurore over mousse and serve remainder separately. Serve with rice.

SWORDFISH IN TOMATO SAUCE   *6 servings*

3 pounds swordfish (2 slices, each 1½ inches thick)
1½ cups finely chopped parsley
½ cup olive oil
1 garlic clove, finely minced
¼ cup lemon juice
2 cups (two 8-ounce cans) tomato sauce
Salt and freshly ground black pepper

1. Preheat oven to hot (425° F.).
2. Cut the fish into serving pieces, if desired, and arrange in one layer in a buttered baking dish.
3. Combine the parsley, oil and garlic in a small skillet and cook for three minutes, stirring occasionally. Add the lemon juice, tomato sauce, and salt and pepper to taste. Heat thoroughly.
4. Pour the sauce over the fish and bake for twenty-five minutes, or until fish flakes easily when tested with a fork.

SWORDFISH WITH CAPERS   *4 servings*

1½ pounds swordfish, about 1½ inches thick
Salt and freshly ground black pepper
¼ cup olive oil
2 tablespoons finely chopped shallots
1 garlic clove, finely minced
3 cups peeled, seeded and chopped ripe or canned tomatoes
⅓ cup dry white wine
1 teaspoon lemon juice
2 tablespoons chopped celery
1 tablespoon chopped parsley
1 tablespoon butter
2 teaspoons flour
1 tablespoon capers

1. Preheat oven to hot (400° F.).
2. Season the fish with salt and pepper to taste and brown quickly on all sides in the oil. Place in a buttered shallow baking dish.
3. Top with the shallots, garlic, tomatoes, wine, lemon juice, celery and parsley. Bake for fifteen to twenty minutes, or until the fish flakes easily when tested with a fork. Transfer the fish to a warm platter.
4. Strain the cooking liquid and add the butter which has been blended with the flour. Heat, stirring, until the sauce thickens. Pour the sauce over the fish and top with the capers.

NIKA HAZELTON'S SPANISH TROUT   *4 servings*

4 whole trout, cleaned
½ lemon
Salt and freshly ground black pepper
2 tablespoons olive oil
½ cup soft fresh bread crumbs
1 garlic clove, minced
2 tablespoons finely chopped parsley
⅓ cup dry sherry

1. Preheat oven to moderate (350° F.).

2. Rub the trout with the lemon, then squeeze the lemon and reserve the juice. Season the fish with salt and pepper.

3. Heat the oil. Remove it from the heat and stir in the bread crumbs, garlic and parsley. Sprinkle half of this mixture over the bottom of a greased shallow baking dish. Place the trout on top. Sprinkle the fish with the remaining bread-crumb mixture. Sprinkle with the reserved lemon juice.

4. Bake the fish for ten minutes, then add sherry. Continue to bake for ten to fifteen minutes, basting occasionally with the sherry. When the fish is done, it should flake easily when tested with a fork.

TROUT WITH BAY LEAF   *6 servings*

6 rainbow trout, fresh or frozen
  Salt and freshly ground black pepper
1 garlic clove
1 teaspoon dried thyme
6 bay leaves

12 slices of bacon
2 tablespoons salad oil
¼ cup melted butter
  Juice of 2 lemons
¼ cup cooked parsley

1. If frozen fish are used, defrost them.

2. Preheat oven to hot (400° F.).

3. Sprinkle the trout inside and outside with salt and pepper. Crush the garlic and thyme together to make a paste. Put some of the paste in each fish. Place one bay leaf in the interior of each fish. Neatly wrap the fish in bacon, using two slices for each fish.

4. Oil a baking dish large enough to hold all the trout and arrange them in it. Sprinkle with melted butter and bake for ten to fifteen minutes, or until bacon and fish are done. Baste the fish as they cook.

5. Transfer the fish to a warm serving platter and sprinkle with lemon juice and parsley. Serve, if desired, with buttered boiled potatoes sprinkled with parsley.

SEAFOOD RING   *About 6 servings*

1½ pounds potatoes, peeled and thinly sliced
6 tablespoons butter
1¼ cups milk, approximately
½ pound mushrooms, sliced
2 tablespoons all-purpose flour
1 egg

¾ cup grated sharp Cheddar cheese
  Salt and freshly ground white pepper
½ pound shrimp, cooked, shelled, deveined and halved
2 cans (7 ounces each) tuna

1. Cook the potatoes in salted water until tender. Drain thoroughly and mash with half of the butter and about one-quarter cup of the milk. The potatoes should be stiff enough to hold shape.

2. Preheat oven to moderate (350° F.).

3. Melt the remaining butter and add the mushrooms. Cook gently until tender. Add the flour and cook, stirring, for about three minutes. Bring one cup of milk to a boil and add to the blend, stirring vigorously until thickened. Add a little of the hot sauce to the egg and mix. Return to the remaining sauce and cook, stirring, for two minutes. Add one-half cup of the cheese and stir until melted. Season to taste.

4. Place layers of the fish and sauce in a buttered baking dish and arrange the potatoes in a ring on top. Sprinkle the surface with the remaining cheese and bake for twenty to thirty minutes, until bubbly.

BROILED WHITING WITH LEMON-MUSTARD SAUCE
4 servings

1½ pounds thawed frozen or dressed fresh whiting
1 teaspoon grated lemon rind
¼ cup lemon juice
¼ cup salad oil
¼ teaspoon salt
⅛ teaspoon freshly ground black pepper

1 tablespoon chopped parsley
2 teaspoons prepared mustard, preferably Dijon
Lemon quarters and parsley sprigs for garnish

1. Split the whiting lengthwise. Combine the rind, juice, oil, salt, pepper, parsley and mustard.

2. Brush the whiting well with the sauce; place skin side down on a greased shallow broiling pan. Broil, four to five inches from the heat, for about eight minutes, brushing frequently with the sauce, until the fish flakes easily when tested with a fork. It is not necessary to turn the fish.

3. Serve garnished with the lemon quarters and parsley sprigs.

NORWEGIAN FISH PUDDING   *6 servings*

1 pound fish fillets, fresh or frozen, cut into small pieces
1½ cups milk
2 tablespoons potato starch or cornstarch

2 eggs
1 cup heavy cream
¼ teaspoon grated nutmeg

1. Preheat oven to moderate (325° F.).

2. Into the container of an electric blender put the fish fillets, one cup of the milk, the starch and eggs. Cover and blend on high speed for two minutes. Remove the cover and, with the motor on, gradually add the remaining milk. Pour in the cream, add the nutmeg, and turn off the motor.

3. Pour the mixture into a buttered one-quart mold. Set the mold in a pan containing warm water about one inch deep and bake for one hour. Turn out and serve with Sauce Hollandaise (page 485) or Sour-Cream and Dill Sauce (page 489).

OVEN-BREADED FISH   *4 to 6 servings*

1 tablespoon salt
1 cup milk
3 fish fillets (about 1½ pounds)
¾ cup fine dry bread crumbs
½ teaspoon finely chopped fresh rosemary

¼ teaspoon ground thyme
¼ cup butter, melted
Paprika and lemon wedges

1. Preheat oven to very hot (525° F.).
2. Add the salt to the milk. Cut the fillets into serving pieces and dip first into the milk and then into the crumbs mixed with the rosemary and thyme.
3. Arrange the fish pieces in a well-greased baking dish and pour the butter over them evenly. Bake on the top shelf of the oven for about twelve minutes. Sprinkle with paprika and serve with lemon wedges.

. . . .

SHELLFISH

. . . .

BURGUNDIAN CLAMS   *4 or 5 servings*

20 large clams
½ cup butter, at room temperature
¼ cup fine dry bread crumbs
1 tablespoon finely chopped parsley
2 garlic cloves, finely minced
2 teaspoons finely chopped shallots or green onions
Freshly ground black pepper

3 tablespoons finely chopped Swiss cheese
Grated Parmesan cheese or bacon (optional)

1. Have clams opened and leave them on the half shell.
2. Preheat oven to hot (425° F.).
3. Combine the butter, bread crumbs, parsley, garlic, shallots, pepper to taste and Swiss cheese, and work the mixture to a paste.
4. Using a small spatula, spread the mixture over the opened clams. If desired, sprinkle with grated Parmesan cheese or top each with bits of bacon. Arrange the clams on pie plates and bake for eight to ten minutes, until the clams are thoroughly heated and bubbling. Serve piping hot.

CLAM FRITTERS   *About 3 dozen fritters*

1½ cups sifted all-purpose flour
½ teaspoon salt
½ cup plus 3 tablespoons butter
3 eggs, lightly beaten
¾ cup beer

2 dozen fresh cherrystone clams or
2 cups drained minced canned
   clams
3 egg whites, stiffly beaten
   Lemon wedges and parsley sprigs
   for garnish

1. Place the flour and salt in a mixing bowl. Melt three tablespoons of the butter and add with the eggs to the bowl. Mix well. Gradually stir in the beer. Allow the batter to stand in a warm place, such as atop the stove, for one hour.

2. Open the clams, remove the meat, and chop finely. Reserve the clam liquor for use in chowder. Fold the minced clams and the egg whites into the batter.

3. Heat the remaining butter in a pan, pour off the clear yellow liquid (clarified butter) into a heavy skillet, and discard the sediment. Heat the clarified butter. When it is hot but not smoking, drop in the batter by spoonfuls. When the undersides of the fritters are lightly browned, turn the fritters and brown the other sides. Drain on paper towels.

4. Place fritters on a warm platter and keep warm until all are cooked. To serve, garnish with lemon wedges and parsley sprigs.

CLAMS MEXICAINE   *4 servings*

4 scallions, trimmed and chopped
1 large green pepper, cored, seeded
   and chopped
½ cup olive oil
1 cup uncooked rice
1 cup Italian plum tomatoes,
   drained

1 cup tomato juice
2 cups (two 8-ounce cans) minced
   clams or 2 cups fresh clams,
   chopped, with their juice
   Salt
1 teaspoon chili powder, or more

1. Cook the scallions and pepper in the oil for three minutes. Add the rice and cook, stirring, for three minutes longer.

2. Add the tomatoes, tomato juice and one cup clam juice. If necessary, add enough water to make the cup of liquid. Season the mixture with salt to taste and chili powder; cover. Simmer for twenty minutes, or until rice is tender. Stir in the clams and heat through. Serve immediately.

STEAMED CLAMS   *4 servings*

4 quarts soft-shelled clams
½ cup water
⅔ cup butter
2 tablespoons lemon juice

Salt and freshly ground black
pepper
Dry white wine

1. Wash clams under cold running water until free of sand. Scrub with abrasive sponge or cloth to remove remaining grime.

2. Boil the water in a large pot and add clams. Cover the pot and lower the heat to minimum. Steam until clams barely open. Stir occasionally so that clams get cooked evenly.

3. Remove clams from the pot, reserving broth. Strain the broth through cheesecloth. Place one-half cup broth in a small bowl for each serving. About two cups of broth will be left. Reserve to serve separately.

4. Melt butter and add lemon juice, salt and pepper to taste, and a little white wine if desired. Divide among small bowls and serve with a slice of lemon or a sprig of watercress.

5. Heap clams into soup bowls and serve with dry white wine. Provide fingerbowls and a large bowl for shells.

Note: To prepare the soup to be served after the clams are eaten, reheat the remaining broth. Add two cups hot water and four tablespoons lemon juice. Garnish with watercress just before serving, or cook for one minute with very thin slices of scallions. Stir and serve.

STUFFED QUAHOGS   *8 servings*

2 dozen quahogs (chowder clams)
¼ cup water
¼ cup minced onion
¼ cup finely chopped celery
¼ cup chopped green pepper
2 cups soft fresh bread crumbs
12 slices of bacon, each cut into halves
Parsley for garnish

1. Preheat oven to hot (450° F.).

2. Wash the clams well and place them in a kettle with the water. Steam over moderate heat just until the clams open wide. Remove the meat and reserve half the shells for stuffing. Reserve the clam broth.

3. Remove the meat from the clams and grind it. Combine it with the onion, celery, pepper and bread crumbs. Dampen the mixture with clam broth, just enough to bind. Stuff the twenty-four reserved clam shells.

4. Lay half a slice of bacon across the top of each stuffed clam and arrange the clams on a baking dish. Bake until bacon is crisp. Garnish each stuffed clam with a parsley sprig and serve hot, with lemon wedges if desired.

CRABMEAT CHASSEUR   *6 servings*

3 tablespoons butter
4 large mushrooms, sliced
2 teaspoons finely chopped shallots
2 tablespoons tomato paste
1¼ cups heavy cream, approximately
1 pound lump crabmeat, fresh, canned or frozen
Salt and freshly ground black pepper
2 egg yolks
1 teaspoon chopped parsley
1 teaspoon chopped chives
1 teaspoon chopped fresh tarragon
Cognac (optional)

1. *Crabmeat Chasseur.* Melt three table-spoons butter in a chafing dish. Add four large mushrooms, sliced, and cook, stirring, for five minutes.

2. Add two teaspoons finely chopped shal-lots. Stir until most of the liquid given up by mushrooms evaporates. Add two tablespoons tomato paste and cook for five minutes longer.

3. Pour in approximately one cup of heavy cream and cook, stirring, until ingredients are thoroughly heated.

4. Pick over one pound lump crabmeat. Add it to the mixture and season with salt and pepper to taste. Stir gently and heat well, but do not break up pieces of crab-meat.

5. Mix two egg yolks with one-quarter cup of heavy cream. Add this mixture and one teaspoon each of chopped fresh parsley, chives and tarragon. Heat to thicken slightly but do not allow to come to a boil.

6. To heighten the flavor of the dish, a gen-erous dash of cognac may be added. Keep hot over water bath of chafing dish.

1. Melt the butter in a skillet or chafing dish. Add the mushrooms and cook, stirring, for five minutes.

2. Add the shallots. Stir until most of liquid given up by mushrooms evaporates. Add the tomato paste and cook for five minutes longer.

3. Pour in approximately one cup of the cream and cook, stirring, until ingredients are thoroughly heated.

4. Pick over the crabmeat. Add it to the mixture and season with salt and pepper to taste. Stir gently and heat well, but do not break up pieces of crabmeat.

5. Mix egg yolks with one-quarter cup of the cream. Add this mixture and the chopped herbs to the crabmeat. Heat to thicken slightly but do not allow to come to boil. To heighten the flavor of the dish, a generous dash of cognac may be added.

6. Keep hot over water bath of chafing dish. Serve with rice or buttered toast and tossed green salad.

CRABMEAT DEWEY   6 servings

2 tablespoons butter
3 large mushrooms, finely chopped
½ green pepper, finely chopped
1 tablespoon all-purpose flour
1 cup heavy cream
¼ teaspoon salt
⅛ teaspoon freshly ground white pepper

2 egg yolks
¼ cup dry sherry
1 pound lump crabmeat, fresh or canned, picked over well
2 clams, finely minced, with juice, or ¼ cup chopped canned clams with 2 tablespoons juice

1. Melt the butter in the top of a double boiler and sauté the mushrooms and green pepper in it. Add the flour and blend well. Add the cream all at once, stirring vigorously with a wire whisk. Add salt and pepper.

2. Beat the egg yolks and blend with the sherry. Add to the cream sauce.

3. Add the crabmeat and chopped clams and cook just long enough to heat thoroughly. Do not boil after the egg yolks are added. Serve on toast points in heated individual casseroles.

CRABMEAT SOUFFLÉ   3 or 4 servings

3 tablespoons butter
1 tablespoon grated onion
¼ cup all-purpose flour
¾ cup milk
Salt and freshly ground white pepper

1 tablespoon curry powder
2 tablespoons lemon juice
1½ cups crabmeat
4 eggs yolks, lightly beaten
6 egg whites

1. Preheat oven to moderate (375° F.).

2. Melt the butter, add the onion, and sauté for two or three minutes without browning. Blend in the flour.

3. Gradually stir in the milk, bring to a boil, stirring, and simmer for one minute. Season with salt and pepper to taste and add the curry powder.

4. Add the lemon juice, crabmeat and egg yolks.

5. Beat the egg whites until stiff and fold into the crab mixture. Pour into a buttered two-quart soufflé dish and bake for thirty-five to forty-five minutes, until puffed and brown. Serve at once.

CRAB PILAFF   *4 servings*

4 slices of bacon
2 onions, peeled and chopped
1 garlic clove, minced
2 ripe tomatoes, peeled, seeded and chopped
1 teaspoon crumbled dried basil
Salt and freshly ground black pepper

3 tablespoons tomato purée
1 pound crabmeat
¼ cup cognac
2 cups dry white wine
2 tablespoons chopped parsley
Pinch of sugar

1. Sauté the bacon until crisp. Remove the slices, break into bits, and reserve.

2. In the fat remaining in the pan sauté the onion and garlic; when just soft, add the tomatoes. Sprinkle with the basil and salt and pepper to taste. Cook over low heat until well blended.

3. Stir in the tomato purée and add the crabmeat. Pour the cognac over the mixture and blaze. When the flame dies, add the white wine, parsley and sugar. Cook until well blended, stirring. To serve, garnish with crumbled bacon.

LOBSTER GRATINÉ   *4 servings*

2 cups dry white French vermouth
2 cups water
1 large onion, thinly sliced
1 medium carrot, thinly sliced
1 medium celery rib, thinly sliced
6 parsley sprigs
1 bay leaf
1 tablespoon dried tarragon or 1 fresh tarragon sprig

Salt
4 peppercorns
4 live lobsters (1½ pounds each)
Butter
¼ cup all-purpose flour
½ cup heavy cream
½ cup grated Swiss cheese
Freshly ground black pepper

1. Combine the vermouth, water, onion, carrot, celery, parsley, bay leaf, tarragon, two teaspoons salt and the peppercorns in a fish kettle or steamer. Simmer for fifteen minutes.

2. If possible, tie the lobsters to a rack so they will stay flat during cooking. Add the lobsters to the rapidly boiling liquid. Otherwise, the lobsters may be dropped into the boiling liquid. Cover closely and steam the lobsters for eighteen to twenty minutes, or until head-feelers can be pulled easily from the sockets. Remove the lobsters and set aside. Place the cooking liquid over high heat and reduce to approximately two cups. Strain.

3. Melt one-fourth cup butter in a saucepan and blend in the flour, stirring with a wire whisk. Cook for two minutes but do not brown. Add half of the cooking liquid, stirring vigorously with the whisk. Add the rest of the cooking liquid and cook, stirring, for one minute. Add the cream. When well blended, stir in all but two tablespoons of the cheese. Season with salt and pepper to taste.

4. Cut off the claws and legs and underpart of lobster shells. Remove sacs and spongy tissues near head of lobsters to expose tail meat and green matter. Cut crisscross slashes through tail meat. The tail meat is, of course, left in the shell. Cover tail meat with sauce. Spoon a bit of sauce into chest cavities.

5. Remove the meat from the claws and place the meat in the chest cavities. Cover claw meat with sauce. Sprinkle with remaining cheese and dot with butter. Arrange lobsters in a broiling pan and set under a moderate broiler to heat through and brown the top.

GRILLED LOBSTERS WITH TARRAGON   *4 servings*

4 small lobsters (1¼ pounds each)
1 cup soft fresh bread crumbs
½ cup butter, at room temperature
2 tablespoons finely chopped fresh tarragon or 2 teaspoons dried tarragon
¼ teaspoon chopped fresh thyme

1 tablespoon finely chopped parsley
Salt and freshly ground black pepper
Melted butter
Lemon wedges
Anchovy Butter (page 499)

1. Place the lobsters on their back shells on a wooden board. Quickly sever spinal cord by plunging a sharp knife through to back shell where body and tail of lobster are joined. Chop through the back shell fore and aft to cut into halves. When all lobsters are split into halves, remove and discard small sac below head. Remove and discard intestinal vein running down center of lobster. Remove the soft green liver and orange coral or roe from cavity of lobsters and place in a mixing bowl.

2. To the mixing bowl add the bread crumbs, butter, tarragon, thyme, and parsley. Blend well with the fingers. Season with salt and pepper to taste.

3. Fill the cavity of each lobster half with an equal portion of the mixture. Cover the filled portion with aluminum foil. Brush the exposed tails with butter and sprinkle with salt and pepper.

4. Place cut sides down over hot coals. Place the claws on the grill. Grill

the lobsters on both sides, brushing occasionally with butter. The total cooking time should be fifteen to twenty minutes.

5. At the end remove the foil and gently turn cut side to coals to let stuffing brown lightly. Handle with care or stuffing will fall out. Garnish with lemon wedges and serve hot with anchovy butter.

COLD STUFFED LOBSTER   *30 picnic servings*

8 gallons sea water, if available; if not, plain water
2 cups vinegar, if sea water is used
15 lobsters (1 pound each)
24 eggs, hard-cooked
⅓ cup finely chopped chives
15 shallots, finely chopped
1 cup fresh mayonnaise
¾ cup finely chopped parsley
Salt and freshly ground black pepper
¼ cup mustard (preferably Dijon or Düsseldorf)

1. Combine the water and vinegar in a kettle large enough to hold the lobsters. (If sea water is not available, cook the lobsters in plain water according to any standard recipe.) Bring sea water and vinegar to a boil and add the lobsters. Cook for fifteen minutes.

2. Drain the lobsters. When they are cool, split them into halves. Remove the hard sac near the top of the head of each and discard. Reserve the coral, liver and roe.

3. Put the eggs through a fine sieve and add the chives, shallots, mayonnaise, parsley, salt and pepper to taste and the mustard.

4. Force the coral, liver and roe through a sieve and add to the mixture. Spoon some of the mixture into the cavity of each lobster half; or use a pastry bag to pipe the mixture into the cavities.

SPANISH DEVILED LOBSTER
12 first-course servings or 4 main-course servings

½ cup olive oil
1 garlic clove, fincly minced
2 lobsters, split down the back, cleaned and with the claws cracked
3 tablespoons butter
½ cup finely chopped mushrooms
¼ cup chopped pimiento
1 teaspoon minced fresh tarragon or ½ teaspoon dried tarragon
3 tablespoons sliced ripe Spanish olives
3 tablespoons finely chopped shallots or onion
½ teaspoon salt
Freshly ground black pepper
3 tablespoons Spanish sherry
¾ cup Diablo Sauce (page 487)

1. Heat the oil in a large skillet and add the garlic. Add the lobsters, split side down, and cook, stirring, until the shells turn red. Cover and cook for ten minutes longer.

Shellfish

2. Cool the lobsters, remove the meat from the shells, and discard the shells. Cut the lobster meat into bite-size pieces. Discard the oil in the skillet.

3. Heat the butter in a skillet and add the mushrooms, pimiento, tarragon, olives, shallots, salt, pepper to taste, and lobster meat. Mix thoroughly and cook for five minutes. Add the sherry and the diablo sauce. Heat through and serve immediately.

LOBSTER-STUFFED TOMATOES   *6 servings*

2 cups diced cooked fresh lobster
½ cup diced fresh celery
1½ tablespoons minced green pepper
1 tablespoon minced fresh onion
2 tablespoons chopped green olives
3 tablespoons mayonnaise
3 tablespoons finely chopped fresh tomato
2 teaspoons fresh lime juice

1½ teaspoons salt
1 teaspoon crumbled dried marjoram
⅛ teaspoon freshly ground black pepper
⅛ teaspoon cayenne pepper
6 firm ripe tomatoes
  Bibb lettuce

1. Combine lobster, celery, green pepper, onion and olives. Mix well. Blend together the mayonnaise, chopped tomato, lime juice, salt, marjoram, black pepper and cayenne pepper. Stir dressing into the lobster mixture.

2. Cut a one-inch-thick slice from the bud end of each tomato and reserve the slices. Cut tomatoes into wedges, leaving the wedges attached at the base. Spread the wedges apart to look like flower petals. Fill with some of the lobster mixture, mounding it in the center.

3. Serve on Bibb lettuce, topping each mound of lobster with the reserved slice of tomato.

BROILED BREADED OYSTERS   *4 to 6 servings*

1 cup soft fresh bread crumbs
2 tablespoons finely chopped parsley
1 teaspoon dried tarragon
¼ teaspoon cayenne pepper
  Salt

3 dozen raw oysters, shucked
½ cup melted butter
  Lemon wedges

1. Preheat broiler for fifteen minutes.

2. Combine the bread crumbs, parsley, tarragon, cayenne pepper and salt to taste. Drain the oysters and roll them in the seasoned crumbs. Place them in a single layer in a buttered baking dish.

3. Pour half of the butter over the oysters and broil them briefly, just until they are golden on top. Turn each oyster carefully and pour the remaining butter over them. Broil briefly until brown. Serve with lemon wedges.

ELEANOR HEMPSTEAD'S SCALLOPED OYSTERS
4 to 6 servings

½ cup butter, at room temperature
1½ cups fine crumbs made from soda
    crackers
24 oysters, shucked and drained
    Salt and freshly ground black
    pepper

2 tablespoons finely chopped shal-
    lots
¼ cup grated Parmesan cheese
½ cup heavy cream, approximately

1. Preheat oven to hot (400° F.).
2. Rub the bottom of a flat baking dish with a third of the butter and sprinkle with a third of the crumbs. Arrange a dozen oysters over the crumbs. Sprinkle with salt and pepper and half of the shallots.
3. Make another layer of crumbs and dot with another third of the butter. Arrange the remaining oysters over this. Add remaining shallots. Sprinkle with a final layer of crumbs. Dot with the remaining butter and sprinkle with the cheese.
4. Dribble the cream over the casserole. Add just enough so that the casserole is moist but not soupy. Bake for fifteen minutes.

In the catalogue of the world's choicest delicacies, one of the most de-lectable is the Olympia oyster produced on the West Coast of America. These sweet and tender morsels are so tiny that it takes three hundred of them to make one pint.

OLYMPIA OYSTERS POULETTE   *6 servings*

1 pint Olympia oysters or East Coast
    oysters
2 tablespoons finely chopped shal-
    lots or green onions
½ cup dry white wine
1 cup plus 2 tablespoons heavy
    cream

2 egg yolks
    Salt and freshly ground white
    pepper
¼ teaspoon cayenne pepper
    Juice of ½ lemon
    French Bread Croûtes (page 500)

1. Drain the oyster liquor into a saucepan. Reserve the oysters. Add the shallots and wine to the oyster liquor.
2. Cook oyster liquor over medium heat until the liquid is reduced al-most by half. Add one cup of the cream and simmer for five minutes. Blend the egg yolks with the remaining cream. Spoon a little of the hot sauce into the egg-yolk mixture, stirring. Return all to the saucepan and add the oysters. Add salt and white pepper to taste and cayenne. Stir and heat thoroughly, but do not boil or the yolks may curdle. Add the lemon juice and, if desired, more salt and pepper to taste.
3. Place a French bread croûte in each of six hot soup bowls and spoon the oysters and sauce over the croûtes.

COOKED PERIWINKLES   *About 1 cup periwinkle meats*

1 quart periwinkles   3 tablespoons salt

1. Rinse the periwinkles well and place them in a one-and-one-half-quart saucepan. Add water to cover to the depth of one inch, and the salt.
2. Bring the periwinkles to a boil and simmer until the operculum (a tiny "door" on each periwinkle) falls off. This may require from ten to twenty minutes.
3. Drain the periwinkles and cool them. Remove the meat from each periwinkle with a pin or nutpick. Serve with food picks and cocktail sauce or melted butter on the side.

EUELL GIBBONS'S PERIWINKLE OMELET   *4 to 6 servings*

1 cup periwinkle meats (see above)	Dried marjoram
1/4 cup butter	3 tablespoons finely chopped chives
8 eggs	1 garlic clove, finely minced
1 can (6 ounces) tomato paste	Paprika
1/2 cup water	4 parsley sprigs
1 teaspoon celery salt	

1. Cook the periwinkles in two tablespoons of the butter until lightly browned.
2. Beat the eggs with the tomato paste, water, celery salt, marjoram to taste, chives and garlic. Fold in the periwinkles.
3. Melt the remaining butter in a large omelet pan or skillet. As soon as it sizzles, pour in the omelet mixture. Cook it slowly until the top is set and the bottom delicately browned.
4. Roll out the omelet onto a serving dish. Garnish with paprika and parsley and serve hot.

COQUILLES ALOYSE   *8 servings*

1 pound scallops, washed	6 shallots, very finely chopped
3/4 cup milk	5 tablespoons finely chopped parsley
1/2 cup freshly toasted bread crumbs	1 cup butter, melted
6 mushrooms, thinly sliced	Salt and freshly ground black
8 very thin slices of lemon, halved	pepper
2 garlic cloves, minced	

1. Preheat oven to hot (450° F.).
2. If the scallops are large, cut them into smaller pieces.
3. Scald the milk in a small pan. Add the scallops and bring the mixture to a boil. Remove from heat, cover, and let stand for five minutes. Drain, reserving the liquid. Place scallops in a covered bowl.

4. Place one tablespoon of the bread crumbs in each of eight greased individual scallop shells. Sprinkle with enough of the reserved cooking liquid to moisten crumbs. Discard any remaining liquid.

5. Arrange scallops over the crumbs. Place mushroom slices over the top. Place a half slice of lemon, with the rind facing in, on either side of each shell.

6. Using a mortar and pestle, pound the garlic and shallots to a paste. Add the parsley and mix well. Add the butter and season with salt and pepper to taste. Spoon over the surface of the filled shells, making sure all the scallops are covered.

7. Bake for five minutes, or until sizzling hot. Serve immediately.

PAN-FRIED SCALLOPS   *4 servings*

1½ pounds sea scallops
¾ cup fine dry bread crumbs
½ cup butter
   Salt and freshly ground black pepper

Paprika
2 tablespoons lemon juice
3 tablespoons chopped parsley

1. Roll the scallops in the bread crumbs.

2. Melt half of the butter in a heavy skillet and add the scallops. Cook, turning the scallops gently, until golden brown on all sides. Remove the scallops to paper towels and sprinkle with salt, pepper and paprika.

3. Add the remaining butter to the skillet. When it melts, add lemon juice and parsley. Do not brown. Arrange the scallops on a hot platter. Pour the sauce over them immediately and serve.

SCALLOP CASSEROLE   *4 servings*

2 tablespoons finely chopped shallots
3 tablespoons butter
½ teaspoon salt
¼ teaspoon freshly ground black pepper
1 teaspoon minced fresh rosemary or ½ teaspoon dried rosemary

½ cup finely diced celery
1½ cups sour cream
1½ pounds scallops, cut into bite-size pieces
⅓ cup buttered soft fresh bread crumbs

1. Preheat oven to moderate (350° F.).

2. Sauté the shallots in the butter until tender. Add the salt, pepper, rosemary, celery and one-quarter cup of the sour cream. Cook for three minutes.

3. Add the scallops and transfer to a buttered shallow baking dish. Add the remaining sour cream and top with the buttered crumbs. Bake for fifteen to twenty minutes, or until the scallops are tender.

SCALLOP AND MUSHROOM CASSEROLE   *6 servings*

2 pounds scallops
2 cups dry white wine
¼ cup butter
¼ cup finely chopped shallots
½ pound mushrooms, sliced

2 tablespoons all-purpose flour
2 tablespoons heavy cream
2 tablespoons chopped parsley
½ cup buttered soft fresh bread crumbs

1. Wash the scallops well and cut into bite-size pieces if they are large.

2. Place the scallops and the wine in a skillet with a tight-fitting cover and simmer for about five minutes, or until tender. Drain and reserve the liquid.

3. Melt the butter and sauté the shallots and mushrooms in it for three to five minutes, until tender but not browned. Stir in the flour and gradually stir in the reserved liquid and the cream. Bring to a boil, stirring.

4. Add the scallops and parsley to the sauce and pour into a shallow casserole. Top with the bread crumbs and place under the broiler until the surface is lightly browned.

BAY SCALLOPS WITH WHITE WINE   *4 servings*

2 tablespoons butter
1 pound bay scallops
Salt and freshly ground black pepper
2 tablespoons finely chopped shallots

½ garlic clove, finely minced
4 mushrooms, thinly sliced
¼ cup dry white wine
1 cup heavy cream
1 tablespoon finely chopped parsley

1. Heat the butter in a skillet and add the scallops. Cook quickly, shaking the pan; sprinkle with salt and pepper. Continue cooking and stirring with a wooden spoon and add the shallots, garlic and mushrooms. Cook, stirring, for about one minute, then transfer scallops to a warm dish.

2. Add the wine to the skillet and cook over high heat, stirring, for about one minute. Add the cream and cook over high heat, stirring, for two minutes. Return the scallops to the skillet and sprinkle with parsley. Serve over freshly made noodles or rice.

SCALLOPS AND RICE AU GRATIN   *6 servings*

1 pound fresh scallops
¼ cup chopped onion
¼ cup chopped celery
½ cup chopped green pepper
¼ cup butter
¼ cup all-purpose flour

Salt and freshly ground black pepper
1¼ cups milk
2 cups cooked rice
1 cup grated sharp Cheddar cheese

1. Preheat oven to moderate (350° F.).

2. If sea scallops are used, cut them into quarters or eighths. Pick over the scallops to remove any small bits of shell.

3. Cook the onion, celery and green pepper in the butter until onion is translucent. Blend in the flour and salt and pepper to taste. Gradually add the milk, stirring constantly. When the mixture is thickened and smooth, add the scallops and remove from heat.

4. Arrange half of the rice, scallops and cheese in a well-buttered one-and-one-half-quart casserole, then repeat the layers, ending with a layer of cheese.

5. Bake the casserole until the mixture is thoroughly heated and cheese is golden brown.

BROILED MARINATED SHRIMP   *4 servings*

Juice of 3 lemons
½ cup salad oil
Salt and freshly ground black pepper
Dash of Worcestershire sauce
Dash of Tabasco
2 pounds shrimp (fresh or frozen), shelled and deveined
2 cups fine dry bread crumbs

1. Combine the lemon juice, oil, salt and pepper to taste, Worcestershire and Tabasco. Marinate the shrimp in the mixture for four to five hours.

2. Roll the marinated shrimp in the crumbs. Broil for five minutes on one side; turn and broil for three to five minutes on the other side.

SHRIMP À LA TURQUE   *4 servings*

2 pounds raw shrimp
1 cup vegetable or peanut oil
1½ teaspoons chili powder
1 tablespoon mint vinegar
1 teaspoon dried thyme
1 tablespoon chopped fresh mint or 1 teaspoon dried mint
Salt and freshly ground black pepper
2 tablespoons finely minced shallots
4 lemon wedges

1. Split the shrimp down the back with a sharp knife or with scissors. Rinse the shrimp under cold water to remove the small intestinal vein down the back. Pat dry.

2. Pour the oil into a mixing bowl. Combine the chili powder and mint vinegar to make a paste. Add to the oil along with the herbs, salt and pepper to taste and shallots. Stir well to mix. Add the shrimp and mix well. Let stand for four hours or overnight.

3. Preheat broiler.

4. Pour the shrimp and the marinade into a broiler pan. Broil the shrimp, five or six inches from the source of heat, for six to ten minutes, depending on size. Turn once. Serve, if desired, with a little of the marinade poured over. Garnish with lemon wedges.

CHIVE SHRIMP IN SHELLS   *5 or 6 servings*

1½ pounds raw shrimp
1½ cups dry white wine
½ teaspoon salt
¼ teaspoon white pepper
2 tablespoons butter
2 tablespoons all-purpose flour
1 cup milk

¼ cup chopped mushrooms
2 tablespoons grated Parmesan cheese
1 tablespoon chopped chives
½ cup buttered soft fresh bread crumbs

1. Place the shrimp, wine, salt and pepper in a saucepan and bring slowly to a boil. Simmer for five minutes. Drain, reserving the cooking liquid.
2. Shell and devein the shrimp and cut into bite-size pieces. Melt the butter, blend in the flour, and then gradually stir in the reserved liquid and the milk.
3. Bring to a boil, stirring, and cook until thickened. Add the shrimp, mushrooms, cheese and chives and cook for two minutes longer.
4. Fill buttered shells or ramekins with the mixture; sprinkle with the buttered crumbs. Broil until the surface is lightly browned.

CRAB-STUFFED SHRIMP   *4 to 6 servings*

1½ pounds jumbo shrimp, shelled and deveined
1 teaspoon sugar
4 peppercorns
½ teaspoon dried parsley
2¼ teaspoons salt
½ pound crabmeat, fresh, frozen or canned

2 tablespoons minced celery
1 tablespoon minced scallion
Freshly ground black pepper
1 teaspoon lemon juice
¼ cup mayonnaise or salad dressing

1. Drop shrimp into boiling water containing sugar, peppercorns, parsley and two teaspoons of the salt. Cook for three to five minutes, until shrimp turn pink. Drain. Cool.
2. Split each shrimp down the back, removing a thin wedge of meat to allow room for stuffing. Chop removed shrimp.
3. Drain and flake crabmeat. Combine with chopped shrimp and remaining ingredients. Pack into cavities of shrimp. Chill until ready to use.

CURRIED SHRIMP WITH GRAPES   *6 servings*

1 medium onion, chopped
1 garlic clove, minced
1 celery rib, diced
½ bay leaf
1 parsley sprig
¼ teaspoon dry mustard
1 tart apple, diced
½ cup butter

¼ pound raw ham, chopped
2 tablespoons all-purpose flour
½ teaspoon ground mace
1¼ teaspoons curry powder
2½ cups clam broth or Chicken Stock
   (page 475)
2 cups peeled deveined raw shrimp
1 cup Thompson seedless grapes

1. Combine the onion, garlic, celery, bay leaf, parsley, mustard, apple, butter and ham in a saucepan. Cook for eight minutes, stirring occasionally.

2. Add the flour, mace and curry powder. Cook for four minutes longer.

3. Add the broth and simmer for one hour. Strain the mixture into another saucepan, forcing the solids through a sieve.

4. Add the shrimp to the mixture and simmer for five minutes. Add the grapes. Heat briefly and serve.

SHRIMP RABBIT   *6 servings*

2 pounds shrimp, cooked in the shell
3 tablespoons butter
2 cups grated Gruyère or Swiss cheese
2 cups grated Cheddar cheese
½ cup heavy cream
2 eggs, lightly beaten

1 teaspoon dry mustard
Worcestershire sauce
Salt and freshly ground black pepper
½ cup dry white wine
Toast

1. Peel and devein the shrimp. If small, leave whole; if large, cut into bite-size pieces.

2. Melt the butter in a saucepan and stir in the cheese. Stir until cheese is melted. Add the cream and eggs, then the remaining ingredients except toast. Stir until mixture is thickened slightly and smooth. Stir in the shrimp and heat thoroughly. Serve over hot toast.

SHRIMP WITH TARRAGON   *4 servings*

1 garlic clove
½ teaspoon salt
½ cup butter, at room temperature
2 teaspoons finely chopped parsley
1 teaspoon minced fresh tarragon or
   ½ teaspoon dried tarragon

¾ cup soft fresh bread crumbs
2 tablespoons white rum or dry sherry
1 pound cleaned cooked shrimp

167

1. Preheat oven to hot (400° F.).

2. Chop the garlic and salt together until they are almost a purée. Cream the purée with the butter, parsley, tarragon, bread crumbs and rum. Spread half of the mixture in the bottom of four ovenproof ramekins. Reserve the remaining mixture.

3. Arrange equal portions of shrimp in the ramekins. Spread the remaining butter mixture over the shrimp. Bake until shrimp are heated through and crumbs are browned.

SHRIMP AND CHERRY TOMATOES PROVENÇALE
4 to 6 servings

36 raw shrimp, peeled and deveined
1 cup milk
Salt and freshly ground black pepper
¾ cup all-purpose flour, approximately

¼ cup vegetable oil
¼ cup butter
Juice of 1 lemon
1 recipe Cherry Tomatoes Provençale (page 434)
Chopped parsley

1. Put the shrimp in a bowl and add the milk. Season with salt and pepper.

2. Take the shrimp from the bowl one by one and dip them into flour seasoned with salt and pepper.

3. Heat the oil and butter in a skillet and cook the shrimp for two to three minutes on each side, turning once. They should be golden brown when cooked. Transfer shrimp as they cook to a warm serving dish.

4. Sprinkle the shrimp with the lemon juice and arrange the prepared tomatoes around. Sprinkle liberally with chopped parsley. Serve immediately.

SHRIMP MARENGO   *About 8 servings*

½ pound sliced lean bacon, diced
2 garlic cloves, finely minced
1 cup chopped onions
1 cup chopped celery
1 pound mushrooms, sliced
4½ cups (one 2-pound, 3-ounce can) Italian-style plum tomatoes
1 can (6 ounces) tomato paste
1 teaspoon monosodium glutamate
1½ teaspoons crumbled dried rosemary
1¼ teaspoons crumbled dried basil

1 bay leaf
1 tablespoon salt
¼ teaspoon freshly ground black pepper
1 tablespoon sugar
3 or 4 drops of Tabasco
3½ pounds raw shrimp, shelled and deveined
2 green peppers, seeded and cut into large cubes
Chicken Stock (page 475)

1. Sauté the bacon in a large skillet or Dutch oven until crisp. Remove and reserve.

2. Add garlic and onions to bacon drippings and sauté until tender and golden but not browned. Add celery and mushrooms and cook for five minutes.

3. Return bacon to skillet. Add tomatoes, tomato paste, monosodium glutamate, rosemary, basil, bay leaf, salt, pepper, sugar and Tabasco. Bring to a boil and simmer, uncovered, for twenty to thirty minutes.

4. Add shrimp and green peppers. When mixture comes to a boil, simmer for ten minutes, or until shrimp are tender.

5. If mixture is too thick, it may be thinned by adding stock. If it is too thin, it may be thickened by adding two to three tablespoons flour mixed with one-third cup stock.

Note: This dish may be prepared ahead by making the sauce as directed through step 3. Reserve the sauce. Twenty minutes before serving time, continue with recipe.

SCAMPI   *6 servings*

1 cup butter
¼ cup olive oil
1 tablespoon chopped parsley
¾ teaspoon dried basil
½ teaspoon dried orégano
1 garlic clove, minced
¾ teaspoon salt
1 tablespoon lemon juice
1 pound large fresh shrimp

1. Preheat oven to hot (450° F.).

2. Melt the butter and add the olive oil, parsley, basil, orégano, garlic, salt and lemon juice. Mix well.

3. Peel and devein the shrimp, leaving the tails attached. Split down the inside lengthwise, being careful not to cut through the shrimp. Spread open to simulate butterflies.

4. Place in a shallow baking pan, tail end up. Pour sauce over all. Bake for five minutes. Place under broiler for five minutes longer to brown.

SEAFOOD CASSEROLE   *100 servings, ⅓ cup each*

1½ cups butter
¾ cup sifted all-purpose flour
4½ cups milk
7 cups heavy cream
Salt and freshly ground black pepper
1½ tablespoons paprika
3 cans (10½ ounces each) frozen cream of potato soup
6 cups finely chopped onions
3 pounds fresh mushrooms, thinly sliced
3 pounds fresh or frozen crabmeat, picked over to remove shell and cartilage
8 pounds shrimp, cooked, shelled and deveined
2 pounds diced cooked lobster meat (There should be about five quarts of seafood in bite-size pieces.)

1. Melt half of the butter in a large heavy pan. Blend in the flour, then stir in the milk and three cups of the cream. Season with salt and pepper to taste and the paprika. Bring to a boil, stirring constantly, and simmer for five minutes.

2. Heat the cream of potato soup with two cups of the remaining cream. Combine with the other sauce.

3. Melt the remaining butter and sauté the onions until tender but not browned. Add the mushrooms and cook for about five minutes. Add the remaining cream, cover, and simmer for five minutes, or until the mushrooms are tender. Season with salt and pepper. Add mushroom mixture to the sauce.

4. Add the crab, shrimp and lobster to the sauce and reheat the entire mixture. Keep over simmering water, covered, until serving time.

SEAFOOD WITH TARRAGON   *6 servings*

1 cup cooked lobster meat
1 cup crabmeat
1 cup shrimp, cut into bite-size pieces
1 tablespoon vinegar, preferably tarragon vinegar

¼ cup finely chopped green onions
2 tablespoons finely chopped chives
1 tablespoon minced fresh tarragon, or more
Mayonnaise
Lobster claws for garnish

1. Combine all ingredients except lobster claws. Use just enough mayonnaise to bind the mixture.

2. Serve on a bed of well-chilled Bean Sprouts Vinaigrette (page 437). Garnish with lobster claws.

SEAFOOD-OKRA GUMBO   *6 to 8 servings*

1 pound uncooked shrimp in shells
¼ cup butter
1 pound okra, sliced
2 onions, chopped fine
1½ tablespoons all-purpose flour
1 cup tomatoes
12 oysters in liquor
2 teaspoons salt

1 garlic clove, crushed
Pinch of cayenne, or ¼ pod red pepper
Tabasco
Worcestershire sauce
½ pound crabmeat
Boiled rice

1. Shell shrimp and sauté in two tablespoons of the butter for several minutes, or until they turn a bright coral color. Set aside.

2. Heat the remaining butter in a soup kettle, add the okra, and cook, stirring frequently, until tender.

3. Stir in onions and cook for several minutes, then stir in flour until the mixture is smooth. Add tomatoes and cook the mixture for several minutes longer.

4. Add enough water to the oyster liquor to make two quarts of liquid. Stir this into the okra mixture and add salt, garlic and cayenne or red pepper pod.

5. Simmer for one hour, then add shrimp, and simmer for thirty minutes longer.

6. Fifteen minutes before serving add the oysters and cook over low heat until edges begin to curl. Add Tabasco and Worcestershire sauce to taste and the crabmeat, and heat through. Serve gumbo in soup plates over boiled rice.

ITALIAN-STYLE SQUID WITH TOMATOES   *4 to 6 servings*

2 pounds small fresh squid
1 garlic clove, minced
¼ cup olive oil
½ cup dry sherry
Pinch of dried thyme
¼ teaspoon dried ground red peppers, or more

1 cup canned tomatoes, preferably Italian plum tomatoes
1 tablespoon finely chopped parsley
Salt and freshly ground black pepper

1. Have the squid thoroughly cleaned. Rinse well under cold running water and dry. Cut off and reserve the tentacles and cut the squid into one-inch pieces.

2. Cook the squid and garlic in the olive oil, stirring, for about five minutes. Add the sherry, cover, and cook over low heat for ten minutes. Add the remaining ingredients, cover, and cook for fifteen minutes, or until squid are tender. Serve with rice.

SQUID STIR-FRIED CHINESE STYLE   *4 to 6 servings*

2 pounds small fresh squid
2 tablespoons peanut or vegetable oil
2 scallions, trimmed and cut into 1-inch lengths
2 slices of fresh gingerroot or ½ teaspoon ground ginger

2 tablespoons soy sauce
2 tablespoons dry sherry
1 tablespoon cornstarch
2 tablespoons water

1. Have the squid thoroughly cleaned. Rinse well under cold running water and dry. Cut off and reserve the tentacles and cut the squid into one-inch pieces.

2. Heat the oil; when it is hot, add all the squid. Add the scallions and gingerroot and cook, stirring, for one minute. Add soy sauce and sherry and cook, stirring, for two minutes longer.

3. Mix the cornstarch and water, stir it into the squid, and cook until the sauce is boiling and translucent. Serve immediately.

STUFFED SQUID *4 to 6 servings*

1 tender fresh squid (1 pound)	1 cup tomato sauce
2 or 3 onions, chopped	1 bay leaf, crumbled
2 or 3 garlic cloves, minced	½ cup uncooked rice
½ cup olive oil	Dried currants (optional)
Salt and freshly ground black pepper	Chopped parsley or dill
	1½ cups boiling water

1. To prepare the squid, discard the celluloid backbone, ink sac and head. Chop tentacles and set aside. Wash squid thoroughly and soak in water until ready to use.

2. Brown the onions and garlic in the oil. Add salt and pepper to taste, tomato sauce and bay leaf. Mix well. Add rice, currants and parsley or dill to taste and the chopped tentacles.

3. Stuff the squid with this mixture. Place in an oiled casserole and pour any remaining stuffing on top. Add the boiling water. Simmer, covered, for twenty-five minutes.

A frog is neither a fish nor a shellfish, but an amphibian; however, one finds recipes for this delicacy along with those for other aquatic creatures. The flavor and texture of frogs' legs most closely resembles that of tender young chicken.

SOUFFLÉED FROGS' LEGS *3 or 4 servings*

1 pound frogs' legs	Batter (see below)
Milk	Oil for deep frying
Seasoned flour	

1. Soak the frogs' legs in milk to cover for thirty minutes.

2. Dry the frogs' legs and dredge them with seasoned flour. Dip them into the batter and fry them in deep oil heated to 370° F. on a frying thermometer for about three minutes, until puffed and golden brown. Drain on absorbent paper.

BATTER:

½ cup sifted all-purpose flour	½ cup milk
½ teaspoon baking powder	1 egg, separated
¼ cup oil	

Sift the flour and baking powder into a bowl. Add the oil and combine thoroughly. Pour in the milk and lightly beaten egg yolk. Beat with a rotary beater until smooth. Beat the egg white until stiff but not dry. Fold it gently into the mixture.

. . . .

CHAPTER FOUR

MEATS

A roast beef dinner

A complete timetable for roasting meats will be found on page 263.

. . . .

BEEF

. . . .

STANDING RIB ROAST

An ideal rib roast should be at least two ribs thick and four pounds in weight. The larger the cut of meat, the better it will roast. Estimate one-half pound beef for each serving.

Prepare two or three ribs of beef weighing five and one-half to eight pounds. Season the meat with salt and pepper and place it, fat side up, in a roasting pan without a rack. Do not add water. Insert a meat thermometer so that the bulb reaches the center of the cut and does not touch the bone. See the timetable (below) for temperatures. Or, if a thermometer is not used, use the timetable to estimate the time required for the meat to reach the desired degree of doneness.

Roast the meat, uncovered, in a preheated moderate oven (325° F.). Remove the meat from the oven when the desired degree of doneness is achieved. Place it on a warm platter in a warm place to rest while making the gravy and any other accompaniments.

THIN PAN GRAVY:

Skim off all excess fat from the meat drippings, leaving any meat pieces in the pan. Stir in one-half to one cup of Beef Stock (page 473). Bring to a boil, scraping the bottom of the pan to loosen the meat pieces. Simmer for one minute and season to taste with salt and pepper. Strain the gravy and serve separately.

STANDING RIB ROAST (5 TO 8 POUNDS) ROASTED IN MODERATE OVEN (325° F.)

Degree of Doneness	Minutes per Pound	Meat Thermometer
Rare	23 to 25	140° F.
Medium	27 to 30	160° F.
Well Done	32 to 35	170° F.

BRAISED ROUND ROAST OF BEEF   *About 12 servings*

5 pounds beef round, prepared for roasting
All-purpose flour
¼ cup butter
½ cup chopped onion
½ cup diced carrot
¼ cup diced turnip
¼ cup diced celery
1 garlic clove, crushed (optional)

1 cup dry red wine
1 cup Beef Stock (page 473)
Salt and freshly ground black pepper
1 bay leaf
¼ teaspoon dried marjoram
½ teaspoon dried thyme
4 carrots, cut into quarters
2 white turnips, cut into eighths

1. Preheat oven to moderate (325° F.).

2. Dredge the beef roast with flour. Melt the butter in a Dutch oven and brown the meat on all sides. Remove the meat.

3. Add the chopped onion, diced carrot, the turnip, celery and garlic to the drippings. Cover and cook over medium heat for ten to fifteen minutes.

4. Place the browned meat on top of the vegetables. Add the wine, stock, salt and pepper to taste, bay leaf, marjoram and thyme.

5. Cover and bake in the oven for about three and one-half hours, until the meat is almost tender. Add more wine or stock if needed during the cooking time.

6. Strain the gravy, discard the vegetables, and return the liquid to the pan. Add the quartered carrots and turnips. Cover and bake for twenty to thirty minutes longer, until the vegetables and meat are tender.

7. Place the meat on a warm platter and arrange the vegetables as a garnish. Pour some of the gravy over the meat and serve the remainder separately. If desired, the gravy may be thickened with cornstarch or arrow-root.

BEEF WELLINGTON   *4 to 6 servings*

PASTRY:

4 cups all-purpose flour
1 teaspoon salt
½ cup butter

½ cup shortening
1 egg, lightly beaten
½ cup ice water, approximately

FILLING:

1 fillet of beef (2½ to 3 pounds)
2 tablespoons cognac
Salt and freshly ground black pepper
6 slices of bacon

8 ounces *pâté de foie gras* or Chicken-Liver Pâté (page 83)
3 or 4 truffles (optional)
1 egg, lightly beaten

1. Place the flour, salt, butter and shortening in a bowl and blend with the tips of the fingers or with a pastry blender. Add the egg and enough ice water to make a dough. Wrap in wax paper and chill.

2. Preheat oven to hot (450° F.).

3. Rub the fillet all over with the cognac and season with salt and pepper. Lay the bacon over the top, securing with string if necessary.

4. Place the meat on a rack in a roasting pan and roast for fifteen minutes for rare, for twenty to twenty-five minutes for medium. Remove from the oven; remove the bacon. Cool to room temperature before proceeding.

5. Spread the pâté all over the top and sides of the beef. Cut the truffles into halves and sink the pieces in a line along the top.

6. Preheat oven to hot (425° F.).

7. Roll out the pastry into a rectangle (about 18 x 12 inches) one-quarter inch thick. Place the fillet, top down, in the middle. Draw the long sides up to overlap on the bottom of the fillet; brush with egg to seal.

8. Trim the ends of the pastry and make an envelope fold, brushing again with egg to seal the closure. Transfer the pastry-wrapped meat to a baking sheet, seam side down.

9. Brush all over with egg. Cut out decorative shapes from the pastry trimmings and arrange the pieces down the center of the pastry. Brush the shapes with remaining egg. Bake for about thirty minutes, or until the pastry is cooked. Serve the dish hot with Sauce Madère (page 479), or serve cold on a buffet table.

Note: Puff pastry may be used to wrap the beef, but care should be taken to roll it very thin. Brioche dough may also be used.

POT ROAST WITH WINE   *8 to 10 servings*

1 boneless beef roast (5 pounds)	½ teaspoon dried marjoram
Salt and freshly ground black pepper	¼ teaspoon dried thyme
	1 bay leaf
2 tablespoons vegetable oil	4 allspice berries
1 garlic clove, finely minced	¾ cup dry red wine
1 cup coarsely chopped onions	
1 celery rib, leaves and all, finely chopped	

1. Preheat oven to slow (250° F.).

2. Sprinkle the roast with salt and pepper. Heat the oil in a Dutch oven or other heavy roaster and brown the meat lightly on all sides. Add the garlic, onions, celery, seasonings and wine; cover.

3. Bake for six to eight hours, or until the meat is thoroughly tender. Remove the bay leaf and allspice. Put the gravy through a sieve, or purée it in a blender. Serve with the sliced meat.

POT ROAST JARDINIÈRE (baked in foil)   *6 to 8 servings*

1 beef pot roast (3½ to 4½ pounds)	Salt and freshly ground black
1 small garlic clove	pepper
6 small onions, peeled	½ bay leaf
6 small carrots	Pinch of ground thyme
½ cup chopped celery	1 parsley sprig
½ cup chopped green pepper	½ cup tomato purée or sauce

1. Preheat broiler.

2. Tear off enough heavy-duty aluminum foil to enclose the pot roast and the vegetables. Place the sheet of foil in a shallow roasting pan and place the pot roast in the center. Turn up the edges of the foil slightly. Place the meat under the broiler and brown well, turning once. When the meat is browned, add the garlic, onions and carrots; let the vegetables brown slightly.

3. Remove the pan from the broiler and add the remaining ingredients. Pull up the edges of the foil and seal tightly with a double fold to make an air-tight package.

4. Place the meat in the oven and reduce the oven heat to slow (275° F.). Bake for three and one-half hours. Or the meat may be baked for four hours in a slower oven (250° F.).

5. Open the foil and transfer the meat and vegetables to a heated serving platter. Pour the pan liquids into a saucepan and skim off the fat. Reduce the liquid to the desired consistency. The sauce may be thickened if desired with a little flour and water. Serve separately.

GINGERED BEEF POT ROAST   *8 servings*

4 to 5 pounds bottom or top round of beef	3 tablespoons oil
	2 onions, thinly sliced
2 teaspoons ground ginger	1 garlic clove, finely minced
¼ cup all-purpose flour	1 cup peeled, seeded and chopped
1 teaspoon ground turmeric	tomatoes, fresh or canned
2 teaspoons salt	1 cup Beef Stock (page 473)
¼ teaspoon freshly ground black pepper	⅓ teaspoon ground thyme
	1 dried red pepper, crushed

1. Wipe the meat with a damp cloth.

2. Combine the ginger, flour, turmeric, salt and pepper and dredge the meat with it.

3. Brown the meat on all sides in the oil in a heavy Dutch oven. Add the onions, garlic, tomatoes, stock, thyme and red pepper. Bring to a boil, cover, and simmer gently for about three hours, or until tender.

4. Place meat on a warm platter. Remove surface grease from the liquid left in the pan and thicken, if desired, with one and one-half tablespoons flour mixed with one-quarter cup water. Serve separately.

BRAISED STEAK   *About 5 servings*

2 pounds round, rump or chuck steak, 1 inch thick
¼ cup all-purpose flour
1½ teaspoons salt
½ teaspoon freshly ground black pepper
¼ cup shortening, bacon drippings or butter

1 onion, thinly sliced
1 carrot, cut into rounds
½ green pepper, diced
1 cup canned tomatoes
1 bay leaf

1. Cut the meat into serving pieces. Mix the flour, salt and pepper and rub it into the meat.

2. Heat the fat in a heavy skillet with a tight-fitting lid. Brown the meat well in the fat on both sides.

3. Add the remaining ingredients, cover, and simmer very gently for one and one-half to two hours, until the meat is tender. If preferred, the meat and vegetables may be cooked in a casserole in a preheated slow oven (300° F.) for two to two and one-half hours.

STEAK FROMAGE   *4 or 5 servings*

1 beef round steak, ½ inch thick
¼ cup all-purpose flour
½ teaspoon salt
⅛ teaspoon freshly ground black pepper
3 tablespoons peanut oil

¼ cup chopped onion
1 garlic clove, finely minced
¾ cup Beef Stock (page 473)
⅓ cup grated Cheddar cheese
2 tablespoons chopped parsley

1. Cut the steak into eight or ten pieces. Pound it to one-quarter-inch thickness. Mix together the flour, salt and pepper and dredge the steak with the mixture. Sprinkle any remaining flour over the steak.

2. Brown the steak in the oil in a heavy skillet. Add the onion and garlic to the pan and cook until the onion is golden. Add the stock, cover tightly, and simmer for one and one-half hours, until the meat is tender.

3. Sprinkle the cheese and parsley over the meat, cover, and simmer for two or three minutes, until the cheese is melted.

TROPICAL STEAK   *6 servings*

3 pounds top round steak, 1¼ inches thick
2 tablespoons lime juice
2 tablespoons olive oil
1 onion, finely chopped
1 teaspoon salt

¼ teaspoon freshly ground black pepper
1 large garlic clove, finely minced
¼ teaspoon dried orégano
2 tablespoons butter, melted
1 tablespoon chopped parsley

1. Pound the steak on both sides with the edge of a plate or with a wooden mallet.

2. Combine the lime juice, oil, onion, salt, pepper, garlic and orégano; pour over the steak. Allow to marinate for one to two hours.

3. Preheat broiler or prepare a bed of hot charcoal.

4. Broil the steak three to four inches from the source of heat for five or six minutes on each side, or until the desired doneness is reached. Mix the butter and parsley and pour on the steak.

STEAK AU POIVRE WITH RED-WINE SAUCE   *4 servings*

2½ pounds boneless sirloin steak
  Salt
  2 tablespoons coarsely ground black pepper
  2 tablespoons peanut oil
  3 tablespoons butter
  2 tablespoons finely chopped shallots

¾ cup dry red wine
  2 tablespoons cognac
  1 cup Brown Sauce (page 477) or canned beef gravy
  1 tablespoon lemon juice

1. Sprinkle the steak with salt to taste and rub in the pepper. Brown on all sides in the oil. Cook for thirty or forty minutes, to the desired doneness.

2. Transfer the steak to a warm serving platter and pour off the fat from the skillet. Add one tablespoon of the butter and the shallots to the skillet. Add the wine and stir to dissolve brown particles on the bottom of the pan. Cook until the wine is reduced to one-quarter cup.

3. Add the cognac, cook for one minute, and stir in the brown sauce. Remove the sauce from the heat, add the remaining butter, and swirl pan until butter melts. Add lemon juice and serve with the sliced steak.

MARINATED CUBE STEAKS   *6 servings*

6 cube steaks (6 to 8 ounces each)
½ cup salad oil
  2 garlic cloves, finely minced
  2 scallions, finely chopped
  1 cup (one 8-ounce can) tomato sauce

1 teaspoon Worcestershire sauce
½ teaspoon dried rosemary
½ teaspoon dried thyme
  1 teaspoon prepared horseradish
½ teaspoon salt

1. Place the steaks in a shallow baking dish. Combine the remaining ingredients and pour over the steaks. Marinate for at least three hours, turning once.

2. Cook on a grill over charcoal or under the broiler for five to ten minutes, until cooked to desired degree of doneness.

PEPPER STEAK   *4 servings*

1¼ pounds boneless beef round
¼ cup olive oil
1 garlic clove, finely minced
2 large tomatoes, skinned and chopped
4 medium-size green peppers, seeded and cut into strips

¼ cup soy sauce
¼ teaspoon freshly ground black pepper
½ teaspoon sugar
1¼ teaspoons ground ginger
1¼ cups Beef Stock (page 473)
2 tablespoons cornstarch

1. Cut the meat diagonally across the grain into thin strips.

2. Heat the oil and brown the meat and garlic in it quickly. Stir in the tomatoes and green peppers.

3. Add the soy sauce, pepper, sugar, ginger and three-quarters cup of the stock.

4. Cover and cook for fifteen to twenty minutes, or until the meat strips are tender.

5. Blend the cornstarch with the remaining stock. Stir into the meat mixture, bring to a boil, and simmer for two minutes, stirring constantly.

ROLLED FLANK STEAK WITH CELERY STUFFING   *6 servings*

2 pounds flank steak
  Salt and freshly ground black pepper
2 tablespoons finely chopped onion
1 garlic clove, finely minced
½ cup finely chopped celery
¼ cup butter
2 cups soft fresh bread crumbs

½ teaspoon poultry seasoning
  All-purpose flour
1 tablespoon chopped beef suet or shortening
¾ cup boiling water
1 tablespoon cornstarch
1 tablespoon water
  Pinch of ground ginger

1. Preheat oven to slow (300° F.).

2. Score the steak. Mix salt and black pepper to taste and rub into both sides of meat.

3. Cook the onion, garlic and celery in the butter until limp. Add bread crumbs, poultry seasoning, one teaspoon salt and one-eighth teaspoon pepper; mix lightly. Spread stuffing over steak and roll lengthwise, jelly-roll fashion.

4. Tie the rolled steak with strings or fasten with skewers. Sprinkle lightly with flour and brown on all sides in beef suet or shortening. Place on a rack in a Dutch oven.

5. Add the boiling water and cover. Bake in the oven or simmer on top of the stove for two hours.

6. To serve, place meat on platter. Cut strings and slice crosswise. Serve with gravy made by mixing the cornstarch with the tablespoon of cold water. Add to pan juices and cook until lightly thickened. Season with ginger and salt and pepper to taste.

BARBECUED STUFFED FLANK STEAK   *4 servings*

1½ pounds flank steak
Meat tenderizer
½ teaspoon crumbled dried rosemary
¼ teaspoon ground tarragon
4 whole cloves
½ teaspoon ground thyme

1 bay leaf
1 tablespoon instant minced onion
½ cup salad oil
½ cup water
½ cup red-wine vinegar
Sage Corn-Bread Stuffing (page
314)

1. Cut steak into halves crosswise and make a pocket in each half, cutting the pocket to within one-half inch of the edge of the steak. Or ask the butcher to make the pocket for you.

2. Rub the meat tenderizer over both sides of the meat, applying it as directed on the package. Let stand for one hour. Combine herbs, spices, onion, oil, water and vinegar. Heat for one minute. Cool. Pour over meat.

3. Marinate in the refrigerator for at least four hours or overnight.

4. Remove meat from marinade and wipe dry with paper towels. Fill the pockets with the stuffing. Close openings of the pockets with skewers.

5. Cook on one side over a very slow-burning charcoal fire for twenty minutes, or until brown. Turn and cook on the other side for twenty minutes, basting with marinade as often as the meat looks dry. To serve, cut into one-inch slices across the grain of the meat.

BEEF BIRDS   *6 servings*

1 pound very lean beef, thinly sliced
1 pound lean beef, ground
1 teaspoon potato starch or cornstarch
½ teaspoon ground ginger
¼ teaspoon ground cloves

½ cup milk
¼ pound marrowbone
1 celery rib
1 medium onion, sliced
2 tablespoons all-purpose flour
4 cups boiling water

1. Pound the beef slices until paper thin, using a cleaver or the flat side of a heavy knife.

2. Into the container of an electric blender put half of the ground beef, half of the starch, half of the ginger and cloves and half of the milk. Cover and blend on high speed for one minute. Empty into a bowl and repeat the process, using the remaining ground beef, starch, ginger, cloves and milk.

3. Spread each slice of beef with some of the beef purée, roll into tiny rolls, and tie with thread. Put the birds into a skillet containing one inch of water. Add the marrowbone, celery and onion. Bring the water to a boil and cook until the water has cooked away. Continue cooking until the meat is browned on all sides. Remove the birds from the pan. Discard the marrowbone.

4. Add the flour to the juices remaining in the skillet and stir to blend.

Gradually stir in the boiling water and cook, stirring in all the brown bits from the bottom and sides of the pan.

5. Remove the celery and onion from the pan and place them in the container of the blender. Add one-half cup of the gravy and cover. Turn the blender on high speed. Remove the cover and, with motor on, gradually add the remaining gravy. Pour the gravy back into the skillet. Remove the threads from the beef birds and return the birds to the gravy. Simmer, covered, for one hour. Serve in a deep dish or stack pyramid-fashion.

STUFFED BEEF BIRDS   *5 servings*

2 pounds round steak, ⅜ inch thick
¼ cup all-purpose flour
1½ teaspoons salt
¼ teaspoon freshly ground black pepper
2 tablespoons butter
2 tablespoons chopped onion
1 tablespoon chopped green pepper

½ cup soft fresh bread crumbs
1 can (10½ ounces) whole-kernel corn, drained
¼ teaspoon dried basil
2 tablespoons oil
½ cup Beef Stock (page 473)
1 bay leaf
Chopped fresh parsley

1. Pound the steak with the edge of a plate or a mallet until very thin. Cut it into ten pieces, each approximately 2 × 4 inches.

2. Dredge the meat with the flour, mixed with one teaspoon of the salt and one-eighth teaspoon of the pepper.

3. Melt the butter and sauté the onion for five minutes. Add the green pepper, bread crumbs, drained corn, basil and remaining salt and pepper.

4. Divide the mixture among the pieces of meat and roll up each one to enclose the stuffing. Secure the rolls with fine string or food picks.

5. Heat the oil and brown the rolls on all sides. Add the stock and bay leaf. Cover and simmer for one hour, until the rolls are tender. Garnish with chopped parsley.

ANDALUSIAN BEEF ROLL   *6 servings*

2 pounds round steak, about ½ inch thick
3 hard-cooked eggs, chopped
4 slices of bacon, diced
⅓ cup chopped pimiento-stuffed green olives

2 tablespoons chopped parsley
2 tablespoons capers
Freshly ground black pepper
5 tablespoons melted shortening
2 teaspoons paprika
Salt

1. Pound the steak with a mallet to flatten it slightly.

2. Combine the eggs, bacon, olives, parsley, capers and one-half teaspoon pepper; mix well. Arrange on the steak and roll up the meat jelly-roll fashion. Fasten with string or skewers.

3. Cook in the shortening until browned on all sides. Sprinkle with paprika, salt and pepper. Add enough water to cover the bottom of the pan.

4. Cover and cook over low heat for about one and one-half hours, until beef is tender. Add more water during cooking period if necessary.

ROSEMARY BEEF ROLLS   *4 servings*

1½ pounds beef, cut into four 4-inch squares
 4 thin carrot strips
 4 small slivers of garlic
   Dried rosemary
 ¼ cup all-purpose flour
 ¼ cup vegetable oil or butter
 2 onions, thinly sliced
 1 carrot, sliced
 ½ teaspoon salt
 ¼ teaspoon freshly ground black pepper
 ½ teaspoon ground rosemary
 1 bay leaf
 2 tomatoes, chopped, or 1 cup canned tomatoes
 1 cup Chicken Stock (page 475) or dry white wine
 2 tablespoons finely chopped parsley

1. Pound the meat slices lightly with a mallet or the flat side of a knife. Place one carrot strip and one sliver of garlic in the center of each. Sprinkle lightly with rosemary. Roll the slices and tie with string. Dip the rolls into flour.

2. Heat the oil in a skillet and brown the meat on all sides. Add remaining ingredients except parsley, and cover. Simmer for forty-five minutes, or until meat is tender.

3. Remove the beef rolls to a serving dish and strain the gravy over them. Sprinkle with parsley.

FONDUE ORIENTALE   *6 servings*

This is a dish to be cooked at the table by the guests themselves. A chafing dish or fondue cooker is required. An excellent beverage to serve with the fondue is a chilled dry wine.

½ pound lean beef
½ pound lean veal
½ pound lean pork
 6 lamb kidneys or 3 veal kidneys
 6 tablespoons chopped onion
¾ cup Mayonnaise (page 467)
¾ cup Sauce Béarnaise (page 486)
¾ cup Curried Mayonnaise (page 468)
 6 cups Beef or Chicken Stock (pages 473 and 475) or water

1. Have the butcher slice the beef, veal and pork into wafer-thin, bite-size slices. Or slice the meat at home; this is easier if the meat is slightly frozen.

2. Slice the kidneys into halves and remove the hard cores. Cut the halves into thin slices.

3. Divide the meats, onion and sauces equally among six plates. Provide each guest with a long, wooden-handled, two-pronged fork.

4. Pour the stock into a chafing dish, electric saucepan or deep heatproof serving dish. Bring the stock to a boil in the kitchen, then place it over an alcohol or other burner in the center of the dining table. The stock must continue to boil while the meal is eaten.

5. The object of this exercise in dining is for each guest to spear a piece of meat and lower it into the boiling liquid until cooked to the desired degree of doneness. (Pork must be well cooked.) The cooked meat then is dipped into the chopped onion and sauces.

6. If desired, serve rice as a side dish. After the meat is eaten, the cooking broth is served as a soup course.

SAVORY SHORT RIBS WITH OLIVES   *6 servings*

3 pounds lean short ribs of beef
Salt and freshly ground black pepper
All-purpose flour
1 tablespoon salad oil
4 cups Beef Stock (page 473)
1 cup chopped celery
1 bay leaf
2 onions, sliced
1½ cups ripe olives, halved

1. Sprinkle the meat with salt and pepper and dredge with flour. Brown on all sides in the oil in a heavy skillet or Dutch oven.

2. Add the stock, celery, bay leaf and onions. Season to taste with salt and pepper. Cover, bring to a boil, and simmer for one and one-half hours, or until the meat is tender. Add the olives and cook for fifteen minutes longer. Remove the meat to a warm platter.

3. Mix one and one-half tablespoons flour with a little cold water and add to the broth. Cook, stirring, until thickened. Spoon some sauce over the meat and serve the remainder separately.

BOEUF EN DAUBE   *6 servings*

3 pounds chuck or stewing beef, cut into 2-inch cubes
1½ cups red wine
¼ cup cognac
2 tablespoons peanut oil
Salt and freshly ground black pepper
½ teaspoon ground thyme
1 bay leaf
1 large onion, coarsely chopped
2 garlic cloves, crushed
2 cups thinly sliced scraped carrots
½ cup coarsely chopped celery
½ pound sliced lean bacon, each slice cut into halves
All-purpose flour
2½ cups canned Italian plum tomatoes, or fresh ripe tomatoes, cored, peeled and chopped
2 cups thinly sliced mushrooms
2 cups Beef Stock (page 473)

1. Place the beef in a large mixing bowl and add the wine, cognac, oil, salt and pepper to taste, the thyme, bay leaf, onion, garlic, carrots and celery. Cover and refrigerate for three hours or longer.

2. Preheat oven to moderate (350° F.).

3. Place the bacon in a saucepan and add water barely to cover. Simmer for five minutes and drain.

4. Line a heatproof casserole with three or four pieces of bacon. Drain the beef and reserve the marinade.

5. Dredge each cube of beef with flour; shake to remove excess flour. Arrange a layer of beef in the casserole, add a layer of the marinated vegetables, a third of the tomatoes and a third of the mushrooms. Continue making layers until all the ingredients are used; end with vegetables and bacon. Sprinkle all with salt and pepper. Add the stock and enough of the marinade to cover.

6. Cover the casserole and bring the liquid to a boil on top of the stove. Place in the oven and bake for fifteen minutes. Reduce oven heat to slow (300° F.) and continue to cook for three to four hours. Reduce heat as necessary so that the casserole barely simmers. Cook until meat is fork tender. Skim the fat from the surface and serve with rice or noodles.

BEEF AND VODKA CASSEROLE   *6 to 8 servings*

6 slices of bacon, cut into small dice
4 pounds lean short ribs of beef
1½ cups finely chopped onions
Salt and freshly ground black pepper

1 teaspoon caraway seeds
Pinch of ground thyme
⅓ cup wine vinegar
1 cup boiling Beef Stock (page 473)
⅓ cup vodka

1. Preheat oven to moderate (350° F.).

2. Cook the bacon in a Dutch oven until it starts to brown. Cook the short ribs of beef with the bacon until meat is golden brown all over. Discard all but one tablespoon of the fat.

3. Add the onions and cook, stirring, until they are wilted. Sprinkle with salt and pepper. Add the caraway seeds, thyme, vinegar and stock.

4. Cover closely and bake for two hours, or until meat is fork tender. Five minutes before serving add the vodka and stir.

BEEF GOULASH   *6 to 8 servings*

3 pounds bottom round of beef, cut into 1½-inch cubes
¼ cup butter
4 cups sliced onions
1 veal kidney, cored and diced
1 piece of salt pork (2 inches square), diced

2 tablespoons paprika (sweet rose)
2 tablespoons all-purpose flour
1½ cups Beef Stock (page 473)
1 bay leaf
2 green peppers, seeded and diced

1. Brown the meat in the butter. Add the onions, kidney and salt pork and cook until onions are golden.

2. Sprinkle with the paprika and flour. Cook gently for two or three minutes, stirring.

3. Add the stock, bay leaf and peppers. Cover and simmer slowly for about one and one-half hours, until the beef is tender.

BEEF WITH CHICK-PEAS   *4 servings*

1 pound round steak, cut into ½-inch cubes
2 tablespoons vegetable oil
½ cup Beef Stock (page 473)
6 tablespoons tomato paste
1 lemon
2 cups (one 1-pound can) chick-peas, drained
1 teaspoon dried marjoram
¼ cup finely chopped parsley
½ teaspoon monosodium glutamate
Salt and freshly ground black pepper

1. Preheat oven to moderate (350° F.).

2. Quickly brown the meat in the oil and transfer the meat to a casserole. Add the stock and tomato paste to the casserole. Trim off and discard the ends of the lemon. Slice the lemon wafer thin and discard the seeds. Add the lemon and the remaining ingredients to the beef with seasoning to taste. Cover and bake for one hour, or until meat is fork tender.

CURRY OF BEEF   *6 to 8 servings*

½ cup butter
1 cup chopped onions
1 cup chopped tart apples
2 garlic cloves, minced
3 pounds bottom round of beef, cut into strips (¼ × 1 × 2 inches)
1 tablespoon ground turmeric
1 teaspoon salt
¼ teaspoon freshly ground black pepper
2 bay leaves, crumbled
1 tablespoon ground ginger
1 teaspoon cuminseeds, ground
1 teaspoon coriander seeds, ground
¼ teaspoon ground cardamom
½ teaspoon dry mustard
2 hot chili peppers, ground
2 cups Coconut Cream (page 491)

1. Melt the butter in a large saucepan. Sauté the onions, apples and garlic in the butter until they are tender but not browned.

2. Add the beef strips and toss with the sautéed mixture until the meat changes color. Do not allow to brown.

3. Sprinkle the turmeric, salt, black pepper, bay leaves, ginger, cumin-

seeds, coriander, cardamom, mustard and chili peppers over the meat mixture. Add the coconut cream.

4. Bring the mixture to a boil, cover, and simmer for twenty-five to thirty minutes, or until the beef is tender.

BEEF BRAZILIEN   *6 servings*

¼ cup butter
3 pounds beef round steak, cut into ¾-inch cubes
1 garlic clove, minced
3 onions, sliced
¼ cup all-purpose flour
1 cup dry red wine

2 teaspoons salt
½ teaspoon freshly ground black pepper
¼ teaspoon dried rosemary
¼ teaspoon dried orégano
1 cup strong black coffee

1. Melt the butter in a deep frying pan or chicken fryer. Add steak and brown on all sides. Add garlic and onions. Cook until onions are soft but not brown. Remove meat and onions from pan.

2. Blend flour with butter remaining in pan. Add the wine, seasonings and coffee. Stir until slightly thickened.

3. Return meat and onions to pan. Cover and bring to a boil. Simmer for one and one-half hours, or until meat is tender.

BEEF WITH DUMPLINGS   *4 to 6 servings*

¼ cup clarified butter (see note)
2 cups finely chopped onions
3 pounds beef chuck, cut into 2-inch cubes
All-purpose flour
Salt and freshly ground black pepper
2 tablespoons cognac (optional)
1 large bay leaf
Boiling Beef Stock (page 473) or water

½ pound small fresh mushrooms, left whole, or large mushrooms, quartered
2 cups sour cream
¼ cup all-purpose flour
½ cup finely chopped parsley
Bread-Crumb Dumplings (page 541)

1. Heat the clarified butter in a Dutch oven and cook the onions in it until they are transparent. Remove the onions from the pan and reserve them.

2. Dredge the beef with flour seasoned with salt and pepper. Brown the meat in the same pan in which the onions were cooked. If necessary, add more clarified butter.

3. When the meat is browned on all sides, add the cognac and ignite. When the flames have died down, return the onions to the pan and add the

bay leaf and boiling stock. Cover, reduce the heat, and simmer for about one and one-half hours, until the meat is almost tender. Add the mushrooms and mix gently.

4. Combine the sour cream with the one-quarter cup of flour. When thoroughly blended, add a little of the hot sauce from the skillet, a tablespoon at a time. Stir in the parsley. Spoon the sour-cream mixture over the top of the meat but do not stir.

5. When the sauce starts to bubble around the sides, spoon the dumplings over the top, starting with the outside edges and working toward the center. Cover the pan and continue to cook for thirty minutes longer. The dumplings should puff and be feather light.

Note: To clarify butter, melt butter and skim off the scum as it forms. Pour off the clear yellow portion (the clarified butter); discard the milky sediment.

STEAK AND KIDNEY PUDDING *6 servings*

PASTRY:

2 cups sifted all-purpose flour
¼ teaspoon salt
1 teaspoon baking powder

1 cup very finely grated beef suet
¾ cup cold water, approximately

FILLING:

1½ pounds stew beef, cut into ½-inch cubes
1 small veal kidney, cored and cubed
⅓ cup seasoned all-purpose flour

1 small onion, grated
¾ cup Beef Stock (page 473), approximately
Beef gravy

1. Place the flour, salt, baking powder and suet in a bowl and mix well. Add enough water while stirring to make a fairly soft pastry. Roll out two-thirds of the pastry and line a greased one-quart pudding basin; arrange the pastry so that there are not too many folds.

2. Coat the beef and kidney with the seasoned flour and pile into the basin along with the onion. Pour in the stock until it reaches two-thirds of the way up the bowl.

3. Roll out the remaining pastry, moisten the edge, and fit over the meat. Cover tightly with aluminum foil or wax paper and a piece of cloth.

4. Set the pudding basin in a steamer over rapidly boiling water or on a rack in a pan with boiling water extending two-thirds of the way up the bowl. Cook for three and one-half to four hours, replenishing the water as necessary. Unmold onto a warm dish and serve with beef gravy.

Beef Wellington is a fillet of beef spread with pâté and baked in a pastry crust. It can be served hot for a winter party or cold for a buffet entertainment.

STEAK AND KIDNEY PIE *6 to 8 servings*

PASTRY:

2 cups sifted all-purpose flour
¼ teaspoon salt
¾ cup butter

¾ cup ice water, approximately
½ teaspoon lemon juice

FILLING:

2 pounds stew beef, cut into ½-inch cubes
⅓ cup seasoned all-purpose flour
3 tablespoons rendered beef suet
1 veal kidney, cored and cubed
1 small onion, grated

¾ cup beef gravy or Brown Sauce (page 477)
½ cup Beef Stock (page 473) approximately
½ egg, lightly beaten with 1 tablespoon water

1. Place the flour and salt in a bowl. Cut the butter into half-inch cubes; add the cubes to the flour and toss to coat them on all sides with flour. Mix the water with the lemon juice and add enough to the flour to mix into a soft, but not sticky, dough. Gather into a ball and chill for fifteen minutes. The fat should remain in lumps.

2. Meanwhile, toss the beef in the seasoned flour and brown, a little at a time, in the rendered fat. Place in a one-and-one-half-quart baking dish (10 × 6½ × 2 inches), preferably one with a flat edge around. Coat the kidney with the remaining flour and add to the dish. Add onion, gravy and enough stock to extend two-thirds of the way up the dish. Set aside.

3. Roll out the chilled pastry on a lightly floured pastry cloth into a rectangle (6 × 18 inches). Fold into three, seal seams with light pressure, make a half turn with the pastry, and roll out again in a similar way, taking care to keep all edges and corners neat and squared off. Repeat the rolling and folding four times in all, chilling in between if necessary. Chill for ten minutes.

4. Preheat oven to hot (450° F.).

5. Roll out the pastry about one inch longer than the dish. Cut off a half-inch strip all around, moisten the strip, and line the edge of the dish with the strip. Moisten the rim made and top with remaining pastry. The pastry should not be stretched at any point. Trim and decorate the edge, making a steam hole in the center. Decorate with pastry leaves made from trimmings. Brush with the egg mixture and bake for about twenty minutes, or until well browned.

6. Reduce the oven heat to moderate (325° F.), cover the pastry loosely with aluminum foil, and continue to cook for about one and one-half hours, until the meat is tender. Serve hot.

MEAT ON A STICK   *4 servings*

1½ pounds lean beef, pork or lamb, cut into 1½-inch cubes
1 teaspoon dry mustard
1 teaspoon chili powder
½ teaspoon ground ginger
½ cup finely chopped onion

1 small garlic clove, finely minced
1 teaspoon ground turmeric
¼ cup lemon juice
1 teaspoon honey
Salt and freshly ground black pepper

1. Place the meat in a mixing bowl. Combine the remaining ingredients and seasoning to taste and pour over the meat; mix thoroughly. Let stand for thirty minutes or longer.

2. Thread the meat on skewers. Broil, turning occasionally, until cooked to the desired degree of doneness. Or grill over charcoal. If pork is used, it should be cooked until well done.

BEEF AND BEANS CASSEROLE   *8 to 10 servings*

1 pound dried pea beans	2 pounds boneless stew beef, cut into cubes
6 cups water	
Salt and freshly ground black pepper	½ teaspoon dried rosemary
	1 bay leaf
1 pound smoked pork sausage links	Pinch of dried thyme
2 cups chopped onions	¾ cup chopped tomatoes
3 garlic cloves, finely minced	Chopped parsley

1. Soak the beans in a large quantity of water overnight. Drain them and add the six cups water and salt and pepper to taste. Bring to a boil and simmer for one and one-half hours, until beans are tender without being mushy. Drain the beans and measure the cooking liquid. Reserve one and one-half cups of the liquid.

2. Preheat oven to slow (300° F.).

3. Cut the sausages into quarters and fry them in a skillet until they are lightly browned. Remove them from the skillet and reserve until ready to use.

4. Pour off all but two tablespoons of fat from the skillet and add the onions and garlic. Cook, stirring, until onions are wilted. Remove onions, add a little more fat to the skillet and brown the beef cubes.

5. Place the beef, rosemary, bay leaf and thyme in a three-quart casserole. Add the onions, garlic and tomatoes and cover closely. Bake for two hours.

6. Add the beans, sausage and reserved cooking liquid from the beans. Cover. Bake for one hour longer, or until beans and meat are thoroughly tender. Stir occasionally while casserole bakes. Serve sprinkled with chopped parsley.

There are few meats as versatile as ground beef, or hamburger. The meat must be absolutely fresh. According to federal standards controlling meat that is shipped across state lines, the maximum fat content of hamburger is thirty per cent. Lean meat is preferable to fat meat because hamburger with an excess of fat shrinks too much in cooking. However, a small amount of fat contributes flavor and richness.

If hamburger is not to be used within twenty-four hours, it should be tightly wrapped in freezer paper and frozen.

GRILLED HAMBURGER FOR ONE   *1 serving*

¼ pound round steak, ground
½ teaspoon butter (optional)
   Soy sauce or Worcestershire sauce
   Tabasco
1 teaspoon lemon juice
1 teaspoon freshly chopped parsley
   Salt and freshly ground black pepper

1. Shape the beef into a large patty.
2. Grill the meat over charcoal; or broil under the broiler; or cook in a very hot skillet lightly sprinkled with salt and without the further addition of fat.
3. When cooked, brush lightly with the butter and sprinkle with soy sauce, Tabasco, lemon juice, parsley, and salt and pepper to taste.

ORIENTAL HAMBURGERS   *4 servings*

1 pound round steak, ground
¼ cup finely diced water chestnuts
½ teaspoon freshly grated gingerroot
   or ground ginger
2 tablespoons soy sauce
   Freshly ground black pepper
¼ teaspoon monosodium glutamate
1 tablespoon peanut oil

1. Combine the meat, water chestnuts, gingerroot, soy sauce, pepper to taste and monosodium glutamate in a mixing bowl. Blend well but lightly with the hands. Shape the mixture into four large patties.
2. Brown in the oil and cook to desired doneness.

HAMBURGERS WITH MARROW   *4 servings*

1 marrowbone (5 inches)
1½ pounds round steak, ground
   Salt and freshly ground black pepper
4 teaspoons butter
   Worcestershire sauce
   Tabasco
   Juice of 1 lemon
3 tablespoons cognac (optional)
¼ cup freshly chopped parsley

1. With a long sharp knife cut the marrow from the bone and push it out. Slice the marrow. Drop the slices into barely boiling water and poach for about three minutes. Drain.
2. Chop the marrow and combine with the meat and salt and pepper to taste. Mix lightly with the hands and shape the mixture into four large patties.
3. Grill the hamburgers over charcoal or pan-broil them. To pan-broil, sprinkle a skillet lightly with salt and heat well. Do not add fat to the skillet. Add the patties. When browned well on one side, turn patties and immediately reduce the pan heat. Cook to the desired degree of doneness. (The hamburger should be cooked until the marrow in the middle of the patty has melted.)

4. Remove the skillet from the heat and top each hamburger with a teaspoon of butter. Sprinkle Worcestershire sauce, Tabasco, and lemon juice over the patties.

5. Sprinkle the cognac over all and ignite it. Transfer the hamburgers to toasted buns and spoon the skillet sauce over them. Sprinkle with chopped parsley and serve.

CARAWAY MEAT BALLS   *16 to 20 meat balls*

3 tablespoons butter
¼ cup finely chopped onion
1 pound round steak, ground
½ pound sausage meat
1 tablespoon caraway seeds
1½ cups soft fresh bread crumbs
½ cup milk

¼ cup heavy cream
1 egg, lightly beaten
1½ teaspoons salt
½ teaspoon freshly ground black pepper
All-purpose flour
1 cup Beef Stock (page 473)

1. Melt one tablespoon of the butter and sauté the onion in it until wilted.

2. Place the beef and sausage in a mixing bowl and add the sautéed onion, caraway seeds, bread crumbs, milk, cream, egg, salt and pepper. Shape the mixture into small balls and dredge with flour.

3. Brown the meat balls in the remaining butter, cover, and simmer for ten minutes. Add the stock, cover, and cook for twenty minutes longer.

SWEDISH BEEF BALLS   *6 servings*

1½ pounds ground beef
½ cup soft fresh bread crumbs
½ cup finely chopped green onions, including green part
1 egg
Salt and freshly ground black pepper
1 teaspoon dry mustard
½ teaspoon snipped fresh dill or dried marjoram

1 teaspoon paprika
¼ cup butter
1½ cups Beef Stock (page 473)
1 can (6 ounces) tomato paste
1 teaspoon Worcestershire sauce, or more
2 cups sour cream

1. Combine the meat, bread crumbs, onions, egg, salt and pepper to taste, mustard, dill and paprika. Shape into twelve balls and brown on all sides in the butter.

2. Combine the stock, tomato paste and Worcestershire sauce; bring to a boil. Stir in the sour cream. Pour the mixture over the meat balls and simmer for ten minutes.

ROQUEFORT HAMBURGERS   *4 servings*

½ cup Roquefort cheese
1 tablespoon finely chopped chives
  or scallions
1 pound round steak, ground

¼ cup butter
1 teaspoon Worcestershire sauce
2 tablespoons finely chopped parsley
  Juice of ½ lemon

1. Blend the cheese with the chives and shape into flattened rounds.

2. Divide the meat into eight parts and shape each piece into a patty. Place Roquefort rounds in the center of four meat patties, top with the remaining patties, and seal the edges.

3. Broil the hamburgers to the desired degree of doneness. Combine the remaining ingredients, heat just to simmering, and pour the sauce over the meat. Serve immediately.

SPINACH AND CHEESE HAMBURGERS   *4 servings*

2 pounds spinach
1 pound round steak, ground
¼ cup grated Parmesan cheese
1 garlic clove, finely minced
1 egg, slightly beaten

Pinch of monosodium glutamate
Salt and freshly ground black
  pepper
½ cup soft fresh bread crumbs

1. Trim the spinach and wash it well in several changes of cold water. Drain and place in a kettle with a tight-fitting lid. Do not add additional liquid. Cover and cook, stirring the leaves with a fork until they are all wilted. Cook for three to five minutes, until tender. Set aside to cool. When cool, squeeze and press the spinach to extract as much water as possible. Chop the spinach finely.

2. Combine the spinach, beef, cheese, garlic, egg, monosodium glutamate, salt and pepper to taste and bread crumbs. Shape into eight meat balls.

3. Broil or grill the balls until done, turning occasionally so that they will brown evenly. They should cook for fifteen to twenty minutes.

BURGUNDY BURGERS   *4 servings*

¼ cup butter
1 small onion, finely chopped
1¼ pounds beef round, ground
1 teaspoon dried marjoram
¼ teaspoon ground thyme

¼ teaspoon crumbled dried celery
  leaves
  Salt and freshly ground black
  pepper
½ cup red Burgundy wine

1. Melt two tablespoons of the butter and sauté the onion in it until transparent.

2. In a mixing bowl, mix the meat with the onion, marjoram, thyme, celery leaves, and salt and pepper to taste. Shape the mixture into eight patties, each about one-half inch thick.

3. Melt the remaining butter in the pan. Sauté the patties over high heat for about one minute on a side.

4. Add the wine and cook gently for about two minutes on each side, or until patties reach desired degree of doneness. Season the wine sauce with salt and pepper and serve with the burgers.

BITOCKS À LA RUSSE   *4 servings*

1 pound round steak, twice-ground (or use half veal)	2 tablespoons butter
Salt and freshly ground black pepper	¼ cup Beef Stock (page 473)
	½ cup heavy cream
	¼ teaspoon grated nutmeg
2 tablespoons chopped scallions	2 tablespoons chopped parsley
All-purpose flour	

1. Lightly blend the meat, salt and pepper to taste, and scallions. Shape into four patties and dredge lightly with flour. Brown in the butter.

2. Remove patties and add the stock. Reduce by half and add the cream. Cook for one minute. Add nutmeg and parsley and pour the sauce over the patties.

GREEN PEPPERS WITH MEAT BALLS   *4 servings*

1 pound lean beef, ground	2 tablespoons shortening
1 teaspoon salt	4 cups sliced green peppers
¼ teaspoon freshly ground black pepper	1 cup onion rings
	1 garlic clove, finely minced
½ teaspoon celery salt	2 cups Beef Stock (page 473)
3 tablespoons all-purpose flour	2 tablespoons cold water

1. Combine the beef with the salt, pepper and celery salt. Shape into one-and-one-half-inch balls. Roll in two tablespoons of the flour and brown in the shortening.

2. Add the green peppers, onion rings and garlic and brown lightly. Add the stock, cover, and cook slowly for about fifteen minutes, until tender.

3. Mix the remaining flour with the cold water to form a smooth paste. Add to the pan and cook until the gravy is medium thick. Serve hot.

HAMBURGER PIE   *6 servings*

1 small onion, finely chopped	¼ teaspoon freshly ground black pepper
1 garlic clove, finely minced	
1 tablespoon butter	1 cup tomato sauce
1 pound beef round, ground	1 tablespoon chopped parsley
½ green pepper, finely chopped	Unbaked Pie Pastry, 1-crust (page 637)
¾ teaspoon salt	4 slices of bacon

1. Preheat oven to hot (400° F.).
2. Sauté the onion and garlic in the butter until translucent but not browned. Add the meat and brown lightly.
3. Add the green pepper, salt, black pepper, tomato sauce and parsley. Pour into a nine-inch pie plate lined with the pastry.
4. Arrange the bacon slices over the mixture like the spokes of a wheel. Bake for twenty to twenty-five minutes.

CHEESEBURGER PIE   *4 servings*

2 tablespoons butter
1 pound beef round, ground
1 tablespoon finely chopped onion
2 tablespoons chopped green pepper
¼ cup all-purpose flour
1 teaspoon salt
¼ teaspoon freshly ground black pepper
1 cup (one 8-ounce can) tomato sauce
½ cup chopped celery
1 teaspoon Worcestershire sauce

CHEESE PASTRY:

½ cup shortening
1½ cups sifted all-purpose flour
½ teaspoon salt
½ cup freshly grated Cheddar cheese
3 to 6 tablespoons water

1. Preheat oven to hot (400° F.).
2. Melt the butter in a skillet, add the meat, onion and green pepper, and cook until meat is lightly browned.
3. Stir in the flour, salt and pepper. Add the tomato sauce and cook, stirring, until the mixture thickens. Stir in the celery and Worcestershire sauce. Reheat and pour into a baking dish (8 × 8 × 2 inches).
4. Prepare the cheese pastry by cutting the shortening into the flour and salt. Stir in the cheese and add just enough of the water to make a stiff dough. Roll out the dough on a pastry cloth or lightly floured board to one-quarter-inch thickness. Cut an eight-inch square and place atop the meat mixture.
5. Cut the remaining pastry into strips and arrange them lattice-style over the top of the pastry square. Bake for thirty to thirty-five minutes, or until the pastry is lightly browned.

BEEF MARJORAM LOAF   *6 servings*

2 pounds beef chuck or round, ground
½ cup soft fresh bread crumbs
1 onion, finely chopped
2 tablespoons butter
1 tablespoon dried marjoram
2 teaspoons salt
¼ teaspoon freshly ground black pepper
1 egg, lightly beaten
¼ cup finely chopped parsley

1. Preheat oven to moderate (325° F.).

2. Combine the meat and bread crumbs in a mixing bowl.

3. Sauté the onion in the butter in a skillet until the onion is transparent but not browned. Add to the meat mixture and combine well.

4. Add the marjoram, salt, pepper, egg and parsley. Mix lightly.

5. Pat the mixture into a loaf pan or ring mold. Bake for one and one-half hours.

6. If the ring mold is used, allow the baked meat to set for five to ten minutes before unmolding it onto a warm platter.

7. Fill the center with a vegetable. Serve with Mushroom Sauce (page 479).

ARMENIAN BEEF LOAF *6 servings*

2 pounds fresh spinach or 2 packages (10 ounces each) frozen chopped spinach	½ teaspoon grated nutmeg
	¼ teaspoon ground cinnamon
	1 cup cooked rice
1 pound round steak, ground	2 eggs, slightly beaten
¾ cup finely chopped onions	3 slices of bacon
Salt and freshly ground black pepper	

1. Preheat oven to moderate (350° F.).

2. If fresh spinach is used, rinse it well in several changes of cold water. Drain, place in a kettle, and cook in only the water that clings to the leaves. Chop well. If frozen spinach is used, cook it according to package directions; drain.

3. Combine the spinach, beef, onions, salt and pepper to taste, nutmeg, cinnamon, rice and eggs. Pack the mixture into a buttered loaf pan (9 × 5 inches). Arrange the bacon on top. Bake for one hour, or until firm. Serve with Tomato Sauce II (page 494).

CORNMEAL BEEF CASSEROLE *12 servings*

¾ cup shortening, melted	¼ teaspoon freshly ground black pepper
⅔ cup chopped celery	
⅔ cup chopped green peppers	2 cups sifted all-purpose flour
1 cup chopped onions	4 teaspoons double-acting baking powder
½ garlic clove, finely minced	
3 pounds ground beef	2 teaspoons sugar
2 cups cooked rice	1 teaspoon baking soda
4 cups (four 8-ounce cans) tomato sauce	1½ cups yellow cornmeal
	2 cups buttermilk or sour milk
¼ cup chili powder	4 eggs, well beaten
5 teaspoons salt	

1. Preheat oven to hot (425° F.).

2. Put one-quarter cup of the shortening in a large skillet. Add the celery, green peppers, onions, garlic and beef. Brown the beef well.

3. Stir in the rice, tomato sauce, chili powder, three teaspoons of the salt and the pepper. Simmer while preparing topping.

4. Sift together the flour, baking powder, remaining salt, the sugar and baking soda. Stir in the cornmeal.

5. Combine the buttermilk, remaining shortening and the eggs. Add to the dry ingredients, stirring until all dry particles are moistened.

6. Spoon the meat mixture into two baking pans (9 × 9 × 2 inches). Spoon half of the cornmeal batter onto each pan. Bake for thirty to thirty-five minutes.

INDIVIDUAL MEAT LOAVES   *6 servings*

½ pound lean pork, ground
1½ pounds beef chuck, ground
 1 medium onion, finely chopped
¼ cup chopped celery
¼ cup chopped parsley
 1 cup soft fresh bread crumbs
 1 egg, lightly beaten

¾ cup Beef Stock (page 473), tomato juice or milk, approximately
 1 teaspoon salt
¼ teaspoon freshly ground black pepper
½ teaspoon dried basil

1. Preheat oven to moderate (350° F.).

2. Cook the pork in a skillet until lightly browned. Mix with the remaining ingredients, adding enough liquid to bind and seasonings to taste. Pack the mixture into six individual molds or custard cups and bake for about forty-five minutes. Serve hot or cold.

CHILI CON CARNE   *4 servings*

 1 pound beef round, ground
 1 large onion, minced
 1 garlic clove, minced
 3 tablespoons olive oil
 1 cup tomato sauce, fresh or canned
 1 can (6 ounces) tomato paste
½ teaspoon ground cuminseed

½ teaspoon dried orégano
¼ teaspoon crushed red pepper
 1 bay leaf
 2 tablespoons chili powder, or more
¼ cup chopped fresh basil or 1 tablespoon dried basil
1½ teaspoons salt
 2 cups cooked pinto beans

1. Sauté the beef, onion and garlic slowly in the oil.

2. Add the tomato sauce, tomato paste, and seasonings. Continue simmering over low heat for about ten minutes.

3. Add the beans, cover, and simmer for one hour or longer. If additional liquid is needed, add beef stock so that the mixture has the consistency of soup.

CHILI CON CARNE TEXAS STYLE   *6 cups*

1½ pounds ground beef
2 medium onions, chopped
1½ teaspoons salt
2 teaspoons ground turmeric
1 tablespoon ground coriander
2 tablespoons mole or chili powder

1 teaspoon chopped hot green pepper (fresh or canned)
1 cup peeled Italian plum tomatoes or 4 medium tomatoes, peeled and chopped

1. In a skillet cook all the ingredients except the tomatoes for ten minutes, stirring to break up the meat.
2. Add the tomatoes and simmer, covered, for twenty minutes.

DILLED BEEF KEBABS   *6 servings*

2 pounds lean beef chuck, ground
2 tablespoons dill pickle liquid
2 teaspoons snipped fresh dill
2 teaspoons salt
¼ teaspoon freshly ground black pepper

1 teaspoon Worcestershire sauce
½ teaspoon coriander seeds, freshly ground
3 dill pickles, cut into halves
3 tomatoes, cut into large wedges

1. Mix together the meat, pickle liquid, dill, salt, pepper, Worcestershire sauce and coriander. Shape into one-and-one-half-inch balls and alternate with pieces of dill pickle on skewers.
2. Broil three to four inches from the source of heat in an oven broiler or outdoor grill for three to five minutes, or until browned.
3. Arrange the tomato wedges on separate skewers and broil alongside of the meat, which has been turned, for five to seven minutes longer, until the desired degree of doneness is reached.

BEEF AND CHEESE ROLL   *6 to 8 servings*

3 slices of bread, crusts removed
1½ pounds chopped beef
2 eggs
1 teaspoon salt
1 teaspoon dry mustard
¼ teaspoon freshly ground black pepper
½ teaspoon ground thyme

2 tablespoons grated onion
¼ cup finely chopped parsley
½ pound mozzarella or Swiss cheese, thinly sliced
2 tablespoons butter, melted
1½ cups Tomato Sauce I (page 493) or Brown Sauce (page 477)

1. Preheat oven to moderate (375° F.).
2. Wet the bread, press out excess moisture, and add bread to the meat.
3. Add eggs, salt, mustard, pepper, thyme, onion, and parsley. Mix with the fingers until well blended.

4. On a piece of wax paper press the meat into a thin rectangle. Spread cheese over meat and roll, beginning at a narrow end, using the paper to lift the meat and aid in the rolling.

5. Carefully place the roll in a shallow baking pan with the joined edges of the meat underneath the roll. Brush with the melted butter. Bake for about forty-five minutes. Serve with tomato sauce or brown sauce to which pan drippings have been added.

HERBED MEAT FRITTERS   *6 servings*

6 eggs, separated	1 tablespoon finely chopped chives
1½ cups leftover roast beef, ground	1 onion, grated
½ teaspoon baking powder	Salt and freshly ground black
½ teaspoon lemon juice	pepper
1 tablespoon minced parsley	

1. Beat the egg yolks well. Combine them with the remaining ingredients except the egg whites.

2. Beat the egg whites until stiff and fold them into the batter. Drop by spoonfuls onto a buttered hot griddle or skillet. When puffed and brown around the edges, turn and brown the other side.

BEEF SLICES WITH CAPER SAUCE   *4 to 6 servings*

3 tablespoons butter	1 teaspoon sugar
3 tablespoons all-purpose flour	1 teaspoon paprika
2½ cups milk	2 teaspoons vinegar
1 teaspoon salt	1 small onion, thinly sliced
¼ teaspoon freshly ground black pepper	¼ cup capers
	1 pound cooked beef, thinly sliced

1. Melt the butter and blend in the flour. Add the milk slowly, stirring. Bring to a boil and simmer for one minute, stirring constantly. Add the remaining ingredients except beef.

2. Reheat the mixture while spooning the sauce over the meat slices, but do not allow to boil.

GLAZED CORNED BEEF   *8 to 10 servings*

5 to 6 pounds corned beef brisket	3 bay leaves
3 onions, sliced	1 tablespoon Düsseldorf mustard
2 or 3 garlic cloves, finely minced	⅓ cup light brown sugar
6 whole cloves	

1. Place the corned beef in a Dutch oven. Barely cover corned beef with boiling water.

2. Add the onions, garlic, cloves and bay leaves. Bring the mixture to a boil. Cover the Dutch oven tightly with aluminum foil and the cover. Simmer gently, but do not allow to boil, for fifty minutes per pound of meat, or until meat is tender when pricked with a fork.

3. Preheat oven to moderate (350° F.).

4. Remove the meat from the liquid and drain. Place the meat in a shallow pan, fat side uppermost. Score the fat. Spread the top with the mustard and then with the sugar. Bake for fifteen to twenty minutes, or until well glazed. Serve corned beef hot or cold.

SHEPHERD'S PIE   *6 servings*

5 tablespoons butter
1 onion, finely chopped
4 cups ground cooked roast beef
2 cups beef gravy
2 teaspoons Worcestershire sauce
½ teaspoon monosodium glutamate
1 teaspoon salt

¼ teaspoon freshly ground black pepper
10 medium potatoes, peeled
⅓ cup light cream or milk, heated
1 egg, lightly beaten, or 2 tablespoons melted butter

1. Preheat oven to hot (425° F.).

2. Melt one tablespoon of the butter and sauté the onion until tender but not browned.

3. Remove from the heat and add the beef, gravy, Worcestershire sauce, monosodium glutamate, one-half teaspoon of the salt and the pepper.

4. Boil the potatoes in boiling salted water until tender. Drain and mash, together with the remaining butter and salt and the cream or milk. Beat until fluffy by hand or electric mixer.

5. Place the meat mixture in the bottom of a greased deep one-and-one-half-quart casserole. Top with mashed potatoes, mounded into a dome. Brush with beaten egg or melted butter.

6. Bake for fifteen to twenty minutes, until heated through and lightly browned.

CORNED-BEEF HASH CHEZ SOI   *4 to 6 servings*

2 cups finely cubed cooked corned beef (about ¾ pound)
3 medium potatoes, cooked and very finely cubed
2 tablespoons butter, melted
¾ cup heavy cream

1 teaspoon Worcestershire sauce, or more
3 tablespoons finely chopped parsley
1 tablespoon finely chopped chives
4 to 6 freshly poached eggs

1. Combine the corned beef and the potatoes in a mixing bowl.

2. Combine the butter, cream, Worcestershire sauce, parsley and chives. Pour the mixture over all. Toss gently but do not mash the potatoes. Press the mixture into four to six large patties.

3. When ready to serve, brown the patties in butter and cook until thoroughly heated.

4. Make an indentation in each cake and fill with a trimmed poached egg that has been drained on paper towels.

CORNED-BEEF CASSEROLE   *4 to 6 servings*

4 cups corned-beef hash
5 tablespoons butter
¾ cup chopped onions
1 garlic clove, finely minced

1 green pepper, seeded and chopped
½ cup finely chopped parsley
½ cup soft fresh bread crumbs
¾ cup grated Cheddar cheese

1. Preheat oven to hot (400° F.).

2. Flake the corned-beef hash with a fork.

3. Melt four tablespoons of the butter in a skillet and cook the onions, garlic and green pepper in it until onions are wilted. Add the corned-beef hash.

4. Spoon half of the mixture into a buttered casserole and sprinkle the layer with the parsley. Spoon the remaining corned-beef mixture into the casserole.

5. Toss the bread crumbs in the remaining butter and sprinkle the crumbs and cheese over the top of the casserole. Bake for twenty-five to thirty minutes, until casserole is brown and bubbly.

CHIPPED BEEF AND CHEESE   *4 servings*

2 tablespoons finely minced onion
1 garlic clove, finely minced
2 tablespoons butter
4 ounces fine noodles, cooked and drained
1 cup pitted ripe olives, cut into wedges

1 cup cottage cheese
1 cup sour cream
1 cup chipped beef, shredded
Freshly ground black pepper
½ cup buttered soft fresh bread crumbs

1. Preheat oven to moderate (350° F.).

2. Sauté the onion and garlic in the butter. Combine the onion mixture with all the remaining ingredients except the bread crumbs.

3. Turn into a greased one-and-one-half-quart casserole. Sprinkle with the bread crumbs and bake for twenty to twenty-five minutes, or until hot, bubbly and lightly browned.

CREAMED CHIPPED BEEF WITH NUTMEG   *6 servings*

2 jars (4 ounces each) chipped beef
¼ cup butter
¼ cup all-purpose flour
1½ cups milk, scalded
½ cup heavy cream

Freshly ground black pepper
¼ teaspoon cayenne pepper
Worcestershire sauce (optional)
½ teaspoon grated nutmeg

1. Place the chipped beef in a colander and pour boiling water over it. Pull beef apart with the fingers and let stand until ready to use.

2. Melt the butter and stir in the flour with a wire whisk. Add the milk, stirring rapidly with the whisk. When the mixture is thickened and smooth, cook, stirring, for three or four minutes. Add the cream and seasonings to taste. Add the chipped beef and stir just enough to mix the meat with the sauce. Heat thoroughly and serve on toast points.

. . . .

VEAL

. . . .

Veal of the best quality is milk-fed veal. This is the flesh of a calf that is eight to ten weeks old when slaughtered. In its prime condition for cooking, it is fine grained and velvety in texture and has a delicate pink-white color, the whiter the better. Europeans in general have a special fondness for veal. Some of the most elegant preparations in Italian, Austrian and French cooking are based on veal. Veal is a year-round meat and may be eaten hot or cold.

BRAISED LEG OF VEAL   *About 8 servings*

½ cup plus 2 tablespoons butter
1 garlic clove, finely minced
1 teaspoon salt
¼ teaspoon ground rosemary
  Pinch of dried thyme
  Freshly ground black pepper
1 small leg of veal (about 5 pounds), boned and tied
2 cups thinly sliced onions

2 celery ribs, trimmed and cut into 2-inch lengths
1 carrot, scraped and cut into 1-inch lengths
1 bay leaf
  Veal or Chicken Stock (pages 474 and 475)
1 tablespoon cornstarch
¼ cup dry sherry

1. Preheat oven to moderate (375° F.).

2. Cream two tablespoons of the butter with the garlic, salt, rosemary, thyme and pepper to taste. Rub this over the meat.

3. Place the remaining butter, the onions, celery, carrot and bay leaf in a heavy casserole or Dutch oven. Put the meat on the bed of vegetables and cover. Bake for about two hours, until meat is very tender. Turn the meat

several times as it cooks. If necessary add a little stock to keep it from becoming dry.

4. Remove the meat and strain the broth. Measure it and add enough stock to make two cups. Boil the liquid rapidly. Blend the cornstarch with the wine and stir it into the boiling sauce. Cook, stirring, until smooth. Serve the meat with the sauce.

BRAISED BONED VEAL   *8 to 10 servings*

3 tablespoons vegetable oil
1 loin of veal (4½ pounds), boned, rolled and tied
3 tablespoons butter
2 onions, peeled and cut into ¼-inch slices
2 carrots, scraped and cut into ¼-inch rounds
3 parsley sprigs
1 bay leaf
1 garlic clove
3 slices of bacon
Salt and freshly ground black pepper
2 cups Veal or Chicken Stock (pages 474 and 475), approximately

1. Preheat oven to moderate (325° F.).
2. Heat the oil in a heavy casserole and brown the veal on all sides. Remove veal and keep warm. Discard browned oil and add the butter to the casserole. Add the onions, carrots, parsley, bay leaf and garlic. Cover and cook slowly for five minutes.
3. Blanch the bacon in boiling water for three minutes and drain.
4. Sprinkle the browned veal with salt and pepper and place it atop the vegetables. Arrange the blanched bacon on top. Add one-half cup of the stock and cover.
5. Bake the veal for two hours, basting frequently and adding more stock as necessary. Serve the veal with the strained pan juices.

ROAST VEAL WITH LEMON-RICE STUFFING   *6 servings*

1 breast of veal (3 to 4 pounds), boned
Salt and freshly ground black pepper
¼ teaspoon ground ginger
2 cups cooked rice
⅓ cup raisins
1 teaspoon grated lemon rind
½ teaspoon dried basil
2 tablespoons butter
¼ cup finely chopped onion
1 garlic clove, finely minced
8 slices of bacon

1. Preheat oven to moderate (325° F.).
2. Spread the veal flat on a board. Season it with salt and pepper to taste and the ginger.
3. Combine the rice, raisins, lemon rind and basil. Melt the butter and sauté the onion and garlic until tender. Add to rice mixture.

4. Place the stuffing over half of the meat, fold over the other half, and sew together or skewer with food picks.

5. Put the meat in a shallow baking pan and cover with the bacon slices. Bake for twenty-five to thirty minutes per pound, or until meat is tender, about two hours.

POITRINE DE VEAU FARCIE AUX OLIVES   *6 to 8 servings*

1 breast of veal (4 pounds), boned, with bones reserved
½ pound lean pork, ground
2 cups soft fresh bread crumbs
⅓ cup milk
12 pitted black olives, coarsely chopped
6 parsley sprigs, chopped
1 garlic clove, finely minced
½ teaspoon dried basil

¼ teaspoon salt
¼ teaspoon freshly ground black pepper
⅛ teaspoon grated nutmeg
1 egg, lightly beaten
2 tablespoons olive oil
1 onion, sliced
2 tomatoes, skinned and chopped
1 cup white wine
1 cup Chicken Stock (page 475)

1. Preheat oven to moderate (325° F.).

2. Wipe the veal and spread out flat. Mix together the pork, bread crumbs, milk, olives, parsley, garlic, basil, salt, pepper, nutmeg and egg. Spread this mixture over the veal. Roll up and tie securely.

3. Heat the oil in a heavy casserole. Sauté the onion in it until tender but not browned. In the same casserole brown the veal lightly on all sides.

4. Add the tomatoes and wine and bring to a boil. Add the stock and veal bones and bring to a boil again.

5. Cover the casserole with aluminum foil and the casserole lid. Bake for three hours, or until tender.

6. Remove the veal to a serving platter. Discard the bones and reduce the liquid in the casserole by one third. Season to taste and serve separately.

Note: If the veal is to be served cold, allow it to cool in the liquid.

BRAISED VEAL SHANKS   *6 servings*

6 veal shanks
All-purpose flour
Salt and freshly ground black pepper
½ teaspoon dried orégano
3 tablespoons butter
3 tablespoons salad oil
¾ cup finely chopped onions

¾ cup finely chopped celery
¾ cup finely chopped carrots
1 garlic clove, finely minced
Pinch of dried thyme
¾ cup tomato purée
¾ cup dry white wine
½ cup Brown Sauce (page 477)

1. Preheat oven to moderate (350° F.).

2. Wipe the veal shanks well with a damp cloth. Combine flour, salt and pepper to taste and the orégano and dredge the meat with the mixture. Brown in the butter and oil and transfer to a large casserole or Dutch oven.

3. Add the vegetables, garlic and thyme to the skillet and brown, stirring, for five minutes. Transfer to the casserole and arrange around the meat.

4. Pour the tomato purée, wine and brown sauce over the meat and cover closely. Bake for one and one-half hours, or until the meat is tender.

GINGERED VEAL STEAKS   *6 servings*

2 tablespoons all-purpose flour
1½ teaspoons salt
1 teaspoon ground ginger
1½ teaspoons dry mustard
3 veal shoulder steaks, ½ to ¾ inch thick

2 tablespoons butter
2 onions, sliced
1 cup Chicken Stock (page 475)
1 cup light cream or evaporated milk

1. Mix together the flour, salt, ginger and mustard. Pound this seasoned flour into the veal steaks.

2. Brown the steaks in the butter. Pour off the drippings. Cover the steaks with the sliced onions, add the stock, cover tightly, and cook for forty-five minutes to one hour, until the meat is tender.

3. Remove the meat to a platter and keep it warm. Add the cream to the cooking liquid and heat it thoroughly. Strain the sauce and serve it separately.

PULPETAS (stuffed veal steaks)   *6 servings*

1 cup chopped ham
1 cup chopped pork
1 hard-cooked egg, chopped
⅓ cup chopped pimiento-stuffed green olives
2 small garlic cloves, minced
¼ cup chopped parsley
⅛ teaspoon grated nutmeg

2 tablespoons sherry
1 raw egg
6 boned veal steaks, about ⅛ inch thick
¼ cup olive oil or melted butter
1 medium onion, chopped
¼ cup chopped blanched almonds
2 cups (one 1-pound can) tomatoes

1. Preheat oven to moderate (350° F.).

2. Combine the ham, pork, hard-cooked egg, olives, half of the garlic, half of the parsley, the nutmeg, half of the sherry and the raw egg. Mix thoroughly. Spread on the veal steaks, roll the steaks in jelly-roll fashion, and fasten with food picks.

3. Heat the olive oil. Add the rolled steaks, onion, almonds and remaining garlic and parsley. Cook until the steaks are browned on all sides.

4. Place the veal rolls in a baking pan (12 × 7 × 2 inches). Combine the onion mixture, tomatoes and remaining sherry. Pour over the steaks and bake for about one hour, until the meat is tender.

There are few dishes in anyone's repertoire more easily prepared than the thin slices of veal called scaloppine *by the Italians,* escalopes de veau *by the French,* Wienerschnitzel *by the Austrians, and veal scallops by us. In each country there are many versions of the basic dish. Because these thin slices may be quickly sautéed, they are ideal for summer menus.*

WIENERSCHNITZEL FOR ONE   *1 serving*

2 thin slices of veal cut from the leg (½ pound)
Salt and freshly ground black pepper
2 tablespoons all-purpose flour
1 egg, lightly beaten

½ cup fine bread crumbs made from day-old bread
3 tablespoons butter
2 thin slices of lemon
Chopped fresh parsley

1. Pound the veal slices thin. Sprinkle them lightly with salt and pepper and flour.
2. Dip the slices into the beaten egg, then into the bread crumbs.
3. Heat the butter in a skillet large enough to accommodate the slices. Cook quickly until golden on one side, then turn and cook until golden on the other. It may be necessary to add more butter to the skillet.
4. Transfer the meat to a warm plate and garnish with lemon slices and chopped parsley.

VEAL CHATEAUBRIAND   *2 servings*

4 thin slices of veal (about ¾ pound)
¼ cup butter
2 teaspoons finely chopped shallots
2 mushrooms, finely chopped
Pinch of dried thyme
⅓ bay leaf

½ cup white wine
½ teaspoon finely chopped fresh tarragon or ¼ teaspoon dried tarragon
Chopped parsley

1. Bone the veal slices and pound until thin. Heat half of the butter in a skillet and quickly brown the slices of veal on both sides. Transfer them to a warm platter while preparing the sauce.
2. Add to the skillet the shallots, mushrooms, thyme, bay leaf and remaining butter. Cook, stirring, but do not brown. Add the wine and tarragon. Cook for three or four minutes to reduce slightly.
3. Return the veal to the skillet. Spoon the sauce over the slices. When thoroughly hot, remove the bay leaf. Serve the veal sprinkled with parsley.

VEAL SCALOPPINE CAMILLO   *4 servings*

1 cup soft fresh bread crumbs
1 teaspoon dried orégano
  Salt and freshly ground black pepper

¼ cup olive oil, approximately
8 boneless veal scallops
3 tablespoons butter

1. Preheat broiler.
2. Mix the bread crumbs with the orégano and salt and pepper to taste. Add the olive oil gradually while tossing the crumbs with a two-pronged fork. The bread crumbs should be coated with oil but should remain flaky.
3. Pound the veal scallops until thin. Sprinkle them lightly with salt and pepper. Cook the scallops in the butter on one side only until they are golden brown.
4. Remove the scallops from the skillet. Using a spatula, spread the uncooked side with the oiled bread crumbs.
5. Broil four inches from the source of heat until the crumb mixture is golden brown. Do not overcook. Serve immediately with sautéed zucchini rounds.

SALTIMBOCCA   *4 servings*

8 slices of boneless veal (4 ounces each)
  Salt and freshly ground black pepper
8 fresh sage leaves, or dried sage

12 thin slices of prosciutto (dry-cured Italian ham)
¼ cup butter
¼ cup Marsala wine or sweet vermouth

1. Place the veal slices between pieces of wax paper and pound slices thin with a mallet or rolling pin. Sprinkle the slices on both sides with salt and pepper. Top each slice with a leaf of fresh sage or sprinkle with dried sage to taste. Cover with a slice of prosciutto. Skewer with food picks.
2. Melt the butter in a skillet and brown the meat quickly in it on both sides. Add the wine to the skillet, cook rapidly to reduce slightly, and serve the meat hot with pan gravy over all.

ESCALOPES DE VEAU À LA PROVENÇALE   *6 servings*

12 small slices of veal cut from the leg or shoulder (about 2 pounds)
⅓ cup all-purpose flour
1 teaspoon salt
⅓ cup olive oil
1 onion, chopped
1 garlic clove, minced

1 cup canned tomatoes
½ cup Chicken Stock (page 475)
1 green pepper, seeded and cut into strips
1 pound spaghetti, cooked
6 rolled anchovies

1. Dredge the veal with the flour mixed with the salt.

2. Heat the oil in a skillet and sauté the onion and garlic in it until onion is golden. Sauté the veal in the oil until golden on both sides.

3. Add the tomatoes, stock and green pepper. Simmer, covered, for thirty minutes.

4. Arrange the veal on a bed of cooked spaghetti, spoon the sauce over the meat, and garnish with anchovies.

BRACIOLETTE RIPIENE (stuffed veal rolls)   *4 to 6 servings*

12 small slices of veal cut from the leg	Salt and freshly ground black pepper
12 small thin slices of lean ham	2 tablespoons olive oil
3 tablespoons pine nuts	2 tablespoons butter
1 cup chopped parsley	½ cup dry white wine
2 tablespoons raisins	
2 tablespoons grated Parmesan cheese	

1. Pound the veal slices until flattened. Place a slice of ham on each slice of veal. Combine the pine nuts, parsley, raisins, cheese and salt and pepper to taste. Place a spoonful of the mixture in the center of the ham. Roll the veal, ham, and filling in jelly-roll fashion. Skewer or tie with strings.

2. Brown the stuffed rolls on all sides in the oil and butter. Add the wine to the skillet, cover, and simmer for fifteen to twenty minutes. Remove the skewers or string from the rolls.

VEAL CHOPS WITH SAUCE SOUBISE   *4 servings*

4 large veal chops, loin or rib	3 medium onions, chopped
6 tablespoons all-purpose flour	⅛ teaspoon grated nutmeg
½ cup butter	1 cup milk
Salt and freshly ground black pepper	¼ cup heavy cream
	¾ cup grated Swiss cheese

1. Coat the chops with three tablespoons of the flour and brown on both sides in three tablespoons of the butter. Sprinkle with one-half teaspoon salt and one-eighth teaspoon pepper. Cover and simmer for about twenty minutes, until tender.

2. Meanwhile, place the onions and two tablespoons of the butter in a saucepan. Cover and cook gently, without browning, until onions are tender.

3. Melt the remaining butter and blend in the remaining flour and the nutmeg. Stir in the milk and cream, bring to a boil, stirring, and cook for two minutes. Add one-half cup of the cheese. Season with salt and pepper to taste. Add the onions to the sauce.

4. Arrange the chops in a heatproof serving dish. Top each with some of the sauce and sprinkle with the remaining cheese. Brown lightly under the broiler.

STUFFED VEAL CHOPS   *4 servings*

4 double-rib veal chops
4 small thin slices of boiled ham
4 slices of Gruyère cheese
  Salt and freshly ground black pepper

Vegetable oil (about ¼ cup)
4 shallots, minced
Dry white wine (about ½ cup)
Parsley and chives, finely chopped

1. Have the butcher split the meaty part of the chops all the way to, but not through, the bone.
2. Preheat oven to moderate (350° F.).
3. Place a slice of ham and a slice of cheese into the slit in each chop. Close the opening with food picks so it will not come open while cooking.
4. Season the chops with salt and pepper and brown quickly in the oil in a heavy casserole. During the last few minutes of browning add the shallots.
5. Pour around the chops one-quarter cup of wine or more if necessary to keep chops from sticking to the pan. Transfer the casserole to the oven. Bake, uncovered, for about forty-five minutes.
6. Remove the chops to a serving platter and keep warm. Scrape the sides and bottom of the pan and add enough additional wine to make a sauce. Pour sparingly around the chops. Sprinkle with parsley and chives.

VEAL CHOPS WITH MUSHROOM STUFFING   *6 servings*

½ pound fresh spinach
2 tablespoons butter
¼ cup finely chopped prosciutto (dry-cured Italian ham)
3 tablespoons finely chopped onion
2 tablespoons finely chopped shallots or green onions
½ cup chopped mushrooms
½ garlic clove, finely minced
3 tablespoons soft fresh bread crumbs

⅓ cup grated Parmesan cheese
  Salt and freshly ground black pepper
1 egg yolk
¼ teaspoon grated nutmeg
6 double-rib veal chops
⅓ cup vegetable oil
½ cup Chicken or Veal Stock (pages 474 and 475)

1. Trim the spinach and wash thoroughly. Place the drained spinach in a saucepan with a tight-fitting lid. Do not add additional water. Simmer, covered, for three to five minutes, until spinach is wilted.
2. Drain the spinach and let cool. When cool enough to handle, press it between the hands, then chop.

A choice of chops

3. Melt the butter and add the prosciutto, onion, shallots, mushrooms and garlic. Simmer, uncovered, until almost all the liquid has evaporated. The mixture should be lightly browned.

4. Add the spinach and stir well. Add the bread crumbs, cheese, and salt and pepper to taste. Remove the saucepan from the heat and let cool slightly. Add the egg yolk and nutmeg and mix rapidly. Use the mixture to stuff the veal chops.

5. Season the chops with salt and pepper and brown quickly in the oil in a heavy casserole.

6. Add enough stock to the casserole to keep chops from sticking to the pan. Transfer the casserole to the oven. Bake, uncovered, for about one hour. Add more stock if the pan becomes too dry.

7. Transfer the chops to a warm serving platter. Add the remaining stock to the casserole. Scrape the bottom and sides and cook over high heat for two minutes. Pour the pan juices over the chops.

VEAL CHOPS WITH MUSTARD SAUCE   *6 servings*

6 veal chops, each 1 inch thick	¼ cup heavy cream
3 tablespoons butter	3 tablespoons olive oil
3 tablespoons vinegar	Salt and freshly ground black
2 teaspoons prepared mustard, preferably Dijon or Düsseldorf	pepper
	Chopped fresh parsley

1. Cook the veal chops in two tablespoons of the butter until they are golden brown. Reduce the heat and cook the chops to the desired degree of doneness.

2. Meanwhile, melt the remaining butter and combine with the vinegar, mustard, cream, olive oil, and salt and pepper to taste. Blend thoroughly.

3. Remove the chops to a warm serving platter and keep them hot. Add the sauce to the skillet in which the chops were cooked. Heat thoroughly, stirring in the brown pan juices. Pour the sauce over the chops and sprinkle with parsley.

VEAL CHOPS AU VIN BLANC   *4 servings*

4 thin veal chops	2 tablespoons chopped parsley
Salt and freshly ground black pepper	½ cup Chicken Stock (page 475)
1 tablespoon butter	½ cup dry white wine
3 slices of lean bacon, finely diced	2 egg yolks, beaten
2 tablespoons finely chopped shallots or onion	1 teaspoon lemon juice

1. Sprinkle the chops with salt and pepper.

2. Cook the butter and bacon over low heat, stirring, for two minutes. Add the chops and cook for twenty to twenty-five minutes, turning occasionally. When done, transfer the chops and bacon bits to a warm platter.

3. Pour off most of the fat from the pan and add the shallots. Cook, stirring, for about two minutes, then add the parsley, stock and wine. Stir to dissolve the brown particles that cling to the bottom and sides of the pan. Cook over high heat briefly until liquid is slightly reduced. Season with additional salt and pepper to taste.

4. Remove the skillet from the heat. Add a little of the hot liquid to the egg yolks, then pour the yolk mixture into the skillet, stirring rapidly. Gently reheat the sauce, stirring constantly, but do not boil.

5. Return the veal and bacon bits to the sauce and heat thoroughly, but do not boil. Stir the lemon juice into the sauce and serve immediately.

VEAL AND TUNA LOAF   *6 servings*

1 pound veal, ground
2 cans (7 ounces each) tuna, drained
2 eggs
½ cup fine dry bread crumbs
¾ cup chopped parsley
¼ cup finely chopped green onions

1 teaspoon dried rosemary (optional)
¼ cup finely chopped green pepper
1 teaspoon salt
  Freshly ground black pepper
3 slices of bacon

1. Preheat oven to moderate (350° F.).

2. In a mixing bowl combine all the ingredients except the bacon slices. Blend well.

3. Line a nine-inch pie plate with aluminum foil. Shape the meat mixture into an oval loaf. Place the loaf on the foil and arrange the bacon slices on top.

4. Bake for one and one-half hours. Serve with Tomato Sauce III (page 494).

VEAL GOULASH   *6 to 8 servings*

3 pounds shoulder or rump of veal, cut into 1½-inch cubes
  Beef suet
1 bay leaf
1 tablespoon caraway seeds
1 tablespoon dill seeds
1 tablespoon salt
½ tablespoon black peppercorns

2 cups Veal or Beef Stock (pages 474 and 473)
3 cups onions rings
3 tablespoons butter
¼ cup all-purpose flour
⅓ cup cold water
2 tablespoons paprika, or more
1 cup sour cream

1. Brown the meat in rendered beef suet in a deep saucepan or Dutch oven.

2. Add the bay leaf, caraway seeds, dill seeds and salt. Tie the pepper-corns in a cheesecloth bag and add along with the stock. Cover and cook slowly for one to one and one-half hours, until meat is tender.

3. Meanwhile cook the onion rings in the butter until they are wilted. Add them to the meat twenty minutes before the end of cooking time.

4. Blend the flour with cold water and stir it into the cooking liquid. Stir until thickened. Discard the bag of peppercorns and remove the veal from the heat. Stir in the paprika and sour cream and heat thoroughly but do not boil.

VEAL LOAF WITH ANCHOVIES   *8 servings*

3 pounds veal, ground
4 slices of day-old bread, crusts removed and roughly torn
1 bunch of parsley, stems removed
3 celery ribs, roughly chopped
½ cup water
1½ teaspoons salt
½ teaspoon freshly ground black pepper
2 eggs, lightly beaten
1 tablespoon lemon juice
1 can (2 ounces) flat anchovy fillets
Lemon slices and additional anchovies for garnish

1. Preheat oven to moderate (325° F.).

2. Place the veal in a large bowl. Put half of the bread, parsley, celery and water in a blender and blend until well minced. Add to the meat. Repeat with the remaining bread, parsley, celery and water. (Ingredients may be finely chopped if blender is not available.)

3. Add the salt, pepper, eggs and lemon juice to the mixture; mix lightly but well.

4. Pack half of the meat mixture into a loaf pan (9 × 5 × 3 inches). Arrange the anchovy fillets over the surface and top with the remaining meat mixture.

5. Bake for two hours, or until done. Unmold onto a warm platter and garnish with lemon slices and anchovies.

VEAL SUCCOTASH   *6 to 8 servings*

⅓ cup olive oil
2 garlic cloves, finely minced
2 cups thinly sliced onions
1 pound veal, ground
1 small eggplant, peeled and cut into large cubes
¼ cup all-purpose flour
3 zucchini, trimmed and cut into 1-inch slices
3 green peppers, cored, seeded and cut into cubes
Salt and freshly ground black pepper
5 firm ripe tomatoes, peeled and chopped
2 cups fresh corn cut from the cob
¼ cup finely chopped parsley

1. Preheat oven to moderate (375° F.).

2. Heat two tablespoons of the oil in a skillet and cook the garlic and onions in it until onions are wilted. Add the veal and cook, stirring with a wooden spoon to break up bits of meat, until veal loses its red color. Transfer the mixture to a heatproof casserole.

3. Heat the remaining oil in the skillet. Dredge the eggplant with the flour and brown it on all sides in the oil.

4. Add the browned cubes to the casserole along with the remaining ingredients. Gently fold the vegetables into the veal and onions. Cover. Bake for about one hour, or until done. Sprinkle with parsley.

FRIKADELLER (Danish meat balls)   *About 6 meat balls*

½ pound raw boneless veal
½ pound raw boneless lean pork
2 tablespoons all-purpose flour
1½ cups milk
1 egg, lightly beaten

1 medium onion, grated
Salt and freshly ground black pepper
Butter

1. Using the finest knife of a grinder, grind the veal and pork several times, until the meats are very smooth and well blended.

2. Add the flour, milk, egg, onion, and salt and pepper to taste. Mix well. Shape into flat oval cakes about three inches long and one inch thick.

3. Heat the butter in a heavy skillet and brown the cakes slowly on both sides.

Like many good things in the world of cuisine, croquettes began in a French kitchen. The name derives from croquer, which means to crunch; and of course a successful croquette has a crunchy exterior hiding the tender and flavorful contents. Croquettes are an ideal way to use leftover cooked foods. Serve croquettes with a favorite sauce for a luncheon or supper dish.

VEAL CROQUETTES   *4 to 6 servings*

1½ cups cold cooked veal
1½ cups Veal Stock (page 474) or milk
6 tablespoons butter
1 medium onion, finely chopped
1 teaspoon salt
½ teaspoon finely ground black pepper

1 garlic clove, finely minced
¾ cup all-purpose flour
1 egg, beaten with a little milk or water
1 cup fine fresh bread crumbs
Fat for deep frying

1. Cut the meat into small pieces. Put it with the stock into an electric blender and blend to a purée.

2. Over low heat melt the butter and add the onion. Cook gently for four or five minutes. Add the salt, pepper and garlic. Stir in one-half cup of the flour and cook, stirring, until the mixture is a smooth paste.

3. Add the blended meat to the pan. Mix and stir over low heat until all is quite thick. Pour the mixture into a shallow dish and chill.

4. Form the chilled mixture into round cakes or cylinders. Roll them in the remaining flour, dip them into the beaten egg, and roll in the crumbs. Chill the cakes again until they are firm.

5. Fry the croquettes in deep fat heated to 360° F. on a frying thermometer. When they are nicely browned, drain on paper towels. Serve with Tomato Sauce III (page 494) or Mustard Hollandaise Sauce (page 485).

Note: This recipe may be used to make croquettes of fish, chicken, or beef, as well as vegetable croquettes. The seasoning may be varied accordingly and any appropriate flavorful sauce may be served with the croquettes.

. . . .

PORK
. . . .

ROAST LOIN OF PORK   *6 to 8 servings*

1 loin of pork (5 pounds)
Salt and freshly ground black pepper
1 teaspoon sugar
½ teaspoon cayenne pepper, or more

1 teaspoon dried rosemary
1 to 2 cups dry white wine
½ cup Beef Stock (page 473)
1 tablespoon butter

1 Preheat oven to hot (450° F.).

2. Rub the pork loin with a mixture of salt and pepper, the sugar and cayenne. Place it on a rack and roast for ten minutes.

3. Reduce the oven heat to slow (300° F.). Sprinkle the roast with rosemary and pour around it half of the wine. Continue to roast for two to two and one-half hours, basting frequently and adding more wine as necessary.

4. When done, remove the roast to a hot platter. Strain the juices from the pan into a saucepan. Skim off and discard fat. Bring to a boil and add the stock and butter. Serve the sauce separately.

ROAST PORK WITH GRENADINE GLAZE   *About 8 servings*

1 loin of pork (6 pounds)
3 teaspoons salt
1 teaspoon freshly ground black pepper

1 teaspoon dried thyme
½ teaspoon ground mace or nutmeg
1 cup grenadine syrup

1. Preheat oven to hot (450° F.).

2. Rub surface of the pork with a mixture of salt, pepper, thyme and mace.

3. Place the pork in a shallow roasting pan and roast for fifteen minutes. Reduce heat to moderate (350° F.) and continue to roast for three hours (thirty to thirty-five minutes per pound). Baste frequently with heated grenadine. Serve the grenadine sauce separately in a warm sauceboat.

JUNE PLATT'S ROAST LOIN OF PORK *6 to 8 servings*

1 loin of pork (6 pounds)	1 garlic clove, crushed
3 teaspoons salt	2 whole cloves
1 teaspoon freshly ground black pepper	2 celery ribs, chopped
1 teaspoon dried thyme	1 bay leaf
½ teaspoon grated nutmeg	1¼ cups dry white wine
2 carrots, cut into ½-inch slices	1¼ cups Beef Stock (page 473)
2 medium onions, peeled and thinly sliced	½ lemon
	½ cup water

1. Preheat oven to very hot (475° F.).

2. Wipe the meat with a damp cloth and rub it with a mixture of the salt, pepper, thyme and nutmeg.

3. Arrange the carrots, onions, garlic, cloves, celery and bay leaf over the bottom of a roasting pan. Put the roast on top of the vegetables. Pour one-half cup each of the wine and stock over the roast.

4. Put the roast in the oven and bake for twenty minutes, until the roast is golden brown. Reduce the heat to moderate (350° F.) and continue to roast for three to four hours, basting occasionally.

5. Fifteen minutes before the roast is done, transfer it to a hot platter and squeeze the lemon over it. Return to the oven while making the gravy.

6. Pour off the fat from the roasting pan and add the remaining stock and wine and the water. Boil rapidly, stirring and scraping the bottom and sides of the pan. Cook until the gravy is thickened and only about one cup remains. Strain the gravy. Serve the meat hot and the gravy in a separate dish.

ROAST CROWN OF PORK FLORIDA STYLE *6 to 8 servings*

1 crown roast of pork made from 12 to 14 ribs	1 teaspoon salt
2 tablespoons butter	¼ teaspoon freshly ground black pepper
3 tablespoons chopped onion	1 teaspoon grated orange rind
3 tablespoons chopped celery	4 oranges, sectioned and halved
1½ cups cooked rice	1 large grapefruit, sectioned and halved
2 cups toasted tiny bread cubes	
1 tablespoon crumbled dried sage	

1. Preheat oven to hot (450° F.).

2. Cover the ends of the rib bones with small pieces of aluminum foil. Place the roast in a roasting pan. Place in the oven and immediately reduce the temperature to moderate (350° F.). Roast for forty minutes per pound.

3. Melt the butter and sauté the onion and celery in it until tender. Add the remaining ingredients and toss to mix.

4. One hour before roast is done spoon the stuffing into the hollow formed by the ribs. Baste twice during the last hour with drippings in the pan.

A Chinese dinner of Batter-Fried Shrimp with dipping sauce, Steamed Chinese Dumplings with Mustard Sauce and plum sauce, Barbecued Spareribs, Hot and Sour Soup, and the inevitable pot of tea.

GHOUROUNAKI PSITO (roast stuffed suckling pig)   *6 servings*

1 suckling pig (10 to 12 pounds)
Salt and freshly ground black pepper
Dried orégano
½ cup lemon juice
¾ cup olive oil
2 pounds feta cheese, crumbled
½ cup chopped parsley
½ lemon

1. Carefully clean the suckling pig, wash inside and outside with cold water, and dry thoroughly. Rub inside and outside with salt, pepper, orégano, half of the lemon juice and one-quarter cup of the oil. Allow the pig to stand for about one hour.

2. Preheat oven to hot (425° F.).

3. Combine the cheese and parsley and stuff the pig with the mixture.

4. Pull front legs of the pig forward and tie together. Wedge the mouth open with a small piece of wood. Combine the remaining lemon juice and olive oil and rub the entire pig generously with the mixture. Place pig on a rack in a roasting pan and roast for thirty minutes.

5. Reduce the oven temperature to moderate (325° F.). Continue to roast for four to five hours longer, basting often with the lemon half dipped into the pan drippings.

6. To serve, untie the legs, remove the wedge of wood, and put a shiny red apple in the mouth.

PORK, APPLES AND SAUERKRAUT   *4 servings*

4 pork shoulder steaks, each ½ inch thick
2 tablespoons butter or drippings
1 teaspoon salt
⅛ teaspoon freshly ground black pepper
1 tablespoon prepared mustard
1 tablespoon prepared horseradish
3½ cups (one 1-pound 13-ounce can) sauerkraut, drained
2 medium apples, chopped
½ cup chopped onion
1 teaspoon caraway seeds

1. Preheat oven to moderate (350° F.).

2. Brown the pork steaks in the butter. Pour off the excess fat. Season the steaks with salt and pepper. Combine the mustard and horseradish and spread over the steaks.

3. Combine the sauerkraut, apples, onion and caraway seeds and place in a two-quart baking dish. Arrange the steaks over the top, cover tightly, and bake for thirty minutes. Uncover and bake for thirty minutes longer.

PORK CHOPS BERMUDIANA   *4 servings*

4 pork chops, each 1½ inches thick
  Salt and freshly ground black
  pepper
1 tablespoon butter
¼ cup uncooked rice
4 slices of peeled tomato
4 slices of green pepper

4 thick slices of Bermuda onion
1 cup Chicken or Beef Stock (pages
  475 and 473)
1 tablespoon finely chopped parsley
1 tablespoon finely chopped chives
½ bay leaf

1. Preheat oven to moderate (350° F.).
2. Sprinkle the pork chops with salt and pepper. Brown the chops on all sides in the butter and transfer them to a baking dish.
3. Spoon one tablespoon of raw rice atop each chop. Top each with a slice of tomato, green pepper and onion and sprinkle with salt and pepper.
4. Pour the stock around the chops and sprinkle with parsley and chives. Add the bay leaf and cover. Bake for one hour.

PORK CHOPS PIQUANTE   *4 servings*

4 thick loin pork chops
2 tablespoons butter
½ cup finely chopped onion
1½ cups tomato purée
1 cup dry white wine
  Pinch of ground thyme

½ bay leaf
  Salt and freshly ground black
  pepper
½ cup finely chopped parsley
2 garlic cloves, finely minced
2 teaspoons grated lemon rind

1. Brown the pork chops on both sides in the butter in a skillet. Transfer chops to a platter and keep warm. Pour off most of the fat.
2. To the fat remaining in the skillet add the onion and cook briefly, stirring until onion is wilted. Add the tomato purée, wine, thyme, bay leaf, and salt and pepper to taste.
3. Return the chops to the skillet and turn them in the sauce. Cover and bake for one hour, basting occasionally, until chops are fork tender.
4. Mix the parsley, garlic and lemon rind together and sprinkle over the chops. Cover and keep warm until ready to serve.

PORK CHOPS WITH CAPER SAUCE   *4 servings*

4 rib or loin pork chops, each about
  1 inch thick
3 tablespoons all-purpose flour
2 tablespoons butter
½ teaspoon salt
⅛ teaspoon freshly ground black
  pepper

½ cup Beef Stock (page 473)
2 teaspoons prepared mustard
3 tablespoons capers
¼ cup water
½ cup sour cream

1. Sprinkle the chops with two tablespoons of the flour. Brown chops in the butter. Pour off the drippings. Season the chops with the salt and pepper.

2. Add the stock to the pan along with the mustard and capers. Cover tightly and simmer for forty-five minutes to one hour. Remove the chops to a warm platter.

3. Add the remaining flour to the drippings and mix well. Add the water and cook, stirring constantly, until thickened. Stir in the sour cream and cook just until heated through. Serve the sauce over the chops.

BARBECUED PORK CHOPS   *2 servings*

4 pork chops
2 tablespoons fat
2 cups (two 8-ounce cans) tomato sauce
½ teaspoon salt
¼ teaspoon freshly ground black pepper

⅓ cup diced celery
1 small onion, thinly sliced
½ cup water
Juice of ½ lemon
2 tablespoons brown sugar
½ teaspoon dry mustard

1. Preheat oven to moderate (350° F.).

2. Brown the pork chops on both sides in the fat. Transfer the chops to a shallow baking dish.

3. Combine the remaining ingredients and pour over the chops. Bake, covered, for one and one-quarter hours, basting occasionally.

MARINATED PORK CHOPS   *6 servings*

8 whole cloves
½ teaspoon salt
¾ teaspoon ground thyme
3 tablespoons finely chopped onion
1 teaspoon curry powder
1½ tablespoons fresh lemon juice

1 cup Beef Stock (page 473)
6 loin pork chops, each ½ inch thick
Flour
Shortening
2 tablespoons butter

1. Combine the cloves, salt, thyme, onion, curry powder, lemon juice and stock in a saucepan. Mix well and heat.

2. Place pork chops in a close-fitting pan. Add the warm sauce. Cool. Cover. Let stand in the refrigerator for several hours, turning chops in the sauce three or four times.

3. Remove chops from sauce and drain well. Reserve sauce. Sprinkle the chops lightly with flour and brown in shortening over medium heat. Add reserved sauce. Cover and cook slowly for about forty-five minutes, until chops are tender. Remove chops from the pan and keep warm.

4. Blend the butter and two tablespoons flour. Stir, bit by bit, into the simmering sauce. When thickened, serve hot with the chops.

COUNTRY PORK CHOPS   *6 servings*

6 loin or rib pork chops, each 1 inch thick
Salt and freshly ground black pepper
½ cup finely diced carrot
½ cup finely diced celery
¼ cup finely diced onion
½ cup Beef Stock (page 473)
½ cup tomato sauce
2 tablespoons prepared mustard
2 teaspoons Worcestershire sauce
Chopped parsley

1. Preheat oven to moderate (350° F.).
2. Lightly grease the bottom of a large skillet with a little fat trimmed from chops. Season chops on both sides with salt and pepper. Brown chops well on both sides for about fifteen minutes altogether.
3. Sprinkle carrot, celery and onion in a shallow two-quart casserole. Arrange browned chops on top. Pour excess fat from skillet. Add stock, tomato sauce, mustard and Worcestershire sauce to the skillet. Blend together. Pour mixture over chops; cover. Bake for fifty minutes; remove cover. Continue to bake for fifteen minutes longer. Sprinkle with chopped parsley.

STUFFED PORK CHOPS   *6 servings*

1 large onion, finely chopped
½ cup finely chopped celery
¼ cup chopped nuts
2 tablespoons butter
¾ cup soft fresh bread crumbs
¼ cup chopped parsley
¼ teaspoon salt
⅛ teaspoon grated nutmeg
1 egg, lightly beaten
Freshly ground black pepper
6 double loin pork chops, with pockets
1 cup Beef Stock (page 473)

1. Preheat oven to moderate (350° F.).
2. Sauté the onion, celery and nuts in the butter until the onion is soft but not brown. Remove from the heat.
3. Add the bread crumbs, parsley, salt, nutmeg and egg to the onion mixture. Add pepper to taste. Mix well.
4. Stuff the pork chops with the bread-crumb mixture. Place the chops in a shallow baking dish and bake for about one hour, until well browned. Place the chops on a hot platter and keep them warm.
5. Add the stock to the pan in which the meat cooked and heat, while scraping loose any browned particles that cling to the bottom and sides of the pan. Remove excess fat and pour the sauce around the chops. Serve immediately.

DEVILED STUFFED PORK CHOPS   *6 servings*

2 tablespoons butter
6 tablespoons chopped onion
1 cup soft fresh bread crumbs
¼ cup chopped celery
2 tablespoons chopped parsley
1½ tablespoons grated orange rind
2 teaspoons chili powder
1¼ teaspoons salt
⅛ teaspoon freshly ground black pepper

6 double loin pork chops, with pockets
2 tablespoons olive oil
⅓ cup vinegar
1½ cups orange juice
3 tablespoons chopped green pepper
2 garlic cloves, crushed
1½ tablespoons all-purpose flour

1. Preheat oven to moderate (350° F.).
2. Melt the butter and sauté half of the onion in it until tender. Add the bread crumbs, celery, parsley, orange rind, half of the chili powder, one-quarter teaspoon salt and the black pepper. Stuff chops with the mixture.
3. Brown chops in the olive oil. Place in a shallow casserole.
4. Mix the vinegar, orange juice, green pepper and garlic and add the remaining onion, chili powder and salt. Pour the mixture over the chops. Cover the casserole and bake for one hour, or until done.
5. Mix the flour with a little water. Add to the casserole and bake just long enough to thicken.

STUFFED SPARERIBS   *6 servings*

6 slices of bacon
1 onion, finely chopped
1 garlic clove, finely minced
3 cups fine dry bread crumbs
½ cup pine nuts
½ teaspoon salt
⅛ teaspoon freshly ground black pepper

½ teaspoon dried thyme
2 tablespoons chopped parsley
2 racks of spareribs (6 to 7 pounds altogether)
½ cup red wine
1 bay leaf
½ cup honey
1 teaspoon dry mustard

1. Preheat oven to moderate (350° F.).
2. Cook the bacon until crisp, reserving the bacon fat in the pan. Crumble the bacon pieces.
3. Sauté the onion and garlic in the reserved bacon fat and add to the bread crumbs. Add the bacon, nuts, salt, pepper, thyme and parsley. Mix well.
4. Spread the stuffing over one of the spareribs racks, top with the second, and secure with skewers or string. Place in a roasting pan and add the wine and bay leaf; cover. Bake for about three hours, or until tender.
5. Remove cover and increase oven heat to hot (425° F.). Combine the honey and mustard and spread over the ribs. Bake until meat is glazed.

LEMON-BARBECUED SPARERIBS   *4 servings*

3 to 4 pounds spareribs
⅓ cup fresh lemon juice
⅓ cup catchup or chili sauce
1 teaspoon prepared horseradish
1 teaspoon salt
  Dash of Tabasco
1 tablespoon Worcestershire sauce

½ cup fresh orange juice
2 teaspoons dry mustard
½ teaspoon paprika
¼ cup honey or brown sugar
1 garlic clove, finely minced
2 unpeeled lemons, sliced

1. Preheat oven to hot (450° F.).

2. Cut the ribs into serving pieces, place them in a roasting pan, and brown them for fifty minutes in the oven. Drain off fat.

3. Combine the remaining ingredients except the sliced lemons; mix well. Brush this sauce over the spareribs. Place a slice of lemon on each piece of meat.

4. Reduce the oven temperature to moderate (350° F.) and cook the meat for one hour, basting frequently with the sauce.

BARBECUED SPARERIBS   *6 servings*

2 racks of spareribs
2 teaspoons monosodium glutamate
2 tablespoons catchup
2 tablespoons soy sauce
2 tablespoons Hoisin sauce (available in Chinese grocery stores; optional)

2 garlic cloves, crushed
2 tablespoons medium sweet or dry sherry
1 tablespoon grated fresh gingerroot or ½ teaspoon ground ginger
1 tablespoon honey

1. Preheat oven to slow (300° F.).

2. Cut the spareribs into individual ribs and arrange them on a rack in a baking pan. Sprinkle with the monosodium glutamate. Bake for forty-five minutes.

3. Combine the remaining ingredients and brush the spareribs lightly with the mixture. Bake for thirty minutes longer and turn the spareribs. Brush with more sauce and bake for thirty minutes longer, or until ribs are nicely browned.

WARWICKSHIRE PORK PIE   *8 servings*

Unbaked Pie Pastry, 2-crust (page 637)
3 pounds boned fresh pork shoulder
2 tablespoons grated onion
2 teaspoons salt
½ teaspoon freshly ground pepper

¼ cup cold water
1 egg, lightly beaten
1 envelope unflavored gelatin
2 cups Pork Broth or Chicken Stock (pages 474 and 475)

1. Preheat oven to moderate (350° F.).

2. Reserve one-quarter of the pastry for the pie cover. Roll the remainder to one-eighth-inch thickness and line a loaf pan (9 × 5 × 3 inches) or a round pâté form (5½ inches in diameter). Take care not to stretch the pastry and not to have overlapping folds at the corners.

3. Cut the pork into one-and-one-half- to two-inch cubes and mix with the onion, salt, pepper and three tablespoons of the water.

4. Pack the mixture into the pastry-lined pan. Roll out the remaining pastry for a cover. Moisten the pastry edges and seal the cover onto the sides. Decorate the edges.

5. Make a hole in the center of the cover to allow the steam to escape. Cut pastry leaves from the scraps, moisten the undersides, and place around the steam hole. Cut an oblong of pastry four inches long and one-half inch wide. Roll up lengthwise and pinch one end to make a rosette.

6. Mix the egg with the remaining water and brush the top of the pie and the rosette with the mixture. Place both on a baking sheet and bake for two hours, or until the internal temperature registers 185° F.

7. Soften the gelatin in one-quarter cup of the broth. Heat the remaining broth, add the gelatin mixture, and stir to dissolve. Cool and chill until partially set.

8. As the pie cools add the jellied broth at intervals through the hole in the crust until the pie will hold no more. Chill the pie for several hours before removing from the pan to serve. Cover the hole with the rosette.

PANAMANIAN STEW   *6 to 8 servings*

2 pounds boneless lean pork	2 cups cubed yellow squash or pumpkin
1 pound boneless beef stew meat	¼ cup finely chopped fresh parsley
½ cup diced ham	1 pound chorizo (Spanish-style sausage)
1 bay leaf	
1 tablespoon salt	1 teaspoon freshly ground black pepper
2 garlic cloves, minced	
4 cups water	1 teaspoon ground coriander
2 medium onions, shredded	⅛ teaspoon cayenne pepper
3 tablespoons fresh lemon or lime juice	2 plantains (optional)
3 medium potatoes, peeled and cubed	

1. Trim excess fat from the boneless pork and beef. Cut into one-inch cubes. Place in a three-quart saucepan with the ham, bay leaf, salt, garlic and water. Cover and cook for one and one-half hours.

2. Add the onions, lemon or lime juice, potatoes, squash and parsley. Cut the sausage into one-quarter-inch slices and add, along with the black pepper, coriander and cayenne. Cover and cook for about twenty minutes, until the vegetables are almost tender.

3. Cut the plantains into one-half-inch slices and add to the stew. Cover and cook for ten minutes longer. Serve hot in deep soup plates.

SWEDISH MEAT AND ONION CASSEROLE   *4 servings*

¼ cup butter
4 large onions, thinly sliced
⅓ pound pork, ground
¼ pound veal, ground
⅓ cup soft fresh bread crumbs
¾ cup heavy cream

¾ cup milk
1 teaspoon salt
¼ teaspoon white pepper
2 tablespoons chopped fresh dill or 1 teaspoon dried dill
¾ cup Chicken Stock (page 475)

1. Preheat oven to moderate (375° F.).

2. Melt the butter in a skillet and sauté the onions in it until golden brown.

3. Mix the meat, bread crumbs, cream and milk together until smooth. Season with salt, pepper and dill.

4. Cover the bottom of a casserole with some of the onions, spread the meat on top, and cover with remaining onions. Pour stock over all, making holes in the meat mixture to let stock run down. Bake for twenty-five minutes. Cover if the crust becomes too brown. Serve very hot.

SPICY MEAT BALLS IN WINE SAUCE   *5 servings*

1 pound lean pork
½ pound beef round
1 garlic clove
2 small onions
2 parsley sprigs
½ teaspoon grated nutmeg
¼ teaspoon ground cinnamon
¼ teaspoon ground allspice
1 teaspoon salt

¼ teaspoon freshly ground black pepper
2 eggs, lightly beaten
¾ cup dry sherry
3 tablespoons butter
¾ cup Chicken Stock (page 475)
2 whole cloves
2 tablespoons brown sugar

1. Grind the pork, beef, garlic, onions and parsley together. Add the nutmeg, cinnamon, allspice, salt, pepper, eggs and two tablespoons of the sherry. Mix well.

2. Form the mixture into balls one inch in diameter. Brown the balls on all sides in the butter in a large skillet. Drain the meat balls.

Choucroute Garnie

3. Deglaze the pan with the remaining sherry. Add the stock, cloves and brown sugar and bring to a boil.

4. Return the meat balls to the pan, cover, and simmer for ten to fifteen minutes, until fully cooked.

PORK LOAF   *6 servings*

2 pounds lean pork, ground
½ cup soft fresh bread crumbs
2 eggs, lightly beaten
½ cup pistachio nuts
2 teaspoons salt

¼ teaspoon freshly ground black pepper
1 tablespoon dried sage rubbed through the fingers

1. Preheat oven to moderate (325° F.).
2. Mix all the ingredients together lightly. Pack into a loaf pan (9 × 5 × 3 inches) or form into a loaf shape and place in a baking pan. Bake for one and one-half to two hours. Serve with Tomato Sauce III (page 494) or Mushroom Sauce (page 480).

HAM

GLAZED BAKED HAM   *12 to 16 servings*

1 ready-to-eat or tenderized bone-in ham (8 to 10 pounds)

Whole cloves
Ham Glaze (see below)

1. Preheat oven to moderate (325° F.).
2. Place the ham on a rack in a large baking pan. Score the ham diagonally in one-inch diamonds. Stud each diamond with a whole clove.
3. Bake the ham, uncovered, for twenty to twenty-five minutes to the pound if it is tenderized; for ten to fifteen minutes per pound if it is a ready-to-eat ham.
4. Spread the glaze over the ham thirty minutes before the end of baking time. Baste the ham with glaze several times.

GRENADINE HAM GLAZE:

¾ cup grenadine syrup
1 cup cider vinegar

½ tablespoon prepared mustard

Heat the grenadine and vinegar together and stir in the mustard. Keep the glaze hot while basting the ham.

ORANGE HAM GLAZE:

1½ cups brown sugar
1 teaspoon dry mustard
½ cup vinegar

¼ cup orange juice
1 tablespoon grated orange rind

Combine all the ingredients to make a smooth mixture. This glaze is particularly good spread over a canned ham before it is placed in the oven to heat.

CRANBERRY HAM GLAZE:

1 cup cranberry jelly
⅓ cup prepared mustard

1 tablespoon water

Melt the jelly over low heat. Do not let it scorch. Stir in the other ingredients and mix well.

SHERRY HAM GLAZE:

1 teaspoon dry mustard
1 cup brown sugar

¼ cup sweet sherry

Combine the mustard and brown sugar. Add the sherry and mix to a spreading consistency.

HAM STEAK IN WHITE WINE   *4 or 5 servings*

1 ready-to-eat ham steak (about 2 pounds)
¾ teaspoon dry mustard
½ teaspoon freshly ground black pepper

2 tablespoons butter
3 shallots or 1 large onion, finely chopped
¾ cup dry white wine
Chicken Stock (page 475)

1. Remove most of the fat from the ham. Blend the mustard and pepper and rub this mixture into both sides of the ham.
2. Melt the butter in a large skillet over moderate heat and brown the ham on both sides. Remove the ham from the skillet. Add the shallots or onion and cook for three minutes.
3. Stir in the wine and return the ham to the skillet. Cover and simmer for about one hour, until the ham is well glazed. If more liquid is needed, add a few tablespoons of stock.

HAM AND MUSHROOM CASSEROLE   *4 servings*

½ cup butter
½ pound mushrooms, sliced
3 tablespoons all-purpose flour
1¼ cups milk
2 egg yolks

1½ cups Swiss or natural Gruyère cheese, grated
½ teaspoon salt
Pinch of cayenne pepper
8 thin slices of smoked ham

1. Preheat oven to moderate (350° F.).

2. Melt six tablespoons of the butter. Cook the sliced mushrooms in the butter until tender but not dry. Blend in the flour and gradually stir in the milk. Bring to a boil, stirring, and simmer for two minutes.

3. Stir a little of the hot mixture into the egg yolks and then return egg-yolk mixture to the pan. Add one cup of the cheese, the salt and cayenne and stir until cheese melts.

4. Spread one tablespoon of the mushroom and cheese sauce over each slice of ham and roll into a cigar shape.

5. Spread about half of the sauce over the bottom of a greased shallow baking dish. Arrange the ham rolls atop the sauce. Spoon the remaining sauce over the rolls.

6. Melt the remaining butter. Sprinkle the casserole with the remaining cheese and butter. Bake for fifteen to twenty minutes, until all is hot and bubbly and the cheese on top golden brown.

HAM AND NOODLE CASSEROLE   *4 servings*

¼ cup butter
¼ cup chopped green onions
¼ cup all-purpose flour
¼ teaspoon salt
⅛ teaspoon freshly ground black pepper
½ teaspoon dry mustard

2½ cups milk
1 cup grated Cheddar cheese
4 drops of Tabasco
6½ ounces noodles, cooked according to package directions
8 slices (½ inch thick) smoked pork butt (approximately ¾ pound)

1. Preheat oven to moderate (350° F.).

2. Melt the butter in a saucepan. Sauté the onions in it until tender. Blend in the flour, salt, pepper and mustard. Slowly stir in the milk. Bring to a boil, stirring, and simmer for one to two minutes. Add the cheese and Tabasco and blend well.

3. Rinse and drain the noodles and put them in a shallow two-quart casserole. Pour the cheese sauce over the noodles and mix gently. Arrange the ham slices over the top. Bake for thirty minutes, or until all is hot and bubbly.

HAM STEAKS WITH CRANBERRY STUFFING   *6 servings*

½ cup raw cranberries
3 slices of day-old bread
2 tablespoons sugar
1 teaspoon salt
1 teaspoon grated orange rind
¼ teaspoon poultry seasoning
¼ cup chopped celery

1 tablespoon chopped parsley
2 ready-to-eat ham steaks (about 1½ pounds each)
¼ cup salad oil
¼ teaspoon freshly ground black pepper

1. Preheat oven to moderate (350° F.).

2. Chop the cranberries with a chopping knife, or put through a food chopper, or chop in an electric blender.

3. Crumble the bread and toast it in the oven until golden. Add to the cranberries along with the sugar, salt, orange rind, poultry seasoning, celery and parsley; mix well.

4. Trim most of the fat from the ham steaks. Brown them, one at a time, in the oil in a large skillet.

5. Oil a baking dish about the same size as the ham steaks. Arrange one steak in it and sprinkle with half of the pepper. Spread the stuffing evenly over the ham steak and cover with the second steak. Sprinkle with remainder of pepper.

6. Cover the baking dish. Bake the stuffed ham in the oven for about one hour.

CALIFORNIA HAM BAKE   *6 servings*

2 California oranges, peeled and sliced into cartwheels	½ cup Chicken Stock (page 475) or water
5 tablespoons brown sugar	1 cup fresh orange juice
6 slices of ready-to-eat ham	½ teaspoon dried marjoram
¼ cup salad oil	2 medium onions, peeled and sliced
2 teaspoons cornstarch	2 tablespoons chopped parsley

1. Preheat oven to moderate (350° F.).

2. Sprinkle the orange slices with three tablespoons of the brown sugar. Set aside.

3. Trim extra fat from the ham slices. Cut the edges of the slices to keep the slices from curling. Heat the oil in a large skillet and brown the ham in it on both sides. Place the browned slices in a greased flat baking dish.

4. Blend the cornstarch with the stock, orange juice, marjoram and re-maining brown sugar. Pour the mixture over the ham. Place the onion slices on top of the ham and sprinkle with the parsley. Cover and bake for forty minutes.

5. Remove baking dish from the oven and arrange the orange slices on top of the ham slices. Return to oven and heat until oranges and ham are well glazed.

HAM AND PORK BALLS   *6 servings*

¾ cup brown sugar	1 pound smoked ham, ground
¼ cup vinegar	½ pound pork, ground
¼ cup water	1½ cups soft fresh bread crumbs
¼ cup pineapple juice	2 eggs, beaten
½ teaspoon dry mustard	½ cup milk

1. Preheat oven to moderate (325° F.).

2. Combine the sugar, vinegar, water, pineapple juice and mustard. Stir until sugar dissolves.

3. Mix the ham, pork, bread crumbs, eggs and milk together. Form into balls, allowing one-half cup of the mixture for each ball. Place the balls in a single layer in a shallow baking dish. Pour the sugar syrup over. Bake for one hour. Baste three or four times with syrup in the pan.

HAM AND VEGETABLE CASSEROLE   *6 servings*

¼ cup butter
¼ cup chopped onion
1½ tablespoons all-purpose flour
1 cup milk
1 cup diced cooked potatoes
1 cup sliced cooked carrots
1 cup cooked green beans

2 cups diced cooked ham
Salt and freshly ground black pepper
2 fresh tomatoes, cut into ½-inch slices
½ cup soft fresh bread crumbs
2 tablespoons bacon drippings

1. Preheat oven to hot (400° F.).

2. Melt the butter in a saucepan and add the onion. Cook until the onion is transparent. Blend in the flour. Bring the milk to a boil and add. Stir and cook until slightly thickened. Add vegetables, ham, one teaspoon salt and one-quarter teaspoon pepper. Mix lightly.

3. Turn the mixture into a buttered one-and-one-half-quart casserole. Arrange tomato slices over the top. Sprinkle with additional salt and pepper. Combine the bread crumbs with the bacon drippings and sprinkle onto the casserole.

4. Bake the casserole for thirty minutes, or until the mixture is hot and the crumbs are brown.

HAM LOAF   *4 or 5 servings*

1 egg
½ cup milk
1 pound smoked ham, ground
½ pound fresh pork, ground
¼ teaspoon freshly ground black pepper

½ teaspoon dried sage
½ cup soft fresh bread crumbs
Ham Glaze (pages 229 and 230)

1. Preheat oven to moderate (350° F.).

2. Beat the egg in a mixing bowl. Stir in the milk, meats, pepper and sage. Stir in the bread crumbs. Mix well and shape into a loaf.

3. Grease a loaf pan (9 × 5 × 3 inches). Place the loaf in the pan. Bake for about forty-five minutes.

4. Prepare whichever ham glaze you are using. Spoon some of it over the loaf, covering the entire surface. Bake the loaf for thirty minutes longer, basting frequently with the glaze.

HAM AND CELERY LOAF   *8 servings*

1½ pounds lean smoked ham
½ pound lean pork
½ pound beef round
2 eggs
1¼ cups tomato juice
½ onion, finely chopped

1 cup finely chopped celery
¾ teaspoon freshly ground black pepper
2 cups soft fresh bread crumbs
Horseradish Sauce (page 489)

1. Preheat oven to moderate (350° F.).
2. Grind the meats together. Beat the eggs in a mixing bowl and add the tomato juice, onion, celery and pepper. Mix in the ground meat and the bread crumbs.
3. Grease a loaf pan (9 × 5 × 3 inches). Pack the mixture into the pan. Bake for one and one-half hours. Serve with horseradish sauce.

HAM AND TONGUE MOUSSE   *6 servings*

3 tablespoons finely chopped shallots
1 tablespoon butter
2 envelopes unflavored gelatin
⅓ cup dry white wine
2 cups hot Chicken Stock (page 475)
2⅓ cups small cubes of cooked smoked ham

2 tablespoons cognac
1½ tablespoons tomato paste
Salt and freshly ground black pepper
½ cup finely diced cooked tongue
1½ tablespoons minced fresh dill (optional)
¾ cup heavy cream, whipped
Salad greens

1. Sauté the shallots in the butter for two or three minutes. Soak the gelatin in the wine.
2. Add the hot stock to soaked gelatin and stir until gelatin is dissolved. Add shallots.
3. Pour one-half cup of the hot liquid into an electric blender. Add one-third cup ham and blend. Stop the motor once and stir down mixture with a rubber spatula. Finish blending. Pour mixture into a large bowl. Repeat process until all liquid and ham are blended.
4. Stir in cognac and tomato paste. Season with salt and pepper to taste. Cool the mixture.
5. When mixture starts to thicken, stir in the diced tongue, dill and whipped cream. Pack into a one-and-one-half-quart mold. Chill for several hours or overnight.
6. Arrange salad greens on a platter. Unmold the mousse onto greens.

Garnish with black and green olives, tomato halves filled with peas, and tiny carrots. Serve with Sour-Cream and Horseradish Sauce (page 489).

HAM MOUSSE   *6 servings*

2 envelopes unflavored gelatin
2 tablespoons white Dubonnet
1 teaspoon lemon juice
½ cup hot Chicken Stock (page 475)
2 eggs, separated

½ cup mayonnaise
5 dashes of Tabasco
1 cup diced cooked ham
½ cup heavy cream

1. Into the container of an electric blender put the gelatin, Dubonnet, lemon juice and hot stock. Cover and blend on high speed for one minute.

2. Add the egg yolks, mayonnaise, Tabasco and ham. Cover and blend on high speed for twenty seconds longer.

3. Uncover and, with the motor on, gradually pour in the cream.

4. In a mixing bowl beat the egg whites until stiff. Pour the blended mixture over the egg whites and fold gently until mixed.

5. Pour into a four-cup mold and chill for about one hour, until set.

LAMB

Lamb is eaten less than other meats in the United States. Historically, it has been considered a spring delicacy, a notion that probably developed from its growth patterns in other days when lamb was a tender meat that appeared at the time of the first jonquil. After the season passed, it was allowed to grow into mutton. Today the quality of lamb in the United States is fairly standard from one season to the other and tender legs of lamb are generally available whenever they are desired. Here the term "spring lamb" refers to those animals that are three to five months old when slaughtered.

Lamb is a wonderfully versatile meat, from riblet to chop to roast, and it deserves greater popularity. It is the basis for countless stews of many nationalities.

ROAST LEG OF SPRING LAMB   *6 servings*

1 oven-ready leg of spring lamb (5 to 6 pounds)
2 garlic cloves
6 tablespoons butter
Salt and freshly ground black pepper
½ cup chopped scallions

½ cup diced carrot
¼ cup diced green pepper
⅓ cup diced celery
2 cups dry white wine
1 cup Lamb or Chicken Stock (pages 474 and 475)

1. Preheat oven to moderate (325° F.).

2. Loosen the skin around the bone of the leg of lamb and insert the garlic cloves. Rub two tablespoons of the butter over the surface and sprinkle with salt and pepper.

3. Sauté the scallions, carrot, green pepper and celery in two tablespoons of the butter for five minutes. Spread in a roasting pan.

4. Place the lamb atop the mixture and pour one cup of the wine over the meat. Roast for twenty minutes per pound, basting occasionally with the liquid in the pan.

5. About forty minutes before the end of the cooking time, remove and discard the vegetables. Brush the remaining butter over the lamb, add the remaining wine and the stock, and complete the roasting. Serve the meat on a warm platter. Serve the gravy separately.

ROAST LAMB WITH CHERRIES   *6 to 8 servings*

1 oven-ready leg of lamb (7½ to 8 pounds)
2 large garlic cloves, cut into quarters
1 tablespoon salt
1 teaspoon sugar
¼ teaspoon freshly ground black pepper

2 small onions, halved
4 small celery ribs with leaves, diced
2 small carrots, diced
2 cups (one 1-pound can) pitted red sour cherries, packed in syrup

1. Preheat oven to hot (400° F.).

2. Make several small slits over the surface of the lamb and insert the garlic pieces. Blend the salt, sugar and pepper together and rub well into the lamb.

3. Place the lamb in a roasting pan and roast for thirty minutes. Drain off all the fat from the roasting pan. Add the onions, celery and carrots and baste with some of the cherry syrup. Reduce the oven temperature to moderate (325° F.) and continue to roast for about three hours, until the lamb is tender. Baste frequently, using all of the cherry syrup. Remove the lamb to a hot platter and keep it warm.

4. Discard the vegetables from the roasting pan and skim the fat off the drippings. Add the cherries to the pan and bring the sauce to a boil. Season with additional salt and pepper to taste and serve the sauce separately.

JAMES BEARD'S BRAISED SHOULDER OF LAMB   *4 servings*

1 shoulder of lamb (2 to 3 pounds), boned and rolled
2 garlic cloves, slivered
½ cup olive oil
½ cup soy sauce

½ cup dry sherry
¼ cup grated fresh gingerroot or 2 teaspoons ground ginger
2 onions, studded with cloves
1 parsley sprig

1. Wipe the lamb with a damp cloth and slash the flesh in several places. Insert slivers of garlic and rub the lamb well with two tablespoons of the oil.

2. Mix the soy sauce, sherry and gingerroot in a large bowl. Add the meat and let it marinate for four hours, turning occasionally.

3. Preheat oven to slow (300° F.).

4. Remove the lamb from the marinade and wipe it with paper towels. Reserve the marinade. Brown the lamb in remaining olive oil in a heavy kettle or Dutch oven. When it is browned on all sides, add the onions, parsley and the reserved marinade.

5. Cover the pan and simmer the meat in the oven for two hours. Remove the lamb to a hot platter and pour the juices over it.

ROAST LAMB WITH HERB SAUCE   *5 or 6 servings*

This preparation for leg of lamb, which starts by marinating it in wine and herbs, makes an excellent dish for a January menu.

1 oven-ready leg of lamb (6½ to 7 pounds)	2 fresh mint sprigs or 1 teaspoon dried mint
4½ cups dry white wine	1 teaspoon dried thyme
2 small onions, peeled and stuck with cloves	¼ cup salad oil
	Freshly ground black pepper
2 garlic cloves, crushed	2 tablespoons finely chopped shallots
12 peppercorns	
12 juniper berries	3 tablespoons butter
Salt	1 cup Brown Sauce (page 477)
2 carrots, scraped and quartered	½ cup Beef Stock (page 473)
4 parsley sprigs	¼ cup chopped parsley
2 bay leaves	

1. Wipe the leg of lamb with a damp cloth. Place it in a stainless-steel, ceramic or enamelware container.

2. Mix the wine with the onions, garlic, peppercorns, juniper berries, 2 teaspoons salt, carrots, parsley, bay leaves, mint and half of the thyme. Pour the mixture over the lamb. Let the lamb marinate in the refrigerator for two days. Turn it occasionally in the marinade.

3. Preheat oven to hot (450° F.).

4. Remove the lamb from the marinade and dry it well. Reserve the marinade. Place the lamb on a rack in a roasting pan and rub it with the oil. Sprinkle with additional salt and pepper.

5. Roast the lamb for fifteen minutes, then reduce the oven heat to moderate (350° F.), and continue to roast for fifteen minutes to the pound, or longer if well-done meat is desired. Turn the lamb occasionally as it cooks.

6. Strain the marinade and place it in a saucepan. Cook it over high heat until it is reduced nearly, but not quite, by half.

7. Cook the shallots in the butter until they start to turn golden, then

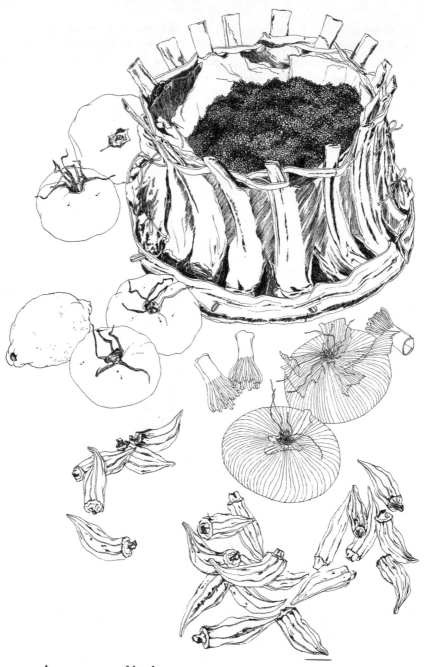

A crown roast of lamb

add one cup of the hot marinade. Add the remaining ingredients and simmer for five to ten minutes. Season with additional salt and pepper, if necessary, and serve hot with the lamb.

CROWN ROAST OF LAMB WITH OKRA   *8 servings*

1 crown roast of spring lamb (prepared by the butcher), about 16 chops
Lemon juice
Salt and freshly ground black pepper
2 pounds young okra
2 cups wine vinegar
⅓ cup olive oil
¼ cup butter
1½ cups finely minced onions
4 large ripe tomatoes, peeled, seeded and chopped
2 tablespoons chopped fresh parsley
½ teaspoon sugar

1. Preheat oven to moderate (350° F.).
2. Rub the crown of lamb on all sides with lemon juice, salt and pepper. Cover the tips of the roast with aluminum foil to prevent burning.
3. Place the roast in a roasting pan fitted with a rack and bake for one hour and twenty minutes. Remove the roast from the oven and discard the aluminum foil. Keep warm while preparing okra. Pour off fat from roasting pan but do not wash the pan. It will be used to cook the okra.
4. Rub the okra with salt but do not bruise the vegetable. The salt will remove most of the fuzz from the okra. Wash the okra in cold running water and trim off stems but do not cut away too much of the pod or the juices will escape. Place the okra in a bowl and cover with the vinegar. Let stand for thirty minutes. This solidifies the okra.
5. Heat the oil and butter and cook onions in it until golden yellow. Add the tomatoes, parsley, sugar and salt and pepper to taste. Cook for fifteen minutes.
6. Drain the okra and rinse the vegetable with cold water. Place the okra in the roasting pan and pour the tomato mixture over it. Cover closely with aluminum foil and place the pan in the oven. Bake for thirty minutes. Remove the foil and continue to cook for twenty minutes longer, or until okra is tender. Do not stir, but shake the pan from side to side occasionally.
7. Place the lamb on a deep round serving platter. Spoon the cooked okra into the center and around the base of the roast. Cover the tips of the chops with paper frills and serve.

BARBECUED LAMB RIBS   *6 servings*

6 pounds breast of lamb, left whole or cut into small pieces
2 quarts water
1 cup cider vinegar
1 onion, sliced
2 bay leaves
1 garlic clove, finely minced
1 teaspoon salt
1 cup Barbecue Sauce (page 497)

1. Place the ribs in a heavy pan and add the water, vinegar, onion, bay leaves, garlic and salt. Bring to a boil, cover, and simmer for forty-five to sixty minutes, or until lamb is tender.

2. Drain the ribs and arrange on broiler pan. Brush with barbecue sauce and broil slowly until crisp and brown.

STUFFED LEG OF LAMB   *6 to 8 servings*

1 leg of lamb (6 to 7 pounds), boned
Salt and freshly ground black pepper
¼ cup butter
1 medium onion, chopped
2 tablespoons finely chopped shallots

1 garlic clove, finely minced
1½ cups soft fresh bread crumbs
¼ cup finely chopped parsley
½ teaspoon dried thyme
1 egg, beaten
1 bay leaf
4 small onions, peeled

1. Preheat oven to hot (400° F.).

2. Place the lamb, boned side up, on a flat surface. Sprinkle with salt and pepper.

3. Melt the butter in a large heavy skillet and cook the onion, shallots and garlic, stirring, until onion is translucent. Remove from the heat and add the bread crumbs, parsley, thyme and beaten egg. Mix well and season with salt and pepper.

4. Spread the filling into the boned cavity of the leg. Roll the leg and tie with soft string or use a skewer.

5. Place the meat in a baking pan and sprinkle with more salt and pepper. Add the bay leaf and onions. Bake for thirty-five to forty minutes per pound. If meat seems to cook too fast, reduce heat to moderate (350° F.). Baste the meat with the pan juices as it cooks.

6. When the lamb is done, transfer it to a heated serving platter and slice it. Discard the bay leaf. Pour most of the fat from the baking pan and strain the remaining pan juices over the lamb slices.

BRAISED LAMB SHANKS   *4 servings*

4 lamb shanks
½ cup butter
2 onions, thinly sliced
½ cup dry white wine
½ cup tomato juice

1 teaspoon paprika
1 teaspoon ground ginger
1 cup Chicken Stock (page 475)
Salt and freshly ground black pepper

1. Preheat oven to slow (250° F.).

2. Remove most of the fat from the lamb. Brown the shanks on all sides in the butter and transfer to a large casserole.

3. Add the onions to the skillet in which lamb was browned and cook, stirring, until wilted. Add remaining ingredients and bring to a boil. Season with salt and pepper to taste. Pour the liquid over the lamb shanks; cover. Bake for three hours, or until meat is very tender.

LAMB PILAU   *8 to 10 servings*

2 pounds lean lamb shanks
½ cup yoghurt
2½ teaspoons salt
2 tablespoons butter
4 whole cardamom pods
6 whole cloves

1 cinnamon stick (2 inches long)
¼ teaspoon caraway seeds
1 bay leaf
2 cups uncooked rice
½ cup (one 4-ounce can) mushrooms

1. Trim off all excess fat from the lamb shanks. Marinate the meat in the yoghurt for thirty minutes. Add two cups cold water and one teaspoon of the salt. Cover and simmer for three hours.

2. Cool the meat and stock. Trim all lean meat from the bones. Discard the bones and reserve the meat.

3. When stock is cold, lift off all the hardened fat and discard it. Add enough water to the stock to make four cups. Reserve the stock.

4. Melt the butter in a four-quart saucepan. Tie the spices in a cheesecloth bag and add to the butter. Sauté for two minutes.

5. Put the rice in the saucepan and cook, stirring, for three to four minutes. Add the reserved stock, the remaining salt, the reserved meat and the mushrooms.

6. Cover the saucepan. Bring the liquid to a boil and boil for fifteen minutes, until the rice is tender and the grains stand apart. Do not stir. Lift out the spice bag and discard. Serve the pilau hot.

LAMB CHOPS MARIA   *6 servings*

6 lamb chops, each 1½ to 2 inches
  thick, trimmed
1 garlic clove, halved
¼ cup chopped parsley

½ teaspoon dried thyme
1 bay leaf
½ cup water
2 tablespoon cold butter

1. Brown the lamb chops on all sides in a hot skillet without fat; there will be enough fat on the lamb. Add the garlic to the skillet. Pour off any fat as it accumulates in the pan. Cooking time will depend on the thickness of the chops and the desired degree of doneness.

2. Just before the chops are done, add the parsley, thyme and bay leaf to the skillet.

3. Stir the chops around in the skillet, then transfer them to a warm serving platter. Add the water to the skillet and let it boil for one minute. Discard the garlic and bay leaf.

4. Remove the skillet from the heat. Add the butter to the sauce and swirl it around without boiling. Pour the sauce over the chops and serve immediately.

BRAISED LAMB CHOPS   *4 servings*

4 thick shoulder lamb chops	4 green pepper rings
2 tablespoons olive oil	½ cup tomato sauce
4 thin slices of lemon	¼ teaspoon dried thyme
4 thin slices of onion	2 tablespoons chopped parsley

1. Brown the chops on both sides in the oil. Top each with a lemon slice, onion slice and green pepper ring. Add the tomato sauce and sprinkle with the thyme.

2. Cover and simmer slowly for about forty-five minutes, or until the chops are tender. Garnish with the chopped parsley.

ESAU'S LAMB   *4 servings*

3 pounds lean lamb, cubed	½ bay leaf
2 tablespoons vegetable oil	3 cups Lamb Stock (page 474)
3 cups finely chopped onions	1 cup dried lentils
2 garlic cloves, finely minced	¼ cup uncooked rice
1 cup finely chopped celery	½ cup finely chopped parsley
½ teaspoon dried thyme	
Salt and freshly ground black pepper	

1. Brown the lamb in the oil in a large skillet. Transfer the lamb to a casserole and pour off most of the fat from the skillet.

2. Add the onions, garlic and celery to the skillet and cook, stirring, until onions are wilted. Sprinkle with the thyme and salt and pepper to taste. Add bay leaf and one cup of the stock. Bring to a boil, stir the mixture around, then pour it over the lamb.

3. Bring the casserole to a boil, cover, and simmer for one hour.

4. Rinse the lentils and add them to the casserole along with the rice. Add remaining stock and cook, covered, for one hour longer, or until lamb and lentils are tender. Pour the stew into a serving dish and sprinkle with parsley.

TUNISIAN COUSCOUS   *8 to 10 servings*

1 cup dried chick-peas
3 to 4 pounds cubed leg of lamb
1 cup olive oil
1 teaspoon salt
½ teaspoon freshly ground black pepper
1 can (6 ounces) tomato paste
2 garlic cloves, finely minced
3 quarts Lamb Stock (page 474)
1 tablespoon caraway seeds, crushed in a mortar
3 or 4 hot red peppers, crushed
½ teaspoon ground cuminseed, or more

2 cups cracked wheat (couscous)
½ cup water
6 turnips, cut into pieces
6 small white onions
12 carrots, cut into pieces
2 small zucchini, sliced
½ small head of cabbage, cut into wedges
1 large green pepper, seeded and cut into strips
Sauce Piquante (page 487)

1. Soak the chick-peas in water overnight. Drain.

2. Place the lamb cubes, olive oil, salt, black pepper and tomato paste in a large deep kettle or in the bottom part of a large steamer. Cook for ten to fifteen minutes over medium heat, stirring occasionally.

3. Add the garlic, stock, caraway seeds, hot peppers, cuminseed and drained chick-peas. Bring the mixture to a boil, cover, and cook for one to two hours.

4. Meanwhile, spread the cracked wheat on a large tray or platter and sprinkle with the water. Mix lightly with the fingers until all the grains are moistened. Line with muslin the top of the steamer or a colander that will fit over the kettle. Drop the moistened grain into the prepared container. Do not pack down.

5. About one hour before the meat and chick-peas are done, lower the grains into the top of the steamer or kettle. Cover tightly. The grains will cook in the steam from the lamb and will absorb the flavors. Stir once or twice during the cooking to break up any lumps.

6. Add the turnips, onions and carrots to the lamb. Cook for fifteen minutes longer. Add the zucchini, cabbage and green pepper. Cook for ten minutes, or until vegetables are tender. Taste the sauce; if necessary, adjust the seasoning.

7. Spread the cooked cracked wheat on a large deep serving platter. Gradually add the liquid from the lamb stew, stirring the couscous until it will not absorb any more. Cover and let stand for five to seven minutes. Add more liquid from the stew to the couscous, again stirring until it will not absorb any more.

8. Push the grain into a rounded mound in the center of the tray. Arrange the lamb and vegetables in an attractive pattern around the mound. Serve with sauce piquante.

Note: If canned chick-peas are used, add them (two cups, or a one-pound can, drained) when adding the zucchini and cabbage.

LAMB AND TOMATOES WITH CRACKED WHEAT
4 servings

1½ pounds lamb, cut into 2-inch cubes
Salt and freshly ground black pepper
1 tablespoon lamb fat or peanut oil
1 cup chopped onions
3 tablespoons butter
2 cups Italian plum tomatoes, drained
3 cups water
1 cup cracked wheat

1. Sprinkle the lamb with salt and pepper and brown on all sides in the lamb fat or peanut oil. Add the onions and cook until they are light brown.

2. Add the butter, tomatoes and water. Season with salt and pepper to taste and bring to a boil. Simmer for forty minutes to one hour, until the lamb is almost tender.

3. Rinse the cracked wheat under cold water and squeeze it to remove excess moisture. Add it to the kettle and cook for twenty minutes longer, or until all the liquid has been absorbed.

LAMB À LA SUÈDE   *4 to 6 servings*

2 pounds leg of lamb, cut into 1½-inch cubes
1½ teaspoons salt
2 small white onions, peeled
1 garlic clove, peeled
10 peppercorns
3 fresh dill sprigs or 1 teaspoon dried dill
¼ cup butter
¼ cup all-purpose flour
1½ tablespoons vinegar
½ teaspoon sugar
Freshly ground black pepper
¼ cup finely chopped fresh dill or 1 teaspoon dried dill

1. Put the lamb in a large saucepan and add cold water to cover. Add the salt, onions, garlic, peppercorns and dill sprigs. Bring to a boil and simmer for one and one-half to two hours, until lamb is thoroughly tender.

2. Measure two cups of the cooking liquid for making sauce. Leave lamb cubes in remaining broth.

3. Melt the butter in a saucepan and blend in the flour with a wire whisk. When blended, stir in the two cups of lamb broth. When mixture is thickened and smooth, continue to cook for five minutes. Stir in the remaining ingredients and, if desired, add more salt.

4. Drain the lamb cubes and add them to the sauce. Heat thoroughly. Serve with buttered boiled potatoes.

NEW-POTATO LAMB FRICASSEE   *6 servings*

2½ pounds boneless shoulder of lamb
1 teaspoon salt
½ teaspoon freshly ground black pepper
2 tablespoons butter
¼ teaspoon minced fresh garlic
1 teaspoon grated lemon rind

2 teaspoons fresh lemon juice
1 bay leaf
5 anchovy fillets
3 cups Lamb Stock (page 474)
12 small new potatoes
2 cups sliced fresh mushrooms
3 tablespoons all-purpose flour
¼ cup water

1. Trim the lamb and discard excess fat. Cut meat into one-inch pieces. Mix the salt and pepper and rub into meat. Brown the meat in the butter.

2. Add the garlic, lemon rind and juice, bay leaf, anchovies and stock. Cover and cook slowly for about one hour. Add the potatoes and mushrooms and cook for thirty minutes longer.

3. Blend the flour with the water and add to the stew. Cook for one to two minutes, or until thickened.

LAMB STEW WITH ZUCCHINI   *6 servings*

2 tablespoons vegetable oil
2½ pounds lean shoulder of lamb, cubed
3 medium onions, chopped
2 garlic cloves, minced
1½ teaspoons salt
Freshly ground black pepper

2 cups tomato purée
1 cup water
½ teaspoon dried orégano
Pinch of dried thyme
1 bay leaf
2 pounds zucchini, thickly sliced

1. In a heavy kettle heat the oil and brown meat on all sides. Add the onions and garlic and cook until onions are lightly browned.

2. Add the salt, pepper to taste, tomato purée, water and seasonings. Simmer for one and one-half hours.

3. Arrange the zucchini on top of the meat. Cover and simmer for about one hour longer, or until meat and vegetables are tender. Serve with noodles.

ANDALUSIAN LAMB STEW   *6 servings*

2 pounds breast of lamb
⅓ cup all-purpose flour
2 tablespoons cooking oil or butter
1 medium onion, chopped
3 cups hot water
1 bay leaf
3½ teaspoons salt
½ teaspoon black peppercorns

½ cup chopped green pepper
½ cup uncooked rice
2 cups (one 1-pound can) tomatoes
1 cup frozen peas, thawed
1 egg, beaten
1 teaspoon olive oil
½ teaspoon cider vinegar

1. Wipe the lamb and cut it into one-and-one-half-inch pieces. Dredge with the flour.

2. Brown the lamb in the oil or butter in a large skillet. Add the onion and cook until wilted. Add the hot water, bay leaf, salt and peppercorns. Cover and cook for about one and one-half hours, until the lamb is almost tender.

3. Add the green pepper and rice. Simmer for twenty minutes. Add the tomatoes and peas and simmer for ten minutes longer.

4. Mix the egg, olive oil and vinegar. Add to the stew, stirring until thickened. Serve hot.

LAMB AND SPINACH STEW   *6 servings*

2 pounds boneless shoulder of lamb
½ cup chopped onion
1½ cups boiling Lamb Stock (page 474)
1 bay leaf
3 pounds fresh spinach, washed and cut into large pieces
3 cups diced tomatoes
1¾ teaspoons salt
1 teaspoon dried rosemary
½ teaspoon freshly ground black pepper
2 tablespoons all-purpose flour
2 tablespoons butter

1. Trim excess fat from lamb. Cut meat into one-inch cubes. Brown on all sides in fat trimmed from lamb in a saucepan. Pour off all but one tablespoon fat.

2. Add the onion and cook briefly. Add the boiling stock and bay leaf. Cover and cook for one hour, or until meat is tender.

3. Add spinach, tomatoes, salt, rosemary and pepper to lamb. Cook for ten to fifteen minutes, or until spinach is done.

4. Blend the flour with the butter and add the mixture bit by bit to the stew, stirring constantly. Cook for about one minute, only until slightly thickened.

CHELLO KEBAB   *8 servings*

This is one of the best dishes in Iranian cuisine. To be authentic, use powdered sumac instead of chopped mint.

3 to 4 pounds boned leg or shoulder of lamb
2 cups yoghurt
2 medium onions, grated
1 tablespoon ground saffron
Salt and freshly ground black pepper
1 cup butter, at room temperature
8 cups cooked Chello (Persian rice, page 341)
8 raw egg yolks
Chopped mint
Tarragon pickles, chopped green onions, and sliced radishes

1. Cut the lamb into strips one and one-half inches wide, five inches long and one-half inch thick.

2. Marinate the strips overnight in the yoghurt mixed with the onions and saffron.

3. Thread the strips on skewers and season with salt and pepper. Broil over charcoal or under a preheated broiler for fifteen to twenty minutes, turning several times.

4. Divide the butter among eight plates. Mound one cup of chello on each plate. Make a small hole in the center and drop in an egg yolk. Mix thoroughly with a fork.

5. Arrange the lamb pieces around the chello and sprinkle with the mint. Serve with side dishes of pickles, green onions and radishes.

LAHM MASHWI (an Arab version of lamb on skewers)　　*6 servings*

3 pounds lean lamb, cut into 1-inch cubes
1 tablespoon salt
Freshly ground black pepper
1 teaspoon dried thyme
2 tablespoons chopped fresh mint
½ cup olive oil
Juice of 2 lemons
18 cherry tomatoes
18 small onions
18 mushroom caps

1. Put the lamb cubes in a large mixing bowl and add the salt, pepper to taste, thyme, mint, oil and lemon juice. Let stand for three hours, turning occasionally to marinate well.

2. Arrange the meat on six skewers, alternating each cube with a cherry tomato, onion and mushroom cap.

3. Grill the meat over charcoal or in an oven broiler three or four inches from the source of heat, rotating the skewers occasionally, until the lamb reaches the desired degree of doneness. Serve piping hot.

NARGISI KEBABS　　*6 servings*

2 cups ground cooked lamb
¼ teaspoon ground ginger
¼ teaspoon ground cuminseed
¼ teaspoon ground coriander
¼ teaspoon ground turmeric
Dash of cayenne pepper
¼ teaspoon ground cinnamon
Dash of ground cloves
1¼ teaspoons salt
1 raw egg
6 hard-cooked eggs
Shortening or oil for shallow frying
Fresh lime or lemon juice

1. Put the lamb again through a food chopper, using the finest blade. Grind it almost to the consistency of paste. To this add the spices, salt and raw egg.

2. Using the fingers, coat the hard-cooked eggs with the meat-spice mixture. Fry in shallow hot shortening or oil until the meat-coated eggs are browned on all sides.

3. Sprinkle with fresh lime or lemon juice. Serve whole or sliced into lengthwise halves. Serve either hot or cold.

MINTED LAMB PATTIES WITH FRESH PINEAPPLE
4 servings

1½ cups soft fresh bread crumbs
¼ cup Chicken Stock (page 475)
1¼ pounds lean lamb (shoulder, neck or shank), ground
1 teaspoon salt
¼ teaspoon freshly ground black pepper
1 egg, lightly beaten
1½ tablespoons minced onion

1 garlic clove, minced
1 tablespoon chopped fresh mint
1 tablespoon chopped parsley
2 thick slices of fresh pineapple with the skin, eyes and core removed
1 tablespoon butter
1 tablespoon brown sugar

1. Preheat broiler.

2. Soak the bread crumbs in the stock. Add the lamb, salt, pepper, egg, onion, garlic, mint and parsley; mix together and shape into eight patties.

3. Broil the patties three to four inches from the source of heat for eight to ten minutes. Turn and broil for four minutes longer. Top each patty with a quarter of a pineapple slice. Dot with the butter and sprinkle with the sugar. Broil for four or five minutes more, or until done.

NAVARIN D'AGNEAU   *6 servings*

The most famous of all lamb stews is the navarin d'agneau *of French cuisine. A* navarin *is a savory ragout with vegetables.*

3 pounds lean lamb shoulder, cut into serving pieces
3 tablespoons olive oil
1 tablespoon sugar
Salt and freshly ground black pepper
3 tablespoons all-purpose flour
2 to 3 cups Lamb Stock (page 474)
2 tomatoes, peeled, seeded and chopped
2 garlic cloves, finely minced
¼ teaspoon dried thyme

1 bay leaf
12 small potatoes, peeled
6 carrots, scraped and cut into 1½-inch lengths
6 small white turnips, peeled and halved
12 small white onions
1 cup shelled fresh peas or 1 package (10 ounces) frozen green peas
1 cup green beans, cut into ½-inch lengths

1. Preheat oven to moderate (375° F.).

2. Brown the meat on all sides, a few pieces at a time, in the oil. Transfer to a heavy heatproof casserole.

3. Sprinkle the meat with the sugar and place the casserole over moderately high heat for four or five minutes. Season the meat with salt and pepper and sprinkle with the flour. Cook for three to five minutes longer, stirring constantly.

4. Add enough stock to cover the meat. Add the tomatoes, garlic, thyme and bay leaf and bring to a boil. Cover and bake in the oven for one to one and one-half hours, or until meat is almost tender.

5. Remove the meat to a clean casserole. Strain the sauce, skim off excess fat, and pour the sauce over meat.

6. Add the potatoes, carrots, turnips and onions. Cover and bake for twenty-five minutes, or until vegetables are almost tender.

7. Add the peas and beans and bake for ten minutes longer. If frozen peas are used, add them only for the last five minutes of the baking time.

KOOFTAH CURRY   *6 servings*

3 tablespoons chopped onion	$\frac{1}{2}$ cup thinly sliced onion
$1\frac{1}{2}$ pounds lamb, ground	1 teaspoon ground turmeric
$2\frac{1}{2}$ teaspoons salt	1 cup water
$\frac{1}{4}$ teaspoon ground cinnamon	2 tablespoons tomato paste
$\frac{1}{8}$ teaspoon ground cloves	2 teaspoons ground coriander
1 egg, beaten	$\frac{1}{2}$ teaspoon ground cuminseed
$\frac{1}{4}$ cup melted shortening or oil	$\frac{1}{8}$ teaspoon cayenne pepper

1. Combine the chopped onion, lamb, one and one-half teaspoons of the salt, the cinnamon, cloves and beaten egg. Shape into eighteen balls and set aside.

2. Heat two tablespoons of the shortening or oil. Brown the onion slices in it. Add the turmeric and cook for two or three minutes. Remove the onion slices from the pan and reserve them.

3. Add the remaining shortening or oil to the pan and heat it. Add the meat balls and cook them until browned on all sides.

4. Mix the browned onions, water, tomato paste, remaining salt, the coriander, cuminseed and cayenne and add to the pan. Cover and cook over moderate heat for twenty minutes.

LAMB AND EGGPLANT BALLS   *5 servings*

1½ pounds lamb, ground
 1 tablespoon finely chopped parsley
 2 cups chopped peeled eggplant
    (1 small eggplant)
⅓ cup soft fresh bread crumbs
 1 egg, lightly beaten
1½ teaspoons cornstarch
1¼ teaspoons salt
¼ teaspoon freshly ground black
    pepper

¾ cup finely chopped onions
 3 tablespoons olive oil or butter
 1 cup (one 8-ounce can) tomato
    sauce
⅛ teaspoon dry mustard
½ teaspoon ground cinnamon
¼ teaspoon ground cloves

1. Mix together the lamb, parsley, eggplant, bread crumbs, egg, corn-starch, one teaspoon of the salt, one-eighth teaspoon of the pepper and one-half cup of the onions.

2. Shape the mixture into twenty balls and brown them on all sides in the oil or butter. Pour off the drippings. Combine the remaining ingredients and pour over the lamb balls.

3. Cover and simmer gently for thirty minutes. Uncover and cook for fifteen minutes longer.

COMBINATION DOLMA   *6 servings*

 3 small green peppers
 3 firm tomatoes
1½ pounds lean lamb, ground
 3 small green squash
 3 small long eggplants
    Salt and freshly ground black
    pepper

½ cup uncooked rice
 3 medium onions, finely chopped
 3 tablespoons minced parsley
 2 tablespoons chopped mint

1. Cut a slice from each pepper and discard the seeds. Cut a slice from each tomato and scoop out the center. Chop the pulp and add it to the ground lamb. Cut a slice from each squash and eggplant, scoop out the centers, chop the centers, and add to the lamb. Sprinkle the vegetables with salt and pepper.

2. Mix the ground meat and vegetables with the rice, onions, parsley and mint until thoroughly blended.

3. Fill scooped-out vegetables, not too tightly, with the mixture and arrange them in rows in a kettle or baking dish. Add water just to cover the bottom of the pan. Cover tightly.

4. Cook over moderate heat on top of the stove; or bake in a moderate oven (350° F.) for about one hour, until the vegetables are tender. If necessary, add a little more water.

SPECIALTY MEATS

ROSEMARY SAUSAGE   *4 to 6 servings*

2 pounds pork chops
Salt
½ teaspoon coarsely ground black pepper

1 teaspoon dried sage
1 fresh rosemary sprig or 6 dried rosemary leaves

1. Each pork chop should have a good layer of fat. Trim off all the lean meat and fat from the bones and put this twice through the fine blade of a meat grinder. (This may be done by the butcher, but not all butchers will grind pork.)

2. In a mixing bowl blend the pork, salt to taste and pepper. Chop the sage and rosemary and blend the mixture well with the hands. If more highly spiced sausage is desired, add more sage or rosemary or both.

3. Shape the mixture into four or six patties and place them in a cold skillet. Cook, turning once or twice, for twenty-five to thirty-five minutes, until golden brown on all sides and cooked through.

SAUSAGE AND NOODLE CASSEROLE   *6 servings*

1½ pounds pork sausage links
2 tablespoons water
4 ounces noodles, cooked
1 package (10 ounces) frozen peas, partly defrosted
½ cup thinly sliced onion

½ teaspoon dried orégano
1½ cups canned tomatoes
1½ teaspoons salt
¼ teaspoon freshly ground black pepper

1. Preheat oven to moderate (350° F.).

2. Place the sausage links and water in a pan. Cover and cook for five minutes. Remove the cover and brown the links.

3. Arrange half of the links in a casserole. Combine the noodles, peas, onion, orégano, tomatoes, salt and pepper. Spoon into the casserole. Arrange the rest of the sausages on top, cover, and bake for forty-five minutes.

SAUSAGE CREAM PIE   *6 servings*

Pastry for a 10-inch 1-crust pie
1 tablespoon butter
2 tablespoons finely chopped onion
1 tablespoon all-purpose flour
1 cup milk
6 whole eggs or 12 yolks

2 cups heavy cream
Salt and freshly ground black pepper
12 small link sausages, imported chipolatas preferably

1. Preheat oven to hot (450° F.).

2. Line a ten-inch pie pan with pastry and flute the edges. Bake for ten minutes; remove from the oven and reserve.

3. Melt the butter in a saucepan and cook the onion until it wilts. Stir in the flour and gradually add the milk, stirring constantly with a wire whisk.

4. When the mixture is thickened and smooth, cook, stirring frequently, for about twenty minutes. Remove the sauce from the heat and let it cool slightly.

5. Beat the eggs or egg yolks and blend with the cream. Add the sauce, a little at a time, to the egg mixture. Season with salt and pepper to taste.

6. Cook the sausages according to package directions; drain them on paper towels. Arrange them symmetrically over the bottom of the partly baked pie shell.

7. Strain the cream-and-egg mixture over the sausages. Bake the pie for about thirty minutes, until the custard is set. Serve hot.

Variety meats, when properly prepared, can be delicious. These specialty cuts have a high nutritive value and most of them are relatively inexpensive.

CALF'S BRAINS VINAIGRETTE   *2 servings*

1 calf's brains, trimmed
Juice of 1 lemon
1 tablespoon vinegar
1 bay leaf
Salt

1. Rinse the brains. Place them in cold water to cover, add the lemon juice and soak for one hour.

2. Drain the brains and add fresh cold water to cover, the vinegar, bay leaf and salt to taste. Bring to a boil and simmer gently for about twenty minutes, until done. Let brains cool slightly in the cooking liquid. Remove and slice. Serve with browned butter.

CALF'S HEAD VINAIGRETTE   *8 servings*

1 calf's head, boned, including brains and tongue
½ cup all-purpose flour
4 small onions, each stuck with 1 clove
3 garlic cloves
2 leeks, trimmed and washed well
2 parsley sprigs
12 peppercorns
1 bay leaf
Pinch of dried thyme
1 celery rib, halved
3 tablespoons salt, approximately
8 potatoes, steamed
Chopped parsley
1¼ cups Vinaigrette Sauce I (page 488)

1. Separate the brains and tongue. Prepare the brains according to the recipe above. Trim the tongue.

2. Cut the head into large serving pieces and drop them into a kettle of boiling water. When the water returns to a boil, cook for five minutes, then drain. Rinse the meat under several changes of cold water.

3. Rinse out the kettle in which the meat was cooked. Return the meat to the kettle and add cold water to cover. Make a paste of the flour with about one-half cup water, adding the water a little at a time. Add the flour mixture to the kettle and stir until dissolved.

4. Add the onions and garlic to the kettle. Tie the leeks, parsley, pepper-corns, bay leaf, thyme and celery into a bundle with string. Add to the kettle. Add the salt and tongue and cover the kettle. Bring to a boil and simmer gently for two hours.

5. Arrange the drained pieces of calf's head on a large platter. Peel the tongue and slice it. Add it, the sliced brains, and steamed potatoes to the platter. Sprinkle with chopped parsley. Serve vinaigrette sauce separately.

HERBED KIDNEY RAGOUT   *6 servings*

3 teaspoons salt
2 pounds veal, lamb, or beef kidneys
¼ cup chopped onion
¼ cup butter
2 cups canned tomatoes
1 tablespoon celery flakes
1 tablespoon sweet-pepper flakes
1 teaspoon sugar
1 cup sliced mushrooms
½ teaspoon dried orégano
½ teaspoon dried basil
⅛ teaspoon freshly ground black pepper

1. Rub one teaspoon of the salt over the kidneys and let them stand for two hours. (This removes some of the strong flavor.) Remove membranes and white tubes, and cut kidneys into one-quarter-inch slices.

2. Sauté the kidneys and onion in three tablespoons of the butter for five minutes. Add tomatoes, celery and sweet-pepper flakes, remaining salt and the sugar. Cover and simmer for thirty minutes.

3. Sauté the mushrooms in remaining butter until wilted. Add them with the seasonings to the stew and cook for ten minutes longer.

KIDNEY TRIFOLATI   *4 servings*

2 pounds lamb or veal kidneys
All-purpose flour
3 garlic cloves, crushed
3 tablespoons olive oil
Salt and freshly ground black pepper
8 anchovy fillets
1 tablespoon butter, softened
2 tablespoons lemon juice
1 tablespoon chopped parsley

1. Remove fat, membranes and cores from kidneys. Wash them and pat dry. Cut into thin slices and dredge lightly with flour.

2. Lightly brown the garlic in the oil, add the kidney pieces, and sauté quickly until browned on the outside. Take care not to overcook or kidneys will be tough. Season with salt and pepper to taste.

3. Mash the anchovies with the butter until they make a paste. Add this to the kidneys and stir well. When butter is melted, remove the pan from the heat, stir in the lemon juice, and sprinkle with the parsley.

ROGNONS DE VEAU EN CASSEROLE   *4 servings*

7 tablespoons butter
3 veal kidneys, trimmed
1 tablespoon minced shallots
½ cup dry white wine
1 tablespoon lemon juice
1½ tablespoons prepared mustard, preferably Dijon

½ cup beef gravy
Salt and freshly ground black pepper
3 tablespoons minced parsley

1. Heat four tablespoons of the butter in a flameproof casserole. Sauté the kidneys in the butter for about ten minutes, turning them occasionally. Remove them to a hot plate.

2. Add the shallots to the pan in which the kidneys were cooked. Cook the shallots for one minute. Add the wine and lemon juice. Bring to a boil, scraping the drippings, and cook until the liquids have been reduced to one-quarter cup. Remove the pan from the heat.

3. Mix the mustard with remaining butter and add by teaspoons to the reduced liquid, stirring. Add the beef gravy and salt and pepper to taste.

4. Cut the sautéed kidneys into very thin crosswise slices. Sprinkle them lightly with additional salt and pepper and add them, with their juices, to the pan. Cook over low heat to warm them, without allowing the sauce to boil, for a minute or two. Shake the pan occasionally. Sprinkle with the parsley and serve in the casserole.

LAMBURGER MIXED GRILL   *6 servings*

6 lamb kidneys
6 small pork sausages
1 medium onion, chopped
1½ pounds lamb, ground
2 tablespoons chopped parsley
1¼ teaspoons salt
⅛ teaspoon freshly ground black pepper

2 tablespoons melted butter
¼ teaspoon dry mustard
¼ teaspoon dried rosemary
Dash of cayenne pepper
¼ teaspoon Worcestershire sauce
3 large tomatoes, halved
3 green-tipped bananas, halved lengthwise

1. Trim the kidneys and split them into halves.
2. Cook the sausages until almost done. Drain them and discard all but

one tablespoon of the fat. Sauté the onion in the fat remaining in the pan until tender.

3. In a bowl mix the onion with the lamb, parsley, one teaspoon of the salt and the pepper. Shape into six oval patties. Place patties and kidneys on a broiler rack.

4. Mix together the butter, mustard, rosemary, cayenne, Worcestershire and remaining salt and brush over the meat. Broil for ten minutes on each side, brushing frequently with the butter mixture.

5. Place the sausages, tomato halves and bananas on the broiler rack, brush with remaining butter sauce, and broil for five minutes longer, or until lightly browned and hot.

BRAISED LIVER   *6 servings*

1½ pounds beef or pork liver, ½ inch thick
¼ cup all-purpose flour
1½ teaspoons salt
¼ teaspoon freshly ground black pepper

5 tablespoons butter
2 cups thinly sliced carrots
1 cup finely chopped onions
1 medium green pepper, diced
¼ cup Beef Stock (page 473)

1. Cut the liver into serving pieces and dredge the pieces with the flour mixed with the salt and pepper.

2. Brown the liver in the butter in a heavy skillet. Arrange the carrots, onions and green pepper on top of the liver. Add the stock, cover, and cook slowly for thirty-five minutes, or until tender.

CALF'S LIVER WITH AVOCADO   *6 servings*

12 thin slices of calf's liver
3 avocados, thinly sliced
½ cup all-purpose flour
1½ teaspoons salt
¼ teaspoon freshly ground black pepper

1 cup butter
Juice of 2 lemons
½ cup Beef Stock (page 473)
½ teaspoon dried thyme
Chopped parsley

1. Dredge the liver and avocado slices with the flour seasoned with the salt and pepper. Heat half of the butter and sauté the liver and avocados very quickly on both sides. Transfer to a warm platter and keep hot.

2. Heat the remaining butter in a saucepan until lightly browned. Add the lemon juice, stock and thyme. When hot, pour over the liver and avocados. Sprinkle with parsley.

CALF'S LIVER WITH PARSLEY SAUCE   *4 servings*

1 garlic clove, finely minced	2 tablespoons lemon juice
3 tablespoons bacon fat	¼ cup chopped parsley
¾ pound calf's liver, thinly sliced	½ cup Brown Sauce (page 477)
1 teaspoon Worcestershire sauce	8 slices of bacon, cooked until crisp

1. Sauté the garlic in the bacon fat in a skillet for two or three minutes. Add the liver slices and cook quickly over high heat for about one and one-half minutes on each side. Remove to a warm platter.

2. Add the Worcestershire, lemon juice, parsley and brown sauce to the skillet. Swirl around and bring to a boil. Pour over the liver. Garnish with bacon slices.

SWEETBREADS WITH MADEIRA   *6 servings*

3 pairs of sweetbreads	¼ cup butter
Salt	3 shallots, chopped
1 tablespoon vinegar or lemon juice	1½ cups Brown Sauce (page 477)
18 small white onions	½ cup Madeira
3 carrots, cut into strips	Freshly ground black pepper

1. Soak the sweetbreads in cold water for several hours; drain. Bring them to a boil in one quart water with one teaspoon salt and the vinegar. Lower the heat and simmer for four minutes. Drain and place in cold water. When cool, remove connective tissues and tubes but not the top membrane. Press under a weight for several hours.

2. Preheat oven to moderate (350° F.).

3. Brown the onions and carrots lightly in half of the butter in a skillet. Turn them into a shallow baking dish. Arrange the sweetbreads over the vegetables.

4. In the same skillet, heat the shallots in the remaining butter and add the brown sauce. Add the wine and pour the mixture over the sweetbreads. Season with salt and pepper to taste.

5. Bake for about one hour, basting frequently with the liquid in the pan.

SWEETBREADS IN INDIVIDUAL CASSEROLES
4 main-course servings or 8 first-course servings

3 pairs of sweetbreads	1¼ cups Chicken Stock (page 475)
2 tablespoons lemon juice	½ cup dry white wine
2 teaspoons salt	¼ cup heavy cream
1 small onion, minced	Salt and freshly ground black
⅓ pound mushrooms, sliced	pepper
2 tablespoons butter	Soft fresh bread crumbs
3 tablespoons all-purpose flour	Melted butter

1. Soak the sweetbreads in ice water for forty-five minutes; drain. Cover with boiling water containing the lemon juice and salt. Simmer for fifteen to twenty minutes.

2. Drain the sweetbreads and cool immediately in ice water. Drain again, and break into small pieces, removing all connective tissues, membranes and tubes.

3. Sauté the onion and mushrooms in the butter until tender. Add the flour and cook over very low heat for a few minutes.

4. Preheat oven to very hot (500° F.).

5. Add stock and wine to the mushrooms. Let the sauce thicken over low heat for ten minutes. Add the cream and sweetbreads, season with salt and pepper, and continue to cook for another six minutes.

6. Spoon the mixture into individual casseroles. Sprinkle with bread crumbs and moisten with melted butter. Bake in the oven until the crumbs are golden brown.

BRAISED TONGUE   *8 servings*

1 fresh beef tongue (4 pounds)	3 tablespoons butter
½ cup diced carrot	3 tablespoons all-purpose flour
½ cup diced onion	Salt and freshly ground black
½ cup diced celery	pepper
¼ cup diced white turnip	¼ cup sour pickles, chopped

1. Wash the tongue, cover with water, and simmer for about two hours. Drain the tongue and cool it. Reserve the cooking liquid.

2. Preheat oven to moderate (350° F.).

3. Remove the skin, bones, roots and gristle from the tongue and place the meat in a deep casserole. Add the vegetables.

4. Melt the butter and blend in the flour. Stir in three cups of the cooking liquid slowly and bring to a boil. Add salt and pepper to taste and the pickles and pour the sauce over the tongue.

5. Bake for two hours. Serve on a hot platter with the strained sauce from the casserole.

TONGUE WITH ALMONDS AND GRAPES   *8 to 10 servings*

1 beef tongue (4 pounds), cooked	1 teaspoon lemon juice
1 tablespoon butter	2 cups beef gravy
2 ounces almonds, blanched and shredded	1 teaspoon tomato paste
4 ounces small seedless grapes or drained canned grapes	2 tablespoons Madeira or sherry
Salt and freshly ground black pepper	Chopped parsley for garnish

1. Cool the tongue; skin and trim it. Slice the tongue, allowing two or three slices per person. Return the slices to the cooking liquid to keep warm.

2. Melt the butter, add the almonds, and sauté until light brown. Add the grapes. Season with salt and pepper to taste and the lemon juice.

3. Add the gravy, tomato paste and wine and heat to the boiling point. Place the tongue slices in the sauce to reheat but do not boil. Serve on a heated platter and sprinkle with parsley.

BRAISED TRIPE   *12 to 16 servings*

8 large cabbage leaves	1½ tablespoons salt
4 onions, cut into rings	Freshly ground black pepper
2 cups sliced carrots	2½ cups butter
4 whole cloves	4½ pounds tripe, cut into 3-inch
2 large bay leaves	squares
½ teaspoon dried thyme	2 calf's feet, split

1. Preheat oven to moderate (350° F.).

2. Arrange two cabbage leaves in the bottom of each of two six-quart casseroles.

3. Arrange the vegetables, seasonings, butter and tripe in layers on top of the cabbage leaves. Put one calf's foot in the center of each casserole. Cover with the remaining cabbage leaves. Cover with a tight-fitting lid.

4. Bake for thirty minutes. Lower heat to slow (225° F.). Bake for nine hours. Remove the tripe pieces to another casserole and strain the sauce over them. Reheat to serve.

TRIPE À LA CREOLE   *4 to 6 servings*

2 pounds honeycomb tripe	½ cup chopped celery
1 teaspoon salt	1 garlic clove, minced
½ teaspoon sugar	¼ teaspoon freshly ground black
2 cups canned tomatoes	pepper
1¼ cups (one 10-ounce can) tomato	Dash of cayenne pepper
purée	½ cup boiled ham, minced
1 green pepper, diced	1 pound mushrooms, sliced
2 medium onions, diced	

1. Wash the tripe several times under running water. Cut it into julienne strips. Place the strips in a large pan and cover with cold water. Bring to a boil and add one-half teaspoon of the salt and the sugar. Cover and simmer for about three hours, until the tripe is tender. Drain.

2. Add the tomatoes, tomato purée, green pepper, onions, celery, garlic, remaining salt, the black pepper and cayenne to the tripe. Cover and simmer for twenty minutes.

3. Add the ham and mushrooms. Cover and simmer for fifteen minutes longer.

OXTAIL RAGOUT   *8 servings*

4 oxtails, skinned and cut into pieces
¼ cup butter
¼ cup vegetable oil
2 cups finely chopped celery
¼ cup finely chopped parsley
2 garlic cloves, finely minced
1 bay leaf
2 carrots, scraped and chopped
2 tablespoons all-purpose flour
1 cup Beef Stock (page 473)

1 cup dry red wine
3 tablespoons cognac
1 pound ripe tomatoes, peeled, seeded and chopped, or 2 cups Italian plum tomatoes, drained and chopped
Juice of ½ lemon
¼ teaspoon grated nutmeg
1 cup Madeira
Freshly ground black pepper

1. Preheat oven to moderate (350° F.).

2. Brown the oxtails well in the butter and oil in a large skillet.

3. Line a buttered casserole with the celery and parsley. Add the garlic and bay leaf. Transfer the oxtails to the casserole.

4. Add the carrots to the skillet in which the oxtails cooked. Cook them, stirring, until lightly browned. Sprinkle with the flour; when it starts to brown, add a little stock. Stir to dissolve brown particles and scrape this mixture into the casserole.

5. Add the remaining stock to the casserole with the red wine, cognac and tomatoes. Cover. Bake for two and one-half to three hours. Transfer the oxtails to a hot deep serving dish.

6. Strain the gravy but press as much as possible of the cooked vegetables through the sieve. Bring the strained sauce to a boil and add the lemon juice, nutmeg, and Madeira. Add pepper to taste. Simmer for five minutes. Pour the sauce over the oxtails and sprinkle them with additional chopped parsley. Serve with boiled potatoes or noodles.

. . . .

GAME

. . . .

BRAISED KID   *6 to 8 servings*

1 small leg of kid (leg of lamb may be substituted)
2 tablespoons butter
1 tablespoon olive oil
1 large onion, sliced
1 large carrot, diced
1 tablespoon water
2 celery ribs, diced

2 teaspoons chopped parsley
1 teaspoon salt
½ teaspoon freshly ground black pepper
1 cup dry white wine
1 cup Lamb Stock (page 474) or water

1. Place the leg of kid, one tablespoon of the butter and the olive oil in a Dutch oven. Brown meat slowly but thoroughly on all sides. When brown, remove to a dish and keep warm.

2. Place the onion, carrot, water, celery, parsley and remaining butter in the Dutch oven. Brown vegetables well without burning, adding a little more water if necessary.

3. Arrange the kid over the braised vegetables and pour over it any juice that drained from it while it was standing. Add the salt, pepper and wine. Cook until wine evaporates. Add the stock. Cover and cook slowly for two hours, or until meat is tender.

REINDEER ROAST   *15 to 20 servings*

1 reindeer roast (about 12 pounds)
1 pound fresh mushrooms, washed, drained and sliced
⅓ cup dry vermouth
⅔ cup corn oil
6 celery ribs with leaves, chopped
½ pound Norwegian blue cheese

1. Preheat oven to moderate (325° F.).
2. Cut off any tough membrane on the roast and puncture any pockets holding fluids. Wash the meat well and place it on a sheet of heavy-duty aluminum foil large enough to cover the meat completely.
3. Combine the mushrooms, vermouth and one-third cup of the oil in the container of an electric blender and blend until smooth. Remove from the blender.
4. Put the celery and the remaining oil in the container of the blender and blend until smooth. Combine with the mushroom mixture. Pour over the meat. Enclose the meat completely with the foil and tuck in the ends.
5. Set the foil package in a shallow roasting pan and place in the oven. Roast for four hours without disturbing. Remove the roast to a warm platter.
6. Combine half of the juices in the foil wrapper with the blue cheese and blend until smooth in the blender. Remove from the blender. Mix the remaining pan juices in the blender. Reheat the two blended sauces separately over water. Do not allow either to boil. Serve the sauces separately with the sliced meat.

SAVORY GAME STEW   *8 to 10 servings*

4 pounds chevon (goat), cut into 2-inch cubes
¼ cup butter
4 onions, diced
2 cups canned tomatoes
4 medium potatoes, diced
1 green pepper, diced
½ teaspoon ground sage
1 bay leaf
2 tablespoons lemon juice
1 tablespoon celery salt
Dash of Tabasco
Pinch of dried thyme

1. Brown the meat in two tablespoons of the butter in a skillet. Remove meat to a platter.

2. Add the remaining butter and other ingredients to the skillet. Simmer for ten minutes.

3. Return the meat to the skillet and spoon the vegetable mixture over it. Cover tightly and simmer for about two and one-half hours, or until meat is tender. Skim off the fat before serving.

Venison is considered the most desirable of game and it may be prepared in many ways. The flesh of a very young deer is as tender as beef; young venison steak, for example, is delicious when sautéed briefly in butter and sprinkled with parsley. With older deer, it is better to marinate the meat for several hours or several days in a well-seasoned marinade. This has the effect not only of flavoring the meat but of making it tender as well.

VENISON CHOPS WITH MUSHROOMS   *4 to 8 servings*

8 tender venison chops
Salt and freshly ground black pepper
½ cup butter
½ pound mushrooms, thinly sliced
⅓ cup dry white wine
¾ cup Brown Sauce (page 477)
8 thin slices of ham

1. Sprinkle the venison chops with salt and pepper. Heat half of the butter in a large heavy skillet and brown the chops in it on both sides. Preferably the chops should be served rare, particularly if the venison is tender. Transfer the chops to a warm serving platter.

2. Add two more tablespoons of the butter to the skillet and add the mushrooms. Cook, stirring, until mushrooms are wilted. Sprinkle with pepper and add the wine. Stir to dissolve the brown particles clinging to the bottom and sides of the skillet. Stir in the brown sauce and simmer briefly.

3. Meanwhile, heat the ham in the remaining butter. Top each chop with a slice of ham. Pour the sauce over the chops and serve immediately.

BIGOS   (Polish hunter's stew)   *8 servings*

½ ounce dried mushrooms
1 cup boiling water
2½ pounds sauerkraut
3 slices of lean bacon
1 large onion, finely chopped
½ cup chopped parsley
1 tablespoon all-purpose flour
2 cups canned tomatoes, drained
½ pound kielbasa (Polish sausage), cut into ⅛-inch slices
1½ pounds leftover cooked game, cut into 1½-inch cubes
1 cup leftover meat gravy
Salt and freshly ground black pepper
2 teaspoons sugar (optional)
1 cup Madeira

1. Wash the mushrooms and pour the boiling water over them. Let stand for thirty minutes.

2. Wash and drain the sauerkraut and place it in a large heavy kettle with a tight-fitting lid. Pour the liquid in which the mushrooms soaked over the sauerkraut. Cut the mushrooms into strips. Add the mushrooms to the sauerkraut and cover. Simmer slowly for thirty minutes.

3. Cook the bacon slightly and add the onion and parsley. Cook until the onion is golden but do not let the bacon become crisp. Add the flour and stir in a little juice from the kettle containing the sauerkraut. Pour the mixture into the sauerkraut and mix well. Add the tomatoes.

4. Fold the meats into the sauerkraut and add the gravy. Add seasoning to taste, the sugar and Madeira. Bring to a boil. Remove from the heat and let stand in a cool place, or refrigerate. Traditionally, this dish is served on the second day, reheated, with boiled potatoes. It may be kept and served several days later.

SAUCE VENAISON   *About 3 cups*

1 quart chopped bones and trimmings from venison or other game
¾ cup chopped carrots
¾ cup chopped onions
½ cup chopped celery
⅓ cup salad oil or lard
¼ cup all-purpose flour
5 cups boiling Beef Stock (page 473)
1 cup dry white wine or red wine or ⅔ cup dry white vermouth

3 tablespoons tomato paste
4 parsley sprigs
1 bay leaf
¼ teaspoon dried thyme
1 teaspoon peppercorns, coarsely ground, or more
½ cup red currant jelly
½ cup heavy cream

1. Brown the bones, trimmings, carrots, onions and celery in the oil or lard in a large skillet. Using a slotted spoon remove them to a platter and reserve.

2. Add the flour to the skillet and brown it slowly, stirring. If necessary, add more fat. Remove the skillet from the heat and stir in the stock, wine and tomato paste.

3. Pour the sauce into a kettle. Add the browned bones and trimmings. Bring to a boil. Tie the parsley, bay leaf and thyme in a cheesecloth bag and add it to the sauce. Simmer, skimming occasionally to remove fat and foam, for about three hours. Strain the sauce through a sieve lined with cheesecloth.

4. Let the sauce cool and skim off all remaining fat. When ready to use, bring the sauce to a boil and add the black pepper. At this point the sauce is called *poivrade*. Also, at this point the sauce may be frozen. To freeze, simply pour the sauce into airproof plastic bags or other freezer containers. Cover or seal, leaving a small amount of air space for expansion and freezing. Defrost the sauce before proceeding.

5. Stir the jelly into the sauce. When it is melted and thoroughly blended, stir in the cream. Heat the sauce to the boiling point and serve. Serve with roasted or broiled venison or other game.

TIMETABLE FOR ROASTING MEATS
(Courtesy National Live Stock and Meat Board)

CUT	APPROX. WEIGHT (POUNDS)	OVEN TEMPER-ATURE CONSTANT	INTERIOR TEMPERATURE WHEN REMOVED FROM OVEN	APPROX. COOKING TIME (MIN. PER LB.)
BEEF				
Standing rib*	6 to 8	300°–325° F.	140° F. (rare)	23 to 25
			160° F. (medium)	27 to 30
			170° F. (well)	32 to 35
	4 to 6	300°–325° F.	140° F. (rare)	26 to 32
			160° F. (medium)	34 to 38
			170° F. (well)	40 to 42
Rolled rib	5 to 7	300°–325° F.	140° F. (rare)	32
			160° F. (medium)	38
			170° F. (well)	48
Delmonico (rib eye)	4 to 6	350° F.	140° F. (rare)	18 to 20
			160° F. (medium)	20 to 22
			170° F. (well)	22 to 24
Tenderloin, whole	4 to 6	425° F.	140° F. (rare)	45 to 60 (total)
Tenderloin, half	2 to 3	425° F.	140° F. (rare)	45 to 50 (total)
Rolled rump (high quality)	4 to 6	300°–325° F.	150°–170° F.	25 to 30
Sirloin tip (high quality)	3½ to 4	300°–325° F.	150°–170° F.	35 to 40
VEAL				
Leg	5 to 8	300°–325° F.	170° F.	25 to 35
Loin	4 to 6	300°–325° F.	170° F.	30 to 35
Rib (rack)	3 to 5	300°–325° F.	170° F.	35 to 40
Rolled shoulder	4 to 6	300°–325° F.	170° F.	40 to 45
PORK, FRESH				
Loin				
Center	3 to 5	325°–350° F.	170° F.	30 to 35
Half	5 to 7	325°–350° F.	170° F.	35 to 40
Blade loin or sirloin	3 to 4	325°–350° F.	170° F.	40 to 45
Picnic shoulder	5 to 8	325°–350° F.	185° F.	30 to 35
Rolled	3 to 5	325°–350° F.	185° F.	40 to 45
Cushion style	3 to 5	325°–350° F.	185° F.	35 to 40
Boston Shoulder	4 to 6	325°–350° F.	185° F.	45 to 50
Leg (fresh ham)				
Whole (bone in)	10 to 14	325°–350° F.	185° F.	25 to 30
Whole (boneless)	7 to 10	325°–350° F.	185° F.	35 to 40
Half (bone in)	5 to 7	325°–350° F.	185° F.	40 to 45

TIMETABLE FOR ROASTING MEATS (*Continued*)

CUT	APPROX. WEIGHT (POUNDS)	OVEN TEMPER- ATURE CONSTANT	INTERIOR TEMPERATURE WHEN REMOVED FROM OVEN	APPROX. COOKING TIME (MIN. PER LB.)
PORK, SMOKED				
Ham (cook before eating)				
Whole	10 to 14	300°–325° F.	160° F.	18 to 20
Half	5 to 7	300°–325° F.	160° F.	22 to 25
Shank or butt portion	3 to 4	300°–325° F.	160° F.	35 to 40
Ham (fully cooked)**				
Half	5 to 7	325° F.	130° F.	18 to 24
Picnic shoulder	5 to 8	300°–325° F.	170° F.	35
Shoulder roll	2 to 3	300°–325° F.	170° F.	35 to 40
Canadian style bacon	2 to 4	300°–325° F.	160° F.	35 to 40
LAMB				
Leg	5 to 8	300°–325° F.	175°–180° F.	30 to 35
Shoulder	4 to 6	300°–325° F.	175°–180° F.	30 to 35
Rolled	3 to 5	300°–325° F.	175°–180° F.	40 to 45
Cushion	3 to 5	300°–325° F.	175°–180° F.	30 to 35

* *Ribs which measure 6 to 7 inches from chine bone to tip of rib.*
** *Allow approximately 15 minutes per pound for heating whole ham to serve hot.*

CHAPTER FIVE

. . . .

POULTRY

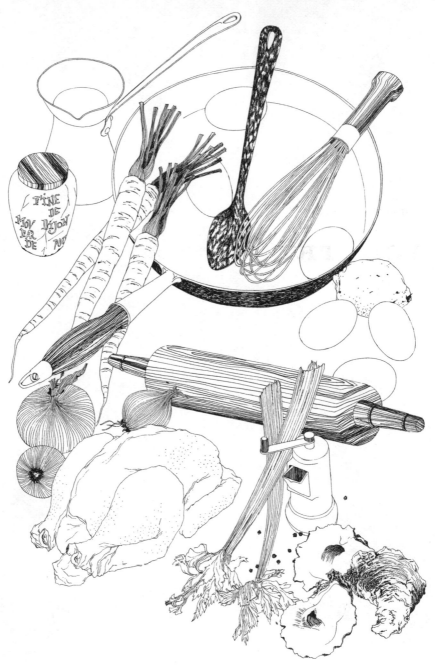

Assembling a chicken and oyster pie

CHICKEN

STUFFED ROAST CHICKEN *6 servings*

1 roasting chicken (3 to 4 pounds)
  Salt and freshly ground black
  pepper
  Stuffing

2 tablespoons soft butter
2 tablespoons butter, melted
1 tablespoon oil

1. Preheat oven to hot (425° F.).

2. Singe the bird if necessary. Wash under running water and dry thoroughly with paper towels.

3. Sprinkle the inside of the bird with salt and pepper and fill the cavity three-fourths full with the stuffing of your choice. Close the opening by sewing or by using small skewers and crisscrossing fine string between. Truss the bird to hold the wings and legs securely (see step photographs on page 279). Rub the skin with the softened butter.

4. Place the chicken, breast up, in a roasting pan and cook for about ten minutes, until the breast is lightly browned, basting once with a mixture of the melted butter and oil.

5. Turn the chicken on one side, baste, and cook for ten minutes longer. Turn to the other side and repeat.

6. Reduce oven heat to moderate (350° F.). Leave the chicken on its side, baste frequently, and cook for about thirty minutes longer. Sprinkle the chicken lightly with salt and turn onto the other side. Cook for another fifteen minutes. Turn breast side up, baste, and cook for a further fifteen minutes. Total roasting time for a four-pound chicken is approximately one and one-half hours.

7. The chicken is done when the drumstick moves easily in the socket and juices coming from the joint are no longer pink. When done, discard trussing strings, thread, pins, etc., and place the bird on a hot platter. Allow the bird to rest for five to ten minutes before carving.

Note: Chickens may be roasted without stuffing. If they are to be served cold, this is the preferred way. Also, several frying chickens may be roasted in place of a single larger bird.

CIRCASSIAN CHICKEN   *6 servings*

1 roasting chicken (4 to 5 pounds)	12 peppercorns
1 onion, peeled	3 quarts water
1 carrot, scraped	2 cups walnut meats
1 celery rib with leaves	3 slices of day-old white bread, with
3 parsley sprigs	crusts trimmed
½ bay leaf	1 to 2 tablespoons paprika
Salt	Cayenne pepper

1. Place the chicken in a large kettle and add the onion, carrot, celery, parsley, bay leaf, salt to taste, peppercorns and water. Bring to a boil and simmer for one to one and one-half hours, or until chicken is tender.

2. Remove the chicken, bring the stock to a boil, and cook over high heat until it is reduced by half. Strain the stock and let it cool to lukewarm.

3. Grind the walnuts twice. Soak the bread with a little chicken stock, then squeeze it dry. Add the bread to the walnuts. Add the paprika and cayenne to taste and put this mixture through the grinder. Place in a mixing bowl.

4. Beat the mixture well with a wire whisk, adding the lukewarm chicken stock gradually. Add two cups or more, until the mixture has the consistency of thin mayonnaise.

5. Remove the skin and bones from the chicken. Cut the meat into bite-size pieces and mix with a little of the walnut sauce. Place the chicken in a serving dish and cover it evenly with the remaining sauce. Sprinkle with paprika and serve.

CHICKEN AND OYSTER PIE   *6 or more servings*

1 roasting chicken or capon (6 to 7 pounds), trussed, with giblets removed	1 onion, peeled
	2 parsley sprigs
	½ cup butter
1 teaspoon salt	½ cup sifted all-purpose flour
10 peppercorns	5 egg yolks, beaten lightly
1 celery rib, trimmed and cut into halves	24 fresh oysters, shucked
	Rich pastry for 1-crust deep-dish
1 carrot, trimmed and quartered	pie, unbaked

1. Place the chicken in a deep kettle and add water to cover. Add salt, peppercorns, celery, carrot, onion and parsley. Bring to a boil and cover partially. Simmer for one and one-half to two hours, or until chicken is tender. Cool chicken and broth and refrigerate overnight. When broth is cold, remove the fat.

2. Take the meat from the bones and reserve. Return the bones and skin to the kettle with the broth. Bring to a boil and cook until broth is reduced.

The broth should have a good, strong flavor. Cut the chicken meat into bite-size pieces and reserve. Season with salt, if necessary. Strain the broth and reserve four cups of it.

3. Preheat oven to hot (425° F.).

4. Melt the butter and stir in the flour with a wire whisk. Using the whisk and stirring vigorously, add the reserved four cups broth. When the mixture is thickened and smooth, continue to cook, stirring occasionally, for five to ten minutes. Remove the sauce from the heat.

5. Add a little of the hot sauce to the egg yolks, then pour this mixture into the sauce, stirring rapidly. Add the chicken pieces and oysters to the sauce and pour into a deep casserole or deep pie dish.

6. Roll out the pastry into a circle and prick it with a fork to allow steam to escape. Fit the pastry over the casserole and flute the edges. Bake for thirty to forty minutes, or until pastry is golden brown.

CHICKEN IN A BAG   *5 or 6 servings*

1 roasting chicken (5 pounds)	½ teaspoon ground cuminseed
1 teaspoon salt	¼ cup olive oil
¼ teaspoon freshly ground black pepper	½ teaspoon paprika
	1 garlic clove, finely minced
1 teaspoon fresh rosemary or ½ teaspoon dried rosemary	

1. Truss the chicken.

2. Combine the salt, pepper, rosemary, cuminseed, oil, paprika and garlic. Set this mixture aside for about thirty minutes.

3. Preheat oven to moderate (325° F.).

4. Rub the entire surface of the chicken with the seasoned oil mixture. Put chicken into a heavy brown paper bag, close the bag, and put it in a roasting pan. Bake for two and one-half to three hours, or until done.

Note: If a well-browned surface on the chicken is desired, the paper bag may be removed for the last thirty minutes of roasting.

BROWN CHICKEN FRICASSEE   *4 servings*

1 roasting chicken (4 pounds), cut into serving pieces	1 celery rib
All-purpose flour	4 cups Chicken Stock (page 475; not too salty since it will later be reduced)
Salt and freshly ground black pepper	
¼ cup butter	1 bay leaf
1 onion stuck with 4 cloves	¼ teaspoon dried thyme
	¾ cup heavy cream

1. Dredge the chicken with flour seasoned with salt and pepper.

2. Heat the butter in a casserole or Dutch oven. Add the chicken pieces and brown on all sides. Add the onion, celery, stock, bay leaf and thyme. Bring the mixture to a boil and simmer for about one hour, until chicken is tender. Remove the chicken from the casserole and reserve.

3. Boil the cooking liquid over high heat until it is reduced to two cups; strain. Bring again to a boil and add the cream and the chicken pieces. Bring to a boil and serve immediately.

Note: If a thickened sauce is desired, knead three tablespoons butter with three tablespoons flour and stir the mixture, bit by bit, into the simmering sauce.

CHICKEN WITH ARTICHOKES   *6 servings*

1 package (9 ounces) frozen artichoke hearts
1 cup dry white wine
1 roasting chicken (5 pounds), cut into serving pieces
2 celery ribs
1 tablespoon salt
½ cup finely chopped onion
½ cup butter
½ cup all-purpose flour
1 cup heavy cream
1 cup milk
2 egg yolks
1 cup sliced mushrooms, sautéed

1. Cook the artichokes in boiling salted water until tender. Drain, cover with the wine, and let stand for several hours or overnight.

2. Heat two cups water to boiling in a large kettle. Add the chicken, celery, salt and onion. Cover and simmer for two hours, until tender. When the chicken is cool enough to handle, remove the skin and bones. Cut the chicken into cubes.

3. Strain the broth and skim off the fat. Heat the butter in a large saucepan. Blend in the flour and add chicken broth, cream and milk. Cook, stirring vigorously with a wire whisk, until thickened and smooth.

4. Beat the egg yolks. Drain the wine from the artichokes and blend the wine with the yolks. Stir the yolk mixture into the chicken sauce. Cook slowly, stirring constantly, for about five minutes. Do not boil.

5. Add the artichoke hearts, mushrooms and cubed chicken to the sauce. Heat thoroughly and serve over noodles. If desired, white seedless grapes may be added just before serving.

POULE AU POT   *6 to 8 servings*

French cookery is celebrated for its elaborate creations, but equally famous is the famed bourgeois dish, the poule au pot. *In the French provinces it is a traditional Sunday dinner dish that is as nourishing as it is delicious.*

4 pounds beef (brisket, rump, shin, plate, chuck or round)
2 onions, each stuck with 1 whole clove
2 celery ribs
14 leeks, washed well
12 carrots, scraped and cut into thirds
4 parsley sprigs
1 bay leaf
¼ teaspoon dried thyme
2 garlic cloves
12 peppercorns
Salt
1 roasting chicken (5 pounds), stuffed and trussed
6 to 8 potatoes, peeled and halved
12 small white turnips, peeled

1. Place the beef in a heavy kettle and add water to cover by three inches. Add the onions, celery, two of the leeks and two of the carrots. Tie the parsley, bay leaf, thyme, garlic and peppercorns in a piece of cheesecloth and add it to the kettle. Add about one tablespoon of salt. Bring the mixture to a boil, skimming frequently. Reduce the heat and simmer, covered, for three to four hours, depending on the cut of beef.

2. Wash the chicken and dry thoroughly. Sprinkle inside with salt and pepper. Stuff the bird with Sausage Stuffing for Chicken (page 313) or with any flavorful stuffing. Sew the openings tightly and truss the bird.

3. About an hour and a half before the beef is done, remove it from the kettle. Strain the broth and discard the cooked vegetables and the spice bag. Return broth and meat to the kettle. Add the chicken, cover, bring to a boil, and simmer for one hour.

4. Tie the remaining carrots and leeks in bundles to help retain their shape. Add them to the kettle with the potatoes and turnips. Adjust the seasoning if necessary. Continue to cook for thirty minutes longer, until the chicken and beef are cooked and the vegetables tender but not mushy.

5. Slice the beef and carve the chicken. Arrange the meats on a large platter and surround them with the vegetables in neat piles. Serve with Sauce Gribiche (page 491).

Note: If desired, the broth may be served as soup at the same meal. If not, save it for other uses as it will be a rich and flavorful stock.

POACHED CHICKEN   *1 chicken*

1 frying chicken (2 to 3 pounds), trussed
1 small onion, studded with 2 cloves
½ bay leaf
Pinch of dried thyme
1 parsley sprig
1 celery rib, trimmed and quartered
1 carrot, scraped and quartered
Salt
10 peppercorns

1. Place the chicken in a small kettle or a large saucepan and add cold water to cover.

2. Add the remaining ingredients and bring to a boil. Reduce heat, cover partly and simmer until the chicken is tender, thirty minutes or longer depending on size.

3. Use the chicken in any recipe that calls for cooked chicken. Strain the broth and save for sauces or soups. To give more flavor to the broth, it may be cooked over high heat, uncovered, until reduced as desired.

CHICKEN SUPREME   *1 or 2 servings*

½ Poached Chicken (page 271)
2 tablespoons butter
2 tablespoons all-purpose flour

1 cup Chicken Stock (page 475) or broth from Poached Chicken (page 271)

1. Remove the chicken meat from the bones. If desired, cut the meat into bite-size pieces.

2. Melt the butter in a saucepan and stir in the flour, using a wire whisk. When blended, add the stock, stirring vigorously with the whisk. When thickened and smooth, continue to cook for about five minutes, stirring occasionally.

3. The sauce may be served at this point, but it will taste better if a little heavy cream is added. It may be seasoned with freshly ground black pepper or a little grated nutmeg. It may be enriched with an egg yolk beaten with a little light cream and lemon juice; add this to the sauce, stirring with the whisk, and heat thoroughly but do not boil.

4. When the sauce is finished, the chicken may be added to it; or the sauce may be served spooned over the chicken.

CHICKEN PUFF   *4 servings*

1⅓ cups sifted all-purpose flour
3 teaspoons salt
¼ teaspoon freshly ground black pepper
1½ teaspoons crushed dried sage
1 frying chicken (2 to 3 pounds), cut up

½ cup melted butter
1 teaspoon baking powder
3 eggs, lightly beaten
1½ cups milk

1. Preheat oven to hot (400° F.).

2. Mix one-third cup of the flour, two teaspoons of the salt, the pepper and sage. Coat chicken pieces with the mixture. Brown chicken on all sides in one-quarter cup of the butter. Place pieces, skin side up, in a well-greased baking dish.

3. Combine the remaining flour and salt, the baking powder and eggs in a bowl. Gradually beat in the milk and remaining butter to make a smooth batter. Pour over the chicken and bake for thirty-five to forty minutes, or until the top is well browned.

CHILI FRIED CHICKEN   *4 servings*

1 frying chicken (3½ pounds), cut into serving pieces
Milk
2 tablespoons chili powder
2 cups peanut oil
½ cup butter
¾ cup sifted all-purpose flour
1 teaspoon freshly ground black pepper
1 teaspoon salt

1. Place the chicken in a mixing bowl and add milk barely to cover. Sprinkle with chili powder, stir briefly, and let stand in the refrigerator overnight.

2. Heat the oil and butter in a large skillet.

3. Place the flour, pepper and salt in a paper bag. Take the chicken pieces from the milk, drain briefly, and dip them, one at a time, into the seasoned flour. Drop them into the fat and cook until brown on one side. Turn and cook until brown on the other side. Total cooking time should be twenty to twenty-five minutes.

4. Drain the chicken pieces on paper towels and serve hot or cold.

CHICKEN ALLA ROMANA   *4 servings*

1 frying chicken (3½ pounds), cut into serving pieces
Salt and freshly ground black pepper
¼ cup olive oil
1 slice of bacon, diced
1 garlic clove, split
1 teaspoon chopped fresh rosemary or ½ teaspoon dried rosemary
½ cup dry white wine
2 teaspoons tomato paste
½ cup hot Chicken Stock (page 475)

1. Sprinkle the chicken with salt and pepper.

2. Heat the oil and bacon and add the garlic. Cook briefly and add the chicken. Cook until chicken is golden on all sides. Sprinkle with the rosemary and add the wine. Cover and continue to cook for ten to fifteen minutes, until the chicken is tender.

3. Remove the garlic and stir in the tomato paste and stock. Cook, uncovered, until the sauce is reduced by half. Serve the chicken with the sauce.

POULET EN CASSEROLE   *4 servings*

1 frying chicken (2½ to 3 pounds), cut up
2 tablespoons butter, melted
¼ pound salt pork, diced
1 chicken liver
4 small white onions
8 potato balls
4 carrots, roughly cut
¼ pound mushrooms, halved if large
1 teaspoon tomato paste
1 cup Chicken Stock (page 475)
⅓ cup dry white wine
1 tablespoon cornstarch
¼ cup cold water
Salt and freshly ground black pepper

1. Preheat oven to moderate (325° F.).

2. Wipe the chicken and brown on all sides in the melted butter in a saucepan. Remove the chicken to a heavy casserole.

3. Brown the salt pork and the liver in the saucepan. Remove the liver, dice it, and reserve.

4. Add the onions, potatoes and carrots and brown on all sides. Add the mushrooms and cook for two minutes longer. Blend in the tomato paste, stock and wine. Bring to a boil and pour over the chicken.

5. Cover the chicken with aluminum foil and the casserole cover. Bake for thirty minutes, or until tender.

6. Blend the cornstarch with the water and add to the casserole, stirring. Simmer for one minute. Season with salt and pepper to taste. Serve in the casserole. Garnish with the reserved chicken liver.

NINETTE LYON'S POULET FLAMBÉ   *4 servings*

¼ cup peanut oil
1 frying chicken (3 pounds), cut into serving pieces
Salt
½ cup butter
⅓ cup Scotch whisky or cognac
Freshly ground black pepper

1 cup heavy cream
½ teaspoon cornstarch
1 tablespoon cold water
1 tablespoon Dijon mustard
Juice of ½ lemon
½ teaspoon *glace de viande* or meat extract

1. Add half of the peanut oil to a skillet. Brown the chicken in it on all sides. Sprinkle the pieces with salt.

2. Combine the butter and remaining oil in another skillet and transfer the browned chicken to this skillet. Cook, uncovered, over low heat for about fifteen minutes, turning occasionally. Cover and cook for thirty to forty minutes longer, or until chicken is tender.

3. Pour the Scotch over the chicken and ignite it. When the flame dies, transfer the chicken to a warm serving dish. Add pepper and adjust seasonings.

4. Add the cream to the skillet and let it boil up, stirring. Continue to cook for about five minutes, then stir in the cornstarch mixed with the water. When the mixture thickens slightly, remove the sauce from the heat. Stir in the mustard and lemon juice and the *glace de viande*. When the glaze melts, pour the sauce over the chicken and serve. Serve with rice.

TARRAGON CHICKEN   *4 to 6 servings*

2 frying chickens (2½ pounds each)
Salt and freshly ground black pepper
4 to 6 fresh tarragon sprigs or 3 teaspoons dried tarragon
½ cup butter

1 cup Chicken Stock (page 475) or half stock and half dry white wine
1½ tablespoons all-purpose flour
1 cup heavy cream
Parsley for garnish

1. Sprinkle the chicken cavities with salt and pepper. Place one or two tarragon sprigs or one teaspoon dried tarragon inside each chicken.

2. Melt six and one-half tablespoons of the butter in a heavy casserole large enough to accommodate both chickens. Brown the chickens thoroughly and evenly on all sides. Add the stock and cover tightly. Cook over low heat for about one hour, until the birds are very tender.

3. Melt the remaining butter in a saucepan and stir in the flour, using a wire whisk.

4. Transfer the chickens to a warm serving platter and add the drippings in the casserole to the butter-flour mixture, stirring constantly. When the mixture is thickened and smooth, add the cream and bring to a boil. Add additional salt and pepper if desired.

5. Chop the remaining tarragon leaves and add them, or one teaspoon dried tarragon, to the sauce. Let the sauce stand over low heat until ready to serve. To serve, garnish the chickens with parsley and serve the sauce separately.

CHICKEN AND NOODLE CASSEROLE   *6 servings*

1 frying chicken (3 pounds)
1 celery rib with leaves
1 carrot, scraped and halved
Salt
6 tablespoons butter
1 onion, finely chopped
1 garlic clove, finely minced
3 firm ripe large tomatoes, peeled and coarsely chopped
1 tablespoon finely chopped parsley
½ teaspoon dried tarragon
Freshly ground black pepper
8 ounces noodles
¼ cup heavy cream
Grated Parmesan cheese

1. Put the chicken in a kettle with water to cover. Add the celery and carrot and salt to taste. Cover and simmer for about one hour, until chicken is tender. Let the chicken cool in the broth.

2. Remove chicken and take the meat from the bones. Strain broth and reserve it to cook the noodles or use it for another purpose.

3. Preheat oven to hot (400° F.).

4. Melt half of the butter in a saucepan and cook the onion and garlic in it until onion is transparent. Add the tomatoes, parsley, tarragon, and pepper and salt to taste. Cook briefly, but do not cook the tomatoes to a pulp. Strain tomato juice into a saucepan and reserve the tomatoes. Cook the juice rapidly until it is reduced by half. Add the strained tomatoes.

5. Cook the noodles in the reserved broth or cook them in water according to package directions. Drain. Toss noodles lightly with the remaining butter, the tomato sauce and chicken. Pour the mixture into a one-quart casserole and pour the cream over it. Sprinkle with the cheese and bake for ten to fifteen minutes, or until lightly browned and bubbling.

CHICKEN AND RICE CASSEROLE   *4 servings*

1 frying chicken (3 pounds), cut into serving pieces
Salt and freshly ground black pepper
⅛ teaspoon ground ginger
½ cup butter
1 garlic clove, finely minced
⅓ cup finely chopped celery
1 onion, finely chopped
½ bay leaf
⅓ cup dry white wine
⅔ cup uncooked rice
2½ cups (one 1-pound 3-ounce can) tomatoes
¼ cup Chicken Stock (page 475)
¼ pound mushrooms, sliced
1 pimiento, chopped
½ cup cooked peas
½ green pepper, chopped
2 tablespoons chopped parsley

1. Season the chicken with salt and pepper to taste and sprinkle with the ginger. Melt one-third cup of the butter in a heavy skillet and brown the chicken in it on all sides.

2. Add the garlic, celery, onion, bay leaf and wine. Bring to a boil and simmer, covered, for twenty minutes.

3. Preheat oven to moderate (350° F.).

4. Sauté the rice in the remaining butter until translucent but not browned. Add the tomatoes, stock, mushrooms, pimiento, peas, green pepper, and salt and pepper to taste.

5. Place the rice mixture in the bottom of a large casserole, top with the chicken, and pour the liquid from the chicken pan over all. Cover tightly and bake for twenty to twenty-five minutes, or until chicken and rice are tender. Check once during the cooking and add more stock if necessary. Serve garnished with chopped parsley.

CHICKEN AND KIDNEY-BEAN CASSEROLE   *10 servings*

1 pound dried red kidney beans
6 cups cold water
2 teaspoons salt
2 frying chickens (3½ pounds each), cut into serving pieces
¼ teaspoon freshly ground black pepper
¼ cup butter
1 onion, sliced
2 garlic cloves, finely minced
3 canned green chilies, chopped
1 cup tomato sauce
1 bay leaf
¼ teaspoon dried thyme
Chicken Stock (page 475)

1. Pick over the beans, wash thoroughly, and cover with the water. Allow to soak overnight; or bring to a boil, simmer for two minutes, and allow to stand for one to two hours before proceeding.

2. Add one teaspoon of the salt, bring to a boil, cover, and simmer for about one and one-half hours, or until the beans are tender. Drain and reserve the liquid.

3. While the beans are cooking, season the chicken pieces with the remaining salt and the pepper and brown on all sides in the butter in a heavy skillet. Transfer to a large heavy Dutch oven or casserole.

4. Sauté the onion and garlic in the butter remaining in the skillet until soft but not browned. Add the chilies, tomato sauce, bay leaf and thyme. Stir to loosen the brown pieces adhering to the pan. Pour over the chicken and add the drained beans. Measure the reserved bean liquid and add enough chicken stock to measure three cups. Add to the casserole. Cover, bring to a boil, and simmer gently for about forty-five minutes, or until chicken is tender. Any excess liquid may be removed by boiling rapidly with the cover off or may be absorbed by mashing some of the beans.

CURRIED CHICKEN   *4 servings*

1 frying chicken (3½ pounds), cut into serving pieces
2 tablespoons butter
2 tablespoons vegetable oil
2 onions, chopped
1½ cups Chicken Stock (page 475)
2 garlic cloves, finely minced
  Salt and freshly ground black pepper
1 teaspoon red-pepper flakes, or more

1 teaspoon ground turmeric
1 teaspoon ground coriander
1 teaspoon ground cuminseed
4 whole cloves
½ cinnamon stick
1 bay leaf
  Pinch of dried thyme
2 large tomatoes, cored, peeled and chopped
½ cup yoghurt

1. Sauté the chicken in the butter and oil until golden. Transfer the chicken to a heatproof casserole.

2. Brown the onions in the same skillet in which chicken cooked and stir in one-half cup of stock. Pour this mixture over the chicken. Add the garlic, salt and pepper to taste, pepper flakes, turmeric, coriander, cuminseed, cloves, cinnamon stick, bay leaf and thyme. Cover closely and cook over low heat, stirring occasionally, for thirty minutes.

3. Combine the tomatoes and yoghurt and add to the chicken. Add salt to taste. Cover again and cook for fifteen minutes longer. Uncover and add the remaining stock. Cook, uncovered, over moderately high heat until sauce is reduced to about two cups.

LEMON CHICKEN SAUTÉ   *3 or 4 servings*

1 frying chicken (3 pounds), cut into serving pieces
  Salt and freshly ground black pepper
⅓ cup butter

⅓ cup chopped shallots or onion
¼ cup chopped parsley
½ teaspoon dried marjoram
⅓ cup fresh lemon juice

1. Sprinkle the chicken with salt and pepper and brown it on all sides in hot butter.

2. Sprinkle the pieces with chopped shallots, parsley and marjoram. Pour the lemon juice over, cover the skillet, and simmer for about fifteen minutes, until the chicken is tender. Serve hot or cold.

CHICKEN IN SOUR CREAM   *4 servings*

1 frying chicken (2½ to 3 pounds), cut up
¼ cup olive oil
½ cup all-purpose flour
1 teaspoon salt
½ teaspoon freshly ground black pepper

¼ cup finely chopped onion
¼ teaspoon dried thyme
2 teaspoons paprika
¾ cup sour cream

1. Wash and dry the chicken pieces. Heat the oil in a skillet.

2. Mix the flour with half of the salt and half of the pepper. Dredge the chicken with the mixture.

3. Fry the chicken in the oil until well browned on all sides. Remove chicken and drain.

4. Sauté the onion in the oil remaining in the skillet until tender but not browned.

5. Return the chicken to the pan and sprinkle with the thyme. Cover and cook gently for thirty minutes, or until done.

6. Sprinkle the chicken with the paprika and the remaining salt and pepper. Stir in the sour cream. Reheat, but do not boil.

CHICKEN IN PEACH SAUCE   *4 servings*

¼ cup shortening
1 frying chicken (2½ to 3 pounds), in serving pieces
1 teaspoon salt
½ teaspoon freshly ground black pepper
¼ teaspoon paprika
½ teaspoon poultry seasoning

2 cups water
¼ cup butter
1 medium onion, finely chopped
3 tablespoons lemon juice
4 large firm peaches
2 tablespoons lime juice
½ cup sugar

1. Melt the shortening in a large skillet and sauté the chicken together with the seasonings until browned. Add one and one-quarter cups of the water and simmer over low heat for about twenty-five minutes.

2. Melt half of the butter in a second skillet and sauté the onion until golden. Remove the onion from the skillet and pour one tablespoon of the lemon juice over it. Let stand.

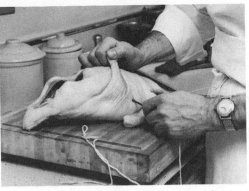

1. *Trussing Poultry*. Hold both legs with one hand and press them down toward tail end of bird as shown. Push a threaded trussing needle through the fleshy portion of one thigh, the cavity and out through the other thigh.

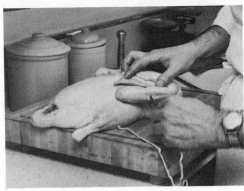

2. Pull the thread through, leaving three inches extending where needle first was inserted. Weave needle through the second wing bone, main wing bone, wing tip and skin. Thread through wing on other side similarly; pull the thread through.

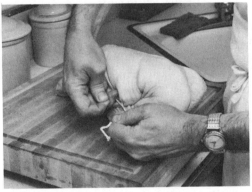

3. With scissors or knife cut off thread, leaving enough thread to tie the two ends together neatly. The thread should be fairly taut when ready to tie the two ends together but not so much so that it tears the flesh of the poultry.

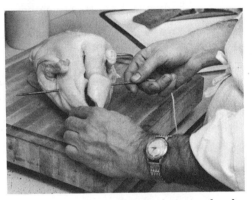

4. To truss the tail opening, push the threaded needle through the thin tail bone on both sides of the bird as shown. Pull the needle through and snip off the thread to leave a length of about one foot threaded through the bird.

5. Bring the length of thread up and tie securely to enclose both the legs and the cavity. Snip off loose ends of thread. The poultry is now ready to be cooked. After cooking, it is easy to remove trussing thread. Just snip and pull.

3. Wash the peaches well and remove the fuzz. Cut them into halves and remove the pits. Slice them. Melt the remaining butter in a skillet and sauté the peaches until they are golden.

4. Add the onion to the chicken and arrange the peaches over. Mix the lime juice with the remaining lemon juice and the sugar and add it to the chicken mixture. Add the remaining water, cover, and simmer over low heat for twenty minutes. Serve with Chello, Persian rice (page 341).

BAKED CHICKEN SUMMER STYLE   *4 servings*

1 frying chicken (3 pounds), cut into 6 serving pieces
2 tablespoons olive oil
2 tablespoons butter
3 slices of bacon, cut into halves
6 slices of fresh ripe tomatoes
2 teaspoons chopped fresh basil
2 teaspoons chopped parsley
1 garlic clove, finely minced
Salt and freshly ground black pepper
½ cup dry white wine

1. Preheat oven to moderate (350° F.).

2. Brown the chicken on all sides in the oil and butter. Transfer the chicken to a baking dish and cover each piece with one-half slice of bacon and a slice of tomato. Sprinkle with a mixture of the basil, parsley, garlic, and salt and pepper to taste. Add the wine to the pan and place the chicken in the oven.

3. Bake the chicken for thirty minutes, basting occasionally with the fat in which the chicken was browned. The chicken is done when it is tender when pricked with a fork.

MEXICAN CHICKEN   *6 servings*

1 frying chicken (3 pounds), cut into serving pieces
3 tablespoons butter
3 medium tomatoes, peeled and quartered
¼ cup chopped onion
1 garlic clove, finely minced
2½ teaspoons salt
1 tablespoon chili powder
⅛ teaspoon freshly ground black pepper
¼ cup chopped pimiento
1 tablespoon all-purpose flour

1. Brown the chicken in the butter. Add the tomatoes, onion, garlic, salt and one-half cup water. Cover and simmer for about thirty minutes, until the chicken is tender.

2. Add the chili powder, pepper and pimiento ten minutes before the end of the cooking time. Remove the chicken to a serving dish and keep warm.

3. Mix the flour with one tablespoon water to a smooth paste and stir it into the gravy left in the pan. Heat for about one minute to thicken. Pour the gravy around the chicken. Serve hot, with rice.

CHICKEN IN SAFFRON CREAM SAUCE   *4 servings*

1 frying chicken (3½ pounds)
Salt and freshly ground black pepper
3 tablespoons butter
¼ teaspoon dried thyme

½ bay leaf
½ teaspoon ground saffron or crumbled saffron shreds
1 cup heavy cream
2 teaspoons tomato paste

1. Season the chicken with salt and pepper and brown it on all sides in butter. Sprinkle with thyme and add the bay leaf, saffron and cream. Stir in the tomato paste until smooth.

2. Cover the skillet and simmer for twenty-five to thirty minutes, or until chicken is tender. Taste the sauce for seasoning and add more salt and pepper if necessary.

BROILED CHICKEN FOR ONE   *1 serving*

½ broiling chicken (1 to 1½ pounds)
Salt and freshly ground black pepper
¼ cup lemon or lime juice or equal parts lemon juice and dry white wine

¼ cup salad oil
1 teaspoon dried tarragon
¼ teaspoon Tabasco

1. Preheat broiler.

2. Sprinkle the chicken with salt and pepper on both sides. Place the chicken, skin side up, on a broiler rack. Place the rack four to six inches from the source of heat.

3. Cook, basting at frequent intervals with a combination of the juice, oil, tarragon and Tabasco, until chicken is brown.

4. Turn the chicken with tongs and continue to broil and baste for forty minutes to one hour, depending on the size of the chicken. It may be necessary to reduce the heat as the chicken cooks. Serve with rice and garnish with watercress.

MOROCCAN-STYLE CHICKEN   *4 servings*

1 lemon
1 frying chicken (3 pounds), cut into serving pieces
Salt and freshly ground black pepper
¼ cup butter

2 tablespoons olive oil
2 shallots or scallions, finely chopped
½ teaspoon finely minced garlic
¾ cup Chicken Stock (page 475)
¼ cup chopped parsley
1 teaspoon dried orégano

1. With a swivel-bladed paring knife pare away half of the lemon rind and cut it into very thin strips. Reserve. Squeeze the lemon and reserve the juice.

2. Sprinkle the chicken parts with salt and pepper. Heat half of the butter and the oil in a skillet. Brown the chicken pieces in it on all sides and transfer them to a warm plate.

3. Add the shallots and garlic to the skillet in which the chicken was browned. Cook, stirring, until golden. Add one-quarter cup of the stock and stir to dissolve all brown particles clinging to the bottom and sides of the skillet. Cook until the liquid is almost evaporated. Reduce the remaining stock to one-third cup.

4. Return the chicken to the skillet and sprinkle with the parsley, orégano, lemon rind, lemon juice and the reduced stock. Cover and cook slowly for about thirty minutes, until the chicken is tender. Stir the remaining butter into the sauce and serve immediately.

COLD CHICKEN IN ASPIC   *12 servings*

1 stewing chicken (5 pounds) or 2 frying chickens (3 pounds each), cut into pieces
4 cups water
1 onion, sliced
1 carrot, diced
2 celery ribs, chopped
2 teaspoons salt
¼ teaspoon freshly ground black pepper

3 fresh tarragon sprigs or 1 teaspoon dried tarragon
2 envelopes unflavored gelatin
1 cup Madeira or Port
1 cup carrot rounds, cooked until barely tender and cooled
Sliced stuffed olives
Salad greens

1. Place the chicken in a Dutch oven or large heavy pan. Add the water, onion, diced carrot, celery, salt and pepper.

2. Cover, bring to a boil, and simmer gently until chicken in tender, about one and one-half hours for the fowl and forty-five to sixty minutes for the fryers. Strain the liquid and return it to the pan. Skim off as much surface fat as possible.

3. Discard the bones and skin and cut the chicken into long strips or bite-size pieces. Cool and chill.

4. Reduce the cooking liquid to three cups by boiling rapidly. Add the tarragon. If fresh tarragon is used, reserve a few sprigs for garnish. Simmer gently for five minutes. Strain the liquid and discard the tarragon.

5. Soften the gelatin in the wine for five minutes. Add to the hot broth, stirring to dissolve. Adjust the seasoning. Chill the broth until just beginning to set.

6. Lightly oil a loaf pan (9 × 5 × 3 inches). Pour a one-eighth-inch layer of the gelatin mixture into the bottom of the pan. Chill until set.

7. Dip the carrot rounds, reserved tarragon leaves and olive slices into the remaining aspic. Arrange them in a pattern over the set layer in the pan. Spoon more aspic over the decorations and chill to set.

8. Half fill pan with chicken pieces. Arrange two rows of sliced olives the length of the pan. Cover with remaining chicken. Pour in the rest of the aspic (which should barely be beginning to set), cover, and chill for several hours or overnight. Unmold onto a chilled plate and garnish with salad greens.

BARBECUED CHICKEN   *4 servings*

2 broiling chickens (2 pounds each), halved for broiling
Vegetable shortening
1 bottle (14 ounces) tomato catchup
½ teaspoon chili powder, or more
½ cup butter
½ teaspoon ground cuminseed
Juice of 1 lemon
3 lemon slices, unpeeled
1 tablespoon Worcestershire sauce, or more
Tabasco
1 garlic clove, flattened
1 cup Chicken Stock (page 475)
Salt and coarsely cracked black pepper

1. Rub all surfaces of the chicken with shortening.

2. Combine the remaining ingredients and simmer briefly until butter is melted.

3. Place chicken, bony side down, on a grill over a charcoal fire. Using a pastry brush, baste chicken with the sauce during broiling, turning chicken several times. To achieve a slight crust on the chicken, place grill closer to coals toward end of cooking time.

4. When chicken is thoroughly cooked, remove it to a heatproof platter and spoon any remaining sauce over it.

Note: The cooked chicken may be kept hot in a very slow oven (200° F.) for one hour.

ROSEMARY BROILED CHICKENS   *4 servings*

2 broiling chickens (2½ pounds each), split for broiling
Salt and freshly ground black pepper
½ cup butter
½ cup lemon juice
1 teaspoon chopped fresh rosemary
¼ teaspoon Tabasco
1 teaspoon Worcestershire sauce

1. Preheat broiler.

2. Sprinkle the chickens on all sides with salt and pepper.

3. Melt the butter and add the lemon juice, rosemary and Tabasco to make a basting sauce.

4. Place the chickens, bony side down, on the broiler rack. Brush chickens with the sauce and place them under the broiler. Cook the chickens for thirty-

five minutes to one hour, until they are done, basting and turning them often. Do not let the chickens burn. Adjust the broiler heat as necessary while they cook. When cooked, the chickens should be nicely browned on all sides.

5. Transfer the chickens to a hot serving platter. Add the Worcestershire sauce to the liquid in the broiler pan. Stir lightly. Pour the sauce over the chickens and serve.

BREADED CHICKEN BREASTS   *6 servings*

3 whole chicken breasts
Salt and freshly ground black pepper
All-purpose flour
2 eggs

1 teaspoon water
2 cups soft fresh bread crumbs
½ cup butter
Lemon wedges and parsley

1. Have the butcher split the breasts into halves and remove the bones. This will produce six pieces of boned chicken breast. Place each breast half between pieces of wax paper and pound thin with the flat side of a heavy knife.

2. Sprinkle the chicken with salt and pepper and dredge with flour. Combine the eggs with the water and beat lightly with a fork. Dip the chicken into the egg mixture and then into the bread crumbs. Pound lightly with the flat side of a knife to make the crumbs adhere. The breaded chicken may be placed on a rack and dried briefly in the refrigerator.

3. Melt the butter in a large skillet and cook the chicken over moderate heat until it is golden brown on all sides. If the chicken breasts are thin enough, further cooking will not be necessary. If they are relatively thick, place them in a preheated moderate oven (350° F.) for five to ten minutes. Serve hot, garnished with lemon wedges and parsley.

CHICKEN IN GREEK PASTRY   *12 servings*

2 whole chicken breasts
5 medium onions, peeled
2 carrots, coarsely chopped
2 parsley sprigs
Salt and freshly ground black pepper

2 celery hearts
2 cups butter
6 eggs
½ teaspoon grated nutmeg
10 sheets of *phyllo* pastry (Greek strudel leaves)

1. Place the chicken breasts in a large saucepan and add cold water to cover. Add two onions cut into quarters, the carrots, parsley, and salt and pepper to taste. Bring to a boil and simmer for twenty to thirty minutes, until chicken is tender. Do not overcook. Remove the chicken from the broth and let it cool. Reserve the broth.

2. When chicken is cool, remove the meat from the bones and discard

the bones and skin. Chop the meat until it is very fine. Cook the chicken broth until it is reduced to less than half. Strain it.

3. Preheat oven to moderate (350° F.).

4. Chop the remaining onions until they are finely minced. Chop the celery until it is finely minced. Cook the celery in one-half cup of the butter for five minutes; add the onions. Continue to cook until onions are tender but not browned. Add the chopped chicken and one cup of the chicken broth. Cook until the liquid is absorbed. Remove the mixture from the heat and cool.

5. Beat the eggs with a rotary beater until they are frothy; add the nutmeg. Fold the eggs into the chicken mixture.

6. Melt the remaining butter. Brush five sheets of *phyllo* pastry, one at a time, with half of the butter. Place the pastry in layers, one sheet atop another. Spread half of the chicken mixture evenly along the bottom of the pastry sheets and carefully roll the sheets like a jelly roll. Press in each end of the roll so that the filling does not escape. Repeat with the remaining pastry and chicken filling.

7. Place the rolls on baking sheets with edges. Bake for forty minutes, or until pastry is browned and crisp. Let cool slightly, cut into slices, and serve warm.

CHICKEN BAKE   *6 servings*

3 whole chicken breasts, halved
2 eggs, lightly beaten
1 teaspoon salt
¼ teaspoon freshly ground black pepper
1 cup soft fresh bread crumbs
½ cup olive oil
6 slices of boiled ham
6 slices of mozzarella cheese
1 cup Tomato Sauce I (page 493)
¼ teaspoon dried orégano

1. Preheat oven to moderate (350° F.).

2. Dip the chicken pieces into the eggs mixed with the salt and pepper. Coat each piece with bread crumbs.

3. Brown the chicken in the olive oil. Arrange the pieces in a single layer in a buttered baking dish. Place a slice of ham and a slice of cheese over each piece of chicken. Pour the sauce mixed with the orégano over all. Bake for twenty minutes, or until chicken is tender.

CHICKEN BREASTS VÉRONIQUE   *6 servings*

3 whole chicken breasts
1 cup cracker crumbs
½ teaspoon salt
¼ teaspoon freshly ground black pepper
¼ teaspoon dried tarragon
7 tablespoons butter
¼ cup finely chopped onion
½ cup Chicken Stock (page 475)
½ cup dry white wine
½ pound mushrooms, sliced
2 cups seedless or seeded green grapes

1. Preheat oven to moderate (375° F.).

2. Remove the skin from the chicken breasts and halve them. Coat the pieces with the crumbs mixed with the salt, pepper and tarragon. Brown the chicken on all sides in four tablespoons of the butter in a skillet. Place the pieces in a single layer in a shallow baking pan.

3. Add the onion to the butter left in the skillet and cook until tender. Pour in the stock and wine and bring to a boil. Pour around the chicken. Bake, uncovered, for thirty minutes.

4. Sauté the mushrooms in the remaining butter and add along with the grapes to the chicken. Bake for eight to ten minutes longer.

BREAST OF CHICKEN VIRGINIENNE   *6 servings*

3 whole chicken breasts, boned and skinned, but with main wing bone left intact
Salt and freshly ground black pepper
½ cup heavy cream
¾ cup all-purpose flour
⅓ cup butter

6 slices of freshly made toast, buttered
6 slices of broiled ham, preferably Virginia or country-style
6 large mushrooms caps, sautéed in butter
2 cups Sauce Suprême (page 481)

1. When the chicken breasts are prepared, have them cut into halves. This will leave six halves, each with a main wing bone attached.

2. Sprinkle the chicken with salt and pepper and dip into the cream. Dredge lightly with flour and cook on all sides in the butter until golden brown. Cook over low heat until cooked through.

3. To serve, place a slice of toast on each of six warm plates. Top with a piece of ham, then with a piece of the sautéed chicken. Garnish with a mushroom cap and spoon the sauce suprême over.

CHICKEN SATE   *4 to 6 servings*

3 whole chicken breasts, boned and skinned
1 cup Coconut Cream (page 491)
1 garlic clove, crushed
½ teaspoon salt
¼ teaspoon freshly ground white pepper

1 cup unsalted shelled skinned peanuts
2 small hot green or red peppers, seeded and chopped

1. Cut the chicken breasts into one-quarter-inch slices. Marinate the slices in the coconut cream containing the garlic, salt and pepper at room temperature for two to three hours.

2. Preheat broiler.

3. Thread the slices on individual metal or wooden skewers. Broil three to four inches from the source of heat, turning two or three times, for about ten minutes, or until chicken is tender.

4. Place the peanuts, coconut-cream marinade and peppers into the container of an electric blender. Blend at high speed for thirty seconds. Heat and serve as a dipping sauce for the chicken strips.

STUFFED BREAST OF CHICKEN MOLIÈRE   *6 servings*

6 small whole chicken breasts
¼ pound sausage meat
12 ounces *pâté de foie gras*
3 small black truffles, sliced
½ cup butter
4 cups Chicken Stock (page 475) or enough to cover the chicken breasts

1 cup Brown Sauce (page 477)
½ cup Madeira
Salt and freshly ground black pepper

1. When buying the chicken breasts, have the butcher split them into halves and remove all bones except the main wing bone. Or this may be done with a sharp paring knife in the home.

2. Combine the sausage meat with the *foie gras*. Spoon equal portions of the mixture onto the underside of six of the halved chicken breasts. Arrange a few truffle slices over the stuffing.

3. Top with remaining chicken breasts and sew the two halves together with a large needle and heavy thread.

4. Melt the butter in a large skillet and brown the stuffed breasts on all sides.

5. Bring the stock to a boil and pour it over the chicken breasts. Let simmer for fifteen to twenty minutes, until the chicken is tender. Transfer the chicken to a hot serving platter and skim off the fat from the poaching liquid. Bring the liquid quickly to a boil over high heat and simmer until reduced by half.

6. Add the brown sauce and Madeira to the skillet. Adjust the seasoning to taste. Spoon part of the sauce over each chicken breast and serve with wild rice.

CHICKEN HOLLANDAISE   *4 servings*

2 tablespoons butter
2 teaspoons finely chopped shallot or scallion
½ cup finely chopped celery
3 tablespoons cornstarch
1½ cups Chicken Stock (page 475)

2 teaspoons lemon juice
Salt
1½ cups cubed cooked chicken
2 egg yolks
Buttered toast triangles
Paprika or chopped fresh parsley

1. Heat the butter and add the shallot and celery. Cook, stirring, for four or five minutes.

2. Add the cornstarch and gradually add the stock, stirring constantly. When the mixture is thickened and smooth, add lemon juice, salt to taste and cubed chicken. Heat thoroughly.

3. Beat the egg yolks well and blend them into the chicken mixture. Cook over low heat for about one minute. Serve over toast triangles and sprinkle with paprika or chopped parsley.

NASI GORENG   *6 servings*

3 onions, cut into thin slices
2 garlic cloves, finely minced
  Peanut oil
2 cups cubed raw chicken
¼ cup *bumbu nasi goreng* (mixed spices)
8 cups steamed rice (about 1 pound raw)
1 pound shrimp, cooked, peeled, deveined and cut into bite-size pieces

4 eggs, lightly beaten
¼ cup water
  Salt and freshly ground black pepper
1 sweet red pepper, cut into strips
1 sweet Italian-style green pepper, cut into strips
½ cup shredded cooked ham

1. Sauté two of the onions and the garlic in three tablespoons peanut oil until soft and tender.

2. Add the chicken cubes and cook over high heat, stirring frequently, for five minutes.

3. Barely cover the *bumbu nasi goreng* with hot water and simmer for fifteen minutes. Add to the chicken mixture.

4. Add the rice and shrimp and heat gently, stirring.

5. Pour two teaspoons oil into a small skillet. Combine the eggs, water, and salt and pepper to taste and pour one-quarter of the mixture into the skillet. Tilt the pan so that the egg covers the bottom. Cook until set. Remove and cut into strips. Repeat with the remaining egg mixture. Add three-quarters of the egg strips to the chicken mixture. Season with salt and pepper to taste.

6. Fry the red and green pepper strips in one tablespoon oil. Separate the remaining onion slices into rings and fry the onion rings in one tablespoon oil until browned.

7. Pile the rice in the center of a dish. Ring with remaining egg strips. Top with the ham, fried red and green pepper strips, and fried onion slices.

CHICKEN-ALMOND CROQUETTES   *9 or 10 croquettes*

3 tablespoons butter
⅓ cup all-purpose flour
1 cup milk or ½ cup milk and ½ cup light cream
1½ cups minced cooked chicken
¼ cup almonds, blanched and shredded
1 tablespoon minced onion
2 tablespoons chopped parsley
2 eggs
2 tablespoons sherry
Salt and freshly ground black pepper
1 tablespoon water
Sifted fine dry bread crumbs
Fat for deep frying

1. Melt the butter, blend in the flour, and add the milk. Cook, stirring with a wire whisk, until the mixture boils and thickens.
2. Add the chicken, almonds, onion, parsley, one egg, the sherry, salt and pepper. Cook, stirring, until thickened. Chill.
3. Use one-quarter cup of the mixture to shape a croquette—cone or cylinder or as desired. Continue until all the mixture is used. Beat remaining egg lightly with the water. Coat the croquettes with crumbs, then with beaten egg, and again with crumbs. Dry on a rack for thirty minutes.
4. Fry in fat heated to 380° F. on a frying thermometer. Drain on paper towels. Serve with Onion-Pimiento Sauce (page 481) or Sauce Poulette (page 481).

SCALLOPED CHICKEN   *4 servings*

2¼ cups Chicken Stock (page 475)
6 tablespoons butter
1 tablespoon chopped onion
⅓ cup uncooked rice
¼ pound mushrooms, sliced
3 tablespoons all-purpose flour
½ cup heavy cream
¼ teaspoon salt
⅛ teaspoon freshly ground black pepper
¼ teaspoon dried thyme
2 cups diced cooked chicken or turkey
¼ cup chopped pimiento
¼ cup sliced pitted ripe olives
⅓ cup buttered soft fresh bread crumbs

1. Preheat oven to moderate (350° F.).
2. Place three-quarters cup of the stock, one tablespoon of the butter, the onion and the rice in a small pan. Cover and bring to a boil. Reduce the heat and simmer gently for about fifteen minutes, or until the liquid has been absorbed and the rice is tender. Add one-half cup additional stock. Set rice aside, covered.
3. Sauté the sliced mushrooms in two tablespoons of the butter and add to rice.

4. Melt the remaining butter and blend in the flour. Stir in remaining stock and the cream. Bring to a boil, stirring, and cook for two minutes. Add the salt, pepper, thyme, chicken or turkey, pimiento and olives. Mix well.

5. Alternate layers of the chicken mixture with the rice mixture in a buttered one-and-one-half-quart casserole, ending with the chicken mixture. Top with buttered crumbs and bake for about thirty minutes, or until hot, bubbly and lightly browned.

CHICKEN LOAF NIVERNAISE   *6 to 8 servings*

CHICKEN MOUSSE:

1 envelope unflavored gelatin	¼ teaspoon grated nutmeg
2 chicken bouillon cubes	¼ teaspoon freshly ground black pepper
⅓ cup boiling water	
½ very small onion	½ teaspoon salt
½ garlic clove	¼ teaspoon dried tarragon
1 cup cubed cooked chicken (6½ ounces)	1 cup heavy cream

1. Into the container of an electric blender put the gelatin, bouillon cubes, boiling water, onion and garlic. Cover and blend on high speed for forty seconds.

2. Add the remaining ingredients, cover, and blend on high speed for ten seconds.

3. Pour the mixture into a loaf pan (9 × 5 × 3 inches) and chill until set.

CARROT MOUSSE:

1 envelope unflavored gelatin	3 tablespoons mayonnaise
⅓ cup boiling water	⅛ teaspoon freshly ground black pepper
2 cups sliced cooked carrots	

1. Put the gelatin and boiling water into the container of an electric blender. Cover and blend on high speed for forty seconds.

2. Add the carrots, mayonnaise and pepper. Cover and blend on high speed for ten seconds longer.

3. Pour the mixture into the loaf pan over the chicken mousse and chill until set.

4. When ready to serve, unmold on a cold serving platter and garnish with salad greens and small cutouts of sliced cooked carrot. Serve with mayonnaise.

Chicken Livers en Brochette served with homemade tomato sauce.

CHICKEN LIVERS EN BROCHETTE   *6 servings*

 1 pound chicken livers
12 medium-size mushrooms
 6 slices of bacon
 6 cherry tomatoes
 6 white onions, cooked
¼ cup all-purpose flour

⅓ cup olive oil
½ teaspoon salt
¼ teaspoon freshly ground black pepper
 1 teaspoon Dijon mustard

1. Preheat broiler.
2. On each of six small skewers alternate chicken livers with mushrooms, folded half strips of bacon, tomatoes and onions.

3. Roll the skewers in the flour. Brush livers and vegetables lightly with the olive oil mixed with the salt, pepper and mustard.

4. Broil the filled skewers three inches from the source of heat until browned on all sides, turning frequently and basting with remaining olive oil if necessary. Serve the skewers atop a bed of rice with a homemade tomato sauce.

CHICKEN LIVERS MADEIRA   *18 servings*

3 pounds chicken livers	8 shallots, diced
1 cup butter	4 cups Chicken Stock (page 475)
Salt and freshly ground black pepper	3 tablespoons chopped parsley
7 tablespoons all-purpose flour	¾ cup Madeira

1. Trim, wash, and dry the chicken livers. Cut them into halves. Sauté the livers in the butter and season with salt and pepper. Cook over high heat, shaking the pan frequently so the livers do not stick. Do not overcook; the livers should be tender, but not dry.

2. Sprinkle the livers with the flour, add the shallots, shake the pan, and let cook for one-half minute.

3. Add the stock and bring to a boil, stirring gently. Add the parsley, wine and additional salt and pepper to taste.

CHICKEN-LIVER TIMBALES   *4 servings*

1½ tablespoons butter	2 egg yolks
2 tablespoons all-purpose flour	⅛ teaspoon freshly ground black pepper
1 cup milk, scalded	6 tablespoons heavy cream
½ teaspoon salt	2 tablespoons cognac
½ pound chicken livers	Sauce Poulette (page 481)
2 whole eggs	

1. Preheat oven to moderate (350° F.).

2. Melt the butter, blend in the flour, stir in the milk slowly, and add one-quarter teaspoon of the salt. Bring the mixture to a boil, stirring, and simmer for one minute. Cool, stirring occasionally.

3. Place the livers, whole eggs, egg yolks, pepper and remaining salt in a blender. Blend for one minute.

4. Add the cooled sauce, cream and cognac and blend for fifteen seconds. Strain the mixture into eight buttered half-cup molds.

5. Set the molds on a rack in a pan of hot water. Bake for twenty-five to thirty minutes, or until set.

6. To serve, run a knife around the edge of each timbale and unmold onto a warm platter. Top each with a spoonful of sauce poulette. Serve the remaining sauce separately.

BROILED CHICKEN LIVERS   *6 servings*

18 chicken livers
   Salt and freshly ground black pepper
10 slices of bacon
¾ cup fine dry bread crumbs

¼ cup butter
1 tablespoon lemon juice
2 tablespoons finely chopped parsley

1. Cut the livers into quarters or thirds depending on size. Sprinkle with salt and pepper.
2. Cook the bacon in a skillet for about one minute, turning once. Reserve bacon drippings. Cool the bacon and cut each slice into sixths.
3. Alternate pieces of liver and bacon on skewers. Brush with bacon fat and sprinkle with bread crumbs.
4. Melt the butter and add the lemon juice and parsley.
5. Broil liver and bacon under the broiler or over hot coals, turning occasionally, until done. Brush with butter sauce and serve.

CHICKEN LIVERS WITH BELGIAN ENDIVE   *6 servings*

6 heads of Belgian endive
½ cup boiling salted water
1 tablespoon lemon juice
½ cup butter
1 pound chicken livers

1 cup sliced mushrooms
½ cup dry sherry
½ cup heavy cream
1 teaspoon salt

1. Cut endive into quarters lengthwise and then tie into bundles with strings. This will help them keep their shape. Add the boiling salted water and lemon juice and simmer for thirty minutes. Drain and remove strings.
2. Melt the butter in a skillet and sauté the endive in it for fifteen minutes. Remove from skillet and keep warm.
3. Cut up the chicken livers and sauté them with the mushrooms in the butter remaining in skillet for ten minutes. Add sherry, cream and salt. Simmer, stirring frequently, but do not boil.
4. Return endive to sauce and simmer gently until the entire mixture is piping hot.

CHICKEN LIVERS HONGROISE   *6 servings*

2 tablespoons butter
½ cup finely chopped onion
1½ pounds chicken livers, trimmed
2 tablespoons finely chopped parsley

¼ teaspoon dried thyme
1 cup sour cream
½ cup Chicken Stock (page 475)
   Salt and freshly ground black pepper

1. Melt the butter and cook the onion in it until translucent. Add the chicken livers, shake the skillet, and cook over high heat until livers are browned. Do not overcook.

2. Reduce the heat, sprinkle the livers with parsley and thyme, and stir in the sour cream. Bring to a boil, stirring constantly. When the boiling point is reached, stir in the stock and simmer for about three minutes. Season with salt and pepper to taste and serve hot.

TURKEY

ROAST TURKEY

The high-temperature method of roasting turkey requires frequent basting and will result in a bird with a crisp browned surface and juicy meat.

The low-temperature method produces a less crisp skin and meat that is also juicy, but some people find a turkey prepared in this way has a more steamed than roasted flavor. This method is easier on the cook because it requires basting only once or twice.

The procedure used obviously depends on taste. In either case, the turkey should not be stuffed until just before it is roasted.

HIGH-TEMPERATURE METHOD:

Preheat oven to hot (425° F.). Season turkey with salt and place it on its side in a roasting pan. Spread the bird generously with butter and place slices of salt pork over the breast; or instead of the salt pork and butter arrange a piece of cheesecloth soaked in melted chicken fat over the breastbone and top of the turkey. Cook for fifteen minutes, then turn on the other side and cook for fifteen minutes longer.

Lower the oven temperature to moderate (375° F.) and continue to roast, turning the bird from side to side and basting often with drippings from the pan. If the fat tends to burn, add a few tablespoons of water to the pan.

Roast the turkey for fifteen to twenty minutes a pound if unstuffed; for twenty to twenty-five minutes a pound if stuffed. If the turkey weighs eighteen to twenty-five pounds, roast at 325° F. for thirteen to fifteen minutes a pound.

Place the turkey on its back for the last fifteen minutes of cooking time. Pierce thigh to test for doneness. If the juice that runs out is clear with no tinge of pink, the bird is done.

LOW-TEMPERATURE METHOD:

Preheat oven to moderate (325° F.). Place turkey breast side up on a rack in an open roasting pan. Grease the surface well with shortening and on top lay a fat-moistened cheesecloth, large enough to drape down over the sides of the bird.

Roast at a constant temperature. Do not add water. Baste only once or twice with fat or drippings from the pan. Remove the cloth for the last half hour of cooking time to allow the turkey to brown.

When the turkey is lightly browned, cover with a loose tent of aluminum foil to avoid overbrowning.

To test for doneness, move the leg joint up and down. It should give readily or break. Another test for doneness is to place a meat thermometer in the center of the inside thigh muscle or the thickest part of the breast muscle; it should register 185° F.

TIMETABLE FOR ROASTING TURKEY BY LOW-TEMPERATURE METHOD

READY-TO-COOK WEIGHT	AMOUNT OF STUFFING	TOTAL COOKING TIME AT 325° F.
(pounds)	(quarts)	(hours)
6 to 8	1 to 1½	2 to 2½
8 to 12	1½ to 2¼	2½ to 3
12 to 16	2 to 3	3 to 3¾
16 to 20	3 to 3¾	3¾ to 4½
20 to 24	3¾ to 4½	4½ to 5½

THAWING TURKEY:

Frozen turkeys need to be defrosted before roasting. There are two methods for doing this.

Here are the approximate thawing times for frozen whole turkeys.

POUNDS	IN REFRIGERATOR	UNDER COLD RUNNING WATER IN WATERTIGHT WRAPPER
4 to 10	1 to 2 days	4 to 6 hours
10 to 20	2 to 3 days	6 to 8 hours
20 to 24	3 to 4 days	8 to 12 hours

CURRIED TURKEY AND HAM *50 servings*

1 turkey (12 to 15 pounds), cut into pieces
4 quarts milk
3 cups heavy cream
1 cup chopped green peppers
1 cup chopped onions
1 cup salad oil
¾ cup butter

2 cups sifted all-purpose flour
3 to 4 tablespoons curry powder
2 tablespoons salt
½ teaspoon freshly ground white pepper
1 quart (1 pound, 4 ounces) cubed cooked ham

1. Simmer the turkey, tightly covered, in enough salted water almost to cover for about two hours, until tender.

2. Remove the turkey; cool it. Remove the meat from the bones, discarding the skin and bones. Cube the meat and strain the broth. Reserve four cups of the broth. There should be about two and one-half quarts of turkey meat.

3. To prepare the sauce, use a three- or four-gallon double boiler. If one is not available, improvise one by using two pots. Scald the milk with the reserved turkey broth and the cream over boiling water.

4. In a skillet sauté the green peppers and onions in the salad oil and butter until tender but not browned. Add the flour, curry powder, salt and pepper. Stir and cook for one minute.

5. Gradually add the flour mixture to the milk mixture and whip vigorously with a wire whisk until the sauce is thickened and smooth.

6. Add the turkey meat and the ham and cook, covered, stirring occasionally, for fifteen minutes. Adjust the seasonings. Serve on rice.

ROAST TURKEY WITH PORK STUFFING   *8 to 12 servings*

½ pound small pork sausages	½ teaspoon dried thyme
1 turkey liver	½ cup dry white wine
2 slices of bread, dried in oven	1 cup Brown Sauce (page 477)
1 pound pork, finely ground	1 tablespoon minced parsley
Salt and freshly ground black pepper	1 cup cooked chestnuts
	1 truffle, sliced (optional)
1½ cups chopped onions	1 turkey (11 pounds), prepared for stuffing
2 garlic cloves, minced	
1 turkey gizzard, ground	Butter
2 teaspoons dried sage or 1 teaspoon ground sage	1 carrot, coarsely chopped
	1 onion, sliced
½ teaspoon dried rosemary	¾ cup turkey broth or Chicken Stock (page 475)
1 bay leaf, crumbled	

1. Preheat oven to moderate (350° F.).

2. Cook the sausages until done. Grind the liver with the dried bread.

3. Cook the ground pork in a skillet. Season with salt and pepper to taste, add the chopped onions and one garlic clove, and cook for five minutes, stirring occasionally. Add the gizzard and cook for ten minutes. Add the sage, rosemary, half of the bay leaf and half of the thyme. Pour in half of the wine and half of the brown sauce and sprinkle with the parsley. Stir. Bake the stuffing, uncovered, for thirty minutes, stirring occasionally.

4. Remove from oven. Stir in the chestnuts, liver mixture and truffle. Drain the sausages and fold them into stuffing.

5. Increase the oven temperature to hot (425° F.).

6. Stuff and truss turkey. Spread generously with butter. Sprinkle with salt and pepper. Place turkey in a large roasting pan, breast side up, and

roast for fifteen minutes; turn on the other side and bake for fifteen minutes longer.

7. Reduce oven to 375° F. and continue to roast, turning turkey from side to side and basting often with fat from the pan. If skin becomes too brown, cover with aluminum foil. If fat tends to burn, add a little water. Roast turkey for twenty minutes a pound.

8. Forty-five minutes before turkey is done, sprinkle the carrot and onion in the roasting pan along with the remaining garlic, thyme and bay leaf.

9. Untruss turkey and place it on a serving platter. Pour most of the fat from the pan and place pan over high heat. Add remaining wine and swirl around. When the sauce is reduced by half, add the stock and remaining brown sauce; stir well. Cook for five minutes, strain, and serve hot.

TURKEY DIVAN   *6 servings*

¼ cup butter
3 tablespoons all-purpose flour
2 cups milk
½ teaspoon grated nutmeg
1 bunch of broccoli (2 pounds)
1 cup grated Parmesan cheese, approximately

3 cups shredded cooked turkey
½ cup Hollandaise Sauce (page 485)
½ cup heavy cream, whipped
3 tablespoons sherry
1 teaspoon Worcestershire sauce

1. Make a white sauce: Melt the butter in a saucepan, add the flour, and stir with a wire whisk until blended. Bring the milk to a boil and add all at once to the butter-flour mixture, stirring vigorously with the whisk until the sauce is thickened and smooth. Stir in the nutmeg. Keep the sauce hot.

2. Cook the broccoli in boiling salted water until tender and drain. Arrange broccoli on a deep ovenproof serving platter. Sprinkle lightly with some of the grated cheese. Arrange the turkey meat on the broccoli.

3. Preheat broiler.

4. Combine the hollandaise sauce with the white sauce. Add the whipped cream, sherry and Worcestershire sauce. Pour over the turkey and broccoli and sprinkle with the remaining cheese.

5. Place about five inches below high heat in the broiler and broil until browned and bubbly.

TURKEY STEW   *4 servings*

¼ cup butter
1 cup chopped onions
1 cup chopped celery
1½ cups ½-inch diagonal pieces of carrots
1¼ cups Beef Stock (page 473)
1½ plus ⅓ cups water

1½ teaspoons salt
1½ cups cut green beans or 1 package (10 ounces) frozen green beans
1½ cups diced cooked turkey
¼ cup all-purpose flour
1 teaspoon Worcestershire sauce

1. Melt the butter in a heavy Dutch oven. Add the onions, celery and carrots. Cover and simmer for ten minutes. Add the stock, one and one-half cups of the water and the salt. Cover and simmer gently for about fifteen minutes, or until the vegetables are tender.

2. Add the green beans and turkey and cook for five minutes. Blend the flour with the remaining water and stir into the vegetable mixture. Add the Worcestershire and bring to a boil, stirring. Cook for five minutes. Serve with Herb Dumplings (page 541).

Note: The dumplings may be cooked atop the turkey stew.

TURKEY-FILBERT CASSEROLE   *6 servings*

½ cup butter
½ pound mushrooms, sliced
3½ tablespoons all-purpose flour
1 cup milk
1 cup light cream
Salt and freshly ground black pepper
¼ teaspoon celery seeds

2 cups noodles, cooked and drained
2 cups coarsely diced cooked turkey
5 thin slices of Bermuda onion, separated into rings
½ lemon, sliced very thinly
⅓ cup sliced or chopped filberts, toasted
½ teaspoon paprika

1. Preheat oven to moderate (350° F.).

2. Melt two tablespoons of the butter and sauté the mushrooms in it until tender.

3. Melt four tablespoons of the butter and blend in the flour. Gradually stir in the milk and the cream. Bring to a boil, stirring. Add the mushrooms and season with salt and pepper to taste.

4. Add the celery seeds to the noodles and place half of them in a greased shallow casserole. Top with the turkey and half of the mushroom sauce. Add remaining noodles and arrange the onion rings and lemon slices over the top.

5. Pour the remaining sauce over all. Dot with the remaining butter and the filberts and sprinkle with paprika. Bake for thirty minutes, or until hot and bubbly.

TURKEY PIE WITH SAGE CORNMEAL PASTRY   *6 servings*

⅓ cup butter
½ cup chopped onion
1 garlic clove, finely minced
⅓ cup all-purpose flour
1½ cups turkey broth
1 cup light cream
2 cups diced cooked turkey

1⅛ teaspoons salt
¼ teaspoon ground sage
⅛ teaspoon freshly ground black pepper
⅛ teaspoon ground mace
1 teaspoon lemon juice
Sage Cornmeal Pastry (page 299)

1. Preheat oven to hot (425° F.).

2. Melt the butter in a saucepan and cook the onion and garlic in it until golden. Blend in the flour. Remove from the heat and stir in the turkey stock and cream. Cook, stirring, until the mixture is medium thick. Add the turkey, seasonings and lemon juice. Turn into a one-quart casserole.

3. Top the casserole with sage cornmeal pastry. Trim, turn under, and flute the edges of the pastry. Cut two or three gashes in the top to allow for escape of steam. Bake for about twenty minutes, until brown.

SAGE CORNMEAL PASTRY: *Pastry for the top of a 1-quart casserole*

½ cup sifted all-purpose flour
½ cup cornmeal
1 tablespoon ground sage

½ teaspoon salt
⅓ cup shortening
3 tablespoons water

In a mixing bowl mix together the flour, cornmeal, sage and salt. Add shortening and cut it in until the mixture resembles coarse crumbs. Add the water. Mix lightly to form a ball. Turn out onto a lightly floured board. Roll to one-eighth-inch thickness and one inch larger than the circumference of the casserole.

. . . .

DUCK AND GOOSE

. . . .

People will turn to duck as main fare in the winter months more than at other seasons. It is a versatile meat, which can be roasted with a wide variety of seasonings or turned into a fine ragout.

ROAST DUCK   *4 or 5 servings*

1 duck (5 pounds)
Salt and freshly ground black pepper
¼ teaspoon dried thyme

5 small onions, peeled
1 carrot, scraped and cut into ¼-inch rounds

1. Preheat oven to hot (450° F.).

2. Sprinkle the duck inside and outside with salt and pepper. Sprinkle cavity with the thyme and add one of the onions. Truss the duck and place it, breast side up, in a roasting pan.

3. Arrange the carrot rounds and remaining onions around duck. Roast for fifteen minutes. It is not necessary to baste duck as it cooks.

4. Reduce the oven heat to moderate (350° F.).

5. Turn duck on its side and roast for thirty minutes longer. Remove most of the fat from pan as it accumulates.

6. Turn duck on its other side. Roast for fifteen minutes and turn duck breast side up again. Roast for fifteen minutes longer. Lift duck so that the juices in the cavity run into the pan. When the thigh is pricked and the juices run pale yellow, the duck is done.

DUCKLING WITH OLIVES   *4 servings*

1 duckling (5 to 6 pounds)	⅛ teaspoon ground thyme
2½ cups pimiento-stuffed olives	2 parsley sprigs
1 tablespoon all-purpose flour	1 celery rib
½ cup Chicken Stock (page 475)	1 small bay leaf
½ cup dry Madeira	
¼ teaspoon freshly ground black pepper	

1. Preheat oven to hot (425° F.).
2. Stuff the duckling with one and one-half cups of the olives. Truss to hold the wings and legs closely to the body. Prick the duckling all over with the tines of a fork. Place on a rack in a shallow roasting pan and roast for ten minutes.
3. Lower the oven temperature to moderate (350° F.) and roast for twenty minutes longer. Remove the duckling from the pan and keep it warm.
4. Pour off all the drippings except two tablespoons. Add the flour to the drippings in the pan and blend. Cook, stirring constantly, over low heat until the flour is golden brown. Add the stock and wine and cook, stirring vigorously with a wire whisk, until the sauce is thickened and smooth.
5. Add the pepper, thyme, parsley, celery and bay leaf to the sauce. Return the duckling to the pan; cover. Return the bird to the 350° F. oven and roast for forty-five minutes to one hour, until tender. Remove the duckling and arrange on a hot platter.
6. Discard the parsley, celery and bay leaf from the sauce. Slice the remaining olives and add them to the sauce. Pour over the duckling and serve immediately.

ROAST DUCK WITH GRAPES   *4 servings*

⅓ cup chopped onion	1 teaspoon ground thyme
¼ cup butter	⅓ cup Duck Stock (page 301)
4 cups toasted bread cubes (croutons)	1 cup Thompson seedless grapes
2 tablespoons chopped fresh parsley	1 ready-to-cook duck (4 to 5 pounds)
1 cup chopped celery	½ lemon
Salt and freshly ground black pepper	

1. Preheat oven to moderate (325° F.).

2. Sauté the onion in the butter. Mix bread cubes with onion, parsley, celery, one teaspoon salt, one-half teaspoon pepper, the thyme, stock and grapes.

3. Sprinkle inside of duck with salt and pepper. Fill crop and body cavity with grape stuffing. Close opening with skewers. Lace tightly with a strong string. Rub the outside of the skin with the lemon.

4. Place duck on a rack in a shallow pan, such as a jelly-roll pan. Bake for two to two and one-half hours. Serve with Giblet Gravy (see below).

DUCK STOCK:

Put duck neck and giblets in two cups water with one-half teaspoon salt, three peppercorns and a parsley sprig. Cook, covered, until tender. Lift out the cooked giblets and strain the stock.

GIBLET GRAVY:

Blend one tablespoon flour with stock made from giblets. Stir and cook until slightly thickened. Chop giblets and add. Season with salt and freshly ground black pepper to taste.

DUCK À L'ORANGE   *4 servings*

1 duck (4 to 5 pounds dressed weight)
Salt and freshly ground black pepper
2 tablespoons sugar
2 tablespoons white vinegar
1 orange
1 lemon
½ cup Brown Sauce (page 477)
1 tablespoon red currant jelly
1 tablespoon orange liqueur (Cointreau, Grand Marnier or Triple Sec), optional

1. Preheat oven to moderate (375° F.).

2. Sprinkle the inside of the duck with salt and pepper. Place the bird on a rack in a roasting pan, place in oven, and roast for fifteen to twenty minutes per pound, depending on the doneness desired. Baste frequently with pan drippings and pour fat from the pan as it accumulates.

3. Meanwhile, combine the sugar and vinegar in a saucepan. Cook over moderate heat until the sugar caramelizes and becomes amber in color; do not overcook.

4. Peel the orange and lemon with a swivel-bladed potato peeler. Using a sharp knife, cut the orange rind and half of the lemon rind into the thinnest possible strips. Discard the remaining lemon rind but save the fruits.

5. Combine the slivers of orange and lemon rinds in a saucepan and cover with water. Bring to a boil, remove from the heat, and let stand for three minutes. Drain and reserve the rinds.

6. Squeeze the juice from the orange and combine it with one tablespoon lemon juice; reserve.

7. Pour off any fat remaining in the roasting pan. Remove the duck and keep it warm on a hot serving platter. Add a little water to the roasting pan and swirl it around to dissolve any brown particles clinging to the bottom and sides of the pan. Pour this mixture over the caramelized sugar and bring to a boil. Cook over high heat for three minutes; strain.

8. Add the orange and lemon juices and the brown sauce to the strained mixture. Cook over high heat for ten minutes. Add the orange and lemon rinds and the currant jelly. Cook until the jelly dissolves. Add the orange liqueur.

9. If desired, the duck may be cut into quarters before serving. Spoon part of the orange sauce over the bird and serve the rest in a sauceboat. Garnish the platter with peeled orange slices and watercress sprigs.

Duck à l'Orange garnished with peeled orange slices and watercress sprigs is served with wild rice and the orange-flavored sauce.

CHINESE ROAST DUCK   *4 servings*

1 duck (4 to 5 pounds)
Salt
2 tablespoons chopped onion
2 tablespoons finely chopped celery
1½ teaspoons sugar
¼ teaspoon ground cinnamon

⅛ teaspoon whole aniseeds
⅓ cup plus 1½ teaspoons soy sauce
2 cups plus 2 teaspoons water
2 tablespoons honey
2 tablespoons cider vinegar
1 teaspoon cornstarch

1. Preheat oven to moderate (325° F.).
2. Wash the duck and remove excess fat from the body and neck cavities. Rub the inside lightly with salt.
3. Combine the onion, celery, sugar, cinnamon, aniseeds, one-third cup soy sauce and one cup of the water. Bring to the boiling point.
4. Tie up the duck's neck tightly with a string so the sauce will not seep out while cooking. Pour the hot sauce inside the duck. Sew up the vent tightly. Rub the outside of the duck with a little salt. Place breast side up on a rack in a roasting pan. Roast for twenty minutes.
5. Heat one cup water with the honey, vinegar, remaining soy sauce and one tablespoon salt. Brush this mixture over the skin of the bird. Continue to cook until the duck is done, about one and one-half hours, basting at twenty-minutes intervals with this sauce.
6. Remove the duck from the oven. Drain the sauce into a saucepan and thicken it with cornstarch mixed with the two teaspoons water. Cook until slightly thickened. Serve separately as gravy.

DODINE OF DUCK   *6 to 8 servings*

2 ducks (4 pounds each)
Salt
2 small onions, thinly sliced
1 carrot, chopped
3 tablespoons finely chopped shallots or green onions
1 cup dry red wine

¼ teaspoon dried thyme
1 bay leaf
1 tablespoon chopped parsley
2½ cups Brown Sauce (page 477)
2 tablespoons cognac
Freshly ground black pepper
10 Liver Canapés (page 304)

1. Preheat oven to hot (450° F.).
2. Sprinkle the ducks with salt inside and outside and truss them. Reserve necks, gizzards, hearts and livers. Roast ducks for one and one-half to two hours, pouring off fat as it accumulates in roasting pan.
3. To prepare the sauce, pour one tablespoon fat from the pan into a large saucepan. Add the necks, gizzards and hearts, and cook, stirring, until brown. Add the onions, carrot and shallots. Cook for ten minutes. Add the wine, thyme, bay leaf, parsley and brown sauce. Simmer for one hour, stirring occasionally.

4. Put one of the duck livers through a food mill or sieve. (Reserve the other liver for liver canapés.) Remove sauce from the heat and add the cognac, salt and pepper to taste, and the puréed liver. Put the sauce through a food mill or fine sieve. Heat the sieved mixture thoroughly, but do not boil.

5. Untruss the roasted ducks and cut them into serving pieces. Arrange the pieces on a hot serving platter and pour the sauce over all. Surround with liver canapés and serve immediately.

LIVER CANAPÉS: *10 canapés*

10 rounds of white bread, 2½ inches across
6 tablespoons melted butter
1 duck liver
2 tablespoons butter

Salt and freshly ground black pepper
1 tablespoon finely chopped shallots
½ garlic clove, finely minced

1. Preheat oven to moderate (350° F.).

2. Using a pastry brush, brush the bread rounds top and bottom with the melted butter. Place them on a baking sheet and bake until golden brown on both sides, turning once.

3. Meanwhile, cook the liver in two tablespoons butter. Add salt and pepper to taste, the shallots and garlic. The liver should not be overcooked or it will become dry.

4. Put the mixture through a food mill or sieve and stir well. Spread on the toast rounds and serve hot with Dodine of Duck.

DUCK IN SAVORY SAUCE   *4 servings*

1 duck (3 to 4 pounds), cut into serving pieces
1 celery rib, diced
1 small onion, chopped
1¼ cups Chicken Stock (page 475)
½ cup dry sherry
1 bay leaf

¼ teaspoon freshly ground black pepper
1½ tablespoons cornstarch
¼ cup lemon juice
1 can (2 ounces) flat anchovy fillets, chopped
2 tablespoons chopped parsley

1. Skin the duck and remove most of the fat. Render some of the fat in a Dutch oven and brown the duck pieces in it on all sides.

2. Add the celery and onion and cook for three minutes longer. Add one cup of the stock, the sherry, bay leaf and pepper. Bring to a boil, cover, and simmer gently for about one hour, or until the duck is tender.

3. Place the duck on a warm platter. Mix the cornstarch with the remaining stock and the lemon juice and add to the cooking liquid after removing surface fat. Bring to a boil, stirring. Add the anchovies and cook for three minutes. Pour over the duck and sprinkle with the parsley.

ANISE DUCK AND RICE CASSEROLE   *4 servings*

1 duck (4 pounds), cut into quarters
2 tablespoons butter
¾ cup finely chopped onions
1 garlic clove, finely minced
3 cups boiling Chicken Stock (page 475)

Salt and freshly ground black pepper
½ teaspoon aniseeds, crushed
¼ teaspoon cayenne pepper
1 cup uncooked long-grain rice

1. Brown the duck in the butter, then transfer it to a heavy Dutch oven. Pour off most of the fat from the skillet and add the onions and garlic. Cook, stirring, until onions are wilted.

2. Add the hot stock to the skillet. Stir with a wooden spoon to dissolve the brown particles which cling to the bottom and sides of the skillet.

3. Pour the liquid over the duck and add salt and pepper to taste; cover. Cook for about one hour, until duck is almost tender. Remove excess fat. Add the remaining ingredients, cover, and cook for twenty minutes, or until rice is tender.

ROAST GOOSE WITH CHESTNUT STUFFING   *6 to 8 servings*

1 goose (12 pounds), with liver and heart
¾ cup chopped onions
1 pound ground bulk sausage
1 teaspoon crumbled dried rosemary
½ teaspoon crumbled dried thyme
1 bay leaf, finely chopped, or ½ teaspoon ground bay leaf
1 garlic clove, finely minced
3 green cooking apples, peeled, cored and chopped

½ cup Chicken Stock (page 475)
3 cups cooked chestnuts
Salt and freshly ground black pepper to taste
½ cup soft fresh bread crumbs
2 tablespoons chopped parsley
1 tablespoon applejack or Calvados (optional)

1. Wash the goose and remove any large pieces of interior fat. Render enough to make two tablespoons fat. Grind the liver and heart of the goose and set aside.

2. Preheat oven to hot (450° F.).

3. Heat the rendered goose fat and cook the onions in it until wilted. Add the sausage and break up with a wooden spoon. Add rosemary, thyme, bay leaf and garlic.

4. When sausage has lost its reddish color, remove some of the excess fat. Add ground goose liver and heart and cook, stirring, for five minutes.

5. Add the apples and stock. Stir in the remaining ingredients. When blended, cool.

6. Stuff the goose with the mixture. Skewer the openings or sew with string. Rub the outside with a little salt.

7. Place the bird on a rack in an uncovered pan and roast for ten minutes.

8. Reduce heat to moderate (350° F.) and continue to cook for twenty-five minutes to the pound, until the goose is well browned and crisp and the drumstick moves up and down easily. Pour off fat as it accumulates.

.   .   .   .

GAME BIRDS

.   .   .   .

Unlikely though it may seem to those who have drowsed on the steps of the New York Public Library, pigeons in their time are one of the greatest delicacies in the world of cuisine. Before they fly, pigeons are squabs and there is scarcely a bird that is more delicious, even though they are an expensive delicacy.

ROAST SQUABS WITH MADEIRA SAUCE   *6 servings*

6 squabs, with livers	¼ cup Brown Sauce (page 477)
2 tablespoons butter	2 tablespoons cold butter
¼ cup Madeira or port	

1. Preheat oven to hot (400° F.).

2. If the birds are not trussed by the butcher, truss them. Fold the wing tips back under the bird. Then take a length of twine and tie the legs tightly together at the ends. Make a tight loop around the tail. Cross the strings over the back and bring string across the wings to hold them firmly to the body. Make another loop to tie the neck skin.

3. Select a large skillet that can be placed in the oven. Heat the butter in the skillet and cook the squabs in it until they are golden brown on all sides.

4. Place each squab on its side and place the skillet in the oven. Roast for ten minutes, basting once or twice, then turn each squab on the other side. Roast for ten minutes longer, basting once or twice, then turn each squab on its back. Add squab livers.

5. Turn off the oven heat. Using a two-pronged fork, drain the liquid from the cavity of each squab into the skillet. Remove the trussing strings and transfer birds to a heatproof serving platter. Return them to the oven but leave oven door ajar.

6. Place the skillet on the stove. Chop the livers, add them to the skillet, and add the Madeira and brown sauce. Stir to blend. Turn off the heat under the skillet and add the cold butter to the sauce. Swirl the butter around until it melts and is well incorporated in the sauce. Place the squabs on toast and serve immediately with the sauce.

STUFFED SQUABS   *6 servings*

6 matzohs
½ cup chopped celery
½ cup diced onion
    Chicken fat
½ pound chicken livers
4 eggs, beaten

1 teaspoon salt
½ teaspoon freshly ground black
    pepper
1 tablespoon chopped parsley
6 squabs, ready for stuffing

1. Preheat oven to hot (400° F.).
2. Soak the matzohs in water and squeeze almost dry. Cook the celery and onion in one tablespoon chicken fat until wilted.
3. Grind the chicken livers and combine with the matzohs, celery and onion, eggs, salt, pepper and parsley. Sprinkle the insides of the squabs with salt and stuff them with the chicken-liver mixture.
4. Roast the squabs for forty-five minutes, basting occasionally with chicken fat and pan juices. Reduce the heat if necessary to prevent burning. Thicken the drippings if desired with a little potato starch mixed with cold water.

JEANNE OWEN'S SQUAB PIE   *4 servings*

4 squabs, split into halves, with livers and gizzards
    Salt and freshly ground black pepper
¼ cup butter
2 ounces cognac, warmed
8 small white onions, peeled

½ cup cubed very lean ham
½ cup red Burgundy
2 tablespoons finely chopped carrot
½ cup Chicken or Veal Stock (pages 475 and 474)
    Rich short crust or flaky pastry

1. Preheat oven to hot (450° F.).
2. Sprinkle the pieces of squab with salt and pepper. Melt the butter in a heavy skillet and brown the squabs in it. Cover and cook for ten to twelve minutes.
3. Pour the cognac over the birds and ignite it. When the flame dies, add the onions, ham and wine. Cook for three or four minutes longer.
4. Arrange the pieces of squab, the onions and ham in a baking dish. Add the chopped carrot. Chop the livers and add them and the whole gizzards. Pour all the juices from the skillet into the baking dish. Add the stock.
5. Cover the dish with short crust or flaky pastry. Do not make slits in the crust as the cooking must be done by steaming. Brush the crust with egg, if desired.
6. Bake for ten minutes, then lower the oven temperature to moderate (350° F.) and bake for thirty-five to forty minutes longer.

POTTED SQUABS   *6 servings*

6 squabs
All-purpose flour
Salt and freshly ground black pepper
⅓ cup butter
1 small onion, chopped

1 carrot, scraped and diced
1 celery rib, chopped
¼ teaspoon ground thyme
1 bay leaf
1 cup Chicken Stock (page 475)

1. Preheat oven to moderate (350° F.).
2. Mix a little flour with salt and pepper and dredge the squabs with it. Brown the birds on all sides in the butter and place them in a casserole or Dutch oven.
3. Add onion, carrot, celery, thyme and bay leaf to the skillet in which squabs were browned. Cook, stirring, for about three minutes. Add the stock. Bring the mixture to a boil and pour it over the squabs.
4. Cover the casserole closely and bake the birds for forty-five minutes to one hour. Strain the sauce and serve it with the squabs. Serve with steamed white rice or wild rice, and peas.
5. The sauce may be thickened with a little flour blended with an equal quantity of butter. Add the mixture to the simmering sauce a little at a time, stirring after each addition. Sour cream may also be added to the sauce after it is finished, but the sauce should not boil after sour cream is added.

PHEASANT SMITANE   *4 servings*

¼ teaspoon ground thyme
1 garlic clove
1 pheasant, trussed
Salt and freshly ground black pepper
3 thick slices of bacon

¼ cup finely chopped shallots
⅓ cup dry white wine
⅓ cup heavy cream
⅔ cup sour cream
1 tablespoon butter

1. Preheat oven to hot (450° F.).
2. Put the thyme and garlic in the cavity of the pheasant. Sprinkle the bird with salt and pepper and place it on a rack in a baking dish. Cover with the bacon. Roast for ten minutes, basting occasionally.
3. Reduce the heat to moderate (350° F.) and continue to roast for about thirty-five minutes. Baste the pheasant and turn it occasionally as it cooks. Do not let the bacon burn. If the bacon starts to get too brown, remove it from the oven and reserve.
4. When pheasant is cooked and golden brown all over, remove it from the oven. Cut it into serving pieces and keep warm.
5. Pour off most of the fat from the pan and add the shallots. Cook, stirring with a wooden spoon, until they are translucent. Add the wine and continue to cook and stir until liquid is reduced almost by half.

6. Add the cream and sour cream and stir, shaking pan, until sauce boils once. Do not overcook or sauce may curdle. Quickly add the butter and shake the pan in a swirling motion until it is incorporated into the sauce. Strain the sauce over the pheasant, garnish with bacon, and serve immediately.

DOVES PONTCHARTRAIN   *4 servings*

12 doves, dressed
   Salt and freshly ground black pepper
12 slices of bacon
   Boiling Chicken Stock (page 475)

Worcestershire sauce
1 lemon, seeded and finely chopped
4 slices of toast
Chopped parsley

1. If desired, remove legs and wings from the doves. Sprinkle the doves with salt and pepper and wrap each in a slice of bacon. Secure bacon with food picks.
2. Brown the bacon-wrapped doves on all sides in a kettle or casserole. When browned, pour off most of the fat. Add the boiling stock to a depth of one-half inch. Add Worcestershire sauce to taste and the lemon. Cover and simmer gently for forty-five minutes.
3. Taste the sauce and adjust the seasonings if necessary. Arrange the doves, three to a person, on toast and sprinkle with parsley. Strain the sauce and serve it separately.

WILD DUCKS WITH MADEIRA   *About 8 servings*

4 wild ducks
   Olive oil or melted butter
   Salt and freshly ground black pepper
4 apples, peeled, cored and cut into eighths
4 onions, peeled and cut into eighths
1 cup chopped celery

4 slices of bacon, each halved
2 tablespoons A.1. Sauce
4 orange slices
4 lemon slices
2 celery ribs with leaves, quartered
½ cup Madeira
2 tablespoons all-purpose flour

1. Preheat oven to slow (275° F.).
2. Clean the ducks well and rub them with oil or butter. Sprinkle inside and outside with salt and pepper. Stuff the cavities with equal quantities of apple, onion and chopped celery. Truss the ducks and place them side by side, breast up, in a roasting pan just large enough to hold them.
3. Arrange two pieces of bacon on each breast and add water to the pan. There should be only about one-half inch of water around the ducks. Stir in the A.1. sauce and arrange the orange and lemon slices and the celery around the ducks. Bake for about three hours, basting occasionally, or until birds are tender.

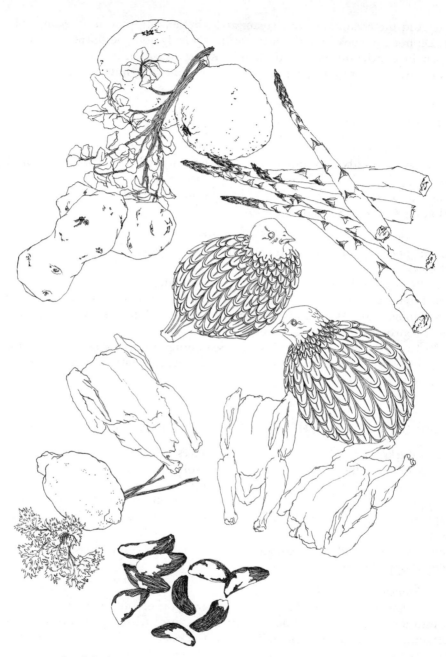

Quail Smitane

4. Thirty minutes before ducks are done, remove the bacon strips and add the Madeira. Baste frequently.

5. When done, remove ducks to a serving platter and strain the juices. Blend the flour with about two tablespoons of the juice to make a paste. Stir this into the sauce, using a wire whisk, until sauce boils up and is thickened. Season with salt and pepper to taste and serve with the ducks.

GAME PÂTÉ   *6 to 8 servings or 15 appetizer servings*

1 pound boned pheasant, wild duck or other feathered game, including the liver
4 thin slices of pork fat back (approximately) or 4 slices of bacon (approximately)
2 truffles, coarsely chopped (optional)
¼ cup cognac
Salt and freshly ground black pepper
2 tablespoons butter
½ cup finely chopped shallots or onions

¾ pound lean veal, finely ground
¾ pound lean pork, finely ground
½ pound pork fat back, finely ground
½ cup shelled fresh pistachio nuts (optional)
½ cup Madeira or cognac
2 eggs
½ teaspoon dried thyme
½ teaspoon ground allspice
1 garlic clove, finely minced
1 bay leaf

1. Cut the game and game liver into slices or cubes. Simmer the fat back or bacon for five minutes, drain it, and dry between paper towels.

2. Combine the game, truffles and one-quarter cup cognac in a bowl. Season with salt and pepper. Let stand in the refrigerator for at least one hour.

3. Preheat oven to moderate (325° F.).

4. Melt the butter. Cook the shallots in it for about five minutes. Combine the shallots, ground meats, ground fat, pistachio nuts, Madeira or cognac, eggs, thyme, allspice and garlic in a bowl. Drain the liquid from the game and add the liquid to the ground meats. Beat well with a wooden spoon.

5. Line the bottom and sides of a two-quart baking dish or pâté mold with a thin layer of the pork fat or bacon slices. Reserve the remaining slices.

6. Divide the ground meat mixture into thirds. Spoon one third into the baking dish. Cover with half of the marinated game. Add another third of the ground meat mixture, top with the remaining game, and add the remaining ground meat. Place the bay leaf on top and cover with the remaining pork or bacon slices. Cover with aluminum foil.

7. Set the baking dish in a larger pan with boiling water halfway up the sides of the baking dish. Bake for one and one-half hours, or until the pâté has shrunk slightly from the edge of the baking dish.

8. Remove the pâté from the oven, leaving the baking dish in the larger pan. Place a pan that is slightly smaller than the pâté dish on top of the

baked pâté. Fill the pan with heavy objects to act as weights and do not remove these until the pâté is completely cooled. Refrigerate the pâté until served.

QUAIL SMITANE   *6 servings*

½ cup fine dry bread crumbs
½ cup finely ground Brazil nuts or hazelnuts
Grated rind of 1 lemon
¼ cup dry sherry
6 quail
Salt and freshly ground black pepper

½ cup butter
2 tablespoons cognac, warmed
½ cup Chicken Stock (page 475)
½ cup dry white wine
1 cup sour cream
Chopped fresh parsley

1. Combine the bread crumbs, Brazil nuts and grated lemon rind. Add the sherry and squeeze the mixture dry.

2. Stuff each quail with equal parts of the bread-crumb mixture and sew up the cavities. Rub the quail with salt and pepper.

3. Heat the butter in a large skillet and brown the birds in it on all sides. Pour the warm cognac over the quail and ignite it. When the flame dies, transfer the quail to a flameproof casserole or Dutch oven.

4. Add the stock and white wine to the skillet in which the quail were browned. Bring the liquid to a boil, stirring to dissolve all brown particles that cling to the bottom and sides of the pan. Pour the liquid over the birds and cover the casserole tightly.

5. Simmer the quail for about thirty minutes, until tender. Add the sour cream and heat for ten minutes longer without boiling. Serve the quail in the sauce and sprinkle with chopped parsley.

.   .   .   .

POULTRY STUFFINGS

.   .   .   .

A well-seasoned stuffing enhances the flavor of roast poultry. An electric blender is useful in preparing ingredients for stuffing, but if a blender is not available, there are other ways to achieve the same purpose. Fresh or dried bread may be crumbled in an old-fashioned grater. Other stuffing ingredients may be finely chopped or may be put through a food grinder. The texture of the stuffing will be slightly different, but the flavor will be unimpaired.

BREAD CRUMBS

Freshly made bread crumbs are superior to packaged crumbs. Some stuffing recipes call for very small bread cubes, but crumbs are even smaller.

SOFT FRESH BREAD CRUMBS:

Trim the crusts from slices of fresh bread and tear the bread into small pieces. Drop the pieces (about two slices at a time) into the container of an electric blender. Cover and blend at high speed for about six seconds.

If no blender is available, bread from a firm loaf may be crumbled in an old-fashioned grater. Trim off the crusts and rub the bread through the coarse side of the greater. If the loaf is soft, allow it to dry for a day or two before grating.

Note: Do not use a food grinder to make fresh bread crumbs. The moisture in the fresh bread will make it come out of the grinder more like a paste than crumbs.

FINE DRY BREAD CRUMBS:

Trim the crusts from slices of fresh bread and arrange the slices in a single layer on a baking sheet. Bake the bread in a slow oven (250° to 275° F.) until the bread is very dry, but do not let it brown at all. When the bread is dry, crumble it in a blender.

If no blender is available, put the dried bread through the fine side of a grater, or put it through a food grinder.

SAUSAGE STUFFING FOR CHICKEN   *1½ to 2 cups*

1 chicken liver, finely chopped
¼ pound fresh sausage meat
1 tablespoon finely chopped shallots
  or green onion
1 tablespoon chopped onion
2 tablespoons chopped parsley

1 garlic clove, finely minced
¾ cup soft fresh bread crumbs
1 egg
3 tablespoons dry white wine
  Salt and freshly ground black
  pepper

Combine the chicken liver and sausage meat and cook until meat loses color. Mix with remaining ingredients.

SAUSAGE STUFFING FOR TURKEY
Enough for a 10- to 12-pound turkey

2 quarts cubes of day-old bread with
  crusts removed
½ pound sausage meat
½ cup butter
1 cup finely chopped onions
¾ cup finely chopped celery, including leaves

¾ teaspoon dried thyme
1 teaspoon ground sage
  Salt and freshly ground black
  pepper

1. Preheat oven to moderate (350° F.).

2. Spread the bread cubes on a baking sheet and bake until dried. Do not brown.

3. In a skillet cook the sausage meat, stirring, until it loses color. Pour off most of the fat.

4. Melt the butter and cook the onions and celery in it until onions are transparent. Add the sausage, bread cubes, herbs, and seasoning to taste. Mix well and let cool.

CORN-BREAD STUFFING   *Enough for a 12- to 15-pound turkey*

1 pound sausage meat
2 pans of Corn Bread (page 529)
4 medium onions, chopped fine
4 celery ribs, chopped fine
½ teaspoon ground sage

½ teaspoon dried thyme
1 teaspoon salt
Dash of freshly ground black pepper

1. Fry the sausage meat over low heat until lightly browned, then break it into pieces with a fork.

2. Crumble the corn bread and add the crumbs to the sausage; mix together. Remove from heat.

3. Cook the chopped onions in a little sausage fat until limp. Add to the mixture, then add the chopped celery and all remaining ingredients, mixing well.

SAGE CORN-BREAD STUFFING   *About 4 cups*

3 cups crumbled Sage Corn Bread (page 530)
1 cup ¼-inch cubes of dried bread
¾ teaspoon ground sage
1 teaspoon instant minced onion
¼ teaspoon salt

⅛ teaspoon freshly ground black pepper
2 tablespoons butter
⅓ cup Beef or Chicken Stock (pages 473 and 475)

Combine corn-bread crumbs, bread cubes, sage, onion, salt and pepper. Add butter and stock and mix lightly but well.

APPLE AND PRUNE STUFFING
Enough for a 10-pound goose; two 5- to 6-pound ducks or chickens

10 slices of white bread
3 medium tart apples, cored and sliced
2 medium onions, quartered
3 celery ribs, chopped
½ cup melted butter
2 teaspoons salt

¼ teaspoon freshly ground black pepper
½ teaspoon dried thyme
½ teaspoon dried marjoram
1 cup dried prunes, cooked, cooled and pitted

1. Tear two slices of the bread and drop the pieces into the container of an electric blender. Cover and blend on high speed for six seconds. Empty into a bowl. Repeat with remaining bread.

2. Place half of the apples, onions and celery in the blender. Fill the blender container with cold water to within one inch of the top; cover. Blend on high speed for four seconds. Drain, and empty the chopped in-gredients into the crumbs. Repeat with remaining apples, onions and celery.

3. Place the butter, seasonings and prunes in the blender. Cover and blend on high speed for fifteen seconds. Empty into the crumbs and mix lightly.

WILD-RICE STUFFING
Enough for a 10-pound goose; two 5- to 6-pound ducks or chickens

½ green pepper, cut into strips	½ cup oil
3 celery ribs, chopped	1½ cups uncooked wild rice
2 medium onions, quartered	2 teaspoon salt
¼ pound mushrooms, sliced	½ teaspoon freshly ground black
2 cups Chicken Stock (page 475)	pepper

1. Place half of the vegetables in the container of an electric blender. Add stock, cover, and blend on high speed for four seconds, or until vegetables are chopped. Drain; reserve stock.

2. Repeat with remaining vegetables, re-using stock. Drain; reserve stock.

3. Heat the oil in a skillet. Add the rice and sauté for ten minutes. Stir in the reserved stock and the salt and pepper. Cover, bring to a boil, and cook for forty-five minutes. Add the chopped vegetables.

BRAZIL-NUT STUFFING   *Enough for a 12-pound turkey*

16 slices of white bread	2 medium onions, quartered
2 cups Brazil nuts	1 teaspoon dried thyme
¾ cup melted butter	2 teaspoons salt
½ cup boiling water	½ teaspoon freshly ground black
1 cup coarsely cut celery	pepper

1. Tear two slices of the bread and drop the pieces into the container of an electric blender. Cover and blend on high speed for six seconds. Empty into a bowl. Repeat with remaining bread.

2. Grate the Brazil nuts in the blender, one cup at a time. Empty the nuts into the bowl with the bread crumbs.

3. Place the remaining ingredients in the container of the blender, cover, and blend on high speed for ten seconds, or until the mixture is blended to a paste. Pour into the bread-crumb mixture and toss until well mixed.

POTATO STUFFING
Enough for a 10-pound goose; two 5- to 6-pound ducks or chickens

½ cup melted butter
2 teaspoons salt
½ teaspoon freshly ground black pepper
½ teaspoon ground sage

2 medium onions, quartered
¼ cup parsley clusters
6 cups diced cooked potatoes (see note)

1. Place the butter, salt, pepper, sage, onions and parsley in the container of an electric blender. Cover and blend on high speed for twenty seconds, or until smooth.

2. Pour the sauce over the potatoes and mix lightly.

Note: Select potatoes that are of the same size so that the cooking time will be the same for all. Wash them well, cover with water, and add two teaspoons salt for each quart of water. Cook until tender. Peel and dice.

CALIFORNIA WALNUT STUFFING
Enough for a 10-pound turkey

½ cup shortening or butter
1 cup chopped onions
1 cup chopped celery
8 cups ½-inch cubes of soft bread
½ cup diced cooked turkey liver
1 cup chopped walnuts

1½ teaspoons salt
¼ teaspoon freshly ground black pepper
1 tablespoon poultry seasoning
½ cup water (optional)
½ cup brandy (optional)

1. Melt the shortening or butter in a large skillet. Add the onions and celery and sauté for fifteen minutes.

2. Combine bread cubes, liver, walnuts and seasonings. Add to onion-celery mixture. This gives a dry stuffing. For a moist stuffing, add the water and brandy.

WINE AND HERB STUFFING　　*Enough for a 4-pound chicken*

½ cup butter
¾ pound mushrooms, thinly sliced
1½ tablespoons finely chopped shallots
1 chicken liver, coarsely chopped
¼ cup Madeira
¼ cup chopped celery

½ cup dry white bread crumbs
2 tablespoons chopped parsley
½ teaspoon dried tarragon
¼ teaspoon salt
⅛ teaspoon freshly ground black pepper

1. Melt half of the butter. Add the mushrooms and shallots and sauté for about eight minutes, until tender. Place in a bowl.

2. Melt the remaining butter and sauté the chopped chicken liver for two minutes. Add it to the mushroom mixture.

3. Pour the wine into the skillet and bring to a boil, scraping to loosen the drippings. Reduce the liquid to one tablespoon and scrape all into the bowl.

4. Add the remaining ingredients and toss lightly. Allow to cool before stuffing the chicken.

NOODLE STUFFING   *Enough for a 5-pound chicken*

4 ounces very fine egg noodles
2 tablespoons butter
¼ cup chopped parsley
½ cup fine white bread crumbs
¼ cup pine nuts

¼ cup chopped fennel or celery
½ teaspoon dried orégano
½ teaspoon salt
¼ teaspoon freshly ground black pepper

1. Cook the noodles in boiling salted water for about eight minutes. Do not overcook. Drain and rinse thoroughly with cold water.

2. Toss the noodles lightly with the butter. Add remaining ingredients and mix lightly. Cool before using to stuff chicken.

COOKED CHESTNUTS

Chestnuts make an excellent addition to poultry stuffings. Four cups of chestnuts in the shell will yield about three cups of cooked chestnuts.

1. Use a paring knife to cut a cross on the flat side of the shell of each chestnut. Cover the chestnuts with water and bring to a boil. Simmer for about five minutes and drain.

2. Peel the chestnuts. If they are hard, add water to cover. Bring to a boil and simmer for about five minutes, until tender. Cooking time will depend on the age of the chestnuts and really fresh ones will often require no further cooking. Peel off the brown skins.

. . . .

CHAPTER SIX

EGGS, CHEESE, RICE AND PASTA

Eggs Forestière

EGG DISHES

HARD-COOKED EGGS

Put enough water in a saucepan to cover the eggs to be cooked. Bring the water to a rapid boil. Lower the eggs into the water one at a time. Reduce the heat until the water barely simmers. Leave the eggs in the water for ten minutes, drain immediately, and plunge into cold water.

CREAMED EGGS WITH OLIVES   *6 servings*

¼ cup butter
¼ cup all-purpose flour
2 cups hot Chicken Stock (page 475)
1 cup heavy cream
¾ teaspoon salt

Cayenne pepper
½ teaspoon crushed dried dill
8 hard-cooked eggs, quartered
½ cup sliced ripe olives
3 tablespoons sherry

1. In a saucepan melt the butter, add the flour, and blend. Add the stock while stirring briskly. Add the cream and cook, stirring, until mixture boils. Season with salt, cayenne to taste, and dill.

2. Add eggs, olives, and sherry. Turn into a chafing dish. Reheat before serving.

EGGS FORESTIÈRE   *4 servings*

6 tablespoons butter
2 tablespoons all-purpose flour
2 cups milk
8 extra-large mushroom caps
4 hard-cooked eggs
   Salt and freshly ground black pepper

½ cup grated Gruyère or Swiss cheese
⅛ teaspoon grated nutmeg
⅓ cup soft fresh bread crumbs
2 tablespoons grated Parmesan cheese

1. Preheat oven to hot (400° F.).

2. In the top of a double boiler melt two tablespoons of the butter; blend in the flour. Gradually stir in the milk. Bring to a boil, stirring, and set over simmering water; cover and let cook for ten to fifteen minutes.

3. Remove the stems from the mushrooms. Chop the stems and sauté them in two tablespoons of the butter until they are tender and most of the moisture has evaporated.

4. Halve the eggs lengthwise, remove the yolks, mash them, and add to the cooked stems. Dot the mushroom caps with the remaining butter, sprinkle with salt and pepper, and broil for three minutes.

5. Stir the Gruyère cheese and nutmeg into the sauce and season with salt and pepper to taste. Add the bread crumbs and enough sauce to moisten to the mixture of egg yolks and mushroom stems.

6. Stuff the egg whites with the mixture. Place one egg-white half, stuffed side down, on each broiled mushroom cap. Pour remaining sauce over all, sprinkle with the Parmesan cheese, and bake for about ten minutes, until lightly browned and bubbly hot. If preferred, the dish may be browned and reheated under a broiler instead of in the oven.

BARBECUE EGGS   *6 servings*

Arrange six sliced hard-cooked eggs on six toast rounds. Blend three-quarters cup chili sauce with one teaspoon Worcestershire sauce, two tablespoons butter and two teaspoons lemon juice. Add salt and pepper to taste. Bring to a boil and spoon over eggs.

STUFFED EGGS AU GRATIN   *4 to 6 servings*

6 hard-cooked eggs	½ cup heavy cream
1 tablespoon anchovy paste	½ teaspoon paprika
½ teaspoon onion juice	12 medium shrimp, cooked and
½ cup butter	shelled
Salt and freshly ground black pepper	½ pound fresh mushrooms, sliced
	2 tablespoons dry sherry
¼ cup all-purpose flour	Grated Parmesan cheese
1 cup milk	

1. Cut the eggs lengthwise into halves and remove the yolks. Reserve the whites. Mash the yolks with the anchovy paste, onion juice and two tablespoons of the butter. Blend well, beating with a wire whisk. Season with a little salt and pepper to taste. Use the mixture to stuff the egg whites. Place the stuffed eggs in a warm baking dish so that they fit snugly.

2. Heat four tablespoons of the remaining butter and blend in the flour. Bring the milk to a boil and add it all at once to the butter-flour mixture,

stirring vigorously with a whisk. When the mixture is thickened and smooth, stir in the cream and cook, stirring occasionally, over low heat for fifteen minutes. Season the sauce with paprika and salt to taste. Stir in the shrimp and keep warm.

3. Meanwhile, cook the sliced mushrooms in the remaining butter until they are wilted and the natural liquid evaporates. Add the mushrooms to the shrimp sauce, bring to a boil, and stir in the sherry.

4. Pour the sauce over the stuffed eggs and sprinkle generously with the cheese. Place the dish under the broiler until golden brown. Serve immediately.

BRENNAN'S EGGS SARDOU   *1 serving*

1 cup hot creamed spinach	2 poached eggs
2 cooked artichoke bottoms	Hollandaise Sauce (page 485)

1. Spoon spinach onto a hot plate and top with artichokes.
2. Place one egg on each artichoke. Cover with sauce.

EGGS MOLLET

Plunge as many eggs as desired into a saucepan of boiling water and maintain the water just below simmering for five or six minutes, depending on the size of the eggs. The whites should be set and the yolks still runny.

Cool the eggs immediately by plunging them into cold water. When the eggs are cool enough to handle, tap them all over with the back of a knife until the shells are mapped with cracks. Hold each egg in the palm of the hand and carefully peel off the shell and inner skin. Small particles of shell adhering to the egg may be removed by dipping the egg into cold water.

To keep the peeled eggs warm until ready to use, place them in hot water.

Eggs mollet may be used in most dishes in which poached eggs are generally used.

EGGS MORNAY   *6 servings*

5 tablespoons butter	¾ cup grated Cheddar cheese
6 tablespoons all-purpose flour	2 tablespoons grated Parmesan
2 cups hot milk	cheese
½ cup heavy cream	6 rounds of buttered toast
Salt and freshly ground black pepper	6 eggs mollet, peeled
	Paprika

1. Melt the butter in a saucepan. Stir in the flour. Add the milk and cream, stirring vigorously with a wire whisk. When the sauce is thickened and smooth, cook, stirring, for five minutes.

2. Season the sauce with salt and pepper and stir in cheeses. When ready to serve, reheat, but do not boil.

3. Place one round of toast on each of six warm plates and top each with one egg. Spoon the hot sauce over the eggs and dust with paprika.

EGGS MOLLET WITH SPINACH PURÉE   *6 servings*

3 pounds fresh spinach, well washed and trimmed
¼ cup minced onion
2 tablespoons butter or 3 slices of bacon, diced
½ teaspoon salt
¼ teaspoon freshly ground black pepper
⅛ teaspoon grated nutmeg
6 eggs mollet, peeled
Toast points

1. Cook the spinach, covered, in a small amount of boiling salted water until just tender. Drain thoroughly. Chop well or put through a food mill.

2. Sauté the onion in the butter or together with the bacon until tender. Add to the spinach purée.

3. Season spinach with the salt, pepper and nutmeg and spread it in a warmed dish.

4. Make six depressions in the purée and place an egg in each. Garnish with the toast points.

MUSTARD BAKED EGGS   *4 servings*

¼ pound sharp Cheddar cheese
4 eggs
6 tablespoons light cream
1 teaspoon dry mustard
Dash of cayenne pepper
½ teaspoon salt
2 tablespoons butter

1. Preheat oven to moderate (350° F.).

2. Shred the cheese and sprinkle it over the bottom of a buttered nine-inch pie plate.

3. Break the eggs over the cheese, being careful not to break the yolks. Combine the cream, mustard, cayenne pepper and salt and pour over the eggs. Dot with butter and bake for fifteen to twenty minutes, or until eggs are set. Do not overbake. The yolks should remain runny inside.

FRESH HERB OMELET   *1 serving*

3 eggs
1 tablespoon cold water
¼ teaspoon salt
1 tablespoon butter
2 teaspoons chopped chives
1 teaspoon chopped parsley
½ teaspoon chopped fresh tarragon
1 fresh parsley sprig

1. Break the eggs into a small bowl. Add the water and salt and beat until light and foamy.

2. Heat the omelet pan. Quickly add the butter and swirl it around. Pour the egg mixture into the pan. Shake the pan back and forth while stirring the eggs clockwise with a fork.

3. When the eggs are set on the bottom but still moist on the top, sprinkle with the chives, parsley and tarragon. Tip the pan and roll the omelet with the fork onto a warm plate. Garnish with parsley.

OEUFS APTOS   *4 servings*

4 teaspoons melted butter	Tabasco
2 shallots, chopped	8 eggs
1 green pepper	Chopped chives or parsley
1 tomato	8 teaspoons sweet cream
Salt, freshly ground black pepper, and cayenne pepper	

1. Preheat oven to moderate (350° F.).

2. Place one teaspoon of melted butter and half of a chopped shallot into each of four individual shirred-egg dishes. Mix well and place in the oven briefly.

3. Peel and chop the green pepper and divide it among the four dishes. Mix well and return to the oven.

4. Peel and slice the tomato and place an equal number of slices in each dish. Season with salt, black pepper, cayenne and Tabasco to taste. Return to the oven and allow the tomatoes to cook for five minutes, or until they begin to soften.

5. Remove the dishes from the oven. Break two eggs into each dish, being careful to keep the yolks whole. Sprinkle with chopped chives or parsley, and with additional salt, pepper, cayenne and Tabasco if desired.

6. Pour one teaspoon cream over each yolk and return to the oven until the whites begin to set.

7. Place under the broiler for a minute or two, until the cream browns, taking care that the eggs remain soft.

HAM AND PEPPER OMELET   *4 servings*

¼ cup butter	½ cup finely chopped baked ham
8 eggs, lightly beaten	1 tablespoon chopped parsley
1 can (4 ounces) pimientos, diced	½ cup milk
¼ cup finely chopped scallions	2 tablespoons water
¼ cup finely chopped green pepper	

1. Heat the butter in a large heavy skillet. Combine remaining ingredients and pour into skillet.

2. Cook over medium heat, stirring gently with a fork, until the mixture starts to set. Raise heat slightly and cook until lightly browned on the bottom. With a spatula, fold the omelet over and slide it onto a warm platter.

CHICKEN-LIVER OMELET   *2 servings*

⅓ cup butter
1 onion, finely chopped
2 mushrooms, sliced
8 chicken livers
2 tablespoons dry sherry
¼ teaspoon dried marjoram
   Salt and freshly ground black pepper

½ cup sour cream at room temperature
1 tablespoon chopped parsley
1 omelet (6 eggs), freshly cooked
   Hot brown gravy

1. Melt the butter in a heavy skillet and sauté the onion until tender. Add the mushrooms and cook for three minutes.

2. Increase the heat, add the chicken livers, and cook quickly until browned on all sides. Add the sherry and stir to loosen the browned-on particles. Season with the marjoram and salt and pepper to taste.

3. Remove the pan from the heat and stir in the sour cream and parsley. Use half of the mixture to fill the omelet. Add enough hot gravy to the remaining chicken-liver mixture to make a sauce to serve over the omelet.

CHAWANMUSHI   *4 servings*

3 eggs
½ teaspoon monosodium glutamate
2 teaspoons sugar
¼ teaspoon salt
1 teaspoon Japanese soy sauce
2½ cups hot Chicken Stock (page 475)

1 raw breast of chicken, skinned and cut into bite-size pieces
8 raw shrimp, peeled and deveined
½ cup cooked peas

1. Beat the eggs together to blend well. Add the monosodium glutamate, sugar, salt, soy sauce and hot stock. Blend well.

2. Divide the chicken pieces among four large custard cups or traditional *chawanmushi* cups. Add two shrimp and two tablespoons peas to each cup. Pour the hot liquid into the cups.

3. Set the cups in a pan containing simmering water extending halfway up the sides of cups. Cover cups very tightly and simmer gently for about thirty minutes, or until set.

CUSTARD FOR TIMBALES   *4 servings*

1 cup Chicken Stock (page 475)
½ cup heavy cream
4 eggs, lightly beaten
½ teaspoon salt

½ teaspoon paprika
⅛ teaspoon grated nutmeg
1 tablespoon chopped parsley (optional)

1. Preheat oven to moderate (325° F.).

2. Combine all the ingredients and beat well. Fill four greased individual molds two thirds full.

3. Set the molds on a rack in a pan of hot water with the water extending to the level of the mixture. Bake for twenty minutes, or until firm. Unmold and serve with a creamed vegetable.

Among the most versatile of pies and among the most substantial are those made with a savory custard. They may be made with seafood, meats, cheese, poultry or vegetables, and the seasoning may include a pinch or more of almost any spice on the herb shelf.

Savory custards may be served either as a luncheon course, cut into thin wedges for cocktail service, or served as the first course for the evening meal. If done gently, the pies may be reheated without ill effect.

PIE SHELL FOR CUSTARD PIES   *1 pie shell*

1½ cups sifted all-purpose flour
¼ teaspoon salt
¼ teaspoon sugar
6 tablespoons butter

2 tablespoons shortening
3 tablespoons cold water, approximately

1. Place the flour, salt and sugar in a bowl. Add the butter and the shortening and rub in with the tips of the fingers or with a pastry blender until the texture is like that of coarse oatmeal.

2. Sprinkle the water over the surface and mix gently with a fork. Use just enough water to make the dough stick together. Chill for thirty minutes.

3. Roll out the pastry on a pastry cloth or a lightly floured board into a circle two inches larger than the pan. Fit it into the pan without stretching, fold under excess pastry around the edge, and decorate. Chill for thirty minutes at least.

4. Preheat oven to hot (400° F.).

5. Prick the pie shell, line with foil, and fill with dried beans or rice. Bake for eight minutes, or until the pastry is set. Carefully remove the foil and beans and bake for three minutes longer, or until the pastry is firm but barely browned. It will be partially baked and the baking will be finished when the filling is baked.

SALMON CUSTARD PIE   *6 to 8 servings*

2 tablespoons butter
2 tablespoons finely chopped shallots
1 can (1 pound) red salmon, skinned, boned and flaked
3 tablespoons snipped fresh dill
¼ teaspoon freshly ground black pepper

¼ cup salmon liquid
1 cup heavy cream, scalded
4 eggs, lightly beaten
1 partially baked pie shell (8 to 9 inches)

1. Preheat oven to moderate (375° F.).
2. Melt the butter in a small pan and sauté the shallots in it until tender but not browned.
3. Place the salmon, dill, pepper and salmon liquid in a bowl and mash with a fork until well mixed. Add the sautéed shallots.
4. Pour the hot cream over the eggs while beating. Gradually beat the egg mixture into the salmon mixture and pour all into the pie shell. Bake for thirty minutes, or until set in the middle.

SPINACH CUSTARD PIE   *6 to 8 servings*

2 tablespoons butter
2 tablespoons finely chopped onion
4 cups finely chopped spinach
¼ teaspoon salt
⅛ teaspoon freshly ground black pepper

¼ teaspoon grated nutmeg
¾ cup grated Parmesan cheese
1¼ cups heavy cream, scalded
4 eggs, lightly beaten
1 partially baked pie shell (8 to 9 inches)

1. Preheat oven to moderate (375° F.).
2. Melt the butter in a large skillet and sauté the onion until tender but not browned.
3. Add the spinach, cover, and cook for five minutes. Turn onto a board and chop again. Place spinach in a bowl and add the salt, pepper, nutmeg and one-half cup of the cheese; mix well.
4. Pour the hot cream over the eggs while beating. Gradually beat into the spinach mixture and pour all into the pie shell. Sprinkle with remaining cheese. Bake for thirty minutes, or until set. Serve warm.

GROUND BEEF AND TOMATO CUSTARD PIE   *6 to 8 servings*

2 tablespoons butter
1 bunch of scallions, sliced
1 pound beef round, ground
1 large tomato, skinned, seeded and chopped
1¼ teaspoons salt
½ teaspoon freshly ground black pepper

½ teaspoon dried marjoram
¼ teaspoon dried thyme
1¼ cups heavy cream, scalded
4 eggs, lightly beaten
1 partially baked pie shell (9 inches across, 2 inches deep)

1. Preheat oven to moderate (375° F.).

2. Melt the butter in a skillet and sauté the scallions and the ground beef until the meat loses its color, breaking the meat up with a fork as it cooks.

3. Add the tomato, salt, pepper, marjoram and thyme and cook for two or three minutes longer.

4. Pour the hot cream over the eggs while beating. Add the meat mixture to the egg mixture and pour all into the pie shell. Bake for thirty minutes, or until set.

. . . .

CHEESE DISHES

. . . .

RACLETTE   *6 to 8 servings*

½ wheel of bagnes or bogne cheese
16 new potatoes, cooked in their jackets and peeled

Pickled onions
Sour gherkins

1. Place the cut portion of the cheese against the heat of a raclette grill or before any upright hot grill, whether charcoal, gas or electric. Turn the cheese two or three times to prevent the melted cheese from dripping. When the cheese is at the bubbling stage, scrape it with a knife onto a hot plate. This is one serving. Repeat until the guests have had sufficient servings.

2. When the cheese is served, pass a bowl of hot potatoes and trays of pickled onions and sour gherkins. Accompany the raclette with dry white wine or beer.

MALAKOFF   *4 to 6 servings*

1½ cups all-purpose flour
1 teaspoon salt
¾ cup beer
¼ cup water
2 egg whites, stiffly beaten

Fat for deep frying
1 pound natural Gruyère cheese, cut into fingers (¾ × ¾ × 2 inches)

1. Blend the flour with the salt and add the beer and water; blend well. Fold in the stiffly beaten egg whites.

2. Heat the fat to 380° F. Spear each finger of cheese on a metal skewer and dip into the beer batter.

3. Fry the cheese in the fat for two or three minutes, until brown and crisp. Serve hot.

CHEESE SOUFFLÉ   *4 servings*

¼ cup butter
¼ cup all-purpose flour
1½ cups milk

2 cups grated Cheddar cheese
Salt and cayenne pepper
4 eggs, separated

1. Preheat oven to moderate, 375° F. for a moist soufflé, 325° F. for a drier one.
2. Melt the butter and blend in the flour. Meanwhile, bring the milk to a boil and add all at once to the butter-flour blend, stirring vigorously with a wire whisk. Cook, stirring, until the sauce is thickened and smooth.
3. Remove the sauce from the heat and add the cheese, stirring until the cheese is melted. Add salt and cayenne pepper to taste. Beat in the egg yolks, one at a time. Let cool.
4. Beat egg whites until stiff and fold them gently into the cooled sauce. Turn into a two-quart casserole with straight sides and bake for about thirty minutes at 375° F. or for about fifty minutes at 325° F., until golden brown and firm.

POTATO-CHEESE SOUFFLÉ   *6 servings*

2 cups mashed potatoes
½ cup hot milk
¾ teaspoon salt
¼ teaspoon freshly ground pepper

1 tablespoon butter
1 tablespoon finely chopped onion
¾ cup grated sharp Cheddar cheese
2 eggs, separated

1. Preheat oven to moderate (350° F.).
2. Mash the potatoes again until very smooth. Add the milk, salt, pepper, butter and onion and beat until fluffy. Stir in the cheese and add the beaten egg yolks. Beat the egg whites until they stand in soft peaks and carefully fold into potato mixture.
3. Turn into an ungreased one-quart casserole and bake for about one hour, until well puffed and firm in the center. Serve at once.

In its most basic sense, Welsh rabbit is a combination of melted cheese and beer. It is seasoned in various ways, however, depending on the cook. However they are made, rabbits are excellent fare for casual entertaining in fall or winter. Ideally, they are made at the table in a chafing dish or a decorative double boiler. They are best served over dry or buttered toast, and the choicest beverage to accompany rabbits is a dry white wine or beer.

WELSH RABBIT   *4 servings*

2 tablespoons butter
1 pounds sharp Cheddar cheese, cut into small cubes
½ teaspoon salt
1 teaspoon dry mustard

Cayenne pepper
1 cup beer or ale
2 egg yolks, lightly beaten
1 teaspoon Worcestershire sauce
4 slices of buttered toast

1. Melt the butter in a saucepan with a heavy bottom. Add the cheese, salt, mustard and cayenne pepper to taste. Stir with a wooden spoon until cheese starts to melt.

2. Continue stirring while gradually adding the beer.

3. When all is blended, remove the saucepan from the heat and add the egg yolks, stirring vigorously. Cook gently until mixture thickens and is smooth. Do not overcook or yolks will curdle.

4. Stir in Worcestershire sauce and serve the rabbit hot over the toast.

GOLDEN BUCK   *4 servings*

1 recipe Welsh Rabbit (see above)
4 poached eggs

8 flat anchovy fillets
Chopped parsley

1. Prepare the rabbit and spoon it onto the four slices of buttered toast.

2. Top each serving with a hot poached egg. Garnish each egg with two crossed anchovy fillets and sprinkle with parsley.

TOMATO RABBIT   *4 servings*

2 tablespoons butter
2 tablespoons all-purpose flour
½ teaspoon dry mustard
¾ cup heavy cream
¾ cup crushed cooked tomatoes
⅛ teaspoon baking soda

2 cups finely cubed Cheddar cheese
2 eggs, lightly beaten
Salt and cayenne pepper
4 slices of buttered toast
Chopped parsley

1. Melt the butter and add the flour and mustard. Blend with a wire whisk. Add the cream, stirring vigorously with the whisk. Cook until mixture is thickened and smooth.

2. Blend the tomatoes and soda and stir them into the sauce.

3. Add the cheese, eggs, and salt and cayenne to taste. Cook, stirring, until cheese is melted. When smooth, serve on buttered toast. Garnish each serving with chopped parsley.

CARAWAY MACARONI RABBIT   *4 servings*

8 ounces elbow macaroni
2 tablespoons butter
1 pound sharp Cheddar cheese
1 teaspoon dry mustard

¾ cup milk
1 tablespoon caraway seeds
Freshly ground black pepper
1 teaspoon paprika

1. Cook macaroni according to package directions. Do not overcook. Drain and rinse.

2. Melt butter in a saucepan or chafing dish over hot water. Shred the cheese and add it. Stir in mustard and milk. Stir and cook until cheese has melted and mixture has the consistency of heavy cream. Add the caraway seeds, black pepper and macaroni. Mix lightly with a fork and sprinkle with paprika.

Cheese is not only one of the most nourishing of foods but also one of the most versatile. Each of these dishes has cheese as the ingredient which gives it the characteristic flavor: Cheese and Parsley Pie, Welsh Rabbit, Gratin Dauphinois and Gougère.

MEXICAN RABBIT *4 servings*

1 tablespoon butter
2 tablespoons finely chopped green pepper
2 teaspoons finely chopped onion
1 garlic clove, finely minced
1 teaspoon chili powder, or more
½ teaspoon ground cuminseed
½ cup drained canned Italian-style plum tomatoes

¾ pound Cheddar cheese, grated or finely cubed
Salt
½ teaspoon cayenne pepper
1 egg beaten with 2 tablespoons milk
4 slices of buttered toast

1. Melt the butter in a saucepan and cook the green pepper, onion and garlic in it for about three minutes, stirring with a wooden spoon. Add the chili powder and cuminseed.

2. Add the tomatoes and simmer for five minutes. Add the cheese, salt to taste, and cayenne.

3. When the cheese is melted, stir in the egg beaten with milk. Do not overcook or egg will curdle. Serve over the toast.

GOUGÈRE   *8 servings*

1 cup water
6 tablespoons butter
1 teaspoon salt
⅛ teaspoon freshly ground black
   pepper

1 cup sifted all-purpose flour
4 eggs
1 cup finely diced Gruyère cheese

1. Preheat oven to hot (425° F.). Lightly grease a baking sheet.

2. Place the water, butter, salt and pepper in a saucepan and heat until the butter is melted and mixture is boiling rapidly.

3. Add the flour to the butter mixture all at once and continue to cook, stirring, until the mixture forms a ball and leaves the sides of the pan clean. Remove the pan from the heat.

4. Beat in the eggs, one at a time, incorporating each thoroughly before adding the next. Stir in all but two tablespoons of the cheese.

5. Place rounded tablespoons of the dough on the prepared baking sheet in the shape of a ring about eight inches in diameter, leaving a space in the center about two inches in diameter.

6. Sprinkle the dough with the remaining cheese and bake for forty to forty-five minutes, or until well puffed and golden brown.

CHEESE AND RICE AVOCADOS   *6 servings*

½ cup finely chopped onion
2 tablespoons butter
½ cup uncooked rice
1 cup Chicken Stock (page 475)
¼ teaspoon salt

½ cup chopped parsley
2 cups grated Cheddar cheese
1 egg, lightly beaten
3 avocados
Lemon juice

1. Sauté the onion in the butter until tender but not browned. Add the rice and cook for three minutes, stirring occasionally.

2. Add the stock and salt, cover, and cook slowly for about twenty minutes, or until rice is tender. Add the parsley, one cup of the cheese and the egg, and stir until the cheese melts.

3. Halve the avocados; skin them and remove seeds. Brush with lemon juice and place in a shallow pan.

4. Fill the halves with the rice mixture, sprinkle with the remaining cheese, and broil four to five inches from the source of heat until the cheese just melts.

CHEESE AND PARSLEY PIE *6 to 10 servings*

Unbaked Pie Pastry, 1-crust (page 637)
1 onion, thinly sliced
2 tablespoons butter
3 tablespoons chopped parsley
1 cup cubed Gruyère or other Swiss cheese
¼ cup grated Parmesan cheese

4 eggs, lightly beaten
2 cups heavy cream or 1 cup each of milk and heavy cream
¼ teaspoon grated nutmeg
¼ teaspoon salt
¼ teaspoon freshly ground white pepper

1. Preheat oven to hot (450° F.).
2. Roll out pastry to a circle ten inches in diameter. Line a nine-inch pie plate with the pastry and flute the edges. Bake for five minutes.
3. Sauté the onion in the butter until onion is transparent.
4. Sprinkle the onion, parsley, Gruyère and Parmesan over the partly baked pastry shell.
5. Combine the eggs, cream, nutmeg, salt and pepper. Strain over the onion-cheese mixture. Bake for fifteen minutes.
6. Reduce oven temperature to moderate (350° F.).
7. Bake the pie for about ten minutes longer, or until a knife inserted one inch from the pastry edge comes out clean. Serve immediately as main course or hors d'oeuvre.

. . . .

RICE AND OTHER GRAINS

. . . .

In the Far East rice is coveted as the staff of life. The Italians rave about risotto, and rice is the accepted ne plus ultra *accompaniment for fried chicken in the Deep South. Rice originated in India and China a few millennia ago and came to Europe via Egypt and Greece. Oddly enough the French were among the last to appreciate its virtue, the reason being, according to gastronomic theory, that the early Gallic chefs succumbed to the temptation to stir it too often and cook it long.*

There are dozens of kinds of rice including the long grain, short grain, oval grain and round grain, each bearing a different name. Wild rice is not botanically rice at all, but another sort of cereal, and it is native to the United States. Genuine rice of Eastern origin was introduced to this country in 1694.

The peoples of the world who depend on rice as a major nourishment eat it cooked from rough unpolished grains; that way it is more nutritious. When polished rice is used and cooked in a great quantity of water, the vitamins and whatever else go down the drain. Rice should be cooked in a minimum of stock or water, just enough for the grains to absorb and become tender. As the rice cooks, it should not be uncovered or disturbed with fork or spoon. According to the Chinese the rice is done when "eyes" form on the surface of the rice, about twenty minutes.

BOILED RICE FOR ONE   *About 1 cup*

1 cup water
½ cup uncooked rice

Salt

1. Place the water in a saucepan with a close-fitting cover and bring to a boil.
2. Pour in the rice, add a little salt, and stir once with a fork. Cover closely and cook, without raising the lid, for exactly twenty minutes. Remove from the heat and serve immediately.

PAPRIKA RICE   *4 servings*

1 cup uncooked long-grain rice
2 cups water
2 tablespoons butter
2 cups Chicken Stock (page 475)

½ teaspoon salt
1½ teaspoons paprika
¼ teaspoon freshly ground black pepper

1. Soak the rice in the water for thirty minutes.
2. Drain the rice and sauté in the butter in a saucepan until rice is dry and begins to stick to the bottom of the pan. Add the stock, salt, paprika and pepper. Stir only until well blended. Cover, bring to a boil, and cook for twelve to fifteen minutes, or until rice is almost tender.
3. Remove rice from heat and let stand, covered, until ready to serve. The rice will absorb all the stock.

SAFFRON RICE   *4 servings*

2 tablespoons butter
1 small onion, finely chopped
½ bay leaf
¼ teaspoon ground saffron

1 cup uncooked rice
2 cups boiling Chicken Stock (page 475)

1. Melt the butter in a saucepan with a tight-fitting cover. Cook the onion in it, stirring, until onion is translucent. Stir in the bay leaf, saffron and rice.
2. Pour the stock over the rice and stir once. Cover and cook without removing the lid for twenty minutes. Remove bay leaf and serve.

LAUREL RICE   *4 servings*

2 tablespoons butter
1 tablespoon finely minced onion
½ teaspoon finely minced garlic

1 cup uncooked rice
1½ bay leaves
2¼ cups Chicken Stock (page 475)

1. Melt the butter in a saucepan and cook the onion and garlic in it without browning. Add the rice and bay leaves and cook, stirring, for about two minutes.

2. Meanwhile, bring the stock to a boil. Add it to the rice; cover. Simmer for exactly twenty minutes. Discard bay leaves.

Note: The rice may be made thirty minutes before serving.

RICE WITH PEAS   *4 to 6 servings*

¼ cup wild rice
¾ cup white rice
1 teaspoon salt
¼ cup butter
2 shallots, finely minced, or 3 tablespoons finely chopped onion

1 garlic clove, finely minced
1½ pounds fresh green peas, shelled
Salt and freshly ground black pepper

1. Place the wild rice in a saucepan and add boiling water to cover. Let stand for two minutes and drain. Add water, let stand, and drain three times.

2. Add the white rice, salt and two and one-half cups water to the wild rice. Cover and cook over low heat for twenty-five to thirty minutes, or until the water is absorbed and rice is tender.

3. In a small saucepan melt the butter and cook the shallots and garlic in it for about two minutes. Simmer the peas in water without salt until tender.

4. Combine the rice, butter and peas and toss briefly. Season with salt and pepper to taste and serve hot.

RISOTTO FOR ONE   *About 1 cup*

1 tablespoon butter
2 tablespoons finely chopped onion
¼ garlic clove, finely minced

½ cup uncooked rice
1 cup boiling Chicken Stock (page 475)

1. Heat the butter in a small saucepan with a tight-fitting cover. Add the onion and garlic and cook, stirring, until the onion is translucent. Add the rice and cook, stirring, until rice is golden.

2. Add the stock and cover. Cook, without uncovering, for exactly twenty minutes. Remove from the heat and let stand until ready to serve.

RISOTTO RING   *About 8 servings*

1½ cups uncooked rice
6 tablespoons butter
½ cup minced onion
4 cups Chicken Stock (page 475)

Salt and freshly ground black pepper
1½ cups grated Parmesan cheese

1. Cook the rice in the butter in a heavy ten-inch skillet over medium heat, stirring constantly, until yellow. Add the onion and continue to cook, stirring, until the onion is limp.

2. Add the stock and bring to a boil, stirring occasionally. Lower the heat and simmer, covered, until the rice is tender.

3. Season with salt and pepper to taste. Add the cheese and mix.

4. Turn into a well-buttered five- to six-cup ring mold and press the rice down gently. Turn out at once on a serving plate or keep warm in a pan of hot water until ready to serve.

PILAFF   *8 servings*

⅓ cup finely chopped onion
6 tablespoons butter
2¼ cups uncooked rice
4½ cups boiling Chicken Stock (page 475)

Salt and freshly ground black pepper

1. Preheat oven to moderate (375° F.).

2. Sauté the onion in the butter in a heavy casserole until tender and transparent but not browned.

3. Add the rice and continue to cook over low heat, stirring occasionally, until rice grains turn opaque. Do not allow rice to brown.

4. Add the stock and season with salt and pepper to taste. Cover tightly and bake for five minutes. Reduce the heat to 350° F. and bake for fifteen to twenty minutes longer, or until rice has absorbed all the stock.

VARIATIONS:

Mushroom pilaff: Sauté one-half pound mushrooms, sliced, in one-quarter cup butter, and add to pilaff before serving.

Nut pilaff: Add one-quarter cup toasted cashew nuts to pilaff before serving.

EGG PILAU   *6 to 8 servings*

2 cups uncooked rice
4 cups Chicken Stock (page 475)
Salt

6 eggs
½ cup melted butter
Freshly ground black pepper

1. In a saucepan combine the rice, chicken stock and salt to taste. Bring to a boil and cover. Reduce the heat and cook slowly for about twenty minutes, until all the liquid is absorbed.

2. Beat the eggs with a whisk or rotary beater and add them all at once to the rice. Add the butter immediately. Stir well without returning the pan to the heat. The heat of the rice will set the eggs. Season with pepper to taste and serve immediately.

RICE AND OLIVE CASSEROLE   *4 servings*

2 cups cooked rice
½ cup finely chopped parsley
1 small onion, finely chopped
1 garlic clove, finely minced
1 cup milk
2 eggs, lightly beaten

Salt and freshly ground black pepper
⅓ cup sliced pimiento-stuffed green olives
¼ cup grated Parmesan cheese

1. Preheat oven to moderate (375° F.).

2. In a mixing bowl combine the rice, parsley, onion, garlic, milk, eggs, and salt and pepper to taste. Mix well and turn into a buttered one-quart casserole.

3. Arrange the sliced olives over the top of the casserole and sprinkle with the grated cheese. Bake for forty minutes.

CURRIED RICE   *6 servings*

5 tablespoons butter
1 cup finely chopped onions
3 tablespoons curry powder
2 tablespoons all-purpose flour

1½ cups Chicken Stock (page 475)
1 cup heavy cream
½ cup milk
3 cups cooked rice

1. Melt the butter in a large skillet. Sauté the onions in it until golden. Blend in the curry powder and flour and stir until a smooth paste forms.

2. Gradually add the stock, cream and milk. Mix well, stirring, until the sauce is thickened and smooth.

3. Add the rice, turning it over gently in the sauce until all the liquid is absorbed. Cook lightly for five minutes. Serve very hot, with a sprinkling of curry powder.

BAKED RICE   *4 to 6 servings*

3 cups cooked rice
1 cup grated sharp Cheddar cheese
1 egg, lightly beaten
1 green pepper, finely chopped

½ garlic clove, minced
2 tablespoons oil
½ cup light cream

1. Preheat oven to moderate (350° F.).

2. Combine all ingredients and mix well. Turn into a casserole and bake for thirty minutes, turning once. If the mixture becomes too dry, cover the casserole.

NASI   (Indonesian boiled rice)   *6 servings*

1 cup uncooked rice   2 cups water

Combine rice and water in a saucepan. Bring to a boil and cover tightly. Cook, without stirring, for exactly twenty minutes.

A Japanese dinner of Shioyaki (salmon with salt), beef teriyaki, Chicken Soup with Mushrooms, Japanese Rice and Chawanmushi (custard with peas).

PINK RICE   *9 to 12 servings*

1 cup butter
3 cups uncooked rice
⅔ cup finely chopped onions
½ cup chopped peeled tomato
2½ cups tomato juice

2 cups Chicken Stock (page 475)
1 teaspoon salt
¼ teaspoon freshly ground black pepper

1. Preheat oven to moderate (375° F.).
2. Melt the butter in a heavy skillet. Add the rice and cook until the butter bubbles briskly. Add the onions, tomato, tomato juice and stock. Stir once and add the seasonings.
3. Cover the skillet, place it in the oven, and bake for thirty minutes. Separate the rice grains with a fork, replace cover, and bake for twenty minutes longer.

JAPANESE RICE   *4 servings*

1 cup uncooked rice

1½ cups water

1. Wash the rice well by rinsing it through several changes of water. Drain rice and place it in a heavy one-quart saucepan.
2. Add the one and one-half cups water. Cover and bring to a rolling boil, then reduce heat to moderate. Let cook for ten minutes. Reduce heat to very low and steam rice for ten minutes longer. At no time during cooking should rice be stirred. Saucepan must be kept covered during entire process and until rice is ready to be served.

FRIED RICE   *4 servings*

¼ cup peanut oil
2 eggs
Salt
½ cup coarsely chopped scallions
4 cups cold cooked rice

3 tablespoons soy sauce
¼ teaspoon sugar
¼ teaspoon monosodium glutamate
½ cup finely chopped ham
½ cup cooked green peas

1. Heat one tablespoon of the oil in a skillet. Break the eggs into a bowl and beat well but not to a froth. Add them to the skillet and cook, stirring, just until they start to set. Do not overcook; they must remain moist. Sprinkle with salt and set aside.
2. In another skillet heat the remaining oil and add scallions, stirring a few times. Add the rice and stir rapidly so that rice will not stick to the pan. Add the soy sauce, sugar and monosodium glutamate.
3. Add the ham and peas and cook, stirring. Break up the eggs into small pieces. Add them to the rice and cook until all ingredients are thoroughly hot. Serve immediately.

Note: Although any good-quality ham may be used, this dish is, more often than not, made with Smithfield or Virginia ham in Chinese-American kitchens.

KOREAN RICE WITH BEEF *6 to 8 servings*

3 tablespoons vegetable oil
½ cup finely chopped onion
2 cups uncooked rice
¼ pound beef, ground
¼ pound mushrooms
3 tablespoons imported soy sauce

3 tablespoons toasted sesame seeds (see note)
½ teaspoon crushed red pepper, or more
Salt
3 cups Beef Stock (page 473)

1. Heat two tablespoons of the oil in a large saucepan and add the onion and rice. Cook, stirring, for five minutes, but do not brown the onion. Add the beef and the remaining oil and cook, stirring, until meat loses its pink color. Add the mushrooms and stir in remaining ingredients.

2. Cover the rice and bring mixture to a boil. Reduce heat and cook for twenty minutes, or until rice is tender.

Note: To toast sesame seeds, spread them out in a shallow pan. Roast them in a preheated moderate oven (350° F.) for twenty minutes, or until seeds are golden brown.

CHELLO (Persian rice) *4 servings*

2½ cups uncooked long-grain rice
3½ tablespoons salt

½ cup butter, melted

1. Rinse the rice three times in lukewarm water and then put it in cold water to cover, to which one and one-half tablespoons of salt have been added. Soak the rice overnight.

2. Boil two quarts of water to which two tablespoons of salt have been added. Drain the rice and add it to the boiling water. Boil for ten to fifteen minutes, stirring occasionally to keep the grains from sticking together. Pour the rice and water into a strainer and rinse with lukewarm water.

3. Pour one-third of the melted butter into the bottom of the pan in which the rice cooked. Add two tablespoons water to the butter in the pan. Drop a spoonful of rice at a time into the pan, distributing it evenly. Allow it to mound in the shape of a cone. Pour the rest of the melted butter over the rice, distributing it evenly.

4. Put paper towels over the pan. Cover and place two or three dish towels on the lid. Cook over medium heat for ten to fifteen minutes. Lower the heat and cook for thirty-five to forty minutes longer. If cooked at the right temperature, the rice will form a crust at the bottom of the pot which will

become crisp and turn a golden brown, while the rest of the rice remains white. If desired, add more melted butter before serving.

Note: Place the pan in a basin filled with cold water for a few minutes before serving to make it easier to remove the crust.

ISRAELI RICE *4 servings*

1 onion, finely chopped
¼ cup olive oil
1 teaspoon curry powder
1 teaspoon salt

1 cup uncooked rice
2 cups hot Beef Stock (page 473)
¼ cup pine nuts

1. Sauté the onion in two tablespoons of the oil until tender but not browned.
2. Add the curry powder, salt, rice and stock. Cover, bring to a boil, and simmer gently for twenty minutes, or until rice is tender.
3. Sauté the pine nuts in the remaining oil until they are just lightly browned. Add them to the rice and toss to distribute.

BARLEY AND MUSHROOM CASSEROLE *4 servings*

1 large onion, chopped
½ pound mushrooms, sliced
5 tablespoons butter

1 cup pearl barley
2 cups Beef or Chicken Stock (pages
 473 and 475)

1. Preheat oven to moderate (350° F.).
2. Cook the onion and mushrooms in the butter until onion is wilted and mushroom juices have evaporated. Add the barley and brown lightly. Pour the mixture into a buttered casserole. Pour one cup of the stock over the barley and cover. Bring to a boil.
3. Bake the casserole, covered, for twenty-five to thirty minutes. Add remaining stock. Continue to cook, covered, for fifteen minutes or longer, until liquid is absorbed and barley is tender.

CRACKED-WHEAT PILAFF *4 servings*

1 cup bulgur (cracked wheat)
5 tablespoons butter
½ cup chopped onion
2 cups Beef or Chicken Stock (pages
 473 and 475)

Salt and freshly ground black pepper

1. Preheat oven to moderate (350° F.).
2. Cook the dry bulgur in four tablespoons of the butter, stirring, until the wheat is thoroughly coated. Cook the onion separately in the remaining butter until it is soft.

3. Combine the onion with the grains and stock in a covered casserole. Add salt and pepper to taste. Bake for thirty minutes; stir gently with a fork. Bake for fifteen minutes longer. At the end of the baking time, all of the liquid should be absorbed and the cracked wheat should be moist but fluffy.

Cornmeal is more widely revered in the American South and Southwest than in other sections of the country, but one exception is the famed scrapple, or pawn, *of the Pennsylvania Dutch. Italians, particularly those of southern Italy, have a keen appetite for polenta, which is made of cornmeal mush and served with cheese, tomato sauce, or other savory adornments.*

POLENTA   *4 to 6 servings*

4 cups water
1 teaspoon salt
1 cup yellow cornmeal
1 egg, lightly beaten

½ cup grated Parmesan or Romano cheese
½ cup butter, melted
2 cups Tomato Sauce III (page 494)

1. Bring two and one-half cups of the water to a boil in the top of a double boiler. Stir in the salt.
2. Mix the cornmeal with the remaining water and add it, stirring, to the boiling water. Cook, stirring, until mixture thickens.
3. Place the mixture over boiling water and cook, covered, for forty-five minutes, stirring occasionally. Pour the mush into a lightly greased pan (9 × 9 × 2 inches). Spread mush quickly with a spatula. Cool, then chill thoroughly.
4. Using a sharp knife, cut the chilled polenta into diamonds or, using a small cookie cutter, cut polenta into rounds.
5. Preheat oven to moderate (375° F.).
6. Dip the polenta shapes into the beaten egg and then coat with grated cheese.
7. Arrange the pieces in a shallow baking dish, overlapping the pieces if desired. Drizzle the butter over the polenta and bake for fifteen to twenty minutes, or until very hot and lightly browned. Serve with hot tomato sauce.

POLENTA WITH MUSHROOMS   *6 to 8 servings*

2 cups cornmeal
2 cups cold water
6 cups boiling water
3 teaspoons salt
4 cups sliced fresh mushrooms
½ cup diced onion
1 garlic clove, minced

2 teaspoons lemon juice
¼ cup butter
⅛ teaspoon freshly ground black pepper
⅓ cup light cream
¾ cup grated Parmesan cheese
6 mushroom caps (optional)

1. Combine the cornmeal and cold water. Pour into a saucepan containing the boiling water and two teaspoons of salt, stirring constantly. Cook until thickened, stirring frequently. Cover and continue to cook over low heat for ten minutes. Turn into a loaf pan (9 × 5 × 3 inches) and let stand until cold and firm.

2. Preheat oven to moderate (350° F.).

3. Sauté the mushrooms, onion and garlic in the lemon juice and butter. Add the remaining teaspoon of salt and the pepper.

4. Remove the cold cornmeal mush from the pan. Split lengthwise into halves to form two layers. Return the lower half to the pan. Cover with the sautéed mushroom mixture and pour the light cream over all. Sprinkle with the grated cheese. Top with remaining cornmeal layer.

5. Bake for thirty minutes. If desired, ten minutes before the baking time is up, dip mushroom caps into melted butter and arrange over the top of the polenta as a garnish. Serve as a main dish.

CHEESE AND CORNMEAL CASSEROLE   *8 servings*

1½ cups yellow cornmeal
5 cups boiling water
1½ teaspoons salt
2 medium onions, chopped
2 garlic cloves, minced
½ cup butter

2 cans (2 ounces each) flat anchovy fillets
2 cups creamed cottage cheese
Freshly ground black pepper
2 cups Tomato Sauce II (page 494)

1. Add the cornmeal gradually to the boiling salted water while stirring. Cook over medium heat, stirring constantly, until very thick. Cover and set aside.

2. Preheat oven to moderate (350° F.).

3. Lightly brown the onions and garlic in half of the butter. Add the anchovies with their oil and cook, while mashing, until the mixture is well blended. Add cottage cheese and pepper to taste.

4. In a greased six-quart baking dish, arrange layers of cornmeal mush and the anchovy-cheese mixture, having bottom and top layers of cornmeal.

5. Dot the top with bits of the remaining butter and bake for about thirty minutes, until lightly browned. Turn out of mold and serve with tomato sauce.

SPOON BREAD   *8 servings*

4 cups milk
1 cup white cornmeal
1 teaspoon salt

¼ cup butter
5 egg whites
4 egg yolks

1. Preheat oven to moderate (350° F.). Butter a three-quart soufflé dish.

2. Scald two and one-half cups of the milk. Mix remaining milk with the cornmeal and stir into the scalded milk. Cook over low heat, stirring constantly, until mixture is a thick mush. Mix in the salt and butter.

3. Beat egg whites until stiff. Beat yolks well. Add a little mush to the yolks; add this mixture to remaining mush. Fold in egg whites.

4. Bake for about fifty minutes, until puffy and brown.

SPOON BREAD WITH HAM AND MUSHROOMS   *8 servings*

Spoon Bread (page 344)
¼ cup butter

4 medium mushrooms, minced
½ cup finely chopped ham

1. Prepare spoon bread through step 2.

2. Melt the butter and sauté the mushrooms in it for three minutes. Add the ham and cook for two minutes longer. Add to the cornmeal mixture.

3. Finish preparing the spoon bread, pour into the prepared soufflé dish, and bake for about one hour.

FRESH-CORN SPOON BREAD   *6 to 8 servings*

3 ears of fresh corn, approximately
⅓ cup cornmeal
2 cups hot milk
¼ cup butter
2 teaspoons sugar

1½ teaspoons salt
⅛ teaspoon freshly ground black pepper
1 tablespoon minced fresh onion
2 eggs, separated

1. Split each row of corn grains with a sharp knife. Cut off about one-third of the grains all around each ear. Repeat the cutting. Scrape the cob with a tablespoon to get the remaining pulp and milk. Measure. There should be one and one-half cups.

2. Preheat oven to moderate (325° F.). Butter the bottom but not the sides of a one-and-one-half-quart casserole.

3. Mix the corn with the cornmeal and stir in the hot milk. Cook, stirring, over moderate heat for about five minutes, until thickened. Remove from the heat and blend in the butter, sugar, salt, pepper and onion.

4. Beat the egg yolks, add a little of the hot mixture, and return to the remaining hot mixture in the pan. Beat the egg whites until stiff and fold them into the corn mixture.

5. Turn the mixture into the prepared casserole and set it in a pan of hot water. Bake for about one hour, until a knife inserted into the center comes out clean. Serve immediately.

TAMALES À LA ANITA KNIBERG   *12 servings*

1½ pounds smoked slab bacon
1 cup ground fresh onions
3 garlic cloves, ground
½ cup ground green pepper
1½ pounds yellow cornmeal
8 cups (four 1-pound cans) cream-style yellow corn

1½ cups milk
⅓ cup tomato sauce
5 teaspoons salt, or more
½ teaspoon freshly ground black pepper
¾ teaspoon ground cuminseed
Juice of 1 lemon

1. Remove and discard rind from the bacon. Cut bacon into cubes (¾ inch). Place cubes in a skillet and fry until bacon is golden brown and most of the fat has been rendered. Transfer bacon cubes to a bowl large enough for mixing tamales.

2. Discard all but one-third cup of the fat in the skillet. Cook onions and garlic in remaining fat for about five minutes. Add vegetables to the fried bacon. Stir in the green pepper, cornmeal, creamed corn, milk, tomato sauce, salt, black pepper and cuminseed.

3. Cut heavy-duty foil into twenty-four squares (7½ inches). Spoon some of the cornmeal mixture along the center of each square. Leave room all around the mixture so that the square of foil may be securely sealed, envelope fashion, before boiling.

4. Bring the edges of the foil together and fold them down, over and over, three times. Fold each end over and over, making certain that each little package is securely closed. The finished packet should allow room for the cornmeal to expand slightly as it cooks.

5. Place the tamales in a large kettle and cover with boiling water containing the juice of one lemon to prevent discoloration of the foil. Boil for one hour.

6. To serve, open the top and side seams of the foil envelopes and turn back the foil. The tamales are to be eaten with a fork from the foil.

. . . .

PASTA DISHES

. . . .

Pasta is a food with a welcome versatility. There are, of course, hundreds of shapes that pasta may take, from acini di pepe *(peppercorns) to* ziti. *The roster includes* amorini *(little cupids),* capelli di prete *(priests' hats),* lancette *(little spears),* lingue di passero *(sparrows' tongues),* occhi di lupo *(wolf's eyes),* fusilli, tufoli, *and the kind known as* vermicelli *(little worms). The* vermicelli *come in strands even thinner than spaghettini, which are a slender version of spaghetti, which means "little strings."*

All forms of pasta possess character only when embellished with a sauce, and there are doubtless as many sauces for pasta as there are names by which pasta is identified. These may range from a simple butter and cheese sauce to an elaborate tomato mixture with many ingredients.

HOMEMADE EGG NOODLES *6 servings*

3 cups sifted all-purpose flour
4 eggs

1 tablespoon salt

1. Place flour in a bowl, add eggs, and mix with the hands until the dough can be gathered into a rough ball.
2. Turn out on a smooth surface and knead until all crumbly particles have been incorporated. The dough should be very stiff. If necessary, work a little additional flour into the mixture.
3. Knead the dough and divide it into thirds. Press each into a flat rectangle. Put one third at a time through the roller of a noodle cutter. Repeat several times, proceeding from the widest to the lowest opening. Adjust the size of the opening by turning the wheel designed for the purpose. It may be necessary to put the dough through one of the larger openings several times to get a smooth consistency. When the dough is satin smooth and has been put through the smallest opening, put it through the noodle-cutting blades. Hang the noodle strands on strings or clotheslines to dry briefly before cooking.
4. To cook, bring three quarts water to a boil and add one tablespoon salt. When it is boiling vigorously, add the noodles and cook, stirring occasionally, for four to six minutes, until the noodles are tender.
5. Drain quickly, turn into a heated ovenproof platter, and dress with any sauce desired.

PARSLEYED NOODLES *6 servings*

1 pound wide noodles, cooked according to package directions and drained
1/4 cup melted butter

Salt and freshly ground black pepper
1/4 cup finely chopped parsley

Combine all the ingredients, toss gently, and serve.

NOODLES WITH FRESH MUSHROOMS *6 servings*

1 pound mushrooms, thinly sliced
6 tablespoons butter
Salt
1/4 teaspoon freshly ground black pepper

1 cup soft fresh bread crumbs
8 ounces egg noodles
2 tablespoons finely minced parsley

1. Cook the mushrooms in five tablespoons of the butter until they are lightly browned. Sprinkle with salt and pepper.

2. In a small skillet cook the bread crumbs in the remaining tablespoon of butter, stirring, until browned.

3. Cook the noodles according to package directions and drain. Turn them onto a hot platter and toss with the mushrooms. Sprinkle with bread crumbs and parsley and serve immediately.

NOODLES WITH CREAM CHEESE   *6 to 8 servings*

1 cup chopped celery	½ teaspoon salt
2 tablespoons butter	½ cup chopped stuffed olives
2 tablespoons all-purpose flour	8 ounces noodles, cooked according
2 cups hot milk	to package directions
6 ounces cream cheese	

1. Put the celery in a saucepan and add boiling salted water to cover. Cook briefly, until celery is just tender. Drain and reserve.

2. Melt the butter and stir in the flour. Stir in the milk and cook, stirring, until sauce is thickened and smooth. Add the cheese and continue to cook and stir until cheese is melted.

3. Add the salt, celery and olives to the sauce. Stir until blended. Serve over hot noodles and toss to blend.

NOODLES WITH SPINACH   *6 servings*

1 pound Homemade Egg Noodles (page 347) ¼ inch wide	1 cup light cream
1½ pounds fresh spinach	Salt and freshly ground black pepper
1 tablespoon lemon juice	⅛ teaspoon grated nutmeg
3 tablespoons butter	½ cup finely chopped prosciutto or cooked ham
1 tablespoon finely chopped onion	½ cup buttered soft fresh bread crumbs
1 garlic clove, finely minced	
3 tablespoons all-purpose flour	

1. Preheat oven to moderate (350° F.).

2. Cook the noodles until barely tender and drain.

3. Wash the spinach carefully and cook in a covered pan in only the water clinging to the leaves until just tender. Drain and chop or put through a food mill. Add the lemon juice.

4. Melt the butter and sauté the onion and garlic in it until tender. Blend in the flour. Gradually stir in the cream and bring to a boil, stirring. Season with salt and pepper to taste and the nutmeg.

5. Add the spinach to the sauce and mix well. Toss the noodles, spinach mixture and ham together and place in a buttered shallow casserole. Top with the crumbs. Bake for fifteen to twenty minutes, or until very hot and lightly browned.

NOODLE CASSEROLE   *4 servings*

½ cup butter, melted
¼ cup olive oil
1 garlic clove, finely minced
½ cup finely chopped onion
2 tablespoons tomato paste
2½ cups (one 1-pound 4-ounce can) Italian-style plum tomatoes

Salt and freshly ground black pepper
½ teaspoon dried orégano
1 pound Homemade Egg Noodles (page 347) ¼ inch wide
½ pound mozzarella cheese, cubed
¼ cup grated Parmesan cheese

1. Preheat oven to moderate (350° F.).
2. Place half of the butter and the oil in a heavy skillet and sauté the garlic and onion in it until tender but not browned.
3. Add the tomato paste, tomatoes and salt and pepper to taste. Bring to a boil and simmer, uncovered, for twenty minutes. Force through a food mill or strainer. Add the orégano.
4. Cook the noodles until barely tender and drain.
5. Mix the noodles with the mozzarella cheese and the remaining butter. Place in the bottom of a buttered casserole. Pour the sauce over the top and sprinkle with the Parmesan cheese. Bake for fifteen to twenty minutes, or until the dish is bubbly hot.

OYSTER NOODLE CASSEROLE   *4 to 6 servings*

1 pint oysters
3 tablespoons butter
3 tablespoons finely chopped onion
2 tablespoons finely minced green pepper
3 tablespoons all-purpose flour
1¼ cups milk

Salt and freshly ground black pepper
¼ teaspoon cayenne pepper
1½ cups noodles, cooked according to package directions
½ cup soft fresh bread crumbs
3 tablespoons melted butter

1. Preheat oven to moderate (350° F.).
2. Drain the oysters and reserve their liquor.
3. Heat the butter and cook the onion and green pepper in it until onion wilts. Add the flour, stirring with a wire whisk. When blended, add the milk, stirring vigorously with the whisk. When the mixture is thickened and smooth, stir in the reserved oyster liquor and season with salt and black pepper to taste and the cayenne.

4. Butter a one-and-one-half-quart casserole and add half of the noodles. Cover with oysters, sprinkle lightly with salt and pepper, and add remaining noodles. Pour the sauce over the noodles and cover with bread crumbs. Pour the melted butter over the crumbs and bake the dish for thirty minutes, or until browned.

CARAWAY NOODLE RING WITH TUNA   *6 servings*

8 ounces noodles	2 cans (6 ounces each) tuna fish
1 tablespoon caraway seeds	¾ teaspoon salt
5 tablespoons butter	Freshly ground black pepper
3 tablespoons all-purpose flour	and cayenne pepper
1 cup milk	¼ teaspoon dried thyme
¾ cup heavy cream	Parsley sprigs

1. Cook the noodles according to package directions; drain. Add the caraway seeds and two tablespoons of the butter. Toss lightly and turn into a buttered one-and-one-half-quart ring mold. Set the mold in a pan of hot water to keep warm.

2. Melt the remaining butter in a saucepan and stir in the flour. Add the milk, stirring with a wire whisk. When the mixture is thickened and smooth, add the cream. Simmer for five minutes, stirring occasionally.

3. Drain the tuna and flake it. Add it to the sauce. Add the seasonings and mix well. Turn out the noodle ring on a hot platter and fill the center with tuna and sauce. Garnish with parsley.

LINGUINE WITH WHITE CLAM SAUCE   *6 servings*

¼ cup butter	Salt and freshly ground black pepper
1 large garlic clove, finely minced	pepper
2 tablespoons all-purpose flour	1½ teaspoons dried thyme
2 cans (7 ounces each) minced clams	1½ pounds linguine, cooked *al dente* and drained
1½ cups bottled clam juice, approximately	Grated Parmesan cheese (optional)
¼ cup chopped parsley	

1. Melt the butter and sauté the garlic in it for three minutes. Blend in the flour.

2. Drain the clams, reserving them. Pour the juice from the clams into a measuring cup. Measure out two cups, adding as much additional bottled clam juice as necessary. Slowly add to the butter and flour mixture, stirring.

3. Add the parsley, salt and pepper to taste and the thyme. Bring the

mixture to a boil and simmer for ten minutes. Add the reserved clams and reheat. Serve over the linguine. Top with grated cheese if desired.

NOODLE SOUFFLÉ   *8 servings*

3 eggs, separated
½ cup melted butter
2 tablespoons sugar
1 pound creamed cottage cheese
1 cup sour cream

8 ounces medium noodles, cooked and drained
½ cup soft fresh bread crumbs
Butter

1. Preheat oven to moderate (375° F.).
2. Beat the egg yolks until light. Add the melted butter and sugar and beat until well mixed. Fold in the cottage cheese, sour cream and drained noodles.
3. Beat the egg whites until stiff and fold into the egg-yolk mixture. Place the mixture in a buttered two-quart casserole. Sprinkle the top with the bread crumbs and dot generously with butter. Bake for forty-five minutes.

TAGLIARINI   (beef and macaroni casserole)   *8 servings*

¼ cup olive oil
⅓ cup finely chopped onion
2 garlic cloves, finely minced
1½ cups diced celery
1½ pounds beef chuck, ground
1 pound fresh mushrooms, sliced
½ cup Beef Stock (page 473)
1 can (6 ounces) tomato paste
2½ cups (one 1-pound 3-ounce can) Italian-style tomatoes
2 teaspoons salt

½ teaspoon freshly ground black pepper
½ teaspoon dried orégano
½ teaspoon dried basil
8 ounces small elbow macaroni, cooked and drained
1 package (10 ounces) frozen spinach, cooked and drained
½ cup buttered soft fresh bread crumbs
⅓ cup grated Parmesan cheese

1. Heat the oil in a large heavy skillet. Sauté the onion and garlic in it until tender and golden. Add the celery and beef and cook until the meat loses its red color.
2. Add the mushrooms, stock, tomato paste, tomatoes, salt and pepper. Bring mixture to a boil and simmer for one to one and one-half hours, stirring occasionally. Add more stock if the mixture becomes too thick.
3. Preheat oven to moderate (350° F.).
4. Mix the sauce with the orégano, basil, macaroni and spinach and pour into a buttered three-quart casserole. Top with the crumbs mixed with the cheese. Bake for thirty minutes, or until bubbly hot and lightly browned.

Note: The casserole may be prepared ahead of time up to the point of baking. It should be stored in the refrigerator. When ready to proceed, bake the casserole for forty-five minutes to one hour, or until thoroughly heated.

MACARONI AND MEAT PUFF   *4 to 6 servings*

2 tablespoons butter
2 tablespoons finely chopped onion
2 tablespoons finely chopped green pepper
½ pound round steak, ground
Salt and freshly ground black pepper

1 cup cooked macaroni
1 tablespoon finely chopped parsley
1 cup soft fresh bread crumbs
3 egg yolks
1½ cups hot milk or half milk and half light cream
3 egg whites, beaten

1. Preheat oven to moderate (350° F.).
2. Melt the butter and cook the onion and green pepper in it until onion is translucent. Add the steak, break it up with a wooden spoon, and cook until the meat loses color. Spoon the mixture into a mixing bowl. Add salt and pepper to taste.
3. Add the macaroni, parsley, bread crumbs and egg yolks to the meat. Pour in the hot milk, then add half of the egg whites. Stir quickly but thoroughly. Gradually fold in the remaining egg whites.
4. Pour the mixture into a buttered two-quart casserole. Bake the mixture for about forty-five minutes, or until it is set.

ALMOND AND MACARONI CASSEROLE   *6 to 8 servings*

1 pound round steak
1 pound pork chops
2 tablespoons olive oil
2 garlic cloves, finely minced
½ cup chopped onion
4 cups canned Italian tomatoes
1 can (6 ounces) tomato paste
Salt and freshly ground black pepper

1 teaspoon dried basil
½ teaspoon dried orégano (optional)
½ cup blanched almonds
1 pound macaroni, cooked according to package directions
1 cup grated Parmesan or Romano cheese

1. Preheat oven to moderate (350° F.).
2. Cut the steak into four pieces. Brown the steak and the pork chops in the olive oil and add the garlic and onion to the skillet. Cook until the onion is golden. Remove the meats and vegetables from the skillet.
3. Add the tomatoes, tomato paste, salt and pepper to taste, and the herbs to the skillet and bring to a boil. Return the meats and vegetables to the skillet and simmer until tender.

4. Meanwhile, place the almonds on a baking sheet and toast in the oven, stirring occasionally.

5. Put the meats and almonds through a meat grinder.

6. Arrange alternate layers of macaroni, sauce, meat and grated cheese in a buttered casserole. Repeat until the casserole is filled, ending with a layer of cheese and tomato sauce. Bake, covered, for thirty minutes.

MEXICAN MACARONI CASSEROLE   *4 to 6 servings*

1 pound pork sausage	2 tablespoons sugar
¾ cup diced onions	1 tablespoon chili powder
¾ cup diced green peppers	1 teaspoon salt
3½ cups canned tomatoes	8 ounces elbow macaroni
2 cups sour cream	

1. In a large skillet brown the sausage, onions and green peppers. Drain off excess fat.

2. Stir in the tomatoes, sour cream, sugar, chili powder and salt. Add the macaroni, cover the skillet, and simmer for about thirty minutes, until the macaroni is tender.

The most popular form of pasta is spaghetti in one form or another. It is one of the easiest of dishes to prepare. Add a few drops of oil to the kettle of boiling water to keep the strands from sticking together or onto the bottom of the kettle. Do not overcook the spaghetti, but cook it just to the al dente stage, the point at which the pasta becomes tender yet remains a little resilient to the bite.

Everything connected with the cooking and serving of spaghetti must be piping hot. It must be cooked in vigorously boiling water, drained immediately, poured onto an oven-hot platter, and served with a steaming sauce on plates hot enough to scorch the fingers.

SPAGHETTI WITH BACON AND MUSHROOM SAUCE
4 servings

8 slices of bacon, cut into small cubes	½ cup dry white wine or dry vermouth
¼ cup butter	Salt and freshly ground black pepper
1 cup thinly sliced mushrooms	
2 cups canned tomatoes, preferably Italian plum tomatoes, drained and chopped	¼ teaspoon crushed red pepper
	1 pound spaghetti, cooked and drained
¼ cup finely chopped parsley	

In a kettle large enough to hold six quarts of water with room to spare, bring the six quarts of water to a full rolling boil. Add one tablespoon salt. Add the spaghetti, using a long-handled, two-pronged fork to bend it into the water.

Stir constantly. As the pasta begins to soften, fold it gingerly over and over in the water. Continue this action until the water boils again.

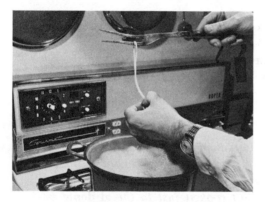

Stir the spaghetti from the bottom frequently. Occasionally lift up a strand and test it with the fingers or bite into it.

As soon as the pasta is done, add a cup of cold water at once. This will stop the cooking process and keep the pasta from getting mushy.

Drain the spaghetti immediately into a colander. Return it to the kettle and add butter or oil. Stir to coat all the strands.

1. Cook the bacon in a skillet until it is rendered of most of its fat. Pour off all but one tablespoon of the fat and add the butter. Cook the mushrooms in it, stirring, until wilted.

2. Add the tomatoes, parsley, wine, salt and pepper to taste and the red pepper to the skillet. Simmer for thirty minutes.

3. Taste the sauce and, if desired, add more salt. Combine the sauce with the spaghetti and serve immediately.

CHICKEN-LIVER AND MUSHROOM SPAGHETTI   *6 servings*

¼ cup butter
1 onion, finely chopped
½ cup finely chopped celery
2 garlic cloves, finely minced
½ bay leaf
¼ teaspoon dried thyme
    Cayenne pepper
2 cups Italian plum tomatoes, chopped

½ teaspoon sugar
½ pound chicken livers, trimmed and quartered
1 cup thinly sliced mushrooms
2 tablespoons all-purpose flour
1 cup Beef or Chicken Stock (pages 473 and 475)
1 pound spaghetti

1. Melt half of the butter in a saucepan and add the onion, celery and garlic. Cook, stirring, until onion is translucent. Add the bay leaf, thyme, cayenne pepper to taste, tomatoes and sugar. Simmer, stirring occasionally, for about thirty minutes.

2. Meanwhile, heat the remaining butter and cook the chicken livers and mushrooms in it, stirring, until chicken livers are lightly browned.

3. Sprinkle with flour and stir in the stock. Bring to a boil. When thickened and smooth, add the mixture to the tomato sauce. Continue to cook for fifteen minutes.

4. Cook the spaghetti according to package directions and serve hot with the sauce.

PAULINE TRIGÈRE'S MUSHROOM SPAGHETTI   *6 servings*

4 medium onions
6 tablespoons butter
2 pounds fresh mushrooms, sliced
1½ teaspoons salt

Freshly ground black pepper
¼ teaspoon freshly grated nutmeg
1 cup heavy cream
1 pound spaghetti

1. Cut the onions into very thin slices. Melt half of the butter in a heavy skillet and add the onions. Cook, stirring, until the onions have a delicate brown color.

2. Cover the skillet and cook the onions for one hour over very low heat. Stir occasionally.

3. In a second skillet melt the remaining butter and sauté the mushrooms in it until tender. Season with salt and pepper to taste and add to the onions.

4. Add the nutmeg and keep the sauce hot until ready to serve. Five minutes before serving add the cream and heat, but do not boil or the sauce will curdle.

5. Cook the spaghetti according to package directions and mix thoroughly with the sauce at the last minute. Serve hot, with grated Parmesan cheese if desired.

SPAGHETTI WITH MEAT BALLS   *4 servings*

½ pound beef, pork or veal, ground
½ teaspoon salt
  Freshly ground black pepper
1 cup finely chopped onions
1 garlic clove, finely minced
¼ pound mushrooms, sliced
¼ cup olive oil

1 can (6 ounces) tomato paste
1½ cups water
1 tablespoon chopped fresh basil or
  1 teaspoon dried basil
½ bay leaf
½ pound spaghetti or vermicelli
½ cup grated Parmesan cheese

1. Combine the meat with salt and pepper to taste but do not overwork it. Shape the meat into balls about one inch in diameter.

2. Cook the meat balls, onions, garlic and mushrooms in the olive oil, shaking the pan gently so that the meat balls will cook on all sides without breaking. When the onions are golden yellow, add the tomato paste, water, basil and bay leaf. Simmer for about thirty minutes, until the sauce is thickened.

3. Cook the spaghetti according to package directions; drain. Dress it with the meat balls and sauce and serve the grated cheese separately.

SPAGHETTI WITH CRABMEAT   *4 to 6 servings*

½ cup butter
½ cup chopped onion
½ cup chopped celery
2 garlic cloves, finely minced
2 tablespoons finely chopped parsley
2 fresh tomatoes, peeled, seeded and
  chopped
1 cup tomato sauce

  Salt and freshly ground black
  pepper
1 teaspoon paprika, or more
1 pound crabmeat, picked over to
  remove bits of shell and cartilage
1 pound spaghetti
  Grated Parmesan cheese

1. Heat the butter in a saucepan. Add the onion, celery and garlic. Cook until onion is wilted. Add the parsley, tomatoes, tomato sauce, salt and pepper to taste and the paprika. Simmer for twenty minutes, stirring occasionally.

2. Add crabmeat and heat thoroughly.

3. Cook the spaghetti according to package directions; drain. Dress the spaghetti with the sauce and serve the cheese separately.

SPAGHETTI ALLA CARBONARA   *6 servings*

6 slices of bacon, cut into ½-inch strips
1 cup 2-inch strips of prosciutto or baked ham
2 egg yolks

1 cup grated Parmesan cheese
1 pound spaghetti, cooked and drained
1 or 2 white truffles, thinly sliced (optional)

1. Sauté the bacon in a skillet until bacon is lightly browned and crisp. Do not drain the bacon fat. Add the prosciutto or baked ham and cook for three to five minutes longer, until the ham is lightly browned.

2. Mix the egg yolks with one-quarter cup of the cheese. Toss the spaghetti with the egg mixture.

3. Add the bacon and ham and, if desired, the truffles. Toss again. Sprinkle with the remaining cheese or serve cheese separately.

SHRIMP AND CHEESE SPAGHETTI   *4 servings*

½ cup chopped onion
3 tablespoons butter
¼ cup chopped green pepper
2¼ cups cooked tomatoes
1½ teaspoons salt
¼ teaspoon paprika

1 teaspoon Worcestershire sauce
4 ounces spaghetti, cooked according to package directions
½ pound cooked fresh shrimp
1 cup grated Parmesan cheese

1. Preheat oven to moderate (350° F.).

2. Cook the onion in the butter until the onion is light yellow. Add the green pepper, tomatoes, and seasonings. Cook slowly for ten minutes.

3. Add the spaghetti and shrimp and half of the grated cheese. Pour into a casserole and sprinkle with the remaining cheese. Bake for about twenty minutes, until the cheese is melted.

Stuffed noodle dumplings appear in four cuisines that are otherwise unrelated. The four dishes are the wonton *of China, the* pelmeny *of Russia, the* kreplach *of Jewish cookery, and the* ravioli *of Italy. Each of the dishes is made with a wafer-thin dough that is used to envelop such foods as meat or cheese. The dumplings are then simmered in broth or water and are served either as soup garnish or with a sauce. All of these dishes are delicious and hearty and are particularly suited to winter menus.*

357

NOODLE DOUGH FOR DUMPLINGS   *About 1 pound*

Although the ingredients for this dough are similar to those for home-made noodles, the method of preparing the dough is different.

3 cups sifted all-purpose flour   4 eggs

1. Place the flour on a board and make a depression in the center. Break the eggs into the hole.

2. With the hands, work the eggs into the flour until dough forms a ball. Knead the dough until it is smooth and elastic. Let it stand, covered with a towel, for one hour.

3. Roll the dough out on a lightly floured board until it is very thin. Stretch it over the rolling pin until it is paper-thin and translucent.

WONTON   *4 servings, 16 wonton*

½ pound Noodle Dough for Dump-   ½ teaspoon sugar
    lings (above)   ¼ teaspoon monosodium glutamate
½ pound pork, ground   3 quarts boiling water
1 tablespoon dry sherry   ½ cup cold water
2 tablespoons soy sauce   3 cups Chicken Stock (page 475)
1½ teaspoons salt   1 scallion, chopped

1. Roll out the dough until it is paper-thin. Cut into four-inch squares.

2. Mix together the pork, sherry, one tablespoon of the soy sauce, one-half teaspoon of the salt, the sugar and monosodium glutamate.

3. Place one teaspoon of the mixture in the middle of each square. Fold over at the center, pressing the edges together. Fold lengthwise again. Pull the corners one over the other and press them together with a little water. When properly folded, the wonton resembles a nurse's cap.

4. Drop the wrapped wonton into the boiling water and bring to a boil again. Wontons will rise to the surface. Add the cold water and bring to a boil again to make sure that the filling is cooked. Drain and reserve.

5. Heat the stock. Add the remaining soy sauce and salt. Drop the reserved wontons and the scallion into the broth and serve as soup.

SIBERIAN PELMENY
3 dozen 3-inch pelmeny, 5 dozen 2-inch pelmeny

1 pound Noodle Dough for Dump-   ½ teaspoon salt
    lings (above)   ¼ teaspoon freshly ground black
¾ pound beef round, ground   pepper
⅓ cup chopped kidney fat   4 cups Beef Stock (page 473)
½ onion, finely chopped   1 egg white

1. Roll out the dough until it is paper-thin. Cut into two- or three-inch circles.

2. Mix together the beef, kidney fat and onion and put through the fine blade of a food grinder. Season with salt and pepper and moisten with one or two tablespoons of the stock.

3. Place one teaspoon of the filling in the center of each circle, moisten the edges with the egg white, and fold over to form a crescent shape.

4. Bring remaining stock to a rolling boil and drop in the pelmeny. Cook for about fifteen minutes. The pelmeny may be eaten in the soup or served separately with melted butter or sour cream.

KREPLACH   *About 7 dozen*

½ pound Noodle Dough for Dump-   1 cup Cheese Filling (see below)
  lings (page 358)   4 cups vegetable stock

1. Roll out the dough and cut it into one-and-one-half-inch squares. Place one-half teaspoon of the cheese filling in the center of each square and pinch together into triangular puffs.

2. Bring the stock to a rolling boil. Drop in the kreplach and cook for ten to fifteen minutes. When cooked, kreplach will rise to the surface. Serve in the soup.

CHEESE FILLING: *About 1 cup*

1 cup ricotta or pot cheese   Dash of freshly ground black
1 egg   pepper
¼ teaspoon salt   2 tablespoons fine dry bread crumbs

Mix all the ingredients together with a fork.

RAVIOLI   *6 dozen 2-inch ravioli, 12 dozen 1-inch ravioli*

1½ chicken breasts, boned   ¾ cup milk, scalded
¼ cup butter   ¼ cup heavy cream
 3 chicken livers   Salt and freshly ground white
 5 slices of prosciutto or thin slices   pepper
   of cooked ham   1 pound Noodle Dough for Dump-
½ cup grated Parmesan cheese   lings (page 358)
 2 tablespoons all-purpose flour   3 quarts boiling water

1. Sauté the chicken breasts in half of the butter until lightly browned.

2. Sauté the chicken livers briefly in the same skillet. Grind the chicken breasts, livers and ham, using the finest blade of a food grinder. Add the cheese; mix.

3. Melt the remaining butter in a small pan and stir in the flour. Gradually stir in the milk and bring to a boil, stirring. Add the cream and season with salt and pepper to taste.

4. Add enough of the sauce to the chicken mixture to moisten it.

5. Roll out dough until it is paper-thin. Cut into one- or two-inch squares or circles. Place one teaspoon of the filling in the middle of each piece of dough, top with another piece, and seal the edges.

6. Drop ravioli into the boiling water. Cook one-inch ravioli for eight minutes, two-inch ravioli for about twelve minutes.

Note: Large ravioli may be served with tomato sauce and freshly grated Parmesan cheese. Small ravioli may be served in the same way, or as a garnish for soup.

VEAL FILLING FOR RAVIOLI   *Enough for 8 dozen ravioli*

2 pounds braised veal
¾ pound cooked fresh salami (available in Italian markets)
1 pound spinach, cooked, pressed dry and chopped

2 eggs
2 tablespoons grated Parmesan cheese
Salt and freshly ground black pepper

1. Grind the veal and salami. Put the mixture in a mixing bowl and add the spinach.

2. Add the eggs, cheese, and salt and pepper to taste. Blend the mixture. Use to fill ravioli.

STUFFED MANICOTTI   *4 to 6 servings*

¾ pound beef round, ground
1 cup cream-style, small-curd cottage cheese
1 garlic clove, finely minced
2 teaspoons salt
2 cups canned tomatoes
1 can (6 ounces) tomato paste

2 teaspoons dried basil
¼ teaspoon freshly ground black pepper
18 manicotti (about 8 ounces)
2 tablespoons grated Parmesan cheese

1. Brown the meat in a skillet, remove from the heat, and add the cottage cheese, garlic and one teaspoon of the salt. Cover and refrigerate while preparing the sauce.

2. Combine the tomatoes, tomato paste, basil, pepper and remaining salt in a pan. Bring to a boil and simmer gently, uncovered, for about thirty minutes, until slightly thickened.

3. Meanwhile, cook the manicotti in boiling salted water for about twenty minutes, until almost tender. Drain and rinse with cold water until cool enough to handle.

4. Preheat oven to moderate (350° F.).

5. Fill each of the manicotti loosely with some of the beef and cheese filling. Arrange in a lightly greased shallow baking dish. Pour the tomato sauce over all. Sprinkle with the Parmesan cheese and bake for twenty-five to thirty minutes, or until hot and bubbly.

CHICKEN CANNELLONI   *6 servings*

3½ cups Mushroom and Cheese Sauce (page 485)
3½ cups Tomato Sauce II (page 494)
1 Poached Chicken (page 271)
½ teaspoon grated nutmeg, or more
½ cup finely chopped fresh parsley
1½ cups sifted all-purpose flour
2 eggs
2 cups grated Parmesan cheese

1. Prepare the sauces and the chicken.

2. Preheat oven to moderate (350° F.).

3. Remove the skin and bones of the chicken. Grind the chicken meat. Add the nutmeg and parsley and one-half cup of the mushroom and cheese sauce. Mix well with a spoon and set aside.

4. Combine half of the tomato sauce with the remaining mushroom and cheese sauce and blend well. Reserve the remaining tomato sauce.

5. Place the flour on a board and make a well in the center. Break the eggs into the well. With the hands work the mixture until the dough forms a ball. Knead until smooth and elastic. Let the dough stand, covered with a towel, for one hour.

6. Roll out half of the dough on a lightly floured board until it is very thin and almost transparent. Cut the dough into squares (4 by 4 inches). Roll out the rest of the dough in the same fashion and cut it into squares. Or the noodles may be made with a home noodle machine.

7. Drop the noodle squares into a kettle of boiling salted water and simmer for two or three minutes. Drain immediately and rinse under cold water.

8. Arrange the squares on a flat surface. Spoon chicken filling along one edge of each square. Roll the dough around the filling to enclose it, making a cigar-shaped roll. Use the same amount of filling for each square so all the rolls will be of the same size.

9. Spoon a layer of the combined sauces over the bottom of a large shallow baking dish. Arrange the stuffed cannelloni over the sauce and cover with the remaining combined sauces. Sprinkle one-half cup or more of the cheese over the top.

10. Bake the cannelloni for thirty minutes, or longer, until the top of the dish is golden brown. Serve with the reserved tomato sauce and the remaining cheese.

STUFFING FOR PASTA   *Enough for 1 pound pasta*

1 medium onion, chopped
1 garlic clove, minced
2 tablespoons butter
1 pound beef, chopped
½ pound ricotta or cottage cheese
1 cup finely chopped mozzarella or Gruyère cheese
¼ cup grated Parmesan cheese
½ cup coarsely chopped pistachios or blanched almonds
2 eggs
1½ teaspoons salt
¼ teaspoon freshly ground black pepper
¼ teaspoon dried basil or orégano

Brown the onion and garlic in the butter, add the meat, and cook until the meat has lost its red color. Add all remaining ingredients and mix thoroughly, using the fingers. Use to stuff manicotti, zitoni, tufoli, or rigatoni.

Another example of a filled dough is the Chinese dish we call "egg roll." Chinese think of these as "spring rolls" because the rolls are a dish served at the New Year, and the old-style Chinese New Year coincided roughly with the appearance of spring.

EGG–SPRING ROLL DOUGH I   *8 to 10 rolls*

2 eggs, lightly beaten
½ cup water
½ teaspoon salt
¾ cup sifted all-purpose flour
Shortening

1. Reserve one teaspoon of the eggs for sealing rolls. Mix remainder of eggs with the water and add to the salt and flour. Beat until smooth.
2. Heat a heavy five-inch skillet slowly. Brush with a light coating of shortening. While rotating the pan in the left hand, pour in two to three tablespoons of the batter to give a very thin layer. Cook until set but not browned on the bottom. Transfer to a damp towel. Repeat process until all the batter is used.
3. Place one tablespoon filling (see recipes below) on each round roll, tucking in the sides and sealing the ends with the reserved egg.
4. Fry the rolls, two or three at a time, in deep fat heated to 350° F. on a frying thermometer, until golden brown on all sides. Drain on paper towels.

EGG–SPRING ROLL DOUGH II   *16 rolls*

1 egg, lightly beaten
2 cups sifted all-purpose flour
1 teaspoon salt
½ cup ice water

1. Reserve one teaspoon of the egg for sealing rolls. Combine the remaining egg and other ingredients to make a dough. Cover with a towel and allow to stand for ten minutes. Knead until smooth and elastic. Divide the dough into sixteen pieces and roll each out into a very thin six-inch square.

2. Place one tablespoon filling (see recipes below) on each square, tucking in the sides and sealing the ends with the reserved egg.

3. Fry the rolls, two or three at a time, in deep fat heated to 350° F. on a frying thermometer until golden brown on all sides. Drain on paper towels.

GRACE CHU'S SHRIMP FILLING FOR EGG ROLLS
Enough for 16 rolls

½ pound raw shrimp
1 teaspoon sherry
2 teaspoons salt
½ teaspoon monosodium glutamate
½ teaspoon cornstarch
½ pound fresh bean sprouts (available in Chinatown) or 1 cup canned bean sprouts

3 tablespoons peanut oil
4 cups finely diced celery
½ teaspoon sugar
⅓ cup finely chopped mushrooms

1. Shell, devein, rinse, and dry the shrimp. Cut them into one-half-inch pieces. Combine them with the sherry, one-half teaspoon salt, one-quarter teaspoon monosodium glutamate and the cornstarch. Set aside.

2. If canned bean sprouts are used, drain and rinse them in cold water two or three times. If fresh bean sprouts are used, wash and drain them.

3. Heat one tablespoon of the oil in a skillet and cook the shrimp mixture over high heat until shrimp just turn pink. Remove from heat and set aside.

4. In another skillet heat the remaining oil. Cook the celery in it, stirring, for about two minutes. Add remaining salt and monosodium glutamate and the sugar. Mix well. Cook for five minutes over medium heat.

5. Add the mushrooms and mix thoroughly. Add bean sprouts and blend. Add the shrimp mixture and turn mixture into a colander. Cool before using as a filling for egg rolls.

SHRIMP AND PORK FILLING FOR EGG ROLLS
Enough for 15 to 20 rolls

1 cup finely chopped raw shrimp
1 teaspoon sherry
1 tablespoon soy sauce
¼ teaspoon monosodium glutamate
1 tablespoon peanut oil or corn oil
½ cup thinly sliced roast pork

½ cup finely chopped green onions
3 water chestnuts, finely diced
6 mushrooms, thinly sliced or chopped (see note)
Salt

1. Combine the shrimp with the sherry, soy sauce and monosodium glutamate. Heat the oil in a heavy skillet and cook the shrimp, stirring, until they turn pink.

2. Blend the shrimp with the remaining ingredients and use the mixture as a filling for egg rolls.

Note: Fresh mushrooms may be used in this recipe, but dried Chinese mushrooms, available in Chinese markets, are preferable. To prepare the mushrooms, cover them with hot but not boiling water and let stand for fifteen to twenty minutes. Before using the mushrooms, drain and squeeze them to remove most of the water.

STEAMED CHINESE DUMPLINGS   *18 to 24 dumplings*

1¼ pounds fresh lean pork, ground
1 can (5 ounces) water chestnuts, finely chopped
1 teaspoon soy sauce
½ teaspoon sesame oil
½ teaspoon cornstarch

2 scallions, including green parts, finely chopped
1½ cups wheat starch
½ cup tapioca flour
1½ cups boiling water

1. Combine the pork, water chestnuts, soy sauce, sesame oil, cornstarch and scallions, and refrigerate.

2. Sift together the wheat starch and tapioca flour into a large bowl. Add the boiling water gradually, stirring. Knead the dough with a little oil until firm. Let stand for ten minutes. Lightly oil a board.

3. Break off the dough in small pieces and roll into rounds about three inches in diameter. Brush one side of a flat cleaver with a little oil and flatten each ball.

4. Spoon two or three tablespoons of filling into the center of each circle, then bring up the edges of the dough to form a pastry cup open at the top. Press around the sides of the "cup" with a dinner knife to give a crimped effect.

5. Arrange the dumplings on a lightly oiled plate or rack and set the plate on a bowl in a large kettle with two to three inches of boiling water in the bottom.

6. Steam the dumplings for about twenty minutes. Serve with hot Mustard Sauce (page 486) and apricot or plum sauce thinned with a little water.

· ·

CHAPTER SEVEN

VEGETABLES

Medley of summer vegetables

One of the highest compliments that has been paid to French cooks is the thought that they could make a thistle palatable. Appropriately enough, the artichoke, much esteemed in French cuisine, is a member of the thistle family. This unusual vegetable is said to be one of the oldest foods known to man; it has been known and cultivated in the Mediterranean region for thousands of years.

COOKING WHOLE ARTICHOKES

Wash six artichokes. Cut off the stems of the artichokes with a sharp knife, leaving flat bottoms that will permit the artichokes to sit upright on a plate. Rub the bottoms with lemon juice. Break off the tough leaves around the base and trim the tips of the other leaves with scissors. Rub all cut portions with lemon juice. Drop the artichokes into a mixing bowl filled with two tablespoons vinegar or lemon juice for each four cups water.

Bring eight quarts of water to a boil in a stainless-steel kettle. Add about half a cup of salt and then add the drained artichokes. Cover with cheesecloth and simmer, uncovered, for about forty minutes, or until the leaves can easily be pulled off and the bottoms are tender. Turn the artichokes upside down and drain immediately.

ARTICHOKES WITH BUTTER SAUCE *4 servings*

4 large artichokes
½ lemon
   Salt
3 tablespoons lemon juice

½ cup melted butter
½ teaspoon dry mustard
   Dash of Tabasco

1. Wash and trim the artichokes and rub all cut portions with the lemon half.

2. Cook the artichokes in salted water to cover with two tablespoons of the lemon juice. When artichokes are tender, turn them upside down to drain.

3. Combine the remaining ingredients and serve hot with the hot artichokes.

MARINATED ARTICHOKES   *6 servings*

6 small artichokes	2 parsley sprigs
2 garlic cloves	Pinch of dried thyme
1 teaspoon salt	Juice of 1 lemon
2 cups water	3 tablespoons olive oil
1 celery rib with leaves	10 peppercorns
1 bay leaf	

1. Trim the artichokes and cut off the sharp points with kitchen shears.

2. Mash the garlic with the salt and place in a kettle with the artichokes and water.

3. Cut the celery rib into halves and tie it into a neat bundle with the bay leaf and parsley. Add to the kettle along with the remaining ingredients. Bring to a boil and simmer until artichokes are tender, twenty minutes or longer, depending on the size of the artichokes. Let the artichokes cool in the marinade. Discard the celery bundle. Serve artichokes well chilled, each with a little of the marinade.

STUFFING ARTICHOKES

1. Prepare the artichokes as in Cooking Whole Artichokes (page 367). Reserve the cut-off stems. They may be peeled and cooked and, when they are tender, used in the filling. Sprinkle all cut portions with lemon juice.

2. Using a sharp knife or scissors, cut off the top third of the vegetables. Open the center leaves carefully. Turn the artichokes over on a flat surface and press down firmly at the base to spread the leaves open further.

3. Turn the artichokes right side up and pull the yellow and yellow-white leaves from the centers. Using a sturdy spoon, carefully scrape and pull all of the fuzzy and prickly portion from the hearts of the artichokes. Sprinkle the scraped hollows with additional lemon juice.

4. Stand the artichokes in a deep kettle or saucepan so that they fit snugly together, or tie with soft strings so that they retain their shape. Add boiling water to cover and one quarter-cup lemon juice and two tablespoons salt for each two quarts water. Cook, covered, for twenty to thirty minutes, or until partly tender.

5. Using two spoons, remove artichokes from the water and turn upside down to drain. When partly cool, fill the centers with stuffing and bake as directed.

ARTICHOKES STUFFED WITH VEAL AND PEPPERS
4 servings

4 artichokes
¼ cup olive oil
1½ pounds veal cutlet, diced
1 large green pepper, diced
1 medium onion, chopped
1 garlic clove, crushed

1 teaspoon salt
¼ teaspoon freshly ground black pepper
2 medium tomatoes, diced
⅓ cup grated Parmesan cheese

1. Prepare the artichokes for stuffing (page 368) and cook until tender in salted water to which lemon juice has been added. Drain, but keep warm.

2. Meanwhile, heat the oil in a skillet. Add the veal and cook over medium heat, stirring occasionally, until the meat is browned on all sides. Add the green pepper, onion, garlic, salt and pepper. Mix well. Cook for ten minutes, stirring occasionally. Add the tomatoes and cheese. Mix well. Cover and cook over low heat, stirring occasionally, for twenty to twenty-five minutes.

3. Fill the drained cooked artichokes with the veal mixture and serve hot.

ARTICHOKES STUFFED WITH PORK AND PINE NUTS
4 servings

4 medium artichokes
1 tablespoon shortening
¾ pound lean pork, ground
¼ cup finely minced onion
1 cup soft fresh bread crumbs
2 tablespoons chopped parsley
½ teaspoon salt
¼ teaspoon freshly ground black pepper

¼ teaspoon grated nutmeg
3 tablespoons pine nuts, finely chopped
1 egg, lightly beaten
1 tablespoon lemon juice
Oil

1. Prepare the artichokes for stuffing (page 368) and cook until partly tender in salted water to which lemon juice has been added. Drain.

2. Preheat oven to moderate (350° F.).

3. Melt the shortening in a skillet and sauté the pork and onion until lightly browned. Remove from the heat; add the bread crumbs, parsley, salt, pepper, nutmeg, pine nuts and egg.

4. Pile the stuffing into the prepared artichokes and tie them to retain their shape.

5. Place them in a small baking dish and pour boiling water around to a depth of one inch. Add the lemon juice to the water. Brush the artichokes generously with oil. Cover with foil and bake for thirty minutes.

COOKING ARTICHOKE BOTTOMS

4 large artichokes
1 lemon, halved

2 teaspoons flour
1½ teaspoons salt

1. Trim off the tough outer leaves of the artichokes. Using a sharp kitchen knife, slice off the stems of the artichokes. Immediately rub cut surface with the lemon. Neatly slice through the vegetables parallel to the base to leave an artichoke bottom less than one inch thick. Immediately rub cut surface with lemon.

2. Squeeze the remaining lemon juice into a saucepan. Add the flour and blend well with a wire whisk to make a paste. Add water, a little at a time, stirring until flour is thinned and well blended. Drop the artichoke bottoms into the pan and add enough water to cover them. Add salt. Bring to a boil, cover, and simmer for twenty-five minutes or longer, until artichokes are tender. Drain.

3. When the artichokes are cool enough to handle, remove the fuzzy "choke" from the center by pulling and scraping with a spoon. If artichoke bottoms are to be served hot, they may be reheated in hot salted water before serving.

ARTICHOKES CLAMART   8 servings

8 artichoke bottoms, freshly cooked
and hot

1 cup puréed green peas
¼ cup melted butter

1. Preheat oven to hot (450° F.).
2. Arrange the artichoke bottoms in a buttered shallow baking dish. Spoon a heaping tablespoon of puréed peas into the center of each. Pour the butter over the purée.
3. Bake until artichokes are thoroughly heated and peas are slightly brown on top.

ARTICHOKES WITH FOIE GRAS   8 servings

2 tablespoons butter
8 artichoke bottoms, freshly cooked
and hot

8 tablespoons foie gras, approximately
1 cup Hollandaise Sauce (page 485)

1. Preheat oven to hot (450° F.).
2. Melt the butter in a shallow baking dish in the oven. When butter is melted, add the artichoke bottoms. Cover with aluminum foil. Bake for three to five minutes, or just until bottoms are thoroughly heated.
3. Remove the foil and spoon one tablespoon of foie gras into each bottom. Spoon enough hot hollandaise sauce over each to mask the foie gras and fill the cavity.

4. Immediately place the dish under the broiler and cook just until a brown glaze forms on the hollandaise. Do not overcook. Serve with buttered toast as a first course or as a vegetable dish.

ARTICHOKES MOCK BENEDICT   *4 servings*

4 rounds of buttered toast or toasted
   English muffins
4 small slices of ham, preferably
   Smithfield
4 artichoke bottoms, freshly cooked
   and hot

4 eggs, poached
2 cups Cheese Sauce (page 484)
Paprika
Watercress for garnish

Place a toast round on each of four hot plates and top each with a slice of ham. Place a cooked artichoke bottom on the ham and fill the center with a poached egg. Spoon cheese sauce over each serving and sprinkle with paprika. Garnish with watercress and serve immediately.

ALCACHOFAS CON SETAS ITURBI   *6 servings*
(artichoke hearts and mushrooms Iturbi)

2 packages (9 ounces each) frozen
   artichoke hearts
¼ cup butter
1 pound unpeeled mushrooms, sliced
½ cup Chicken Stock (page 475) or
   half sherry and half stock

Salt and freshly ground black
pepper
Pinch of dried orégano

1. Defrost the artichoke hearts by heating them with the butter in a skillet over low heat.
2. Add the mushrooms when the artichoke hearts are tender. Add the stock and cook for ten minutes or less, until the mushrooms are done. Season with salt and pepper to taste and orégano.

ASPARAGUS WITH BROWN BUTTER SAUCE   *6 servings*

½ cup butter
3 tablespoons lemon juice, or more

2 pounds fresh asparagus, steamed
Chopped fresh parsley for garnish

Heat the butter in a small saucepan until it just starts to turn a hazelnut brown. Add the lemon juice and pour the sauce over the hot asparagus. Garnish with chopped parsley.

ASPARAGUS, MILANESE STYLE   *6 servings*

2 pounds fresh asparagus
1½ teaspoons salt
2 tablespoons butter

¼ teaspoon freshly ground black pepper
¼ cup grated Parmesan cheese

1. Preheat oven to moderate (350° F.).

2. Wash the asparagus; remove the hard ends of the stalks and the scales. Place in a saucepan with one-half inch of boiling water and one teaspoon of the salt. Bring to the boiling point and cook, uncovered, for five minutes. Drain.

3. Place a layer of the cooked asparagus in a buttered one-quart casserole. Dot with butter and sprinkle with black pepper. Repeat, using remaining asparagus, butter and black pepper. Sprinkle the top with remaining salt and the Parmesan cheese. Bake for five minutes. Serve hot.

ASPARAGUS AND EGGPLANT MORNAY   *6 servings*

6 large slices of eggplant, ½ inch thick
3 teaspoons salt
⅛ teaspoon freshly ground black pepper

Flour
½ cup salad oil
2 pounds fresh asparagus
Sauce Mornay (page 484)

1. Sprinkle the eggplant slices with two teaspoons of the salt and the black pepper. Dust lightly with flour. Sauté in the oil, turning to brown both sides. Arrange on a serving platter.

2. Cut the asparagus stalks into four-inch lengths and wash thoroughly. Tie them in six bundles. Place in a saucepan with one-half inch of boiling water and the remaining salt. Cover and cook for ten to fifteen minutes. Drain.

3. Place a bundle of asparagus over each slice of sautéed eggplant. Serve with Sauce Mornay.

ASPARAGUS WITH TOMATO SAUCE AND SOUR CREAM
4 servings

½ cup chopped onion
1 garlic clove, finely minced
¼ cup butter or olive oil
2 celery ribs, coarsely chopped
½ cup coarsely chopped green pepper
2 large tomatoes, peeled and chopped

½ teaspoon dried thyme
1 bay leaf
Salt and freshly ground black pepper
1 tablespoon capers
24 asparagus stalks, trimmed
½ cup sour cream

1. In a saucepan cook the onion and garlic in half of the butter until golden brown.

2. In a small skillet cook the celery and green pepper in the remaining butter for about two minutes, stirring occasionally. The vegetables should remain crisp.

3. Add the tomatoes, the celery and green pepper to the saucepan containing the onion and garlic. Season with the thyme, bay leaf, and salt and pepper to taste. Simmer, stirring occasionally, for about twenty minutes, until thickened slightly. Add the capers. Remove and discard the bay leaf.

4. Place the asparagus in a skillet with cold salted water to cover. Bring to a boil and simmer for ten to twelve minutes, until the asparagus is barely tender. Drain.

5. To serve, place the asparagus on warm dinner plates and spoon the sauce over each serving. Top with sour cream and serve immediately.

ASPARAGUS PUDDING   *6 servings*

2 cups 1-inch pieces of asparagus
2 cups milk
½ teaspoon salt
  Dash of cayenne pepper

  Dash of grated nutmeg
3 eggs, slightly beaten
2 tablespoons melted butter

1. Cook the asparagus in boiling salted water until tender. Drain.
2. Preheat oven to moderate (350° F.).
3. Add the milk, salt, cayenne and nutmeg to the eggs. Add asparagus and butter and pour the mixture into a baking dish. Set the baking dish in a pan of water and bake for forty to fifty minutes, until the custard is set.

ASPARAGUS CHEESE PUDDING   *8 servings*

1½ pounds fresh asparagus
3 slices of white bread
1 cup shredded sharp Cheddar cheese
2 eggs, lightly beaten

2 cups milk
1 teaspoon salt
½ teaspoon freshly ground black pepper
1 tablespoon butter

1. Preheat oven to moderate (325° F.).
2. Wash the asparagus and cut two-inch tips from eight of the stalks. Reserve for use later. Cut the remaining asparagus into one-inch pieces.
3. Toast the bread and cut it into one-inch squares. Arrange alternate layers of toasted bread cubes, asparagus pieces and cheese in a buttered baking dish (10 × 6 × 2 inches). Combine the eggs, milk, salt, pepper and butter. Heat the custard mixture and pour it into the baking dish. Set the dish in a pan of hot water and bake for about one hour, until the custard is set.
4. Meanwhile, wrap the eight asparagus tips in aluminum foil and bake them until tender.

5. Arrange the asparagus tips over the top of the pudding for garnish. Serve hot.

HERBED GREEN BEANS   *4 servings*

1 pound fresh green beans, cut into 1-inch lengths
¼ cup butter
¼ cup minced onion
½ garlic clove, minced

¼ cup minced celery
¼ teaspoon dried rosemary
¼ teaspoon dried basil
¾ teaspoon salt

1. Soak the green beans in cold water for fifteen minutes.
2. Melt the butter in a one-and-one-half-quart saucepan. Sauté the onion, garlic and celery in it until tender.
3. Add the drained beans, cover, and cook over low heat for fifteen to twenty minutes. Add seasonings.

GREEN BEANS, ITALIAN STYLE   *4 servings*

1 pound whole fresh green beans or 1 package (9 ounces) frozen green beans
2 tablespoons butter

½ garlic clove, minced
½ teaspoon dried orégano
1 cup Tomato Sauce II (page 494)
Chopped parsley

1. Steam the fresh beans in a little boiling salted water, or cook the frozen beans according to package directions. Drain; keep hot.
2. Heat the butter in a saucepan and add the garlic and orégano. Cook until the garlic starts to turn golden. Add the tomato sauce and simmer for five minutes. Pour the sauce over the beans and toss well. Serve sprinkled with chopped parsley.

GREEN BEANS WITH DILL   *4 servings*

1 pound fresh green beans
2 tablespoons peanut oil
3 tablespoons butter, melted

Salt
1 teaspoon lemon juice
1 tablespoon finely chopped dill

1. Trim the beans, pinching off the tips at both ends. Break or cut the beans into two-inch lengths. Rinse the beans and drain.
2. Put the oil into a saucepan with a tight-fitting lid and add the beans. Do not add other liquid. Cover and cook over low to medium heat, shaking the saucepan frequently. Cook for fifteen to twenty minutes, until the beans are crisp-tender. Pour the beans into a vegetable dish and pour the butter over them. Add salt to taste and the lemon juice and sprinkle with the chopped dill.

CHILLED GREEN BEANS   *4 servings*

1 pound fresh green beans   1 teaspoon salt

1. Pinch off the tips of the beans. Rinse and drain the beans. Lay beans on a flat surface and cut them, a few at a time, into relatively even lengths from two to four inches, depending on the size of beans. The even lengths allow for even cooking and the finished beans have a better appearance. Tie beans securely with soft string into four bundles. Place in a saucepan.

2. Add the salt and cover with boiling water. Bring beans to a boil, cover, and simmer for five to ten minutes, until tender but still crisp. Drain beans, discarding strings. Chill. Use for salads and cold vegetable combinations.

SAMBAL GORENG BUNTJIES (green-bean sambal goreng)
4 servings

1 tablespoon vegetable oil
1 medium onion, sliced
2 garlic cloves, sliced
1 tablespoon diagonal slices of hot red pepper
1 teaspoon shrimp paste (available in Chinese markets)

1 cup Coconut Milk (page 491)
1 tablespoon sugar
2 bay leaves
Salt
2 cups 1-inch slices of green beans
1 tablespoon tamarind juice (see note)

1. Heat the oil in a saucepan and sauté the onion, garlic, red pepper and shrimp paste in it for two minutes. Add coconut milk, sugar, bay leaves and salt to taste. Bring to a boil, reduce heat, and simmer for five minutes.

2. Add the beans and simmer for twenty minutes. Two minutes before serving, add tamarind juice.

Note: To prepare tamarind juice, soak two tablespoons shelled tamarind (available in Puerto Rican markets) in one cup water for thirty minutes. Stir until dissolved. The juice may be stored in the refrigerator until ready to use.

SNAP BEANS IN CASSEROLE   *6 servings*

3 slices of bacon, chopped
½ cup chopped onion
2 cups 2-inch pieces of cooked snap beans, green or yellow
4 large tomatoes, cubed

¼ teaspoon salt
⅛ teaspoon freshly ground black pepper
¼ cup grated Parmesan cheese

1. Preheat oven to moderate (350° F.).

2. Fry the bacon and remove it from the skillet. Sauté the onion in the bacon fat until just tender.

3. Combine the onion, bacon, beans, tomatoes, salt and pepper. Place in a greased casserole, top with grated cheese, and bake until the cheese is brown.

PURÉE OF LIMA BEANS   *6 servings*

2 packages (10 ounces each) frozen large lima beans
3 tablespoons heavy cream
3 tablespoons butter
Freshly ground black pepper
Chopped parsley

1. Cook the lima beans according to package directions. Drain, reserving about one-quarter cup of the cooking liquid. Rub the beans through a food mill or blend in an electric blender. If a blender is used, blend only a small quantity of beans at a time, adding a little of the reserved liquid as necessary and stirring down occasionally with a rubber spatula.

2. Transfer the purée to the top of a double boiler and keep hot. Add the cream and butter and season with black pepper to taste. The purée should have the consistency of mashed potatoes. Serve sprinkled with chopped parsley.

Note: Other beans, such as kidney beans, black beans and navy beans may be prepared in the same way.

FRIJOLES REFRITOS (crisp fried beans)   *8 servings*

1 pound dried red kidney beans
6 cups water
1 teaspoon salt
½ cup bacon drippings or lard, approximately
2 chorizos (Spanish sausage)
4 ounces Cheddar cheese, cubed or grated

1. Pick over the beans, wash thoroughly, and cover with the water. Allow to soak overnight; or bring to a boil, simmer for two minutes, and allow to stand for one to two hours before proceeding.

2. Add the salt, bring to a boil, cover, and simmer for about two hours, or until the beans are tender. Mash the beans with a potato masher, add the drippings, and heat the mixture until all the fat is absorbed, stirring frequently.

3. Skin the sausages, break them into pieces, and fry in a small amount of drippings.

4. Add the cheese and sausages to the beans. Reheat until crisp around the edges.

FRIJOLES FRITOS (fried black beans)   *12 servings*

4 cups dried black beans
2½ quarts water
3 teaspoons salt
¾ cup ground fresh onions (about 2 medium onions)
1 tablespoon salad oil
3 tablespoons butter
3 tablespoons grated Parmesan cheese
½ teaspoon grated nutmeg
½ teaspoon freshly ground black pepper

1. Wash beans well and soak overnight in one quart of the water.

2. Drain off any water that remains after soaking overnight. Add remaining water and cook, covered, for three hours, or until beans are tender, adding the salt for the last ten minutes of cooking time. Remove beans from heat and cool.

3. Put beans through a food chopper using the coarse blade, or mash with a potato masher.

4. Sauté onions in the oil until they are translucent. Add the butter and cook for five minutes, stirring. Add to beans along with the cheese, nutmeg and pepper. Stir and cook over medium heat for ten minutes, or until beans are dry.

5. Turn into a serving dish. Garnish with grated Parmesan cheese and chopped pimiento. Serve with corn chips or tortillas.

PURÉE OF BLACK BEANS WITH SOUR CREAM
About 8 cups purée

2 cups dried black beans
6 cups water
1 large onion, chopped
1 green pepper, chopped
2 garlic cloves, minced
½ cup olive oil
1 bay leaf

1 teaspoon salt
¼ teaspoon freshly ground black pepper
3 tablespoons wine vinegar
Sliced Italian red onions
Sour cream

1. Pick over and wash the beans. Boil the beans in the water for two minutes. Remove from the heat, cover, and let stand for one to two hours.

2. Sauté until wilted the onion, pepper and garlic in the olive oil. Add to beans.

3. Add bay leaf and salt and pepper and cook, covered, for about two hours, until the beans are tender. Add water as needed to prevent sticking. Beans should be fairly dry when done.

4. Add vinegar to the beans and purée the mixture in a blender or sieve. Reheat. Serve with red onions and sour cream.

LOUBIA (savory white beans)
10 or more servings as accompaniment; 3 or 4 servings as vegetable

1 cup dried Italian *cannellini* (white kidney beans)
7 garlic cloves, peeled
1 parsley sprig
Salt
3 tablespoons olive oil
1 large tomato, unpeeled and quartered

Freshly ground black pepper
1½ tablespoons all-purpose flour
1 tablespoon ground cuminseed, or more
2 tablespoons paprika, or more

1. Soak the beans overnight in four cups water.

2. Drain the beans; add fresh water to come one inch above the beans. Add two of the garlic cloves, the parsley and two teaspoons salt. Cover and cook until the beans are tender. Remove the parsley and garlic.

3. Heat the oil and add the tomato and two more garlic cloves and cook over high heat until slightly thickened. Sprinkle with salt and pepper. Remove the garlic and stir in the flour. Stir the sauce well and add a little of the cooking liquid from the beans. Add this sauce to the beans.

4. Crush a few of the beans with the back of a spoon. Add the cumin-seed and salt and pepper to taste. Mince the remaining garlic and stir into the beans with the paprika. Serve as an accompaniment to Couscous (page 582).

NEW ENGLAND BAKED BEANS   *About 12 servings*

4 cups dried navy (pea) beans	¼ teaspoon ground ginger
1 piece (8 ounces) salt pork, streaked with lean	2 tablespoon sugar
	¼ cup molasses
1 teaspoon dry mustard	2 cups boiling water, or more
2 teaspoons salt	

1. Pick over the beans, discarding split or discolored ones and any foreign matter. Wash the beans well, cover them with water, and let stand overnight.

2. Drain the beans, cover them with fresh water, and cook slowly until the skins wrinkle when a few in a spoon are blown upon. Rinse the beans with cold water and place in a four-quart bean pot.

3. Preheat oven to slow (250° to 300° F.).

4. Pour boiling water over the salt pork, scrape the rind until white, and score in half-inch strips without cutting through the skin. Press the pork gently into the top of the beans.

5. Mix seasonings well and add one and one-half cups boiling water. Pour over beans and cover pot.

6. Bake for about nine hours, adding a little boiling water about every hour or when needed. The water should never cover the beans but should appear as tiny bubbles above the beans.

Note: If desired, an onion may be placed in the bean pot before the beans are added.

LENTILS À L'INDIENNE   *4 servings*

2 cups dried lentils	Freshly ground black pepper
1 onion, stuck with 2 cloves	1 teaspoon ground cuminseed, turmeric or curry powder
1 bay leaf	
1 teaspoon salt	

1. If unprocessed lentils are used, soak them overnight in seven cups water. Drain. If quick-cooking lentils are used, they need not be soaked. Cover the lentils with water and add the onion, bay leaf, salt and a dash of pepper. Bring to a boil and simmer for thirty to forty-five minutes, until lentils are tender.

2. Discard the onion and bay leaf and stir in the spice. Add more salt and pepper if necessary.

MARIA'S LENTILS   *8 to 10 servings*

1¾ pounds lean pork, cubed
 1 large onion, coarsely chopped
 2 garlic cloves
 4 medium tomatoes, peeled, seeded and chopped
1½ cups dried lentils

Salt and freshly ground black pepper
 2 barely ripe bananas, cut into 1-inch chunks
1½ cups pineapple cubes
Cilantro (fresh coriander leaves) (optional)

1. Simmer the pork barely covered with water in a deep skillet. Cook until the liquid evaporates and pork browns.

2. Add onion and garlic and cook gently until golden brown. Add tomatoes. Simmer.

3. Meanwhile, cook the lentils in four cups water for about forty minutes, until almost tender. Pour into pork mixture and mix well. Season to taste. Simmer for thirty minutes longer.

4. Five minutes before serving, add bananas, pineapple and, if desired, cilantro leaves.

BEETS À LA CRÈME   *6 servings*

2 tablespoons butter
2 tablespoons all-purpose flour
1 cup Chicken Stock (page 475)
1 onion slice
 Salt and freshly ground black pepper

½ cup heavy cream
 3 cups sliced peeled cooked fresh beets
 Chopped fresh parsley

1. Melt the butter and stir in the flour. Add the stock, stirring with a wire whisk. When thickened and smooth, add the onion and seasoning to taste. Simmer for five minutes, then discard the onion.

2. Stir in the cream, simmer for two minutes longer, and stir in the beets. Heat thoroughly. Serve sprinkled with chopped parsley.

BEETS IN ORANGE-BUTTER SAUCE   *4 servings*

¼ cup fresh orange juice
1 teaspoon fresh lemon juice
2 tablespoons butter
½ teaspoon salt

3 cups shredded peeled fresh beets
1 teaspoon cornstarch
1 teaspoon water

1. Combine the orange juice, lemon juice, butter and salt in a one-quart saucepan. Bring to the boiling point.

2. Add the beets, cover, and cook for about five minutes, until the beets are tender.

3. Mix the cornstarch with the water and add to the cooked beets. Cook, stirring, for about one-half minute, only until the sauce has thickened. Serve hot.

POLISH BEETS   *6 servings*

1 small onion, finely chopped
1 tablespoon butter
1 tablespoon all-purpose flour
½ cup yoghurt
5 medium beets, cooked, peeled and shredded

2 to 3 tablespoons prepared horse-radish
½ teaspoon sugar
Salt and freshly ground black pepper
2 tablespoons chopped parsley

1. Sauté the onion in the butter for three to five minutes. Stir in the flour. Add the yoghurt and heat to just below the boiling point.

2. Add the beets, horseradish and sugar, and heat thoroughly. Season with salt and pepper to taste and sprinkle with the parsley.

PICKLED BEETS   *12 servings*

1 cup vinegar
1 teaspoon salt
1 garlic clove, finely minced
½ cup brown sugar

2 teaspoons mixed whole pickling spices
8 to 12 medium beets, cooked, cooled, and sliced or quartered

Combine the vinegar, salt, garlic, sugar and spices in a saucepan. Bring to a boil, simmer for two or three minutes, and pour over the beets. Cool and chill.

Note: The pickled beets may be stored in the refrigerator for periods of up to two weeks.

BROCCOLI WITH ANCHOVY-CHEESE SAUCE   *6 servings*

1 bunch of broccoli (about 1½ pounds)
1 teaspoon salt

Anchovy-Cheese Sauce (page 485)
Anchovies for garnish

1. Wash and trim the broccoli, remove stem ends, and cut into portions of similar size.

2. Place broccoli in a saucepan with one inch of boiling water containing the salt. Bring to a boil and cook, uncovered, for five minutes. Cover and boil for ten to fifteen minutes longer, or until broccoli is barely tender. Drain.

3. Top with anchovy-cheese sauce. Garnish with anchovies.

CREOLE FRESH BROCCOLI   *6 servings*

2 tablespoons butter
1 cup diced fresh tomatoes
½ cup diced celery
1 garlic clove
¼ cup chopped onion
½ cup diced green pepper

1 teaspoon salt
1 teaspoon sugar
⅛ teaspoon freshly ground black pepper
1 bunch of broccoli (about 2 pounds)
1 teaspoon cornstarch

1. Melt the butter in a ten-inch skillet. Add the tomatoes, celery, garlic, onion, green pepper, salt, sugar and black pepper. Mix well. Remove from the heat.

2. Wash and trim the broccoli. Place over the vegetables in the skillet. Cover tightly and cook over medium heat for fifteen to twenty minutes, until tender.

3. Place the broccoli on dinner plates. Stir the cornstarch into the juice and vegetables left in the pan. Cook until slightly thickened. Discard the garlic. Serve a spoonful of the sauce over each serving of broccoli.

BROCCOLI RING   *6 servings*

1 bunch of broccoli (about 2 pounds)
1 garlic clove
2 tablespoons butter
2 tablespoons all-purpose flour
1 cup heavy cream

4 eggs, separated
Pinch of grated nutmeg
Salt and freshly ground black pepper

1. Preheat oven to moderate (350° F.).

2. Wash and trim the broccoli and cut it into smaller pieces. Cook the broccoli and garlic in water to cover until tender. Discard the garlic. Chop the broccoli until fine and reserve.

3. Melt the butter and stir in the flour, using a wire whisk. When blended, add the cream, stirring vigorously with the whisk. When thickened and smooth, combine with the broccoli. Remove from the heat and stir in the slightly beaten egg yolks, the nutmeg, and salt and pepper to taste.

4. Beat the egg whites until thick and fold them into the broccoli mixture.

5. Generously butter a one-quart ring mold and lightly flour it. Pour the mixture into the mold and set the mold in a larger pan. Pour about one inch of boiling water around the bottom of the mold. Bake the ring for thirty minutes, or until puffed and set. Serve with Cheese Sauce (page 484) or Sauce Hollandaise (page 485).

BROCCOLI AND LOBSTER MORNAY   *4 to 6 servings*

1 bunch of broccoli (1½ pounds) or 1 package (10 ounces) frozen broccoli
1 pound cooked lobster meat
¼ cup butter
5 tablespoons all-purpose flour
1 cup milk
1 cup heavy cream
1 cup grated Gruyère or sharp Cheddar cheese
Salt and freshly ground black pepper
2 tablespoons dry sherry
¼ cup grated Parmesan cheese
Buttered soft fresh bread crumbs

1. Cook the broccoli until it is just done; do not overcook. Separate it into flowerets. Cut the lobster meat into bite-size chunks.

2. Preheat oven to hot (400° F.).

3. Heat the butter in a saucepan and blend in the flour with a wire whisk. Meanwhile, bring the milk and cream to a boil and add all at once to the butter-flour mixture, stirring vigorously with the whisk. When the mixture is thickened and smooth, stir in the Gruyère cheese. When it melts, season with salt and pepper to taste. Add the sherry.

4. Arrange the broccoli and lobster in a baking dish and pour the sauce over them. Sprinkle with Parmesan cheese and bread crumbs. Bake for ten to twenty minutes, until the sauce bubbles and the crumbs are lightly browned.

BRUSSELS SPROUTS POLONAISE   *4 to 6 servings*

1 quart Brussels sprouts
2 teaspoons salt
Freshly ground black pepper
3 tablespoons melted butter
1½ cups soft fresh bread crumbs
2 tablespoons grated Parmesan cheese

1. Wash and trim the sprouts. Soak them in four cups cold water containing one teaspoon of the salt for twenty minutes. Drain.

2. Place the sprouts in a saucepan with one inch of fresh boiling water containing the remaining salt. Bring to a boil and cook, uncovered, for five minutes. Cover and cook for ten minutes longer, or only until crisp-tender. Drain. Sprinkle with black pepper.

3. Combine butter, bread crumbs and cheese. Mix lightly. Stir and cook until golden. Sprinkle over Brussels sprouts. Serve hot.

BRUSSELS SPROUTS À LA CRÈME   *4 to 6 servings*

1 quart Brussels sprouts
2½ teaspoons salt
2 tablespoons butter
2 teaspoons finely chopped onion
3 tablespoons all-purpose flour
1 cup Chicken Stock (page 475)

½ cup light cream
⅛ teaspoon freshly ground white pepper
Dash of grated nutmeg
1 teaspoon chopped parsley

1. Wash and trim the sprouts. Soak them in four cups cold water containing one teaspoon salt for twenty minutes. Drain.

2. Cook the sprouts, uncovered, in one inch of fresh boiling water containing one teaspoon salt for five minutes. Cover and continue cooking for ten to fifteen minutes, until tender. Drain.

3. Melt the butter in a saucepan and cook the onion in it until soft but not brown. Add the flour and stir and cook until it turns golden.

4. Stir in the stock, cream, remaining salt, the white pepper and nutmeg. Cook over low heat, stirring constantly, until thickened. Stir in chopped parsley. Serve the cream sauce over the Brussels sprouts.

BRUSSELS SPROUTS CREOLE   *4 to 6 servings*

1 quart Brussels sprouts
Salt
¼ cup finely chopped onion
¼ cup chopped green pepper
2 tablespoons butter

2 cups diced fresh or canned tomatoes
Freshly ground black pepper
¼ teaspoon poultry seasoning

1. Wash and trim the sprouts. Soak them in four cups cold water containing one teaspoon salt for twenty minutes. Drain.

2. Sauté the onion and green pepper in the butter. Add the tomatoes, sprouts, pepper, poultry seasoning and salt to taste. Stir and cook for five minutes, uncovered. Cover and continue cooking for ten to fifteen minutes, or until sprouts are tender. Serve immediately, with additional butter if desired.

BRUSSELS SPROUTS WITH WATER CHESTNUTS   *8 servings*

2 quarts Brussels sprouts
Salt
¼ cup butter

2 tablespoons finely chopped onion
1 can (5 ounces) water chestnuts, drained and slivered

1. Remove the wilted outer leaves and the stems of the sprouts. Cut a crosswise gash into the stem end. Soak the sprouts in two quarts cold water containing two teaspoons salt for about ten minutes. Drain.

2. Steam or boil the sprouts rapidly in a small quantity of lightly salted water for about fifteen minutes, or until barely tender.

3. Melt the butter, add the onion and slivered water chestnuts, and sauté gently until the onion is soft but not browned. Pour over the Brussels sprouts.

BRUSSELS SPROUTS WITH CELERY KNOB   *4 to 6 servings*

1 quart Brussels sprouts
1 medium celery knob, peeled and roughly chopped
3 tablespoons butter
1 small onion, finely chopped
2 tablespoons all-purpose flour
1 cup milk

¼ teaspoon salt
⅛ teaspoon freshly ground black pepper
¼ cup soft fresh bread crumbs
2 tablespoons grated Parmesan cheese

1. Preheat oven to moderate (375° F.).
2. Wash and trim the sprouts. Soak them in four cups cold water containing one teaspoon salt for twenty minutes.
3. Steam the sprouts and the celery knob in a small quantity of boiling salted water, covered, until the sprouts are barely tender. Drain. Place the vegetables in a shallow baking dish.
4. Melt two tablespoons of the butter. Sauté the onion in it until tender. Sprinkle the flour over the onion and gradually stir in the milk. Heat to boiling, stirring, and season with the salt and pepper.
5. Pour the sauce over the vegetables. Melt the remaining butter, combine it with the bread crumbs, and sprinkle the mixture over the sauce. Sprinkle with the cheese. Bake for fifteen minutes, or until lightly browned on top and bubbling hot.

BRUSSELS SPROUTS WITH SAUTÉED MUSHROOMS
4 to 6 servings

1 quart Brussels sprouts
2 teaspoons salt
¼ pound fresh mushrooms
¼ cup butter

2 tablespoons lemon juice
⅛ teaspoon freshly ground black pepper

1. Wash and trim the sprouts. Soak them in four cups cold water containing one teaspoon salt for twenty minutes. Drain.
2. Place the sprouts in a saucepan with one inch of boiling water and one teaspoon salt. Boil, uncovered, for three minutes. Cover and cook for twelve to fifteen minutes, until crisp-tender. Drain if necessary.
3. Wash and slice the mushrooms. Sauté them in the butter and one tablespoon of the lemon juice. Combine them with the cooked sprouts, the remaining lemon juice and the pepper. Add additional salt to taste. Serve at once.

BRUSSELS SPROUTS WITH CHESTNUTS   *6 servings*

1 quart Brussels sprouts
1½ teaspoons salt
1 tablespoon finely chopped onion
  Boiling Beef or Chicken Stock
  (pages 473 and 475)

¼ cup butter
⅔ cup cooked chestnuts

1. Wash and trim the sprouts. Soak them in four cups cold water containing one teaspoon salt for twenty minutes. Drain.
2. Place in a saucepan with the onion, stock and remaining salt. Bring to a boil and cook, uncovered, for five minutes. Cover and cook for ten to twelve minutes longer, or until sprouts are tender. Drain.
3. Melt the butter, add the chestnuts, and cook until butter is golden. Pour over sprouts and toss lightly to mix sprouts and chestnuts.

CREAMED CABBAGE   *6 servings*

2 cups milk or Chicken Stock (page 475)
6 cups finely shredded green cabbage
3 tablespoons butter

3 tablespoons all-purpose flour
1 cup light cream
1 teaspoon salt
Freshly ground white pepper

1. Heat the milk or stock, add the cabbage, and cook for three minutes.
2. Melt the butter in a separate saucepan. Blend in the flour and add the cream all at once, stirring with a wire whisk. Add the salt and pepper to taste and continue to cook, stirring constantly, until the sauce is thickened and smooth.
3. Add the cream sauce to the cabbage and cook, stirring constantly, for three or four minutes.

CABBAGE IN CARAWAY CREAM   *4 servings*

1 small firm green cabbage
2 tablespoons butter
1 teaspoon salt
1 garlic clove, finely minced

1 teaspoon caraway seeds
1 teaspoon sugar
1½ tablespoons vinegar
½ cup sour cream

1. Trim the cabbage and shred it coarsely.
2. Heat the butter in a skillet. Add the cabbage, salt and garlic and stir well. Cover tightly and steam for ten minutes. Water is not necessary if the cover is tight enough.
3. Remove cover and add the caraway seeds, sugar and vinegar. Mix well. Stir in the sour cream and heat thoroughly but do not boil. Serve immediately.

HOT CABBAGE SLAW   *4 servings*

3 cups shredded green or white cabbage
1 teaspoon salt
1 tablespoon butter

½ cup milk
1 teaspoon caraway seeds
½ teaspoon dried tarragon, or more
Freshly ground black pepper

1. Put the cabbage in a one-quart pan. Rinse and drain. Sprinkle with the salt, cover, and place over medium heat. When the cover is hot to the touch, reduce the heat to low and cook for five minutes.

2. Add butter, milk and caraway seeds. Add the tarragon and pepper to taste and stir to blend. Bring to a boil. Serve hot.

STEWED RED CABBAGE   *6 servings*

1 medium head of red cabbage
¼ cup butter
1 tablespoon sugar
¼ cup water

½ teaspoon grated orange rind
¼ cup orange juice
½ cup red currant jelly
Salt

1. Remove the outer leaves of the cabbage and shred the tender inner portion.

2. Simmer together for three minutes the butter, sugar, water, orange rind and juice.

3. Add the cabbage, cover tightly, and cook, stirring occasionally, for one hour or longer, until the cabbage is tender.

4. Just before the cabbage is done, add the jelly, salt to taste and additional orange juice to taste. Continue to simmer until the cabbage is dry, glossy and tender.

RED CABBAGE WITH VERMOUTH   *6 servings*

1 small red cabbage (about 1½ pounds)
2 tablespoons butter
½ cup diced onion
7 tablespoons sweet vermouth
1 tablespoon brown sugar

¾ teaspoon salt
1½ cups Thompson seedless grapes, halved if large
1 teaspoon lemon juice
1 teaspoon cornstarch

1. Remove outside leaves of cabbage and shred the cabbage coarsely. Set aside.

2. Melt the butter in a two-quart saucepan. Add the onion and sauté until limp. Add cabbage, four tablespoons of the vermouth, the sugar and salt. Mix lightly. Cover and cook for eight minutes, or until cabbage is barely tender.

3. Add the grapes and lemon juice. Cover and cook for one minute. Blend cornstarch with remaining vermouth and add to cabbage. Cook for one minute, or until juice thickens slightly.

BRAISED RED CABBAGE   *About 6 servings*

2 onions, sliced
2 tablespoons oil or bacon drippings
1 red cabbage, finely shredded
2 large tart apples, peeled and diced
½ cup red currant jelly
1 bay leaf

6 allspice berries
 Salt and freshly ground black pepper
⅔ cup red wine, or more
24 fresh chestnuts, peeled (see page 317)

1. Preheat oven to moderate (325° F.).
2. Sauté the onions in the oil in a heavy stainless-steel or porcelainized-iron casserole until tender.
3. Add the shredded cabbage, apples, jelly, bay leaf, allspice berries, salt and pepper to taste, and one-half cup of the wine.
4. Cover tightly and bake for two hours, adding more of the wine if necessary to prevent sticking. Stir occasionally.
5. Add the chestnuts about one hour before the end of cooking time. Add a little more wine if cabbage seems dry. Remove the bay leaf and allspice berries before serving.

When winter is without and the appetite rages within, there are few things more gratifying to the taste buds than the aromatic flavor of sauerkraut. The most famous sauerkraut dish is choucroute garnie, *or garnished sauerkraut. Almost any smoked meat product can be used in this dish. A characteristic seasoning is juniper berries, and a dry white Alsatian wine is often used as the cooking liquid. Either champagne or cold beer can accompany* choucroute garnie. *It is customary to accompany the dish with various kinds of mustards, including the mustards of Düsseldorf or Dijon, tarragon-flavored mustards, hot mustards made with a paste of dry mustard and water or beer, and mild mustards.*

ALSATIAN SAUERKRAUT   *6 servings*

2 quarts sauerkraut, fresh or canned
 Pork rind or salt pork
2 garlic cloves, minced
 Freshly ground black pepper

Dry white Alsatian wine
1 onion, studded with 4 cloves
 Frankfurters or other meats (see note)

1. Wash the sauerkraut, drain, and squeeze out the liquid.
2. Line a heavy kettle with pork rind or thin slices of salt pork. Add the

sauerkraut, garlic, pepper to taste and enough wine to cover. Add the onion. Cover tightly.

3. Cook in a preheated moderate oven (325° F.) or simmer gently on top of the stove for three and one-half to four hours. Add more wine as necessary.

Note: Many combinations of meats may be used in the preparation of this dish: pigs' knuckles: cook on top of the sauerkraut for four hours; Polish sausage or Italian coteghino: add for the last thirty-five minutes of cooking; knackwurst: add for the last fifteen or twenty minutes of cooking; cooked ham slices: heat through in a little white wine; frankfurters: cook on top of the sauerkraut for five minutes.

PIERRE FRANEY'S CHOUCROUTE GARNIE   *About 8 servings*

3 to 3½ pounds sauerkraut, fresh or canned

12 thin slices of fat back (available at pork stores and many meat markets)

1 bottle dry white wine

½ teaspoon ground cuminseed

2 cups Chicken or Veal Stock (pages 475 and 474)

2 small onions, each stuck with 4 cloves

2 large carrots, trimmed and scraped

1 bay leaf

12 juniper berries

12 peppercorns

Pinch of dried thyme

1 garlic clove

2 pounds smoked pork shoulder butt

1 pound lean bacon, in one piece, with rind removed

1 garlic sausage

8 frankfurters

1. Preheat oven to moderate (325° F.).

2. Drain the sauerkraut and empty it into a basin of cold water. Rinse well and squeeze dry. Pull the sauerkraut apart to loosen any lumps.

3. Line a large kettle with fat back and add the sauerkraut. Add the wine, cuminseed, stock, onions and carrots. Tie the bay leaf, juniper berries, peppercorns, thyme and garlic in a small cheesecloth bag. Add it to the kettle. Bring the sauerkraut to a boil, cover, and place the kettle in the oven. Simmer for about three hours.

4. About one and one-quarter hours before the sauerkraut is done, put the pork butt, bacon and garlic sausage in a large saucepan. Add cold water to cover, bring to a boil, and cover. Simmer for one hour, or until pork butt is tender.

5. Fifteen minutes before serving, drop the frankfurters into boiling water to cover, remove from the heat, and let stand until ready to serve.

6. Remove the onions and cheesecloth bag from the sauerkraut and discard them. Spoon the sauerkraut onto a hot serving platter and garnish with sliced pork butt, sliced bacon, sliced garlic sausage and drained frankfurters. Slice the carrots and use as a garnish.

GLAZED CARROTS   *6 servings*

1½ pounds carrots
1½ cups Beef Stock (page 473)
  2 tablespoons sugar
    Salt and freshly ground black
    pepper

6 tablespoons butter
Chopped parsley

1. Scrape the carrots and cut them lengthwise into quarters. Cut the quartered carrots into two-inch lengths.

2. Combine the carrots, stock, sugar, salt and pepper to taste and the butter in a saucepan. Cover and bring to a boil. Simmer for twenty-five to thirty minutes, or until the carrots are tender. When done, there should be almost no liquid remaining and the carrots should have a syruplike coating. Any excess liquid may be evaporated by simmering gently without a cover. Before serving, sprinkle the carrots with parsley.

ORANGE-GLAZED CARROTS   *5 servings*

3 tablespoons fresh orange juice
1½ tablespoons sugar
¼ cup butter
6 whole cloves

¼ teaspoon salt
4½ cups hot cooked sliced carrots
Chopped fresh parsley

Combine the orange juice, sugar, butter, cloves and salt in a saucepan. Cook until the butter is melted and the sauce is hot. Remove and discard the cloves. Pour the mixture over the carrots and serve garnished with the parsley.

CARROT TZIMMES   *6 to 8 servings*

2 pounds carrots
½ teaspoon salt
¾ cup honey

1 tablespoon lemon juice
2 tablespoons all-purpose flour
2 tablespoons butter, melted

1. Scrape the carrots and slice them into very thin rounds. Cook the carrot rounds in salted water to cover for about eight minutes, until they are almost tender.

2. Add the salt, honey and lemon juice. Simmer until the liquid in the pan is reduced to about half of its original volume.

3. Blend the flour into the butter. Add to the carrots, stirring. Bring the mixture to a boil and simmer for one minute.

Note: If this recipe is prepared for the menu for Rosh Ha-Shanah, instead of butter use vegetable shortening or chicken fat.

CARROTS AND POTATOES MOUSSELINE   *4 to 6 servings*

6 carrots, scraped and quartered
3 medium potatoes, peeled
3 tablespoons butter

½ cup heavy cream
Freshly grated nutmeg

1. In separate saucepans cook the carrots and potatoes in boiling salted water until tender. Drain.

2. Force the vegetables through a food mill and return them to one of the saucepans. Add the butter and beat with a wooden spoon. Add the cream while beating and season with a little nutmeg. Serve hot.

CARROTS WITH ARTICHOKE HEARTS   *6 servings*

½ pound fresh mushrooms, quartered
1 tablespoon olive oil
1½ tablespoons butter
  Salt and freshly ground black pepper
2 tablespoons minced shallots or green onions

1 package (9 ounces) frozen artichoke hearts, cooked
1½ pounds carrots, braised in butter
⅓ cup Beef Stock (page 473)
2 tablespoons minced parsley, or a combination of parsley, chervil and chives

1. Sauté the mushrooms in the oil and butter in a skillet for four or five minutes, until very lightly browned. Season with salt and pepper.

2. Stir the shallots and artichoke hearts into the mushrooms and toss for two or three minutes over moderately high heat. Fold in the carrots.

3. Add the stock to the mixture. Cover and cook slowly for four or five minutes, until the stock has almost completely evaporated. Correct seasoning if necessary.

4. Put the vegetables in a hot serving dish and sprinkle with the parsley.

Cauliflower, broccoli, Brussels sprouts, cabbage and kale are cousins under the leaf. The finest heads of cauliflower are firm to the touch and range in color from chalk to creamy white. The outer leaves should be firm, fresh and green. The leaves are thoroughly edible. Good taste in cauliflower has nothing to do with size and relative sizes have little to do with age.

Marie Jeanne Bécu, the Countess du Barry, the court favorite of Louis XV, gave her royal name to many dishes made with cauliflower. The name du Barry on a menu almost invariably denotes cauliflower in some form.

CAULIFLOWER WITH MUSTARD SAUCE   *4 to 6 servings*

1 medium cauliflower
¾ cup heavy cream
¾ cup fresh mayonnaise
  Salt

1½ tablespoons prepared mustard, preferably Dijon or Düsseldorf
  Juice of ½ lemon, or more
  Paprika

1. Remove the stem and leaves from the cauliflower. Steam the cauliflower whole until it is barely tender. Drain and keep warm.

2. Whip the cream and set aside briefly.

3. In a mixing bowl combine the mayonnaise, salt to taste, mustard and lemon juice. Whip until blended; fold in the whipped cream. Pour the sauce over the cauliflower or serve it separately. Sprinkle with paprika.

CONFETTI CAULIFLOWER   *4 to 6 servings*

1 medium cauliflower	2 tablespoons chopped fresh parsley
¼ cup butter	½ teaspoon salt
½ cup toasted dry bread crumbs	1 hard-cooked egg, finely chopped
¼ cup grated raw carrot	

1. Remove the stem and leaves from the cauliflower. Cut several slashes in the bottom of the head and soak it in cold salted water for thirty minutes.

2. Place the cauliflower in a one-and-one-half-quart saucepan, rinse the vegetable, and drain it. Cover and place over medium heat. When the lid is hot to the touch, reduce the heat to low and cook for fifteen minutes longer.

3. Melt the butter and add the crumbs, carrot, parsley and salt. Sprinkle the mixture over the cooked cauliflower and garnish with the chopped egg.

CAULIFLOWER WITH CAPER SAUCE   *6 servings*

1 large cauliflower	⅛ teaspoon freshly ground black pepper
1¼ teaspoons salt	1 teaspoon ground turmeric
Cornstarch	2 tablespoons capers
3 tablespoons butter	Chopped parsley
3 tablespoons lemon juice	
1 tablespoon grated onion	

1. Remove the stem and leaves from the cauliflower. Place the cauliflower in a saucepan with one inch of boiling water containing one teaspoon of the salt. Bring to a boil and cook, uncovered, for five minutes. Cover and cook for twenty minutes longer, or until cauliflower is tender, turning once.

2. Drain the liquid from the cauliflower and measure it. There should be about one cup. Blend in one teaspoon cornstarch for each one-half cup liquid.

3. Add the butter, lemon juice, onion, pepper, turmeric and remaining salt to the liquid. Cook, stirring, until sauce has thickened. Add the capers. Pour the sauce over cauliflower and garnish with parsley.

CAULIFLOWER MORNAY   *6 servings*

1 large cauliflower, cut into flowerets
¼ cup butter
2 tablespoons all-purpose flour
1 cup Chicken Stock (page 475)
1 cup heavy cream

Salt and freshly ground white
pepper
2 egg yolks, lightly beaten
2 tablespoons grated Parmesan
cheese

1. Cook the cauliflowerets in salted water until just tender. Drain well.
Turn into a hot serving dish or casserole.

2. While the cauliflower is cooking, make a sauce of two tablespoons of
the butter, the flour, stock and cream. Season with salt and pepper to taste.

3. Mix egg yolks with a bit of the sauce and add, stirring, to the sauce.
Add the cheese and remaining butter. Mix until the cheese has melted.

4. Serve over the cauliflower; or use a heatproof casserole, sprinkle the
top with extra grated cheese, and broil to a golden brown.

*In the United States celery is rarely thought of as a vegetable to cook. The
French, however, serve braised celery often as an accompaniment for roast
meats.*

*The celery growers of this country have waged a campaign to unify the
terms used to identify the parts of the celery plant. A stalk or bunch refers
to the whole plant. A stalk of celery consists of ribs.*

CELERY BRAISED IN WHITE WINE   *4 to 6 servings*

6 celery hearts
2 tablespoons olive oil
2 tablespoons butter
½ teaspoon salt

⅛ teaspoon freshly ground black
pepper
½ cup dry white wine
¼ cup Chicken Stock (page 475)

1. Cut off most of the leaves and remove the rough outer ribs of the
celery. Cut each heart lengthwise into halves. Wash thoroughly and drain on
paper towels.

2. Heat the oil and butter in a skillet large enough to hold all the celery
pieces in one layer. Arrange the pieces, flat side down, in the skillet and cook
over low heat until lightly browned. Turn the pieces over and sprinkle with
half of the salt and pepper. Brown the rounded side, turn over, and sprinkle
with the remaining salt and pepper. Add more oil and butter to the skillet if
it becomes too dry.

3. Pour the wine and stock into the pan, cover, and simmer gently until
the celery is tender. Remove the celery to a heated serving plate. Reduce the
cooking liquid a little and spoon some of it over the celery. Sprinkle with
chopped parsley or chives or paprika.

CELERY KNOB PARMIGIANA   *6 servings*

4 celery knobs
1 tablespoon lemon juice
2 teaspoons salt

6 tablespoons butter, melted
½ cup grated Parmesan cheese
2 tablespoons chopped parsley

1. Preheat oven to hot (425° F.).

2. Peel the celery knobs and cut them into thin little sticks about two inches long. Drop the pieces into boiling water to cover with the lemon juice and salt added. Cook for about ten minutes, or until just tender. Do not overcook. Drain.

3. Butter a baking dish large enough to hold the celery knobs. Arrange a layer of the drained pieces and sprinkle with some of the melted butter and some of the cheese. Continue to fill the dish with drained pieces, butter and cheese. If desired, each layer may be sprinkled with a little black pepper and paprika.

4. Bake for fifteen minutes, or until the cheese is golden brown. Sprinkle a border of parsley around the edge and serve the celery knob in the baking dish.

CORN ON THE COB WITH PEPPER BUTTER   *6 servings*

½ cup butter, at room temperature
2 teaspoons peppercorns or 1 teaspoon coarsely ground black pepper

Salt
12 ears of fresh corn

1. Place the butter in a mixing bowl. Grind the peppercorns in a mortar or crush them carefully with the flat side of a skillet. Blend the butter with the pepper and add salt to taste. Spoon into a serving bowl and chill until ready to serve.

2. Shuck the corn just before cooking.

3. Heat enough water in a large kettle to cover the ears of corn. When the water reaches a full rolling boil, drop the ears of corn into it. Let the water return to a boil and immediately turn off the heat. Cover the kettle and let the corn stand for at least five minutes before serving. The corn may be left to stand in the water for as long as fifteen minutes. Serve corn with the chilled pepper butter.

CORN IN CREAM   *6 servings*

12 ears of fresh corn, shucked
¼ cup butter
Salt and freshly ground black pepper

½ to ¾ cup heavy cream

1. Cut or grate the kernels from corn cobs. Heat butter in a saucepan and add the corn kernels. Cook for three to five minutes.

2. Season corn with salt and pepper to taste and stir in the cream. Heat thoroughly and serve.

CORN CREOLE   *4 to 6 servings*

6 ears of fresh corn
3 tablespoons butter
2 scallions, trimmed and sliced
2 tablespoons chopped green pepper

1 large tomato, peeled and finely chopped
Salt and freshly ground black pepper

1. Cut the corn kernels from the cobs. Heat one tablespoon of the butter and add the corn, scallions and green pepper. Cook for three minutes.

2. Add the tomato and salt and pepper to taste. Cover and cook for five minutes, or until the corn is tender. Stir in the remaining butter and serve.

CORN AND MUSHROOM SAUTÉ   *6 servings*

1 cup sliced fresh mushrooms
1 teaspoon finely chopped onion
2 tablespoons butter or bacon drippings
3 cups fresh corn, cut off the cobs (6 to 8 ears)

1 teaspoon sugar
1 teaspoon salt
¼ teaspoon coarsely ground black pepper

1. Sauté the mushrooms and onion in the butter in a saucepan for ten minutes.

2. Add the corn, sugar, salt and black pepper. Stir and cook for five minutes. Serve hot.

SHAKER GREEN CORN PUDDING   *6 servings*

2 cups grated green corn
3 eggs
¼ cup sugar
Dash of grated nutmeg
½ teaspoon salt
⅛ teaspoon freshly ground black pepper

2 cups milk
½ cup buttered soft fresh bread crumbs
2 tablespoons butter

1. Preheat oven to slow (250° F.).

2. Place the corn in a buttered baking dish. Beat the eggs well. Add the sugar, nutmeg, salt, pepper and milk; blend. Pour the mixture over the corn

and sprinkle the top with buttered bread crumbs. Dot with the butter. Set the baking dish in a pan of boiling water and bake for one hour.

CORN AND CHEESE PUDDING   *6 servings*

¼ cup all-purpose flour
¼ cup butter, melted
1½ cups milk
1½ cups sharp Cheddar cheese
1½ cups fresh corn, cut off the cobs
  (3 or 4 ears)
1 cup soft fresh bread crumbs

1¼ teaspoons salt
1 teaspoon dry mustard
½ teaspoon sugar
½ teaspoon coarsely ground black
  pepper
4 eggs, beaten

1. Preheat oven to moderate (325° F.).
2. Blend the flour with the butter in a saucepan. Gradually stir in the milk. Stir and cook over low heat until thickened.
3. Remove the mixture from the heat and add the remaining ingredients. Mix well and turn into a buttered two-quart casserole.
4. Set the casserole in a pan of hot water and bake in the water bath for one hour and fifteen minutes, or until a knife inserted into the center comes out clean. Serve hot.

CORN AND TOMATO CASSEROLE   *6 to 8 servings*

4 cups fresh corn, cut off the cobs
  (about 8 ears)
1 cup sliced fresh okra
1 cup soft fresh bread crumbs
¼ cup finely chopped onion
3½ teaspoons salt
2 teaspoons sugar
½ teaspoon freshly ground black
  pepper

¼ cup bacon drippings or butter or
  margarine
2 cups milk
4 large eggs, lightly beaten
6 medium or 3 large tomatoes
2 tablespoons butter, melted

1. Preheat oven to moderate (350° F.).
2. Combine vegetables, crumbs, onion, seasonings, drippings and milk in a saucepan. Stir and cook for five minutes, or until thickened. Remove from heat and stir a little of the hot mixture into the eggs, then add eggs to the remaining hot mixture. Turn into a buttered two-quart casserole.
3. Bake for one hour and ten minutes, or until the mixture is firm.
4. Wash tomatoes and cut into one-half-inch slices. Arrange slices over the top of the casserole fifteen minutes before end of baking time. Brush top with melted butter and sprinkle with additional salt and pepper.

SPANISH CORN CASSEROLE   *4 to 6 servings*

½ cup olive oil
½ cup finely chopped onion
1½ cups finely chopped green peppers
1 medium tomato, chopped
2 cups fresh corn, cut from the cobs (about 4 ears)
½ teaspoon freshly ground black pepper

1 tablespoon sugar
2 egg yolks
½ cup pimiento-stuffed green olives, chopped
½ cup seedless raisins
2 hard-cooked eggs, chopped
¼ teaspoon ground thyme

1. Preheat oven to moderate (350° F.).

2. Heat half of the olive oil. Add half of the onion and one cup of the green peppers. Cook until the onion is tender. Add the tomato and cook for ten minutes. Add the corn, black pepper, sugar and egg yolks and cook, stirring occasionally, for ten minutes longer.

3. Meanwhile, heat the remaining olive oil. Add the remaining onion and green pepper. Cook until the onion is tender. Add the olives, raisins, eggs and thyme; mix well.

4. Spread half the corn mixture in the bottom of a greased one-and-one-half-quart baking dish. Top with the olive mixture, then with the remaining corn mixture. Garnish with additional olives. Bake for twenty minutes.

TORTILLAS DE MAÍZ (corn tortillas)   *6 tortillas*

1¼ cups fresh corn, cut off the cobs (about 2 ears)
½ cup salad oil
6 large eggs
1½ teaspoons all-purpose flour

1½ teaspoons salt
Freshly ground black pepper
Butter
Sour cream and chopped parsley

1. Cut the corn off the cobs according to the method in Torrejas de Maíz (page 397). Drain the cut corn on paper towels to absorb excess moisture.

2. Heat the oil in a skillet. Add the corn and fry for about fifteen minutes, until golden brown. Drain on paper towels.

3. Make one tortilla at a time. For each, place in a small mixing bowl one egg, one-quarter teaspoon flour, one-quarter teaspoon salt and a dash of black pepper. Beat lightly and add about one-sixth of the fried corn.

4. Melt one teaspoon butter in a five-inch skillet. Pour in the egg mixture and cook until the edges are lightly browned and curled. As the mixture sets, gently pull the edges toward the center with a fork and tip the pan so the uncooked mixture flows under the cooked portion. Turn to cook the other side. Turn onto a plate and roll in jelly-roll fashion.

5. Repeat for each tortilla, adding additional butter to the skillet as needed. Serve topped with sour cream and chopped parsley.

TORREJAS DE MAÍZ TIERNO (fresh corn fritters)
24 two-inch fritters

6 ears of fresh corn
¼ cup all-purpose flour
2 tablespoons sugar
½ teaspoon salt
⅛ teaspoon freshly ground black pepper

1 egg, lightly beaten
2 tablespoons shredded mild Cheddar cheese
Fat or oil for deep frying

1. Cut the corn off the cob by running the point of a sharp knife lengthwise down the middle of each row of kernels, cutting the kernels into halves. Shave a thin layer of kernels off the entire cob. Repeat, taking off another layer. Clean off the remainder by scraping the cob with the bowl of a tablespoon.

2. Mix the corn with the flour, sugar, salt and pepper. Blend in the egg and cheese.

3. Heat the fat to 365° F. on a frying thermometer. Drop the mixture into the fat by teaspoons. Cook until golden brown. Drain on paper towels.

TAMALES DE MAÍZ TIERNO (corn tamales)   *6 servings*

6 ears of fresh corn
½ cup all-purpose flour
1 egg, lightly beaten
½ cup shredded mild cheese
3 tablespoons sugar

½ teaspoon salt
⅛ teaspoon freshly ground black pepper
¼ cup raisins

1. Remove the shucks and silks from the corn ears. Reserve twelve large strips of shucks for use later. Cut the corn from the cob according to directions in the recipe for Torrejas de Maíz (above). Reserve three of the scraped cobs for use later.

2. Combine the cut corn, flour, egg, cheese, two tablespoons of the sugar, the salt, pepper and raisins. Mix well.

3. For each tamale, use two large shucks, placing them side by side lengthwise, overlapping the edges about one inch. Place one-quarter cup of the corn mixture in the center of each. Fold the lengthwise edges over the top. Fold the ends under.

4. Place the tamales in a saucepan with the three scraped corn cobs, the remaining sugar and boiling water to cover. Cook slowly, covered, for about one hour and fifteen minutes, until the filling is firm. Discard cobs.

CUCUMBERS AU GRATIN   *6 servings*

3 cucumbers
1½ teaspoons salt
¼ teaspoon freshly ground black pepper

¾ cup shredded sharp American cheese
2 tablespoons butter
¾ cup soft fresh bread crumbs

1. Preheat oven to moderate (350° F.).
2. Wash the cucumbers and cut into one-quarter-inch slices. Place them in a saucepan with one inch of boiling water containing one-half teaspoon of the salt. Cover and simmer for three minutes. Drain.
3. Place the cucumbers in a casserole (10 × 6 × 2 inches). Sprinkle with the remaining salt, the pepper and cheese. Toss lightly.
4. Melt the butter and mix it with the bread crumbs; sprinkle over the top of the cucumbers. Bake for about thirty-five minutes, until the crumbs are brown.

STUFFED CUCUMBERS   *3 servings*

3 large cucumbers
¼ cup butter
2 tablespoons finely chopped onion
¼ cup soft fresh bread crumbs
½ cup minced cooked chicken
1 tablespoon slivered toasted almonds

¼ teaspoon salt
⅛ teaspoon freshly ground black pepper
¼ teaspoon ground thyme
Chicken Stock (page 475)

1. Preheat oven to moderate (375° F.).
2. Peel the cucumbers, cut them into two-inch lengths, and scoop out the seeds with an apple corer or small sharp knife. Place the cucumbers in boiling salted water, simmer for three minutes, and drain.
3. Melt two tablespoons of the butter, add the onion, and sauté until tender but not browned. Add the bread crumbs, chicken, almonds, salt, pepper and thyme. Moisten the chicken mixture with a little stock.
4. Stuff the cucumber tubes with the chicken mixture and arrange them in a buttered casserole. Sprinkle the remaining butter, melted, over the cucumbers. Add stock to casserole to come halfway up the cucumber pieces.
5. Bake for about twenty minutes, until the cucumbers are just tender.

HERB-BAKED CUCUMBERS   *8 servings*

8 cucumbers
2 tablespoons vinegar
1½ teaspoons salt
¼ cup melted butter
1 tablespoon finely chopped shallots

2 teaspoons chopped fresh dill or ½ teaspoon dried dill
2 tablespoons chopped chives
⅛ teaspoon freshly ground black pepper
1 tablespoon chopped parsley

1. Peel the cucumbers and cut into quarters. Remove the seeds and cut the quartered cucumbers into strips about two inches long and half an inch wide.

2. Place the cucumber strips in a bowl and sprinkle with the vinegar and salt. Let stand for thirty minutes. Drain and dry.

3. Preheat oven to moderate (375° F.).

4. Place the cucumbers in a baking dish and sprinkle with the butter, shallots, dill, chives and pepper. Do not cover. Bake for about forty-five minutes. Turn into a hot serving dish, add salt and pepper to taste, and sprinkle with parsley.

EGGPLANT SLICES WITH PARMESAN   *About 4 servings*

2 eggs, lightly beaten	1 cup fine dry bread crumbs
1 teaspoon water	2 tablespoons grated Parmesan cheese
1 teaspoon salt	1 large eggplant
Freshly ground black pepper	About 2 cups vegetable oil

1. Combine the eggs, water, salt, and pepper to taste in a mixing bowl. Combine the crumbs and cheese in a shallow plate.

2. Cut the unpeeled eggplant into thin slices, about one-eighth inch thick. Dip them into the egg mixture, then into the cheese-crumb mixture, coating as thoroughly as possible.

3. Pour the oil into a skillet to the depth of one-quarter inch. Heat the oil. Cook the eggplant, a few slices at a time, on both sides until golden brown. Add more oil when necessary to keep slices from sticking. Drain on paper towels.

EGGPLANT WITH SOUR CREAM   *6 servings*

1 large eggplant	1 tablespoon butter
1½ teaspoons salt	½ cup sour cream
¼ teaspoon freshly ground black pepper	Paprika and chopped fresh parsley for garnish
1 tablespoon finely chopped onion	

1. Peel the eggplant and cut it into one-half-inch slices, then into cubes. Place in a saucepan with one-half inch of boiling water containing one teaspoon of the salt. Cook, covered, for four or five minutes, until the cubes are tender but still retain their shape. Drain.

2. Add the remaining salt, the pepper, onion, butter and sour cream to the eggplant cubes. Cook only until the sour cream is hot, but do not allow to boil. Serve garnished with paprika and parsley.

BAKED MARINATED EGGPLANT   *4 to 6 servings*

¾ cup olive oil
3 tablespoons lemon juice or vinegar
Salt and coarsely ground black pepper
½ teaspoon finely minced garlic

2 tablespoons anchovy paste (optional)
1 large eggplant
¾ cup grated sharp Cheddar cheese

1. Preheat oven to hot (400° F.).
2. Combine the oil, lemon juice, salt and pepper to taste, garlic and anchovy paste. Beat with a fork or rotary beater until well blended.
3. Pare the eggplant and slice it crosswise into half-inch rounds. Pour the oil mixture over the slices and let stand for fifteen minutes, turning occasionally. If necessary, baste occasionally with the mixture.
4. Place the slices on a baking sheet lined with aluminum foil and bake for ten to fifteen minutes, turning once. Sprinkle with the cheese and place under the broiler until cheese melts.

FRENCH-FRIED EGGPLANT STICKS   *6 servings*

1 large eggplant
¾ cup fine dry bread crumbs
6 tablespoons grated Parmesan cheese
2½ teaspoons salt
¼ teaspoon freshly ground black pepper

2 eggs, beaten
2 tablespoons milk
Fat or oil for deep frying
Celery salt

1. Peel the eggplant and cut it into one-half-inch crosswise slices. Cut each slice into one-half-inch strips. Set aside.
2. Combine the bread crumbs, cheese, salt and pepper. Beat the eggs with the milk. Dip eggplant sticks into bread-crumb mixture, then into egg mixture, and again into bread-crumb mixture.
3. Fry sticks in deep fat or oil preheated to 375° F. on a frying thermometer. Sprinkle with celery salt. Drain on brown paper or on paper towels. Serve hot.

EGGPLANT AND CHICKEN-LIVER CASSEROLE   *6 servings*

2 medium eggplants
¼ cup butter
½ pound chicken livers
¼ pound fresh mushrooms
Salt and freshly ground black pepper

2 eggs
⅓ cup heavy cream
½ cup freshly grated Parmesan cheese
½ teaspoon grated nutmeg, or more
½ cup fine dry bread crumbs
Melted butter

1. Preheat oven to moderate (350° F.).

2. Peel the eggplants and cut them into one-inch cubes. Cook until tender in boiling salted water barely to cover. Drain well and mash with a fork.

3. Melt half of the butter and cook the livers until done but not over-cooked. Melt the remaining butter in a separate skillet and cook the mush-rooms until wilted. Season both livers and mushrooms with salt and pepper. Chop the livers fine.

4. Beat the eggs, cream, cheese and nutmeg together until well blended. Combine the eggplant, chopped livers, mushrooms and the egg mixture. Mix well and spoon into a buttered one-quart casserole. Cover with bread crumbs and sprinkle with a little melted butter. Bake for twenty to thirty minutes.

EGGPLANT BALLS   *6 servings*

1 large eggplant
1¾ teaspoons salt
¼ cup chopped onion
¾ cup finely chopped green peppers
1½ cups fine dry bread crumbs
2 eggs
1 tablespoon grated sharp Cheddar cheese

1 teaspoon paprika
¼ teaspoon freshly ground black pepper
All-purpose flour
Olive oil or other cooking oil
Tomato Sauce III (page 494)

1. Peel and cube the eggplant. Place cubes in a saucepan with one inch of boiling water containing one-half teaspoon of the salt. Cover and cook for fifteen minutes, or until tender. Drain off water and discard it.

2. Chop the eggplant. Mix the pulp with the onion, green peppers, one-half cup of the bread crumbs, one egg, the cheese, paprika, black pepper and the remaining salt. Cool until thoroughly chilled, two to three hours or overnight.

3. Drop a heaping teaspoon of the mixture into flour and roll to coat completely. Beat the other egg. Using two forks, dip the eggplant ball into the beaten egg, then into the remaining bread crumbs, being careful to keep the ball as round as possible. Continue with the rest of the mixture in the same way.

4. Fry the balls in hot oil until browned. Drain on brown paper. Serve with tomato sauce.

MILDRED KNOPF'S EGGPLANT CASSEROLE   *12 servings*

2 small eggplants
2 cups olive or vegetable oil
3 cups tomato sauce or chili pepper sauce (available canned in Italian grocery stores)

Salt and freshly ground black pepper
2 cups freshly grated Parmesan cheese
½ pound mozzarella cheese, sliced

1. Preheat oven to hot (400° F.).

2. Wash the eggplants but do not peel. Cut into one-quarter-inch slices. Season the slices with salt and pepper. Brown slices lightly on both sides in the oil in a large skillet. As the slices brown, drain them on paper towels.

3. Pour one cup of the tomato sauce onto the bottom of a large casserole. Sprinkle with one-half cup of the Parmesan cheese. Cover with slices of the eggplant. Top with slices of the mozzarella, then with another one-half cup of the Parmesan, then with another cup of the tomato sauce. Repeat this pattern until all the ingredients are used, topping with the last of the mozzarella and Parmesan cheeses.

4. Bake, uncovered, for twenty minutes. Serve hot.

ITALIAN EGGPLANT   *4 to 6 servings*

1 large eggplant
2 slices of bacon, cubed
1 onion, finely minced
1 large tomato, peeled, seeded and chopped
½ cup chopped celery
1 egg, beaten
Salt and freshly ground black pepper

8 black olives, pitted and sliced (imported black olives are best)
6 flat anchovy fillets, chopped
¾ cup soft fresh bread crumbs
½ cup grated Parmesan or Romano cheese

1. Preheat oven to moderate (325° F.).

2. Peel and cube the eggplant. Steam the cubes over hot water for five to ten minutes, or until nearly tender.

3. Cook the bacon until crisp. Mix the crisp pieces with the eggplant, onion, tomato, celery, egg, salt and pepper to taste, the olives, anchovies and half of the bread crumbs.

4. Pour the mixture into a greased baking dish. Combine the remaining bread crumbs with the cheese and sprinkle over the top of the casserole. Bake for thirty minutes.

BRAISED ENDIVE   *4 servings*

12 heads of endive
Juice of ½ lemon
5 tablespoons butter

1 teaspoon salt
⅓ cup water
1 teaspoon sugar

1. Trim off and discard any discolored leaves from the outside of the endive. Place the heads in a kettle and add the lemon juice, two tablespoons of the butter, the salt, water and sugar. Cover and bring to a boil. Cook over moderate heat for thirty to forty minutes, until endive are tender.

2. Drain the endive and press gently to remove any excess moisture.

3. Heat the remaining butter in a large skillet and brown the endive in it on all sides. They should be a light caramel color when cooked. Serve with roast meats.

SAUTÉED ESCAROLE   *4 servings*

2 pounds escarole
¼ cup olive oil
1 garlic clove, finely minced

Salt and freshly ground black pepper
Olive oil and vinegar (optional)

1. Trim the escarole and discard any tough or bruised leaves. Trim off the root end. Cut the head of escarole into quarters. Rinse well. Shake escarole to remove any excess moisture.

2. Heat the oil in a large saucepan and add the garlic. Let it cook briefly, then add the escarole. Do not add any water except that which clings to the leaves. Cover and cook for ten to fifteen minutes, stirring occasionally so that the cooking will be even.

3. Sprinkle with salt and pepper. Serve with olive oil and vinegar, if desired. Sautéed escarole may also be served cold with oil and vinegar.

ESCAROLE WITH PINE NUTS   *4 to 6 servings*

2 pounds escarole
½ garlic clove, minced
1 tablespoon olive oil

¼ cup pine nuts
1 teaspoon salt

1. Wash and shred the escarole.

2. Sauté the garlic in the oil in a three-quart pan for one minute. Add pine nuts, escarole and salt. Cover, reduce heat to low, and cook for ten minutes.

The pungent and pleasing flavor of anise or licorice found widely in Italian and Scandinavian cuisine usually comes from the seeds, leaves and bulbous stems of the fennel plant, an aromatic herb of the parsley family. The seeds of the common fennel are used in sweet pickles, cookies, apple pies and candy. The chopped feathery green leaves add color and flavor to sauces for fish, particularly herring, mackerel and salmon, and the leaves make an excellent addition to salads.

Fennel may be eaten raw, like celery. To serve it raw, trim the coarse outer leaves and cut the bulb into quarters, slices or julienne strips.

Fennel is also delicious cooked, and it may be substituted in any recipe for celery.

FENNEL AU GRATIN   *4 servings*

1 large head of fennel
5 tablespoons butter
3 tablespoons all-purpose flour
1½ cups milk
½ teaspoon salt

¼ teaspoon freshly ground black pepper
¼ cup grated Parmesan cheese
½ cup soft fresh bread crumbs

1. Preheat oven to moderate (375° F.).
2. Wash the fennel, trim it, and cut it into one-inch lengths. Steam the fennel over boiling water for about ten minutes, or until barely tender.
3. Melt three tablespoons of the butter, blend in the flour, and gradually stir in the milk. Season with the salt and pepper and bring to a boil, stirring. Add the cheese and stir to melt.
4. Spread half of the crumbs over the bottom of a greased shallow one-quart casserole. Place the steamed fennel pieces over the top and pour the sauce over all. Top with remaining crumbs and dot with remaining butter. Bake for twenty minutes, or until bubbly hot.

BATTER-FRIED FENNEL   *About 8 servings*

6 small heads of fennel
2 eggs
6 tablespoons all-purpose flour
¾ cup milk

½ teaspoon salt
⅛ teaspoon freshly ground black pepper
Salad oil

1. Trim the leaves and any tough outside stalks from the heads of fennel. Wash heads well. Steam over boiling water for about ten minutes, or until barely tender.
2. Cut each head into quarters. Combine the eggs, flour, milk, salt and pepper in a bowl to make a smooth batter.
3. Pour oil into a heavy skillet until it reaches a depth of one inch. Heat slowly to just below the smoking point.
4. Dip the pieces of fennel into the batter and fry them in the hot oil until browned on all sides. Drain on paper towels.

COLCANNON WITH KALE   *6 servings*

2 pounds white potatoes
2½ teaspoons salt
3 cups finely cut kale
3 tablespoons minced onion

3 tablespoons butter
⅛ teaspoon freshly ground white pepper
1 to 2 tablespoons milk

1. Preheat oven to hot (400° F.).
2. Peel the potatoes and cut them into quarters. Place in a saucepan with one inch of boiling water containing one-half teaspoon of the salt. Cover

and cook for fifteen to twenty minutes, until the potatoes are tender. Drain and mash.

3. Meanwhile, cook the kale until tender in one inch of boiling water containing one-half teaspoon of the salt. Drain.

4. Sauté the onion in half of the butter. Combine the onion with the mashed potatoes, drained kale, remaining salt, the pepper and milk. Beat until smooth.

5. Turn the mixture into a shallow baking dish, dot with the remaining butter, and place in the oven. Heat for fifteen to twenty minutes.

LEEKS WITH RED WINE   *6 servings*

3 bunches of leeks
¼ cup olive oil
¼ teaspoon salt

½ cup red wine
3 tablespoons Beef Stock (page 473)

1. Clean the leeks thoroughly, trim, and slice lengthwise almost to the white part. Lightly brown the leeks on both sides in the olive oil. Add the salt.

2. Pour the wine and stock over the leeks. Cover and cook, turning once, for about ten minutes, or until leeks are tender.

3. Place leeks in a shallow serving dish. Reduce the sauce, if necessary, and pour over the leeks.

SWISS MUSHROOMS   *4 to 6 servings*

1 tablespoon chopped shallots or green onions
7 tablespoons butter
1 pound mushrooms
Juice of ½ lemon
1 tablespoon chopped parsley
1 egg yolk

¼ cup all-purpose flour
1 cup milk
1 cup light cream
¼ teaspoon grated nutmeg
Salt and freshly ground black pepper
¾ cup grated Gruyère or Swiss cheese

1. Preheat oven to moderate (350° F.).

2. Cook the shallots in three tablespoons of the butter, stirring, for about three minutes. Do not brown.

3. Chop the mushrooms fine and add them to the skillet. Sprinkle them immediately with the lemon juice and stir in the parsley. Cook, stirring, for about fifteen minutes, until almost a paste. Remove from the heat. When slightly cool, stir in the egg yolk.

4. Melt the remaining butter in a saucepan and stir in the flour, using a wire whisk. When mixture is blended, add the milk and cream, stirring rapidly with the whisk. When mixture is thickened and smooth, season with the nutmeg and salt and pepper to taste. Stir in the mushrooms.

5. Make a layer of the mushroom mixture in a buttered casserole. Cover with half of the cheese. Add remaining mixture and sprinkle with remaining cheese. Bake for fifteen to twenty minutes, until lightly browned and heated through. Final browning may be done under the broiler.

SPICY MUSHROOMS   *4 servings*

1 pound fresh mushrooms
2 whole cloves
3 tablespoons butter
1 teaspoon salt

2 tablespoons chopped fresh parsley
2 tablespoons all-purpose flour
Freshly ground black pepper

1. Clean and slice the mushrooms. Place them in a one-and-one-half-quart pan. Rinse, drain, and cover.
2. Place the pan over medium heat and when the cover is hot, reduce the heat to low and cook for five minutes.
3. Crush the cloves in a mortar and blend with the remaining ingredients. Add to the mushrooms and boil for one minute, or until the sauce is thickened. Serve over toast points.

MUSHROOMS IN SOUR CREAM ON TOAST   *6 servings*

4 cups sliced fresh mushrooms
½ cup diced onion
2 teaspoons caraway seeds
2 teaspoons lemon juice
⅓ cup butter
1 teaspoon salt
⅛ teaspoon freshly ground black pepper

¼ cup all-purpose flour
1 cup sour cream
½ cup milk
½ cup chopped fresh parsley
6 slices of toast
Paprika

Sauté the mushrooms, onion and caraway seeds in the lemon juice and butter. Stir in the salt, pepper, flour, sour cream and milk. Heat only until hot. Just before serving, stir in the chopped parsley. Serve on toast. Sprinkle with paprika.

MUSHROOMS AU GRATIN   *4 servings*

1 pound fresh mushrooms
¼ cup butter
3 tablespoons all-purpose flour
¾ cup Chicken Stock (page 475)
¼ teaspoon dried marjoram
1 tablespoon chopped parsley
¼ teaspoon salt

⅛ teaspoon freshly ground black pepper
¼ cup heavy cream
1 tablespoon sherry
2 tablespoons grated Parmesan cheese
¼ cup soft fresh bread crumbs

1. Preheat oven to moderate (350° F.).

2. Wash the mushrooms and remove the stems. Chop the stems fine and slice the caps.

3. Melt the butter in a large skillet and cook the mushroom stems and caps in it for fifteen minutes, stirring occasionally.

4. Stir in the flour and blend well. Gradually stir in the stock. When the sauce is smooth, add the marjoram, parsley, salt and pepper and cook, stirring, for five minutes. Stir in the cream and sherry and cook, stirring, for three minutes longer.

5. Put the mushrooms and sauce into a small casserole. Sprinkle with the cheese mixed with bread crumbs. Brown in the oven for fifteen minutes.

MUSHROOMS IN OIL WITH PARSLEY   *4 servings*

1 pound large mushrooms	¼ cup chopped parsley
¾ cup olive oil	1 garlic clove, finely minced
1 teaspoon salt	1 shallot, finely minced
¼ teaspoon freshly ground black pepper	¼ cup soft fresh bread crumbs

1. Wash and slice the mushrooms, cutting through caps and stems. Marinate the mushrooms for one hour in one-half cup of the olive oil containing the salt and pepper.

2. Heat the remaining oil in a heavy skillet. Drain the mushrooms and sauté them in the hot oil for about five minutes, until just tender.

3. Add the remaining ingredients and toss lightly. Serve immediately.

SHERRIED MUSHROOMS   *4 servings*

12 large mushroom caps	¼ teaspoon grated nutmeg
Lemon juice	2 tablespoons finely chopped parsley
¼ cup butter	1 tablespoon finely chopped chives (optional)
1 garlic clove, finely minced	Salt and freshly ground black pepper
2 tablespoons grated Gruyère or Parmesan cheese	
6 tablespoons soft fresh bread crumbs	¼ cup dry sherry, approximately

1. Preheat oven to moderate (350° F.).

2. Remove the stems from the mushrooms. Chop the stems and sprinkle the caps with lemon juice.

3. Melt half of the butter in a small saucepan and cook the chopped stems until wilted. Add the garlic. Stir in the cheese, bread crumbs, nutmeg, parsley, chives, and salt and pepper to taste.

4. Stuff the caps with this mixture. Arrange them in a buttered baking dish. Sprinkle lightly with sherry and dot with remaining butter. Bake for fifteen minutes.

MUSHROOMS FLORENTINE   *4 to 6 servings*

12 to 16 large mushrooms
½ cup butter, melted
1½ tablespoons finely minced onion
1 garlic clove, finely minced
¾ cup puréed cooked spinach
½ cup minced cooked chicken or ground cooked pork

¼ teaspoon grated nutmeg
½ teaspoon salt
⅛ teaspoon freshly ground black pepper
2 tablespoons grated Parmesan cheese
Toast rounds (optional)

1. Preheat oven to moderate (375° F.).
2. Wash the mushrooms and remove the stems. Dip the caps into six tablespoons of the melted butter and place them upside down in a buttered baking dish.
3. Chop the mushroom stems and sauté them, along with the onion and garlic, in the remaining butter for about ten minutes, until soft but not browned.
4. Add the spinach, chicken or pork, nutmeg, salt and pepper to the sautéed mixture.
5. Fill the mushroom caps with the spinach mixture. Sprinkle the grated cheese over the top of the filling. Bake for fifteen minutes. Serve hot, on rounds of toast if desired.

PARSLEYED WHITE ONIONS   *4 to 6 servings*

24 small white onions, unpeeled
¾ cup Chicken Stock (page 475) water or dry white wine
6 tablespoons butter
½ bay leaf
2 parsley sprigs

¼ teaspoon dried thyme
Salt and freshly ground black pepper
3 tablespoons finely chopped parsley

1. Place the onions in a saucepan with a tight-fitting cover. Add the stock, two tablespoons of the butter, the bay leaf, parsley, thyme, and salt and pepper to taste. Cover and simmer for forty-five to fifty minutes, until onions are tender. Shake the saucepan from time to time as the onions cook.
2. Remove pan from the heat, uncover, and let stand until onions are cool enough to handle. Peel the onions and put them in another saucepan.
3. Add remaining butter, heat the onions thoroughly, and sprinkle with the chopped parsley.

BATTER-FRIED ONION RINGS   *6 servings*

3 large onions
1 cup sifted all-purpose flour
½ teaspoon salt
½ cup undiluted evaporated milk
6 tablespoons water

2 tablespoons peanut or vegetable oil
1 egg white, stiffly beaten
Fat for deep frying

1. Peel the onions and cut them into one-quarter-inch slices. Separate the slices into rings.
2. Combine the flour, salt, evaporated milk, water and oil in a mixing bowl. Blend lightly but thoroughly. Fold in the egg white.
3. Heat the fat to 375° F. on a frying thermometer. Dip the onion rings into the batter. Fry them, a few at a time, turning once, for about one minute, until they are golden brown. Drain on paper towels and keep hot until all are finished.

ALVINA MATTES'S ONION SCALLOP   *6 servings*

¼ cup butter
3 tablespoons all-purpose flour
1 teaspoon salt
⅛ teaspoon freshly ground black pepper
⅛ teaspoon grated nutmeg
1 cup milk
½ cup light cream

12 medium onions, cooked and drained well
1 cup diced celery, cooked and drained well
½ cup blanched almond halves
Paprika or buttered bread crumbs
Freshly grated Parmesan cheese (optional)

1. Preheat oven to moderate (350° F.).
2. Make a cream sauce by melting the butter and stirring in the flour, salt, pepper and nutmeg. Cook gently, stirring, until mixture is bubbly. Slowly add milk and cream. Continue to cook, stirring, until thickened.
3. Arrange layers of onions, celery and almonds in a buttered casserole. Pour cream sauce over the vegetables and sprinkle the top with paprika or buttered crumbs. Sprinkle with Parmesan cheese if desired. Bake until sauce is brown and bubbly.

BAKED ONIONS   *4 servings*

8 onions, each 2 inches in diameter
¾ teaspoon salt
⅛ teaspoon freshly ground black pepper
2 tablespoons butter

½ cup Beef or Chicken Stock (pages 473 and 475)
1 tablespoon all-purpose flour
2 tablespoons cold water
Fresh parsley for garnish

1. Preheat oven to moderate (375° F.).

2. Peel the onions. Place them with the salt and boiling water to cover in a saucepan. Bring to the boiling point, cover, and cook for five minutes. Drain the onions and place them close together in a one-quart casserole. Sprinkle with pepper, dot with butter, add the stock, and bake for about forty-five minutes, until tender.

3. Mix the flour and cold water to a smooth paste and blend with the liquid around the onions. Bake for about five minutes longer, until the sauce is slightly thickened. Garnish with parsley.

BAKED ONIONS WITH PORK AND SCALLIONS
4 to 8 servings

4 large onions
3 tablespoons butter
1 garlic clove, finely minced
¼ pound lean pork, ground
½ cup soft fresh bread crumbs
¼ cup chopped scallions, including
green parts

1 tablespoon chopped parsley
Salt and freshly ground black
pepper
Tomato sauce (optional)

1. Preheat oven to moderate (350° F.).

2. Peel the onions and cut them into halves crosswise. Scoop out part of the inside but leave a thick shell and cavity for stuffing. Chop the scooped-out onion.

3. Melt one tablespoon of the butter and cook the chopped onion and garlic in it briefly, stirring.

4. Combine the pork, bread crumbs, scallions, parsley, and salt and pepper to taste in a mixing bowl. Add the onion and garlic mixture and blend well. Sprinkle the eight onion halves with salt and stuff them with equal amounts of the filling.

5. Rub the bottom of a baking dish with the remaining butter. Arrange the stuffed onions on it and cover closely with aluminum foil.

6. Bake for one hour, until onions are tender and meat is thoroughly cooked. Serve as is or, if desired, with a tomato sauce.

PEAS IN LETTUCE   *4 servings*

2 pounds fresh peas or 1 package
(10 ounces) frozen peas
2 large outside leaves of lettuce

½ teaspoon salt
1 tablespoon butter
½ garlic clove

1. Shell the fresh peas, or break the block of frozen peas into several pieces.

2. Place one leaf of lettuce in the bottom of a one-quart pan. Add peas, salt, butter and garlic. If using fresh peas, add one-quarter cup water. Cover with the other lettuce leaf and the lid. Place over medium heat.

3. When the lid is hot to the touch, reduce the heat, and cook for thirty minutes if using fresh peas, for fifteen minutes if using frozen peas. Remove lettuce and garlic.

MOUSSE OF GREEN PEAS   *4 servings*

1 envelope unflavored gelatin
1 cup boiling water
2 cups cooked peas, fresh or frozen

½ teaspoon salt
⅛ teaspoon white pepper
1 cup sour cream

1. Into the container of an electric blender put the gelatin and boiling water. Cover and blend on high speed for forty seconds.

2. Add the peas, salt and pepper; cover and blend for forty seconds longer.

3. Remove the cover and, with the motor on, add the sour cream. Pour the mousse into a three-cup mold and chill until firm.

Note: If desired, the liquid in which the peas were cooked may be used in place of the boiling water, but the liquid must be boiling when added to the container of the blender.

FRIED GREEN PEPPERS   *6 servings*

12 green peppers
¼ cup butter
3 tablespoons olive oil

Salt and freshly ground black pepper
Dried orégano

1. Wash the peppers and cut them into quarters. Remove stems, seeds and membranes.

2. Heat the butter and olive oil in a large skillet and add the quartered peppers. Cook, stirring occasionally, for twenty to thirty minutes, until the peppers are tender.

3. Season with salt, pepper and orégano to taste. Serve immediately.

RICE-STUFFED GREEN PEPPERS   *6 servings*

6 large green peppers
¼ cup finely chopped onion
2 tablespoons butter
4 cups cooked rice
¼ cup finely chopped parsley

1 cup grated Cheddar cheese
Salt and freshly ground black pepper
⅓ cup Chicken Stock (page 475)
Tomato sauce (optional)

1. Preheat oven to moderate (350° F.).

2. Hollow out the peppers and remove the seeds. Place the peppers in a colander or sieve and lower into a large pan of boiling water. Leave them in the water for about five minutes. Drain.

3. Sauté the onion in the butter until tender. Combine the onion with the rice, parsley, cheese, and salt and pepper to taste. Stir in the stock and fill the pepper cases with the mixture.

4. Place the filled peppers in a buttered baking dish, add one-quarter cup water, and bake for about fifteen minutes, or until peppers are barely tender and filling is piping hot. Serve with tomato sauce if desired.

CRABMEAT-STUFFED PEPPERS   *4 servings*

4 medium green peppers	2 tablespoons lemon juice
1½ cups fresh crabmeat or 1 can (6½ ounces) crabmeat	1 tablespoon chopped onion
	½ teaspoon curry powder
2 eggs, lightly beaten	¼ teaspoon salt
1 cup cooked rice	Dash of cayenne pepper
3 tablespoons butter, melted	1 cup soft fresh bread crumbs

1. Preheat oven to hot (400° F.).

2. Cut the peppers lengthwise into halves and remove the seeds. Cook in boiling salted water for five minutes. Drain.

3. Flake and pick over the crabmeat. Combine it with the eggs, rice, two tablespoons of the butter, the lemon juice, onion, curry powder, salt and cayenne. Fill the pepper halves with the mixture.

4. Combine the bread crumbs with the remaining butter and sprinkle over the mixture in the pepper shells. Bake for fifteen minutes.

BRAZILIAN STUFFED PEPPERS   *6 to 8 servings*

6 to 8 large green peppers	1 tablespoon minced onion
1 pound beef, ground	½ cup undiluted evaporated milk
1 teaspoon salt	¾ cup soft fresh bread crumbs
¼ teaspoon freshly ground black pepper	1 egg
	2 cups (two 8-ounce cans) tomato sauce
¼ teaspoon dried thyme	
⅓ cup chopped Brazil nuts	½ teaspoon dried basil
1 tablespoon chopped parsley	

1. Preheat oven to hot (400° F.).

2. Cut a crosswise slice from the stem end of each pepper and discard. Remove the seeds from the peppers.

3. Sprinkle the ground beef with the salt, pepper and thyme. Add the remaining ingredients except the tomato sauce and basil. Toss gently with a

fork to blend. Stuff the mixture into the peppers and place the peppers close together in a deep saucepan.

4. Combine the tomato sauce, basil and one-half cup water; blend. Pour over the stuffed peppers. Place the saucepan over medium heat and bring to a boil. Cover with a tight-fitting lid and place in the oven. Bake for forty-five to sixty minutes, until the peppers are crisp tender.

SCALLOPED POTATOES WITH SOUR CREAM   *4 servings*

4 medium potatoes
1 cup sour cream
2 eggs, well beaten
2 tablespoons milk
3 tablespoons chopped chives

½ teaspoon salt
Dash of freshly ground black pepper
1 cup shredded sharp Cheddar cheese

1. Preheat oven to moderate (350° F.).
2. Cook the potatoes in lightly salted water until just tender. Allow to cool slightly, then peel and slice. There should be three cups of sliced potatoes. Arrange the potatoes in a buttered shallow one-and-one-half-quart baking dish.
3. Combine the sour cream with the beaten eggs, milk, chives, salt and pepper. Pour over the potatoes in the baking dish and sprinkle with the shredded cheese.
4. Bake for about thirty minutes, until heated through and lightly browned.

ROSEMARY POTATOES WITH CHEESE   *6 to 8 servings*

8 medium potatoes, peeled
⅓ cup plus 1 tablespoon butter
1 cup minced onions
1½ cups grated Cheddar cheese
¾ cup hot milk

Salt and freshly ground black pepper
1 teaspoon chopped fresh rosemary or ½ teaspoon dried rosemary
2 eggs, well beaten

1. Preheat oven to moderate (375° F.).
2. Peel the potatoes and cook them in boiling salted water to cover. Drain and mash them.
3. Melt one tablespoon of the butter and add the onions. Cook, stirring, until onions are translucent.
4. Combine the mashed potatoes, onions, remaining butter, the cheese, milk, salt and pepper to taste and rosemary.
5. Fold in the beaten eggs and pour the mixture into a lightly buttered casserole. Bake for forty-five minutes, until puffy and brown. Serve immediately.

SWEDISH POTATO CAKES   *6 servings*

2 cups hot seasoned mashed
  potatoes
1 egg
1 tablespoon finely minced onion

1 tablespoon finely minced fresh dill
  or parsley
⅛ teaspoon grated nutmeg
¼ cup butter

1. Mix the potatoes and egg and beat thoroughly until mixture is fluffy. Blend in the onion, dill and nutmeg and shape into six flat cakes.
2. Heat the butter in a large skillet and brown the cakes in it until crisp and brown on both sides.

DEVONSHIRE POTATO-MUSHROOM PIE   *6 servings*

3 cups seasoned mashed potatoes
1½ cups sliced fresh mushrooms
¼ cup chopped onion
2 tablespoons butter
1 teaspoon lemon juice

¼ teaspoon salt
  Dash of freshly ground white
  pepper
½ cup sour cream

1. Preheat oven to moderate (350° F.).
2. Place half of the mashed potatoes in a buttered nine-inch pie pan.
3. Sauté the mushrooms and onion in the butter. Add the lemon juice and salt and pepper and spoon over the potato layer. Spread with sour cream. Top with remaining potatoes.
4. Bake for forty-five minutes, until browned. To serve, cut into wedges.

GERMAN FRIED POTATOES   *6 servings*

3 tablespoons salad oil
4 cups thinly sliced raw potatoes

1 large onion, sliced
1 teaspoon salt

Heat the salad oil in a large skillet. Add the sliced potatoes and onion. Cover the skillet and cook, turning occasionally, until the potatoes are tender and golden. Season with salt.

POTATO AND TOMATO PIE   *5 servings*

3 medium potatoes
1 cup all-purpose flour
  Salt and freshly ground black
  pepper
½ cup olive oil

1 cup canned tomatoes, drained
½ pound mozzarella cheese, diced
¼ cup grated Parmesan cheese
1 tablespoon chopped fresh orégano
  or ½ teaspoon dried orégano

1. Preheat oven to hot (400° F.).
2. Boil the potatoes and mash them until they are very smooth. Mix them with the flour and season with salt and pepper to taste.

3. Press the potato mixture in a half-inch-thick layer in the bottom of an oiled shallow baking dish. Spoon half of the oil over the potatoes.

4. Arrange the tomatoes over the oil. Top with the cheeses and sprinkle with orégano and remaining oil. Bake for twenty-five minutes, until the surface is lightly browned.

POTATO PUFFS   *6 to 8 servings*

4 medium potatoes
2 teaspoons salt
2 tablespoons butter
¼ teaspoon grated nutmeg
¼ teaspoon freshly ground black
   pepper

1 egg, separated
Fat for deep frying
Fresh parsley for garnish

1. Wash and peel the potatoes. Place in a saucepan with one inch of boiling water containing one teaspoon of the salt. Cover and cook until the potatoes are tender but not mushy.

2. Drain the potatoes if necessary and mash until fluffy with the butter, nutmeg, remaining salt, the pepper and egg yolk. Beat the egg white until it stands in soft peaks and fold it into the potato mixture.

3. Put enough fat in a heavy skillet to make a layer one-half inch deep; heat. Drop the potato mixture, a heaping teaspoon at a time, into the hot fat. Fry until brown. Drain on paper towels. Garnish with fresh parsley.

CARAWAY POTATOES   *6 to 8 servings*

¼ cup butter
4 cups (two 1-pound cans) small potatoes
2 tablespoons caraway seeds
2 tablespoons grated onion

1 teaspoon salt
¼ teaspoon freshly ground black
   pepper
½ teaspoon paprika

Melt the butter in a pan. Add the potatoes and remaining ingredients and heat, occasionally shaking the pan, until the potatoes are lightly browned.

BAKED POTATO FOR ONE   *1 serving*

1 large potato for baking
   Bacon fat or vegetable oil
1 tablespoon butter

Salt and freshly ground black
   pepper

1. Preheat oven to hot (425° F.).

2. Wash the potato and dry well. Rub the outside of the potato with bacon fat or vegetable oil and place it on a rack in the oven. Bake for forty

minutes to one hour, depending on the size of the potato. To test for doneness, press into the sides of the potato, guarding the fingers with a heavy cloth.

3. Make a large deep gash down the center of the potato, loosen the
flesh with a fork, and fill the opening with the butter. Sprinkle the potato
with salt and pepper to taste and serve immediately.

Note: Sour cream and chopped chives may be substituted for the butter.

STUFFED POTATO FOR ONE   *1 serving*

Bake a large potato. When baked, split it into halves, scoop out the flesh,
and reserve one of the scooped-out shells. Put the flesh through a ricer and
season with butter, salt, pepper and a touch of grated nutmeg. Add a little
heavy cream, blend well, and use the mixture to stuff the reserved shell.
Sprinkle with about one-quarter cup grated sharp Cheddar cheese and place
in a small baking dish. Bake in a moderate oven (350° F.) until the potato
is heated through and the cheese is melted.

STUFFED POTATOES AÏOLI   *6 servings*

6 large baking potatoes	Freshly ground black pepper
½ cup sour cream	2 hard-cooked eggs, chopped
1¾ teaspoons salt	⅓ cup half and half cream, heated
1 garlic clove, finely minced	6 tablespoons butter
½ teaspoon ground cuminseed	

1. Preheat oven to hot (450° F.).

2. Scrub the potatoes and bake them for at least one hour, or until done.

3. Cut a small slice from the top of each potato. Discard slices. Scoop
out the insides of the potatoes into a warm mixing bowl. Leave the potato
shells intact and reserve.

4. Combine the sour cream, salt, garlic, cuminseed, pepper to taste, eggs
and cream. Add to the potato mixture and beat quickly and briskly. Stuff
the potato shells with the filling and top each with a tablespoon of butter.
Return the potatoes to the oven for ten minutes, until thoroughly hot.

POTATOES-IN-THE-SHELL SOUFFLÉ   *6 servings*

6 large baking potatoes	3 tablespoons hot milk
1½ teaspoons salt	1 egg, separated
⅛ teaspoon freshly ground black pepper	Finely grated sharp aged Cheddar cheese
Dash of grated nutmeg	Fresh parsley for garnish
2 tablespoons butter	

1. Preheat oven to hot (400° F.).

2. Scrub the potatoes. Prick the potatoes with a knife or skewer and bake them for about one hour, until tender.

3. Cut a slice off the top of each potato; discard slices. Scoop out the insides and mash until fluffy with the seasonings, butter and hot milk. Beat in the egg yolk. Beat the egg white until stiff and fold into the potato mixture. Refill potato shells with this mixture. Sprinkle with grated cheese.

4. Lower the oven temperature to moderate (350° F.) and bake the potatoes for about twenty-five minutes, until browned. Garnish with fresh parsley.

BAKED POTATOES WITH SOUR CREAM AND SCALLIONS
6 servings

6 large baking potatoes	¾ cup sour cream
Bacon fat or vegetable oil	½ cup finely chopped scallions
6 teaspoon butter	
Salt and freshly ground black pepper	

1. Preheat oven to hot (425° F.).

2. Scrub and dry the potatoes. Rub the outsides of the potatoes with fat and place them on an oven rack. Bake for forty-five minutes to one hour, depending on size.

3. Make a deep gash down center of each potato and loosen the pulp with a fork. Stir a teaspoon of butter into each, and season with salt and pepper. Blend sour cream with scallions and spoon the mixture onto the potatoes.

POTATO BOATS   *24 servings*

24 large potatoes	3 teaspoons salt
1½ cups hot light cream, approximately	½ teaspoon freshly ground black pepper
½ cup melted butter	1 teaspoon baking soda
4 cups finely chopped corned beef or ham	24 eggs
¼ cup finely chopped green pepper (optional)	

Early in the day:

1. Preheat oven to hot (425° F.).

2. Scrub and dry the potatoes. Bake them for about one hour, or until done.

3. Cut a slice from the top of each potato; discard slices. Scoop out the insides of the potatoes into a mixing bowl, taking care not to break the skins. Reserve shells.

4. Add the hot cream and butter to the potatoes, beating vigorously until the mixture is smooth and fluffy. Stir in the corned beef or ham, green pepper, salt, pepper and baking soda. (The soda is added to prevent darkening.) Pile the mixture into the shells and place them in large shallow baking pans. Make a slight depression in the top of each filled potato. Cover and set aside.

5. Thirty to forty minutes before serving time, preheat oven to moderate (375° F.).

6. Bake the filled potato shells for twenty to twenty-five minutes, or until thoroughly heated. Break an egg into each depression and return shells to the oven. Cook for seven to ten minutes, until the eggs are set.

POTATO-CHEESE CHARLOTTE   *6 servings*

½ cup chopped onion
2 tablespoons butter
3 cups grated raw potatoes
2 eggs, beaten
1½ teaspoons salt

1 teaspoon paprika
⅛ teaspoon pepper
1 cup grated sharp Cheddar cheese
2 slices of white bread

1. Preheat oven to moderate (350° F.). Butter a one-quart casserole.

2. Sauté the onion in the butter until limp. Mix with the potatoes, eggs, salt, paprika, pepper and cheese.

3. Soak the bread in water until soft. Squeeze dry and add to the potato mixture. Mix well.

4. Turn into the prepared casserole and bake for one hour.

GRATIN DAUPHINOIS   *6 servings*

4 cups very thinly sliced potatoes
1 teaspoon salt
¼ teaspoon freshly ground black pepper
⅛ teaspoon grated nutmeg
1 garlic clove, finely minced

1¼ cups grated Gruyère cheese
¼ cup butter
2 eggs, lightly beaten
1 cup heavy cream
2 tablespoons grated Parmesan cheese

1. Preheat oven to moderate (375° F.).

2. Sprinkle the potatoes with half of the salt, half of the pepper, the nutmeg and garlic.

3. Place a layer of potatoes in a greased shallow baking dish, sprinkle with one third of the Gruyère cheese, and dot with one third of the butter. Alternate layers of potatoes, cheese and butter until all are used, ending with cheese.

4. Combine the eggs, cream and remaining salt and pepper. Pour over potatoes. Sprinkle with Parmesan cheese. Bake, covered, for thirty to forty

minutes, or until potatoes are almost tender. Uncover and bake until well browned and set.

GRATIN SAVOYARD   *6 to 8 servings*

6 large baking potatoes
1 large or 2 small celery knobs
  Butter
1¼ cups grated Gruyère or Swiss cheese

1 teaspoon salt
  Freshly ground black pepper
¾ cup Beef or Chicken Stock (pages 473 and 475)

1. Preheat oven to moderate (375° F.).
2. Peel potatoes and celery knobs and cut them into even slices about one-eighth inch thick.
3. Butter a baking dish well and arrange alternate layers of celery knob, potato, and cheese, using about one cup of the cheese. Begin and end the layers with potatoes. Sprinkle with salt and pepper and pour the stock over all.
4. Bake for one to one and one-quarter hours, until potatoes are tender and most of the liquid is absorbed. Sprinkle with remaining cheese and return to the oven until cheese melts.

Like fresh asparagus and shad, new potatoes are evidence of spring.

BRAISED NEW POTATOES AND CARROTS WITH DILL
6 servings

12 medium-size new potatoes
 1 teaspoon salt
 3 tablespoons butter

⅓ cup water
2 cups ¼-inch slices of carrots
1 tablespoon chopped fresh dill

1. Wash and scrape the potatoes; leave them whole. Place them in a saucepan with the salt, butter and water. Cover and cook for twenty minutes over low heat.
2. Add the carrots. Cover and cook for fifteen minutes longer, or until carrots and potatoes are tender. Add dill and mix lightly. Serve hot.

NEW POTATOES, FRENCH STYLE   *6 to 8 servings*

2 pounds small new potatoes
  Chicken or Beef Stock (pages 473 and 475)
½ teaspoon salt
1 tablespoon butter

¼ teaspoon freshly ground black pepper
1½ teaspoons cornstarch
1 tablespoon water
  Chopped fresh parsley

1. Wash and scrape the potatoes; leave them whole. Pour one inch of stock into a saucepan and bring to a boil. Add the potatoes and salt, cover,

and bring again to a boil. Cook for fifteen to twenty minutes, depending on the size of the potatoes.

2. Add the butter and pepper. Mix the cornstarch with the water and add to the liquid around the potatoes. (There will be only a little.) Cook for one minute, or until slightly thick and transparent. Turn potatoes out onto a serving dish and garnish with chopped parsley.

SWEET POTATOES MOUSSELINE   *6 to 8 servings*

4 medium sweet potatoes (about 2 pounds)	2 tablespoons butter
	1 egg, well beaten
½ teaspoon grated nutmeg	¼ cup heavy cream
¾ teaspoon salt	1 tablespoon grated orange rind
Dash of ground cloves	½ teaspoon grated lemon rind
¼ cup sugar	2 tablespoons light brown sugar

1. Preheat oven to hot (450° F.).

2. Cook the unpeeled whole sweet potatoes in boiling water to cover for twenty to thirty minutes, until tender. Slip off the skins and mash the potatoes until smooth.

3. Add the nutmeg, salt, cloves, sugar, one tablespoon of the butter, the egg, cream and grated rinds to the mashed potatoes. Beat until fluffy.

4. Turn the mixture into a buttered one-quart casserole. Melt the remaining butter and brush the top of the mixture. Sprinkle with brown sugar. Bake for about thirty-five minutes, until browned.

CANDIED SWEET POTATOES   *6 servings*

4 to 6 sweet potatoes	¼ cup water
1 cup granulated brown sugar	¼ teaspoon ground cinnamon
1 teaspoon salt	⅛ teaspoon grated nutmeg
2 tablespoons butter	

1. Preheat oven to moderate (350° F.).

2. Parboil the sweet potatoes for fifteen minutes; peel and slice them. Place in a buttered one-and-one-half-quart round baking dish.

3. Make a syrup by combining sugar, salt, butter, water and spices and boiling for three minutes. Pour syrup over potatoes.

4. Bake for one and one-quarter hours, basting frequently.

SWEET POTATOES À LA ANN SERANNE   *6 servings*

3 pounds sweet potatoes	1 teaspoon ground cinnamon
½ cup butter	Cream
¼ cup sherry	Salt and freshly ground black pepper
¼ teaspoon grated nutmeg	

1. Preheat oven to moderate (325° F.).

2. Cook the potatoes in boiling water to cover for thirty to forty minutes, until tender.

3. Cool the potatoes slightly, then peel, and put the pulp through a potato ricer.

4. Beat in half of the butter, the sherry, nutmeg and half of the cinnamon. If the potatoes are dry, beat in enough cream to moisten; season with salt and pepper to taste.

5. Put the potatoes into a one-and-one-half-quart casserole. Dot with remaining butter and sprinkle with remaining cinnamon. Bake for thirty minutes.

GLAZED SWEET POTATOES WITH WALNUTS   *6 to 8 servings*

6 sweet potatoes, boiled or baked
1½ cups dark brown sugar
3 tablespoons water
3 tablespoons butter

1 teaspoon grated lemon rind
½ cup walnut halves or chopped walnuts

1. Preheat oven to moderate (350° F.).

2. Peel the potatoes, halve them, and place in a baking dish.

3. Combine the sugar, water, butter and lemon rind in a saucepan. Bring the mixture to a boil and pour it over the sweet potatoes.

4. Bake for ten to fifteen minutes, basting several times during cooking. Remove from the oven and sprinkle with the nuts.

Note: One-half cup of the brown sugar may be replaced with one-half cup honey.

SWEET-POTATO SOUFFLÉ   *6 to 8 servings*

2 pounds sweet potatoes
½ teaspoon grated nutmeg
Pinch of ground cloves
¼ teaspoon salt

¼ cup light brown sugar
2 tablespoons butter
¼ cup heavy cream
3 eggs, separated

1. Preheat oven to hot (400° F.).

2. Cook the sweet potatoes in boiling water until tender. Drain, peel, and mash until smooth.

3. Add the spices, salt, sugar, butter and cream. Beat together. Add the egg yolks. Beat the egg whites until stiff and fold them into the mixture.

4. Bake in a buttered soufflé mold or casserole for about thirty-five minutes, or until soufflé is well risen and brown. If desired, brush the top of the soufflé with melted butter and sprinkle lightly with light brown sugar before baking.

The French use the name "Florentine" for almost all spinach dishes, supposedly because the fields around Florence once were green with the vegetable. When one sees eggs Florentine, fish Florentine, or mushrooms Florentine on a menu, it is safe to assume that the foods in question are served on a bed of spinach, either puréed or en branche.

The water content of spinach is formidable, and because of this it should be cooked only in the water which clings to its leaves after it is washed. Use a saucepan or casserole with a tight-fitting cover.

CREAMED SPINACH   *4 to 6 servings*

3 pounds fresh spinach
¼ cup butter or chicken fat
¼ cup all-purpose flour
1 tablespoon grated onion
2 cups Chicken Stock (page 475) or milk

1 teaspoon salt
¼ teaspoon freshly ground black pepper
Hard-cooked eggs

1. Wash the spinach several times in cold water to remove all sand; discard any tough stems. Place the spinach in a kettle with only the water that clings to the leaves; cover. Cook until spinach is wilted, then drain and chop very fine.

2. Heat the butter in a skillet. Add the flour and onion and cook, stirring, until brown. Gradually add the stock or milk, stirring constantly until thickened and smooth.

3. Add the spinach, salt and pepper; simmer for several minutes. Garnish with chopped egg whites and riced egg yolks.

SPINACH WITH ORÉGANO   *4 servings*

2 pounds fresh spinach
1 teaspoon salt

1 teaspoon dried orégano
¼ cup butter

1. Wash and shred the spinach. Place in a four-quart saucepan, rinse, and drain.

2. Cover the pan and place over medium heat. When the cover is hot, reduce the heat to low and cook for five minutes. Add remaining ingredients.

SPINACH WITH SESAME SEEDS   *4 servings*

2 pounds fresh spinach
¼ cup sesame seeds
3 tablespoons soy sauce
¼ cup butter

Juice of ½ lemon
Salt and freshly ground black pepper

1. Preheat oven to moderate (350° F.).

2. Wash the spinach and discard any tough stems. Place the spinach in a saucepan with only the water that clings to the leaves. Do not season. Cover, bring to a boil, and cook just until leaves wilt, stirring once or twice. Drain well and keep warm.

3. Meanwhile, scatter the sesame seeds in a small skillet and bake for five to ten minutes, until they are brown, stirring occasionally. Remove from the oven.

4. Place spinach in a serving dish and add toasted sesame seeds and remaining ingredients.

SPINACH AND ROQUEFORT   *4 servings*

2 pounds fresh spinach or 2 packages (10 ounces each) frozen spinach
2 tablespoons butter
2 tablespoons all-purpose flour
1 cup heavy cream
1½ ounces Roquefort cheese, crumbled
Salt and freshly ground black pepper

1. Wash the spinach and discard any tough stems. Cook the spinach until just tender in the water that clings to the leaves, or cook the frozen spinach according to package directions. Drain the spinach and chop it; or if it is very young and tender, leaves may be left whole.

2. Melt the butter, blend in the flour, and add the cream, stirring with a wire whisk. Bring to a boil, stirring, and cook until the mixture is thickened and smooth.

3. Add the Roquefort to the spinach; add the sauce and salt and pepper to taste. Reheat, but do not boil, and serve immediately.

SPINACH WITH SAUTÉED MUSHROOMS   *4 or 5 servings*

2 small onions, chopped
2 tablespoons butter
2 pounds fresh spinach
⅓ cup sliced fresh or canned mushrooms
2 teaspoons lemon juice
1¼ teaspoons salt, or more
¾ teaspoon sugar
⅛ teaspoon freshly ground black pepper

1. Sauté the onions in one tablespoon of the butter.

2. Wash the spinach and cut off and discard the root ends and any tough stems. Chop the spinach coarsely and add to the onions. Cover and cook over medium heat for ten minutes.

3. Sauté the mushrooms in the lemon juice and remaining butter. Add to the spinach along with the seasonings. Toss lightly. If desired, garnish with additional sautéed sliced mushrooms. Serve immediately.

Clockwise from top left: puréed fennel, chestnuts, potatoes, mushrooms and carrots
Copyright © 1965 The New York Times Company.

SPINACH CASSEROLE   *6 servings*

2 pounds fresh spinach or 2 packages (10 ounces each) frozen
chopped spinach
8 ounces cream cheese
½ cup butter

Salt and freshly ground black
pepper
1 cup soft fresh bread crumbs
¾ teaspoon ground sage

1. Preheat oven to moderate (350° F.).
2. Wash the fresh spinach and discard root ends and any tough stems.
Cook in the water clinging to the leaves for five to eight minutes, drain, and
chop; or cook the frozen spinach according to package directions and drain.
3. Mix the spinach with the cheese, half of the butter, and salt and
pepper to taste. Stir to mix well. Pour into a one-and-one-half-quart casserole.
4. Melt the remaining butter. Toss with the bread crumbs and sage;
sprinkle the mixture over the spinach.
5. Bake for twenty to thirty minutes, until bubbly hot and lightly
browned.
Note: This casserole may be made through Step 4 several hours in advance and refrigerated until time to bake it.

SPINACH MOLD   *6 servings*

3 cups chopped drained cooked
spinach
⅔ cup fine dry bread crumbs
½ cup finely minced onion
5 tablespoons butter
⅛ teaspoon freshly ground black
pepper

½ teaspoon salt
⅛ teaspoon grated nutmeg
½ cup grated Swiss cheese
5 eggs
1 cup milk, scalded

1. Preheat oven to moderate (325° F.). Generously oil a one-quart ring
mold.
2. Combine the spinach and bread crumbs in a mixing bowl.
3. Cook the onion in two tablespoons of the butter in a covered skillet
for ten minutes. Add to the spinach mixture. Add the pepper, salt, nutmeg
and cheese.
4. Lightly beat the eggs. Melt the remaining butter in the hot milk and
add to the eggs, stirring constantly. Add to spinach mixture and mix well.
5. Pour the mixture into the prepared mold and set the mold in a pan
of hot water. Bake for thirty-five minutes, or until a knife plunged into the
center comes out clean.
6. Allow the mold to rest for five minutes before unmolding onto a warm
serving platter.

PALAVER SAUCE (spinach stew)   *4 to 6 servings*

2 cups palm oil or salad oil
3 cups thinly sliced onions
¼ pound salt cod, soaked overnight in water to cover, and drained
¼ pound salt beef, soaked overnight in water to cover, and drained (dried beef may be substituted)

2 pounds spinach, cooked, drained and chopped, or 2 packages (10 ounces each) frozen chopped spinach
3 tomatoes, peeled and chopped
1 cup Beef Stock (page 473) or water
2 cans (7 ounces each) tuna
Coarsely ground red pepper flakes

1. Heat the oil in a saucepan and add the onions. Cook until onions are wilted. Add the salt cod and beef. Add the spinach, tomatoes and stock and simmer for forty-five minutes, stirring occasionally.

2. Ten minutes before the stew is done, add the tuna. Sprinkle with red pepper flakes to taste just before serving.

For vegetable lovers, the squash family is a bountiful blessing, for this genus of edible gourd includes such diverse members as white pattypans or cymlings, yellow crooknecks and dark green zucchini. The small green acorn squash, the giant blue-gray Hubbards and even the familiar orange pumpkins are relatives. One may use any one of the orange-fleshed fall varieties in place of another and they can be glazed or candied in the same way that sweet potatoes are prepared. The smaller species, such as zucchini, cymlings and acorn squash, with their seed-filled hollow centers, are well designed for stuffing preparations and their bland flavors combine successfully with a wide variety of seasonings.

CYMLINGS STUFFED WITH VEAL   *8 servings*

4 cymlings (white pattypan squash)
¼ cup olive oil
1 onion, finely chopped
2 garlic cloves, finely minced
1 pound veal, ground
2 tart green apples, peeled, cored and diced

1 cup soft fresh bread crumbs
¼ cup grated Parmesan cheese
2 tablespoons pine nuts, chopped
½ teaspoon dried thyme
Salt and freshly ground black pepper
Chicken Stock (page 475)

1. Preheat oven to moderate (350° F.).

2. Wash the squash. Cut a small slice from both stem and blossom ends and cut the squash into halves horizontally. Steam in a colander over a pan of boiling water for ten minutes. Scoop out the seeds and discard them. Scoop out some of the squash to enlarge the hollow, but do not cut through the bottom. Chop the scooped-out vegetable. Turn the hollowed-out halves upside down to drain.

3. Heat the oil in a skillet and sauté the onion and garlic until tender but not browned. Add the veal and cook until the meat loses its color, stirring occasionally.

4. Add the apples, crumbs, cheese, nuts, thyme, salt and pepper to taste and the chopped squash. Mix well. Fill the squash halves with the mixture.

5. Place the filled cymlings in a shallow baking dish. Pour in the stock until it reaches a depth of one inch. Bake for twenty-five minutes, or until the cymlings are tender and the stuffing hot.

BAKED ACORN SQUASH   *6 servings*

3 acorn squash
Grated nutmeg or ground ginger
Salt and freshly ground black pepper

3 teaspoons brown sugar, or more
6 teaspoons butter
6 teaspoons sweet sherry (optional)

1. Preheat oven to moderate (325° F.).
2. Split the squash into halves and scoop out the fibers and seeds.
3. Sprinkle the cavity of each half with nutmeg, salt, pepper, brown sugar and a teaspoon of butter. Bake for thirty to forty-five minutes, or until flesh is tender. Five minutes before serving, add a teaspoon of sherry to each cavity.

BUTTERNUT SQUASH HAWAIIENNE   *4 servings*

1 butternut squash (2 pounds)
2 tablespoons butter
2 teaspoons brown sugar or maple syrup

½ cup crushed sweetened pineapple, fresh, frozen or canned
¼ teaspoon salt
Heavy cream

1. Peel the squash and cut it into slices of even thickness. Remove the seeds.
2. Place the squash slices on a rack in a pot with a tight-fitting cover. Add enough water to cover the bottom of the pot, and steam, covered, for fifteen to twenty minutes, until tender.
3. Drain the squash and mash it, or put it through a food mill. Add the butter, brown sugar, pineapple, salt and enough heavy cream to make the mixture soft and fluffy. Reheat before serving.

SUMMER SQUASH WITH ORÉGANO   *4 servings*

1½ pounds yellow summer squash
1 garlic clove, sliced
1 tablespoon olive oil
1 large tomato, peeled and quartered

1½ teaspoons salt
½ teaspoon dried orégano
Freshly ground black pepper
2 tablespoons chopped parsley

1. Scrub the squash with a stiff brush and slice crosswise into thin slices.

2. Sauté the garlic in the oil in a one-and-one-half-quart pan for one minute. Add the sliced squash and continue to cook for one minute while turning the slices gently in the oil. Stir in the tomato, salt and orégano.

3. Cover and cook over low heat for twelve to fifteen minutes. Sprinkle with pepper to taste and garnish with parsley.

SQUASH AND ONION CASSEROLE   *4 to 6 servings*

1 cup finely chopped onions	½ cup sour cream
¼ cup butter	Freshly ground black pepper
2 pounds yellow summer squash	½ cup soft fresh bread crumbs
1 teaspoon salt	2 tablespoons melted butter

1. Preheat oven to moderate (350° F.).

2. Cook the onions in the butter until golden, stirring almost constantly.

3. Scrub and trim the squash and cut them into cubes. Cook squash in one inch of boiling water containing the salt for fifteen minutes, or until tender. Put the squash through a food mill or ricer.

4. Combine the puréed squash, onions and sour cream and season the mixture with additional salt and pepper to taste. Spoon it into a casserole and top with bread crumbs. Dribble the butter over it.

5. Bake for ten to fifteen minutes, or until the casserole starts to bubble. Place it briefly under the broiler until crumbs are brown.

ZUCCHINI AND CORN CASSEROLE   *6 servings*

6 zucchini	1 cup grated sharp Cheddar cheese
½ teaspoon salt	5 eggs, well beaten
½ cup butter	1 cup drained whole-kernel corn,
1½ cups finely chopped onions	canned or frozen
1 garlic clove, finely minced	
1 green pepper, cored, seeded and finely chopped	

1. Preheat oven to moderate (350° F.).

2. Place the zucchini in a pan with a tight-fitting cover. Add about one cup water and the salt; cover. Steam the zucchini for about ten minutes, until barely tender; do not overcook.

3. Drain the zucchini; when they are cool enough to handle, chop or grind them.

4. Melt two tablespoons of the butter and cook the onions, garlic and green pepper until onions are wilted. Blend with the zucchini. Add the cheese, eggs, remaining butter and the corn. Pour the mixture into a one-and-one-half-quart casserole and bake for one hour.

ZUCCHINI WITH HERBS   *6 servings*

3 large or 6 small zucchini
3 tablespoons butter
1 tablespoon finely minced shallots or
  onion

1 teaspoon finely minced fresh tarragon or ½ teaspoon dried tarragon

1. Wash and dry the zucchini. Trim off the ends and cut the zucchini into one-inch lengths. Cut each length through the center into two.

2. Drop the zucchini into boiling salted water to cover and simmer for twelve to fifteen minutes, until zucchini are tender but not mushy. Drain well in a colander.

3. Melt the butter in a large skillet, add the shallots, and cook briefly. Add the tarragon. Toss the zucchini in the skillet until coated with butter. Serve immediately.

ZUCCHINI AND CUCUMBER IN SOUR CREAM   *6 servings*

2 medium zucchini
1 medium cucumber
¾ teaspoon salt
½ cup chopped green onions
2 tablespoons butter

½ cup sour cream
⅛ teaspoon freshly ground black
  pepper
Chopped fresh parsley

1. Cut squash and cucumber into crosswise slices one-quarter-inch thick. Place squash in a saucepan with one-half inch of boiling water containing the salt. Cover and bring to a boil. Reduce heat and cook for twelve minutes longer, or until almost tender.

2. Add the cucumber and cook only until crisp-tender, about three minutes. Drain, if necessary.

3. Sauté the green onions in the butter. Add to saucepan along with sour cream and black pepper. Mix lightly. Heat, but do not boil. Serve sprinkled with parsley.

ZUCCHINI CHEESE CUSTARD   *4 servings*

4 small zucchini
2 medium onions
¼ cup melted butter
3 eggs, lightly beaten
⅔ cup light cream

Pinch of grated nutmeg
1½ cups grated sharp Cheddar cheese
Salt and freshly ground black
  pepper

1. Preheat oven to moderate (350° F.).

2. Peel the zucchini and cut them into two-inch rounds. Peel the onions and cut them into thin rings.

3. Cook the zucchini and onions in the butter until light golden. Do not brown and do not let the zucchini become soft.

4. Spoon the zucchini and onions into a shallow casserole. Combine the eggs, cream, nutmeg and half of the cheese. Pour the mixture over the vegetables. Sprinkle with salt and pepper and the remaining cheese.

5. Set the casserole in a baking dish, pour boiling water around it, and bake for thirty-five to forty minutes, until custard is set.

BAKED ZUCCHINI AND TOMATOES   *6 to 8 servings*

2 cups onions
1 green pepper, cored, seeded and chopped
½ cup chopped celery
2 garlic cloves
¼ cup butter
4 cups chopped peeled tomatoes, fresh or canned
1 bay leaf
1 tablespoon chopped fresh basil or 1 teaspoon dried basil
¼ cup chopped parsley
Salt and freshly ground black pepper
4 zucchini
½ cup all-purpose flour
¾ cup olive oil
¾ cup soft fresh bread crumbs
¼ cup grated Parmesan cheese

1. In a medium-size kettle cook the onions, pepper, celery and garlic in three tablespoons of the butter until onions are translucent. Add the tomatoes, bay leaf, basil, parsley, and salt and pepper to taste. Simmer for thirty minutes.

2. Preheat oven to hot (450° F.).

3. Scrub and trim the zucchini and cut them into one-inch rounds. Dredge the rounds with flour, then shake to remove excess flour. Quickly brown the rounds in the oil and transfer to paper towels to drain. Add the drained slices to the tomato mixture and continue to cook for about ten minutes, until zucchini are tender. Do not let vegetable become mushy.

4. Pour the mixture into a two-quart baking dish and sprinkle with a mixture of the bread crumbs and cheese. Dot with remaining butter. Bake until thoroughly hot and bubbling. The top should be golden brown. The leftover dish may be eaten cold.

GLAZED PUMPKIN   *6 to 8 servings*

1 pumpkin (3 pounds)
¼ cup orange juice
¾ cup firmly packed brown sugar
¾ teaspoon ground cinnamon
½ teaspoon salt
¼ cup melted butter

1. Peel and seed the pumpkin. Cut it into chunks and steam it on a rack in a pot with a tight-fitting cover for twenty minutes, until the pumpkin is nearly tender. Drain the chunks well.

2. Preheat oven to hot (400° F.).

3. Arrange the pumpkin chunks in one layer in a greased shallow baking dish. Mix the orange juice, sugar, one-half teaspoon of the cinnamon and the salt and spoon the syrup over the pumpkin. Drizzle with the melted butter.

4. Bake for twenty-five minutes, until the pumpkin is tender and glazed. Sprinkle the remaining cinnamon over the pumpkin before serving.

FRIED GREEN TOMATOES   *4 to 6 servings*

¼ cup all-purpose flour
1 tablespoon cornmeal
½ teaspoon salt
4 large green tomatoes, unpeeled

¼ cup oil
¼ cup butter
Sugar
Freshly ground black pepper

1. Mix flour, cornmeal and salt. Wash and core the tomatoes and slice them. Coat the slices with the flour mixture.

2. Brown on one side in hot oil and butter; sprinkle with sugar. Using a spatula, carefully turn each slice over to brown the other side. Sprinkle the browned side with pepper. Do not overcook or the slices will fall apart. Serve immediately.

CUCUMBER-STUFFED TOMATOES   *6 servings*

2 cucumbers
2 teaspoons grated onion
4 teaspoons lemon juice
¼ cup butter
¼ cup water

Salt and freshly ground black
  pepper
6 tomatoes
Buttered soft fresh bread crumbs

1. Preheat oven to hot (400° F.).

2. Peel the cucumbers and cut them into half-inch cubes. Add the onion, lemon juice, butter, water and seasonings to taste. Simmer for five minutes.

3. Remove the seeds and pulp from the tomatoes and drain them. Fill the tomatoes with the cooked cucumber mixture. Sprinkle with bread crumbs. Bake for about ten minutes, until the tomatoes are tender and the crumbs are brown.

TOMATO SOUFFLÉ   *6 servings*

2 tablespoons butter
1 garlic clove, finely minced
2 tablespoons all-purpose flour
2 cups milk
1 teaspoon salt

1 teaspoon Worcestershire sauce
1 bay leaf
6 tablespoons tomato paste
  Pinch of sugar (optional)
6 eggs, separated

1. Preheat oven to moderate (350° F.).

2. Melt the butter in a saucepan. Add the garlic and cook for one minute. Blend in the flour and add the milk gradually. Cook over low heat, stirring vigorously with a wire whisk, until the sauce is thickened and smooth. Add the salt, Worcestershire, bay leaf, tomato paste and sugar. Cook for five minutes, then remove the bay leaf.

3. Beat the egg yolks lightly and add a small amount of the hot mixture to the yolks. Combine the egg yolks with the remaining hot mixture. Beat the egg whites until stiff and carefully fold them into the hot mixture.

4. Pour the soufflé mixture into a three-quart soufflé dish and set the dish in a pan of hot water. Bake for fifty to sixty minutes, until the soufflé is puffed and brown. Serve immediately.

MUSHROOM-STUFFED TOMATOES   *6 servings*

6 large firm ripe tomatoes
Salt and freshly ground black pepper
½ pound mushrooms
Juice of ½ lemon
¼ cup butter

2 tablespoons tomato purée
2 egg yolks, lightly beaten
1 teaspoon chopped fresh basil or ½ teaspoon dried basil
Fine dry bread crumbs

1. Preheat oven to moderate (350° F.).

2. Trim the tops of the tomatoes. Remove the cores and the seeds. Sprinkle the insides with salt and pepper and invert on a rack to drain.

3. Chop the mushrooms fine and sprinkle with lemon juice. Season with salt and pepper and cook in the butter, stirring frequently, until most of the natural juices evaporate. This will take several minutes. Remove from the heat.

4. Blend the tomato purée and egg yolks and add to the mushrooms. Add the basil and mix.

5. Stuff the tomatoes with the mushroom mixture, sprinkle with bread crumbs, and dot with additional butter. Bake for ten to fifteen minutes, until the tomatoes are tender, yet firm, and the crumbs are browned.

TOMATOES STUFFED WITH VEGETABLES   *6 servings*

6 large firm tomatoes
2 small carrots
½ green pepper, seeded
1 small onion
2 large celery ribs
2 cups raw spinach, washed well
2 parsley sprigs
2 tablespoons butter

1 egg, beaten
¾ cup fine dry bread crumbs
½ cup milk
½ teaspoon salt
⅛ teaspoon freshly ground black pepper
Grated Parmesan cheese

1. Preheat oven to hot (400° F.).

2. Wipe the tomatoes and cut a thin slice from the stem end of each. Scoop out the seeds and pulp. Wash the remaining vegetables and parsley and put through a food chopper.

3. Melt the butter, add the chopped vegetables, and cook until almost all the liquid evaporates. Chill slightly. Add the egg, bread crumbs, milk and seasonings; mix thoroughly.

4. Fill the tomatoes with the chopped vegetable mixture and sprinkle with the cheese. Place in a buttered pan and bake for about twenty minutes, until the tomatoes are tender.

TOMATOES STUFFED WITH TONGUE   *6 servings*

6 large firm ripe tomatoes
1 garlic clove, crushed
　Salt and freshly ground black
　pepper
4 chicken livers
¼ cup butter

½ cup finely chopped onion
½ cup soft fresh bread crumbs
2 cups chopped cooked tongue
1 tablespoon chopped parsley
3 tablespoons sour cream
¼ cup grated Parmesan cheese

1. Cut the tops off the tomatoes and scoop out the seeds and pulp. Rub the inside of each tomato with the garlic and season with salt and pepper.

2. Brown the chicken livers quickly on all sides in two tablespoons of the butter in a skillet. Remove livers and dice them.

3. Add the remaining butter to the skillet and sauté the onion in it until transparent. Combine with the diced livers, bread crumbs, tongue, parsley and sour cream. Season with salt and pepper to taste.

4. Fill the tomatoes with the mixture and sprinkle with the cheese. Broil at least four inches from the source of heat until hot and lightly browned.

TOMATOES STUFFED WITH CHICKEN LIVERS   *8 servings*

8 firm tomatoes
　Salt and freshly ground black
　pepper
½ pound fresh mushrooms
¼ cup butter

1 medium onion, minced
½ cup soft fresh bread crumbs
1 tablespoon chopped parsley
1½ pounds chicken livers
2 tablespoons dry white wine

1. Preheat oven to moderate (350° F.).

2. Wash and dry the tomatoes. Cut off a thin slice from the stem end of each tomato and scoop out the pulp. Season the tomato shells lightly with salt and pepper and reserve; reserve half of the pulp.

3. Wipe the mushrooms and reserve eight of the caps. Chop the remaining mushrooms. Melt two tablespoons of the butter and in it sauté the mushroom caps briefly. Remove mushrooms from the pan and set aside. Add the

onion and chopped mushrooms to the butter left in the pan and cook for three minutes. Add the bread crumbs, reserved tomato pulp, parsley, one teaspoon salt and one-eighth teaspoon pepper. Cook for three minutes longer.

4. Cut the chicken livers into bite-size pieces and sauté them in the remaining butter. Add them to the bread-crumb mixture along with the wine; blend well. Fill the tomato shells generously with the mixture. Dot with additional butter and top with the mushroom caps.

5. Place in a well-buttered baking pan and bake for twenty minutes.

Note: If desired, the dish can be completely assembled and refrigerated overnight before baking.

TOMATOES AND GREEN BEANS À LA FRANÇAISE   *4 servings*

2 ripe tomatoes
1 recipe Chilled Green Beans (page 375)
½ cup finely chopped red or Bermuda onion
Salt and freshly ground black pepper
¼ cup wine vinegar
¾ cup olive or vegetable oil
½ cup finely chopped parsley

1. Wash and dry the tomatoes, leaving the skin intact. Trim away and discard the stem end of each tomato and a thin slice from the base of each. Slice the tomatoes.

2. Arrange the tomatoes and green beans in separate serving dishes.

3. Sprinkle the tomatoes and beans with the onions and salt and pepper to taste. Pour half of the vinegar and oil over the tomatoes, and half over the beans. Sprinkle with chopped parsley and serve.

CHERRY TOMATOES PROVENÇALE   *6 servings*

36 ripe cherry tomatoes
⅓ cup soft fresh bread crumbs
2 garlic cloves, finely minced
2 tablespoons finely chopped green onions
3 tablespoons finely chopped parsley
Pinch of dried orégano
3 tablespoons olive oil
Salt and freshly ground black pepper
Butter

1. Remove the stems from the tomatoes. Cut a slice from the top of each tomato and scoop out the pulp with a melon-ball cutter. Put the pulp through a coarse sieve to remove the seeds. Reserve the pulp.

2. Preheat oven to hot (400° F.).

3. Combine the bread crumbs, garlic, green onions, parsley, orégano and olive oil. Add salt and pepper to taste. Add enough of the tomato pulp to make the mixture moist. Use this mixture to stuff the tomatoes.

4. Place the tomatoes in an oiled pan. Dot the filling with butter. Bake for ten minutes, until the tomatoes are heated through and bread crumbs are golden brown.

TURNIPS WITH POULETTE SAUCE   *6 servings*

2 pounds white or yellow turnips
½ teaspoon salt

Sauce Poulette (page 481)
Chopped fresh parsley

1. Peel the turnips and cut them into half-inch slices. Cut the slices into half-inch strips.
2. Place strips in a saucepan with one inch of boiling water containing the salt. Bring to the boiling point, uncovered, and boil for five minutes. Cover and cook for about fifteen minutes, until tender.
3. Drain the turnips and toss them lightly with poulette sauce. Garnish with parsley.

RUTABAGA PUDDING   *6 servings*

2 cups mashed cooked rutabagas (yellow turnips) (about 1¼ pounds)
2 tablespoons butter
1 cup soft fresh bread crumbs
¼ teaspoon ground mace
⅛ teaspoon freshly ground black pepper

1 teaspoon salt
1 tablespoon sugar
⅛ teaspoon ground ginger
½ cup milk
1 egg, beaten
1 tablespoon melted butter

1. Preheat oven to moderate (350° F.).
2. Combine the rutabagas, butter, bread crumbs, mace, pepper, salt, sugar, ginger and milk. Beat in the egg. Turn the mixture into a buttered one-quart casserole and brush the top with the melted butter. Bake for about forty-five minutes, until brown.

VEGETABLE MEDLEY   *4 servings*

2 tablespoons olive oil
½ garlic clove, crushed
½ cup chopped green pepper
½ cup chopped onion
2 cups sliced yellow squash
1 cup cut green beans

1 cup whole-kernel corn
1 teaspoon salt
1 teaspoon chili powder
1 tablespoon lemon juice
Freshly ground black pepper

1. Heat the oil in a one-and-one-half-quart saucepan. Add the garlic, green pepper and onion; sauté for three to five minutes.
2. Add the squash, green beans and corn. Cover the pan and cook over low heat for twenty minutes. Add salt, chili powder, lemon juice and black pepper to taste.

PETJEL   (mixed vegetables with peanut sauce)   *6 servings*

3 tablespoons peanut butter	1 tablespoon lemon juice
1½ cups water	Salt
1 teaspoon shrimp paste	1 cup sliced cabbage
1 garlic clove, minced	1 cup diced green beans
1 tablespoon brown sugar	1 pound spinach
1 tablespoon ground hot red pepper	1 cup bean sprouts

1. Combine the peanut butter, water, shrimp paste, garlic, brown sugar, red pepper and lemon juice in a saucepan. Bring to a boil, reduce heat, and simmer for two minutes. Add salt to taste. Cool.

2. Boil the cabbage and beans in salted water to cover for twenty minutes. Add the spinach and simmer for five minutes. Add the bean sprouts and cook, stirring, for one minute. Drain. Place vegetables on a large serving dish. Top with the sauce and serve immediately.

STEAMED VEGETABLES

Vegetables steamed with very little water lose a minimum of vitamin and mineral content and consequently retain most of the flavor. This is the method of choice if the vegetable is to be chilled and served with a sauce such as vinaigrette.

Leafy greens such as spinach and kale should be washed thoroughly in several waters, drained, and steamed in only the water that clings to the leaves. Asparagus, green and yellow snap beans, broccoli, cauliflower, fennel, leeks, yellow summer squash and zucchini are particularly delicious steamed. Wash and trim the vegetables; asparagus and leeks need careful cleaning to remove any sand. Separate broccoli and cauliflower into flowerets. Very small squash may be cooked whole, and larger squash may be halved, quartered, sliced, or cut into uniform cubes. Asparagus, snap beans and leeks should be tied into bundles with soft string.

Put the prepared vegetable in a large skillet or saucepan with a tight-fitting cover; a double-boiler bottom with the top reversed is ideal for whole asparagus stalks. Add one-half to two inches (depending on the depth of the vessel) of boiling salted water, enough to fill the pan with steam. Add a little more boiling water during the cooking if the pan becomes dry, but there should be very little water remaining in the pan when the vegetable is done. Steam the vegetable until just tender, for five to eight minutes if the vegetable is cut up, for ten to fifteen minutes if it is whole.

VEGETABLES VINAIGRETTE

Chilled cooked vegetables with vinaigrette sauce make an excellent vegetable dish for summer menus. They can also be served as a salad course or as one of the dishes in a selection of appetizers. Some of the vegetables which are well suited to this preparation are asparagus, celery knobs, leeks, onions, potatoes and spinach *en branche*. Raw mushrooms in vinaigrette sauce make an excellent appetizer as well as a flavorful accompaniment to cold meats.

Vegetables to be served this way should be cooked in boiling salted water, or steamed, until just tender, not mushy, then chilled. Spoon Vinaigrette Sauce I or II (page 488) over them and serve. Or, for a more pronounced flavor, marinate the vegetable in the sauce for thirty minutes or longer before serving.

For salads, arrange the prepared vegetable on a bed of endive or shredded lettuce or on several whole leaves of romaine or Boston lettuce.

ARTICHOKES VINAIGRETTE: *4 servings*

1 package (9 ounces) frozen arti-   ½ cup vinaigrette sauce
choke hearts, or 4 fresh artichokes

If frozen artichokes are used, cook them according to package directions. If fresh artichokes are used, trim them and cook in lightly salted water with a little lemon juice until tender. Drain and chill artichokes. Arrange them on chilled plates and spoon the sauce over them.

GREEN BEANS VINAIGRETTE: *4 servings*

Prepare one recipe of Chilled Green Beans (page 375) and marinate the bundles in one-half cup, or more, vinaigrette sauce. Before serving remove the strings and arrange a narrow strip of pimiento across each bundle of beans.

KIDNEY BEANS VINAIGRETTE: *4 to 6 servings*

2 cups (one 1-pound can) red kidney   1 cup vinaigrette sauce
beans   1 cup finely shredded iceberg lettuce
¼ cup chopped onion
Salt and freshly ground black
pepper

Drain the kidney beans in a sieve. Rinse well under cold running water and drain well. Pour the kidney beans into a salad bowl and sprinkle with the chopped onion and salt and pepper to taste. Add the sauce and toss well. Chill until ready to serve. Then add the shredded lettuce and toss. Serve immediately.

BEAN SPROUTS VINAIGRETTE: *6 servings*

Drain four cups (two one-pound cans) bean sprouts, rinse, and drain again. Pour one cup vinaigrette sauce over the sprouts and toss gently. Marinate and chill for one hour, or longer. Drain before serving.

TOMATOES VINAIGRETTE: *4 servings*

2 or 3 large ripe tomatoes   ¾ cup vinaigrette sauce

Dip the tomatoes, one at a time, into rapidly boiling water for exactly ten seconds. Remove each tomato and peel. Cut away the stem ends and slice the tomatoes. Arrange the slices on chilled plates and spoon the sauce over them. Marinate and chill for thirty minutes before serving.

. . . .

CHAPTER EIGHT

SALADS AND
SALAD DRESSINGS

Assorted salad greens

SALADS

MIXED GREEN SALAD   *6 servings*

1 egg yolk
1 teaspoon prepared mustard (preferably Dijon)
2 tablespoons wine vinegar
6 tablespoons salad oil
1 tablespoon finely chopped shallots or sweet onion
Salt and freshly ground black pepper
4 cups mixed salad greens (escarole, romaine, watercress), in bite-size pieces

Combine the egg yolk with the mustard and beat in the wine vinegar with a fork. Add the oil, shallots, and seasoning to taste and stir rapidly until well blended. Pour the sauce over the salad greens and toss well. Serve on chilled plates.

MIMOSA SALAD   *6 servings*

4 cups mixed salad greens
Watercress sprigs
French Dressing (page 464)
2 small eggs or 1 large egg, hard-cooked

1. Place the salad greens and watercress sprigs in a bowl and sprinkle with French dressing. Toss well and distribute on chilled salad plates.
2. Peel the eggs, chop the whites, and sieve the yolks. Combine the mixture and sprinkle on the salad. Serve immediately.

SALAD FOR ONE   *1 serving*

1½ to 2 cups salad greens, cut into bite-size pieces
Salt
1 garlic clove, halved
½ teaspoon dry mustard

2 teaspoons wine vinegar, approximately
2 tablespoons olive oil, approximately
Freshly ground black pepper

1. Rinse the greens in cold water and drain well.
2. Sprinkle the bottom of a salad bowl with salt and rub with garlic halves. Discard the garlic.
3. Add the mustard and vinegar. Let stand for ten minutes. Add the greens, toss lightly, and sprinkle with oil. Toss, sprinkle with pepper, and serve.

WATERCRESS AND RADISH SALAD   *4 servings*

2 bunches of watercress
1 bunch of red radishes
1 teaspoon salt
1 garlic clove, halved

1 teaspoon dry mustard
1 tablespoon wine vinegar
¼ cup olive oil

1. Rinse the watercress under cold water and shake well to remove excess moisture. Trim the radishes well, wash, and dry.
2. Place the salt in the bottom of a salad bowl and rub it with the garlic clove around bottom and sides of bowl. Discard garlic. Add mustard and vinegar and stir to blend. Let stand for ten minutes to develop mustard flavor. Add the oil and blend with a fork.
3. Chop the tops and part of the stems of the watercress and place in the bowl. Slice the radishes and add them. Toss well and serve immediately.

WATERCRESS AND ORANGE SALAD   *6 servings*

2 bunches of watercress
3 heads of Belgian endive
2 oranges, peeled and sectioned
2 shallots, finely chopped

½ cup olive oil
2 tablespoons lemon juice
Salt and coarsely ground black pepper

1. Wash the watercress and trim off the stems. Place the watercress tops in a large salad bowl. Trim off the ends of the endive and cut into one-inch lengths. Add to the watercress. Top with the orange sections.
2. Combine the shallots, oil and lemon juice in a measuring cup and add salt and pepper to taste. Blend well with a fork. Pour the sauce over the greens and toss gently.

BELGIAN SALAD   *6 servings*

6 heads of Belgian endive
½ cup fresh walnut meats, whole or broken
2 firm sweet apples

Juice of 1 lemon
6 tablespoons olive oil, approximately
Salt

1. Trim away a little of the end of each head of endive. Cut the endive into bite-size bits and place in a colander or salad basket. Rinse thoroughly in cold water, then shake colander to dry endive.

2. Put the endive in a salad bowl and sprinkle with the walnuts.

3. Core and peel the apples and cut them into bite-size bits or thin slices. Add the apples to the salad bowl and immediately sprinkle with lemon juice. Toss.

4. Add the oil and salt to taste and toss again. If desired, add more oil. Serve immediately.

CURLY ENDIVE WITH BACON DRESSING   *4 to 6 servings*

1 head of curly endive
1 scallion, finely chopped, including green part
3 slices of bacon
½ cup heavy cream
2 egg yolks, well beaten

Salt and freshly ground black pepper
1 teaspoon sugar
3 tablespoons wine vinegar
Chopped parsley

1. Remove the core from the endive and cut the leaves into bite-size pieces. Drop them into cold water and rinse well. Drain in a salad basket or on paper towels. Place the endive in a salad bowl, sprinkle with scallion, and set aside.

2. Cut the bacon into small cubes and cook in a skillet until bacon is crisp but not burned. With a slotted spoon remove the bacon and dry on paper towels. Sprinkle the bacon over the salad greens.

3. Blend the cream and egg yolks and pour the mixture into the skillet. Add salt and pepper to taste, the sugar and vinegar and cook over very low heat, stirring constantly, until mixture thickens slightly. Do not boil or it may curdle. Cool slightly. Pour the sauce over the endive and toss. Sprinkle with parsley.

AVOCADO AND GRAPEFRUIT SALAD   *4 servings*

1 large ripe avocado
1 large grapefruit
Boston, romaine or Bibb lettuce leaves
1 tablespoon lemon juice
½ teaspoon dry mustard

¼ cup olive oil
1 shallot, finely chopped, or 1 tablespoon finely chopped chives
½ teaspoon finely minced garlic
Salt and freshly ground black pepper

1. Peel and pit the avocado and cut it into strips. Peel the grapefruit and cut it into sections; remove any pits.

2. Line four salad plates with a single layer of Boston, romaine or Bibb lettuce leaves. Arrange alternate strips of avocado and grapefruit sections symmetrically over the lettuce. Chill.

3. Combine the lemon juice and mustard and let stand for ten minutes. Combine with the oil, shallot and garlic and blend well, beating with a small fork. Adjust the seasonings to taste.

4. When ready to serve, spoon the sauce over the avocado and grapefruit. This is an excellent salad to serve with highly spiced dishes such as chile con carne or curries.

ASPARAGUS SALAD   *6 servings*

2 pounds asparagus, cut into 4-inch lengths	2 teaspoons chopped parsley
	Chicory
½ cup olive oil	2 hard-cooked egg yolks, sieved
2 tablespoons wine vinegar	1 tablespoon capers
¼ teaspoon salt	Ripe olives
⅛ teaspoon freshly ground black pepper	

Early in the day:

Cook the asparagus until barely tender. Cool. Place it in a shallow dish. Combine the oil, vinegar, salt, pepper and parsley and pour the mixture over the asparagus. Chill in the refrigerator.

Just before serving:

Place the asparagus on a bed of chicory. Sprinkle the cut ends with the egg yolks and top with the capers. Garnish with the olives.

MEXICAN AVOCADO SALAD   *6 servings*

2 tablespoons olive oil	2 tablespoons lemon juice
2 tablespoons vinegar	Crisp salad greens
⅛ teaspoon salt	1 medium orange, peeled and sliced
Dash of freshly ground black pepper	1 small onion, thinly sliced
3 medium avocados	¼ cup sliced pimiento-stuffed green olives

1. Combine the olive oil, vinegar, salt and pepper; blend well.

2. Cut the avocados into halves and peel them. Brush all over with the lemon juice.

3. Arrange avocados on the salad greens. Top with orange, onion and olive slices. Pour the dressing over the salad.

BEET SALAD   *6 servings*

6 medium beets, cooked
2 cups shredded dandelion greens
6 heads of Belgian endive, cut up

½ cup French Dressing (page 464)
Salt and freshly ground black pepper

Drain and cool the beets, peel them, and cut them into thin slices. Put the slices in a bowl with the greens, pour the dressing over all, and toss gently. Add salt and pepper to taste.

BEET AND ONION SALAD   *6 servings*

6 medium beets, cooked
1 medium onion, sliced tissue-thin
3 whole cloves
1 teaspoon sugar, or more

3 tablespoons cider vinegar, or more
¼ cup olive oil
Salt and freshly ground black pepper

1. Drain and cool the beets, trim them, and slip off the skins with a paring knife. Cut the beets into thin slices and chill them.
2. Add the onion slices to the beets and toss with the remaining ingredients and seasoning to taste.

BROCCOLI SALAD   *5 or 6 servings*

1 bunch of broccoli (1½ to 2 pounds)
½ cup French Dressing (page 464)
Romaine lettuce leaves

⅓ cup mayonnaise
¾ teaspoon lemon juice
Anchovy fillets for garnish

1. Cook the broccoli until just tender, drain, and chill. Marinate the broccoli in the French dressing for one hour or longer.
2. Arrange the romaine leaves on individual salad plates. Place the marinated broccoli on the romaine just before serving.
3. Combine the mayonnaise with the lemon juice and spoon the mixture over the broccoli. Garnish with anchovy fillets.

CAULIFLOWER SALAD NAPOLITANA   *6 servings*

1 medium head of cauliflower
1¾ teaspoons salt
2 tablespoons olive or salad oil
1 cup wine vinegar
½ teaspoon freshly ground black pepper

¼ teaspoon dried basil
6 anchovy fillets, diced
2 tablespoons capers
¼ cup chopped black olives

1. Break the cauliflower into flowerets. Place in a saucepan with one inch of boiling water containing one teaspoon of the salt. Simmer, uncovered, for five minutes. Cover and cook for five to six minutes longer, only until flowerets are crisp-tender. Drain the flowerets and rinse in cold water. Place in a salad bowl.

2. Combine the oil, vinegar, pepper, basil and remaining salt. Mix well and pour over cauliflower. Add anchovies, capers and olives. Toss lightly. Sprinkle with additional capers, if desired, before serving.

CORN SALAD, MEXICAN STYLE   *6 servings*

4 to 6 ears of fresh corn	Lettuce
½ cup diced green pepper	Fried bacon rind (available in
¼ cup diced pimiento	plastic bags)
1 cup diced fresh tomatoes	Red-onion rings
1 teaspoon salt	
¼ cup Vinaigrette Sauce II (page 488)	

1. Boil the ears of corn for six to eight minutes before cutting the kernels off the cobs. Measure out two cups corn and combine it with the green pepper, pimiento and tomatoes.

2. Just before serving, add the salt and salad dressing. Toss lightly. Turn into a salad bowl lined with lettuce. Sprinkle the top with the bacon rind and garnish with onion rings.

SWEDISH CUCUMBERS   *6 servings*

3 large cucumbers	¼ cup vinegar
¾ teaspoon salt	Freshly ground black pepper
1 teaspoon sugar	Chopped parsley

1. Peel the cucumbers, leaving a bit of the skin on for color. Halve the cucumbers lengthwise and scoop out the seeds. Slice thin and sprinkle with the salt. Refrigerate for at least one hour. Drain.

2. Sprinkle cucumbers with the sugar and pour vinegar over them. Sprinkle with pepper and parsley to taste.

CUCUMBER MAYONNAISE

Peel cucumbers and scrape out the seeds with a spoon or melon-ball cutter. Slice cucumber flesh as thin as possible or dice it finely. Combine with mayonnaise, using two cups mayonnaise to each cucumber. Season with salt, cayenne pepper and lemon juice to taste.

This makes a notable accompaniment for cold salmon and other fish.

SALATA MELITZANAS (eggplant salad)   *6 to 8 servings*

1 large eggplant
1 small onion, chopped
  Salt and freshly ground black
  pepper

½ cup olive oil
1½ tablespoons vinegar
  Chopped parsley, tomato wedges
  and black olives for garnish

1. Preheat oven to moderate (350° F.).
2. Bake the eggplant for about one hour, or until soft.
3. Remove the skin from the eggplant and chop the flesh. Combine the eggplant, onion, salt and pepper to taste, olive oil and vinegar. Mix well. Garnish with parsley, tomato wedges and olives.

EGGPLANT AND SESAME SALAD   *4 servings*

2 tablespoons sesame seeds
¼ cup olive oil
1 large eggplant
2 garlic cloves, finely minced
2 tablespoons lemon juice

Chopped fresh dill
Salt and freshly ground black
pepper
Parsley

1. Preheat oven to hot (400° F.).
2. Sauté the sesame seeds in one tablespoon of the oil until they are lightly browned. Set aside.
3. Bake the eggplant for about forty-five minutes, or until tender. Wash under running water and remove the skin very carefully. Let the eggplant drain.
4. Chop or mash the eggplant with a wooden spoon or blend in an electric blender. Add the garlic, lemon juice and remaining oil to the eggplant. Season with dill, salt and pepper to taste. Top with the sesame seeds and a sprinkling of parsley.

SALADE FORESTIÈRE   *6 servings*

1 pound fresh white mushrooms
¼ cup fresh lemon juice, or more
¼ cup chopped parsley
½ cup olive oil

Salt and freshly ground black
pepper
4 cups mixed salad greens (chicory,
endive and Boston lettuce)

1. Trim the stems of the mushrooms but do not peel the mushrooms. Wash carefully and dry thoroughly. Slice the mushrooms through caps and stems into very thin slices.
2. Pour the lemon juice over the slices and add the parsley, oil, and salt and pepper to taste. Chill the mushrooms.
3. Toss mushrooms and marinade with the greens and serve.

HEART OF PALM AND AVOCADO SALAD   *12 servings*

1 large head of romaine
1 large head of escarole
6 scallions or 2 medium onions
4 ripe avocados
4 cups (two 1-pound cans) hearts of
palm

Pimiento strips
Tarragon French Dressing (page
465)

1. Wash salad greens, drain well, and wrap in a clean towel to absorb all the water. Tear salad greens into bite-size pieces and place in a large salad bowl.

2. Wash scallions and slice them, green part and all. Arrange them in center of the salad; if onions are used, slice thin and arrange them in center of salad.

3. Peel avocados and cut lengthwise into one-quarter-inch slices. Cut drained hearts of palm into one-quarter-inch rounds.

4. Arrange avocados and palm hearts on the greens. Garnish with the pimiento strips. Just before serving, toss with the dressing.

ENSALADA DE CEBOLLA BURRIANA (onion salad, Burriana style) *6 servings*

Slice three or four sweet Spanish onions (or sweet red Italian onions) very thin. Soak them in salted water with ice cubes for thirty minutes. Drain the onions and wring out in a linen towel. Arrange in a large salad bowl, sprinkle with oil and wine vinegar, and garnish with anchovy fillets and pitted ripe black olives.

SPINACH MIMOSA   *6 servings*

2 pounds fresh spinach
1 tablespoon lemon juice
2 teaspoons grated onion
½ teaspoon dry mustard
½ teaspoon crumbled dried basil

1½ teaspoons salt
⅛ teaspoon freshly ground black
pepper
2 tablespoons chopped pimiento
3 hard-cooked eggs, finely chopped

1. Wash the spinach but do not dry it. Cook it in a covered saucepan with only the water that clings to the leaves until wilted and tender. Drain, if necessary.

2. Chop the spinach fine. Add the lemon juice, onion, mustard, basil, salt, pepper, pimiento and two of the eggs. Mix well.

3. Fill six oiled half-cup molds with the spinach mixture, firmly packed. Refrigerate for two to three hours or overnight.

4. Just before serving, unmold and decorate with the remaining hard-cooked egg.

SPINACH AND ENDIVE SALAD   *12 servings*

2 pounds baby leaf spinach
¾ pound Belgian endive
1 cup Italian olive oil
½ cup tarragon vinegar
1 tablespoon lemon juice
1 tablespoon coarsely ground black Java pepper
½ tablespoon Hungarian paprika
1 tablespoon dried orégano
1 tablespoon dried sweet basil
2 tablespoons mayonnaise
½ tablespoon Worcestershire sauce
1 tablespoon salt
⅛ pound Roquefort cheese, crushed

1. Wash the spinach in several changes of water to make certain that no sand clings to the leaves. Cut the large leaves into bite-size pieces. Cut the endive into bite-size pieces.

2. Combine the remaining ingredients and blend well. Pour enough salad dressing over the salad greens to coat greens lightly. Toss well. There should be no dressing in the bottom of the bowl when the salad is served.

SPINACH AND BACON SALAD   *6 servings*

1½ pounds fresh spinach
3 tablespoons wine vinegar
5 tablespoons peanut oil
5 tablespoons olive oil
Salt and freshly ground black pepper
2 teaspoons Dijon or Düsseldorf mustard
1 small garlic clove, finely minced
½ cup chopped parsley
8 slices of bacon

1. Trim off and discard any tough stems or bruised spinach leaves. Wash the spinach thoroughly in several changes of cold water. Drain and shake off excess water or pat with paper towels.

2. Combine the vinegar, oils, salt and pepper to taste, mustard, garlic and parsley. Blend well.

3. Cut the bacon into small cubes and fry until crisp. Drain on paper towels. Crumble it.

4. When ready to serve, toss the spinach with the dressing and sprinkle with the crumbled bacon.

SPINACH AND MUSHROOM SALAD   *6 servings*

10 ounces fresh spinach
6 slices of lean bacon, broiled until crisp
1 bunch of scallions, washed, trimmed and sliced
¼ pound mushrooms, sliced
2 tablespoons lemon juice
6 tablespoons olive oil
¾ teaspoon salt
⅛ teaspoon freshly ground black pepper
1 garlic clove, finely minced
⅛ teaspoon dry mustard
¼ teaspoon sugar
1 egg yolk

1. Trim and thoroughly wash the spinach. Dry carefully in a towel. Place spinach in a salad bowl.

2. Crumble the bacon over the spinach and add the scallions and mushrooms. Chill.

3. Combine the dressing ingredients; blend well; chill. Use to dress the salad.

CREOLE SALAD   *6 to 8 servings*

6 small zucchini	½ teaspoon sugar
3 tomatoes, chopped	1 teaspoon salt
1 green pepper, finely chopped	½ teaspoon freshly ground black
1 avocado, peeled and cubed	pepper
2 scallions, chopped	

Wash the zucchini thoroughly. Do not peel, but cut it into wafer-thin slices. Toss with remaining ingredients and let sit for one hour. Serve with olive oil and wine vinegar to taste.

Not only is the tomato the most versatile of vegetables; there is none other with more perceptible differences in flavor and texture. Off season they are tasteless, but when summer comes they are something to feast upon. The small cherry tomatoes which are available even during the winter months have a surprising depth of flavor and make a colorful garnish for almost any green salad.

The most elegant way of serving any tomato, large or small, is to peel it in advance. This is easily done if the tomatoes are dipped quickly into boiling water and allowed to stand for precisely ten seconds. If they stand longer than that, they start to cook and their texture is spoiled. Remove them from the water and skin them with a paring knife. The operation is not as tedious as it may sound.

HERBED TOMATO SALAD   *4 servings*

¼ cup olive oil	½ garlic clove, finely minced
3 tablespoons fresh lemon juice	1 teaspoon paprika
¾ teaspoon salt	1 teaspoon fresh or dried mint
Freshly ground black pepper	3 large ripe tomatoes, sliced
1 tablespoon chopped onion	

Combine oil, lemon juice, salt, pepper to taste, onion, garlic, paprika and mint. Beat with a fork and refrigerate for thirty minutes. Chill the tomatoes. Pour the dressing over the tomatoes and serve.

TOMATO AND ONION SALAD *4 servings*

1 cup sliced onions
3 ripe medium tomatoes, sliced
¼ cup olive oil
2 teaspoons fresh lemon juice
2 teaspoons wine vinegar
½ cup chopped fresh parsley

1 teaspoon chopped fresh basil or ½ teaspoon dried basil
½ teaspoon sugar
Salt and freshly ground black pepper

Arrange alternate slices of onions and tomatoes on a chilled serving dish and sprinkle with remaining ingredients, which have been mixed well. Chill briefly and serve.

TOMATO AND SPINACH SALAD *6 servings*

1 pound fresh spinach
4 large ripe tomatoes
¼ cup chopped onion

½ cup French Dressing (page 464)
6 anchovy fillets, sliced
2 tablespoons chopped parsley

1. Wash the spinach carefully in several waters to remove all sand. Trim the spinach and discard any tough stems or bruised leaves.
2. Remove the stems from the tomatoes and peel them. Cut the tomatoes into wedges.
3. Put the spinach leaves, tomato wedges and onion in a salad bowl. Pour the dressing over, add the chopped anchovies, and toss well. Sprinkle parsley over the top.

SALADE PROVENÇALE *6 servings*

2 medium heads of Boston or romaine lettuce
2 large ripe tomatoes, cut into bite-size wedges
1 onion, thinly sliced
1 or 2 garlic cloves, finely minced
2 tablespoons finely chopped chives
1 tablespoon chopped fresh basil
1 dozen pitted green olives

1 dozen pitted black olives
1 teaspoon prepared mustard, preferably Dijon or Düsseldorf
2 tablespoons wine vinegar
7 tablespoons olive oil
Salt and freshly ground black pepper
Radishes for garnish

1. Core the lettuce and cut or tear the leaves into bite-size pieces. Place them in a salad bowl and add the tomatoes, onion, garlic, chives, basil and the green and black olives.
2. Blend the mustard with the vinegar and sprinkle over the salad. Toss lightly, then add the oil and salt and pepper to taste and toss again. If desired, add more vinegar, oil, or both, and toss again. Garnish with radishes.

CHERRY-TOMATO AND SOUR-CREAM SALAD
6 or more servings

1 pint cherry tomatoes
1 teaspoon dry mustard
¾ cup sour cream
Salt
Cayenne pepper

2 tablespoons finely chopped fresh basil
¼ cup finely chopped scallions, including green parts

1. Remove the stems from the tomatoes and peel them.
2. Place the mustard in a mixing bowl and stir in a little of the sour cream to form a paste. Blend in the remaining sour cream. Add salt and cayenne pepper to taste. Gently stir in the cherry tomatoes. Chill. When ready to serve, sprinkle with chopped basil and scallions.

SABRA SALAD   *6 servings*

2 large tomatoes
1 large cucumber
1 bunch of red radishes
1 bunch of scallions
1 dill pickle
¼ cup olive oil

¼ cup chopped parsley
2 tablespoons lemon juice
Salt and freshly ground black pepper
2 garlic cloves, finely minced
Lettuce leaves

1. Cut the tomatoes, cucumber, radishes, scallions and pickle into small cubes. Add the oil and parsley.
2. Mix the lemon juice, salt and pepper to taste and garlic, and pour the mixture over the salad. Serve on lettuce leaves.

Note: Seeded and diced green peppers, diced celery and grated fresh kohlrabi may be added to or substituted for any of the vegetables listed above. For those who prefer their salad piquant, hot red peppers may be added.

MOLDED ROQUEFORT SALAD WITH VEGETABLES
6 to 8 servings

2 envelopes unflavored gelatin
1½ tablespoons all-purpose flour
2½ teaspoons salt
1 teaspoon dry mustard
2 tablespoons sugar
Dash of freshly ground black pepper
Dash of paprika
2 cups milk

2 eggs, separated
6 tablespoons cider vinegar
2 ounces Roquefort cheese
1 medium green pepper, chopped
2 teaspoons minced onion
½ cup chopped celery
1 cup chopped cucumber
½ cup heavy cream, whipped
Watercress for garnish

1. Mix the gelatin, flour, salt, mustard, sugar, pepper and paprika. Blend with the milk in the top of a double boiler.

2. Beat the egg yolks and add to the double boiler. Cook over boiling water, stirring constantly, until thick. Add the vinegar. Cool.

3. When the mixture begins to thicken, mash the Roquefort cheese and stir it into the milk mixture. Add the green pepper, onion, celery and cucumber.

4. Whip the egg whites until stiff. Fold the egg whites and whipped cream into the milk mixture.

5. Pour into a one-and-one-half-quart mold and chill until firm. Unmold and garnish with watercress and any desired raw or cooked vegetables. Serve with mayonnaise.

MOLDED CANTALOUPE SALAD   *8 servings*

3 envelopes unflavored gelatin
¾ cup cold water
1 cup hot water
½ cup sugar
¼ cup lemon juice
¼ teaspoon salt

2 cups Sauternes
3 cups cantaloupe balls (about 2 cantaloupes)
¾ cup pineapple wedges
¾ cup fresh strawberries
¼ cup kirsch (optional)

1. Soften the gelatin in the cold water. Stir it into the hot water. Add the sugar, lemon juice, salt and wine. Chill until the mixture begins to thicken.

2. Fold in the cantaloupe balls and turn into a lightly oiled six-cup ring mold. Chill.

3. Marinate the pineapple wedges and strawberries in the kirsch for one hour.

4. Unmold the ring and spoon the fruit into the center.

CANTALOUPE FLOWER SALAD   *6 servings*

1 large cantaloupe
2 cups mixed fresh fruits (pitted cherries, blueberries, strawberries, raspberries or pineapple wedges)

Belgian endive leaves
Fresh peach, pear or apricot slices
Orange French Dressing (page 465)

1. Slash the cantaloupe part of the way down in six sections so that it slightly opens out like the petals of a flower. Remove the seeds and chill the fruit.

2. Place the melon on a serving plate and fill it with the mixed fresh fruits. Surround it with endive leaves and overlapping slices of peaches, pears or apricots.

3. Serve a slice of melon with mixed fruit and endive and pour some dressing over each serving.

FRUIT SALAD *18 servings*

8 seedless oranges	Juice of 1 lemon
2 lemons	2 Spanish melons
4 cups sugar	2 ripe pineapples
2½ cups water	1 bunch of black grapes
4 grapefruits	1 bunch of white grapes
8 bananas	2 pints strawberries

1. With a vegetable peeler; peel off the skins of the oranges and lemons. Discard the lemon pulp or reserve for another use. Cut the peel into the thinnest possible strips. Add to the sugar and water in a saucepan. Simmer for about thirty minutes, until the rinds are transparent. Chill.

2. Peel the grapefruits. Section the grapefruits and oranges. Score the bananas with fork tines and cut into thick slices. Marinate the grapefruits, oranges and bananas in the juice of one lemon for ten minutes.

3. Cut the melons into balls and the pineapples into chunks. Skin and pit the black grapes; skin the white grapes. Combine with the strawberries and add to the marinated fruits. Chill.

4. Mix all the fruits with the sugar and citrus-rind sauce just before serving.

GRAPEFRUIT AND GREENS TOSSED SALAD *6 to 8 servings*

1 bunch of watercress, trimmed	1 teaspoon salt
2 heads of Belgian endive	¼ cup salad oil
½ head of curly endive	2 tablespoons lemon juice
1 cup fresh grapefruit sections	Additional fresh grapefruit sections, cucumber slices and onion rings for garnish
½ cup sliced cucumber	
½ cup diced green pepper	
¼ cup onion rings	

Cut the greens into bite-size pieces and combine them with the grapefruit, cucumber, green pepper, onion rings, salt, salad oil and lemon juice. Toss lightly. Garnish as desired with additional fresh grapefruit sections, cucumber slices and onion rings.

CHICK-PEA SALAD *6 to 8 servings*

4 cups (two 1-pound cans) chick-peas	¾ cup olive oil
¼ cup lemon juice	1 garlic clove, finely minced
¼ cup red-wine vinegar	¼ cup finely chopped green onions
¾ cup peanut oil	2 tablespoons finely chopped parsley

1. Drain the chick-peas thoroughly. Combine the remaining ingredients and stir well. Add the chick-peas.

2. Let marinate in the refrigerator for two or three hours. Serve on beds of Boston lettuce leaves, sprinkled with additional chopped parsley. Leftover chick-peas may continue to marinate in the refrigerator for several days.

BEAN AND MUSHROOM SALAD   *6 servings*

1 package (10 ounces) frozen lima beans or 2 cups (one 1-pound can) red kidney beans
½ pound fresh mushrooms
6 scallions, finely chopped
1 tablespoon chopped fresh parsley
½ teaspoon dried marjoram
3 tablespoons wine vinegar
⅓ cup olive oil
1 garlic clove, finely minced
½ teaspoon salt
¼ teaspoon freshly ground black pepper
⅛ teaspoon dry mustard
Salad greens

1. Cook the lima beans according to package directions and drain; or drain the kidney beans. Trim the mushrooms, wash and dry thoroughly. Cut the mushrooms into thin slices.

2. Combine the beans, scallions, parsley, marjoram, vinegar, oil, garlic, salt, pepper and mustard. Allow to marinate for at least thirty minutes.

3. Add the mushrooms and toss lightly. Pile the mixture atop salad greens.

WINTER SALAD   *6 to 8 servings*

1 cup cooked lima beans (fresh or frozen)
1 cup cooked green beans, cut into 1-inch lengths
1 cup cooked field peas, speckled beans or black-eyed peas
½ cup thinly sliced water chestnuts
1 medium red onion, chopped or cut into thin rings
¼ cup wine vinegar
½ to 1 garlic clove, finely minced
¾ cup plus 2 tablespoons olive oil
Salt and freshly ground black pepper
24 cherry tomatoes
¼ cup chopped parsley

1. The vegetables for this dish should be freshly cooked and not over-cooked. They should be tender but still somewhat crisp. Combine the lima beans, green beans, field peas, water chestnuts and onion in a bowl.

2. Combine the vinegar, garlic, oil, and salt and pepper to taste. Beat with a wire whisk until well blended. Pour the sauce over the vegetables and refrigerate for several hours or overnight.

3. When ready to serve, toss lightly but thoroughly. Garnish with cherry tomatoes and sprinkle with chopped parsley.

Potatoes generally have either a mealy texture or a firm waxy texture when cooked. For salads select the thin-skinned waxy potatoes for they will not crumble when they are sliced or cubed; or use new potatoes. Cook the potatoes in the skins to retain the most flavor and cool them only until they can be handled before peeling and slicing them. If the dressing is added to the potatoes while they are still warm, the salad will be much more flavorful.

POTATO SALAD   *6 servings*

3 tablespoons olive oil
1 tablespoon wine vinegar
  Salt and freshly ground black pepper
2 cups cubes of warm cooked potatoes

2 hard-cooked eggs, coarsely chopped
1 cup finely chopped celery
1 tablespoon minced shallots
3 tablespoons minced parsley
1 tablespoon dry mustard
⅓ cup mayonnaise

1. Combine the oil, vinegar, and salt and pepper to taste. Pour the dressing over the warm potatoes. Toss lightly and chill.
2. Add the remaining ingredients and toss again.

SPRING POTATO SALAD   *8 servings*

1 pound new potatoes, cooked and peeled
2 tablespoons fresh lemon juice
1 tablespoon vinegar
1 tablespoon salad oil
1½ teaspoons salt
¼ teaspoon freshly ground black pepper

½ head of Boston lettuce
½ head of romaine
3 scallions with tops, chopped
1 cup diced celery
½ cucumber, sliced
2 tablespoons mayonnaise
2 medium tomatoes for garnish

1. Dice the potatoes while still warm and combine with one tablespoon of the lemon juice, the vinegar, salad oil, salt and pepper. Let the potatoes marinate in the refrigerator for at least one hour.
2. Tear the lettuce and romaine into bite-size pieces and place in a salad bowl along with the scallions, celery, cucumber and marinated potatoes. Mix the remaining lemon juice with the mayonnaise. Add to the salad and toss tightly. Garnish with tomato slices or wedges.

POTATO SALAD WITH ANCHOVIES   *12 servings*

5 pounds new potatoes
1 bunch of scallions, chopped
1 can (5 ounces) pimientos, drained and cut into strips
3 cans (2 ounces each) flat anchovy fillets, diced

¼ cup wine vinegar
1 tablespoon lemon juice
¼ cup olive oil
  Salt and freshly ground black pepper

1. Cover the potatoes with boiling salted water, bring to a boil, and simmer for about twenty minutes, until barely tender. Drain, peel, and cut into quarter-inch slices.

2. While potatoes are still warm, place them in a large bowl. Add the scallions, pimientos and anchovies along with the oil from the can.

3. Combine the remaining ingredients and pour over the salad. Toss to mix and chill for at least two hours.

POTATO AND AVOCADO SALAD   *6 servings*

3 pounds new potatoes
2 ripe avocados
1 bunch of scallions, trimmed and chopped
1/4 cup olive oil
2 tablespoons wine vinegar
1 teaspoon salt

1/8 teaspoon freshly ground black pepper
3 hard-cooked eggs, coarsely chopped
1 cup mayonnaise
2 tablespoons lemon juice
1 tomato, skinned and sliced, for garnish

1. Scrub the potatoes and place them in hot salted water to cover. Cover and simmer for about twenty-five minutes, until tender. Allow the potatoes to cool until they can be handled.

2. Peel the potatoes while still warm and slice them into a bowl. Peel the avocados and slice them into the bowl. Add the scallions. Combine the oil, vinegar, salt and pepper and pour over the potato mixture. Toss gently and chill.

3. Add the eggs. Blend the mayonnaise with the lemon juice and stir gently into the salad. Adjust the seasonings and garnish with tomato slices.

RICE AND PEAS SALAD   *6 servings*

1 cup cooked rice
1 cup cooked green peas
1/4 cup finely minced parsley
1/4 cup finely minced onion
2 tomatoes, peeled, seeded and cubed
1 tablespoon finely chopped fresh basil or 1 teaspoon finely chopped fresh mint

Salt and freshly ground black pepper
1/2 cup olive oil
3 tablespoons vinegar, or less

Combine all the ingredients in a mixing bowl. Mix well and chill thoroughly before serving.

Midsummer feast for porch or patio might include Cold Borscht with Cucumbers, Seafood with Tarragon, cold stuffed tomatoes, Mixed Green Salad, crusty bread and fruits with custard.

RICE SALAD À LA FRANÇAISE   *6 servings*

1 cup cooked rice, chilled
2 tomatoes, cored, peeled and cut into small cubes
6 radishes, trimmed and thinly sliced
½ cup finely chopped onion
½ cup finely chopped celery heart
4 small beets, cooked, peeled and cut into thin strips
¼ cup sliced green olives
Salt and freshly ground black pepper

½ teaspoon curry powder
1 teaspoon mustard, preferably Dijon or Düsseldorf
2 tablespoons wine vinegar, approximately
7 tablespoons olive oil, approximately

1. In a salad bowl combine the rice with the tomatoes, radishes, onion, celery heart, beets and olives. Sprinkle with salt and pepper.

2. Combine the curry powder, mustard and vinegar and sprinkle the mixture over the salad. Toss salad briefly and sprinkle with the oil. Toss again. If desired, add more vinegar, oil, or both.

A substantial salad often serves as the main course of a light supper. These main dishes are well suited for informal summertime entertaining. Often they can be prepared ahead of time. Also, these dishes can be garnished attractively and used as the basis for a summer buffet. Serve with hot rolls and cold drinks or, for an added touch of elegance, accompany the meal with a chilled white wine.

HOT CRAB SALAD   *6 servings*

2 cans (7½ ounces each) Alaska king crab
¼ cup finely chopped green pepper
2 tablespoons chopped shallots or scallions
½ cup diced celery
2 tablespoons chopped parsley

2 tablespoons lemon juice
¼ teaspoon salt
Dash of Tabasco
½ cup mayonnaise
½ cup buttered soft fresh bread crumbs

1. Preheat oven to hot (400° F.).

2. Drain the crab, slice the leg sections, and pick over for cartilage. Combine the crab with the remaining ingredients except the buttered crumbs.

3. Spoon the mixture into shells or individual ramekins. Top with the buttered crumbs and bake for ten minutes, or until heated through and lightly browned.

CURRIED LOBSTER SALAD   *6 servings*

3 lobsters (1½ to 2 pounds each)
1 package (9 ounces) frozen artichoke hearts
1 cup diced celery
1 cup mayonnaise
¼ cup lime juice

1 teaspoon curry powder, or more
¼ teaspoon dry mustard
Salt and freshly ground black pepper
Salad greens
Radish roses

1. Plunge the lobsters into a large kettle of boiling water. Boil for fifteen minutes, or until tender. Remove and cool.

2. Cook the artichoke hearts according to package directions. Cool. Cut each heart into six pieces.

3. Split lobsters into halves. Remove and reserve the meat, liver and coral from each. Remove and discard the sac and large vein from each, but retain the shells.

4. Dice the lobster meat and coral, and toss with the liver, artichoke hearts and celery. Mix mayonnaise with lime juice, curry powder and mustard. Add to lobster mixture and mix well. Season with salt and pepper to taste.

5. Place the salad greens in a large serving bowl. Pile the lobster mixture into the shells. Arrange shells on the greens, pyramid fashion. Garnish with radish roses.

CHICKEN SALAD WITH ALMONDS   *5 servings*

4 cups lightly packed ¾-inch cubes of cooked chicken meat
2 cups thinly sliced celery
1 to 2 tablespoons minced onion
1 tablespoon lemon juice

¾ cup mayonnaise
¼ cup heavy cream
Salt and freshly ground white pepper
¼ to ½ cup toasted almonds

1. Toss the chicken and celery together.

2. Mix the onion, lemon juice, mayonnaise and cream. Add to the chicken and toss until the pieces of chicken and celery are coated with the dressing.

3. Season with salt and pepper to taste and stir in the almonds, or reserve them to use as a garnish. Chill.

4. Serve on a bed of lettuce or other salad green.

CHICKEN OR SHRIMP SALAD FOR ONE   *1 serving*

1 cup cooked chicken or shrimp
¼ cup mayonnaise, approximately
1 teaspoon capers

3 tablespoons chopped celery
Lemon juice
Freshly ground black pepper

Cut the chicken or shrimp into bite-size pieces. Place in a bowl. Add mayonnaise, capers and celery. Sprinkle lemon juice and pepper to taste over the salad. Stir just to coat chicken or shrimp and blend ingredients. Serve on lettuce leaves.

TURKEY SALAD *100 servings or four 2-quart molds*

2 gallons (10 pounds) diced cooked turkey meat
2¼ quarts finely diced celery
4½ cups toasted blanched almonds
2 cups finely chopped scallions
1 cup wine vinegar
2½ cups olive oil
Juice of 2 lemons
Salt and freshly ground black pepper
½ cup finely chopped parsley
½ cup capers
6½ cups mayonnaise
12 hard-cooked eggs, coarsely chopped
Ripe olives, pimientos and parsley sprigs for garnish

1. Place the turkey in a large bowl; add the celery, almonds and scallions. Add half of the vinegar and chill.
2. Combine the remaining vinegar with the oil, lemon juice, salt and pepper to taste and parsley. Beat to blend well.
3. Pour the dressing over the turkey. Add the capers, mayonnaise and chopped eggs. Adjust the seasonings if necessary.
4. Pack the salad into molds. Chill for several hours. Unmold and garnish with olives, pimientos and parsley. Or arrange the salad on beds of salad greens on large serving platters.

POLLO EN SALSA TONNATO (chicken in tuna sauce)
6 servings

4 large chicken breasts, halved and skinned
1¼ cups dry white wine
1 onion, finely chopped
1 garlic clove, finely minced
1 can (7 ounces) tuna fish
6 anchovy fillets, chopped
½ teaspoon salt
¼ teaspoon freshly ground black pepper
1 teaspoon grated lemon rind
¼ cup olive oil
3 tablespoons lemon juice
4 cups cooked white rice, cold
3 tablespoons chopped parsley
Capers

1. Combine the chicken with the wine, onion, garlic, tuna, anchovies, salt, pepper and lemon rind in a heavy saucepan. Cover, bring to a boil, and simmer gently for twenty-five minutes, or until chicken is tender.
2. Transfer the chicken to a bowl. Put the sauce in which the chicken was cooked into the container of an electric blender and purée it; or put it

through a food mill. Add the oil and lemon juice, and pour over chicken. Cover and let stand overnight.

3. Spread the cold rice on a serving platter. Slice the chicken into large oval pieces, discarding the bones. Place chicken atop rice. Add parsley to the sauce, pour over chicken and rice, and sprinkle with capers.

Note: For a more economical dish, pieces of a frying chicken may be substituted for the chicken breasts.

INDIAN MELON SALAD   *6 servings*

2 cups coarsely cut cooked chicken or turkey
1 can (5 ounces) water chestnuts, sliced
½ pound seedless green grapes
½ cup chopped celery
1 cup mayonnaise
½ teaspoon curry powder
1 tablespoon lemon juice
¼ teaspoon salt
⅛ teaspoon freshly ground black pepper
1 teaspoon soy sauce
1 cup honeydew melon balls
1 cup cantaloupe melon balls
Boston lettuce cups

1. Combine the chicken, chestnuts, grapes and celery.

2. Mix the mayonnaise with the curry powder, lemon juice, salt, pepper and soy sauce. Combine with the chicken mixture.

3. Add the melon balls and toss lightly. Serve in lettuce cups.

CHEF SALAD À L'ADAM   *About 4 servings*

½ cup wafer-thin slices of sweet onion (Bermuda or Italian)
½ cup strips of Gruyère or Swiss cheese (matchlike strips about 1 inch long)
½ cup ham strips (matchlike strips about 1 inch long)
½ cup strips of green pepper (matchlike strips about 1 inch long)
1½ tablespoons wine vinegar
1½ tablespoons olive oil
2 tablespoons peanut oil
Salt and freshly ground black pepper

Combine all ingredients and mix well. Add seasonings to taste. Let stand in the refrigerator overnight. Serve cold.

BEANS AND TUNA VINAIGRETTE   *6 to 8 servings*

2 cups (1 pound) dried pea beans or navy beans
1 garlic clove
2 teaspoons salt
¼ teaspoon freshly ground black pepper
2 cups finely chopped scallions
¾ cup olive oil
2 tomatoes, peeled, seeded and chopped
¼ cup chopped parsley
1 can (7 ounces) tuna fish, flaked
3 tablespoons wine vinegar
3 or 4 drops of Tabasco
Salt and freshly ground black pepper

1. Wash the beans, cover with cold water, and soak overnight. Or cover beans with water, bring to a boil for two minutes, cover, and let stand for one hour.

2. Place the beans in a saucepan with enough of the water they were soaked in just to cover them. Add the garlic, salt and pepper. Bring to a boil and simmer for about forty-five minutes, or until barely tender; drain.

3. Meanwhile, sauté the scallions in one-third cup of the oil until just wilted. Add the tomatoes and cook for one minute longer. Add to the drained beans. Add parsley and tuna fish, gently mix, and chill.

4. Just before serving, combine the remaining oil with the vinegar and Tabasco and pour over the bean salad. Season with salt and pepper to taste.

RICE AND HAM VINAIGRETTE   *6 servings*

1½ cups uncooked long-grain rice
1 cup finely diced cooked ham
½ cup finely chopped parsley
¼ cup finely chopped chives
1 tablespoon chopped capers
½ cup peanut oil

2 tablespoons olive oil
1 egg yolk
3 tablespoons wine vinegar
Salt and freshly ground black pepper

1. Cook the rice in two quarts boiling salted water until it is tender. Drain in a colander, place the colander over boiling water, and steam the rice briefly until it is fluffy and the grains stand apart. Refrigerate the rice.

2. When the rice is thoroughly chilled, combine it with the ham, parsley, chives and capers in a large mixing bowl. Refrigerate while preparing the sauce.

3. Combine the peanut oil, olive oil, egg yolk and vinegar in a small bowl. Whip the mixture with a wire whisk until the sauce reaches the consistency of a thin mayonnaise. Season with salt and pepper to taste.

4. Toss the vinaigrette sauce with the rice-ham mixture until all grains of rice are coated. If necessary, add more oil or vinegar. Adjust seasonings to taste.

STUFFED AVOCADO ANDEAN   *10 servings*

5 avocados
⅓ cup chopped celery
2 tablespoons chopped parsley
1 tablespoon chopped chives
¼ cup chopped green onions
½ cup chopped onion
2½ teaspoons curry powder
½ cup chopped green pepper
½ cup chopped red pepper

⅓ cup chopped cooked carrot
2 medium potatoes, cooked and chopped
1 teaspoon finely minced garlic
3 tablespoons mayonnaise
3 tablespoons salad oil
1 omelet of 5 eggs, chopped
1½ teaspoons salt

1. Wash the avocados. Cut them lengthwise into halves and remove the pits.

2. Combine the remaining ingredients and blend thoroughly. Stuff the filling into the center of the avocado halves. Serve garnished with tomato slices, stuffed olives and radish roses.

SALAD DRESSINGS

FRENCH DRESSING *½ cup*

2 tablespoons cider vinegar
6 tablespoons olive oil
¾ teaspoon salt

¼ teaspoon freshly ground black pepper
¼ teaspoon dry mustard

Combine all the ingredients, blend thoroughly, and chill.

HERBED FRENCH DRESSING *About 1½ cups*

1 teaspoon salt
¼ teaspoon freshly ground black pepper
1 teaspoon dried basil
1 teaspoon paprika
2 teaspoons chopped chives

1 cup salad or olive oil
½ teaspoon dry mustard
1½ teaspoons water
1 teaspoon sugar
5 tablespoons red-wine vinegar
1 garlic clove, finely minced

1. Combine the salt, pepper, basil, paprika, chives and oil.

2. Blend the mustard with the water and let stand for ten minutes to develop flavor. Add mustard to the oil with remaining ingredients. Beat with a rotary beater until well blended. This dressing is particularly good on sliced tomatoes.

MUSTARD FRENCH DRESSING *1¼ cups*

1 cup salad or olive oil
1 teaspoon salt
1 teaspoon sugar
1 teaspoon dry mustard
1 tablespoon finely chopped shallots or scallion

¼ teaspoon freshly ground black pepper
3 tablespoons wine vinegar

1. Combine the oil with the salt, sugar, mustard, shallots and pepper. Let stand for at least one hour.

2. Add the vinegar and beat vigorously with a fork or rotary beater.

TARRAGON FRENCH DRESSING   *½ cup*

5 tablespoons salad oil
3 tablespoons red-wine vinegar
2 teaspoons salt
½ teaspoon crumbled dried tarragon
¼ teaspoon freshly ground black pepper
1 garlic clove

1. Combine oil, vinegar, salt, tarragon and pepper.
2. Peel garlic, cut into halves, and add to dressing. Let the dressing stand for several hours before using.
3. Remove and discard garlic. Mix the dressing well and pour over salad just before serving.

ORANGE FRENCH DRESSING   *1 cup*

½ cup salad oil
¼ cup fresh orange juice
2 tablespoons fresh lemon juice
1 teaspoon sugar
¼ teaspoon dry mustard
⅛ teaspoon salt
Dash of freshly ground white pepper
2 tablespoons shredded fresh apples or pears

Combine all ingredients and beat with a rotary beater or blend in an electric blender for one-half minute. This is an excellent dressing for fruit salads.

GRAPEFRUIT FRENCH DRESSING   *2 cups*

1½ teaspoons salt
1 teaspoon paprika
⅛ teaspoon freshly ground white pepper
1 teaspoon minced fresh tarragon
1 teaspoon sugar
1 cup peanut oil
¾ cup fresh grapefruit juice
3 tablespoons fresh lemon juice

Combine the salt, paprika, pepper, tarragon, sugar and oil. Let stand for one hour. Add the grapefruit juice and lemon juice and store in the refrigerator until serving time.

CHEESE AND VEGETABLE SALAD DRESSING   *About 1½ cups*

½ cup cottage cheese
½ cup milk
Salt
1 teaspoon paprika
2 tablespoons lemon juice
½ teaspoon finely minced garlic (optional)
½ green pepper, finely minced
2 green onions, trimmed and finely chopped
4 radishes, trimmed and thinly sliced

A mortar and pestle make it easy to have freshly ground herbs and spices for salads and sauces.

A melon-ball cutter helps make fruit salads and fruit desserts look festive.

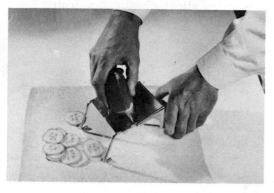

A simple metal slicer will give uniform slices of cucumbers, carrots, beets and the like to make salads as beautiful as they are delicious.

A wire salad basket is valuable for shaking water off salad greens after washing.

1. Place the cheese, milk, salt to taste, paprika, lemon juice and garlic in the container of an electric blender. Cover and blend for ten seconds, or until well blended.

2. Stir the green pepper, onions and radishes into the dressing. Spoon over salad greens.

CARAWAY-SEED AND COTTAGE-CHEESE DRESSING
About 1¼ cups

2 medium radishes, chopped
2 hard-cooked egg yolks, mashed
⅓ cup cottage cheese
1 tablespoon finely chopped green pepper
1 garlic clove, finely minced

1 teaspoon caraway seeds
1 teaspoon salt
½ teaspoon paprika
2 tablespoons lemon juice
½ cup buttermilk

Combine all ingredients and mix well. Serve on green salad.

EGG AND CREAM SALAD DRESSING   *About 1 cup*

4 eggs, hard-cooked
1 teaspoon prepared mustard, preferably Dijon or Düsseldorf
½ cup heavy cream

3 tablespoons lemon juice or tarragon vinegar
Salt and freshly ground black pepper

1. Cut the eggs into halves and put the yolks through a sieve or potato ricer. Blend the yolks with the mustard and stir in the cream. Add the lemon juice and salt and pepper to taste. Chill until ready to serve.

2. When ready to serve toss lightly with salad greens. Chop the egg whites and sprinkle over the salad. Use for salads of watercress or Boston lettuce.

MAYONNAISE   *About 2 cups*

2 egg yolks
1 teaspoon dry mustard
½ teaspoon salt
Pinch of cayenne pepper

¼ cup wine vinegar or lemon juice
1 cup olive oil
1 cup salad oil

1. Beat the egg yolks until thick and lemon colored. Add seasonings and half of the vinegar; beat well.

2. Mix the oils and add, while beating, drop by drop at first and then in a gradually increasing amount as mixture thickens. Do not overbeat.

3. Slowly add the remaining vinegar and beat well. Chill.

BLENDER MAYONNAISE *About 1½ cups*

Juice of 1 lemon
½ teaspoon dry mustard
½ teaspoon salt

1 egg
1 cup olive oil

1. Place the lemon juice, mustard, salt, egg and one-quarter cup of the olive oil in the container of an electric blender. Cover and turn the blender motor on low speed.

2. Immediately remove the blender cover (or center disk, if there is one) and add the remaining olive oil in a steady stream.

Note: This mayonnaise will keep stored in the refrigerator for two or three weeks.

MAYONNAISE ASPIC *2½ cups*

1 envelope unflavored gelatin
¼ cup lemon juice
1 teaspoon salt
¼ teaspoon freshly ground black pepper

1 egg
1 cup salad oil
1 cup heavy cream

1. Sprinkle the gelatin over the lemon juice in a small saucepan and soak for two minutes. Place saucepan over low heat and stir the mixture until the gelatin is dissolved.

2. Pour the gelatin mixture into the container of an electric blender. Add the salt, pepper, egg and one-quarter cup of the oil. Cover and blend on low speed. Remove cover and add one-quarter cup of remaining oil, pouring in a slow stream. Add remaining oil alternately with cream, continuing to blend on low speed. If necessary, stop the motor and use a rubber spatula to stir down the mixture.

3. If mixture starts to thicken before ready to be used, it may be reheated by placing the blender container in hot water and stirring the aspic until it returns to the proper consistency.

GREEN MAYONNAISE *About 2 cups*

Combine one and one-half cups mayonnaise with three-quarters cup finely minced mixed greens. Greens may include a mixture of spinach, watercress, parsley, chives or tarragon. Greens may be pounded in a mortar or puréed in a blender to make a smoother sauce.

CURRIED MAYONNAISE

Add one tablespoon of curry powder (or more to taste) to each cup of mayonnaise.

SEA GODDESS DRESSING   *About 2 cups*

1 garlic clove, finely minced
3 tablespoons minced anchovies
¼ cup finely minced chives
1 tablespoon lemon juice
1 tablespoon tarragon wine vinegar

½ cup sour cream
1 cup mayonnaise
⅓ cup finely chopped parsley
Salt and freshly ground black pepper

Combine the ingredients in the order given. Chill thoroughly. Serve with salads of fish or shellfish.

CHAPTER NINE

SAUCES AND GARNISHES

STOCKS AND ASPIC GARNISHES

BEEF STOCK   *3 quarts*

3 pounds shin of beef
2 marrowbones
3 pounds beef chuck, cut into
  pieces
1½ tablespoons salt
6 peppercorns
1 large onion, studded with 4 cloves

1 large leek
1 bay leaf
½ teaspoon dried thyme
2 carrots, washed and trimmed
2 parsley sprigs
2 celery ribs

1. Remove the meat from the shinbone. Place the shinbone and marrow-bones in boiling water, cook for five minutes, and drain well.

2. Place the bones and all the meat including trimmings in a large kettle. Add five quarts cold water and bring to a boil. Reduce the heat. Skim to remove foam and fat and continue to skim occasionally until foam ceases to rise.

3. Add the salt, peppercorns and onion. Trim the leek and split down the center without cutting through the root end. Wash well to remove any sand. Place the bay leaf in the center of the leek and sprinkle with the thyme. Tie the little bundle together with soft string and add to the kettle. Add remaining ingredients, cover loosely, and simmer gently for four to five hours.

4. Lift the bones and meat from the liquid. (The meat may be used for hash.) Strain the liquid through a double thickness of cheesecloth. If a richer, more concentrated flavor is desired, the stock may be reduced by simmering, uncovered, until it reaches the desired flavor.

5. Cool the stock quickly and chill it. The fat in the liquid will rise to the surface and form a hardened thin layer. Remove this before using the stock in recipes.

Note: Stock made at home is ideal as a basis for other preparations as it may be seasoned and concentrated to taste; however, it is a time-consuming project. Beef broth or bouillon and beef consommé are available in cans, and granules and cubes may be reconstituted to make a liquid stock. Any of these may be substituted for beef stock in recipes, but it may be necessary to adjust the seasoning as the purchased broth may be more salty.

VEAL STOCK   *3 quarts*

1 large veal knuckle (3 to 4 pounds)
1½ pounds veal, cut into pieces
1 tablespoon salt
6 peppercorns
1 large onion, studded with 4 cloves
1 carrot, washed and trimmed
1 celery rib with leaves
3 parsley sprigs
1 large bay leaf

1. Put the veal knuckle in boiling water, cook for five minutes, and drain well.

2. Place the bone and meat in a large kettle. Add five quarts cold water and bring to a boil. Reduce the heat. Skim to remove foam and fat and continue to simmer and skim until foam ceases to rise.

3. Add remaining ingredients, cover loosely, and simmer gently for about three hours.

4. Lift the bones and meat from the liquid. (The meat may be used for hash.) Strain the liquid through a double thickness of cheesecloth.

5. Cool the stock and chill it. Remove the layer of fat from the surface before using the stock in recipes.

Note: If veal stock is to be used for aspic dishes, a calf's foot or two may be added to the kettle to give a greater amount of gelatin. Parboil the calf's feet with the veal knuckle before adding them to the kettle.

LAMB STOCK   *About 3 quarts*

2 to 3 pounds neck of lamb, cut into pieces
Lamb bones
4 quarts water
1½ teaspoons salt
½ teaspoon freshly ground black pepper
2 onions, sliced

1. Place all the ingredients in a large kettle. Bring to a boil, cover, and simmer for three to four hours.

2. Strain, cool, and chill the stock. Before using it, discard the layer of fat which has risen to the top.

PORK BROTH   *About 1 cup*

Put one pound cracked pork bones in two cups lightly salted water. Cover and simmer for one hour. Strain.

CHICKEN STOCK   *6 cups*

6 pounds chicken wings, backs or necks
2½ quarts water
1 small onion, peeled and halved
½ cup chopped celery leaves
¼ cup chopped fresh parsley

1 large bay leaf
6 allspice berries
2 teaspoons salt
⅛ teaspoon freshly ground black pepper

1. Wash the chicken pieces and place them in a saucepan with the water. Add the onion, celery leaves, parsley, bay leaf, allspice, salt and pepper. Simmer, covered, for two and one-half hours.

2. Lift chicken and bones from the stock and strain liquid through a fine sieve. The stock may be further reduced if a concentrated flavor is desired. Cool the stock and chill it. Discard the layer of fat before using.

Note: While nothing is quite as satisfactory as homemade stock, there are many substitutes available. Chicken broth or bouillon is available in jars, cans, granules, and cubes. Canned chicken consommé is sold as well. Any of these may be substituted in the recipes calling for chicken stock. Remember, however, that the purchased broth or bouillon may be more salty than homemade stock and adjust the seasoning in the recipe accordingly.

FISH STOCK   *1½ cups*

Bones, heads, skin, and trimmings from 6 or more flounder, sole or whiting
1 cup dry white vermouth
1 onion, sliced

1 carrot, sliced
8 parsley sprigs
½ bay leaf
½ teaspoon salt

Place bones, heads, skin and trimmings in a large saucepan. Add remaining ingredients and enough cold water to cover. Simmer for thirty minutes and strain. Boil the strained liquid until it is reduced to one and one-half cups.

Note: Fish stock is the easiest of all stocks to make since it does not require such long slow cooking as stocks made of meat. However, if it is not convenient, clam broth may be used instead. This is available bottled. If you prefer to make your own clam broth, a recipe for this appears on page 109.

QUICK ASPIC FOR BEEF   *About 2 cups*

2 cups Beef Stock (page 473)
2 envelopes unflavored gelatin
2 egg shells

2 egg whites
2 tablespoons cognac

1. Combine the stock, gelatin, egg shells and egg whites in a saucepan and bring to a boil, stirring constantly. When the boiling point is reached, remove from the heat.

2. Line a colander or sieve with a clean napkin or a piece of flannel that has been rinsed in cold water and wrung out.

3. Strain the liquid through the cloth and add the cognac. Let stand at room temperature until ready to use. If the mixture gels before it is used, it may be reheated over low heat.

QUICK ASPIC FOR CHICKEN   *About 4 cups*

3 cups Chicken Stock (page 475)
1 cup tomato juice
4 envelopes unflavored gelatin
1 teaspoon sugar
2 egg shells, crushed

2 egg whites, lightly beaten
2 tablespoons cognac
  Salt and freshly ground black pepper

1. Combine stock, juice, gelatin, sugar, egg shells and egg whites in a saucepan. Heat slowly, stirring, until mixture boils up. Remove from heat and stir in cognac and salt and pepper to taste.

2. Strain the mixture through a sieve lined with flannel that has been rinsed in cold water and wrung out.

QUICK ASPIC FOR FISH   *About 2 cups*

1½ cups clam broth
½ cup tomato juice
2 envelopes unflavored gelatin
¼ teaspoon salt
⅛ teaspoon freshly ground black pepper

1 teaspoon sugar
1 egg white, lightly beaten
1 egg shell, crushed
2 tablespoons chopped parsley

1. Combine the clam broth, tomato juice, gelatin, salt, pepper, sugar, egg white and egg shell in a saucepan. Heat the mixture slowly, stirring constantly, until it boils up in the pan.

2. Strain the mixture through a sieve lined with flannel that has been rinsed in cold water and wrung out. Pour into a shallow dish (8 × 8 inches). Chill.

3. When aspic is set, turn onto a chopping board, add the parsley, and chop aspic until fine.

Note: If this aspic is to be used for a shellfish dish such as stuffed clams, reserve any clam liquor to use as part of the clam broth.

ASPIC SHELLS   *About 15 shells*

1. Make Quick Aspic for Chicken or Fish (page 476).
2. When the aspic is cool but still liquid, spoon it into shell-shaped cookie molds. Chill until set.
3. Place the molds on a towel that has been rinsed in hot water and wrung out. Lift aspic shells out carefully with a spatula. Use to garnish cold fish dishes.

SAUCES

SAUCE ESPAGNOLE or BROWN SAUCE   *About 2 quarts*

There is nothing more French than the sauce that is known as espagnole. *It is one of the foundation sauces of French cuisine and is nearly as important as wine, shallots, butter and cream. In most recipes written in English,* espagnole *is translated as "brown sauce." Brown sauce is easy to prepare, but it is time-consuming. It frequently is combined with a reduction of butter, shallots and wine as an accompaniment to grilled meats, poultry and game. It is also used to enrich stews and ragouts.*

There is nothing that is a perfect substitute for brown sauce, but the closest approximation is canned beef gravy, which may be used in any recipe calling for brown sauce.

5 pounds veal bones, cracked	1 teaspoon crushed peppercorns
1 large onion, quartered	3 garlic cloves, unpeeled
2 celery ribs with leaves, coarsely chopped	1 tablespoon salt
5 small carrots, peeled and quartered	½ cup all-purpose flour
	12 cups water
½ teaspoon dried thyme	1¼ cups tomato purée
3 bay leaves	½ cup chopped leeks, green part
	3 parsley sprigs

1. Preheat oven to hot (475° F.).
2. Combine the bones, onion, celery, carrots, thyme, bay leaves, peppercorns, garlic and salt in an open roasting pan. Bake for forty-five minutes. Reduce the oven temperature if necessary to keep the bones from burning, but do not add any liquid to the pan.
3. Sprinkle the bones with the flour. Stir the bones with a two-pronged fork to distribute the flour evenly. Bake for fifteen minutes longer.
4. Transfer the bones to a large kettle. Add two cups water to the roasting pan and cook over moderate heat, stirring to dissolve brown particles that cling to the bottom and sides of the pan.

5. Pour the liquid from the roasting pan into the kettle with the bones. Add the tomato purée and remaining water.

6. Add the leeks and parsley. Bring to a rapid boil and simmer for two hours. Add more liquid if necessary. Skim to remove fat and foam; strain.

7. The sauce may be frozen and defrosted as needed or it may be stored, tightly sealed, in the refrigerator for several weeks.

SAUCE BERCY   *About 2 cups*

⅓ cup finely chopped shallots
3 tablespoons butter
¾ cup plus 2 tablespoons dry white wine

1½ cups Brown Sauce (page 477)
1 teaspoon each of chopped tarragon and parsley

Cook the shallots in one tablespoon of butter until they are golden brown. Add three-quarters cup of the dry white wine and cook until it is reduced by half. Add the brown sauce and cook for ten minutes. Strain through a sieve and bring to the boil. Turn off the heat and stir in the two tablespoons cold butter. Add remaining wine and the herbs. Serve hot.

SAUCE MARCHAND DE VIN   *About 1½ cups*

¼ cup butter
2 tablespoons finely chopped shallots or green onions
⅓ cup dry red wine
1 cup Brown Sauce (page 477)

1 tablespoon cognac
Juice of ½ lemon
Salt and freshly ground black pepper

1. Melt half of the butter in a saucepan. Cook shallots in it for two minutes, stirring. Add wine; cook to reduce by half. Add the brown sauce and simmer for fifteen minutes. Remove from heat.

2. Add cognac and remaining butter. Swirl pan until butter melts. Add lemon juice, salt and pepper. Serve with grilled steak.

SAUCE BORDELAISE: *About 2¼ cups*

½ cup sliced beef marrow
Salt

2 cups Sauce Marchand de Vin (above)

Place the marrow slices in a saucepan and barely cover with water. Add salt to taste and bring to the boil. Cook in barely simmering water for two minutes. Add the poached marrow to the marchand de vin sauce and serve hot. Serve with roasted and sautéed meat dishes.

SAUCE PÉRIGUEUX   *About 2 cups*

2 cups Brown Sauce (page 477)   2 tablespoons cold butter
1 small can (1 ounce) truffles

Heat the brown sauce and add the liquid from the can of truffles. Chop the truffles and add them to the sauce. Bring to a boil and remove from the heat. Stir in the cold butter and serve hot with grilled beef, veal or chicken dishes.

SAUCE MADÈRE   *About 1¾ cups*

⅓ cup chopped shallots   ½ cup plus 3 tablespoons Madeira
3 tablespoons butter   1½ cups Brown Sauce (page 477)

Cook the shallots in one tablespoon of the butter until they are golden brown. Add one-half cup of Madeira and reduce it by half. Add the brown sauce and cook for ten minutes. Strain the sauce through a sieve and bring again to a boil. Turn off the heat and stir in the remaining cold butter. Stir until butter melts, then add remaining Madeira. Serve with roasted and sautéed meat dishes.

SAUCE AU PORTO:

Prepare the sauce as for the Sauce Madère (above) but substitute Port for the Madeira.

MUSHROOM SAUCE (brown)   *About 2½ cups*

½ pound mushrooms   ½ cup Madeira
1 tablespoon finely chopped shallots   1 cup heavy cream
  or green onion   1 teaspoon strong prepared mustard
¼ cup butter   Salt and freshly ground black
¾ cup Brown Sauce (page 477)   pepper

1. Cook the mushrooms and shallots in three tablespoons of the butter until dry.

2. Combine the brown sauce and wine. Cook for ten minutes. Add the cream and cook for five minutes longer. Remove from heat and stir in the mustard, remaining butter, salt and pepper to taste, and the mushrooms and shallots.

Note: For a white mushroom sauce see page 480.

SAUCE BÉCHAMEL   *About 2 cups*

Béchamel, or white sauce, is another of the foundation sauces of French cuisine. It may be made with milk alone or enriched with additional cream, or part of the liquid may be stock.

¼ cup butter
¼ cup all-purpose flour
2 cups milk
2 thin slices of onion
2 parsley sprigs

3 tablespoons heavy cream
Salt and freshly ground white pepper
Dash of grated nutmeg

1. Heat the butter in a saucepan and stir in the flour. Cook, stirring with a wire whisk, until thoroughly blended.
2. Scald the milk with the onion and parsley. Strain it into the butter-flour mixture, stirring constantly with the wire whisk. When the mixture is thickened and smooth, add the cream.
3. Season the sauce with salt and pepper to taste and add a dash of nutmeg.

MUSHROOM SAUCE (white)   *About 2 cups*

¼ cup butter
¼ pound mushrooms, sliced
½ small onion, minced
3 tablespoons all-purpose flour

1¼ cups milk
1 teaspoon salt
⅛ teaspoon freshly ground white pepper

Melt the butter in a saucepan. Add the mushrooms and onion and sauté until the mushrooms are tender. Blend the flour with the milk and add to the saucepan. Cook over low heat, stirring constantly, until thickened. Add salt and pepper.
Note: For a brown mushroom sauce see page 479.

GRAPE SAUCE   *About 1 cup*

2 tablespoons melted butter
1½ teaspoons lemon juice
2 tablespoons all-purpose flour
1 cup Chicken or Fish Stock (page 475)

2 egg yolks, lightly beaten
½ teaspoon salt
⅛ teaspoon freshly ground white pepper
½ cup seedless grapes

1. Combine the butter and lemon juice, blend in the flour, and stir in the stock. Bring the mixture to a boil, stirring, and simmer for two minutes.
2. Pour some of the hot liquid onto the egg yolks. Mix well and return to the pan. Reheat, but do not boil. Stir in the salt, pepper and grapes. Serve over white fish or boiled poultry.

SAUCE SUPRÊME   *About 2 cups*

2 tablespoons butter
2 tablespoons all-purpose flour
1 cup hot Chicken Stock (page 475)
½ cup light cream

Salt
¼ teaspoon grated nutmeg
1 egg yolk, lightly beaten

1. Heat the butter and blend in the flour. Stir in the stock, beating with a wire whisk. When the mixture is thickened and smooth, add the cream. Add salt to taste and the nutmeg. Simmer, stirring frequently, for ten minutes.

2. Remove from the heat. Add a little of the hot mixture to the beaten egg yolk, then return to the sauce in the pan. Reheat for one or two minutes, but do not let the sauce boil after the egg is added.

SAUCE POULETTE   *About 1½ cups*

½ cup sliced fresh mushrooms
1 tablespoon finely chopped onion
3 tablespoons butter
1 teaspoon lemon juice
2 tablespoons all-purpose flour
1 cup Chicken Stock (page 475)

¼ cup heavy cream
1¼ teaspoons salt
Dash of freshly ground white pepper
¼ cup sherry or other white wine
1 egg yolk

1. Sauté the mushrooms and onions in the butter and lemon juice. Blend in the flour. Add the stock and cream and cook, stirring vigorously with a wire whisk, until the mixture is thickened and smooth. Add the seasonings and wine.

2. Beat the egg yolk with a little of the sauce and add to the remaining sauce in the pan. Cook for one minute.

ONION-PIMIENTO SAUCE   *About 2½ cups*

1 medium onion, minced
3 tablespoons butter
3 tablespoons all-purpose flour
1 cup Chicken Stock (page 475)
½ cup heavy cream

2 tablespoons chopped pimiento
2 teaspoons chopped parsley
Salt and freshly ground white pepper

1. Sauté the onion in the butter until tender but not browned. Add the flour and blend with a wire whisk. Add the stock and cream and cook, stirring, until the sauce boils.

2. Add the pimiento, parsley, and salt and pepper to taste. Purée in a blender or sieve.

SAUCE AURORE   *2 cups*

5 tablespoons butter
¼ cup all-purpose flour
1 cup hot milk
½ cup Fish Stock (page 475)
½ cup heavy cream

1 tablespoon tomato paste
Salt and freshly ground black pepper
Lemon juice

1. Heat three tablespoons of the butter in a heavy enamelware or stainless-steel saucepan. Blend in the flour and cook slowly for two minutes. Remove from the heat.

2. Beat in the hot milk with a wire whisk, blending thoroughly. Beat in the fish stock, one-quarter cup of the cream and the tomato paste. Boil, stirring, for one minute. Thin out with remaining cream, adding one tablespoon at a time. Season with salt, pepper and lemon juice to taste. Remove from heat.

3. Just before serving, beat in the remaining butter, one tablespoon at a time. Serve with poached or baked fish.

SHRIMP SAUCE   *About 3 cups*

2 cans (10 ounces each) frozen cream of shrimp soup
½ pound fresh mushrooms, sliced
2 tablespoons butter
⅓ cup heavy cream

⅓ cup sherry
1 cup cooked shrimp, shelled, deveined and chopped
2 tablespoons chopped fresh parsley (optional)

1. Heat the soup, stirring constantly with a wooden spoon.

2. Sauté the mushrooms in the butter for about five minutes, until they are tender.

3. Add the mushrooms and remaining ingredients to the soup and reheat, but do not allow the sauce to boil or it will curdle.

LOBSTER SAUCE   *About 3 cups*

1 tablespoon butter
2 shallots, finely chopped
1 tablespoon all-purpose flour
¾ cup tomato juice
½ cup milk

1 to 1½ pounds cooked lobster meat, cut into small pieces
2 tablespoons sherry
½ cup heavy cream

1. Melt the butter and sauté the shallots in it until they are tender but not browned.

2. Stir in the flour, tomato juice and milk. Bring to a boil, stirring with a wire whisk or wooden spoon, and simmer for one minute.

3. Add the lobster meat, sherry and cream. Reheat but do not boil.

A wire whisk is the best implement for beating eggs or for making smooth sauces.

A double-lined sieve is ideal for straining sauces. A wooden spoon helps press solids through.

EGG SAUCE   *1½ cups*

2 tablespoons butter
2 tablespoons all-purpose flour
1 cup Fish Stock (page 475)
¼ teaspoon salt
⅛ teaspoon freshly ground white pepper

1 teaspoon lemon juice
2 tablespoons butter, in small pieces
2 hard-cooked eggs, chopped

1. Melt the butter and blend in the flour. Stir in the stock and bring to a boil, stirring constantly. Simmer for one minute.

2. Add the salt, pepper, lemon juice and small pieces of butter, swirling them through the mixture.

3. Add the chopped egg and reheat but do not boil. Serve with fish dishes.

CREAMED EGG SAUCE   *About 1½ cups*

3 tablespoons butter
3 tablespoons all-purpose flour
1 cup milk or ½ cup milk and ½ cup heavy cream
Salt and freshly ground black pepper

¼ teaspoon grated nutmeg
2 hard-cooked eggs, peeled and coarsely chopped

Melt the butter in a saucepan and stir in the flour, using a wire whisk. When blended and smooth, add the milk, stirring vigorously. When mixture

483

is thickened and smooth, add salt and pepper to taste, nutmeg and chopped eggs. Heat thoroughly, pour into a warm sauceboat, and serve immediately.

CHEESE SAUCE (Cheddar)   *1 cup*

1 tablespoon butter
1 tablespoon all-purpose flour
1 cup milk
½ teaspoon salt

⅛ teaspoon freshly ground black pepper
¾ cup grated sharp Cheddar cheese
1 teaspoon lemon juice

Melt the butter and blend in the flour. Stir in the milk, salt and pepper. Cook, stirring, until slightly thickened. Add the cheese and lemon juice and cook only until the cheese is melted.

SAUCE MORNAY   *About 2 cups*

¼ cup butter
¼ cup all-purpose flour
1¾ cups light cream or half milk and half cream
Salt and freshly ground white pepper

¼ teaspoon grated nutmeg, or more
½ cup freshly grated Parmesan or Gruyère cheese
2 egg yolks, lightly beaten

1. Melt the butter in a saucepan and stir in the flour. Gradually add the cream, stirring with a wire whisk. When the mixture is thickened and smooth, add salt and pepper to taste and the nutmeg. Remove from the heat and stir in the cheese. When cheese is blended, let sauce cool slightly.

2. Add a little of the sauce to the egg yolks, then blend this mixture with the sauce. Use for vegetables or fish or for dishes that are to be glazed under the broiler just before serving.

MUSTARD-CHEESE SAUCE   *About 2 cups*

1¼ teaspoons dry mustard
¼ cup butter
¼ cup all-purpose flour
2 cups milk
½ teaspoon salt

¼ teaspoon freshly ground black pepper
1 cup shredded Cheddar cheese
1 teaspoon fresh lemon juice

1. Combine the mustard with one teaspoon of cold water and let stand for ten minutes to develop flavor.

2. Melt the butter in a saucepan and blend in the flour. Gradually add milk. Stir and cook until the sauce is of medium thickness.

3. Add the salt, mustard mixture, pepper, cheese and lemon juice. Heat only to melt cheese.

ANCHOVY-CHEESE SAUCE   *About 1 cup*

1½ tablespoons butter
1½ tablespoons all-purpose flour
1½ cups milk

Dash of ground white pepper
¾ cup shredded Cheddar cheese
6 anchovies, chopped

Melt the butter and stir in the flour. Remove from the heat and add the milk, stirring. Cook until thick. Add the pepper, cheese and anchovies. Heat only until cheese is melted.

MUSHROOM AND CHEESE SAUCE   *About 3½ cups*

½ pound mushrooms
¼ cup butter
2 tablespoons finely chopped shallots
5 tablespoons all-purpose flour
1½ cups milk

1 cup heavy cream
1 cup grated Swiss, Gruyère or
   Cheddar cheese
Salt and freshly ground black
   pepper

1. Finely chop the mushrooms.

2. Melt the butter in a saucepan and add the shallots. Cook briefly, stirring, and add the mushrooms. Continue to cook, stirring occasionally, until mushrooms have wilted and most of the liquid has evaporated.

3. Sprinkle with the flour and gradually add the milk and cream, stirring vigorously with a wire whisk. When the sauce has thickened, remove it from the heat and stir in the cheese and salt and pepper to taste.

SAUCE HOLLANDAISE   *About ¾ cup*

4 egg yolks
3 tablespoons hot water
2 tablespoons lemon juice

Salt and freshly ground white
   pepper
½ cup butter

1. In a saucepan beat the egg yolks with a wire whisk until they are thick and pale in color. Add the hot water, lemon juice and salt and pepper to taste, and beat vigorously.

2. Heat the butter just to bubbling in another saucepan. Pour it slowly into the egg mixture, beating rapidly with the whisk.

3. Place the sauce over very low heat and cook, stirring constantly, until sauce is properly thickened. Do not overcook or sauce will curdle. To restore a slightly curdled sauce, add two tablespoons cold light cream and beat quickly, off the heat.

MUSTARD HOLLANDAISE SAUCE   *1 cup*

3 teaspoons dry mustard
1 teaspoon water
¾ cup butter, at room temperature

1½ tablespoons vinegar
3 egg yolks
Salt

1. Combine mustard with water and let stand for ten minutes. Divide the butter into three parts.

2. Place one-third of the butter in the top part of a small double boiler. Add vinegar and egg yolks. Place over hot, not boiling, water and cook slowly, beating vigorously.

3. As mixture begins to thicken, add the second piece of butter, then the third, beating constantly. Stir and cook until thickened. Do not overcook. Add the mustard mixture and mix well. Add salt to taste. If the sauce tends to curdle, place pan over ice and stir vigorously.

SAUCE MALTAISE   *About ¾ cup*

3 egg yolks	½ cup butter, melted and hot, but
1 tablespoon lemon juice	not browned
¼ cup orange juice	1 tablespoon grated orange rind
¼ teaspoon salt	
⅛ teaspoon freshly ground white pepper	

1. Place the egg yolks, lemon juice, one tablespoon of the orange juice, the salt and pepper in an electric blender.

2. Turn the motor on low speed and gradually add the butter in a steady stream. Blend for about fifteen seconds, or until the sauce is smooth and well blended.

3. Remove to a warm sauceboat and fold in the remaining orange juice and the grated rind. Serve over cooked broccoli, asparagus or cauliflower.

MUSTARD SAUCE

Combine one-quarter cup dry mustard with enough water to make a paste. Let the mixture stand for ten minutes to develop flavor. Use for Chinese dishes.

SAUCE BÉARNAISE   *1½ cups*

1 teaspoon chopped shallot	5 egg yolks
1 small tarragon sprig, chopped	¾ cup butter, melted
1 small chervil sprig, chopped	Pinch of cayenne pepper
2 peppercorns	½ teaspoon minced fresh tarragon
Pinch of salt	½ teaspoon minced fresh chervil
¼ cup tarragon vinegar	

1. Simmer the shallot, tarragon sprig, chervil sprig, peppercorns and salt in the vinegar over low heat until the vinegar has been reduced by two thirds. Cool to lukewarm.

2. Add the egg yolks and beat briskly with a wire whisk. Place over low heat and gradually add the butter. Whisk until the sauce thickens. Strain. Season with cayenne and stir in the minced tarragon and chervil.

SAUCE PIQUANTE   *About ½ cup*

3 tablespoons hot-pepper flakes
½ teaspoon cayenne pepper
¼ cup olive oil

1 teaspoon paprika
3 or 4 saffron shreds

Crush the pepper flakes with a mortar and pestle. Add the cayenne pepper and enough boiling water to make a paste. Stir in the remaining ingredients and let stand until ready to use.

DIABLO SAUCE   *¾ cup*

2 tablespoons butter
¼ cup chopped scallions
1 teaspoon dry mustard
1 teaspoon anchovy paste
1 hard-cooked egg yolk, crushed

2 tablespoons olive oil
1 tablespoon tarragon vinegar
2 tablespoons Spanish sherry
Salt and Tabasco

Heat the butter and cook the scallions in it for three minutes. Add the remaining ingredients with salt and Tabasco to taste and bring to a boil. Let stand until ready to use.

CUMBERLAND SAUCE   *About 1½ cups*

½ cup currant jelly
Grated rind and juice of 2 lemons
Grated rind and juice of 1 orange

1 tablespoon grated horseradish (optional)

Beat all the ingredients together. Chill and serve on cold tongue.

LEMON SAUCE   *About 1¾ cups*

¼ cup melted butter
2 tablespoons all-purpose flour
¼ cup lemon juice
1 cup boiling water

¼ teaspoon salt
Dash of Tabasco
½ cup whipped sweet or sour cream, approximately

Melt three tablespoons of the butter in a saucepan. Stir in the flour and let cook for two minutes. Add the lemon juice and boiling water; stir and cook until smooth and thickened. Simmer for five minutes and add salt and Tabasco. Just before serving, add the cream and remaining butter. Serve over asparagus.

VINAIGRETTE SAUCE I   *About 1¼ cups*

3 tablespoons wine vinegar
¾ cup olive oil
½ cup finely chopped parsley
1 tablespoon finely chopped chives
1 tablespoon chopped drained capers

½ teaspoon finely chopped onion
1 teaspoon finely chopped sour pickle (optional)
Salt and freshly ground black pepper

Combine all the ingredients and beat with a fork until well blended. Chill the sauce if it is to be used with chilled vegetables or shrimp. Heat sauce to lukewarm if it is to be used with hot boiled beef, fish or chicken, pigs' feet or calf's head.

VINAIGRETTE SAUCE II   *About 1 cup*

2 tablespoons lemon juice
2 tablespoons cider vinegar
1 garlic clove, minced
¾ teaspoon salt
⅛ teaspoon freshly ground black pepper
1 tablespoon sugar

¾ cup salad oil
1 tablespoon chopped green pepper
1 tablespoon chopped parsley
1 tablespoon chopped cucumber pickles
2 tablespoons chopped pimiento
1 tablespoon chopped capers

Combine all ingredients and stir vigorously before serving. Serve over hot vegetables and with salads.

PARSLEY SAUCE   *About 1¼ cups*

¾ cup olive or vegetable oil
3 tablespoons plus 1 teaspoon lemon juice
Salt and freshly ground black pepper

2 tablespoons finely chopped onion
¼ teaspoon finely minced garlic
¼ cup chopped fresh parsley
¼ teaspoon dried orégano

1. Combine the oil, lemon juice and salt and pepper to taste in a small saucepan. Stir briskly to blend, and heat thoroughly. Do not boil.
2. Remove the sauce from the heat, let cool almost to lukewarm, and add the remaining ingredients. Serve immediately with fish.

HERB SAUCE FOR BOILED BEEF   *About 2 cups*

¼ cup butter
¼ cup all-purpose flour
2 cups Beef Stock (page 473), hot

2 egg yolks, beaten lightly
2 tablespoons chopped capers
1 tablespoon finely chopped parsley

1. Melt the butter and stir in the flour. Add the hot stock, beating vigorously with a wire whisk. When the mixture is thickened and smooth, simmer for five minutes, stirring occasionally.

2. Remove from the heat and add gradually to the egg yolks. Return to the heat and add the capers and parsley. Heat briefly and serve hot with boiled beef.

SOUR-CREAM AND DILL SAUCE   *About 1 cup*

Combine one cup sour cream with one-quarter cup finely chopped fresh dill or two teaspoons dried dill. Heat over simmering water until thoroughly hot.

SOUR-CREAM AND HORSERADISH SAUCE   *About 1 cup*

1 cup sour cream
2 tablespoons prepared horseradish

1 teaspoon prepared mustard

Combine the sour cream with the horseradish and mustard. Chill until ready to serve.

HORSERADISH SAUCE   *About 1 cup*

½ cup heavy cream, whipped
¼ cup grated fresh horseradish

1 teaspoon lemon juice
¼ teaspoon salt

Mix the ingredients together just before serving. Add more salt if desired. Serve with ham or beef.

HOMEMADE CURRY POWDER   *About ½ cup*

2 tablespoons ground turmeric
2 tablespoons cuminseeds, crushed in a mortar
2 tablespoons coriander seeds, crushed in a mortar
1 tablespoon ground ginger

1 tablespoon freshly ground black pepper
2 teaspoons cardamom seeds, crushed
2 teaspoons ground mace
1 teaspoon mustard seeds, crushed
1 teaspoon ground cloves

Combine all the ingredients and mix well. To increase the heat in a curried dish, increase the amount of ginger or pepper in the powder; or add finely chopped hot chilies to the dish instead of adding more of the mixed powder.

CUCUMBER SAUCE   *1½ cups*

1 cup finely chopped peeled cucumbers
½ teaspoon salt
2 teaspoons sugar

1 tablespoon cider vinegar
⅛ teaspoon freshly ground black
  pepper
½ cup heavy cream, whipped

1. Combine the cucumbers and salt. Let stand in a covered jar in the refrigerator for at least one hour.

2. Drain cucumbers and mix with sugar, vinegar and pepper. Just before serving fold in the whipped cream. Serve over fish.

Coconut Cream, made of the liquid and pulp of the coconut, is used in much of the cuisine of the Far East. These dishes include Chicken Sate with dipping sauce made with peanuts, Curry of Beef with rice and condiments, and individual dishes of Molded Coconut Cream.

COCONUT CREAM

1. Preheat oven to hot (400° F.).

2. With an icepick puncture soft spots in two eyes of a coconut. Drain off the coconut water, measure it, and set aside.

3. Bake the drained coconut for fifteen minutes.

4. Gently tap the baked coconut with a hammer until shell falls off easily. Pare off the dark outer skin and cut the meat into one-half-inch cubes. Measure the cubes.

5. Combine the reserved coconut water with enough scalded milk or boiled water to equal one cup liquid for each one cup of the cubes. Mix one cup liquid and one cup cubes and blend in an electric blender for thirty to forty-five seconds; or grate with a hand grater; or allow the mixture to stand for fifteen minutes. Follow the same procedure with the remaining liquid and cubes.

6. Drain the mixture through a double layer of cheesecloth, squeezing out as much liquid as possible. An average coconut will make three to four cups of coconut cream. Use the coconut cream for desserts and in curries.

COCONUT MILK: The used blended or grated coconut may be processed a second time with additional scalded milk or boiled water. This liquid will be thinner and less flavorful, but it can be used in the same way as coconut cream.

Note: Coconut cream and coconut milk may be made with dried coconut. It may be used in exactly the same way. To gain the most flavor, when the milk or water is mixed with the coconut shreds, bring the mixture to a boil and simmer until it is foamy before pressing out the liquid.

Coconut milk as it exists in tropical countries is taken from green coconuts. The liquid, or coconut water, that is found in the ripe coconut is quite different in taste.

SAUCE GRIBICHE   *About 2 cups*

1 egg yolk
Salt and freshly ground black pepper
1 teaspoon prepared mustard, preferably Dijon or Düsseldorf
3 tablespoons wine vinegar
½ cup olive oil
½ cup vegetable oil
2 tablespoons finely chopped shallots
1 tablespoon finely chopped onion
¼ teaspoon dried thyme
3 tablespoons chopped chives
¼ cup finely chopped parsley
1 teaspoon finely chopped fresh tarragon or ½ teaspoon dried tarragon
1 hard-cooked egg, sieved or finely chopped
¼ cup cold water, approximately

1. This sauce is made like a mayonnaise. Place the egg yolk in a mixing bowl and add salt and pepper to taste, the mustard and vinegar. Immediately

begin whipping the mixture with a wire whisk or rotary beater. Add the oil, a few drops at a time, then continue to add it in a steady stream, beating constantly. The sauce should become thicker all the time.

2. Stir in the remaining ingredients, adding only enough water to make a thin sauce.

AÏOLI   (garlic mayonnaise)   *2 cups*

2 to 4 garlic cloves, finely minced
2 egg yolks
½ teaspoon salt

Freshly ground black pepper
2 cups olive oil

1. Place the garlic in a mixing bowl and add egg yolks, salt, and pepper to taste. Beat rapidly with a wire whisk or rotary beater.

2. Gradually add the oil, while beating. Add it drop by drop at first and then in a gradually increasing amount as the mixture thickens. Chill. Serve with cooked artichokes, green beans, carrots, steamed cod or potatoes in jackets.

SAUCE ROUILLE   *About 6 cups*

2 medium potatoes, baked, mashed while warm
3 garlic cloves, finely minced
3 egg yolks
½ teaspoon paprika

½ teaspoon ground saffron
2 cups peanut oil
1 cup heavy cream
Salt and freshly ground black pepper

1. Spoon the mashed potatoes into the mixing bowl of an electric mixer. Add the garlic, egg yolks, paprika and saffron and beat well.

2. Meanwhile, warm the oil and cream and start adding the oil to the potato mixture while beating on low speed. Add the oil and cream alternately until the sauce has the consistency of mayonnaise. Season with salt and pepper to taste, and beat at high speed for thirty seconds. Serve with poached fish.

TARTAR SAUCE   *About 1¼ cups*

1 cup mayonnaise
1 teaspoon mustard, preferably Dijon or Düsseldorf
2 tablespoons finely chopped sour pickles

2 tablespoons finely chopped capers
1 tablespoon finely chopped chives
1 tablespoon finely chopped tarragon (optional)
Lemon juice

Combine mayonnaise and mustard and all the chopped ingredients. Stir in lemon juice to taste. If this sauce seems too thick, it may be thinned by beating a little cold water into it. Serve with fish and shellfish.

SEAFOOD COCKTAIL SAUCE   *About 1 cup*

1 cup tomato catchup
1 tablespoon Worcestershire sauce, or
more

2 tablespoons prepared horseradish
Lemon juice

Combine catchup, Worcestershire, and horseradish. Add lemon juice to taste and chill.

MARINARA SAUCE   *About 2 quarts*

¼ cup olive oil or butter
2 garlic cloves, finely minced
2 cups finely chopped onions
3½ cups (one 1-pound 12-ounce can) Italian plum tomatoes
2 cups (one 15-ounce can) tomato purée
1½ cups (one 12-ounce can) tomato paste

½ cup water or meat stock
1 teaspoon each of dried basil and orégano
½ teaspoon ground sage
1 teaspoon salt
Freshly ground black pepper
1 cup grated Parmesan cheese

1. Heat the oil in a large saucepan and add the garlic and onions. Cook, stirring, until the onions are light brown.
2. Add the tomatoes, tomato purée, tomato paste, water and seasonings. Simmer for one hour, stirring occasionally.
3. Add the cheese and cook for thirty minutes longer. Leftover sauce may be frozen.

TOMATO SAUCE I   *About 2 cups*

3 medium tomatoes (about 1½ pounds)
3 tablespoons butter
1 cup coarsely chopped onions

½ garlic clove, finely minced
½ teaspoon dried thyme
Salt and freshly ground black pepper

1. Peel the tomatoes. Remove the cores. Quarter the tomatoes.
2. Heat the butter in a saucepan and cook the onions and garlic in it until onions are translucent. Add the tomatoes and seasonings and cook for fifteen minutes, stirring occasionally. The tomatoes should retain some of their texture.
3. Strain the liquid from the tomatoes into another saucepan and reduce by half over high heat. Add the tomato pulp and heat thoroughly.
Note: This sauce may be stored for several days in the refrigerator. The sauce may also be frozen.

TOMATO SAUCE II   *3 to 4 cups*

5 large ripe tomatoes
⅓ cup Italian olive oil
1 onion, thinly sliced
1 carrot, thinly sliced

2 garlic cloves, finely minced
2 leaves of sweet basil
½ cup butter

1. Peel the tomatoes. Remove the cores. Cut the tomatoes into eighths.

2. Heat the oil in a saucepan and cook the onion and carrot in it, stirring, until onion is golden brown. Add the garlic, cook briefly, and add the basil and tomatoes. Simmer for thirty minutes.

3. Put the mixture through a food mill. Return it to the pan and add the butter. Simmer for twenty minutes longer and serve hot.

TOMATO SAUCE III   *2½ cups*

½ cup sliced onion
¼ cup butter
3 tablespoons all-purpose flour
1 cup water
1 teaspoon cider vinegar
1 small bay leaf

½ teaspoon salt
¼ teaspoon black peppercorns
2 cups diced peeled fresh tomatoes
¼ teaspoon ground thyme
Dash of cayenne pepper

1. Sauté the onion in the butter until lightly browned. Add the flour and cook over low heat, stirring constantly, until the mixture is light brown in color.

2. Add the water, vinegar, bay leaf, salt, peppercorns and tomatoes. Simmer for ten minutes. Add the thyme and cayenne and simmer for five minutes longer. Strain. Serve with eggplant dishes, veal dishes, and polenta.

TOMATO AND MEAT SAUCE   *50 servings*

4 cups finely chopped onions
2 cups diced celery
1 pound fresh mushrooms, finely chopped
4 garlic cloves, minced
½ cup salad oil
6 pounds beef, ground
3 pounds veal, ground
3 pounds pork, ground
1 teaspoon dried basil or 1 tablespoon chopped fresh basil

1 teaspoon dried thyme
1 teaspoon dried orégano
4 bay leaves
2 tablespoons salt
1 teaspoon freshly ground black pepper
4 quarts canned tomatoes
2½ quarts tomato paste
2 quarts Beef Stock (page 473)

1. Cook the onions, celery, mushrooms and garlic in the salad oil in a heavy saucepan until the vegetables are wilted.

2. Add the ground meats and cook until the moisture is evaporated and the meat begins to brown.

3. Add the remaining ingredients and bring to a boil, stirring frequently. Reduce the heat and simmer for two and one-half to three hours. Stir occasionally from the bottom. Serve with pasta.

TOMATO PASTE   *3 to 4 pints*

6 pounds ripe tomatoes, sliced
2 tablespoons chopped sweet basil leaves
2 teaspoons salt
¾ cup chopped celery
¾ cup chopped carrots
1 large onion, finely chopped
½ teaspoon freshly ground black pepper

1. Combine all the ingredients, bring to a boil, and simmer until the vegetables are soft.

2. Press mixture through a sieve into a heavy-bottomed saucepan. Place the saucepan over an asbestos mat and cook for about three hours, or until the paste is thick.

3. Pour into hot sterilized jars. Seal. Process in a water bath for five minutes.

SALSA FRIA   *About 4 cups*

4 cups peeled fresh tomatoes or canned Italian plum tomatoes
¼ cup canned green chilies
¼ cup wine vinegar
2 tablespoons oil
2 tablespoons finely chopped fresh parsley
2 garlic cloves, finely minced
1 teaspoon fresh or dried thyme
1 teaspoon dried orégano
2 teaspoons chopped fresh basil or 1 teaspoon dried basil
Salt and freshly ground black pepper

Chop the tomatoes and combine with the remaining ingredients. Chill until ready to serve.

MARINADES AND BASTING SAUCES

MARINADE   *About ½ cup*

¼ cup soy sauce
3 tablespoons sherry
1 tablespoon brown sugar
1 teaspoon monosodium glutamate
2 small slices of fresh gingerroot, diced
1 garlic clove, crushed

Combine all the ingredients. Use the mixture to marinate spareribs, shrimp or beef kebabs.

MARINADE FOR SMOKED OR BARBECUED FOODS   *2½ cups*

1 bottle or can (12 ounces) beer or ale
¼ cup salad oil
1 cup soy sauce
1 teaspoon dry mustard

2 tablespoons finely chopped onion
2 tablespoons sugar
2 tablespoons vinegar
½ teaspoon ground ginger
½ teaspoon ground cinnamon

Mix all ingredients in an electric blender. Pour over butterfish, bluefish, salmon or swordfish steaks in a shallow pan. Marinate for two to three hours, stirring occasionally. Drain and smoke. Makes enough marinade for two to three pounds of fish.

BASTING SAUCE FOR DUCK   *About 1¼ cups*

¼ cup honey, Chinese bead molasses, or syrup from a jar of preserved gingerroot
½ cup soy sauce (preferably Japanese)

½ cup sherry
1 garlic clove, finely minced
1 teaspoon freshly grated gingerroot or ½ teaspoon ground ginger

Combine all ingredients in a saucepan, bring to a boil, and remove from the heat. Use to baste a duck, every fifteen minutes, as it roasts or turns on the spit.

AVERY ISLAND BARBECUE SAUCE   *2½ cups*

2 tablespoons butter
1 medium onion, chopped
1 garlic clove, minced
½ cup chopped celery with leaves
¼ cup chopped green pepper
3½ cups (one 1-pound 12-ounce can) tomatoes
1 can (6 ounces) tomato paste
1 bay leaf

3 tablespoons molasses
2 teaspoons dry mustard
⅓ cup vinegar
½ teaspoon ground cloves
½ teaspoon ground allspice
2 slices of lemon
1½ teaspoons salt
2 teaspoons Tabasco

Melt the butter in a saucepan. Add the onion and garlic and cook until the onion is tender but not brown. Add the remaining ingredients and simmer for thirty minutes. Let stand until cool. Strain if desired. Use to brush hamburgers, chicken, spareribs, or frankfurters during baking, broiling or grilling.

BASTING SAUCE FOR SPIT-ROASTED LEG OF LAMB
About 1¼ cups

½ cup olive oil
½ cup red wine
1 bay leaf, crushed
¼ teaspoon dried thyme or 1 fresh thyme sprig
1 teaspoon chopped fresh rosemary or ½ teaspoon dried rosemary
8 juniper berries, crushed (optional)
¼ teaspoon ground ginger
¼ teaspoon cayenne pepper
¼ teaspoon grated nutmeg
1 teaspoon sugar
Salt and freshly ground black pepper

Combine all the ingredients in a saucepan, bring to a boil, and remove from the heat. Use to baste leg of lamb.

BARBECUE SAUCE   *About 4 cups*

4 large onions, sliced
⅓ cup olive oil
1 can (6 ounces) tomato paste or 1 bottle (14 ounces) tomato catchup
1 parsley sprig
1 thyme sprig
1 bay leaf
1 garlic clove, finely minced
½ bottle Worcestershire sauce
2 tablespoons sugar
1 dried hot-pepper pod
2 cups vinegar
Salt and cayenne pepper

Sauté the onions in the olive oil until soft. Add the tomato paste, parsley, thyme, bay leaf and garlic and let simmer for thirty minutes. Add remaining ingredients and let simmer until the desired flavor and thickness are attained. If a smooth sauce is preferred, the sauce may be puréed in an electric blender.

GREEN-PEPPER BARBECUE SAUCE   *1¼ cups*

1 teaspoon dry mustard
1½ teaspoons chili powder
1 teaspoon salt
⅛ teaspoon cayenne pepper
2 tablespoons brown sugar
2 tablespoons finely chopped onion
2 tablespoons chili sauce
½ cup diced green pepper
2 tablespoons salad oil
2 slices of lemon
½ cup cider vinegar

Combine all ingredients in a pan. Cook for three minutes. Use for basting spareribs, chops and chicken.

SOUTHERN BARBECUE SAUCE   *About 2¼ cups*

1 bottle (14 ounces) tomato catchup
½ cup butter
Juice and rind of 1 lemon
1 garlic clove, finely minced
1 tablespoon Worcestershire sauce

Combine all ingredients in a saucepan and bring to a boil. After the butter melts, simmer for five minutes and remove from the heat. Remove the lemon rind and use the sauce for basting poultry, fish or meats.

BARBECUE SAUCE FOR SPARERIBS   *About 2 cups*

1 teaspoon salt	¼ cup vinegar
1 teaspoon chili powder	¼ cup Worcestershire sauce
1 teaspoon celery seeds	1 cup canned tomatoes
1 teaspoon lemon juice	1 medium onion, chopped
2 teaspoons prepared mustard	1 garlic clove, finely minced
¼ cup brown sugar	

Combine all the ingredients in a saucepan and simmer for thirty minutes. Use as a basting sauce for goat or for spareribs.

. . . .

COMPOSED BUTTERS
AND BREAD GARNISHES

. . . .

CLARIFIED BUTTER

To clarify butter, cut it into small pieces and place in a pan over low heat. When the butter has melted, skim off the foam and pour off the clear yellow liquid (which is the clarified butter) into a bowl, leaving the milky residue in the bottom of the pan.

BEURRE BLANC   *About 1½ cups*

6 tablespoons butter	Salt
1 cup heavy cream	1 egg yolk, lightly beaten
¼ teaspoon Tabasco	2 tablespoons lemon juice

1. Place the butter, cream, Tabasco and salt to taste in a small skillet. Bring to a boil and stir gently with a wire whisk until the mixture has the consistency of a rich cream sauce.

2. Remove the skillet from the heat; stirring rapidly with the whisk, add the egg yolk. Continue stirring and return briefly to the heat. Do not let the mixture boil. Remove from heat and stir in the lemon juice. If the mixture boils again it will curdle. Serve immediately.

ANCHOVY BUTTER   *About 1 cup*

12 anchovy fillets
½ cup butter

Juice of 1 lemon
Tabasco

Chop the anchovies until they are almost a paste. Combine the paste, butter, lemon juice and Tabasco to taste. Heat thoroughly. Serve the sauce with grilled lobsters.

MUSTARD BUTTER   *½ cup*

Place one-half cup butter, at room temperature, in a mixing bowl and blend well with three tablespoons prepared mustard, preferably Dijon or Düsseldorf. Use as a spread for sandwiches. Leftover mustard butter may be refrigerated and reserved for later use.

SNAIL BUTTER   *Enough for 12 snails*

1 garlic clove, minced
2 tablespoons finely chopped shallots
2 tablespoons finely chopped parsley

¼ cup butter, creamed
Salt and freshly ground black pepper

Using a mortar and pestle, pound garlic and shallots to a paste. Add the parsley and mix well. Blend with the butter and salt and pepper to taste. Use with snails to fill about twelve snail shells.

DILL BUTTER   *½ to 1 cup*

Chop enough of the feathery leaves of dill to make one-quarter cup. Pour boiling water over them, let stand for one minute, and drain. Pound the leaves to a paste in a mortar; or put them in the container of an electric blender with one tablespoon lemon juice and purée the leaves. Stir the purée into one-half to one cup softened butter. Add additional lemon juice and salt to taste. Serve as a cold butter or as a hot sauce with fish dishes.

TABASCO ROQUEFORT STEAK SPREAD
Enough for two 4-pound steaks

½ teaspoon Tabasco
2 tablespoons butter

3 ounces Roquefort cheese

Cream all ingredients together until well blended. Spread over charcoal-grilled steak.

SESAME-SEED AND LEMON BUTTER   *About ½ cup*

⅓ cup melted butter
1 tablespoon fresh lemon juice
2 tablespoons toasted sesame seeds

Salt and freshly ground black pepper

Combine all ingredients and heat. Serve with hot vegetables.

HERBED CAPER BUTTER   *¼ cup*

¼ cup butter
⅛ teaspoon freshly ground black pepper

½ teaspoon dried orégano
2 teaspoons capers, chopped if large

Combine all ingredients in a small saucepan. Heat until butter is melted. Serve over cooked vegetables such as broccoli, Brussels sprouts, cabbage, cauliflower and snap beans.

SAVORY PECAN BUTTER   *1 cup*

½ cup butter, melted
2 tablespoons chopped chives
½ teaspoon salt
¼ teaspoon freshly ground black pepper

¼ teaspoon dried marjoram
3 tablespoons lemon juice
½ cup chopped pecans

Combine all the ingredients and heat just enough to blend the flavors. Serve over cooked vegetables.

FRENCH BREAD CROÛTES

Preheat oven to hot (400° F.). Place slices of French bread, one-half inch thick, on a baking sheet and butter generously on one side. Bake for ten to fifteen minutes, turning once. The croûtes are done when they are crisp and brown. Use for fish soup or as a base for slices or pieces of other foods.

GARLIC-FLAVORED CHEESE CROÛTES:

Rub the outside of a crusty loaf of French bread with garlic. Cut the bread into slices one-quarter inch thick. Brush the slices with oil and place on a baking sheet. Bake until golden. Turn once. Sprinkle with grated Parmesan or Swiss cheese and bake just until the cheese melts.

TABASCO CROÛTES:

Preheat oven to moderate (375° F.). Cut French bread on the diagonal into half-inch slices. Melt one-quarter cup butter and stir in one garlic clove, minced, and one-quarter teaspoon Tabasco. Brush the mixture on the cut surfaces of the bread. Bake for fifteen to twenty minutes, until hot and toasted.

CROUTONS

Cut slices of bread into half-inch cubes, or into smaller or larger cubes as desired. Dry them in a moderate oven (325° F.); or brush them with butter, oil, or cheese, and toast them in the oven as for croûtes (page 500); or sauté them over moderate heat until golden brown.

Bread garnishes can be cut in other shapes, tiny rounds, triangles, crescents, etc. These little crusts can be prepared in the same way as the cubes.

BREAD CRUMBS

Bread crumbs are used as a finishing garnish on the top of many dishes, and crumbs are an essential of the garnish or sauce called polonaise, which is especially good with vegetables such as asparagus, broccoli, and Brussels sprouts. For directions for making soft fresh bread crumbs and fine dry bread crumbs, see page 313.

. . . .

RELISHES

. . . .

CRANBERRY JELLY   *1 cup*

2 cups fresh cranberries   ¾ cup sugar
½ cup water

Cook the cranberries in the water in a covered saucepan until the skins pop. Sieve the berries, add the sugar, and cook for three to five minutes. Chill until firm.

GINGERED CRANBERRY SAUCE   *2 pints*

4 cups fresh cranberries   Dash of salt
1 cup water   ⅓ cup candied or preserved ginger-
2 cups sugar   root, diced

1. Place the cranberries in a saucepan containing the water. Cover and bring to a boil. Cook for six to eight minutes, until skins burst.

501

2. Remove the cranberry mixture from the heat and stir in the sugar, salt and gingerroot. Mix thoroughly. Cool and chill. Serve with poultry, pork, ham or veal.

CRANBERRY-WALNUT SAUCE   *2 pints*

4 cups fresh cranberries
1 cup orange juice

2 cups sugar
½ cup coarsely chopped walnuts

Combine the cranberries and orange juice in a saucepan. Cover and cook for six to eight minutes, until the skins pop. Add sugar and mix well. Cool and chill. Stir in the walnuts. Serve with turkey.

CRANBERRY-APPLE SAUCE   *2 pints*

1 pound cranberries
2 cups sugar
2 apples, peeled, cored and diced

½ teaspoon ground cinnamon
⅛ teaspoon ground allspice
⅛ teaspoon ground cloves

1. Pick over and wash the cranberries. Place them in a two-quart pan. Add the sugar and apples.

2. Cover the pan and place over medium heat. When the cover is hot to the touch, reduce the heat to low and cook for twelve minutes. Stir in the spices and serve with pork, chicken or turkey.

EGGPLANT RELISH   *7 pints*

2 eggplants (1 pound each)
  Olive or cooking oil
12 cups diced tomatoes (about 12 tomatoes)
1 jar (7 ounces) pitted green olives
1 cup sliced blanched almonds or pine nuts
1½ cups seedless raisins

½ cup capers
4 cups 1-inch pieces of celery
1 tablespoon salt
1 teaspoon freshly ground black pepper
½ cup sugar
1 cup wine vinegar

1. If eggplant is young and tender, do not peel. If not, peel. Cut into half-inch cubes. Fry in hot oil one inch deep. Drain on brown paper. Set aside.

2. Cook the tomatoes for ten minutes, or until soft. Force through a sieve. Cut the olives into quarters. Combine tomatoes, olives, nuts, raisins, capers, celery, salt and pepper. Cook, uncovered, for twenty minutes, until celery is tender, stirring frequently.

3. Add sugar and vinegar. Cook for five minutes. Add the eggplant. Heat only until eggplant is hot.

4. Ladle into hot sterilized jars. Seal at once. Serve cold as a relish and sandwich filling or serve hot as a vegetable.

OLIVE-VEGETABLE RELISH   *About 2 pints*

¼ cup wine vinegar
¾ cup salad or olive oil
1 tablespoon sugar
1 garlic clove, slivered
¼ teaspoon freshly ground black pepper
½ teaspoon paprika
¾ cup pimiento-stuffed olives
½ cup chopped celery

¾ cup diced cauliflower
1 tablespoon capers
½ cup diced carrots
½ cup diced white turnips
½ cup small white onions
½ cup diced green pepper
½ cup diced summer squash
¼ cup chopped canned pimientos

1. Combine the vinegar, oil, sugar, garlic, pepper and paprika in a jar or bottle. Shake well to blend thoroughly.
2. Place the remaining ingredients in a mixing bowl. Pour the liquid mixture over them and mix well. Chill for at least forty-eight hours.

Put summer in a jar with sugar and spices. Almost any vegetable from the garden can be pickled or turned into a relish that will add a piquant touch to winter menus.

PICKLED MUSHROOMS   *2 to 3 cups*

1 pound small fresh mushrooms
¾ cup olive oil
¼ cup tarragon vinegar
¼ cup finely chopped parsley

1 teaspoon dried chervil
1 garlic clove, finely minced
Salt and coarsely cracked black pepper

1. Trim away the mushroom stems and use them for another purpose. Drop the mushroom caps into boiling salted water and simmer, covered, for exactly forty-five seconds. Drain immediately. Put the mushrooms in a glass jar.

2. Combine the remaining ingredients and blend well with a fork. Pour the marinade over the hot mushrooms, cover, and let stand in the refrigerator for two days. Use as a relish or as one of the dishes for antipasto or hors d'oeuvre.

MUSHROOM AND CELERY PICKLES   *3 cups*

1 pound small fresh mushrooms
2 teaspoons salt
2 tablespoons lemon juice
⅔ cup olive or other salad oil
1 garlic clove, split
1 cup sliced celery

2 tablespoons sliced pimiento-stuffed olives
2 tablespoons sliced ripe olives
1 tablespoon chopped fresh parsley
1 tablespoon capers
1 tablespoon wine vinegar

1. Wash the mushrooms and leave them whole. Cook them in one inch of boiling water containing one teaspoon of the salt for ten minutes.

2. Drain the mushrooms. Add remaining ingredients and toss lightly. Refrigerate for several hours, overnight, or for several days before serving. Use as a relish or as one of the dishes for antipasto or hors d'oeuvre.

CUCUMBER YOGHURT RELISH   *About 3 cups*

2 small cucumbers
½ teaspoon salt
2 tablespoons vinegar

¼ cup chopped scallions
2 cups yoghurt

1. Score the skin of the cucumbers lengthwise with a fork. Cut the cucumbers into halves, discard the seeds, and finely chop the cucumbers.

2. Sprinkle the chopped cucumbers with the salt and vinegar and let the mixture stand for twenty mintues. Drain, if necessary. Add the cucumbers and scallions to the yoghurt.

ATJAR KETIMUM (sweet and sour relish)   *8 servings*

2 cucumbers, peeled and cut into 1-inch cubes
Salt

½ cup vinegar
3 tablespoons sugar
¼ cup water

1. Sprinkle the cucumbers lightly with salt and let stand for twenty minutes. Drain.

2. Heat the vinegar, sugar and water and boil for two minutes. Remove from heat and cool.

3. Add the cucumbers and let the mixture stand for several hours before serving.

Note: Halved red and white radishes and sliced bamboo shoots may be substituted for the cucumbers.

SAMBELANS (Indonesian side dishes)   *4 to 6 servings*

SEROENDENG (fried coconut with peanuts) :

1 cup grated fresh coconut	1 onion, finely chopped
1 tablespoon *trasse udang* (shrimp paste)	1 tablespoon sugar
	1 garlic clove, finely minced
2 tablespoons ground hot red peppers, or more	¼ cup chopped peanuts

Combine all ingredients in a heavy skillet and cook gently, stirring constantly, until fairly dry and lightly browned.

SLICED MUSHROOMS FLAVORED WITH TAMARIND:

½ pound mushrooms, sliced	¼ teaspoon *assem* (tamarind)
2 tablespoons peanut oil	2 tablespoons hot water

Sauté the mushrooms in the oil for two to three minutes. Add the tamarind and water and reheat.

GRAPE AND GREEN-TOMATO CHUTNEY   *2 pints*

2 pounds green tomatoes, sliced (about 2 tomatoes)	½ teaspoon crumbled dried red pepper
4 tart apples	1 tablespoon mustard seeds
⅔ cup chopped onions	1 teaspoon dry mustard
2¾ cups dark brown sugar	2 teaspoons ground ginger or 1 teaspoon finely chopped fresh ginger-root
2 cups cider vinegar	
1 cup seedless raisins	
½ teaspoon salt	3 cups Thompson seedless grapes

1. Put the tomato slices in a five-quart saucepan. Peel and dice the apples and add them to the tomatoes. Add the onions, sugar, vinegar, raisins and salt. Mix well. Cook over medium heat for about thirty minutes.

2. Add the red pepper, mustard seeds, dry mustard, ginger and grapes to the hot mixture. Cook for about thirty minutes longer, or until mixture is thickened.

3. Pack chutney into hot sterilized jars, preferably one-cup size. Seal at once.

PICKLED WALNUTS *1 quart*

1 quart unripe white walnuts (butternuts)
1 dill sprig
3 walnut leaves

1 teaspoon mixed pickling spice
1 teaspoon salt
1/4 teaspoon alum
Boiling cider vinegar

1. The walnuts must be of almost maximum size, but they must be gathered before their shells have started to harden. If a nutpick or icepick can be pushed straight through the walnuts, husk and all, they are young and tender enough to pickle.

2. Put the nuts in a large kettle and cover them with boiling water. Boil until water discolors badly. Pour off the water, add fresh boiling water, and continue cooking. Continue boiling and changing water until the water remains clear.

3. Drain the nuts and pack them into a quart jar with the dill, walnut leaves, pickling spice, salt and alum. Add enough boiling cider vinegar to fill the jar. Seal. Let stand for one month.

Note: Pickled walnuts are delicious when served with scrambled eggs, kippered herring, grilled tomatoes and toast.

. . . .

CHAPTER TEN

SANDWICHES

Although the United States could be called a sandwich festival from one end of the year to the other, it is the summer season, naturally, when the fête reaches its zenith. The consensus seems to be that midday, in particular, is the time for a cool brow and a cold stove, and a sandwich with a tall drink just fills the bill.

The club sandwich is probably the original American version of the hero, submarine, torpedo, grinder or what have you, but both styles are popular today.

CLUB SANDWICH   *4 sandwiches*

1 tablespoon dry mustard	4 slices of ham
12 large slices of firm white bread, toasted	8 slices of chicken breast
½ cup mayonnaise	1 cucumber, peeled and thinly sliced
16 slices of crisp bacon	Salt and freshly ground black pepper
2 tomatoes, sliced	Bread and butter pickles
4 lettuce leaves	

1. Blend the mustard with two tablespoons water and let stand for ten minutes to develop flavor. Trim the toast and arrange the slices on wax paper.

2. Combine the mayonnaise and mustard and spread the toast on one side.

3. Arrange four slices of bacon on each of four slices of toast. Place tomato slices on the bacon and top with lettuce leaves. Top this with another slice of toast, mayonnaise side up.

4. Arrange one ham slice on each sandwich and top this with the chicken slices. Add the cucumber and sprinkle with salt and pepper. Finish with the last slices of toast, mayonnaise side down.

5. Using a sharp slicing knife, cut each sandwich diagonally. Secure each half with food picks and serve with chilled bread and butter pickles.

Note: Tomato peelings can make an interesting garnish for sandwiches. Roll them around loosely to resemble roses.

LOBSTER ROLL   *4 sandwiches*

3 tablespoons olive oil
1 tablespoon vinegar
  Salt and freshly ground black pepper
½ cup mayonnaise
2 tablespoons chili sauce
2 teaspoons chopped fresh dill or 1 teaspoon dried dill

2 tablespoons finely chopped scallions
⅔ cup finely chopped celery
  Tabasco
2 cups lobster meat, cut into bite-size pieces
8 hamburger buns, toasted
  Lettuce leaves

1. Combine the oil and vinegar in a mixing bowl and add a sprinkling of salt and pepper. Mix well with a fork.

2. Stir in the mayonnaise, chili sauce, dill, scallions and celery. Add Tabasco to taste and the lobster meat. Blend well.

3. Use as a filling for toasted hamburger buns. Garnish each sandwich with lettuce leaves.

SHRIMP SALAD SANDWICH   *4 sandwiches*

2 cups shelled and deveined cooked shrimp
¼ cup chopped chives
5 tablespoons Dijon or Düsseldorf mustard
2 tablespoons chopped capers
3 tablespoons mayonnaise
2 cans (5 ounces each) water chestnuts, drained and chopped

  Salt and freshly ground black pepper
1 teaspoon lemon juice
  Tabasco
8 large slices of white or dark bread
  Slices of hard-cooked egg
  Watercress and stuffed olives

1. Chop the shrimp coarsely and combine with the chives, mustard, capers, mayonnaise, water chestnuts, salt and pepper to taste and the lemon juice. Add more mayonnaise if necessary to make a spreadable mixture. Add Tabasco to taste and blend well.

2. Spread the filling over half of the bread slices and cover with remaining slices. Garnish the sandwiches with egg slices, watercress sprigs and olives.

Some of the best sources for sandwich fillings are Italian grocery stores which offer such delicacies as thin-sliced prosciutto, hot pickled peppers, assorted salami, tuna fish in olive oil and a multitude of cheeses. These flavorful ingredients make superior hero sandwiches.

TUNA AND PEPERONI HERO   *4 to 6 servings*

1 crusty loaf of French or Italian bread
2 cans (7 ounces each) tuna fish packed in olive oil
8 to 12 pickled peppers (peperoni)
Juice of 1 lemon

1. Slice the bread from one end to the other but do not cut all the way through. Leave one edge of the bread as a "hinge."
2. Empty the undrained tuna fish down the middle of the loaf and arrange the pickled peppers on top. Squeeze the lemon juice over the tuna fish. Close the sandwich, slice into individual portions, and serve.

EGG AND TOMATO HERO   *4 to 6 servings*

1 crusty loaf of French or Italian bread
2 ripe red tomatoes, cored and sliced
   Salt and freshly ground black pepper
3 hard-cooked eggs, sliced
6 flat anchovy fillets
1 onion, thinly sliced
   Wine vinegar and olive oil

1. Slice the bread from one end to the other but do not cut all the way through. Leave one edge of the bread as a "hinge."
2. Arrange the tomato slices down the middle of the bread and sprinkle with salt and pepper. Arrange the sliced eggs over the tomatoes. Cover with the anchovy fillets and onion slices. Sprinkle the filling lightly with vinegar and generously with olive oil. Close the sandwich, slice into individual portions, and serve.

OPEN-FACED TOMATO SANDWICH   *6 sandwiches*

6 slices of firm bread
   Butter, softened
   Mozzarella cheese, sliced
2 large firm ripe tomatoes
½ teaspoon dried orégano
⅛ teaspoon freshly ground black pepper
1 tablespoon butter, melted
   Salt
   Grated Parmesan cheese
18 flat anchovy fillets

1. Spread one side of each bread slice with softened butter. Cover each with slices of mozzarella cheese.
2. Wash the tomatoes and cut into six slices one-half inch thick. Place one slice on each of the sandwiches.
3. Combine the orégano, pepper and melted butter and brush over tomato slices. Sprinkle with salt to taste and the Parmesan cheese. Top each sandwich with three anchovy fillets.
4. Place the sandwiches under the broiler until cheese is melted and bubbly. Serve hot, garnished with parsley.

HAM AND CHEESE HERO   *4 to 6 servings*

1 crusty loaf of French or Italian bread
Mustard Butter (page 499)
½ pound prosciutto or other ham, sliced as thin as possible

½ pound thinly sliced Swiss or Gruyère cheese

1. Slice the bread from one end to the other but do not cut all the way through. Leave one edge of the bread as a "hinge."
2. Spread the bread generously with mustard butter and fill the sandwich from one end to the other with ham and cheese. Close the sandwich, slice into individual portions, and serve.

CAVIAR AND EGG SANDWICHES   *6 sandwiches*

12 slices of toast, freshly made
Butter
6 tablespoons caviar

3 hard-cooked eggs
6 tablespoons sour cream
6 tablespoons chopped onion

1. Trim the toast and spread one side of each slice with butter. Spread half of the slices with one tablespoon of caviar each.
2. Put the hard-cooked egg yolks through a sieve and chop the egg whites. Mix the eggs with the sour cream and onion and spoon the mixture over the caviar. Cover with remaining buttered toast.

PARSLEY BUTTER SANDWICHES   *About 12 dozen sandwiches*

6 loaves of unsliced bread (1 pound each)
3 cups butter, at room temperature
1 cup finely chopped parsley

Juice of 3 lemons
Grated rind of 3 lemons
Salt and cayenne pepper

1. Remove the crusts from the loaves of bread. Slice each loaf lengthwise into about twelve long thin slices.
2. Combine the butter with the parsley, lemon juice and rind, and salt and cayenne pepper to taste. Beat well.
3. Spread half of the slices with the butter mixture and top with the remaining slices, using all the bread and all the filling. Wrap in plastic wrap and chill.
4. Cut the long slices into fancy shapes, or triangles, or fingers. Each slice will make about four small sandwiches.

SMØRREBRØD

Lunch in Denmark is a selection of delicious sandwiches called smørre-brød, *literally butter and bread. These sandwiches do not have tops, for they are too fat, and usually have garnishes as well. The important thing is that they must be made of the finest ingredients, including the freshest butter, and the sandwiches must not only taste but look good. The breads must be firm; rye bread is especially favored. Any of these sandwiches could be made in miniature to serve as canapés, but in the usual size they are as filling as a standard American sandwich for all the daintiness of their appearance.*

SHRIMP SANDWICH:

Butter a thin slice of dark or light rye bread and cover copiously with tiny bay shrimp (may be purchased in jars). Garnish with a small lettuce leaf and a slice of lemon.

SMOKED-EEL SANDWICH:

Butter a thin slice of dark or light rye bread and cover with thin slices of smoked eel. Top with a small spoonful of cold scrambled egg. Garnish with a radish rose and a small lettuce leaf.

MATJES-HERRING SANDWICH:

Butter a thin slice of dark or light rye bread and cover with slices of matjes herring. Garnish with grated orange rind, quartered orange slices, and a thin lettuce leaf.

DANISH-CHEESE SANDWICH:

Butter a thin slice of dark or light rye bread and cover with thin slices of Danish cheese such as Danish blue, Samsø, Havarti, or King Christian IX.

LUMPFISH-CAVIAR SANDWICH:

Butter a thin slice of dark or light rye bread and cover with a spoonful of imported lumpfish caviar (may be purchased in jars). Garnish with a small lettuce leaf and twist of lemon.

ROAST-CHICKEN SANDWICH:

Butter a thin slice of dark or light rye bread and cover with thin slices of roast chicken. Decorate with a liver paste pushed through a pastry tube. Garnish with maraschino cherry half and tiny triangle of pineapple.

FRIKADELLER SANDWICH:

Butter a thin slice of dark or light rye bread and cover with thin slices of *Frikadeller* (page 216). Top with a spoonful of cold orange-flavored red cabbage and/or shredded beets.

SANDWICHES

SMOKED-SALMON SANDWICH:

Butter a thin slice of dark or light rye bread and cover with thin slices of smoked salmon. Garnish with lemon wedges.

LIVER-PÂTÉ SANDWICH:

Butter a thin slice of dark or light rye bread and cover with thin slices of liver pâté, either purchased or homemade. Top with a thin slice of a clear firm aspic and shreds of cooked beets. Garnish with cucumber slices and lettuce.

HAM AND EGG SANDWICH:

Butter a thin slice of dark or light rye bread and cover it with overlapping thin slices of Danish ham. Top with a spoonful of cold scrambled egg. Garnish with white asparagus tips and slivers of tomato.

FRESH-PORK SANDWICH:

Butter a thin slice of dark or light rye bread and cover with thin slices of roast fresh pork. Top with a spoonful of cold orange-flavored red cabbage and a cooked prune. Garnish with quartered thin orange slices.

ROAST-DUCK SANDWICH:

Butter a thin slice of dark or light rye bread and cover with slices of roast duck with crisp skin. Top with a spoonful of cold orange-flavored red cabbage and garnish with quartered thin orange slices.

BISMARCK-HERRING SANDWICH:

Butter a thin slice of dark or light rye bread and cover with bits of Bismarck herring and thin onion rings. Garnish with a thin lettuce leaf, finely chopped parsley and bits of pimiento.

TONGUE SANDWICH:

Butter a thin slice of dark or light rye bread and cover with overlapping thin slices of tongue. Cover this with a spoonful of cold vegetable salad mixed with mayonnaise. Garnish with white asparagus tips, a small lettuce leaf and slivers of tomato.

SARDINE SANDWICH:

Butter a thin slice of dark or light rye bread and cover with small imported sardines in tomato sauce. Garnish with a small lettuce leaf, a twist of lemon and parsley sprigs.

TARTARE STEAK SANDWICH:

Butter a thin slice of dark or light rye bread and cover with a large spoonful of freshly ground raw beef such as sirloin or tenderloin. Garnish with a raw egg yolk in half of an eggshell, grated fresh horseradish, chopped onion, corn-and-mustard relish (optional), capers, anchovy fillets and a small lettuce leaf.

EGG AND TOMATO SANDWICH:

Butter a thin slice of dark or light rye bread, cover with thin slices of hard-cooked egg, and top with thin slices of tomato. Garnish with freshly grated horseradish and a small lettuce leaf.

· ·

CHAPTER ELEVEN

BREADS

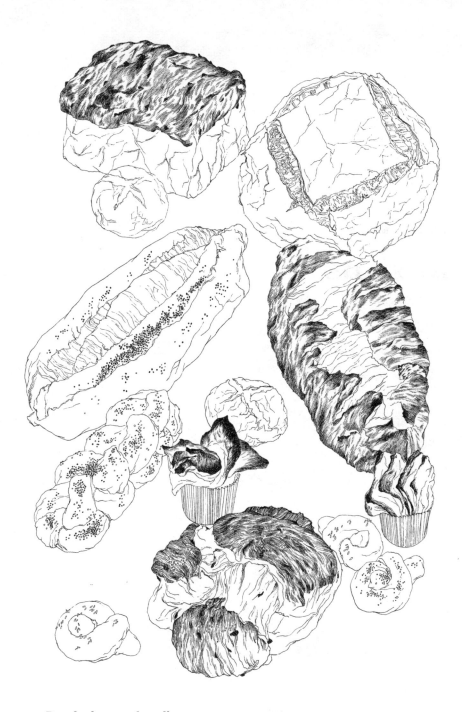

Breads—large and small

YEAST BREADS

WHEATEN BREAD   *2 loaves*

2 packages active dry yeast
2 teaspoons granulated sugar
1⅓ cups lukewarm water
2 tablespoons butter, softened
2 teaspoons salt

¼ cup light brown sugar
1½ cups stone-ground whole-wheat flour
3 cups all-purpose flour

1. Sprinkle the yeast and granulated sugar on the water. Let stand for fifteen minutes.

2. Add the butter, salt, light brown sugar, wheat flour and two cups of all-purpose flour to the yeast mixture. Mix with a wooden spoon until well blended.

3. Put the remaining flour on a board and turn the dough onto it. Knead the dough in the flour until the dough is smooth. Place it in a greased bowl and set in a warm place to rise. Let stand for about three hours, or until dough is doubled in bulk.

4. Grease two loaf pans (4 × 8 inches). Punch down the dough, shape it into two loaves, and place in the pans. With a sharp knife score the top of the loaves as you would a ham. Set in a warm place to rise. Let stand for one and one-half hours, or until doubled in bulk.

5. Preheat oven to moderate (375° F.).

6. Brush the top of the dough with cold water. Bake the loaves for thirty-five minutes, or until they sound hollow when tapped on the bottom. Cool on a rack.

SALT-RISING BREAD   *2 loaves*

2 medium potatoes, peeled and thinly sliced
2 tablespoons cornmeal
½ tablespoon sugar
1 teaspoon salt
2 cups boiling water

2 cups milk, scalded and cooled to lukewarm
⅛ teaspoon baking soda
8 cups sifted all-purpose flour, approximately
¼ cup soft shortening or butter

1. Place the potatoes, cornmeal, sugar and salt in a three-quart bowl. Add the boiling water and stir until the sugar and salt are dissolved. Cover with transparent wrap or foil. Set the bowl in a pan of warm water over the pilot light of a stove, or where it will stay at about 120° F., until small bubbles show in the surface, for twenty-four hours or longer.

2. Remove the potatoes to a sieve and press out excess moisture. Add this liquid to the potato water still in the bowl.

3. Add the milk, baking soda and four cups of the flour to the bowl. Stir until smooth. Set the bowl again in the pan of warm water and let it stand for about two hours, until the sponge is almost doubled in bulk.

4. Chop the shortening or butter into one cup of the remaining flour. Add this to the sponge. Add enough additional flour, about three cups, to make a moderately stiff dough. Knead on a floured surface quickly and lightly. Do not let dough get cold.

5. Return the dough to the bowl, grease the surface of the dough, and let it rise for about two hours, until doubled in bulk.

6. Turn the risen dough out on a lightly floured surface and shape into two loaves. Place in greased loaf pans (9 × 5 × 3 inches) and grease the tops of the loaves. Let rise again for about two hours, until almost doubled in bulk, or slightly above the tops of the pans. Sprinkle the tops with cornmeal if desired.

7. About fifteen minutes before the loaves have finished rising, preheat oven to hot (400° F.).

8. Bake the loaves for fifteen minutes, then lower the oven temperature to moderate (350° F.) and bake for about thirty-five minutes longer, or until the bread shrinks from the sides of the pans and is well browned. Cool on a rack.

RYE BREAD   *3 loaves*

1 package active dry yeast
½ cup warm water
3 cups sifted rye flour
2 tablespoons honey
⅓ cup shortening

1 tablespoon salt
2 cups boiling water
5 to 5½ cups sifted all-purpose flour
1 tablespoon caraway seeds, if desired

1. Soften the yeast in the warm water. Combine rye flour, honey, shortening and salt. Add boiling water and blend well. Cool to lukewarm.

2. Add softened yeast. Gradually stir in all-purpose flour to make a soft dough. Add caraway seeds. Turn out on a floured board and let rest for ten minutes.

3. Knead the dough for about ten minutes, until it is smooth and satiny. Place in a lightly greased bowl and turn once to grease the surface. Cover and let rise until doubled in bulk.

4. Punch dough down, cover, and let rise again until almost doubled in bulk.

5. Divide dough into three parts, form round loaves, and place them on greased baking sheets.

6. Preheat oven to moderate (350° F.).

7. Let loaves rise until almost doubled. Brush them with slightly beaten egg. Bake for thirty-five to forty minutes.

Note: The same recipe made with whole-wheat flour instead of all-purpose flour will make a darker bread.

SWISS CHEESE LOAF   *3 loaves*

1½ cups milk, scalded	2 packages active dry yeast
3 tablespoons sugar	8 cups sifted all-purpose flour, approximately
1½ tablespoons salt	
3 tablespoons butter	1½ cups Gruyère cheese, grated
1 cup cold water	3 teaspoons paprika
½ cup warm water (105° to 115° F.)	1 egg, beaten

1. Pour the milk into a large bowl. Add the sugar, salt and butter. Stir until butter melts. Stir in the cold water.

2. Place the warm water in a small warm bowl. Sprinkle with yeast and stir to dissolve. Add yeast to milk mixture. Add five cups of the flour and beat until smooth. Add enough remaining flour to make a stiff dough.

3. Turn dough out on a lightly floured board and knead for eight to ten minutes. Place in a greased large bowl and grease the top of the dough. Cover and let rise in a warm place, free from draft, for about one hour, until doubled in bulk.

4. Roll one-third of the dough into a rectangle ten by twelve inches. Sprinkle with one third of the cheese and paprika. Roll up on the long side and seal seam and edges. Place in a loaf pan (9 × 5 × 3 inches) and brush with beaten egg. Cover and let rise again for about one hour, until doubled in bulk. Repeat with remaining dough, cheese and paprika.

5. Preheat oven to moderate (375° F.).

6. Bake the loaves for thirty to forty minutes, or until golden brown.

CHEESE-HERB BREAD   *2 loaves*

1½ cups milk, scalded
2 tablespoons sugar
1 tablespoon salt
¼ cup butter
1 teaspoon dried orégano
6 cups sifted all-purpose flour, approximately

8 ounces sharp Cheddar cheese, grated
1 cup lukewarm water
3 packages active dry yeast
1 egg white, lightly beaten
1 teaspoon water

1. Combine the milk, sugar, salt, butter and orégano in a large bowl. Cool to lukewarm. Blend in two cups of the flour. Beat until smooth. Stir in the cheese.

2. Place the lukewarm water in a large warm bowl. Sprinkle with yeast. Stir to dissolve. Blend in the milk mixture. Add enough of the remaining flour to make a soft dough. Knead the dough on a lightly floured board for about ten minutes, until smooth and elastic.

3. Place in greased bowl. Grease top of dough. Cover and let rise in a warm place, free from draft, for about forty-five minutes, until doubled in bulk.

4. Punch dough down. Turn out on a lightly floured board and knead gently for one or two minutes. Halve dough. Shape halves into balls or oblongs. Place balls in greased two-quart casseroles, or oblongs in loaf pans (9 × 5 × 3 inches). Cover and let rise again for about thirty minutes, until doubled in bulk.

5. Preheat oven to hot (400° F.).

6. Brush loaves with egg white mixed with water. Bake for thirty to forty minutes, or until dark golden brown. Loaves should sound hollow when tapped on the bottom.

BLACK-PEPPER CRACKLING BREAD   *2 loaves*

2 packages active dry yeast
½ cup warm water (110° to 115° F.)
4 teaspoons sugar
1 cup milk, scalded
⅓ cup shortening
1 tablespoon salt
1 egg

6 cups sifted all-purpose flour, approximately
Melted butter
2 teaspoons freshly ground black pepper
3 cups pork cracklings (see note)

1. Combine the yeast, warm water and one teaspoon of the sugar. Let stand for five minutes to soften yeast.

2. Combine hot milk and shortening. Cool to lukewarm. Add to yeast mixture. Stir in the salt, egg, two cups of the flour and the remaining sugar. Beat batter until it falls in a sheet from the spoon.

3. Gradually add enough of the remaining flour to make a soft dough, kneading flour in. Continue to knead on a lightly floured board for five to ten minutes, until the dough is smooth and elastic.

4. Place dough in a greased bowl; turn to grease on all sides. Cover with a towel and let rise in a warm place (80° to 85° F.) for about one hour, until doubled in bulk.

5. Punch dough down. Form into two balls of equal size. Cover balls and let rest for ten minutes.

6. Roll each ball of dough into a flat rectangle (½ × 9 × 14 inches). Brush surface of each with melted butter. Sprinkle each with one teaspoon black pepper and one and one-half cups cracklings. Roll up in jelly-roll fashion.

7. Place each loaf in a greased loaf pan (9 × 5 × 3 inches). Brush the surfaces with melted butter. Cover and let rise in a warm place (80° to 85° F.) for about one hour, until doubled in bulk.

8. Preheat oven to moderate (375° F.).

9. Bake the loaves for forty minutes, or until browned.

Note: If cracklings are not available, cut three pounds salt pork into thin slices. Place in a large baking pan and bake for five minutes in a preheated hot oven (450° F.). Reduce heat to moderate (350° F.) and bake for twenty-five minutes longer, or until pork is crisp and brown. Reserve fat for other cooking purposes.

CHEESE BRIOCHE   *1 brioche ring or 12 small brioches*

¼ cup warm water (105° to 115° F.)   ½ teaspoon salt
1 package active dry yeast   3 eggs
2 cups sifted all-purpose flour   ½ cup butter, melted
4 teaspoons sugar   ¼ pound Swiss cheese, shredded

1. Place the warm water in a large warm bowl. Sprinkle with yeast. Stir to dissolve. Add one-half cup of the flour and mix well. Cover and let rise in a warm place, free from draft, for about twenty minutes, until doubled in bulk.

2. Combine remaining flour, the sugar and salt. Stir in eggs and beat until smooth. Stir in butter and the yeast mixture. Beat until smooth. Stir in the cheese. Cover and let rise again for about one hour, until doubled in bulk.

3. Punch dough down; cover with wax paper and a damp towel. Chill overnight.

BRIOCHE RING:

4. Shape chilled dough into a roll. Fit into a greased nine-inch ring mold. Cover and let rise again for about one hour, until doubled in bulk.

5. Preheat oven to moderate (375° F.).

6. Bake for about forty-five minutes, or until golden brown. Remove from pan; cool slightly on rack. Serve warm.

INDIVIDUAL BRIOCHES:

4. Shape twelve tiny balls out of one-sixth of chilled dough. Shape remainder into twelve large balls. Place large balls in greased brioche pans or muffin tins. With a dampened finger, make a depression in each large ball and insert a tiny ball. Cover and let rise in a warm place, free from draft, for about one hour, until doubled in bulk.

5. Preheat oven to hot (450° F.). Proceed as in step 6 above. Bake about fifteen minutes.

RAISIN-OAT CINNAMON BREAD   *2 loaves*

1¼ cups milk, scalded
1 cup uncooked rolled oats, either quick cooking or regular
¼ cup shortening
¾ cup sugar
1¼ teaspoons salt
1 package active dry yeast
1 egg, lightly beaten
2¾ cups sifted all-purpose flour, approximately
½ cup seedless raisins
1 teaspoon ground cinnamon
¼ cup melted butter

1. Pour one cup of the milk over the oats. Stir in the shortening, one-quarter cup of the sugar and the salt, and cool to lukewarm.

2. Cool the remaining milk to lukewarm, add the yeast, and stir until dissolved. Add to the oats mixture.

3. Stir in the egg, flour and raisins and mix to a soft dough. Turn dough out on a lightly floured board and knead until smooth and elastic. Shape into a ball and place in a clean greased bowl, turning once to grease the top.

4. Cover and let rise in a warm place for about one hour, until doubled in bulk. Punch down, cover, and let rest for ten minutes. Divide dough into halves and shape into loaves. Place each in a greased pan (9 × 5 × 3 inches). Cover and let rise again in a warm place for about one hour, until doubled in bulk.

5. Preheat oven to moderate (350° F.).

6. Bake for forty-five to sixty minutes, or until the loaves sound hollow when tapped on the bottom.

7. Combine the remaining sugar with the cinnamon. While the loaves are still hot, brush with the melted butter and sprinkle tops, sides and ends with the sugar mixture.

GOTT VETEBROD (Swedish coffeecake)   *2 coffee rings*

2 packages active dry yeast
½ cup warm water (110° to 115° F.)
1 teaspoon plus ⅓ cup plus ¼ cup sugar
½ cup scalded milk
1 cup butter
1 teaspoon salt
1½ teaspoons ground cardamom
2 large eggs
5 cups sifted all-purpose flour
1½ cups minced glacé fruits
1½ cups seedless raisins
3 tablespoons melted butter

1. Combine the yeast, warm water and one teaspoon of the sugar. Let stand for five minutes to soften.

2. Combine the hot milk, three-quarters cup of the butter, one-third cup of the sugar, the salt and cardamom. Stir to melt the butter. Cool to lukewarm.

3. Add the yeast and one egg to the mixture; mix well. Stir in two cups of the flour. Beat until the batter falls in sheets from a spoon. Add remaining flour to make a soft dough. Knead on a lightly floured board until smooth and satiny.

4. Place in greased bowl, turning dough to bring greased surface to top. Cover and let stand in a warm place (80° to 85° F.) for forty to fifty minutes, until doubled in bulk.

5. Punch down dough, cover, and let rest for ten minutes. Divide dough into halves. Roll each half into a flat rectangle ($\frac{1}{4}$ × 10 × 13 inches). Spread the surface with the remaining butter, softened. Sprinkle with glacé fruits, raisins and remaining sugar.

6. Roll the dough lengthwise in jelly-roll fashion. Twist each roll and place each in a buttered four-and-one-half-cup ring mold.

7. Cut gashes two inches apart through the top of dough almost to the bottom with floured scissors. Brush cut side with melted butter. Cover and let rise for about forty-five minutes, until doubled in bulk.

8. Preheat oven to moderate (375° F.).

9. Beat remaining egg and brush over top of dough. Bake for forty minutes, or until done.

SWEDISH COFFEE LOAVES   *2 loaves*

2 packages active dry yeast or compressed yeast
¼ cup water
⅔ cup butter
⅓ cup sugar
2 teaspoons crushed cardamom seeds or 1 teaspoon ground cardamom

½ teaspoon salt
¾ cup scalded milk
1 egg
3½ to 4 cups sifted all-purpose flour
¾ cup raisins
Beaten egg for glaze

1. Soften active dry yeast in warm water or compressed yeast in lukewarm water.

2. Mix together the butter, sugar, cardamom, salt and hot milk. Cool until lukewarm. Add the egg, softened yeast and two and one-half cups of the flour. Beat thoroughly.

3. Add enough of the remaining flour, a little at a time, to make a soft dough. Set a little aside for kneading. Turn the dough out on a lightly floured surface and knead for about ten minutes, until smooth and elastic.

4. Place dough in a lightly buttered bowl, turning once to grease the

surface. Cover and let rise in a warm place for about one and one-half hours, until doubled in bulk. When light, punch down, turn out on lightly floured surface, and knead lightly.

5. Mix the raisins with the dough and divide the mixture into two. Cut each half into three pieces of equal size. Roll the pieces into long ropes and braid three ropes together for each loaf. Place the loaves on a buttered cookie sheet. Cover with a towel and let rise again in a warm place for about forty-five minutes, until doubled in bulk.

6. Preheat oven to moderate (375° F.).

7. Brush the loaves with beaten egg; sprinkle with sugar and chopped nuts if desired. Bake for twenty to twenty-five minutes.

BABKA   *2 medium-size loaves*

2½ cups milk	16 egg yolks
6 cups sifted all-purpose flour, approximately	¾ cup butter, softened
	1 cup white sultana raisins
4 packages active dry yeast	¼ cup rum
½ cup sugar	Confectioners' sugar
1 teaspoon salt	

1. Bring two cups of the milk to a rolling boil. Add it to one and one-quarter cups of the flour, beating it in hard until the mixture is as fluffy as mashed potatoes. Cool to lukewarm.

2. Add the yeast to the remaining half cup of lukewarm milk. Stir in the sugar and salt and add to the cooled paste. Let the mixture rise for twenty minutes, or until it forms a light sponge. Stir it down.

3. Beat in the egg yolks and enough flour to make a soft sticky dough. Add the butter.

4. Knead the dough in the bowl until it is very smooth, shiny and elastic. The hand should be clean when it is pulled abruptly from the dough. Kneading by hand will take about forty minutes, possibly longer. It is possible to beat this dough in the type of home mixer equipped with a kneading hook (not those with rotary beaters). When the dough has been beaten enough, clean the sides of the bowl, cover with a towel, and let the dough rise in a draft-free place until doubled in bulk.

5. Preheat oven to moderate (375° F.). Grease two small kugelhopf molds or tube pans.

6. Stir the risen dough down. Work in the raisins. Fill the pans halfway, cover with a cloth, and let the dough rise again until almost doubled in bulk. Bake in the preheated oven for thirty to forty-five minutes, until the loaves are a deep golden brown.

7. Remove the loaves from the pans. Sprinkle them with rum and cool. Dust with confectioners' sugar when they are cool.

HOLIDAY FRUIT BREAD   *2 loaves*

2 packages active dry yeast
¼ cup lukewarm water
1 cup milk, scalded
½ cup sugar
2 teaspoons salt
⅓ cup butter
3 eggs

5 cups sifted all-purpose flour, approximately
1 cup raisins
¾ cup chopped candied cherries
¼ cup chopped candied citron
1 tablespoon water

1. Soften the yeast in the lukewarm water.

2. Place the milk, sugar, salt and butter in a mixing bowl and stir to dissolve the sugar and melt the butter. Cool to lukewarm. Stir in the yeast and two of the eggs, lightly beaten.

3. Add enough flour to make a soft dough. Turn the dough out on a lightly floured board and knead for about ten minutes, until smooth and satiny. Place in a clean greased bowl, turning to grease the top of the dough. Cover with a towel and set in a warm place for about one hour, until doubled in bulk.

4. Punch dough down and let rest for ten minutes. Knead in the raisins, cherries and citron until well mixed. Divide the dough into halves and shape into two loaves. Place in two greased loaf pans (4½ × 8½ × 2½ inches). Cover and let rise until doubled in bulk.

5. Preheat oven to moderate (375° F.).

6. Beat the remaining egg with the tablespoon water and brush over the tops of the loaves. Bake for about forty minutes, or until the loaves are golden brown and sound hollow when tapped on the bottom. Cool on wire racks.

Note: The halves of dough may be shaped into braids or into ring shapes to lend variety.

CRANBERRY ANADAMA BREAD   *2 loaves*

1½ cups fresh cranberries
1 tablespoon grated orange rind
¼ cup sugar
2 packages active dry yeast
½ cup warm water (110° to 115° F.)
⅔ cup yellow cornmeal

2½ cups boiling water
3 teaspoons salt
3 tablespoons shortening
½ cup molasses
7½ cups sifted all-purpose flour
1 tablespoon milk

1. Wash the cranberries and put them through a food chopper, using the coarse blade. Add the orange rind and sugar. Let stand.

2. Soften the yeast in the warm water. Set aside.

3. Add the cornmeal to the boiling water. Cook for three minutes, or until thickened. Remove from heat and add the salt, shortening and molasses. Mix well. Cool to lukewarm.

4. Stir in softened yeast and cranberries. Add five cups of flour and mix well. Knead in remaining flour on a pastry board.

5. Continue kneading until dough is smooth and satiny. Place the dough in a greased bowl, turning to grease dough on all sides. Cover and let rise in a warm place for one hour, or until doubled in bulk.

6. Punch down dough, cover, and let rest for ten minutes. Shape dough into two loaves. Place in two greased loaf pans (9 × 5 × 3 inches). Cover and let rise again in a warm place for about forty-five minutes, until dough has doubled in bulk.

7. Preheat oven to moderate (375° F.).

8. Brush the tops of the loaves with the milk. Bake for forty-five minutes, or until done.

ST. LUCIA'S CARDAMOM BUNS   *18 buns*

2 packages active dry yeast	¾ cup scalded milk
½ cup warm water (110° to 115° F.)	1 large egg
⅓ cup sugar	4⅓ cups sifted all-purpose flour
2 teaspoons salt	Raisins
1 teaspoon ground cardamom	1 egg white, beaten only until
½ cup butter	foamy

1. Soften the yeast in the warm water.

2. Place the sugar, salt, cardamom and butter in a large bowl. Add hot milk, mix well, and cool to lukewarm. Stir in the yeast, egg and two cups of the flour. Beat until batter falls in sheets from a spoon.

3. Add remaining flour and knead dough on a lightly floured board for about five minutes, until creamy and satiny.

4. Place in greased bowl, turning dough to bring greased surface to top. Cover and let rise in a warm place (80° to 85° F.) for forty-five to fifty minutes, until dough is doubled in bulk.

5. Punch down dough and shape into a ball. Cover and let rest for ten minutes.

6. Pinch off pieces of dough and roll into twelve-inch lengths one-half inch thick. Curl each end and put two rolls together back to back. Stick a raisin in the center of each curl. If desired, form the rolls of dough in the shape of an S, coiling or curling the ends. Stick a raisin in each coil.

7. Place the buns on a greased baking sheet. Brush with the egg white. Cover and let rise in a warm place (80° to 85° F.) for about forty minutes, until doubled in bulk.

8. Preheat oven to hot (400° F.).

9. Bake the buns for ten to twelve minutes.

QUICK BREADS

BASIC BAKING MIX

12 cups sifted all-purpose flour
 2 tablespoons salt

¼ cup double-acting baking powder
 1 pound vegetable shortening

1. Mix the dry ingredients together.
2. Blend in the shortening, using a pastry blender or the fingertips, until the mixture resembles coarse cornmeal. Store in a cool dry place.

PANCAKES:

Combine two cups mix with two eggs and one to one and one-half cups milk, for a thin batter.

BREAD TWISTS:

Combine two cups mix with one-half to two-thirds cup milk or water for a soft, but not sticky, dough. Shape into rolls one foot long, one inch wide and one-half inch thick. Wrap around two-inch-thick, two-foot-long sticks, pointed at both ends, with the bark removed.

Push sticks into the ground around a hot fire, turning them as bread browns. If the bottom bakes faster than the top, turn sticks upside down.

DUMPLINGS:

Combine two cups mix with two-thirds cup milk or water and drop atop a pot of simmering stew. If desired, dried or fresh herbs may be added. Cook rapidly, uncovered, for ten minutes. Cover and cook for ten to twelve minutes longer.

CORN BREAD   *8 to 10 servings*

1½ cups cornmeal
  2 cups all-purpose flour
  2 tablespoons sugar
  1 teaspoon salt

4 teaspoons baking powder
2 eggs
2 cups milk
¼ cup bacon drippings

1. Preheat oven to hot (450° F.).
2. Grease two nine-inch-square pans.
3. Sift the cornmeal, flour, sugar, salt and baking powder together into a mixing bowl. Stir in the lightly beaten eggs, the milk and bacon drippings until well mixed.
4. Spread in baking pans and bake for thirty minutes. Cool.

SAGE CORN BREAD   *4 or 5 servings*

1 cup yellow cornmeal
1 cup all-purpose flour
¼ cup sugar (see note)
4 teaspoons baking powder
½ teaspoon salt

1 teaspoon ground sage
1 large egg
1 cup milk
¼ cup shortening, melted

1. Preheat oven to hot (425° F.).
2. Combine cornmeal, flour, sugar, baking powder, salt and sage. Add egg and milk. Stir in shortening.
3. Grease well an iron skillet (8 inches) or a shallow baking pan (9 × 9 × 2 inches). Place in the oven to heat. Pour in the batter. Bake for thirty to thirty-five minutes, or until done.

Note: For a less sweet corn bread, reduce the amount of sugar to one tablespoon.

SOUTHERN CORN BREAD   *6 to 8 servings*

2 cups white cornmeal
1 teaspoon salt
½ teaspoon baking soda
2 cups buttermilk

2 eggs
6 tablespoons melted butter, lard or rendered bacon fat

1. Preheat oven to hot (425° F.).
2. Sift the cornmeal, salt and baking soda onto a piece of wax paper. Combine the buttermilk and unbeaten eggs in a mixing bowl and beat in the sifted ingredients. Add half of the melted fat and mix thoroughly.
3. Heat a nine-inch ovenproof iron skillet and pour the remaining fat into it. Pour in the cornmeal mixture.
4. Bake the bread for thirty to forty minutes, or until the mixture just sets and no longer shakes in the middle when the skillet is budged. The corn bread should be well browned on top. Cut the corn bread into wedges like a pie and serve hot or cold with butter.

ORANGE OATMEAL BREAD   *1 loaf*

¾ cup plus 2 tablespoons sugar
1 orange, peeled and thinly sliced, with each slice cut into eighths
1½ cups sifted all-purpose flour
1 teaspoon salt
4½ teaspoons baking powder

¼ teaspoon baking soda
1 cup old-fashioned rolled oats
2 tablespoons melted butter
2 eggs, lightly beaten
⅔ cup water
2 tablespoons grated orange rind

1. Preheat oven to moderate (350° F.).
2. Sprinkle two tablespoons of the sugar over the orange pieces. Set aside.

3. Combine the flour, salt, baking powder, baking soda and remaining sugar in a bowl. Add the oats.

4. Combine the melted butter, eggs, water, orange rind and sweetened oranges and add to the dry ingredients, stirring just until blended. Pour into a greased loaf pan (9 × 5 × 3 inches) and bake for fifty-five to sixty minutes. Cool on a rack.

FENNEL OATMEAL BREAD   *2 loaves*

Fine dry bread crumbs
1½ cups milk
2 tablespoons vinegar
2 eggs, lightly beaten
⅔ cup firmly packed dark brown sugar
2⅔ cups sifted all-purpose flour

1 teaspoon baking powder
1 teaspoon baking soda
1 cup quick-cooking oatmeal
¼ cup wheat germ
1 teaspoon fennel seeds
¼ cup butter, melted and browned

1. Preheat oven to moderate (350° F.). Grease two pans (10 × 5 × 3 inches) and dust with bread crumbs.

2. Place the milk and vinegar in a bowl and let stand for five minutes. Stir in the eggs and sugar.

3. Sift together the flour, baking powder and baking soda. Add to the milk mixture and stir until the flour is dampened.

4. Combine the oatmeal, wheat germ and fennel seeds after crushing them in a mortar. Add to the batter and fold in the browned butter.

5. Pour the batter into the prepared pans and bake for forty minutes, or until done. Turn out on a rack to cool.

BOSTON BROWN BREAD   *2 large or 3 small loaves*

1 cup yellow cornmeal
1 cup rye flour
1 cup whole-wheat flour
2 teaspoons baking soda

1 teaspoon salt
2 cups buttermilk
¾ cup molasses
1 cup seedless raisins

1. Combine the cornmeal, flours, baking soda and salt in a mixing bowl.

2. Mix together buttermilk, molasses and raisins. Add to the dry ingredients; mix well.

3. Fill well-greased pudding molds or cans two-thirds full. (Dough will fill three No. 2 cans or two No. 2½ cans.) Cover with greased mold covers or can lids and then with aluminum foil.

4. Set on a rack in a large kettle with water halfway up the sides. Cover and cook for three hours, replenishing water as necessary.

STEAMED DATE AND HONEY BREAD   *2 large or 3 small loaves*

1 cup yellow cornmeal
1 cup rye flour
1 cup all-purpose flour
½ teaspoon salt
½ teaspoon ground cinnamon
1 teaspoon baking soda

½ cup light molasses
½ cup honey
1½ cups buttermilk, or 1½ cups milk mixed with 1½ tablespoons vinegar or lemon juice
1 cup pitted dates, quartered

1. Combine the cornmeal, rye flour, all-purpose flour, salt, cinnamon and baking soda in a mixing bowl. Stir in the molasses, honey and buttermilk. Fold in the dates.

2. Generously grease two coffee cans or three No. 303 cans fitted with covers (shelled nuts come in these cans). Spoon the batter into the cans, cover tightly with aluminum foil or the can covers.

3. Set the cans on a rack in a large pot or roaster equipped with a tight-fitting cover. Pour enough water into the large pot to come halfway up the height of the cans. Bring to a boil, reduce heat to low, cover the pot, and steam the bread for two and one-half hours in the coffee cans, or for two hours in the smaller cans. Remove from cans immediately and cool on racks.

BANANA WALNUT BREAD   *1 loaf*

¾ cup sugar
¼ cup shortening
2 eggs
1 cup mashed ripe bananas
2 cups sifted all-purpose flour

2 teaspoons baking powder
½ teaspoon salt
¼ teaspoon baking soda
1 cup chopped walnuts

1. Preheat oven to moderate (350° F.).

2. Mix the sugar, shortening and eggs; beat hard until light. Add the mashed bananas.

3. Sift together the flour, baking powder, salt and baking soda. Stir into the banana mixture, beating until smooth. Add the walnuts.

4. Pour the batter into a greased loaf pan (9 × 5 × 3 inches) and bake for sixty to seventy minutes. Cool on a rack.

CRANBERRY-NUT BREAD   *1 loaf*

2 cups sifted all-purpose flour
2 teaspoons baking powder
½ teaspoon salt
½ teaspoon baking soda
¼ cup butter
1 cup sugar

1 egg
1 tablespoon grated orange rind
½ cup chopped nuts
¼ cup chopped citron
½ cup fresh orange juice
1½ cups fresh cranberries

1. Preheat oven to moderate (350° F.).
2. Sift together the flour, baking powder and salt.
3. Add the baking soda to the butter and mix well. Gradually blend in the sugar. Beat in the egg. Stir in the orange rind, nuts and citron. Add the flour mixture alternately with the orange juice.
4. Put the cranberries through a food chopper, using the coarse blade. Stir into the dough.
5. Turn into a well-greased, lightly floured loaf pan (9 × 5 × 3 inches) and bake for one hour and twenty minutes. Cool.

SPICE BREAD   *1 loaf*

1½ teaspoons aniseeds
¾ cup water
½ cup honey
½ cup sugar
½ cup finely chopped citron
2¼ cups sifted all-purpose flour

1½ teaspoons baking soda
½ teaspoon salt
1 teaspoon ground cinnamon
Dash of ground cloves
1 teaspoon freshly grated nutmeg

1. Preheat oven to moderate (350° F.).
2. Combine the aniseeds and water in a saucepan. Bring mixture to a boil. Add the honey, sugar and citron, and stir until sugar is dissolved. Remove from the heat.
3. Sift together the remaining ingredients and fold in the liquid mixture. Turn the batter into a loaf pan (9 × 5 × 3 inches) and bake for one hour. Serve buttered or with cream cheese.
Note: This bread improves if allowed to stand for one day.

WHOLE-WHEAT BACON BISCUITS   *About 14 biscuits*

1 cup whole-wheat flour
1 cup all-purpose flour
1 tablespoon baking powder
¾ teaspoon salt

⅓ cup shortening
½ cup crumbled crisp cooked bacon
¾ cup milk, approximately

1. Preheat oven to hot (450° F.).
2. Mix together the whole-wheat flour, all-purpose flour, baking powder and salt in a bowl. Cut in the shortening.
3. Add the bacon and mix to a soft dough with the milk. Turn out on a lightly floured board and knead for one-half minute so that dough is no longer sticky.
4. Roll out to half-inch thickness, cut into two-inch rounds, and place on an ungreased cookie sheet. Bake for about fifteen minutes.

FRESH-CORN MUFFINS   *15 muffins*

2 eggs, well beaten
1 cup milk
¼ cup shortening, melted
1 cup fresh corn cut from the cobs
  (2 or 3 ears)

1½ cups sifted all-purpose flour
1 teaspoon salt
3 teaspoons baking powder
2 tablespoons sugar
¾ cup yellow cornmeal

1. Preheat oven to hot (400° F.). Grease cupcake pans well with shortening.
2. Combine the eggs, milk, shortening and corn in a mixing bowl.
3. In another bowl sift together the flour, salt, baking powder and sugar. Blend with the cornmeal and stir into the corn mixture.
4. Fill the cupcake pans two-thirds to three-quarters full with the mixture. Bake for twenty-five minutes, or until done. Serve hot.

CHEESE MUFFINS   *About 24 large muffins*

1½ cups sifted all-purpose flour
3 teaspoons baking powder
1 tablespoon sugar
½ teaspoon salt
¼ teaspoon dried orégano

½ cup freshly grated sharp Cheddar
  cheese
1 egg
1 cup milk
3 tablespoons melted butter

1. Preheat oven to moderate (350° F.).
2. Sift together the flour, baking powder, sugar and salt. Add the orégano and cheese and mix well.
3. Combine the egg, milk and butter and stir into the dry ingredients, using only ten to twelve strokes to incorporate. Do not overmix. The dough will be lumpy. Fill greased muffin tins two-thirds full. Bake for twenty to thirty minutes.

CORNMEAL WAFERS   *About 50 wafers*

1 cup white cornmeal
1½ teaspoons sugar
1 teaspoon salt
2½ tablespoons bacon drippings or
  butter

1 to 2 teaspoons grated onion
1½ cups boiling water
1 egg, beaten

1. Preheat oven to hot (400° F.). Grease baking sheets.
2. Mix the cornmeal, sugar, salt, drippings and onion. Add the boiling water and stir until smooth. Add the egg and beat well.
3. Drop the batter by scant teaspoons onto baking sheets, keeping the mounds of batter about one inch apart. Flatten with a spoon. Bake for about fifteen minutes, until crisp and brown around the edges.

ALMOND WAFERS:

Add one-quarter cup chopped almonds to the batter for cornmeal wafers (page 534). After the cakes have been flattened, garnish with slivered almonds.

INDIVIDUAL YORKSHIRE PUDDINGS   *6 servings*

1 cup sifted all-purpose flour	1 cup milk
1 teaspoon salt	6 teaspoons beef drippings
2 eggs	

1. Preheat oven to hot (425° F.).
2. Sift the flour and salt together and make a well in the center. Drop the eggs and one-third cup of the milk into the well and mix to a smooth dough. Add the remaining milk, stirring very well to give a smooth batter.
3. Place one teaspoon of hot beef drippings into each of six deep muffin pans or custard cups. Fill the pans or custard cups half to two-thirds full of batter.
4. Bake for about thirty minutes, until risen and browned.

Note: If desired, make one large Yorkshire pudding by baking all the batter in one pan (8 × 8 × 2 inches). Cooking time will be about forty minutes.

. . . .

PANCAKES AND DUMPLINGS
. . . .

There is an antique German maxim which states, in effect, "In the morning it is best to dine like a king, at midday like a prince and in the evening like a pauper." The thought is sound, and the best of it may be the reference to the matutinal meal, for a well-rounded breakfast makes the noblest foundation for a day.

Breakfast is a pleasure too frequently ignored through haste or other mundane considerations. There is nothing that can gladden an appetite more than pancakes, particularly in winter. Slathered with butter and served hot from a griddle, with a steaming pot of freshly brewed coffee or neatly steeped tea, they are an available luxury. They are, of course, even better of a weekend, when the first meal of the day may embrace the noon hour.

WHOLE-WHEAT PANCAKES   *About 20 pancakes*

¾ cup cake flour	3 tablespoons molasses
1 cup whole-wheat flour	2 eggs, lightly beaten
1 teaspoon salt	¼ cup melted butter or salad oil
2 tablespoons sugar	1 cup milk
1¾ teaspoons baking powder	

1. Combine the flours, salt, sugar and baking powder in a bowl. Mix together the molasses, eggs, butter or oil and the milk. Pour the liquid into the flour mixture and stir to make a fairly smooth batter.

2. Heat a griddle to 350° F., or so that a drop of water sputters when it is dropped onto the griddle. Lightly grease the griddle.

3. Spoon the batter onto the griddle to make cakes about two and one-half inches in diameter. When the surface bubbles and the underside is browned, turn the cakes and brown the other side.

CORNMEAL PANCAKES   *About 20 pancakes*

1⅓ cups cornmeal
¼ cup all-purpose flour
1 teaspoon salt
½ teaspoon baking soda

2 cups buttermilk
2 eggs
¼ cup melted butter

1. Place the cornmeal, flour, salt and baking soda in a bowl. Mix the buttermilk and eggs together and stir into the dry ingredients. Stir in the melted butter.

2. Heat the griddle to about 350° F., or until a drop of water sputters on the surface. Lightly grease the griddle with shortening.

3. Pour or spoon the batter onto the griddle to make two-inch pancakes. When the surface bubbles and the cakes are set and lightly browned on the underside, turn and brown the second side. These are very light pancakes and can only be turned easily if made small.

RAISED BUCKWHEAT PANCAKES   *About 20 pancakes*

2 teaspoons active dry yeast
2 cups milk, scalded and cooled to lukewarm
2 cups buckwheat flour
½ teaspoon salt

2 tablespoons molasses
½ teaspoon baking soda, dissolved in ¼ cup lukewarm water
1 egg
¼ cup salad oil or melted butter

1. Place the yeast in a bowl and gradually add the milk, stirring to dissolve. Stir in the flour and salt until the mixture is smooth. Cover with a towel and let stand at room temperature overnight or for about twelve hours.

2. Stir in the molasses, baking soda, egg, and oil or butter.

3. Heat a griddle to about 350° F., or until a drop of water sputters on the surface. Grease lightly with shortening.

4. Pour or spoon the mixture onto the griddle to make cakes about two and one-half inches in diameter. Cook until surface bubbles and the cakes are set and lightly browned on underside. Turn, and brown the second side.

FRESH-CORN PANCAKES   *16 pancakes*

4 to 6 ears of fresh corn
1 cup milk
2 tablespoons butter, melted
2 eggs, separated

⅔ cup sifted all-purpose flour
1 teaspoon sugar
1 teaspoon baking powder
1½ teaspoons salt

1. Boil the ears of corn for one minute before cutting the kernels off the cobs. Measure out two cups of kernels and combine them with the milk, butter and egg yolks in a saucepan.
2. Sift together the flour, sugar, baking powder and salt. Add to the liquid ingredients and mix well.
3. Beat the egg whites until they stand in soft peaks. Fold into the mixture.
4. Fry the mixture on a hot well-greased griddle, using one-quarter cup batter for each pancake. Turn to brown on both sides. Serve with maple syrup or butter.

MINUTE SCALLION PANCAKES   *2 large pancakes*

½ cup Chicken Stock (page 475)
½ teaspoon salt
¼ teaspoon monosodium glutamate
1 egg
⅔ cup sifted all-purpose flour

⅓ cup minced scallions
1 slice of bacon, cooked and minced, or 1 tablespoon dried shrimp, minced
4 teaspoons vegetable oil

1. Combine the stock with one-quarter teaspoon salt and the monosodium glutamate. Combine the stock mixture with the remaining ingredients except the oil. Mix in a bowl into a thin paste.
2. Place two teaspoons of the oil in a hot skillet over medium heat. Cover the bottom evenly by tipping around or using a spatula. Pour half of the mixture from the bowl into the skillet, spread out flat, and cover the bottom. Cook until edge is lightly browned, then turn to brown the other side.
3. Use the remaining oil and cook the remaining mixture in the same way. Serve hot as a snack or breakfast dish.

RICE AND SESAME PANCAKES   *24 three-inch pancakes*

¾ cup all-purpose flour
1½ teaspoons baking powder
½ teaspoon sugar
¼ teaspoon salt
1 egg, separated

1 cup milk
2 tablespoons melted butter
½ teaspoon vanilla extract
½ cup cooked rice
1 tablespoon toasted sesame seeds

1. Sift the flour, baking powder, sugar and salt together.
2. Combine the egg yolk, milk, butter and vanilla. Stir in the dry ingredients and beat until smooth. Fold in the rice and sesame seeds.

3. Beat the egg white until stiff but not dry and gently fold into the mixture.

4. Preheat a griddle or heavy skillet. Grease lightly with shortening or oil. Spoon the batter in tablespoons onto the hot griddle and cook until lightly browned on the underside. Turn and lightly brown the other side. Serve with preserves and sour cream.

WILD-RICE PANCAKES   *About 16 pancakes*

¼ cup uncooked wild rice	2 tablespoons all-purpose flour
2 eggs	Pinch of salt
1 cup milk	Butter for frying

1. Put the wild rice into the container of an electric blender. Cover and blend on high speed for one minute. Add the eggs, milk, flour and salt. Cover and blend on high speed for thirty seconds.

2. Fry the batter in plenty of butter on a hot griddle until browned on both sides, making small thin pancakes about three inches in diameter. While one batch cooks, stir remaining batter occasionally.

3. Drain the pancakes on absorbent paper, fold them into quarters, sprinkle them with salt, and serve as hors d'oeuvre.

MUSHROOM CRÊPES   *4 to 6 servings*

CRÊPES:

½ cup all-purpose flour	¾ cup milk
2 eggs, lightly beaten	¼ teaspoon salt

FILLING:

1 small onion, finely chopped	½ teaspoon salt
¼ cup butter	¼ teaspoon freshly ground black pepper
1 pound mushrooms, diced	

COATING:

2 eggs, lightly beaten	¼ cup butter
½ cup fine dry bread crumbs	2 tablespoons chopped parsley

1. Combine the flour, eggs, milk and salt and beat to a smooth batter. Set aside at room temperature for one hour.

2. Meanwhile, sauté the onion in the butter until tender but not browned. Add the mushrooms and cook gently for about fifteen minutes, until most of the liquid has evaporated. Season with the salt and pepper.

3. Heat a five-inch crêpe pan and grease lightly with butter. Pour two

to three tablespoons of the batter into the pan, tilting the pan so that the batter covers the bottom evenly. Cook until the top side is dry and the underneath is lightly browned. Remove from the pan and set aside. Repeat until all batter is used.

4. Place one tablespoon of the mushroom stuffing in the middle of each crêpe placed browned side up. Roll up the crêpe by tucking in the edges. Dip into the coating eggs, roll in the bread crumbs, and fry gently in the butter, a few at a time, until browned on all sides. Sprinkle with the parsley.

Note: The stuffed crêpes may be made ahead of time and stored in the refrigerator; they can then be egged, bread-crumbed, and fried just before serving.

MATZOH BALLS   *16 dumplings*

4 large eggs
1 teaspoon salt
½ teaspoon freshly ground white pepper
½ teaspoon ground ginger
⅓ cup vegetable oil
½ cup water
1¼ cups matzoh meal
¼ teaspoon baking powder

1. Combine the eggs, salt, pepper and ginger in a china, glass, or enamelware mixing bowl. Beat well with a wire whisk or use a blender. Beat in the oil, water, matzoh meal and baking powder.

2. Chill the mixture for thirty minutes or longer, or chill overnight.

3. Bring a large quantity of salted water to a boil. Shape the mixture into sixteen balls and drop them into the water. Simmer for thirty minutes. Serve in soup or with pot roasts.

GALUSKA (Hungarian dumplings) *4 or 5 servings*

3 cups sifted all-purpose flour
2 eggs
Salt
2 teaspoons butter

1. Mix the flour, eggs, one teaspoon salt and three-quarters cup water. Beat until bubbles appear on the surface. Fill a saucepan half full of water and add additional salt. Bring to a boil.

2. Put a dumpling machine over the pan and place the dough in it. Move the machine back and forth to give time for the dough to drop slowly into the boiling water. After all the dough is in the water, cook for five minutes. Drain.

3. Turn the dumplings into a casserole containing the butter. Mix well and serve with goulash or chicken paprika. Pour gravy from goulash or chicken over the dumplings.

Galuska (Hungarian dumplings) are shaped by dropping the dough through a dumpling machine into boiling water. These delicate little dumplings make a good accompaniment for Veal Goulash, Brown Chicken Fricassee and other chicken dishes seasoned with paprika.

BREAD-CRUMB DUMPLINGS *About 12 large dumplings*

1 loaf of good-quality sliced white bread
¼ cup water
6 to 8 eggs, beaten

Salt
½ cup finely chopped parsley
½ cup finely chopped onion
½ teaspoon grated nutmeg

1. Trim the crusts from the bread. Use the white part to make bread crumbs. To make the crumbs, tear up and blend a few slices at a time in an electric blender. Or grate them on a hand grater or rub them through a sieve.

2. Sprinkle enough of the water over the crumbs, tossing with a two-pronged fork, barely to moisten. Add the eggs, tossing lightly with the fork. When well blended, add salt to taste and the remaining ingredients.

3. Drop by tablespoons atop bubbling stew or boiling stock. Cover the pan and steam for about thirty minutes. The dumplings should puff up and be very light.

TOMATO DUMPLINGS *12 dumplings*

1 cup sifted all-purpose flour
½ teaspoon salt
1½ teaspoons baking powder

½ teaspoon dry mustard
½ cup tomato juice

Sift the flour with the salt, baking powder and mustard. Gradually stir in the tomato juice. Drop atop bubbling stew or boiling stock; cover. Cook without lifting the lid for fifteen minutes.

HERB DUMPLINGS *About 18 dumplings*

1½ cups sifted all-purpose flour
2 teaspoons baking powder
1 teaspoon salt
½ teaspoon dried thyme

¼ teaspoon dried marjoram
2 tablespoons chopped parsley
1 egg, lightly beaten
⅔ cup milk

1. Mix together the flour, baking powder, salt, thyme, marjoram and parsley. Combine the egg and milk and stir into the flour mixture until flour is moistened.

2. Drop by tablespoons atop bubbling stew or boiling stock; cover. Steam for ten minutes. Uncover and cook for ten minutes longer.

· · · · · · · · · · · · · · · · · · ·

CHAPTER TWELVE

DESSERTS

Summer fruits

FRUIT DESSERTS

ANISE CODDLED APPLES   *6 servings*

1 cup sugar
2 cups boiling water
½ teaspoon aniseeds

¼ teaspoon salt
6 firm baking apples
Whipped cream

1. Combine the sugar, water, aniseeds and salt in a six-cup saucepan. Mix well, bring to a boil, and simmer for five minutes.

2. Peel, quarter, and core the apples. Drop them, two at a time, into the syrup; cover. Simmer for ten to twelve minutes, or until fruit is tender. Lift out apples with a slotted spoon. Cool.

3. When all the apples are cooked, cook the syrup until it is as thick as molasses. Pour it over apples. Serve with whipped cream.

APPLE COMPOTE   *6 servings*

6 medium apples
3 tablespoons lemon juice
2 cups water
½ cup sugar

½ cup dry white wine
Rind of ½ lemon
1 cinnamon stick
⅓ cup currant jelly

1. Peel apples, halve them, and core them. Rub them immediately with lemon juice to prevent discoloration. Drop them into one cup of the water.

2. Combine the remaining water with the sugar, wine and one tablespoon of the lemon juice. Add the apple halves, cover, and simmer until fruit is tender but still firm. Remove fruit, place it in a glass bowl, cover, and let stand until cool.

3. Add the lemon rind and cinnamon stick to the cooking liquid. Simmer until the sauce begins to thicken. Strain it over the apples and chill. Just before serving, dot with currant jelly.

BAKED BANANAS À L'ORANGE   *6 servings*

3 firm ripe bananas
2 teaspoons cornstarch
2 tablespoons granulated sugar
⅓ cup fresh orange juice
1 tablespoon butter

1 tablespoon brown sugar
⅓ cup shredded coconut
Whipped cream or vanilla ice cream (optional)

1. Preheat oven to moderate (375° F.).
2. Peel the bananas and cut crosswise and lengthwise into halves. Arrange in a buttered shallow baking dish.
3. Combine the cornstarch, sugar and orange juice. Pour the mixture over the bananas, coating well. Dot with butter and sprinkle with brown sugar and coconut.
4. Bake for thirty minutes, or until bananas are tender and sauce is slightly thick. Serve topped with whipped cream or ice cream.

BANANAS IN SHERRY   *3 or 4 servings*

3 or 4 firm ripe bananas
2 tablespoons fresh lemon or lime juice

¼ cup honey
¼ cup sherry
2 tablespoons butter

1. Preheat oven to hot (400° F.).
2. Peel the bananas and cut them lengthwise into halves. Brush with lemon or lime juice. Place them in a buttered baking dish (12 × 7½ × 2 inches). Blend the honey and sherry and pour over the bananas. Dot with butter.
3. Bake for twenty minutes; baste with the pan juices. Bake for fifteen minutes longer, or until thoroughly tender.

CHERRY-GRAPEFRUIT PORT-WINE GELATIN   *8 servings*

2 cups (one 1-pound can) Bing cherries
1 cup port
2 envelopes unflavored gelatin
½ cup water
½ cup sugar
1¼ cups strained fresh grapefruit juice

¼ cup lemon juice
⅛ teaspoon salt
Grapefruit sections
½ cup slivered blanched almonds or chopped walnuts

1. Drain the cherries and reserve the juice. Pour the wine over the cherries and allow to steep for at least three hours. Drain and reserve the liquid.

2. Soak the gelatin in the cold water. Add one cup of the reserved cherry juice to the gelatin along with the sugar. Heat the mixture, stirring to dissolve the gelatin.

3. Add the grapefruit juice, lemon juice, reserved port and the salt. Chill the mixture until slightly thickened.

4. Decorate the bottom of a two-quart mold with grapefruit sections and spoon in enough of the chilled gelatin mixture to set the sections in place. Chill.

5. Add the cherries and nuts to the remaining gelatin mixture and pour into the mold. Chill until firm. Unmold. Serve with sweetened whipped cream.

GRAPE AND SHERBET CUP   *6 servings*

3 cups Thompson seedless grapes
¾ cup orange juice

6 scoops lemon sherbet

Place one-half cup grapes in each of six sherbet glasses. Pour two tablespoons orange juice into each glass. Top each with a scoop of sherbet.

FROSTED GRAPES

To frost about two pounds of Thompson seedless grapes, beat one egg white until it is frothy but not stiff. Dip clusters of grapes into the egg white and place on a rack. Sprinkle with granulated sugar and let stand until dry. Use the frosted grapes to decorate desserts or meat platters.

CANTALOUPE WITH HONEYDEW BALLS   *4 servings*

2 small cantaloupes
1 large honeydew
4 teaspoons sugar

4 teaspoons white crème de menthe
Fresh mint sprigs

1. Cut the cantaloupes into halves and remove the seeds and stringy portion. Chill.

2. Cut the honeydew into balls. There should be about two cups. Marinate the honeydew balls in a mixture of the sugar and crème de menthe.

3. Fill the cantaloupe halves with the marinated honeydew balls and garnish with sprigs of fresh mint. Serve as a first course or dessert.

FRUIT-FILLED CANTALOUPE   *4 servings*

2 small cantaloupes
1½ cups fresh strawberries
1 cup fresh blueberries

2 or 3 tablespoons sugar
¼ cup gin
1½ tablespoons lemon juice

1. Cut the cantaloupes into halves and remove the seeds and stringy portion.

2. Wash and hull the strawberries. Cut each berry into halves and combine them lightly with the blueberries, sugar, gin and lemon juice.

3. Spoon the fruit mixture into the cavities of the melon halves. Chill for two hours or longer. Serve as a first course or dessert.

PERLES DE CANTALOUPE AU RHUM   *6 servings*

1 large cantaloupe	2 tablespoons lemon juice
¼ cup sugar	½ cup light rum
½ cup orange juice	

1. Cut the cantaloupe into halves and scoop out the seeds and stringy portion. Cut into melon balls.

2. Combine the sugar, orange juice, lemon juice and rum. Pour over the melon balls. Chill and serve.

CANTALOUPE ROYAL   *6 servings*

6 very small cantaloupes, of uniform size	1 tablespoon kirsch, or more
	Fresh mint leaves
1 pint vanilla ice cream, softened	Fresh berries in season
½ cup heavy cream, whipped	

1. Cut the cantaloupes into halves, remove the seeds, and drain. Scoop out the inside of each cantaloupe, leaving a one-quarter-inch shell. Freeze the shells overnight.

2. Chop one cup of the scooped-out cantaloupe meat very fine and blend it with the softened ice cream. (Any leftover cantaloupe meat can be reserved for use in fruit cups or salads.)

3. Fold the whipped cream and kirsch into the ice-cream mixture. Spoon into the frozen cantaloupe shells. If the ice-cream mixture melts too much, freeze it until it is firm enough to spoon into the shells.

4. Freeze the filled shells until firm. The dessert should have the consistency of ice cream. If it is too hard, let it stand at room temperature for about thirty minutes. Serve garnished with mint leaves and seasonal berries.

FRUIT-FILLED HONEYDEW   *4 to 6 servings*

1 large honeydew melon	¼ cup orange liqueur
1 orange, sectioned	Fresh mint leaves
1 pint strawberries, sliced	
Small bunch of seedless green grapes	

1. Cut off and discard a thin slice from the bottom of the melon so that it will stand evenly.

2. Cutting in sawtooth fashion, remove the top third of the melon. Scrape out and discard the seeds. Carefully make as many melon balls as possible from the flesh.

3. Combine most of the melon balls, the orange sections, strawberries and grapes, reserving the rest for garnish. Pour the liqueur over the fruit mixture and add two or three crushed mint leaves.

4. Fill the melon with the mixture. Garnish with mint leaves and reserved fruit.

MELON DELIGHT   *4 servings*

1 cantaloupe or Persian melon	Juice of ½ lemon
2 peaches, peeled and sliced	½ teaspoon salt
⅓ cup sugar	2 tablespoons rosewater

1. Cut the melon into halves and discard the seeds. Cut the melon into balls.

2. Combine the melon balls and peaches with the sugar, lemon juice and salt. Chill.

3. Add the rosewater thirty minutes before serving. To serve, top each portion with a little crushed ice.

Note: If desired, other fruits such as seedless grapes or nectarines may be added to the dessert before chilling.

PEACHES ROMANOFF   *6 servings*

½ cup plus 3 tablespoons sugar	1 tablespoon butter
⅓ cup water	½ cup rum
Grated rind of 1 lemon	1 to 2 cups heavy cream
½ tablespoon lemon juice	6 fresh peaches, sliced, halved, or
1 egg yolk	poached whole

1. Combine the half cup of sugar and the water. Cook to 240° F. on a candy thermometer, or until a thick syrup forms. Add the lemon rind and juice.

2. Beat the egg yolk with the three tablespoons sugar. Add to the hot syrup. Cook over low heat for five minutes. Add the butter and rum. Cool.

3. Whip the cream. Combine the rum sauce with the whipped cream and serve over chilled peaches.

PEACHES IN WHITE WINE   *4 to 8 servings*

8 unblemished firm ripe peaches
2 cups cold water
2 cups dry white wine

1 tablespoon lemon juice
1 cup sugar

1. Wash the peaches well and dry them, leaving the skin intact. The skin will give the peaches color as they cook.
2. Bring the water, wine, lemon juice and sugar to a boil in an enamelware or stainless-steel saucepan. Simmer until sugar is dissolved.
3. Drop the peaches into the boiling syrup. When the mixture returns to a boil, simmer until peaches are tender. The cooking time will depend on the texture of the peaches. Chill in the syrup.
4. To serve, peel the peaches and serve them in the syrup.

VANILLA POACHED PEARS   *6 servings*

6 firm ripe small pears
1 cup sugar
1 cup water
2 teaspoons lemon juice

$\frac{1}{8}$ teaspoon salt
$1\frac{1}{2}$ teaspoons vanilla extract or 1 piece of vanilla bean (2 inches)

1. Peel pears, leaving them whole with stems intact.
2. Combine sugar, water, lemon juice, salt and vanilla in a saucepan. Bring to a boil, add three pears, and cook, covered, for thirty minutes, or until tender. Remove and reserve. Cook remaining pears.
3. Return the first poached pears to the syrup, and let all stand until cool. Chill. Remove vanilla bean if used.

PEARS CARMELITE   *6 servings*

6 ripe pears
1 cup sugar
2 cups water
Dash of salt
$1\frac{1}{2}$ teaspoons vanilla extract or 1 piece of vanilla bean (2 inches)

3 cups Dessert Rice (page 583) or 6 squares of spongecake
$\frac{1}{2}$ cup mixed glacé fruits, coarsely chopped
3 tablespoons apricot jam
Red currant jelly

1. Peel the pears, leaving them whole with stems intact.
2. Combine the sugar, water, salt and vanilla in a saucepan. Add the pears, cover, and cook for thirty minutes, or until tender. Do not overcook. Remove from syrup and cool. Discard syrup.
3. Cut off stem end of each pear and reserve. Remove cores with an apple corer.

4. Place one-half cup of the rice, or one spongecake square, in each of six dessert dishes. Top each with a pear. Combine glacé fruit and apricot jam. Spoon some into the cavity of each pear. Replace each stem top. Melt currant jelly and spoon over pears.

PEARS BAKED WITH GRAPES AND WINE   *3 or 4 servings*

3 or 4 slightly underripe table pears
1 tablespoon lemon juice
¾ cup dry white wine

⅔ cup sugar, approximately
1 cup white seedless grapes, or more
2 to 3 tablespoons cognac (optional)

1. Preheat oven to moderate (375° F.).
2. Cut the pears into halves and remove the cores. Place, cut side down, in a glass baking dish that contains the lemon juice and wine.
3. Bake, covered, for about twenty minutes, or until the pears are beginning to soften.
4. Turn the pears and sprinkle with the sugar. Fill with grapes. Return to the oven and cook, uncovered, until tender and glazed. Pour the cognac over the pears and serve warm or chilled. If desired, flame the cognac before pouring it over the pears.

PEARS BAKED IN GRENADINE   *3 to 6 servings*

3 firm fresh pears
1 cup grenadine syrup

Juice of ½ lemon
Sour cream

1. Preheat oven to moderate (325° F.).
2. Peel the pears, leaving them whole with stem intact, or cut into halves lengthwise and remove cores. Place in a baking pan, cut side down.
3. Combine grenadine with lemon juice. Pour over pears. Bake the pears for forty-five to fifty minutes, or until tender when tested with a food pick. Baste frequently with the syrup.
4. Chill in refrigerator. Serve with the baking syrup and with sour cream.

PEARS BAKED WITH MINCEMEAT   *6 servings*

3 large ripe pears, peeled
6 heaping teaspoons mincemeat
⅓ cup sugar
½ cup water

Dash of salt
1 tablespoon fresh lemon juice
Cognac (optional)

1. Preheat oven to moderate (375° F.).
2. Halve the pears and core them with a melon-ball cutter. Place the pear halves in a baking dish (10 × 5 × 2 inches). Fill each half with one heaping teaspoon of mincemeat.

3. Combine the sugar, water, salt and lemon juice in a saucepan. Bring to the boiling point, then pour over the pears. Cover the baking dish with aluminum foil. Bake for one hour, or until pears are tender, basting three times with the syrup. Remove the foil and bake for fifteen to twenty minutes longer, basting frequently.

4. Serve one pear half for each serving, with some of the syrup spooned over it. If desired, spoon one teaspoon of cognac over each pear before serving.

PEARS IN PORT WINE   *4 to 5 servings*

8 unblemished ripe pears	1 cup port
1 tablespoon lemon juice	4 cups water
1 orange	1 cup sugar

1. Peel the pears and drop them immediately into water to cover containing the lemon juice.

2. Peel the orange carefully, removing only the outside rind. Reserve the fruit for another use. Cut the rind into thin slivers.

3. Bring the wine, four cups water, the sugar and orange rind to a boil in an enamelware or stainless-steel saucepan. Simmer until sugar is dissolved.

4. Drain pears and add to syrup. Cook until tender. Chill in syrup until ready to serve.

AMBROSIA   *6 servings*

1 ripe pineapple	2 cups grated fresh coconut
6 seedless oranges	1/3 cup kirsch (optional)
1/2 cup confectioners' sugar	

1. Peel the pineapple. Discard the core and cut pineapple flesh into thin uniform slices. Peel the oranges and cut into sections.

2. Place the fruits in a bowl and sprinkle with the sugar. Cover with the coconut and add the kirsch. Chill until ready to serve.

STRAWBERRIES AL ASTI   *6 servings*

1 cup almonds, blanched	3 cups strawberries
2 1/4 cups Asti Spumante or other sparkling white wine	1 cup heavy cream, whipped and sweetened
6 egg yolks	1/3 cup currant jelly
3/4 cup sugar	

1. Preheat oven to moderate (350° F.).

2. Crush the almonds in a mortar or blender. Add two cups of the wine and heat to simmering.

3. Beat the egg yolks with one-half cup sugar. Add the almonds while stirring and turn into a buttered and sugared eight-inch cake pan. Set on a rack in a pan of hot water and cook for about twenty-five minutes, until custard is set. Stand in cold water to cool. Chill.

4. To serve, unmold custard onto a cold plate. Roll the berries in one-quarter cup sugar. Pile in the center of the custard.

5. Using a pastry tube, make a border around the berries with the whipped cream.

6. Mix the jelly and remaining one-quarter cup wine and pour around the custard.

STRAWBERRIES ALEXANDRA   *8 servings*

1 ripe pineapple
¼ cup kirsch or cognac
¾ cup sugar, approximately
3 cups strawberries

½ cup pitted canned apricots
1 cup heavy cream, whipped and sweetened

1. Slice and peel the pineapple. Cut four of the best slices into halves. Add two tablespoons kirsch and two tablespoons sugar to the half slices and chill until ready to use. Dice the remaining pineapple.

2. Reserve one cup of the best strawberries for garnish. Cut remaining berries into quarters and add to the diced pineapple. Sweeten to taste, mix, and chill.

3. Purée the apricots. Add one-quarter cup sugar to the purée and cook, stirring, until the mixture is clear. Add the remaining kirsch and chill.

4. To serve, pile the diced fruits in the center of a serving plate and surround with the half slices of pineapple. Cover the center with whipped cream and garnish with the reserved strawberries. Coat the pineapple slices with the apricot sauce.

STRAWBERRIES WITH RUM CREAM   *6 servings*

1 quart whole fresh strawberries, hulled, rinsed and drained
½ cup granulated sugar
1 cup heavy cream

½ cup grated sweet chocolate
1 tablespoon confectioners' sugar
1 tablespoon light rum

1. Arrange the strawberries in a serving bowl and sprinkle with the granulated sugar. Chill until ready to serve.

2. Whip the cream and fold the chocolate and confectioners' sugar into it. Fold in the rum. Serve the cream with the berries.

FRUIT MÉLANGE   *4 to 6 servings*

Peel two peaches and two pears and cut into small dice. Combine with approximately two cups of berries such as blueberries, strawberries or raspberries. Sprinkle with one tablespoon lemon juice and one-quarter cup sugar. Let stand until sugar dissolves. Add a spirit such as applejack, kirsch or cognac and serve chilled.

COMPOTE OF DRIED FRUITS WITH SAUCE A LA RITZ
6 servings

1 pound dried figs	1 cup sugar
1 pound dried apricots	1 tablespoon grated lemon rind
Water	1 jar (about 8 ounces) brandied
1 cup claret	cherries

SAUCE À LA RITZ:

¼ cup milk	2 tablespoons sugar
¾ cup heavy cream	¼ teaspoon vanilla extract
1 egg yolk	Kirsch

1. Soak the figs and apricots in cold water until they have plumped; drain.
2. Add the claret, one-half cup water, sugar and lemon rind to the fruits and cook slowly until tender. Add the cherries and chill.
3. Scald the milk and one-quarter cup of the cream. Beat the egg yolk with the sugar until light. Gradually beat in the scalded milk and cream.
4. Place the mixture in the top part of a small double boiler and cook over hot water, stirring, until the mixture just coats the back of the spoon. Cool and chill.
5. Whip the remaining cream and fold into the mixture along with the vanilla. Fold in kirsch to taste. Serve the sauce separately from the compote.

ANISE FRUIT COMPOTE   *6 servings*

1 cup sugar	½ cup fresh grapefruit sections
1½ cups water	½ cup seeded fresh grape halves
¼ teaspoon aniseeds	½ cup diced fresh pears
⅛ teaspoon salt	½ cup diced unpeeled raw apples
½ cup fresh orange sections	½ cup diced fresh pineapple

Combine the sugar, water, aniseeds and salt in a saucepan. Mix well, bring to a boil, and cook for three or four minutes. Strain over the mixed fruit, chill, and serve.

FROZEN FRUIT CHUNKS   *About 18 chunks*

1¾ cups pineapple juice or reconstituted frozen lemonade

1 pint fresh strawberries or raspberries

¾ cup orange juice

1. Pour the pineapple juice or lemonade into a chilled ice-cube tray with the divider in place. Allow to freeze partly.

2. Wash the berries and purée them in an electric blender or force them through a sieve.

3. Combine the berries and the orange juice and pour the mixture over the partly frozen pineapple juice. Freeze until partly set.

4. Insert a popsicle stick or wooden fork or spoon into the center of each cube. Freeze until solid. Once removed from the ice-cube trays, the chunks can be stored in plastic bags in the freezer.

. . . .

MOUSSES,
FROZEN DESSERTS AND MERINGUES

. . . .

CHOCOLATE-ORANGE MOUSSE   *6 to 8 servings*

1½ bright-skinned oranges
2 cups boiling water
1 cup plus 1 tablespoon sugar
⅓ cup cold water
1 teaspoon vanilla extract
4 eggs, separated
⅓ cup superfine granulated sugar

¼ cup orange liqueur
6 ounces (6 squares) semisweet baking chocolate
¼ cup strong coffee
¾ cup sweet butter
⅛ teaspoon salt

1. Remove orange rind with a potato peeler and cut into fine julienne strips. Place in the boiling water and simmer for ten minutes. Drain, rinse, and dry.

2. Dissolve one cup sugar in the cold water. Bring to a boil and boil rapidly, uncovered, to 230° F. on a candy thermometer, or to the thread stage. Remove from heat, stir in the dry orange rind and the vanilla, and let stand for at least thirty minutes.

3. Beat the egg yolks and superfine sugar until pale yellow and very thick. Beat in the orange liqueur.

4. Heat chocolate and coffee in the top part of a double boiler over hot water until chocolate melts. Remove from heat and gradually beat in the butter to make a smooth cream.

5. Beat the chocolate cream into the egg-yolk mixture. Beat in one-quarter cup of the orange rind, drained of syrup.

6. Beat the egg whites and salt until soft peaks form. Sprinkle remaining sugar into the egg whites and beat until stiff.

7. Stir one-quarter of the egg whites into chocolate mixture. Gently fold in the remaining egg whites. Pour into serving dishes. Chill for at least two hours. Use any remaining orange rind for garnish.

JACQUELINE CARDELLI'S MOUSSE AU CHOCOLAT
4 servings

¼ pound semisweet chocolate
½ cup sugar
¼ cup water

4 eggs, separated
2 tablespoons rum
Chopped pistachio nuts

1. Melt the chocolate in the top part of a double boiler.

2. Combine the sugar and water and cook for eight to ten minutes, to the syrup stage (when the syrup spins a thread).

3. Stir the syrup into the melted chocolate. Add the egg yolks, one at a time, beating well after each addition. Remove the mixture from the heat and stir in the rum. Cool.

4. Beat the egg whites until stiff. Fold them into the mixture. Heap the mousse into a serving dish or into individual dishes. Serve sprinkled with chopped pistachio nuts.

COFFEE CHARLOTTE   *8 servings*

2 envelopes unflavored gelatin
1 cup milk
1 cup strong coffee
1 cup sugar

2 egg whites
⅛ teaspoon salt
2 cups heavy cream
Ladyfingers

1. Soften the gelatin in the cold milk. Heat the coffee to the boiling point and add it to the milk mixture. Stir until the gelatin is dissolved.

2. Add three-quarters cup of the sugar and stir until the sugar is dissolved. Chill until slightly thickened.

3. Whip the egg whites until soft peaks form. Add the remaining sugar and the salt gradually, beating until stiff and glossy. Fold into the gelatin mixture.

4. Whip one and one-half cups of the cream. Fold into the gelatin mixture. Line eight dessert glasses with ladyfingers. Spoon the gelatin mixture into the glasses and chill until set. Whip the remaining cream and use as a garnish.

GRAPE AND MELON MOUSSE   *8 servings*

2 envelopes unflavored gelatin
½ cup cold water
1 cup hot water
¼ cup sugar
¼ cup lemon juice
⅛ teaspoon salt
½ cup stiffly whipped cream
½ cup sour cream
2 cups Thompson seedless grapes
1 cup Spanish melon balls

1. Soften the gelatin in the cold water. Stir the hot water, sugar, juice and salt into the gelatin until gelatin melts. Chill until mixture begins to thicken.

2. Combine whipped sweet cream and sour cream and fold into the gelatin. Gently fold in fruits. Turn into an oiled one-and-one-half-quart mold. Chill until firm.

3. Unmold the mousse onto a serving plate. Garnish with clusters of green grapes.

RASPBERRY MACAROON MOUSSE   *6 servings*

2 packages (10 ounces each) frozen raspberries
2 egg whites
½ cup sugar
2 cups heavy cream, whipped
⅔ cup crisp macaroon crumbs (see note)

1. Drain the raspberries and place them in the container of an electric blender. Blend on high speed, then strain through a sieve lined with cheesecloth.

2. In a mixing bowl beat the egg whites until stiff, gradually adding the sugar while beating.

3. Fold the raspberries into the whipped cream, then fold in the egg whites. Pour into a mold or a refrigerator freezer tray and freeze. After an hour remove from the freezer and, using a spoon, fold in the macaroon crumbs so that they are streaked through the mousse. Return to the freezer and freeze until firm.

Note: To make macaroon crumbs, break dried macaroons into pieces and blend in an electric blender, a few at a time, until they form crumbs.

FROZEN MOCHA MOUSSE   *8 servings*

3 ounces (3 squares) unsweetened chocolate
⅓ cup water
¾ cup sugar
Pinch of salt
3 egg yolks
1 tablespoon instant coffee powder
½ teaspoon vanilla extract
2 cups heavy cream, whipped

1. *Dacquoise.* Preheat oven to very slow (250° F.). Place five egg whites in a mixing bowl, add one-eighth teaspoon cream of tartar, and beat until frothy. Reserve egg yolks for the buttercream.

2. Gradually add three-quarters cup granulated sugar while beating. Continue to beat until the meringue stands in stiff peaks when the beater is withdrawn from the mixing bowl.

3. Blend one-half cup sugar, one cup ground blanched almonds, one-half cup zwieback crumbs, two tablespoons each of sifted all-purpose flour and cornstarch, and one-half teaspoon vanilla extract. Fold the mixture into the meringue.

4. Cut out two eight-inch circles of parchment paper and place them on a baking sheet. Or grease and flour a baking sheet and mark two eight-inch circles with the help of a layer-cake pan.

5. Spoon the meringue mixture into a pastry bag fitted with a plain tube with a half-inch opening. Pipe the mixture out spirally from the center to cover the prepared circles. Bake the layers for forty-five minutes. Cool.

6. *Buttercream.* Combine one cup sugar and one-third cup water in a saucepan.

7. Heat, stirring, to 236° F. on a candy thermometer, or until the syrup spins a thread.

8. Beat five egg yolks until they are thick and pale. Gradually pour the syrup over them, beating all the time.

9. Beat in one and one-quarter cups butter. Add two tablespoons each of Grand Marnier and instant coffee powder. Chill the mixture until it is just thick enough to spread.

10. Spread the buttercream between the cooled meringue layers. Sprinkle sifted confectioners' sugar and shaved chocolate over the top.

11. Dacquoise in the picture was made by doubling the recipe. This elegant French creation makes a fabulous dessert for spring menus.

1. Place the chocolate and water in a saucepan and gradually bring to a boil, stirring. When chocolate is melted, add the sugar and salt and cook over low heat for two minutes, stirring constantly.

2. Place the egg yolks in a mixing bowl and beat with a whisk. Pour in the chocolate mixture, beating constantly. Add the coffee. Let the mixture cool.

3. Fold in the vanilla and whipped cream. Pour into refrigerator trays. Place in the freezer until firm.

FRESH PINEAPPLE MOUSSE *4 servings*

Juice of ½ lemon
1 cup grated fresh pineapple (prepared on a grater or in an electric blender)
3 egg yolks
½ cup sugar
⅛ teaspoon salt

1½ envelopes unflavored gelatin
½ cup cold milk
1 cup heavy cream, whipped
2 tablespoons Cointreau or kirsch
1 pint fresh strawberries, washed and hulled

1. Add the lemon juice to the grated pineapple.

2. Beat the egg yolks, sugar and salt until thick and lemon-colored. Add the pineapple and mix well. Place in the top part of a double boiler and cook over boiling water, stirring, until the mixture thickens. Do not overcook.

3. Sprinkle the gelatin over the cold milk and add to the hot pineapple mixture. Stir to dissolve the gelatin. Chill the mixture until it reaches the consistency of raw egg white.

4. Fold in the whipped cream and liqueur. Chill until set. Serve in a hollowed-out pineapple shell, a serving dish, or individual sherbet glasses. Garnish with the fresh strawberries.

FROZEN CITRON MOUSSE *About 6 servings*

4 egg yolks
1 cup sugar
⅛ teaspoon salt
1 cup milk
1 cup light cream

¾ cup chopped citron
⅓ cup cognac
½ teaspoon vanilla extract
2 cups heavy cream, whipped

1. Beat the egg yolks, sugar and salt together.

2. Scald the milk and the light cream and gradually pour into the beaten egg yolks while stirring vigorously. Return to the pan and heat, stirring, over medium heat until the mixture coats the back of the spoon. Do not allow to boil. Cool, then chill the custard.

3. Soak the citron in the cognac.

4. When the custard is cold, stir in the vanilla and any cognac not absorbed by the citron. Reserve the citron.

5. Fold the whipped cream into the custard. Pour the mixture into ice-cube trays. Freeze until frozen around the outside but still mushy in the middle. Scrape into a bowl. Beat to blend and stir in the citron.

6. Pour the mixture into a one-quart soufflé dish or other straight-sided dish which has had a collar of wax paper tied around the outside to extend two to three inches above the rim. Freeze until firm. Remove collar before serving.

FROZEN LIME FOAM   *4 to 6 servings*

3 eggs, separated	Juice of 1 or 2 limes
½ cup sugar	1 cup heavy cream, whipped
Grated rind of 1 lime	¾ cup graham-cracker crumbs

1. Combine egg yolks, sugar, lime rind and juice in the top part of a double boiler. Cook over hot water, stirring, until slightly thickened. Cool.

2. Fold in stiffly beaten egg whites. Fold in whipped cream.

3. Sprinkle half of the crumbs into a large refrigerator tray. Pour in lime mixture. Top with remaining crumbs. Freeze until firm.

NO-COOK ICE CREAM   *2 to 3 quarts*

2½ cups sugar	4 cups heavy cream
4 eggs, well beaten	2 tablespoons vanilla extract
6 cups milk	½ teaspoon salt

Gradually add the sugar to the eggs, beating constantly. Continue beating until mixture is thick. Add milk, cream, vanilla and salt. Mix thoroughly. Freeze according to directions for the kind of ice-cream freezer used.

STRAWBERRY, RASPBERRY, PEACH OR BANANA ICE CREAM: Substitute four cups puréed fresh fruit, selected as desired, for four cups of the milk. Omit the vanilla. If desired, substitute almond extract.

NUT ICE CREAM: Add two cups chopped nuts to mixture.

CUSTARD ICE CREAM   *About 3 quarts*

5 eggs, lightly beaten	5 cups milk, scalded
½ teaspoon salt	5 cups heavy cream
1¼ cups sugar	2 tablespoons vanilla extract

Combine eggs, salt and sugar. Slowly add milk. Heat, stirring, until the mixture coats the back of the spoon. Do not allow to boil. Cool and chill. Add cream and vanilla. Freeze according to directions for the kind of ice-cream freezer used.

CHOCOLATE CUSTARD ICE CREAM: Add four ounces (four squares) unsweetened chocolate to the milk before it is scalded.

FROZEN EGGNOG   *About 18 servings*

1 cup sugar
1/3 cup water
Pinch of cream of tartar
4 egg yolks

1/8 teaspoon salt
3 tablespoons rum, cognac, or bourbon
3 cups heavy cream, whipped

1. Combine the sugar, water and cream of tartar in a saucepan. Bring to a boil and cook to 136° F. on a candy thermometer.
2. Put the egg yolks, salt and rum into container of an electric blender. Cover and turn motor on high. Remove cover and, with motor on, gradually pour in the hot syrup. Turn off motor.
3. Chill the mixture until thick. Fold into the whipped cream.
4. Turn the mixture into a six-cup mold, or into eighteen small paper cups. Freeze.

FROZEN MACAROON CREAM   *6 servings*

2 dozen macaroons
1/2 cup bourbon whiskey or cognac
1 quart vanilla ice cream

1 cup heavy cream
1 tablespoon sugar

1. Line a deep dish or silver bowl with all but two of the macaroons. Pour over them all but three tablespoons of the bourbon or cognac. Chill. Spoon the ice cream into the center and place in freezer until ready to serve.
2. Whip the heavy cream and add the sugar and remaining whiskey. Spoon the whipped cream over the ice cream. Crumble the remaining macaroons and sprinkle them over all.

FROZEN CHESTNUT PUDDING   *8 servings*

3 egg whites
1/4 cup sugar
1¾ cups milk, scalded
1½ cups crème de marrons (purchased)

2 tablespoons maraschino or other liqueur
1/2 cup heavy cream, whipped
Chestnuts in syrup (purchased)

1. In the top part of a double boiler beat the egg whites until stiff, adding the sugar gradually. Add the milk and cook, stirring, over simmering water for seven minutes. Add the crème de marrons and the liqueur and cool.

2. Freeze until almost firm. Whip to break up lumps and fold in the whipped cream. Freeze again until firm. Serve garnished with chestnuts in syrup.

PINEAPPLE REFRIGERATOR PUDDING   *About 12 servings*

24 ladyfingers, split
½ cup butter, at room temperature
 1 cup sugar
 4 eggs, separated
 1 teaspoon grated lemon rind
⅓ cup lemon juice

⅓ cup rum
½ cup well-drained shredded canned pineapple
 1 envelope unflavored gelatin
 2 tablespoons cold water

1. Line a two-quart bowl or casserole with wax paper and cover the bottom with split ladyfingers. Stand ladyfingers around sides.

2. Cream together until fluffy the butter and three-quarters cup sugar. Add the egg yolks, one at a time, and beat until thick and light. Add lemon rind and juice, rum and pineapple.

3. Soften gelatin in the cold water and dissolve over hot water. Add while beating to the pineapple mixture. Cool until just beginning to thicken.

4. Beat egg whites until foamy. Add the remaining one-quarter cup of sugar gradually and beat until stiff. Fold into the pineapple mixture.

5. Cover ladyfingers in the bottom of the prepared pan with pineapple mixture, add another layer of ladyfingers, and repeat until all filling has been used. Cover the top with remaining ladyfingers. Cover.

6. Refrigerate for twelve hours or longer. To serve, turn out of mold and garnish with whipped cream.

FROZEN VANILLA CHOCOLATE PIE   *6 servings*

 2 eggs, separated
¾ cup confectioners' sugar
⅓ cup water
1½ ounces (1½ squares) unsweetened chocolate

 2 teaspoons vanilla extract
 1 cup heavy cream, whipped
½ cup vanilla-wafer crumbs or angel-flake coconut

1. Beat the egg yolks with one-quarter cup of the sugar and the water in the top part of a double boiler. Cook, stirring, over hot water until the mixture thickens. Add the chocolate and stir until melted. Add the vanilla. Cool.

2. Beat the egg whites until they stand in soft peaks, adding the remaining sugar gradually. Fold into the cooled custard, along with the whipped cream.

3. Sprinkle half of the vanilla-wafer crumbs or coconut over the bottom and sides of an ice-cube tray. Pour in the chocolate mixture and sprinkle with the remaining crumbs or coconut. Freeze. To serve, cut into wedge-shaped pieces.

Add to the list of foods that team together to multiply in goodness ice cream and old-fashioned meringue. They are a wonderful combination for summer desserts. Common to all meringues is a base of egg whites beaten until stiff, and sweetened. The best-known meringue is that which is annually swirled atop some million pies. The delicate meringues to serve with ice cream are lightweight confections that are baked until crisp and dry, but still as white and unblemished as suburban snow. The oven must be regulated to maintain a constant very low heat (225° F.). At a higher temperature the meringues will brown. In an earlier era, meringues were often left to bake and dry overnight in the retained heat of an oven that had been turned off.

Meringues may be kept for days and even weeks in a dry place. Meringues that are imperfect and broken may be crumbled and combined with whipped cream as a topping for cakes and ice cream.

MERINGUES, INDIVIDUAL AND PIE SHELL
1 meringue pie shell and 9 to 12 individual meringues

7 egg whites, at room temperature	2¼ cups superfine granulated sugar
⅛ teaspoon salt	1 teaspoon vanilla extract

1. Preheat oven to very slow (200° to 250° F.). Grease and lightly flour an eight-inch pie pan, and cover a baking sheet with unglazed paper or parchment baking-pan liner.

2. Beat the egg whites with the salt until stiff. Continue to beat while adding one and one-half cups of the sugar, one tablespoon at a time. Beat until the mixture no longer feels grainy when pressed between the fingers.

3. Fold the vanilla and the remaining sugar into the mixture.

4. Using about half of the mixture, spread a thin layer of meringue over the bottom of the prepared pie pan. Build up the sides with meringue to form a deep pie shell. Do not overlap onto the rim of the pan.

5. Form the remaining meringue into nine to twelve ovals, using two serving spoons to shape them or putting the meringue through a pastry bag fitted with a plain tube. Place the ovals on the prepared baking sheet.

6. Bake the pie shell and the oval meringues for forty-five to sixty minutes, or until dry but not browned. To complete the drying process, turn off the oven and allow the shell and meringues to cool slowly with the oven door ajar. In an oven with a pilot light, the shell and meringues may be left in overnight with the door closed.

STRAWBERRY ANGEL PIE   *8 to 10 servings*

Pile scoops of strawberry ice cream (two quarts) into a baked eight-inch meringue shell (page 564). Garnish with whole fresh strawberries or Strawberry Sauce (page 685), or a combination of both.

MERINGUES GLACÉES

Place one scoop of strawberry ice cream between two individual meringues (page 564). Top with Strawberry Sauce (page 685).

MERINGUE PIE TOPPING   *Topping for a 9-inch pie*

3 egg whites
  Pinch of salt
¼ teaspoon cream of tartar

6 tablespoons sugar
1 teaspoon flavoring, such as vanilla
  extract

1. Preheat oven to hot (425° F.).
2. Beat the egg whites with the salt until light and frothy. Add the cream of tartar and continue to beat until the whites are stiff enough to hold in peaks.
3. Beat in the sugar, one tablespoon at a time, until meringue is stiff and glossy. No grains of sugar should be felt when a small amount of the mixture is rubbed between the fingers.
4. Pile the meringue lightly on cooled pie filling, spreading the meringue until it touches the edges of the pastry to prevent the meringue from shrinking. Bake for five to six minutes, until the top is brown.
Note: This amount of meringue is enough to cover the top and sides of an eight-inch two-layer cake.

BAKED ALASKA   *6 servings*

1 quart ice cream, either brick or
  molded
  Spongecake

1 recipe Meringue Pie Topping (see
  above)
1 tablespoon granulated sugar

1. Place the ice cream in the freezer until ready to use. It must be hard frozen.
2. Trim a layer of spongecake to the shape of the bottom of the ice cream, but have the cake extend an inch around the rim of the ice-cream base.
3. Preheat oven to hot (450° F.).
4. Cover a thick wooden board with heavy unglazed paper and place the trimmed spongecake in the center. Place the ice cream in the center of the spongecake. Cover both ice cream and cake with a layer of meringue. Dust with granulated sugar.

5. Bake the Alaska for about five minutes, or until meringue is delicately browned. The board, paper, cake and meringue are all poor conductors of heat and keep the ice cream from melting. Slip the baked Alaska onto a chilled platter and serve immediately.

MERINGUE PIE   *6 to 8 servings*

5 egg whites, at room temperature
¼ teaspoon cream of tartar
1 cup plus 2 tablespoons sugar
2 teaspoons vanilla extract

1 cup heavy cream
1 tablespoon rum
3 to 4 tablespoons grated unsweetened chocolate

1. Preheat oven to hot (400° F.).
2. Beat the egg whites briefly and add the cream of tartar. Continue to beat the egg whites until they are stiff and dry. Gradually beat in the cup of sugar and one teaspoon of the vanilla extract.
3. Spread the mixture into a nine-inch pie plate and smooth it around with the back of the spoon until it resembles a piecrust. Place the shell in the oven and immediately turn off the heat. Leave the crust in the oven for at least four hours or overnight.
4. Whip the cream and add the remaining sugar and vanilla and the rum. Pour this filling into the baked shell and sprinkle with the grated chocolate. Chill and serve.

DACQUOISE   *6 to 8 servings*

A fabulous dessert for spring menus is this elegant French creation, of unknown origin, made with baked meringue layers filled with buttercream.

5 eggs, separated
⅛ teaspoon cream of tartar
1¼ cups granulated sugar
1 cup ground blanched almonds
½ cup zwieback crumbs
2 tablespoons sifted all-purpose flour

2 tablespoons sifted cornstarch
½ teaspoon vanilla extract
Buttercream (page 567)
Confectioners' sugar
Unsweetened chocolate

1. Preheat oven to very slow (250° F.).
2. Place the egg whites in a mixing bowl. (Reserve the egg yolks for the buttercream, below.) Add the cream of tartar and beat until frothy. Gradually add three-quarters cup granulated sugar while beating. Continue to beat the meringue until it stands in stiff peaks when the beater is withdrawn from the mixing bowl.
3. Blend the remaining sugar, the almonds, zwieback crumbs, flour, corn-starch, and vanilla. Fold the mixture into the meringue.

4. Cut out two eight-inch circles of parchment paper and place them on a baking sheet. Or grease and flour a baking sheet and mark two eight-inch rings on it with the help of a layer-cake pan.

5. Spoon the meringue mixture into a pastry bag fitted with a plain tube with a half-inch opening. Pipe the mixture out spirally from the center to cover the prepared circles. Bake the layers for forty-five minutes. Cool.

6. Spread the buttercream between the cooled layers. Sprinkle sifted confectioners' sugar and shaved chocolate over the top.

BUTTERCREAM:

1 cup sugar
⅓ cup water
5 egg yolks

1¼ cups butter
2 tablespoons Grand Marnier
2 tablespoons instant coffee powder

1. Combine the sugar and water in a saucepan. Heat, stirring, to 236° F. on a candy thermometer, or until the syrup spins a thread.

2. Beat the egg yolks until they are thick and pale. Gradually pour the syrup over them, beating all the time.

3. Beat in the butter. Add the liqueur and coffee powder. Chill the mixture until it is just thick enough to spread.

. . . .

CREAMS, CUSTARDS, PUDDINGS AND SOUFFLÉS

. . . .

ORANGE BAVARIAN CREAM   *8 servings*

2 large juice oranges
1½ envelopes unflavored gelatin
5 eggs, separated
2 additional egg yolks
1 cup plus 1 tablespoon sugar

2 teaspoons cornstarch
1½ cups milk, scalded
⅛ teaspoon salt
½ cup heavy cream, whipped
2 tablespoons orange liqueur

1. Grate the rind from the oranges into a bowl. Squeeze the oranges and add three-quarters cup juice and the gelatin to the rind. Set aside.

2. Lightly beat the egg yolks. Gradually add one cup sugar, beating until thick. Beat in the cornstarch.

3. Gradually add the milk to the egg mixture, beating, and pour into a heavy pan. Heat, stirring, until mixture thickens, but do not allow to boil. Add the orange-juice and gelatin mixture.

4. Whip the egg whites and salt with the remaining sugar until stiff but not dry. Fold into the custard. Cool as quickly as possible, stirring gently several times.

5. When cool but not set, fold in the cream and liqueur. Pour the mixture into a two-quart mold. Cover with wax paper and chill for at least four hours or, preferably, overnight. Unmold and garnish as desired with orange slices and sections.

RASPBERRY BAVARIAN   *6 servings*

4 teaspoons unflavored gelatin
3 tablespoons cold water
⅛ teaspoon salt
1½ cups sieved raspberry purée
  (see note)
1 tablespoon lemon juice

½ cup sugar
2 tablespoons kirsch or framboise
  (optional)
2 egg whites
1 cup heavy cream, whipped

1. Soften the gelatin in the cold water in the top part of a double boiler. Add the salt. Place the mixture over boiling water and stir until gelatin is dissolved.

2. In a mixing bowl combine the raspberry purée, the lemon juice and one-quarter cup of the sugar. Stir in the hot dissolved gelatin. Place the bowl over ice and stir slowly until the mixture begins to thicken. Stir in the kirsch or framboise.

3. Beat the egg whites until stiff but not dry. Add the remaining sugar gradually, beating well after each addition.

4. Fold the meringue and the whipped cream thoroughly into the slightly thickened gelatin.

5. Rinse a two-quart mold with cold water and pour the mixture into it. Chill until set.

6. Unmold on a large serving platter. If desired, garnish with additional whipped cream and raspberries.

Note: Strawberries or blackberries may be substituted for the raspberries in this recipe. Either fresh or frozen fruit may be used. To prepare a purée, the berries may be mashed and pressed through a sieve or they may be puréed in an electric blender at high speed.

CITRUS RUM CHIFFON CREAM   *6 servings*

4 eggs, separated
¾ cup confectioners' sugar
½ cup orange juice
¼ cup lemon juice

2 tablespoons light rum
¼ teaspoon salt
1 teaspoon vanilla extract
18 ladyfingers

1. Beat the egg yolks and one-half cup of the sugar in the top part of a double boiler until thick, fluffy and lemon-colored. Slowly beat in the orange and lemon juices, rum and salt. Cook over hot, not boiling, water, stirring vigorously with a wooden spoon until the mixture thickens. Cool slightly.

2. Beat the egg whites until they stand in soft peaks. Gradually beat in the remaining sugar and the vanilla. Fold into the mixture. Cool. Serve in sherbet glasses, each lined with three ladyfingers.

ORANGE FOAM   *6 servings*

3 eggs, separated
½ cup sugar
2 tablespoons cornstarch

1 tablespoon orange liqueur
Grated rind of 1 orange
2 cups fresh orange juice

1. Place the egg yolks in the top part of a double boiler and beat over barely simmering water until they are lemon-colored.
2. Gradually add the sugar and continue beating until fluffy. Stir in the cornstarch, the liqueur, orange rind and juice. Continue to cook and beat until the mixture has the consistency of mayonnaise. Do not allow the sauce to boil or it will curdle.
3. Beat the egg whites until stiff and fold them gently but thoroughly into the orange mixture. Pour into a glass serving bowl and refrigerate until well chilled.

MOLDED COCONUT CREAM   *6 servings*

½ cup hot Coconut Cream (page 491)
2 envelopes unflavored gelatin
3 egg yolks
⅓ cup sugar
2 teaspoons vanilla extract

1 cup cold Coconut Cream (page 491)
½ cup heavy cream
Crushed ice

1. Put the hot coconut cream and the gelatin into the container of an electric blender. Cover and blend on high speed for forty seconds.
2. Add the egg yolks, sugar and vanilla. Cover and blend on high speed.
3. Uncover and, with motor still running, pour in the cold coconut cream, the heavy cream, and enough crushed ice to bring the liquid to the top of the container.
4. Pour into a one-quart mold and chill for ten minutes.

COFFEE CREAM CHANTILLY   *About 2 cups*

¼ cup sugar
½ cup very strong, hot black coffee

2 egg yolks, lightly beaten
1 cup heavy cream, whipped

1. Dissolve the sugar in the hot coffee. Pour the mixture over the egg yolks and stir to blend. Cook in the top part of a small double boiler over hot water, stirring constantly, until the mixture thickens like a custard.
2. Cool mixture and chill in the refrigerator until ready to use. Just before serving, fold in the whipped cream.

FRESH LIME CREAM   *6 servings*

1 cup sugar
2 tablespoons cornstarch
⅛ teaspoon salt
1 cup water
¼ cup fresh lime juice
1 egg, lightly beaten

1 teaspoon grated lime rind
1 teaspoon vanilla extract
1 cup heavy cream, whipped
Additional whipped cream and grated lime rind for garnish

1. Combine the sugar, cornstarch and salt in a saucepan or in the top part of a double boiler. Gradually stir in the water. Cook over hot, not boiling, water or over low direct heat until thickened, stirring constantly. Add the lime juice and cook until thickened.

2. Add a little of the hot mixture to the beaten egg and then stir it into the remaining hot mixture. Cook for one to two minutes over low heat, stirring constantly. Remove from the heat and add the grated lime rind and vanilla. Cool.

3. Fold in the whipped cream. Serve in sherbet glasses, garnished with additional whipped cream and a sprinkling of lime rind.

CRÈME CELESTE   *4 to 6 servings*

1 cup heavy cream
½ cup sugar
1½ teaspoons unflavored gelatin
3 tablespoons cold water

1 cup sour cream
2 tablespoons cognac or kirsch (optional)
Crushed and sweetened berries

1. Combine the cream and sugar in a saucepan and cook, stirring, until the sugar is dissolved.

2. Soften the gelatin in the cold water and stir it into the cream mixture.

3. When the gelatin is dissolved, beat in the sour cream with a wire whisk or a rotary beater. Stir only until the mixture is thoroughly blended and smooth. Flavor with cognac or kirsch, if desired, and pour into a lightly oiled two-cup mold.

4. Chill for three to four hours, until firm. Unmold. Serve with sweetened crushed strawberries or raspberries.

BOILED CUSTARD   *About 3 cups*

6 egg yolks
¼ cup sugar
⅛ teaspoon salt

2 cups scalded milk
Vanilla extract or sherry to taste

1. Beat the egg yolks until pale but not dry. Add the sugar, salt and milk. Cook and stir in the top part of a double boiler over simmering water. The water must never bubble into a boil.

2. When the custard reaches 175° F. on a candy thermometer, it is done and must be removed from the heat, flavored, and put aside to use. If you do not own a candy thermometer, watch the stirring spoon. When it coats all over with the egg mixture and nothing drips from it, 175° F. has been reached.

CHOCOLATE CUSTARD   *4 servings*

1½ ounces (1½ squares) unsweetened chocolate
1 cup milk
6 tablespoons sugar
1½ tablespoons all-purpose flour

¼ teaspoon salt
1 egg yolk, lightly beaten
½ teaspoon vanilla extract
⅓ cup heavy cream, whipped

1. Add the chocolate to the milk. Heat in the top part of a double boiler over hot water. Beat until the chocolate is blended.
2. Combine the sugar, flour and salt. Add gradually to the chocolate mixture and cook, stirring constantly, until thickened. Continue to cook for ten minutes longer, stirring occasionally.
3. Stir a little of the hot mixture into the egg yolk, then stir the yolk into the hot sauce and cook for two minutes longer. Remove from the heat and add the vanilla. Cool. Before serving, fold in the whipped cream.

MAPLE CUSTARD   *4 servings*

2 cups milk
3 eggs

½ teaspoon salt
1 cup maple syrup

1. Preheat oven to moderate (350° F.).
2. Place the milk in a saucepan and bring just to a boil.
3. Place the eggs, salt and syrup in a mixing bowl and beat thoroughly to combine. Gradually pour the milk over the egg mixture, stirring.
4. Rinse four custard cups in cold water. Pour the custard into the cups and set them in a pan. Pour boiling water to the depth of one inch around them. Bake for about one hour, until firm. Serve with sweetened whipped cream.

RUM CUSTARD   *4 to 6 servings*

1 cup milk
1 cup heavy cream
4 egg yolks

3 tablespoons sugar
1 envelope unflavored gelatin
½ cup rum

1. Combine the milk and cream in a saucepan and bring to a boil.
2. Beat the egg yolks with the sugar and pour the hot liquid over them, stirring constantly.

3. Return the mixture to the saucepan and cook, stirring, over low heat until the custard coats a metal spoon. Do not allow the mixture to boil.

4. Soak the gelatin in the rum and dissolve it in the hot custard. Cool, stirring occasionally, until the custard is thick and begins to set. Pour it into a mold rinsed in ice water. Chill for several hours or overnight. Unmold by loosening the edges with a knife and dipping the bottom of the mold quickly into hot water.

FLAN   (Spanish caramel custard)   *12 servings*

1¼ cups sugar
⅛ teaspoon salt
 2 teaspoons vanilla extract

 7 large eggs
½ cup cold milk
 4 cups hot milk

1. Preheat oven to moderate (325° F.).

2. Stir and cook three-quarters cup of the sugar in a small saucepan over medium heat until it is melted and a light amber color. Pour it into a one-and-one-half-quart casserole, turning to coat all the bottom and as much of the sides as possible. If casserole is very cold, place in a pan of hot water to warm. This prevents the caramel from hardening before bottom and sides are coated.

3. Combine salt, vanilla and remaining sugar. Mix well. Add the eggs and beat lightly with a rotary beater. Stir in the cold milk, then add the hot milk. Mix well.

4. Pour the custard into the caramel-coated casserole. Set in a pan of hot water. Bake in the oven for one hour and twenty minutes.

5. Remove from the oven and cool. Then chill. Just before serving, turn out into a shallow bowl or a slightly cupped serving plate that is about two inches larger than the flan. Slice and serve.

CINNAMON PUMPKIN FLAN   *9 servings*

1¼ cups plus 1 tablespoon sugar
½ teaspoon salt
 1 teaspoon ground cinnamon
 1 cup mashed cooked pumpkin
 5 large eggs, lightly beaten

1½ cups undiluted evaporated milk
⅓ cup water
1½ teaspoons vanilla extract
½ cup heavy cream, whipped
¼ teaspoon ground ginger

1. Melt one-half cup of the sugar over low heat until sugar forms a golden syrup. Stir constantly to prevent burning. Pour immediately into a shallow cake pan (8 × 8 × 2 inches) or a nine-inch pie plate, turning and rolling pan from side to side to coat with caramel. Set aside.

2. Preheat oven to moderate (350° F.).

3. Combine three-quarters cup of the remaining sugar with the salt and cinnamon. Add pumpkin and eggs. Mix well. Stir in the evaporated milk, the water and vanilla extract. Mix well and turn into the caramel-coated pan. Set in a pan of hot water. Bake for one and one-quarter hours, or until a knife inserted into the center of the filling comes out clean. Cool and chill.

4. To serve, run a spatula around the sides of the pan. Turn flan out onto a serving plate. Cut into squares or wedges. Combine the whipped cream with the remaining sugar and the ginger and spread over the squares.

CRÈME BEAU RIVAGE   *8 servings*

There is probably nothing more gratifying to a dessert lover than the velvet-smooth creations made with cream, vanilla and sugar. Not content with such a masterpiece as crème renversée au caramel, *some French chef carried it to a more luxurious conclusion and produced* crème beau rivage. *This is the caramel custard embellished with rolled almond cookies filled with strawberry cream. It is so beautiful to look at, it is almost a shame to eat it.*

6 whole eggs	1¼ teaspoons vanilla extract
2 egg yolks	3 tablespoons granulated sugar
⅔ cup light brown sugar	¾ teaspoon water
3 cups light cream	Strawberry Cream (see below)
1 cup milk	Petits Cornets (page 574)

1. Preheat oven to moderate (350° F.).

2. Beat together the whole eggs and the egg yolks. Stir in the brown sugar, cream, milk and vanilla. Set aside.

3. In a saucepan cook the granulated sugar and the water until a brown and caramelized syrup is formed. Pour the syrup into a warm scalloped ring mold (1½ quarts), tipping it slightly from side to side to coat the bottom evenly. Pour in the custard mixture.

4. Set the mold in a pan of hot water. Bake for forty-five to fifty minutes, until a knife inserted into the center comes out clean. Chill thoroughly.

5. Carefully unmold the chilled caramel custard onto a serving platter with a rim. Fill the center with strawberry cream. Use remaining strawberry cream to fill the *petits cornets*. Place them on and around the custard ring.

STRAWBERRY CREAM: *About 5 cups*

1 package (12 to 14 ounces) frozen strawberries, thawed	1 envelope unflavored gelatin
	2 cups heavy cream, whipped

1. Drain the berries and place the juice in a small pan. Add the gelatin to the juice.

2. Purée the berries either in an electric blender or by forcing them through a sieve.

3. Heat the gelatin mixture gently, stirring until gelatin dissolves. Stir in the purée.

4. Chill the mixture until it begins to thicken but is not completely set. Fold it into the whipped cream.

PETITS CORNETS: *12 to 18 cones*

3 egg whites
½ cup sugar
⅓ cup sifted all-purpose flour
⅓ cup ground blanched almonds

⅓ cup melted butter, cooled
⅛ teaspoon salt
1 teaspoon vanilla extract

1. Preheat oven to moderate (375° F.).

2. Beat egg whites until stiff. Gradually beat in the sugar until mixture is very stiff. Fold in remaining ingredients. Spoon into a pastry bag fitted with a plain tube about one-half inch in diameter.

3. Press out two-inch rounds, one-quarter inch thick, onto a greased and floured cookie sheet. Allow two inches between rounds. Cook only four to six cookies at one time.

4. Bake for eight to ten minutes, until edges of cookies are lightly browned. Immediately remove from the oven and from the cookie sheet. As soon as the cookies are cool enough to handle, but still warm and flexible, bend each into a cone shape, pinching until the shape is retained. Place them, seam side down, on a rack to cool. Continue until all the dough is used.

DOROTHY STANFORD'S LEMON CURD   *4 servings*

¼ cup butter
¾ cup sugar
2 eggs, lightly beaten

Juice of 2 lemons
Grated rind of 2 lemons

1. Cream the butter and gradually beat in the sugar.

2. Beat the eggs into the creamed mixture, then add the lemon juice and grated rind. Cook, stirring, over low heat until mixture thickens. This must be cooked over low heat and stirred constantly to keep it from curdling. If desired, use a double boiler.

3. Serve hot or cold, or use as a dessert filling.

LEMON CREAM   *6 servings*

1 cup sugar
2 tablespoons cornstarch
⅛ teaspoon salt
1 cup water
¼ cup fresh lemon juice
1 egg, lightly beaten

1 teaspoon grated lemon rind
1 teaspoon vanilla extract
1 cup heavy cream, whipped
  Whipped cream and fresh strawberries

1. Combine the sugar, cornstarch and salt in a saucepan or the top part of a double boiler. Gradually stir in the water. Cook over hot water or medium heat, stirring constantly, until thickened.

2. Add the lemon juice and cook until thickened. Add a little of the hot mixture to the egg. Stir into the remaining hot mixture. Cook, stirring constantly, over low heat for one or two minutes.

3. Remove from heat and add the lemon rind and vanilla. Cool.

4. Fold the whipped cream into the mixture. Serve in sherbet glasses, garnished with whipped cream and strawberries.

LEMON FROMAGE WITH BLUEBERRIES   *6 servings*

3 whole eggs	¼ cup lemon juice
2 egg yolks	2 cups heavy cream
½ cup sugar	1 pint blueberries, washed well and
Grated rind of 1 lemon	sweetened to taste
¾ tablespoon unflavored gelatin	

1. Beat the eggs and egg yolks until lemon-colored and frothy. While beating, add the sugar in a slow stream and continue to beat until mixture is thickened. Add the grated rind.

2. Combine the gelatin and lemon juice in a heatproof measuring cup. Place the cup over hot water and stir until gelatin dissolves. Add it to the egg mixture and beat well.

3. Whip the cream until it is stiff and fold it gently into the egg and lemon mixture. Pour the mixture into a one-quart mold and chill for four hours. Unmold and serve with the sweetened blueberries.

The proof of a pudding may be in the eating but it is certainly not in the defining. There must be few things in the world of food so difficult to categorize.

The earliest puddings were encased in the tripe of one animal or another. The most famous of these is the haggis, which Scots are said to dote on, a substantial dish made with the heart, liver and lights of a sheep or calf.

As civilization progressed, puddings of various kinds came to be enjoyed, both savory (as a main dish) and sweet (as a dessert), and following the early method of preparation, most of them were steamed or boiled in a bag or cloth. In the broadest sense a pudding may be made from almost any edible, including meats, fruits, or vegetables, and seasoned at will. The present multitude of dessert puddings includes plum pudding, rice pudding and, the most commonplace of all, bread pudding. Today a pudding can still be so called even if it is not steamed in a bag. It may be baked in a casserole or cooked on top of the stove, or it may even be a cold dish. Hot puddings are excellent fare for winter menus.

VANILLA PUDDING   *5 or 6 servings*

⅓ cup cornstarch
½ cup sugar
⅛ teaspoon salt

3 cups milk
2 egg yolks
1½ teaspoons vanilla extract

1. In a bowl mix the cornstarch, sugar and salt. Add about one-half cup milk and mix. Heat remaining milk almost to simmering in a heavy saucepan over moderate heat.

2. Stir cornstarch mixture to blend it and add about half of the scalded milk to it while stirring. Return to milk in saucepan and cook, stirring, until the mixture boils.

3. Beat the egg yolks lightly. Add a small amount of the pudding mixture to the yolks, stirring all the while. Return all to the saucepan and cook, stirring, until thickened.

4. Add vanilla and turn the mixture immediately into a serving dish or into five or six custard cups. Cool and chill. Serve with a fruit sauce.

CHOCOLATE PUDDING I   *10 servings*

12 ounces (12 squares) semisweet baking chocolate
6 tablespoons strong coffee
½ cup soft butter
5 eggs, separated

1 cup sugar
2 teaspoons vanilla extract
1 cup sifted all-purpose flour.
1 cup very finely ground unblanched almonds

1. Preheat oven to moderate (350° F.). Butter and flour a one-and-one-half-quart ring mold.

2. Heat chocolate and coffee in the top part of a double boiler over hot water, stirring until chocolate is melted. Add butter and stir to melt.

3. Beat the egg yolks until thick and pale. Gradually add the sugar and beat until very thick. Beat in the chocolate mixture and the vanilla. Fold in the flour and ground nuts.

4. Beat the egg whites until stiff but not dry and fold into mixture. Pour into the prepared ring mold.

5. Bake for about forty minutes, until the pudding is done. Serve with hot fudge sauce, whipped cream or hard sauce.

CHOCOLATE PUDDING II   *4 servings*

3 ounces (squares) unsweetened chocolate
1 tablespoon hot water
½ cup sugar
1½ tablespoons all-purpose flour

½ cup melted butter
1½ teaspoons vanilla extract
4 eggs, separated
Mocha Cream Sauce (page 689)

1. Preheat oven to moderate (350° F.).

2. Combine the chocolate and water in the top part of a double boiler. Cook over hot water until the chocolate melts, then slowly stir in the sugar and flour. Blend in the butter and vanilla.

3. Remove the mixture from the heat and add the well-beaten egg yolks. Beat the egg whites until stiff and fold them into the pudding.

4. Scrape the mixture into a well-buttered one-quart soufflé dish. Bake for one hour. Let the pudding cool in the mold, then chill if desired. The dessert will puff in the oven, then fall as it chills. Serve with mocha cream sauce.

BLACK BOTTOM PARFAIT   6 servings

1 cup sugar	1 teaspoon vanilla extract
1¼ tablespoons cornstarch	1 envelope unflavored gelatin
2 cups milk, scalded	¼ cup cold water
4 eggs, separated	¼ teaspoon salt
¾ cup semisweet chocolate pieces, melted	¼ teaspoon cream of tartar

1. In the top part of a double boiler mix one-half cup of the sugar and the cornstarch. Add the milk and bring to a boil, stirring constantly.

2. Beat the egg yolks and add to the milk while stirring. Place over hot water and cook, stirring, for two minutes.

3. Pour one cup of this custard into a small bowl, add the chocolate, and stir until blended. Add one-half teaspoon of the vanilla. Divide among six parfait glasses.

4. Soften the gelatin in the cold water, add to the white custard, and stir until dissolved. Add the remaining one-half teaspoon vanilla. Cool until the mixture is beginning to thicken.

5. Beat the egg whites until foamy with salt and cream of tartar. Gradually add the remaining one-half cup of sugar and whip until stiff. Fold into the white custard. Pour over the chocolate custard in the glasses and cover. Chill until firm. Garnish with grated chocolate.

Note: This gives a bitter chocolate custard. If desired, sweeten to taste before turning into parfait glasses.

STRAWBERRY PARFAIT   6 servings

2 eggs, lightly beaten	1 teaspoon unflavored gelatin
¼ cup plus 1 tablespoon sugar	1 tablespoon cold water
⅛ teaspoon salt	1½ teaspoons vanilla extract
2 cups milk	1½ cups sliced fresh strawberries

Chocolate, one of the world's favorite flavors, is the principal ingredient in these desserts—individual dishes of Mousse au Chocolat, Chocolate Cheesecake, meringue eggs on Chocolate Custard, Chocolate Soufflé.

1. Combine the eggs, one-quarter cup sugar, the salt and one-quarter cup of the milk in a saucepan or the top part of a double boiler. Heat remaining milk and add. Mix well.

2. Cook over hot water or over very low heat until the mixture coats a metal spoon.

3. Soften the gelatin in the cold water and stir into the hot custard. Stir in vanilla and chill.

4. Combine the strawberries and remaining one tablespoon sugar. Just before serving, fill parfait glasses with alternating layers of custard and strawberries, beginning with custard and ending with strawberries.

ALMOND BLANCMANGE   *3 or 4 servings*

¼ pound almonds, blanched
5 or 6 bitter almonds or ¼ teaspoon almond extract
2 cups light cream
¼ cup sugar
Dash of salt
1 envelope unflavored gelatin
¼ cup cold water

1. Put the almonds through the food grinder using the finest blade. Add the cream, mix, and let stand for thirty minutes.

2. Strain the mixture through a fine sieve, pressing out all possible liquid. Add the sugar, salt and if no bitter almonds were used, add the almond extract at this point.

3. Soften the gelatin in the water and heat it gently, stirring until the gelatin is dissolved. Add, while stirring with a wire whisk, to the cream. Turn into a serving dish or individual dessert saucers. Chill until set.

4. If desired, garnish with additional blanched or toasted almonds and shapes of angelica or serve with chocolate sauce or a sweetened fresh fruit.

COCONUT BLANCMANGE   *4 to 6 servings*

1½ envelopes unflavored gelatin
⅓ cup kirsch or rum
½ cup plus 1 tablespoon confectioners' sugar
3⅔ cups Coconut Cream (page 491)
1 teaspoon almond extract

2 tablespoons toasted coconut (optional)
1 pint whole fresh or frozen strawberries
Sugar

1. Sprinkle the gelatin into the kirsch, then stir over hot water until the gelatin dissolves. Stir constantly until clear.

2. Combine confectioners' sugar with coconut cream and stir until thoroughly dissolved. Continue stirring and add kirsch and dissolved gelatin in a thin stream. Add the almond extract. Pour the mixture into a one-quart ring mold which has been rinsed in cold water. Chill until firm.

3. When ready to serve, run a small spatula around the rim of the dessert. Dip the bottom of the mold twice, but briefly, into warm water. Wipe the bottom dry, place a round plate over the mold, and invert it quickly. Sprinkle the blancmange with toasted coconut, if desired, and fill the center with strawberries sweetened with sugar to taste. The strawberries also may be marinated in kirsch or rum if desired.

COCONUT PUDDING   *8 servings*

¾ cup butter
¾ cup sugar
1 whole egg plus 3 egg yolks, beaten
3 cups finely grated fresh coconut
1¼ cups light cream or undiluted evaporated milk

1½ teaspoons vanilla extract
Meringue Pie Topping (page 565)
1½ tablespoons fresh lime juice

1. Preheat oven to moderate (350° F.).

2. Cream together the butter and sugar until fluffy. Add the eggs, coconut, cream and vanilla and mix well.

3. Butter eight individual six-ounce baking dishes and fill three-quarters full with pudding mixture. Set in a pan of hot water. Bake for about forty-five minutes, until firm.

4. Remove and cool. Fold the lime juice into the meringue pie topping and spoon the meringue over the pudding. Return to the oven for twelve to fifteen minutes to brown the meringue.

BREAD-AND-BUTTER PUDDING   *4 to 6 servings*

⅓ cup raisins
6 to 8 very thin slices of bread, buttered
1 tablespoon chopped candied peel (optional)

⅔ cup sugar
3 cups milk
1 cup light cream
1 long curl of lemon peel
4 eggs, lightly beaten

1. Preheat oven to moderate (325° F.).

2. Plump the raisins by covering with boiling water for two or three minutes. Drain.

3. Remove the crusts from the bread slices and cut each slice lengthwise into three pieces.

4. Place a layer of bread strips, buttered side up, in the bottom of a greased shallow baking dish (1½ quarts). Sprinkle with one third of the raisins, one teaspoon of candied peel and one tablespoon of sugar.

5. Repeat with another layer of bread, raisins, candied peel and sugar until the dish is half full and there are about three layers.

6. Heat the milk, cream, lemon peel and remaining sugar to boiling. Pour onto the eggs, stirring.

7. Strain the egg mixture down the side of the dish, not over the bread. Allow to stand for thirty to forty-five minutes before baking, if time permits.

8. Set the baking dish in a deep pan and pour simmering water around it. Bake for one hour, or until the custard is set and the top browned and crusty. Remove the pudding from the water bath. Serve warm or cold.

COFFEE BREAD-AND-BUTTER PUDDING   *8 servings*

1 cup strong coffee
1 cup light cream
2 cups milk
6 thin slices of raisin bread
  Soft butter or margarine

2 eggs
½ cup sugar
½ teaspoon salt
1 teaspoon vanilla extract
¼ teaspoon grated nutmeg

1. Preheat oven to moderate (325° F.).

2. Combine the coffee, cream and milk; bring to scalding point.

3. Spread bread slices lightly with butter or margarine; do not trim off crusts. Cut into half-inch cubes and add to coffee mixture.

4. Beat eggs slightly; add sugar and salt; mix well. Add bread mixture and vanilla.

5. Pour into a one-and-one-half-quart casserole. Sprinkle with the nutmeg.

6. Set the casserole in a pan of warm water. Bake for one hour and fifteen minutes, or until a knife inserted near rim of casserole comes out clean. Chill. Serve with plain or whipped cream.

STEAMED FIG SOUFFLÉ PUDDING   *8 servings*

4 slices of white bread, crusts removed
1 cup milk
½ cup soft butter
8 eggs, separated
¾ cup sugar
¾ cup very finely ground almonds
6 ounces figs, chopped
1 teaspoon vanilla extract
Custard Sauce (page 688)

1. Tear the bread into pieces and drop the pieces into a small saucepan. Add the milk and simmer until mushy. Remove from the heat and add the butter. Cool.

2. Beat the egg yolks until very pale and thick. Gradually beat in the sugar. Fold bread mixture into eggs. Stir in the nuts, figs and vanilla. Fold in the stiffly beaten egg whites.

3. Pour into a buttered and floured three-quart pudding basin. Cover with greased wax paper, then tightly with aluminum foil. Set on a rack in a deep kettle with boiling water extending two thirds of the way up the basin.

4. Steam for one hour and fifteen minutes. Serve immediately; the pudding will shrink far and fast. Serve with custard sauce.

FLAMRI DE SEMOULE   *4 or 5 servings*

½ cup orange juice
½ cup water
3 tablespoons quick-cooking farina
¼ cup sugar
2 tablespoons lemon juice
2 tablespoons dry sherry
1 teaspoon grated orange rind
2 egg whites

1. Heat the orange juice and water to boiling. Stir in the farina and cook, stirring, for two to four minutes.

2. Stir in the sugar, lemon juice, sherry and orange rind. Cool to room temperature.

3. Beat the egg whites until stiff but not dry. Fold into the farina mixture. Pour into four or five oiled individual molds. Chill for at least one hour.

4. Unmold and serve alone or with fresh orange segments or a purée of fresh fruit.

COUSCOUS WITH FRUITS AND NUTS   *10 or more servings*

1 cup seedless grapes
½ cup honey
1 tablespoon orange-flower water
¾ cup raisins
Rind of 1 lemon
Sugar
4 cups buttered steamed couscous (see below)

2 oranges, peeled and cut into sections
½ cup untoasted almonds or walnuts
Candied violets and candied mimosa for garnish

1. Combine the grapes, honey and orange-flower water and set aside.

2. Cover the raisins with warm water and add the lemon rind and one-quarter cup sugar. Set aside.

3. Pile the cold buttered couscous in the center of a round serving tray. Sprinkle lightly with sugar. Arrange over it the honeyed grapes, the drained raisins, orange sections, almonds and candied flowers. Serve at room temperature.

COUSCOUS: *About 6 cups*

2 cups cracked wheat (couscous)
½ cup water

¼ cup butter

1. Spread the wheat grains on a tray and sprinkle with the water. Mix lightly with the fingers to moisten all the grains.

2. Drop grains lightly into a muslin-covered colander or into the top of a steamer. Do not pack solidly. Cover tightly and steam over boiling water for twenty minutes.

3. Stir the grains lightly, breaking up the lumps. Cover and steam for twenty minutes longer. Stir the butter into the grains until it is all absorbed.

INDIAN PUDDING   *8 to 10 servings*

1 cup yellow cornmeal
4 cups milk, heated but not boiling
2 eggs, beaten
3 ounces suet, finely minced
½ cup sugar
⅔ cup molasses

¾ teaspoon salt
¼ teaspoon ground cinnamon
¼ teaspoon ground cloves
¼ teaspoon ground ginger
⅛ teaspoon ground allspice
⅛ teaspoon ground nutmeg

1. Preheat oven to moderate (325° F.). Butter an eight-inch-square baking dish.

2. Gradually stir the cornmeal into the milk. Stir vigorously until mixture thickens. Cool slightly. Add to the beaten eggs. Add remaining ingredients and mix well.

3. Pour the mixture into the prepared baking dish. Bake for two hours. Serve hot, with vanilla ice cream.

DESSERT RICE   *6 servings*

¾ cup uncooked white rice	1 teaspoon salt
2 cups hot milk	⅓ cup sugar
2 tablespoons butter	1½ teaspoons vanilla extract

1. Place the rice, hot milk, butter and salt in a saucepan. Cover and cook over low heat for thirty minutes, or until rice is tender. To insure uniformity in cooking, lift the rice with a fork from the bottom of the pan two or three times during cooking.

2. Remove rice from heat. Add the sugar and vanilla and mix thoroughly. Chill before using with desserts such as Pears Carmelite.

COCONUT RICE   *4 servings*

1 cup uncooked long-grain rice	1 teaspoon salt
2 cups Coconut Cream (page 491)	

Combine all the ingredients in a large heavy pan. Cover and bring to a boil. Simmer for twelve to fifteen minutes, or until the rice is tender and the liquid absorbed.

LEMON RICE   *6 to 8 servings*

3 cups milk	¾ teaspoon salt
½ cup uncooked rice	4 egg yolks, lightly beaten
½ cup sugar	4 egg whites
Grated rind of ½ lemon	2 tablespoons confectioners' sugar
2 tablespoons lemon juice	

1. Place the milk and rice in the top part of a double boiler. Cook over hot water for about thirty minutes, until the rice is soft.

2. Preheat oven to hot (425° F.).

3. Add the sugar, lemon rind, one and one-half tablespoons of the lemon juice, the salt and egg yolks to the rice mixture. Cook, stirring gently, until thickened. Spoon into a well-buttered baking dish. Cool.

4. Beat the egg whites until soft peaks form. Beat in the confectioners' sugar and remaining lemon juice. Spoon over the pudding and bake for about five minutes, just long enough to brown the meringue.

APRICOT RICE PUDDING   *6 servings*

1 cup heavy cream	2 cups cold cooked rice
½ cup sugar	⅓ cup slivered blanched almonds
½ teaspoon vanilla extract	1 tablespoon lemon juice
1 cup drained cooked dried apricots	

1. Combine the cream, sugar and vanilla; chill. Beat until stiff.

2. Cut the apricots into small pieces. Fold into the whipped cream together with rice, almonds and lemon juice. Chill well before serving.

RICE PUDDING   *8 servings*

1⅔ cups uncooked rice
4 cups milk, scalded
½ teaspoon salt
1 tablespoon butter
1 cup sugar
3 tablespoons hot water

¼ cup orange juice
¼ cup lemon juice
2 tablespoons rum
1 cup strawberry or apricot preserves
4 egg whites

1. Place the rice, milk and salt in a pan. Bring to a boil, cover, and simmer slowly for fifteen to twenty minutes, until rice is tender.

2. Place the butter and three-quarters cup of the sugar in a small heavy skillet. Heat slowly, stirring, until mixture is pale amber.

3. Add the hot water slowly, while stirring. Stir in the orange and lemon juices, bring to a boil, and add to cooked rice mixture. Simmer for two minutes.

4. Remove from the heat and add the rum. Cool slightly.

5. Divide rice mixture into three parts. Spread one part in the bottom of a buttered baking dish (8 × 8 × 2 inches). Spread half of the preserves over rice. Repeat with second part of rice and remaining preserves. Top with remaining rice.

6. Preheat oven to moderate (350° F.).

7. Beat the egg whites until frothy; gradually beat in remaining sugar until stiff and shiny. Spread over the top layer of rice.

8. Bake for about fifteen minutes, until lightly browned. Serve with cream.

RICE MALTAISE   *8 servings*

½ cup uncooked rice
2¾ cups milk, scalded
4 eggs, separated
½ cup sugar

1 envelope unflavored gelatin
2 tablespoons orange juice
2 tablespoons orange liqueur
1 cup heavy cream, whipped

ORANGE FILLING:

1 cup sugar
¼ cup water
½ cup orange juice
1 tablespoon grated orange rind

2 tablespoons orange liqueur (optional)
5 seedless oranges, peeled and cut into thin slices

1. Cook the rice in boiling water for five minutes; drain. Place in the top part of a double boiler with two cups of the milk. Cook over boiling water, stirring occasionally, for about thirty-five minutes, or until the rice is tender. Cool.

2. Beat the egg yolks with the sugar and gradually beat in the remaining milk. Heat, stirring, until the mixture thickens but do not allow it to boil.

3. Soften the gelatin in the orange juice and add to the hot custard. Stir to dissolve. Cool.

4. Mix together the rice, cooled custard and orange liqueur. Fold in the stiffly beaten egg whites and the whipped cream. Pour into a lightly oiled six-cup ring mold. Chill.

5. For the filling, combine the sugar, water, orange juice and grated rind in a small pan. Bring to a boil, stirring to dissolve the sugar. Cool, add the liqueur and orange slices, and chill.

6. Unmold the rice pudding. Spoon the orange filling into the center.

APPLE-OATMEAL CRISP   *6 servings*

4 cups sliced tart cooking apples
1 tablespoon lemon juice
2 to 4 tablespoons sugar, depending on the tartness of the apples
⅓ cup all-purpose flour
1 cup rolled oats, either old-fashioned or quick-cooking

½ cup brown sugar
½ teaspoon salt
1 teaspoon ground cinnamon
⅓ cup melted butter

1. Preheat oven to moderate (375° F.).

2. Place the apples in a greased shallow baking dish. Sprinkle with the lemon juice and sugar.

3. Combine the remaining ingredients and sprinkle over the apples. Bake for about thirty minutes, or until apples are tender. Serve hot or warm, with whipped cream.

BANANA PUDDING, ITALIAN STYLE   *4 servings*

½ cup mashed ripe bananas
1 teaspoon lemon juice
1 pound ricotta cheese, strained through a fine sieve
1 cup sifted confectioners' sugar
1 tablespoon milk or orange juice

1 tablespoon almond extract
1 ounce (1 square) unsweetened chocolate, grated
6 ladyfingers or macaroons, finely crumbled

1. Place the bananas, lemon juice, ricotta, confectioners' sugar, milk and almond extract in a bowl. Mix together until fluffy, using medium speed on an electric mixer or a rotary beater. Add the chocolate and stir until well blended.

2. Sprinkle the crumbs in the bottom of a one-and-one-half-quart mold. Pour the banana mixture over the crumbs, place in the refrigerator, and chill until firm.

BLUEBERRY BETTY   *6 servings*

1 quart fresh blueberries	1 cup sugar
1 tablespoon lemon juice	½ cup butter
¼ teaspoon ground cinnamon	1 quart vanilla ice cream
1 cup sifted all-purpose flour	

1. Preheat oven to moderate (375° F.).
2. Wash the berries and drain them in a colander. Place the berries in a one-and-one-half-quart casserole. Sprinkle with the lemon juice and cinnamon.
3. Sift flour and sugar together. With a pastry blender chop in the butter until it is crumbly. Sprinkle the mixture over the berries. Bake for forty-five minutes. Serve with ice cream.

CHERRY-WALNUT PUDDING   *9 servings*

2 cups (one 1-pound can) pitted red sour cherries packed in water	1⅓ cups sifted all-purpose flour
¼ cup shortening	2 teaspoons baking powder
½ teaspoon vanilla extract	½ teaspoon salt
¼ teaspoon almond extract	½ cup milk
¾ cup sugar	½ cup chopped walnuts
1 egg	Cherry Sauce (page 683)

1. Preheat oven to moderate (350° F.). Grease a glass ovenware pan (8 × 8 × 2 inches).
2. Drain the cherries and discard the water or reserve for another use.
3. Thoroughly cream together the shortening, vanilla, almond extract and sugar. Add the egg and beat well.
4. Sift together the flour, baking powder and salt. Add the creamed mixture alternately with the milk, beating until smooth after each addition. Fold in the cherries and walnuts.
5. Pour into the prepared pan. Bake for forty-five to fifty minutes. Cut into squares and serve warm with hot cherry sauce.

GRAND MARNIER PUDDING   *6 to 8 servings*

½ cup butter	1½ cups milk, scalded
½ cup sugar	5 eggs, separated
¾ cup sifted cake flour	½ cup Grand Marnier

1. Preheat oven to moderate (325° F.). Butter a five-cup soufflé dish or casserole.

2. Melt the butter, add the sugar and flour, and cook, stirring with a whisk, until well blended. Add the milk, stirring vigorously, and cook, continuing to stir, until the mixture boils and is very thick.

3. Beat the egg yolks, add the Grand Marnier, and mix. Add the hot paste to the egg yolks, about one quarter at a time, and beat until smooth after each addition. Whip the egg whites until stiff and fold into the pudding.

4. Turn into the prepared baking dish. Bake for about sixty minutes, or until lightly browned. Unmold and serve with a custard sauce flavored with Grand Marnier.

LEMON PUDDING   *4 to 6 servings*

4 eggs, separated
1 cup sugar

⅓ cup lemon juice
2 cups graham-cracker crumbs

1. Beat the egg yolks until light and lemon-colored. Add half of the sugar and beat until well mixed. Add the lemon juice. Cook in the top part of a double boiler over boiling water until thick and smooth, stirring constantly. When the custard is thick, remove from the hot water.

2. Beat the egg whites until stiff, adding the remaining sugar gradually. Fold the beaten egg whites into the hot custard. Pile in a serving dish, making alternate layers of pudding and cracker crumbs. Chill and serve.

LEMON-ORANGE PUDDING   *4 to 6 servings*

½ cup butter
1 cup sugar
4 eggs
2 cups sifted all-purpose flour
2 teaspoons baking powder

Pinch of salt
1½ tablespoons grated lemon rind
½ cup orange juice
Orange slices for garnish

1. Cream the butter and sugar until light and fluffy. Beat in the eggs, one at a time.

2. Sift the flour, baking powder and salt together. Fold the dry ingredients into the batter, a little at a time, along with the lemon rind and alternately with the orange juice.

3. Pour into a buttered one-quart pudding mold. Cover tightly with greased wax paper and then with aluminum foil. Set on a rack in a deep kettle with boiling water two thirds of the way up the mold.

4. Cover the kettle and steam for two and one-half to three hours, replenishing boiling water as necessary. Unmold and garnish with orange slices. Serve with Sabayon Sauce (page 689), Sauternes Custard Sauce (page 689), or Lemon-Nutmeg Sauce (page 688).

LEMON CUSTARD PUDDING   *6 servings*

1½ cups sugar
½ cup sifted all-purpose flour
½ teaspoon baking powder
¼ teaspoon salt
3 eggs, separated

2 teaspoons grated lemon rind
¼ cup lemon juice
2 tablespoons melted butter
1½ cups milk

1. Preheat oven to moderate (350° F.). Butter a two-quart baking dish.
2. Sift together one cup of the sugar, the flour, baking powder and salt. Set aside.
3. Beat the egg whites until stiff, beating in the remaining half cup of sugar gradually. Set aside.
4. Beat the egg yolks until light. Add the lemon rind and juice, butter and milk. Stir into the reserved flour mixture. Beat until smooth. Gently fold in the beaten whites until no flecks show.
5. Pour the mixture into the prepared dish. Set the dish in one-half inch of hot water in a larger pan.
6. Bake for forty-five minutes. Chill for at least one hour. The top of the pudding will be cakelike and the soft lemon custard on the bottom is served as the sauce. If desired, serve with unsweetened whipped cream.

NUT PUDDING BAHIANA   *8 servings*

1 cup fine dry bread crumbs
2 tablespoons butter
2 cups milk, scalded
2 eggs, lightly beaten

6 tablespoons sugar
½ cup ground toasted Brazil nuts
½ teaspoon grated lemon rind
   Apricot Sauce (page 683)

1. Preheat oven to moderate (325° F.).
2. Add the bread crumbs and butter to the hot milk. Cool. Add the beaten eggs to the milk mixture along with the remaining ingredients except sauce.
3. Turn into eight buttered half-cup molds. Set in a shallow baking pan. Pour in boiling water to half the depth of the molds.
4. Bake the puddings for one hour. Cool for five minutes, then unmold. Serve hot or cold, topped with apricot sauce.

PUERTO RICAN PUDDING   *8 servings*

1 cup seedless raisins
¾ cup dry red wine or rum
1½ cups fine dry bread crumbs
1 cup sugar
½ teaspoon salt
2 teaspoons ground cinnamon

½ teaspoon ground cloves
3 large eggs, beaten
¼ cup butter, melted
1 cup milk
1 cup toasted blanched almonds, slivered

1. Soak the raisins in the wine or rum at least overnight, but three to four days is preferable.

2. Preheat oven to moderate (350° F.).

3. Combine the bread crumbs, sugar, salt, cinnamon and cloves. Add the eggs, butter and milk. Mix. Add the almonds and the raisins and liquid in which they were soaked. Turn into a one-quart casserole. Set in a pan of hot water.

4. Bake for one and one-half hours. Serve hot with Clove Whipped Cream (page 683).

QUEEN OF PUDDINGS   *6 servings*

2½ cups soft fresh bread crumbs	2 tablespoons butter
2½ cups hot milk	3 eggs, separated
6 tablespoons sugar	1 teaspoon vanilla extract
Grated rind of 1 lemon	3 tablespoons strawberry preserves

1. Preheat oven to moderate (325° F.).

2. Place the bread crumbs in a bowl. Combine the milk, four tablespoons of the sugar, the lemon rind and butter and pour over the bread crumbs. Stir.

3. Beat the egg yolks lightly, add a little of the hot bread mixture to the egg yolks, return to the bowl, and mix well. Add the vanilla. Pour into a well-greased one-and-one-half-quart casserole.

4. Bake for thirty minutes, or until the pudding is set. Remove from the oven and spread with the preserves.

5. Beat the egg whites until frothy. Gradually add the remaining sugar while continuing to beat until stiff. Spoon the meringue over the preserves. Bake for fifteen minutes longer, or until the meringue is lightly browned. Serve immediately.

STEAMED SPONGE PUDDING   *6 to 8 servings*

½ cup butter	⅛ teaspoon salt
½ cup brown sugar	1 teaspoon ground ginger
½ cup granulated sugar	¾ cup milk
2 eggs	⅔ cup raisins or dried currants or
2¾ cups cake flour	mixed raisins and dried currants
3½ teaspoons baking powder	

1. Cream the butter and the sugars until smooth and fluffy. Beat in the eggs, one at a time.

2. Sift together the flour, baking powder, salt and ginger. Add all but two tablespoons of the dry ingredients alternately with the milk. Mix gently. Mix the remaining dry ingredients with the dried fruit and fold into the

batter. Pour the batter into a well-greased one-and-one-half-quart pudding basin. Cover tightly with aluminum foil.

3. Set on a rack in a pan of boiling water with the water extending two thirds of the way up the sides of the mold. Steam for one and one-half hours, replenishing the water with more boiling water as needed.

4. Unmold the pudding onto a warm plate. Serve with Custard Sauce (page 688) or hot Jam Sauce (page 687).

VARIATIONS:

Omit the ginger, raisins and dried currants. Add one teaspoon vanilla extract to the batter and place three tablespoons of marmalade or preserves in the bottom of the greased mold before adding the batter.

Replace the dried currants and raisins by chopped pitted dates or figs.

Omit the raisins, dried currants and ginger. Add one teaspoon vanilla extract to the batter and two tablespoons cocoa to the dry ingredients. Serve with a sauce flavored with chocolate.

ELIZABETH BORTON DE TREVIÑO'S BEST PUDDING
6 to 10 servings

1 cup dark rum or bourbon
1 cup mixed candied fruit
1 cup sugar
1 cup water
⅓ cup corn syrup

4 cups mashed sweet potatoes or yams, canned or freshly cooked
Grated nutmeg and whipped cream

1. Combine one-half cup of the rum and the candied fruit and let stand for one or two hours.

2. Combine the sugar, water and corn syrup and simmer for five minutes. Whip the sweet potatoes and beat in the syrup and candied fruit. Add the remaining rum.

3. Transfer the mixture to a glass dish. Let it stand in the refrigerator for two days before serving. Just before serving, sprinkle with nutmeg and garnish with whipped cream.

APPLE SOUFFLÉ WITH LEMON-NUTMEG SAUCE   *6 servings*

3 eggs, separated
½ cup sugar
1 teaspoon vanilla extract
⅛ teaspoon almond extract
¼ cup butter
¼ cup all-purpose flour

1 cup milk
1 cup shredded raw apples
1 tablespoon lemon juice
½ cup cookie or cake crumbs
Lemon-Nutmeg Sauce (page 688)

1. Preheat oven to moderate (325° F.).

2. Beat the egg yolks until thick and lemon-colored. Stir in one-quarter cup of the sugar and the vanilla and almond extracts. Set aside.

3. Melt the butter in a saucepan. Stir in the flour and mix until smooth. Add the milk and cook over low heat, stirring constantly, until thick. Gradually stir in the egg-yolk mixture.

4. Combine the shredded apples with the lemon juice and cookie crumbs and fold into the egg-yolk mixture.

5. Beat the egg whites until soft peaks are formed. Gradually add the remaining sugar and continue beating until stiff. Gently fold the meringue into the apple mixture. Turn into an ungreased one-and-one-half-quart casserole or baking dish. Set in a pan of hot water and bake for about one hour, until done. Serve at once with lemon-nutmeg sauce.

CHOCOLATE SOUFFLÉ   *6 servings*

3 ounces (3 squares) unsweetened chocolate	¾ cup hot milk
	⅓ cup sugar
3 tablespoons cold coffee	Dash of salt
3 tablespoons butter	4 egg yolks, lightly beaten
3 tablespoons all-purpose flour	5 egg whites, stiffly beaten

1. Melt the chocolate with the coffee in the top part of a double boiler over hot water.

2. Melt the butter in a saucepan over low heat. Blend in the flour. Gradually add the hot milk, sugar and salt. Cook, stirring constantly, for about five minutes, until the mixture is smooth and thickened.

3. Blend in the chocolate-coffee mixture and the beaten egg yolks. Cool.

4. Fold in the stiffly beaten egg whites.

5. Butter six individual soufflé dishes and sprinkle with sugar; or butter and sugar a one-quart soufflé dish. Turn the mixture into the soufflé dishes, filling them two-thirds full.

6. Bake the individual soufflés in a preheated moderate oven (350° F.) for ten to fifteen minutes. Bake the one-quart soufflé at 375° F. for thirty to forty-five minutes.

Note: If desired, tie a strip of buttered wax paper around each soufflé dish before baking. The paper should extend two inches above the top of the dish. This encourages a high-rising soufflé.

LEMON SOUFFLÉ   *6 servings*

3 tablespoons all-purpose flour	¼ cup granulated sugar
2 tablespoons butter, melted	⅛ teaspoon salt
¾ cup milk	5 egg yolks, well beaten
¼ cup lemon juice	5 egg whites at room temperature
1½ teaspoons grated lemon rind	Confectioners' sugar

1. Preheat oven to moderate (350° F.).

2. Blend the flour and butter in a saucepan. Gradually stir in the milk. Cook, stirring constantly, until the mixture is thickened and smooth. Remove from heat.

3. Stir the lemon juice and rind, granulated sugar and salt into the beaten egg yolks. Blend this mixture into the hot milk mixture.

4. Tie a six-inch-wide strip of buttered wax paper around a well-greased seven-inch soufflé dish to form a collar. Dust dish and collar with granulated sugar.

5. Place the egg whites in a large mixing bowl and beat at highest speed until stiff but not dry. Gradually fold egg-yolk mixture into beaten egg whites. Pour the mixture into the prepared dish.

6. Bake for about forty minutes, or until golden brown. Remove collar at once and sprinkle soufflé with confectioners' sugar. Serve at once, with a custard sauce.

SOUFFLÉ ROTHSCHILD   *12 servings*

2 cups sifted all-purpose flour	1 piece of vanilla bean (1 inch)
1 cup sugar	½ cup butter
4 whole eggs	¾ cup finely cut candied fruit
8 egg yolks	2 tablespoons kirsch (optional)
4 cups milk	10 egg whites, stiffly beaten

1. Preheat oven to moderate (375° F.).

2. Combine the flour, sugar, the whole eggs and three of the egg yolks in the top part of a double boiler.

3. Bring the milk barely to a boil and pour it over the egg mixture, stirring rapidly.

4. Add the vanilla bean and stir with a wire whisk until the sauce is thickened and smooth. Add the butter to the sauce.

5. Stir in the five remaining egg yolks. Sprinkle the candied fruit with kirsch and fold it into the mixture. Discard the vanilla bean.

6. Mix half of the stiffly beaten egg whites into the soufflé mixture with a wire whisk. Fold the mixture into the remaining egg whites.

7. Butter two two-quart soufflé dishes generously and sprinkle the bottoms and sides with sugar. Divide the soufflé mixture between the dishes.

8. Bake the soufflés for thirty to thirty-five minutes, until they are well puffed and browned. Serve immediately, with sweetened whipped cream flavored with kirsch.

GRENADINE ICED SOUFFLÉ   *4 to 6 servings*

1 envelope unflavored gelatin
¼ cup cold water
4 eggs
½ cup sugar
¼ teaspoon salt

½ cup grenadine syrup
1 cup grated unblanched almonds
½ teaspoon almond extract
1 cup heavy cream

1. Sprinkle the gelatin over the cold water to soften.

2. Separate the eggs. Put egg yolks in the top part of a double boiler. Stir in the sugar and salt. Cook over gently boiling water, stirring constantly, until slightly thick and custardy.

3. Remove from heat. Stir in the softened gelatin, the grenadine, grated almonds and almond extract. Cool.

4. Beat egg whites until they stand in peaks. In a separate bowl, whip the cream. Pile egg whites and whipped cream on grenadine mixture. Fold gently until well blended.

5. Pour into a one-quart soufflé dish; the mixture will fill the dish to the brim. Refrigerate until firm.

. . . .

COOKIES

. . . .

ALMOND SQUARES   *16 squares*

½ cup sifted all-purpose flour
½ teaspoon salt
⅛ teaspoon baking soda
1 egg

1 cup light or dark brown sugar
½ teaspoon vanilla extract
1 cup blanched almonds

1. Preheat oven to moderate (325° F.).

2. Sift the flour, salt and baking soda.

3. Beat the egg until it is light and foamy. Add the brown sugar and vanilla and beat well. Stir in the flour mixture and then the almonds.

4. Grease a shallow pan (8 × 8 × 2 inches) and spread the mixture into it with a spatula. Bake for twenty-five to thirty minutes, or until top is firm with a crust. While warm cut into squares, about two inches each. Cool before taking from the pan.

ALMOND THINS   *About 6 dozen*

½ cup sweet butter
¾ cup sugar
1 egg, separated
1 cup sifted all-purpose flour

½ cup finely chopped blanched almonds
½ teaspoon ground cinnamon

1. Preheat oven to hot (400° F.).

2. Cream together the butter and one-half cup of the sugar until very light. Beat in the egg yolk.

3. Sift the flour gradually over the batter, mixing until all flour is incorporated. Using a wet knife or spatula, spread the dough on a greased and lightly floured cookie sheet (14 by 18 inches). Spread batter as thinly as possible.

4. Beat the egg white until stiff and spread it over the dough. Combine the almonds, cinnamon and remaining sugar and sprinkle the mixture over the meringue-topped dough.

5. Bake for ten to fifteen minutes, or until golden brown. Immediately cut the cake into one-and-one-half-inch diamond shapes. Cool.

FRUITED ALMOND COOKIES   *About 3 dozen*

3 eggs, lightly beaten
½ cup sugar
½ cup sifted all-purpose flour
½ teaspoon salt
½ teaspoon ground cinnamon
⅛ teaspoon ground cloves

1½ cups firmly packed finely ground blanched almonds
1 cup semisweet chocolate bits
½ cup finely chopped mixed candied fruits
½ teaspoon grated lemon rind

1. Preheat oven to moderate (350° F.).

2. Beat the eggs and sugar together until thick and pale.

3. Sift together the flour, salt, cinnamon and cloves. Fold into the egg mixture.

4. Stir in the ground almonds, chocolate bits, candied fruits and lemon rind.

5. Drop batter by teaspoons onto foil-lined cookie sheets. Bake for about twelve minutes, until firm and lightly browned. Remove cookies from foil immediately and allow to cool on a rack.

ALMOND GINGER COOKIES   *About 8 dozen*

1 cup vegetable shortening
1 cup sugar
½ cup molasses
1 tablespoon ground ginger
2 teaspoons ground cinnamon

2 teaspoons ground cloves
1 teaspoon baking soda
1 teaspoon salt
1 cup blanched almonds, chopped
3½ cups sifted enriched flour

1. Blend the shortening and sugar. Stir in the remaining ingredients.

2. Turn the dough onto a floured board and knead until smooth. Shape into thick rolls or oblongs, wrap in wax paper, and chill.

3. Preheat oven to moderate (350° F.).

4. Cut dough crosswise into one-quarter-inch slices. Place slices on a greased baking sheet and bake for eight to ten minutes.

COOKIES ANISETTE   *About 8 dozen*

¾ cup butter
1 cup light brown sugar
½ teaspoon crushed aniseeds
2 cups sifted all-purpose flour

1 teaspoon baking powder
⅛ teaspoon salt
1 egg, beaten
2 tablespoons milk

1. Preheat oven to hot (400° F.).

2. Cream the butter until fluffy. Gradually blend in the sugar and ani-seeds. Sift flour with baking powder and salt and add to the butter mixture alternately with a mixture of the egg and milk. Mix well.

3. Fill a cookie press with the dough. Form cookies of any desired shapes on ungreased cookie sheets. Bake for eight to ten minutes.

ANISE FORK COOKIES   *7 dozen*

½ cup butter
1 teaspoon baking soda
1 teaspoon aniseeds
¼ teaspoon salt

1 cup sugar
1 large egg
2¼ cups sifted all-purpose flour
1 teaspoon cream of tartar

1. Preheat oven to moderate (350° F.).

2. Soften the butter. Add the soda, aniseeds and salt. Mix well and gradually blend in the sugar. Beat in the egg. Sift the flour with cream of tartar and stir it into the mixture.

3. Shape the mixture into half-inch balls and place them on ungreased cookie sheets, not too close together. Dip fork tines into flour and press the fork into each cookie in a crisscross pattern. Bake for eight minutes. Cool on wire racks. Store airtight.

BUTTER-SUGAR COOKIES   *About 4 dozen*

1 cup butter
⅔ cup sugar
1 egg
1 teaspoon vanilla extract

2½ cups sifted all-purpose flour
½ teaspoon salt
Royal Icing (page 679)

1. Cream together the butter and sugar. Beat in the egg. Add the vanilla. Combine the flour and salt, and stir into the creamed mixture.

2. Wrap the dough in aluminum foil and chill for three to four hours.

3. Preheat oven to moderate (350° F.).

4. Roll out the dough to one-eighth-inch thickness. Cut into shapes. Place on ungreased cookie sheets. Bake for eight to ten minutes, or until lightly browned.

5. Cool on a rack. When cool, frost with royal icing, using a decorator tube and bag or a spatula.

CRISP CITRON COOKIES   *About 3 dozen*

½ cup butter
1 cup plus 2 tablespoons sugar
2 eggs, separated
½ teaspoon vanilla extract
1 tablespoon milk

1½ cups sifted all-purpose flour
1 teaspoon baking powder
½ teaspoon salt
2 tablespoons finely chopped citron

1. Beat together the butter and one cup of the sugar until creamy. Beat in the egg yolks, vanilla and milk.

2. Sift together the flour, baking powder and salt and blend into the creamed mixture. Wrap in wax paper and chill for two to three hours.

3. Preheat oven to moderate (375° F.).

4. Roll out the dough on a lightly floured cloth or board until thin; cut into shapes with cookie cutters. Arrange the cookies on lightly greased baking sheets. Brush with the unbeaten egg whites. Sprinkle the remaining sugar on the cookies and top with the citron. Bake for about eight minutes, or until lightly browned. Cool on a rack.

SOFT CHOCOLATE COOKIES   *3 dozen*

1 cup shortening
2 cups firmly packed light brown sugar
1 teaspoon salt
1 teaspoon baking soda
¾ teaspoon ground cinnamon
½ teaspoon ground nutmeg

3 ounces (3 squares) unsweetened chocolate, melted
2 eggs
2½ cups sifted all-purpose flour
1 cup sour milk or buttermilk
1 cup chopped nuts
Nut halves for garnish

1. Cream the shortening with the brown sugar. Blend in the salt, baking soda, spices and melted chocolate. Beat in the eggs. Add the flour alternately with the milk; stir in the nuts. Chill the dough for at least one hour.

2. Preheat oven to moderate (375° F.).

3. Drop teaspoons of the dough onto lightly greased cookie sheets. Bake for fifteen to eighteen minutes.

4. Press a nut half into the center of each cookie immediately after removing from the oven. Cool on wire racks.

CHOCOLATE MERINGUES   *About 8 dozen*

6 ounces (1 cup) semisweet chocolate morsels
3 egg whites

1 cup sugar
⅓ cup graham-cracker crumbs
½ teaspoon vanilla extract

1. Preheat oven to moderate (350° F.).
2. Melt chocolate morsels over hot, not boiling, water. Remove from hot water and let cool for five minutes.
3. Beat the egg whites until stiff but not dry. Gradually add the sugar and beat until smooth and glossy. Fold in melted chocolate, the crumbs and vanilla.
4. Drop level teaspoons of the batter onto greased cookie sheets. Bake for fifteen minutes. Serve with custards and ice creams.

CHOCOLATE SQUARES   *20 squares*

½ cup shortening
½ cup sugar
1 teaspoon vanilla extract
½ cup dark corn syrup
2 eggs

2 ounces (2 squares) unsweetened chocolate, melted
½ cup chopped walnuts
½ cup sifted all-purpose flour
½ teaspoon salt

1. Preheat oven to moderate (325° F.).
2. Cream together the shortening, sugar and vanilla until light and fluffy. Add syrup and beat well. Add eggs, one at a time, beating well after each addition.
3. Add the chocolate and walnuts to the mixture, blending well. Fold in flour and salt.
4. Pour mixture into a greased nine-inch-square pan. Bake for forty minutes, or until done. Cut into squares while warm.

BLACK-PEPPER CHOCOLATE COOKIES   *3 dozen*

1½ teaspoons baking powder
¼ teaspoon salt
1½ cups sifted all-purpose flour
¾ cup cocoa
¾ cup butter, at room temperature
½ teaspoon freshly ground black pepper

¾ teaspoon ground cinnamon
¼ teaspoon ground cloves
1½ teaspoons vanilla extract
1 cup sugar
1 egg

1. Preheat oven to moderate (375° F.).

2. Sift together the baking powder, salt, flour and cocoa. Set aside. Mix together butter, spices and vanilla. Blend in sugar. Beat in egg. Gradually stir in flour mixture.

3. Shape dough into one-inch balls. Place one and one-half inches apart on greased cookie sheets Flatten to one-quarter-inch thickness. Bake for twelve minutes. Cool on a rack. Frost, if desired.

SOUR-CREAM CHOCOLATE COOKIES   *4 dozen*

2 ounces (2 squares) semisweet chocolate
⅔ cup butter
1⅓ cups sugar
1 egg
1 teaspoon vanilla extract

½ cup sour cream
2 cups sifted all-purpose flour
½ teaspoon baking powder
½ teaspoon baking soda
½ teaspoon salt
½ cup chopped pecans

1. Preheat oven to moderate (375° F.).

2. Melt the chocolate over hot water. Allow to cool.

3. In a two-quart mixing bowl, cream the butter. Add the sugar gradually, mixing until creamy. Add the egg and vanilla and beat until fluffy.

4. Stir in the cooled chocolate, then the sour cream. Sift together the flour, baking powder, baking soda and salt, and add. Blend well. Add the nuts.

5. Drop teaspoons of the mixture onto greased cookie sheets. Bake for twelve to fifteen minutes.

CRANBERRY BARS   *32 bars*

1½ cups coarsely ground cranberries
1¼ cups sugar
1 teaspoon salt
2 teaspoons vanilla extract
1 teaspoon baking soda
2 teaspoons grated lemon rind
1 cup butter

1 large egg
2½ cups sifted all-purpose flour
2½ cups rolled oats
3 tablespoons lemon juice
¼ cup water
Confectioners' Sugar Icing (page 679)

1. Preheat oven to moderate (375° F.). Grease and flour two nine-inch-square baking pans.

2. Combine berries and one-quarter cup sugar. Reserve.

3. Combine salt, vanilla, baking soda, lemon rind and butter. Blend in remaining sugar. Beat until fluffy. Beat in the egg.

4. Combine flour, oats, lemon juice and water. Add to butter mixture. Stir in the berries.

5. Spread batter in the prepared pans. Bake for forty minutes, or until brown. Cool in pans before cutting. Spread with icing while warm.

FLORENTINES   *4 dozen*

⅓ cup sifted all-purpose flour
  Dash of salt
¼ teaspoon baking soda
¼ cup butter
⅓ cup firmly packed brown sugar

2 tablespoons light corn syrup
1 egg, well beaten
½ teaspoon vanilla extract
½ cup flaked coconut
2 ounces dot chocolate

1. Preheat oven to moderate (350° F.).

2. Sift together the flour, salt and baking soda.

3. Cream the butter and add the sugar gradually, creaming until light and fluffy. Add the corn syrup and egg and beat well.

4. Stir in the flour, vanilla and coconut. Drop teaspoons of the dough about two inches apart onto a greased baking sheet. Spread into thin rounds.

5. Bake for ten minutes. Remove at once from baking sheet. Cool.

6. Heat the chocolate over hot water until partly melted. Remove from

A pastry brush is useful to coat cookies or pastries with butter or beaten egg. It is also handy for basting.

A pastry bag is wonderful for decorating cookies, cakes and pastries.

A rubber spatula is used for folding in egg whites, scraping mixing bowls, and the like.

hot water and stir rapidly until entirely melted. Dribble the melted chocolate in a lacy pattern over the cookies. Let stand for several hours, or until chocolate is firm.

DOUBLE FUDGE BROWNIES   *About 2 dozen*

½ cup plus 2 tablespoons butter
4 ounces (4 squares) unsweetened chocolate
2 cups sugar
4 eggs, lightly beaten

1 cup sifted all-purpose flour
1 teaspoon vanilla extract
1 cup coarsely chopped nuts
12 ounces (2 cups) semisweet chocolate bits

1. Preheat oven to moderate (325° F.).
2. Melt one-half cup of the butter and the unsweetened chocolate over hot water; cool slightly. Beat together the sugar and eggs until thick.
3. Blend the two mixtures. Stir in the flour, vanilla and nuts. Spread the batter in a greased nine-inch-square pan. Bake for forty minutes and cool in the pan.
4. Melt the chocolate bits with remaining butter over hot water and spread over the cooled brownies. Decorate with walnut halves, if desired.

HONEY-CHOCOLATE BARS   *About 50 bars*

2¾ cups sifted all-purpose flour
2 teaspoons ground cinnamon
1 teaspoon ground cloves
1 teaspoon cardamom seeds, crushed in a mortar
1 teaspoon baking soda
1 teaspoon baking powder
1¼ cups sugar
¾ cup honey

2 tablespoons water
2 ounces semisweet chocolate bits
1 cup chopped walnuts
½ cup chopped mixed candied fruits
2 eggs, beaten
¼ cup orange juice
Confectioners' sugar

1. Sift together the flour, cinnamon, cloves, cardamom, baking soda and baking powder. Set aside.
2. Bring the sugar, honey and water to a boil. Cool. Stir in the chocolate bits, walnuts, candied fruit, eggs and orange juice.
3. Blend in the flour mixture. Place dough in a lightly covered dish and store at room temperature for two or three days to ripen.
4. Preheat oven to moderate (325° F.).
5. Spread the dough in a greased pan (1 × 10 × 15 inches). Bake for thirty-five to forty minutes. Cool. Wrap in aluminum foil and store, for up to three weeks, at room temperature until needed. The flavor improves on storing.
6. When ready to use, dust with confectioners' sugar and cut into bars (1 × 3 inches).

CHEWY COCONUT BARS   *24 bars*

1 cup light brown sugar
¼ cup shortening
¼ cup butter
1 cup plus 2 tablespoons sifted all-purpose flour
2 eggs
½ cup light corn syrup

1 teaspoon vanilla extract
1 teaspoon baking powder
½ teaspoon salt
1 cup shredded coconut
1 cup coarsely chopped nuts (walnuts, almonds and/or pecans)

1. Preheat oven to moderate (350° F.).

2. Blend one-half cup of the sugar with the shortening and butter until smooth and fluffy. Stir in one cup of the flour.

3. Pat the mixture into the bottom of an ungreased pan (9 × 9 × 2 inches) and bake for ten minutes.

4. While the mixture bakes, beat the eggs well and blend with remaining sugar. Stir in the corn syrup and vanilla. Add remaining flour, the baking powder and salt; mix well.

5. Stir in the coconut and nuts and spread the mixture over the bottom layer. Return to the oven and bake for twenty-five minutes longer, or until the top is golden brown. Allow to cool in the pan. Cut into finger-length bars.

FYRSTEKAKA (royal cake)   *54 bars (1 x 2 inches)*

2¼ cups sifted all-purpose flour
2 teaspoons baking powder
¾ cup sugar
¾ cup butter

1 large egg yolk
2 tablespoons milk
Cardamom-Almond Filling (see below)

1. Preheat oven to slow (300° F.).

2. Sift together flour, baking powder and sugar. Add the butter and cut it in until the mixture has the consistency of crumbs.

3. Beat the egg yolk with the milk. Add to flour mixture and mix well. Press two thirds of the dough into a one-quarter-inch layer in a baking pan (13 × 9 × 2 inches). Spread with filling.

4. Roll remaining dough into a rectangle one-eighth inch thick. Cut with a pastry cutter into strips one-half inch wide. Place crisscross fashion over filling.

5. Bake for forty-five minutes, or until pastry is browned. Cool. Cut into bars.

CARDAMOM-ALMOND FILLING:

Put one and one-quarter cups unblanched almonds through a food chopper using the fine blade, or use an electric blender. Mix one and one-quarter cups sifted confectioners' sugar with three-quarters teaspoon ground cardamom, one-half teaspoon ground cinnamon, one large egg white and six tablespoons water. Blend well with the chopped almonds.

LEMON NUT WAFERS *About 5 dozen*

½ cup shortening
1 cup sugar
1 egg
1 tablespoon lemon juice
1 tablespoon grated lemon rind
2 cups sifted enriched flour
1 teaspoon baking powder
⅛ teaspoon salt
1 cup finely chopped nuts

1. Preheat oven to moderate (350° F.).
2. Blend the shortening and sugar. Beat in the egg, lemon juice and rind. Stir in dry ingredients and mix well. Stir in the nuts.
3. Shape the dough into rolls, wrap in wax paper, and chill.
4. Slice the dough crosswise thinly, place on greased baking sheets, and bake for twelve to fifteen minutes.

MACAROONS *About 30*

4 egg whites
Sugar
1 cup almond paste
Few drops of almond extract
15 blanched almonds, split

1. Preheat oven to hot (400° F.). Line a baking sheet with unglazed paper.
2. Beat the egg whites until they form soft peaks. Continue to beat while adding one-half cup sugar very slowly, until the mixture is very stiff.
3. Beat the almond paste while gradually adding the meringue. Add the almond extract.
4. Drop teaspoons of the batter onto the prepared baking sheet. Sprinkle with sugar. Top each cookie with a blanched almond half.
5. Bake for about fifteen minutes, until lightly browned. Remove from the paper and cool on a rack.

ITALIAN MACAROONS *About 30*

1 cup almond paste
1 cup sugar
3 egg whites
2 tablespoons sifted all-purpose flour
¼ cup finely chopped mixed candied fruits

1. Work the almond paste with the hands until pliable.
2. Gradually add the sugar and egg whites until well mixed. Add the flour and mix well. Add the fruits.

3. Line cookie sheets with greased aluminum foil. Drop small teaspoons of the mixture about two inches apart onto the foil. Cover lightly with wax paper and let stand in a cool place (not the refrigerator) overnight.

4. Preheat oven to slow (300° F.).

5. Bake the cookies for about twenty-five minutes. Store them, tightly covered, for at least twenty-four hours before serving.

SOFT MOLASSES DROP COOKIES   *About 3 dozen*

½ cup shortening
½ cup brown sugar
½ cup molasses
1 egg
1¾ cups sifted all-purpose flour
1 teaspoon ground cinnamon
1 teaspoon ground ginger
¼ teaspoon ground cloves

½ teaspoon salt
¼ teaspoon baking soda
1½ teaspoons baking powder
1 teaspoon vinegar
2 tablespoons water
¼ cup buttermilk
Chocolate Frosting (page 680)

1. Preheat oven to moderate (350° F.).

2. Beat shortening and sugar until light and fluffy. Beat in molasses, egg and three tablespoons of the flour.

3. Sift together remaining flour and other dry ingredients. Mix together the vinegar, water and buttermilk. Add alternately to the molasses mixture and beat batter until it is very smooth.

4. Drop teaspoons of the mixture onto greased cookie sheets. Flatten dough if desired. Bake for twelve to fifteen minutes. Cool. Top each cookie with a dime-sized round of chocolate frosting.

AUSTRIAN NUT-BUTTER COOKIES   *About 18*

1 cup sifted all-purpose flour
⅓ cup sugar
⅔ cup ground nuts
½ cup soft butter
Chocolate-Butter Filling (page 677)

Apricot preserves
Chocolate Frosting (page 680)
¼ cup slivered or chopped nuts

1. Combine the flour, sugar and ground nuts in a mixing bowl. Blend in the butter with a spoon or pastry blender to form a dough. Chill for one to two hours.

2. Preheat oven to moderate (375° F.).

3. Roll out the dough on a lightly floured pastry cloth or board to one-eighth-inch thickness. Cut into two-inch circles with a floured cutter. Transfer to an ungreased cookie sheet. Bake for seven to ten minutes. Cool on a rack.

4. When cool, sandwich two cookies together with the filling. Spread the top with a thin layer of preserves, coat with the frosting, and sprinkle with the nuts.

NUTMEG DATE BARS   *21 bars*

8 ounces pitted dried dates
1 cup pecans or walnuts
1 cup sifted confectioners' sugar
2 large eggs, beaten
½ teaspoon salt

1 tablespoon butter, melted
1 tablespoon fresh lemon juice
¼ cup all-purpose flour
¾ teaspoon ground nutmeg

1. Preheat oven to moderate (325° F.).
2. Put the dates and nuts through a food grinder using the medium blade. Add the sugar, eggs and salt and mix well. Add the melted butter, lemon juice, flour and nutmeg and mix thoroughly.
3. Spread the batter in a very thin layer in a greased nine-inch-square pan. Bake for thirty minutes.
4. Cool partially. Cut into bars. Roll the bars in additional confectioners' sugar.

NUTMEG HERMITS   *5 dozen*

4 cups sifted all-purpose flour
1 teaspoon baking soda
1½ teaspoons ground nutmeg
½ teaspoon salt
1 cup butter

2 cups soft brown sugar
4 eggs
¼ cup milk
2 cups seedless raisins
1 cup chopped pecans or walnuts

1. Preheat oven to moderate (375° F.).
2. Sift together the flour, baking soda, nutmeg and salt. Cream the butter and brown sugar. Beat the eggs into the butter mixture. Add the flour mixture alternately with the milk. Stir in the raisins and nuts.
3. Drop teaspoons of the batter onto lightly greased cookie sheets. Bake for twelve to fifteen minutes.

NUTMEG PRESSED COOKIES   *5 dozen*

1 teaspoon ground nutmeg
½ teaspoon salt
⅔ cup butter
1 cup sugar

1 large egg
2¾ cups sifted all-purpose flour
½ teaspoon baking powder
2 tablespoons milk

1. Preheat oven to hot (400° F.).
2. Add the nutmeg and salt to the butter. Mix well. Gradually blend in the sugar and beat in the egg.

3. Sift the flour with baking powder and add it to the nutmeg mixture along with the milk. Mix well.

4. Force the dough through a cookie press onto ungreased cookie sheets. Bake the cookies for eight to ten minutes. Cool on wire racks.

NUTMEG SAND TARTS   *7 dozen*

2 cups sifted all-purpose flour
1 cup plus 2 tablespoons sugar
¼ teaspoon ground nutmeg
⅔ cup butter

1 egg
1 tablespoon cold water
½ teaspoon ground cinnamon

1. Preheat oven to hot (400° F.).

2. Combine the flour, one cup sugar and the nutmeg. Cut in butter until mixture resembles coarse meal.

3. Beat egg lightly, mix with the water, and add to the butter mixture. The dough will be stiff, therefore it is best to use fingers for mixing it.

4. Drop the dough onto cookie sheets, one-half teaspoon at a time, two inches apart to allow room for spreading.

5. Flatten to a thickness of one-sixteenth inch with a glass covered with a damp cloth. Combine the two tablespoons sugar with the cinnamon. Sprinkle a little over each cookie.

6. Bake for six to seven minutes. Cool cookies on wire racks. Store in airtight containers.

OATMEAL THINS   *About 2 dozen*

½ cup sifted all-purpose flour
1½ cups rolled oats, either quick-
    cooking or old-fashioned
¼ cup superfine sugar

½ teaspoon baking soda
1 tablespoon maple syrup
½ cup butter

1. Preheat oven to moderate (375° F.).

2. Mix together the flour, oats, sugar and baking soda. Melt the butter with the syrup and add to the dry ingredients.

3. Place teaspoons of the batter two inches apart on greased cookie sheets. Bake for eight to ten minutes. Let stand for one or two minutes before removing to racks to finish cooling.

ORANGE BUTTER COOKIES   *About 4 dozen*

1 tablespoon grated orange rind
1 teaspoon grated lemon rind
1 cup butter, at room temperature
¼ teaspoon salt

1 cup sugar
1 large egg
¼ cup fresh orange juice
2 cups sifted all-purpose flour

1. Preheat oven to moderate (375° F.).

2. Blend the orange and lemon rinds with the butter. Mix in salt and sugar. Beat in the egg and orange juice and stir in the flour. Mix well.

3. Chill the dough until it is stiff enough to handle. Shape the dough into one-inch balls. Place them two inches apart on ungreased cookie sheets. Bake for ten to twelve minutes, or until done. Cool on wire racks.

PEANUT-RAISIN CHEWS   *36 to 48 squares*

1⅛ cups sifted all-purpose flour
¾ teaspoon baking powder
⅛ teaspoon baking soda
⅜ teaspoon salt
3 eggs

1½ cups firmly packed light brown sugar
⅓ cup melted butter
½ cup crunchy peanut butter
¾ cup raisins

1. Preheat oven to moderate (350° F.).

2. Sift together the flour, baking powder, baking soda and salt.

3. Beat the eggs until thick. Gradually add sugar and beat well. Add the butter and peanut butter and mix well.

4. Fold in the flour mixture and the raisins. Pour batter into two greased disposable pans (6 × 6 × 2 inches). Bake for twenty-five to thirty minutes. Cool, then cut into squares. The chews may be frosted with Orange Frosting (page 681).

PECAN BARS   *16 bars*

1 cup plus 3 tablespoons sifted all-purpose flour
½ teaspoon baking powder
⅓ cup plus ¼ cup firmly packed dark brown sugar
¼ cup butter

2 eggs
¾ cup corn syrup
½ teaspoon salt
1 teaspoon vanilla extract
¾ cup chopped pecans

1. Preheat oven to moderate (350° F.).

2. Sift together one cup of the flour and the baking powder. Stir in one-third cup brown sugar. Cut in the butter, using a pastry blender or two knives, until well blended. The mixture should appear dry.

3. Pat evenly into a shallow pan (12 × 8 × 2 inches). Bake for ten minutes. Remove from oven.

4. Blend remaining one-quarter cup brown sugar with remaining three tablespoons flour. Beat the eggs and add to them the syrup, sugar-flour mixture, the salt and vanilla. Mix well.

5. Pour over the partially baked mixture. Sprinkle with chopped nuts. Return to the oven and bake for twenty-five to thirty minutes longer. Cut into bars while warm.

SPICED PECANETTES   *6 dozen*

¾ cup butter
¼ teaspoon ground cloves
½ teaspoon ground mace
½ teaspoon ground ginger
½ cup sugar

1 cup chopped pecans
2 cups sifted all-purpose flour
   Sifted confectioners' sugar   or
   Chocolate Glaze (page 682)

1. Preheat oven to moderate (325° F.).
2. Beat the butter with the spices until fluffy. Add the sugar gradually, mixing well after each addition. Stir in chopped pecans. Gradually add the flour.
3. Shape into one-inch balls. Place on ungreased cookie sheets. Bake for twenty to twenty-five minutes, or until lightly browned around the edges. Do not overbake.
4. Remove from cookie sheets while warm and roll in confectioners' sugar. Cool and roll in confectioners' sugar again. If desired, omit the confectioners' sugar and top cookies with chocolate glaze.

PEPPARKAKOR   *About 6 dozen*

½ cup butter
¾ cup sugar
1 egg
¾ cup molasses
2 teaspoons grated orange rind
3½ cups sifted all-purpose flour

1 teaspoon sugar
1½ teaspoons ground ginger
1½ teaspoons ground cinnamon
1 teaspoon ground cloves
¼ teaspoon ground cardamom
   Ornamental Frosting (page 679)

1. Cream the butter and sugar well. Beat in the egg and then the molasses and orange rind.
2. Sift together the dry ingredients and gradually stir into the creamed mixture. Mix to blend. Wrap in aluminum foil and chill for at least four hours, preferably overnight.
3. Preheat oven to moderate (375° F.).
4. Roll out the dough on a lightly floured board to one-quarter-inch to one-eighth-inch thickness. Cut into shapes with floured cutters and place on greased baking sheets. The cookies may be decorated at this point with sprinkles, raisins, cinnamon candies and silver dragées.
5. Bake for about ten minutes. Cool on wire racks and decorate with frosting.

CAKES

COTTAGE CHEESECAKE   *6 to 8 servings*

1½ cups graham-cracker crumbs
1½ cups sugar
¼ cup butter, melted
4 eggs
¼ cup sifted all-purpose flour
¼ teaspoon salt

2 tablespoons lemon juice
¼ teaspoon lemon rind
¾ cup heavy cream
3 cups cottage cheese, sieved or whipped in a blender

1. Preheat oven to moderate (325° F.).
2. Combine cracker crumbs and one-quarter cup of the sugar. Blend in the butter. Press mixture evenly onto bottom and sides of a greased eight-inch springform pan.
3. Beat eggs until thick and gradually beat in remaining sugar. Beat in flour and salt, then the lemon juice and rind, cream and cottage cheese. Blend well. Turn into lined pan.
4. Bake for one and one-quarter hours. Cool in oven for one hour, then cool on rack. Remove outer rim of pan and chill cake in refrigerator.

PINEAPPLE REFRIGERATOR CHEESECAKE   *6 servings*

2 tablespoons unflavored gelatin
½ cup cold water
3 eggs, separated
1 cup sugar
½ cup milk
Dash of salt
1½ teaspoons grated lemon rind

2 tablespoons lemon juice
4 cups cottage cheese, sieved or whipped in a blender
1 cup heavy cream, whipped
1 cup drained canned crushed pineapple
Crumb Crust (page 609)

1. Sprinkle the gelatin over the cold water and let stand for about five minutes, until softened.
2. In the top part of a double boiler, beat the egg yolks lightly. Gradually add the sugar while beating. Stir in the milk and salt.
3. Cook over boiling water, stirring constantly, until the custard is slightly thickened and coats a metal spoon.
4. Add the gelatin, stirring until it has dissolved. Cool slightly.
5. Add the lemon rind and juice to the cottage cheese and mix well. Add to the slightly cooled custard mixture, beating until thoroughly blended. Let cool until thickened and partially set, then beat until light and foamy. Fold in the stiffly beaten egg whites, the cream and pineapple.

6. Turn the mixture into the crumb-lined pie pan and sprinkle the top with the remaining crumbs. Chill until set.

CRUMB CRUST:

6 ounces zwieback
¼ cup sugar

½ cup butter, melted

1. Roll zwieback into fine crumbs. Combine with the sugar and butter.
2. Reserve one-third cup of the mixture for the top of the cake. Press the remainder evenly onto the bottom and sides of a greased nine-inch pie pan.

CRANBERRY CHEESECAKE   *8 to 10 servings*

1½ pounds cream cheese
5 large eggs
1 cup sugar
¼ teaspoon salt

1½ teaspoons vanilla extract
¼ teaspoon almond extract
Cranberry Topping (see below)

1. Preheat oven to moderate (325° F.). Butter a nine-inch springform pan.
2. Beat the cheese until smooth. Add the eggs, sugar, salt and extracts. Beat until thick and lemon-colored.
3. Pour the cheese mixture into the prepared pan. Bake for one and one-half hours.
4. Cool and chill cake in the pan. To serve, remove sides of pan, place cake on a plate, and spread with the topping.

CRANBERRY TOPPING:

1½ cups fresh cranberries
¼ cup fresh orange juice
¾ cup sugar

1½ teaspoons cornstarch
1 tablespoon water
½ teaspoon grated lemon rind

1. Mix the cranberries, orange juice and sugar in a saucepan. Cover and cook for six to eight minutes, until skins burst.
2. Blend the cornstarch and water and add to cranberries. Cook, stirring, for two minutes, or until mixture thickens.
3. Remove from heat and stir in lemon rind. Chill.

CRANBERRY CHEESE CUPCAKES   *12 cupcakes*

2 cups fine graham-cracker crumbs
¼ cup butter, melted
½ cup plus 3 tablespoons sugar
12 ounces cream cheese
3 large eggs

⅛ teaspoon salt
¼ teaspoon almond extract
1 teaspoon vanilla extract
¾ cup sour cream
Cranberry Topping (see above)

1. Blend graham-cracker crumbs with the butter and two tablespoons of sugar.

2. Line twelve cupcake pans with paper liners. Press the crumb mixture in the bottom and around sides of liners. Refrigerate for one hour.

3. Preheat oven to moderate (325° F.).

4. Beat the cream cheese until smooth and soft. Add the eggs, one-half cup sugar, the salt, almond extract and half of the vanilla. Turn the mixture into the prepared cupcake pans. Bake for thirty-five to forty minutes, or until firm in the center.

5. Remove the cupcakes from the oven and cool in pans on a rack for twenty minutes.

6. Combine the remaining sugar and vanilla and the sour cream. Spoon over the top of the cupcakes. Return the cakes to oven and bake for five minutes longer. Cool. Spoon cranberry topping over the cakes, chill, and serve.

CHEESECAKE DE LUXE   *8 servings*

CRUST:

1 cup sifted all-purpose flour	½ cup butter
¼ teaspoon sugar	1 egg yolk, lightly beaten
1 teaspoon grated lemon rind	¼ teaspoon vanilla extract

FILLING:

2½ pounds cream cheese	¼ teaspoon salt
¼ teaspoon vanilla extract	5 eggs
1 teaspoon grated lemon rind	2 egg yolks
1¾ cups sugar	¼ cup heavy cream
3 tablespoons all-purpose flour	

GLAZE:

2 pounds frozen whole strawberries, thawed	Cherry juice or water
	2 tablespoons cornstarch

1. Preheat oven to hot (400° F.).

2. To prepare the crust, combine flour, sugar and lemon rind. Cut in butter until mixture is crumbly. Add egg yolk and vanilla. Mix. Pat one third of the dough over the bottom of a nine-inch springform pan with sides removed. Bake for about six minutes, or until golden. Cool.

3. Butter the sides of the pan and attach to the bottom. Pat remaining dough around sides to a height of two inches. Increase oven heat to 475° F.

4. To prepare the filling, beat cream cheese until fluffy. Add vanilla and lemon rind.

5. Combine sugar, flour and salt. Gradually blend into cheese mixture. Beat in eggs and egg yolks, one at a time, and the cream. Beat well.

6. Pour mixture into the prepared pan. Bake for eight to ten minutes.

7. Reduce oven heat to very slow (200° F.). Bake for one and one-half hours longer, or until set. Turn off heat. Allow cake to remain in the oven with door ajar for thirty minutes.

8. Cool on a rack. Chill.

9. To prepare the glaze, drain strawberries very well, reserving any juice. Add cherry juice to it until liquid measures two cups. Reserve berries.

10. Slowly mix the cornstarch with the juice in a small pan. Gradually bring to a boil, stirring, and cook for two to three minutes, or until translucent and thick. Cool and chill. Fold in the strawberries. Spread atop chilled cake.

CHOCOLATE CHEESECAKE   *12 to 14 servings*

1½ cups zwieback crumbs
⅓ cup melted butter
¾ cup sugar
8 ounces sweet cooking chocolate
1¼ pounds cream cheese, softened
¼ teaspoon salt

1½ teaspoons vanilla extract
4 eggs, separated
2 cups heavy cream
½ cup sifted all-purpose flour
Shaved chocolate

1. Preheat oven to moderate (325° F.). Lightly grease bottom and sides of a nine-inch springform pan.

2. Mix the crumbs with the butter and two tablespoons of sugar. Sprinkle one-quarter cup of the crumb mixture around the sides of the pan. Press remaining mixture onto the bottom.

3. Melt the chocolate in the top part of a double boiler over hot water. Remove from heat and cool slightly.

4. Mix cream cheese with salt, vanilla and half of remaining sugar. Beat in the egg yolks. Fold in melted chocolate.

5. Beat egg whites until they hold stiff peaks. Beat in remaining sugar, one tablespoon at a time, until well blended and very stiff.

6. Beat one cup of cream until stiff and pour over the egg-white mixture. Add cream-cheese mixture. Sprinkle the flour on top and fold all the ingredients together gently.

7. Pour the mixture into the prepared pan. Bake for one hour and fifteen minutes. Do not open the oven door for one hour. Turn off heat at end of baking time and allow cake to remain in the oven with door closed for three to four hours. The cake may crack, but this is not detrimental to it.

8. Chill the cake. Remove the springform. Whip remaining cream until stiff and spread over top of cake. Decorate with chocolate shavings.

Like country-cured hams and vintage wines, fruitcakes improve with age, so several weeks before Christmas, or sooner, is the time for preparing and storing this specialty that is part and parcel of the holiday season.

The particles of fruit should be sprinkled lightly with flour because this gives better separation and distribution through the batter. It is frequently desirable to marinate the bits of fruit overnight in some wine or spirit such as cognac, sherry or rum.

Only a small amount of batter should be used in proportion to the fruits. It is recommended that the final mixing of the fruit and batter be done by hand, and filling the cake pans as well, to be sure the corners of the pans are filled.

SWEDISH FRUITCAKE   *10 to 12 servings*

1 cup dried currants or seedless raisins	1 cup butter
1½ cups mixed candied fruits	1 cup sugar
1¾ cups sifted all-purpose flour	3 eggs, separated
½ teaspoon baking powder	¼ teaspoon cream of tartar
	Fine dry bread crumbs

1. Preheat oven to slow (300° F.).

2. Rinse currants in cold water. Place in a saucepan, cover with water, and bring to a boil. Drain fruit and dry thoroughly in a towel.

3. Chop candied fruits or slice thin, except the cherries, which should be left whole. Mix fruits thoroughly with one cup of the flour until coated.

4. Sift remaining flour with the baking powder. Cream butter, gradually add sugar, and cream until light and fluffy. Add one egg yolk at a time, beating well after each addition. Stir in floured fruit mixture and sifted ingredients. Mix thoroughly.

5. Beat egg whites for a few minutes. Add cream of tartar and continue to beat until they form moist peaks. Fold egg whites very carefully into the batter.

6. Butter a tube pan (9 × 3½ inches) and sprinkle with fine dry bread crumbs until evenly coated, shaking off any excess. Pour cake batter into the pan. Bake for one and one-half to two hours, or until done.

7. Cool cake for a few minutes before removing from pan. Keep for at least two days before cutting.

Note: This cake will keep moist for many months if it is wrapped in aluminum foil and stored in the refrigerator.

FROZEN FRUITCAKE   *9 to 12 servings*

2 cups milk	2 cups finely crumbled macaroons
½ cup sugar	1 cup white raisins
¼ cup sifted all-purpose flour	1 cup chopped pecans
¼ teaspoon salt	½ cup chopped candied cherries
2 eggs, lightly beaten	1 cup heavy cream, whipped but not stiff
¼ cup light rum	

1. Butter a loaf pan (9 × 5 × 3 inches).

2. Scald one and one-half cups of the milk in the top part of a double boiler. Mix the sugar, flour and salt together and blend in the remaining half cup of milk. Pour the scalded milk onto the sugar mixture.

3. Return the mixture to the pan and heat, stirring, until it reaches boiling. Simmer for five minutes, stirring.

4. Pour some of the hot mixture over the eggs, stirring well. Return to the pan and cook for two to three minutes longer without boiling. Cool.

5. Add the rum, macaroon crumbs, raisins, pecans and cherries; mix well. Fold in the heavy cream carefully.

6. Pour the mixture into the prepared pan, cover with moisture- and vaporproof paper, and freeze for at least twenty-four hours.

7. To serve, turn out onto a serving platter and decorate with cherries and pecans. Allow to soften slightly and cut into three-quarter-inch slices.

Hogmanay, the Scottish New Year's Eve, is the stepping stone between the old and the new and the most important holiday of the year in Scotland, with traditions dating back to the Druidical ceremony of gathering in the mistletoe. The actual derivation of the word "Hogmanay" is lost in antiquity. In ancient times, Guisers, or Mummers, produced plays, danced and sang in return for sweets, shortbread, oatcakes, black bun and currant loaf. The famous New Year's Day parade in Philadelphia is a reminder of this tradition.

The Hogmanay bannock or oatcake, with a hole in the center, is flavored with caraway seeds and, as a reminder of its pagan origin, has notched edges symbolizing the rays of the sun. The black bun is a dark currant cake inside a pastry crust and is thought to be the original Twelfthcake associated with the twelve days of Christmas.

BLACK BUN   *20 servings*

PASTRY:

½ cup butter
3 cups sifted all-purpose flour
¼ teaspoon salt
½ teaspoon baking powder

FILLING:

1¼ pounds (4 cups) dried currants
12 ounces (2 cups) seedless raisins
1 cup almonds, blanched and chopped
1 cup chopped mixed candied fruits
⅔ cup light brown sugar
2 cups sifted all-purpose flour
¼ teaspoon salt
1½ teaspoons ground cinnamon
½ teaspoon ground ginger
¾ teaspoon ground allspice
½ teaspoon freshly ground black pepper
1½ teaspoons baking soda
1½ teaspoons cream of tartar
4 eggs, lightly beaten
¼ cup brandy or milk
1 tablespoon cold water

1. Preheat oven to slow (300° F.).

2. Prepare the pastry by rubbing the butter into the flour, salt and baking powder. Add enough water just to make a stiff dough.

3. Reserve one third of the dough for the top. Roll out the remainder of the dough into a twelve-inch circle. Line a greased deep cake pan (8 × 3 inches) on the bottom and sides with the pastry. A springform pan is ideal for this cake.

4. Mix together the currants, raisins, almonds, fruits and sugar. Combine the flour, salt, cinnamon, ginger, allspice, pepper, baking soda and cream of tartar and add to the fruit mixture.

5. Beat three of the eggs lightly and add with the brandy or milk. Using the hands, mix well until the mixture is all moistened.

6. Fill the lined pan with the cake mixture. Roll out the reserved dough into a nine-inch round and fit it in place over the cake loosely, but secure the edges by pinching together and decorating.

7. Brush the top of the bun with the remaining egg mixed with the water. Prick three or four holes down through the top pastry and to the bottom of the cake mixture.

8. Bake for two and one-half to three hours, or until a cake tester inserted into the cake comes out clean. Remove the cake from the pan and cool on a rack. Brandy may be poured through the holes drop by drop while it is cooling.

BRAZIL BANANA CAKE   *1 cake*

2¼ cups sifted cake flour
1¼ cups sugar
2¼ teaspoons baking powder
½ teaspoon baking soda
½ teaspoon salt
½ cup shortening

2 eggs
1½ cups mashed bananas (4 or 5 medium bananas)
½ cup ground toasted Brazil nuts
1 cup heavy cream, whipped
Toasted Brazil nut slices (see note)

1. Preheat oven to moderate (375° F.).

2. Sift together the flour, sugar, baking powder, baking soda and salt into a mixing bowl. Add the shortening, eggs and one-half cup of the mashed bananas. Mix in an electric mixer at medium speed for two minutes.

3. Add the remaining bananas and the ground Brazil nuts. Beat for one minute.

4. Grease two eight-inch cake pans and line them with wax paper. Turn the batter into the prepared pans. Bake for twenty-five minutes. Cool on a rack, remove from the pans, and finish cooling.

5. Spread whipped cream between the layers and on top of the cake. Decorate the edges with toasted Brazil nut slices.

Note: To slice Brazil nuts, cover the shelled nuts with cold water and bring slowly to a boil. Simmer for five minutes; drain. Slice the nuts lengthwise. To toast, spread the sliced nuts in a shallow pan and toast in a moderate oven (350° F.) for twelve minutes.

SHORTBREAD   *12 to 14 pieces*

½ cup superfine sugar
 3 cups sifted all-purpose flour

¼ teaspoon salt
 1 cup butter, at room temperature

1. Preheat oven to slow (300° F.).
2. Place the sugar, flour and salt on a board and gently mix together.
3. Squeeze the butter in the hands until it is pliable and then very slowly start to incorporate the flour mixture into the butter. Work thoroughly on the board to make sure that the mixture does not crumble. The process will take twenty to twenty-five minutes.
4. Shape the shortbread into an eight-inch round, using the bottom of a layer-cake pan as a guide. Place on an ungreased cookie sheet. Decorate the edge and mark into twelve to fourteen triangular sections.
5. Tie a band of wax paper one inch high, of triple thickness, around the outer edge of the shortbread and secure with a paper clip. Bake for one hour. The shortbread should be firm but very pale in color. Sprinkle immediately with a little sugar. Cool on a rack. Wrap in foil or place in a tin for at least two days before serving. Shortbread texture and flavor improve with storage.

ORANGE PECAN SHORTBREAD   *8 servings*

½ cup butter
⅓ cup sugar
 2 eggs, separated
 1 teaspoon vanilla extract
1¼ cups sifted all-purpose flour
 ¼ teaspoon baking soda

¼ teaspoon salt
 1 cup orange marmalade
½ cup chopped pecans
   Pecan halves for garnish
 1 tablespoon sugar

1. Preheat oven to moderate (350° F.).
2. Cream the butter and sugar until fluffy. Add the egg yolks and vanilla and beat well.
3. Sift together the flour, baking soda and salt. Stir into the creamed mixture. Press into the bottom and sides of a nine-inch pie pan.
4. Spread the marmalade on the shortbread to form a layer of filling. Sprinkle the chopped pecans over the marmalade.
5. Beat the egg whites until stiff but not dry. Spread over the nuts and marmalade. Arrange the pecan halves in an attractive design on top and sprinkle with the sugar. Bake for thirty minutes.

APPLE ORANGE NUT LOAF   *2 loaves*

2 large oranges
1 cup seedless raisins
2 cups applesauce
4 cups sifted all-purpose flour
4 teaspoons baking powder
4 teaspoons baking soda

2 cups sugar
1½ teaspoons salt
1½ cups chopped walnuts or pecans
2 eggs, lightly beaten
6 tablespoons melted butter

1. Preheat oven to moderate (350° F.).
2. Squeeze the oranges. Put the rind of the oranges and the raisins through the medium blade of a food chopper. Add the orange juice and ground orange rind and raisins to the applesauce.
3. Sift together the flour, baking powder, baking soda, sugar and salt. Add the applesauce mixture and the nuts. Mix thoroughly and add the eggs and melted butter.
4. Grease two loaf pans (9 × 5 × 3 inches) and pour in the batter. Bake for one hour and fifteen minutes. Remove the cakes from the pans and cool on a wire rack. Let stand overnight before cutting.

BRAZIL-NUT CAKE   *1 large cake*

1 cup butter
1 cup shortening
1½ cups sugar
1½ teaspoons salt
⅓ cup honey

10 eggs
2 cups crumbs from leftover white or chocolate cake
1¼ cups sifted cake flour
2 cups ground toasted Brazil nuts

1. Preheat oven to moderate (325° F.).
2. Cream together the butter and shortening. Gradually add the sugar and salt and beat until light and fluffy. Blend in the honey. Add the eggs, one at a time, beating well after each addition. Stir in the remaining ingredients.
3. Turn into a greased and floured three-quart ring mold. Bake for one hour and fifteen minutes. Cool for five minutes before removing from the pan.

BRAZIL-NUT TARTLETS   *6 servings*

¼ cup butter
¼ cup shortening
½ cup sugar
½ cup honey
3 eggs
¼ cup semisweet chocolate pieces, melted

2 tablespoons milk
½ cup sifted cake flour
¾ cup crumbs of white or chocolate cake
½ cup ground toasted Brazil nuts
Whipped cream and sliced toasted Brazil nuts

1. Preheat oven to moderate (350° F.).

2. Cream together the butter and shortening. Gradually add the sugar and continue creaming until light and fluffy. Blend in the honey.

3. Add the eggs, one at a time, beating after each addition. Blend in the melted chocolate and milk. Stir in the flour, cake crumbs and ground Brazil nuts.

4. Turn into six four-inch tart pans. Bake for forty minutes. Top with whipped cream and garnish with slices of toasted Brazil nuts.

CRANBERRY CAKE   *8 servings*

2 cups sifted all-purpose flour
1½ teaspoons baking powder
½ teaspoon salt
1½ cups coarsely chopped fresh cranberries
1⅓ cups sugar
½ teaspoon baking soda

1½ teaspoons vanilla extract
½ cup shortening
1 tablespoon grated orange rind
2 whole eggs
2 egg yolks
⅔ cup milk
Cranberry Frosting (page 681)

1. Preheat oven to moderate (375° F.). Grease two eight-inch layer-cake pans. Line the bottoms with wax paper and grease the paper.

2. Sift together the flour, baking powder and salt. Set aside. Blend the cranberries with one-third cup of the sugar. Set aside.

3. Add the baking soda and vanilla to the shortening. Cream well; gradually add remaining sugar and the grated rind. Beat in the whole eggs and egg yolks, one at a time. Add the flour mixture alternately with the milk. Stir in the cranberries.

4. Pour the batter into the prepared pans. Bake for thirty minutes, or until a food pick inserted into the center comes out clean. Cool in pans for ten minutes. Turn out on racks to finish cooling. Spread frosting between layers and over top and sides of cake.

BIRTHDAY BUTTER CAKE   *16 to 18 servings*

2 cups butter
2 cups very fine sugar
10 eggs
2 teaspoons vanilla extract

4 cups cake flour
1½ cups Orange Frosting (page 681)
Candies or chopped nuts

1. Preheat oven to slow (300° F.).

2. Beat the butter and sugar together until fluffy and creamy in texture with no granules of sugar left.

3. Add the eggs, one at a time, beating well after each addition. Beat in the vanilla.

4. Gradually fold in the flour. Pour the batter into a greased nine-inch tube pan or a greased baking pan (13 × 9 × 2⅝ inches) or two loaf pans (9 × 5 × 3 inches). Bake for one and one-quarter to one and one-half hours, or until a cake tester inserted comes out clean. Cool thoroughly.

5. Frost with orange frosting and top with the candies or nuts.

SESAME-SEED BUTTER CAKE   *1 cake*

1½ tablespoons butter
½ cup untoasted sesame seeds
 2 cups sifted all-purpose flour
½ teaspoon salt
 2 teaspoons baking powder
 1 cup sugar

1½ teaspoons vanilla extract
½ cup butter, softened
 2 large eggs
 1 cup milk
   Sesame-Seed Frosting (see below)

1. Preheat oven to moderate (350° F.).

2. Melt one and one-half tablespoons butter in a skillet. Add the sesame seeds. Stir and cook until lightly browned. Set one-quarter cup of the mixture aside to add to the cake batter. Reserve remaining seeds to top the frosting.

3. Sift together the flour, salt and baking powder and set aside. Gradually blend the sugar and vanilla with the softened one-half cup butter. Beat in the eggs. Mix the one-quarter cup toasted sesame seeds with the flour mixture and add alternately with the milk to the butter-sugar mixture. Beat the batter for thirty seconds.

4. Turn the batter into a lightly floured well-greased pan (9 × 9 × 2 inches). Bake for thirty-five minutes, or until a cake tester inserted into the center comes out clean. Cool in the pan for ten minutes. Turn out onto a wire rack to finish cooling. When cold, spread with sesame-seed frosting. Sprinkle top with reserved toasted sesame seeds. To serve, cut into squares.

SESAME-SEED FROSTING:

Heat two tablespoons butter until golden. Remove from the heat and blend in one and one-half cups confectioners' sugar alternately with about two teaspoons milk, adding as much milk as necessary to give the mixture a spreading consistency. Stir in one-half teaspoon vanilla extract and two tablespoons toasted sesame seeds.

CHOCOLATE CAKE   *10 to 12 servings*

½ cup shortening, at room temperature
1¾ cups cake flour
 2 teaspoons baking powder
¼ teaspoon baking soda
 1 teaspoon salt

1½ cups sugar
1¼ cups undiluted evaporated milk
 2 eggs
 1 teaspoon vanilla extract
 2 ounces (2 squares) unsweetened chocolate, melted

1. Preheat oven to moderate (350° F.). Grease a cake pan (13 × 9 × 2 inches) and line the bottom with wax paper.

2. Place the softened shortening in a bowl. Sift together the cake flour, baking powder, baking soda, salt and sugar. Add to shortening.

3. Add one cup of the evaporated milk and mix until the flour is just dampened. Beat in an electric mixer at medium speed for two minutes, or beat by hand for three hundred strokes.

4. Add the eggs, vanilla, melted chocolate and the remaining milk. Beat for one minute longer, or one hundred fifty strokes.

5. Pour the batter into the prepared pan. Bake for thirty-five to forty minutes, or until done. Cool in the pan for five minutes, then top with Coconut Topping (page 682), or turn out onto a rack to cool completely before frosting with Chocolate Frosting (page 680).

CHOCOLATE SKILLET CAKE   *6 servings*

½ cup cold water
½ cup cocoa
1½ cups sifted all-purpose flour
1 teaspoon baking soda
½ teaspoon salt
1¼ cups firmly packed brown sugar

½ cup shortening
3 eggs
½ cup buttermilk
1 teaspoon vanilla extract
4 thin milk-chocolate bars (1 ounce each)

1. Preheat oven to moderate (350° F.).

2. Gradually add the water to the cocoa, beating well after each addition.

3. Sift together the flour, baking soda, and salt. Add the sugar, shortening, eggs and half of the buttermilk. Beat for three minutes. Add the vanilla, remaining buttermilk and the cocoa mixture. Beat for two minutes.

4. Pour the mixture into a well-greased heavy ten-inch skillet. Top the batter with squares of candy bars.

5. Cover the skillet and bake for fifty to sixty minutes. Serve warm or cold, plain, or with whipped cream or ice cream.

COFFEE CREAM CAKE   *10 to 12 servings*

2 eggs
¼ teaspoon salt
1 cup sugar
1 teaspoon vanilla extract
½ cup milk

1 tablespoon butter
1 cup sifted all-purpose flour
1 teaspoon baking powder
Coffee Syrup (page 620)
2 cups heavy cream, whipped

1. Preheat oven to moderate (350° F.). Grease and lightly flour three eight-inch layer-cake pans.

2. Beat the eggs until light. Add the salt, sugar and vanilla. Heat the milk and butter to boiling. Beat into the egg mixture. Sift together the flour and baking powder and beat into the egg mixture.

3. Divide the batter equally among the three prepared pans. Bake for about twenty-five minutes, until a tester inserted into the center comes out clean.

4. Cool the layers and split them horizontally. Spread the cut side of five layers and the uncut surface of one layer with warm coffee syrup. Put the layers together with the whipped cream, using the glazed uncut layer on top. Spread the sides of the cake with whipped cream. Chill for several hours.

COFFEE SYRUP:

Stir one cup sugar and two-thirds cup strong coffee over low heat until the sugar dissolves. Bring to the boiling point and remove from the heat. Stir in one tablespoon rum.

ALICE PETERSEN'S DANISH CREAM CAKE   *1 cake*

1 cup heavy cream	1 cup sugar
2 eggs	2 teaspoons baking powder
¼ cup almond extract	¼ teaspoon salt
1½ cups sifted all-purpose flour	Almond Topping (see below)

1. Preheat oven to moderate (350° F.).

2. Whip the cream until it holds soft peaks. Add the eggs, one at a time, beating thoroughly after each addition. Stir in the almond extract.

3. Sift together the flour, sugar, baking powder and salt. Add this to the cream mixture, folding in until well blended. Pour the batter into a greased and floured eight-inch springform pan. Bake for forty-five minutes, or until lightly browned on top.

4. Spread the cake with almond topping and return it to the oven. Bake for exactly ten minutes longer.

ALMOND TOPPING: *Enough for one 8-inch cake*

2 tablespoons butter	1 tablespoon heavy cream
⅓ cup sugar	1 tablespoon all-purpose flour
¼ cup slivered blanched almonds	

In a small saucepan combine all the ingredients. Stir over low heat until well blended.

LEMON CAKE   *2 cakes*

1 cup butter	½ teaspoon baking soda
3 cups sugar	4 cups sifted all-purpose flour
5 egg yolks, beaten	1 cup milk
Grated rind and juice of 1 lemon	5 egg whites, stiffly beaten

1. Preheat oven to moderate (325° F.).

2. Cream the butter, adding the sugar gradually, until light and fluffy.

3. Add the remaining ingredients except the egg whites, and mix until well blended. Fold in the beaten egg whites. Divide the batter between two loaf pans (9 × 5 × 3 inches). Bake for one hour. Sprinkle with sifted confectioners' sugar and serve with ice cream.

MARBLE CAKE   *1 loaf*

3 cups sifted all-purpose flour	1 cup milk
3 teaspoons baking powder	½ cup unsulphured molasses
¾ teaspoon salt	1½ teaspoons ground cinnamon
¾ cup butter	½ teaspoon ground cloves
1½ cups sugar	¼ teaspoon ground ginger
3 large eggs	

1. Preheat oven to moderate (350° F.).

2. Sift together the flour, baking powder and salt. Set aside.

3. Cream the butter and sugar. Beat in the eggs, one at a time. Add the flour mixture alternately with the milk. Beat batter for thirty seconds.

4. Pour half of the batter into a bowl. Stir in the molasses and spices. Pour the light and dark batters alternately into a lightly floured well-greased loaf pan (13 × 9 × 2 inches). Bake for forty-five minutes, or until done. Cool. Frost, if desired.

NORWEGIAN MOCHA CAKE   *8 to 10 servings*

2 cups strong coffee	½ teaspoon salt
2 cups granulated sugar	2 teaspoons baking powder
2 tablespoons cocoa	½ teaspoon baking soda
1 cup seedless raisins, cut up	1 teaspoon ground cinnamon
½ cup shortening	1 teaspoon ground nutmeg
½ teaspoon vanilla extract	½ teaspoon ground cloves
2 eggs	Confectioners' sugar
2 cups sifted all-purpose flour	

1. Preheat oven to moderate (350° F.).

2. Combine the coffee, one cup granulated sugar, the cocoa and raisins in a saucepan. Bring to a boil and simmer for ten to fifteen minutes. Cool.

3. Cream the shortening and add remaining granulated sugar gradually, creaming until light and fluffy. Add vanilla. Add eggs separately, beating well after each addition.

4. Mix and sift the remaining ingredients except the confectioners' sugar, and stir in. Spoon into a greased and floured pan (10 × 10 × 2 inches). Bake for about one hour.

5. When cool, place paper lace doily on top. Sift confectioners' sugar onto doily; lift off carefully. Cut into squares to serve.

PINEAPPLE UPSIDE-DOWN CAKE   *6 servings*

¾ cup butter
¾ cup brown sugar
 3 slices of fresh pineapple (½ inch thick), halved
¼ cup pecans
½ cup granulated sugar
 1 egg

½ teaspoon vanilla extract
1½ cups sifted all-purpose flour
1½ teaspoons baking powder
½ teaspoon salt
½ cup milk
 Sour cream

1. Preheat oven to moderate (375° F.).
2. Melt one-quarter cup of the butter in a nine-inch-square baking dish and sprinkle with the brown sugar. Arrange the pineapple slices and pecans in a design on top of the sugared butter.
3. Cream the remaining butter with the granulated sugar and beat in the egg and the vanilla. Stir in the sifted flour, baking powder and salt alternately with the milk.
4. Spoon the batter carefully over pineapple slices. Bake for about thirty-five minutes, or until done. Let cake stand for five minutes before inverting onto a serving platter. Serve warm with sour cream.

POUNDCAKE   *2 loaf cakes or 1 tube cake*

According to tradition, the original poundcake was made with four pounds of ingredients. It contained a pound each of butter, sugar, flour and eggs. In whatever manner the poundcake came about, it is a delectable legacy from the standpoint of both flavor and texture. The cake has a firm texture and a tender crumb. The only leavening is provided by stiffly beaten egg whites.

 2 cups butter
 2 cups sugar
10 eggs, separated
 1 teaspoon salt

2 cups chopped mixed glacé fruits
2 teaspoons grated lemon rind
1 teaspoon cream of tartar
4 cups sifted all-purpose flour

1. Preheat oven to moderate (325° F.). Grease two loaf pans (9 × 5 × 3 inches), or line the bottoms with brown paper. Or use one ten-inch tube pan instead.
2. Cream together the butter and one and one-quarter cups of the sugar until mixture is light and fluffy. Add the egg yolks, one at a time, beating well after each addition.

3. Add the salt to the egg whites. Beat until they hold stiff peaks. Add the remaining sugar to the egg whites, one tablespoon at a time, beating well after each addition. Continue to beat until the egg whites are very stiff.

4. Combine the glacé fruits with the lemon rind, cream of tartar and four tablespoons of the flour.

5. Gently fold the beaten egg whites and the remaining flour alternately into the creamed butter mixture. Fold in the fruits.

6. Pour the batter into the prepared pans. Bake until golden brown, about one and one-half hours in the loaf pans or almost two hours in the tube pan.

BISHOP'S BREAD   *10 to 12 servings*

8 eggs	½ cup chopped citron
2¾ cups confectioners' sugar	½ cup chopped candied cherries
2½ cups sifted all-purpose flour	1 cup slivered almonds
½ teaspoon salt	1 cup semisweet chocolate bits

1. Preheat oven to moderate (350° F.).

2. Beat the eggs and sugar until thick and lemon-colored. Because there is no leavening in this cake other than the air beaten into the eggs, it is most important that the eggs be beaten almost to the ribbon stage. Fold in two cups of the flour.

3. Combine the remaining flour with the remaining ingredients and fold the mixture into the batter. Pour into a nine-inch mold or angel-cake pan. Bake for about forty-five minutes, until a cake tester inserted into the mold comes out clean. Remove to a cake rack. When cool, turn out onto the rack. The cake may be iced with Confectioners' Sugar Icing (page 679).

CLOVE CAKES   *6 dozen small cupcakes*

3 cups sifted all-purpose flour	1 cup shortening
½ teaspoon salt	1½ cups sugar
4 teaspoons baking powder	3 large eggs
½ teaspoon ground cloves	1¼ cups milk
1 teaspoon ground cinnamon	Spiced Butter Frosting (page 679)

1. Preheat oven to moderate (375° F.).

2. Sift together the flour, salt and baking powder and set aside.

3. Mix the spices and shortening and gradually blend in the sugar. Beat in the eggs, one at a time. Add the flour mixture alternately with the milk. Beat the batter for thirty seconds. Turn the batter into lightly floured well-greased muffin tins.

4. Bake the cakes for thirty minutes, or until a cake tester inserted into the center comes out clean. Cool in pans for five minutes. Turn out onto wire racks to finish cooling. Frost when cool.

ALL-PURPOSE CHIFFON CAKE   *About 16 servings*

2¼ cups sifted cake flour
1½ cups sugar
 1 tablespoon baking powder
 1 teaspoon salt
 ½ cup salad oil (not olive)
 5 egg yolks

 2 teaspoons grated lemon rind
 ¾ cup water
 2 teaspoons vanilla extract
 1 cup egg whites
 ½ teaspoon cream of tartar

1. Preheat oven to moderate (325° F.). Put the rack in the lower half of the oven.

2. Sift together into a bowl the flour, sugar, baking powder and salt.

3. Make a well in the center of the flour mixture and add the oil, egg yolks, lemon rind, water and vanilla. Stir and beat until smooth.

4. In another bowl beat the egg whites with the cream of tartar until very stiff, much stiffer than for meringue.

5. Pour the egg-yolk mixture gradually over the egg whites, folding gently with a rubber spatula until just blended. Do not stir.

6. Pour the batter at once into an ungreased ten-inch tube pan. Bake for sixty-five to seventy minutes.

7. Immediately turn the pan of cake upside down and place the tube over a funnel or other support so that the cake can hang in the pan free of the table until cool.

8. To remove cake from pan, loosen it from the tube and sides with a spatula and hit the edge of the pan on the table. Serve plain or top with Lemon Glaze (page 682).

CHIFFON LAYERS:

For two square layers (9 × 9 × 1¾ inches), use the recipe for all-purpose chiffon cake and reduce the egg yolks to four. Bake in a moderate oven (350° F.) for about thirty-five minutes.

Use one or both layers for party variety cakes (below) or as basis for other desserts.

PARTY VARIETY CAKES: *24 small cakes*

1 nine-inch layer of All-Purpose Chiffon Cake (see above)
1 recipe Lemon Filling (page 677)
1 recipe Cream-Cheese Frosting (page 680)

Confectioners' sugar
Chopped nuts, colored coconut, candied fruits and candy sprinkles for garnish

1. Bake and cool the chiffon layer. Split it and fill it with lemon filling.

2. Cut the cake into halves and frost each half with the cream-cheese frosting, or frost one half and sprinkle the other with confectioners' sugar.

3. Cut each frosted half-layer into thirds and then cut each of the thirds into four finger-shaped strips. Garnish as desired. Cut the sugar-sprinkled cake into finger-shaped strips, but serve it undecorated.

LEMON CHIFFON CAKE   *12 servings*

2 cups sifted cake flour	2 tablespoons grated lemon rind
1½ cups sugar	¼ cup lemon juice
3 teaspoons baking powder	½ cup water
1 teaspoon salt	½ teaspoon cream of tartar
½ cup salad oil (not olive)	1 cup egg whites
5 egg yolks	

1. Preheat oven to moderate (325° F.).

2. Sift together the flour, sugar, baking powder and salt.

3. Make a well in the center of the dry ingredients and add the oil, egg yolks, lemon rind, juice and water. Beat with a wooden spoon until very smooth.

4. Add cream of tartar to egg whites; beat until stiff. Gently fold egg-yolk mixture into egg whites.

5. Turn into an ungreased ten-inch tube pan. Bake for fifty-five minutes; increase heat to 350° F. and bake for about ten minutes longer. Invert pan to cool.

ORANGE CHIFFON CAKE:

Substitute three-quarters cup orange juice for the lemon juice and water, and orange rind for lemon rind.

SPONGECAKE   *1 cake*

4 eggs, separated	1½ teaspoons baking powder
1 cup sugar	¼ teaspoon salt
¼ cup orange juice	Preserves and confectioners'
1 tablespoon grated orange rind	sugar
1 cup cake flour	

1. Preheat oven to moderate (325° F.).

2. Beat the egg yolks until thick. Gradually beat in the sugar. Beat in the orange juice and add the orange rind.

3. Sift the flour together with the baking powder and salt. Fold into the egg-yolk mixture.

4. Beat the egg whites until stiff but not dry. Fold into the batter.

5. Pour into two nine-inch layer-cake pans, greased on the bottom. Bake for twenty-five to thirty minutes, until done. Cool.

6. Sandwich the layers together with preserves. Sift confectioners' sugar over the cake.

BLOTKAKE   (Norwegian spongecake)   *8 servings*

4 whole eggs	6 tablespoons all-purpose flour
2 eggs, separated	1 teaspoon baking powder
1 cup sugar	2 cups sweetened whipped cream
1 teaspoon vanilla extract	Multerberries or other berries

1. Preheat oven to moderate (350° F.). Grease a round nine-inch cake pan and line the bottom with wax paper. Butter the paper.

2. In a mixing bowl combine the whole eggs with two egg yolks, the sugar and vanilla. Beat until thick and lemon-colored.

3. Sift the flour and baking powder together and fold into the egg mixture.

4. Whip the egg whites until stiff and fold them into the batter.

5. Pour the batter into the prepared pan and bake for ten minutes. Reduce the heat to 325° F. and continue to bake for about fifty minutes longer, until a cake tester inserted into the center comes out clean.

6. Let the cake cool. Slice it into four layers. Spread whipped cream between the layers and around the sides. Garnish the cake with multerberries or other berries.

Note: Multerberries are available in cans wherever Norwegian food delicacies are sold.

VALENTINE CAKE   *3 heart-shaped layers*

2¼ cups sifted cake flour	2 teaspoons lemon juice
1½ cups sugar	¾ cup water
3 teaspoons baking powder	6 egg whites
1 teaspoon salt	½ teaspoon cream of tartar
½ cup salad oil	Strawberry Filling (page 677)
6 egg yolks	Fudge Frosting (page 680)
1 teaspoon grated lemon rind	Buttercream (page 678)

1. Preheat oven to moderate (350° F.).

2. Sift the flour, sugar, baking powder and salt into a mixing bowl. Add the oil, unbeaten egg yolks, lemon rind and juice and the water. Beat until smooth with a hand or electric mixer.

3. Beat the egg whites together with the cream of tartar until very stiff. Fold the egg-yolk mixture into the egg whites until just blended. Do not overblend.

4. Pour the batter into three ungreased heart-shaped pans. Bake for thirty-five minutes. Invert the pans to cool by resting on two other pans. When cool, loosen all around with a spatula and remove from the pan.

Note: Batter not baked immediately should be refrigerated.

ASSEMBLING THE CAKE:

1. Brush off the loose crumbs from two of the layers.

2. Place one layer upside down on a platter or foil-covered cardboard shape. Spread with half the strawberry filling, keeping it one-quarter inch from the edge.

3. Add the second layer. Spread with the remaining filling as before. Top with the third layer.

4. Using a wide spatula, spread the sides of the cake with fudge frosting. Spread the remaining frosting on top of the cake. Smooth the layer of frosting by using a clean spatula dipped into warm water.

5. Place the buttercream in a decorating tube or bag fitted with a star decorating point. Decorate the base and top of the cake.

6. Arrange a cascade of fresh garnet roses (which have been rinsed under running water and drained well on a paper towel) atop the decorated cake.

7. The cake should be stored in the refrigerator until serving time and any left over should be promptly returned to the refrigerator.

SPONGE ROLL   *8 servings*

4 eggs, at room temperature	¾ cup sifted cake flour
¾ teaspoon baking powder	Confectioners' sugar
1 teaspoon salt	1½ cups heavy cream, whipped
¾ cup sugar	2 tablespoons orange liqueur
1 teaspoon vanilla extract	¼ cup pistachio nuts, unsalted

1. Preheat oven to hot (400° F.). Line a greased jelly-roll pan (15½ × 10½ inches) with parchment paper and grease again.

2. Beat the eggs together with the baking powder and the salt until very thick and light colored. Gradually beat in the sugar. The mixture should form a ribbon as it drops from the beaters.

3. Stir in the vanilla and then fold in the flour gently. Pour the batter into the prepared pan, spread evenly, and bake for thirteen minutes, or until done. Turn immediately onto a clean towel that has been generously sprinkled with confectioners' sugar.

4. Quickly remove the paper and roll, jelly-roll style, starting with the long side and enclosing the towel inside. Cool on a rack.

5. Combine the cream, one-quarter cup of confectioners' sugar, the liqueur and the nuts. Unroll the cooled cake and spread with the cream mixture. Reroll. Sprinkle with confectioners' sugar and chill before serving.

VARIATION:

Instead of whipped cream, orange liqueur and pistachios, spread the cake with Mocha Buttercream (page 678). Reroll, and sprinkle with confectioners' sugar and shaved unsweetened chocolate.

LEMON AMBROSIA   *12 servings*

1 Spongecake (page 625), baked in a 9-inch tube pan	¾ cup hot water
	6 eggs, separated
1 package (3 ounces) lemon-flavored gelatin	1½ cups sugar
	Grated rind and juice of 2 lemons

1. Cut the spongecake into halves crosswise and use the bottom half. Reserve the top half for another use.
2. Dissolve the gelatin in the hot water and set aside.
3. In the top part of a double boiler, beat the egg yolks with three-quarters cup sugar, the lemon rind and juice. Cook over hot water until thick, beating constantly. Add to gelatin and set aside.
4. Beat the egg whites until stiff, adding remaining three-quarters cup sugar gradually. Fold gently into the egg-yolk mixture. Pour over spongecake and chill until set.

CHOCOLATE ROLL   *8 servings*

5 large eggs, separated	3 tablespoons strong coffee
⅔ cup sugar	Cocoa
6 ounces (6 squares) semisweet chocolate	1¼ cups heavy cream, whipped

1. Preheat oven to moderate (350° F.). Butter a large baking sheet (8 × 12 inches). Line it with wax paper and butter the paper.
2. Beat the egg yolks and sugar with a rotary beater or electric mixer until thick and pale in color.
3. Melt the chocolate in the coffee over low heat, stirring until chocolate melts. Let the mixture cool slightly, then stir it into the egg yolks. Beat the egg whites until stiff and fold them in.
4. Spread the mixture evenly on the prepared baking sheet. Bake for fifteen minutes, or until a knife inserted into the middle comes out clean. Do not overbake.
5. Remove the pan from the oven and cover the cake with a damp cloth. Let stand for thirty minutes, or until cool. Loosen cake from the baking sheet and dust cake generously with cocoa. Turn the cake out on wax paper, cocoa side down.
6. Carefully remove the paper from the bottom of the cake. Spread the cake with whipped cream, sweetened and flavored to taste, and roll up like

a jelly roll. The last roll should deposit the log, seam side down, on a long board or platter. Dust the top with a little more cocoa.

CRANBERRY SPONGE ROLL *10 to 12 servings*

4 eggs, separated
1 cup sugar
3 tablespoons orange juice
½ teaspoon grated lemon rind
1 cup sifted cake flour

¼ teaspoon salt
1¼ teaspoons baking powder
Cranberry Topping (page 609)
Confectioners' sugar

1. Preheat oven to moderate (350° F.). Lightly grease a jelly-roll pan (15 × 10 inches) and line with wax paper. Grease paper.

2. Beat egg yolks until thick and lemon-colored. Gradually beat in three-quarters cup sugar. Add orange juice and lemon rind.

3. Beat egg whites until they stand in peaks. Gradually beat in remaining sugar. Fold in egg-yolk mixture.

4. Sift the flour with salt and baking powder. Fold into egg mixture and pour into prepared pan. Bake for fifteen minutes.

5. Turn out at once onto a towel sprinkled with confectioners' sugar. Quickly remove paper and roll cake in the towel. Let stand until cold.

6. Unroll cake and spread with the topping. Roll up and sprinkle with confectioners' sugar.

DANISH APPLE CAKE *6 servings*

6 cups diced baking apples
1 cup hot water
1½ cups plus 1 tablespoon sugar
⅛ teaspoon salt
1½ teaspoons vanilla extract

3 cups fine dry bread crumbs
¾ cup butter
½ cup currant jelly or raspberry jam
1 cup heavy cream, whipped

1. Cook the apples in the hot water in a covered saucepan for about ten minutes, until soft but not until they lose their shape. Add one cup of the sugar, the salt and one teaspoon vanilla. Cool.

2. Cook the bread crumbs in the butter over medium heat until well mixed. Add one-half cup sugar and stir. Place two cups of the crumb mixture in the bottom of a buttered seven-inch springform pan. Spread with half of the drained cooked apples. Over this, spread half of the jelly or jam. Repeat, using one cup of the bread mixture and the remaining apples and jelly. Top with the remaining bread crumbs. Chill for several hours or overnight.

3. Before serving, add the remaining sugar and vanilla to the whipped cream. Spread over the top and sides of the cake.

1. *Sponge Roll.* Preheat oven to moderate (350° F.). Grease a jelly-roll pan, line with wax paper, and grease again. Beat egg yolks until they are pale and thick. Gradually beat in sugar.

2. Beat egg whites until they stand in peaks. Fold into egg-yolk mixture. Blend remaining ingredients and fold gently into egg mixture.

3. Pour the mixture into the prepared jelly-roll pan and spread it evenly to all sides and corners of the pan with a rubber spatula. Bake until the cake is lightly browned and rebounds to the touch.

4. Remove the cake from the oven, cover it with a damp cloth, and place on a rack until cool. Remove the cloth and sprinkle the top of the cake with confectioners' sugar. Invert the pan over a large piece of wax paper and carefully peel off the paper in which the cake was baked.

5. Spread the filling you are using evenly over the cake. Carefully roll up the cake from the long side like a jelly roll. Sprinkle the top with more confectioners' sugar.

6. The completed sponge roll presents a handsome appearance and makes a tasty dessert for autumn and winter menus.

In the broadest sense the Viennese Torte is almost any form of cake, but it is generally an inspired confection made from baked meringue or sponge-cake with delicate fillings such as whipped cream or buttercream. Such goodness may be compounded with the addition of ground almonds or hazelnuts and the fillings flavored with perfumed liqueurs such as framboise or kirsch or with chocolate, coffee or rum.

ALLEMANDE TORTE   6 servings

4 eggs, separated
⅓ cup granulated sugar
2 teaspoons grated lemon rind
2 tablespoons lemon juice
⅔ cup quick-cooking farina
¼ cup ground blanched almonds

1 tablespoon confectioners' sugar
1 cup heavy cream, whipped
½ cup sliced fresh fruit, such as berries or peaches
6 unblanched almonds, finely chopped

1. Preheat oven to moderate (350° F.). Grease well an eight-inch-square cake pan and line the bottom with parchment paper or greased wax paper.

631

2. Beat the egg yolks together with the granulated sugar until thick and light colored.

3. Fold in the lemon rind and juice, farina and ground almonds. Beat the egg whites until stiff but not dry and fold in. Pour the mixture into the prepared pan and bake for thirty-five minutes, or until done.

4. Cool on a rack. The cake will shrink as it cools. Fold the confectioners' sugar into the cream.

5. Slice the cake horizontally and fill with the fruit mixed with one-third cup of the cream. Frost with the remaining cream and decorate with the chopped almonds.

BLUEBERRY TORTE   *12 servings*

2 cups crushed graham crackers
1½ cups sugar
⅔ cup butter, melted
1½ pounds cream cheese, at room temperature
4 eggs

2½ teaspoons grated lemon rind
1 pint blueberries
¼ cup water
1 teaspoon cornstarch, mixed with 2 tablespoons water

1. Preheat oven to moderate (350° F.). Grease an eight-inch springform pan.

2. Mix crumbs, one-half cup of the sugar and the melted butter. Press crumbs over bottom and part way up sides of the pan.

3. Beat the cheese. Beat in remaining sugar, the eggs and two teaspoons lemon rind.

4. Pour mixture into prepared pan. Bake for thirty-five minutes. Cool. Chill overnight.

5. Combine berries, water, cornstarch and remaining lemon rind. Simmer for a few minutes. Cool and spread over the torte.

CARROT TORTE   *12 servings*

¾ cup sugar
12 eggs, separated
6 tablespoons grated carrot
6 tablespoons grated almonds
6 tablespoons coarsely grated apple

3 tablespoons matzoh cake flour
1 teaspoon lemon juice
1 teaspoon baking powder
Matzoh meal

1. Preheat oven to moderate (375° F.).

2. Mix the sugar with the egg yolks and beat until light in color and creamy. Add the grated carrot, almonds and apple and fold in the cake flour. Add the lemon juice and baking powder.

3. Beat the egg whites until stiff and fold them into the batter.

4. Grease a ten-inch springform pan and sprinkle it with matzoh meal. Pour in the torte mixture. Bake for about forty-five minutes, until a cake tester inserted into the torte comes out clean.

CHOCOLATE NUT TORTE   *12 to 16 servings*

¾ cup butter
¾ cup sugar
7 eggs, separated
4 ounces sweet cooking chocolate, melted and cooled

1 cup unblanched almonds, finely ground
½ teaspoon baking powder
Chocolate Filling (page 676)
¼ cup unblanched almonds, chopped

1. Preheat oven to moderate (350° F.).
2. Cream the butter and gradually beat in the sugar until the mixture is light and creamy.
3. Beat in the egg yolks, one at a time. Blend in the chocolate. Gently fold in the ground almonds mixed with the baking powder. Fold in the egg whites, beaten until stiff but not dry.
4. Pour the mixture into two well-greased nine-inch layer-cake pans. Bake for about thirty minutes. Cool away from drafts. There will be some shrinkage.
5. Frost between the layers and over the top of the torte with the filling. Sprinkle with the chopped nuts.

FILBERT TORTE   *12 servings*

10 eggs, separated, at room temperature
1½ cups sugar
3 tablespoons cake flour
2 cups finely ground skinned filberts (page 634)

12 ounces apricot preserves
Juice of 1 lemon
2 cups heavy cream
½ cup dark brown sugar
Shaved filberts for garnish

1. Preheat oven to moderate (350° F.). Line the bottoms of three nine-inch layer-cake pans (preferably with removable bottoms) with parchment paper or greased and lightly floured wax paper.
2. Beat the egg yolks until thick. Gradually add the sugar, beating until the mixture is light and fluffy. Fold in the flour and ground nuts.
3. Beat the egg whites until stiff but not dry. Mix one-third of the egg whites into the nut mixture. Fold in the remainder gently.
4. Pour the batter into the prepared pans. Bake for thirty to thirty-five minutes, until browned and set.
5. Remove from the oven and cool slightly. The layers will shrink. Set the layers, still on paper, on racks to cool.

6. Mix the preserves with the lemon juice. Whip the cream with the brown sugar until it reaches spreading consistency.

7. Carefully remove the paper from one layer and place it on a cake plate. Spread with the apricot mixture and then with two tablespoons of the whipped cream. Remove the paper from a second layer and place on top. Repeat the spreading process and finally top with the third layer.

8. Frost the torte all over with the remaining cream. Garnish with shaved filberts and refrigerate.

SKINNING FILBERTS:

Spread the shelled nuts in a shallow pan and bake in a moderate oven (350°) for fifteen to twenty minutes. Remove the filberts from the oven, cover them with boiling water and drain immediately. Rub the nuts back and forth between two towels, loosening the skin. Any skin remaining after this process will not be detrimental to the dishes prepared.

LAURA TORTE   *8 to 10 servings*

5 tablespoons fine dry bread crumbs	5 tablespoons sweet butter
6 egg whites	3 egg yolks
1 cup very fine sugar	1 cup confectioners' sugar
2 cups whole almonds, blanched and grated	1 cup heavy cream, whipped
7 teaspoons instant coffee powder	½ cup slivered toasted blanched almonds
3 tablespoons very strong brewed coffee	

1. Preheat oven to hot (400° F.). Grease two eight-inch layer-cake pans, line with wax paper, and grease the wax paper. Sprinkle each pan with one tablespoon of the bread crumbs.

2. Beat the egg whites until frothy. Very gradually add one-half cup very fine sugar, beating until very stiff. Fold in the remaining very fine sugar, all but three tablespoons of the grated almonds, the remaining bread crumbs and four teaspoons instant coffee powder.

3. Divide the mixture evenly between the two prepared pans. Bake for fifteen to twenty minutes, or until a food pick inserted into the center comes out clean.

4. Remove the layers from the pans and peel off the wax paper. While still hot, sprinkle the undersides with the strong coffee. Cool on racks. The layers will shrink as they cool.

5. Beat the butter, egg yolks and confectioners' sugar together until well blended. Fold in remaining grated almonds, the whipped cream and remaining instant coffee powder.

6. Place one cooled layer on a serving dish. Top with half of the cream mixture. Put remaining layer on top. Cover sides and top with the remaining cream mixture. Sprinkle top and sides with the toasted almonds.

CREOLE PECAN TORTE   *8 to 10 servings*

4 eggs, separated
1 cup sugar
2 tablespoons all-purpose flour
½ teaspoon salt
½ teaspoon baking powder
1 tablespoon orange juice or Jamaica rum

2 cups grated pecans
½ cup cream, whipped
1½ teaspoons grated orange rind
Chocolate Buttercream (page 678)

1. Preheat oven to moderate (350° F.).
2. Beat egg yolks until thick and light, then beat in sugar. Stir in the flour, salt, baking powder, orange juice or rum and pecans. Beat egg whites until stiff and fold in.
3. Pour the mixture into two eight-inch layer-cake pans, greased and lined with wax paper. Bake for twenty-five minutes, or until cake springs back when touched gently with the finger. Cool; then remove from pans.
4. Mix the cream with the orange rind. One to three hours before serving, put the layers together with the orange-flavored cream. Top with chocolate buttercream.

STRAWBERRY-RICE TORTE   *About 12 servings*

PASTRY SHELL:

2 cups sifted all-purpose flour
3 tablespoons sugar
⅔ cup butter
Grated rind of 1 lemon

1 egg yolk, lightly beaten
3 tablespoons water
1 tablespoon lemon juice

1. Preheat oven to moderate (375° F.). Put the rack in the lowest position. Rub an eight-inch springform pan with shortening.
2. Mix or sift the flour with the sugar. Cut the butter into slivers and mix well with the flour, using the fingers. Add lemon rind.
3. Mix the egg yolk, water and lemon juice. Add to the flour mixture, stir to mix, and turn out and knead until smooth. Shape into a roll and chill briefly.
4. Slice the pastry about one-quarter inch thick. Arrange slices over the bottom of the pan and press with the fingers to cover the bottom. Arrange remaining slices around the sides and press them against the pan. Trim off any

pastry that extends over the top and make small gashes with the tip of the knife in the bottom and sides to allow air to escape.

5. Bake for about thirty-five minutes, until the edges are a golden brown. If the pastry in the bottom of the pan puffs up after baking for ten or fifteen minutes, cut small gashes in it again and press it flat again. Cool in the pan on a rack.

FILLING:

½ teaspoon salt
1 cup uncooked long-grain white rice
1 quart fresh strawberries
1 cup sugar

1 envelope unflavored gelatin
1 to 2 tablespoons strawberry jam (optional)
½ to 1 cup heavy cream, whipped

1. Heat two and one-quarter cups water with the salt to boiling. Add the rice, return to boiling, and cover. Cook over very low heat for about twenty minutes, until the rice is tender and water is absorbed. Cool.

2. Wash and hull the strawberries. Drain, add sugar, and cook over medium heat, stirring until juice forms. Continue to simmer until the berries are tender.

3. Soften the gelatin in one-quarter cup water, add to the hot berries, and stir until dissolved. Cool to a syrupy consistency.

4. Add the rice to the berries and, if more sweetness is desired, add the jam. Cool, then chill the mixture until it is almost set. Turn it into the cooled pastry shell, smooth the top, and chill.

5. Garnish with the whipped cream, sweetened and flavored to taste with vanilla. If desired, make a lattice top and border with the cream and fill the spaces with strawberries.

PIES AND PASTRIES

Pies are among the easiest of desserts to prepare because there is such a wide latitude in the crusts and fillings. The shortening, be it butter or lard, can be increased or decreased according to individual taste. The more shortening, of course, the more fragile the pastry and the more difficult to handle. For best results, the dough should be worked as quickly and as little as possible or it will toughen. Many experts recommend placing a dough-lined pie plate in the refrigerator before filling because the chilling helps the dough retain its shape during cooking.

UNBAKED PIE PASTRY   *Pastry for 2-crust 9-inch pie*

2 cups sifted all-purpose flour   ¼ cup ice water
1 teaspoon salt
⅔ cup shortening or ⅓ cup butter
   and ⅓ cup lard

1. Sift the flour and salt into a mixing bowl. Cut in the shortening with a pastry blender or two knives until the mixture resembles coarse cornmeal.

2. Sprinkle the water, one tablespoon at a time, over the mixture. Use only enough to dampen the flour. Mix lightly with a fork until flour is moistened. With the hands, gather dough into a ball.

3. Roll out half of the dough on a lightly floured board to a circle one-eighth inch thick and about one and one-half inches larger in diameter than the pie plate.

4. Roll out the rest of the dough into a circle about one inch larger in diameter than the pie plate. If the dough is not to be used at once, chill until ready to use.

UNBAKED PIE PASTRY   *Pastry for 1-crust 9-inch pie*

1½ cups sifted all-purpose flour   3 tablespoons water
 ½ teaspoon salt
 ½ cup shortening or ¼ cup butter
    and ¼ cup lard

1. Sift the flour and salt into a mixing bowl. Cut in the shortening with a pastry blender or two knives until the mixture resembles coarse cornmeal.

2. Sprinkle with the water, one teaspoon at a time. Mix thoroughly with a two-pronged fork after each addition. When all the flour is moistened, gather the dough into a ball.

3. Roll out the dough into a circle about one-eighth inch thick and about one and one-half inches larger than the pie plate. Chill until ready to use.

BAKED PIE PASTRY   *Pie shell for 9-inch pie*

1. Preheat oven to hot (450° F.).

2. Make the pastry for a one-crust pie (see above). Roll out to a circle of the size needed. Line a pie plate with the dough, pressing against the bottom of the plate without stretching. Prick the bottom, line with aluminum foil, and cover with dried beans or rice. This will keep the pastry from swelling as it bakes.

1. *Lattice Pie Topping*. Prepare any standard dough using two cups of flour. Divide the dough into halves with a knife.

2. Roll out half of the dough. Line an eight- or nine-inch pie plate. Trim dough around sides leaving a one-inch overhanging border.

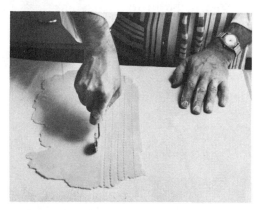

3. Roll out remaining dough. With a pastry cutter, cut the dough into strips about one-half inch wide. Carefully separate strips.

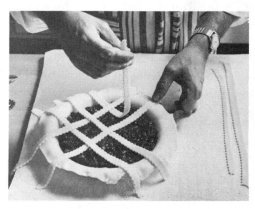

4. Spoon the filling into pastry-lined pan. Place strips over the filling and interweave. Trim off overhanging edges with scissors.

5. Fold edges of bottom dough under. Using the forefingers, press to form a fluted edge, or use a fork to decorate the edge.

6. Mincemeat and fruit fillings make handsome pies when baked with lattice tops.

3. Bake the pastry for ten minutes. Reduce the heat to moderate (350° F.). Remove the foil and beans. Bake for five to ten minutes longer, or until the pastry is golden brown.

SWEET PIE PASTRY   *Pastry for 9- or 10-inch flan ring*

2 cups sifted all-purpose flour
¼ cup sugar
⅛ teaspoon baking powder
5 tablespoons butter
2 tablespoons vegetable shortening, chilled

1 egg
1 teaspoon water
½ teaspoon vanilla extract

1. Place the flour, sugar, baking powder, butter and shortening in a bowl. With the tips of the fingers gently rub the fat into the dry ingredients until the mixture resembles coarse oatmeal.
2. Beat the egg with the water and add with the vanilla to the flour mixture. Blend the dough into a ball with a fork or the fingers. Wrap in wax paper and chill for several hours, until firm. The dough can be kept for several days in the refrigerator, or it may be frozen.

ALMOND SHORT PASTRY   *Pastry for 9- or 10-inch flan ring*

½ cup almond paste
3 raw egg yolks
1¼ cups sifted all-purpose flour
⅔ cup ground unblanched almonds
⅓ cup sugar
½ teaspoon salt

1 teaspoon grated lemon rind
½ cup butter, softened
Pinch of ground cloves
¼ teaspoon ground cinnamon
2 hard-cooked egg yolks, sieved

1. Cream the almond paste with the raw egg yolks.
2. Mix the flour and ground almonds together in a bowl. Make a well in the center and in it place the sugar, salt, lemon rind, butter, spices, hard-cooked egg yolks and the almond-paste mixture.
3. With the finger tips gradually work the ingredients together to form a ball of dough. Chill until firm.

SHAPING AND BAKING A FLAN RING

1. Place a flan ring (9 or 10 inches) on an ungreased baking sheet; or use a cake pan with a removable bottom.
2. Roll chilled dough (Almond Short Pastry or Sweet Pie Pastry, see above) between sheets of wax paper until it is one to two inches larger in diameter than the flan ring and about one-quarter inch thick.

3. Peel off the top paper. Invert the pastry over the flan ring. Peel off the remaining paper. Ease the pastry down into the ring. Do not stretch. Allow the pastry to extend one-eighth inch above the ring or pan and make a decorative edge with the dull edge of a table knife. Refrigerate.

4. Preheat oven to hot (400° F.). Set the rack in the middle of the oven.

5. Line the bottom and sides of the pastry with aluminum foil and weight it with dried beans or rice. Bake for eight or nine minutes, until the pastry is set. Remove the foil and the beans. Prick the bottom of the pastry with a fork to prevent it from rising. Bake for about ten minutes longer, or until the shell is very lightly browned.

6. Remove the flan ring or the rim of the cake pan and cool the shell on a rack.

LATTICE PIE TOPPING

1. Prepare any standard dough using two cups of flour. Divide the dough into halves with a knife.

2. Roll out half of the dough. Line an eight- or nine-inch pie plate with the dough, pressing it against the bottom of the plate without stretching. Trim the dough evenly around the sides, leaving a one-inch border all around.

3. Roll out remaining dough. Use a pastry cutter to cut the dough into strips about one-half inch wide.

4. Spoon the filling into the pastry-lined pie plate. Arrange the dough strips over the filling at even intervals and weave over and under to make a lattice. Trim off the overhanging edges of the strips.

5. Fold under the edges of the bottom dough. Use the forefingers to form a fluted edge, or use the tines of a fork to crimp the edge.

BAKED TART SHELLS   *8 tart shells*

1½ cups sifted all-purpose flour	1 teaspoon grated lemon rind
⅓ cup sifted confectioners' sugar	½ cup butter
⅛ teaspoon salt	3 tablespoons milk

1. Preheat oven to moderate (350° F.).

2. Sift together into a mixing bowl the flour, sugar and salt. Add lemon rind and butter and cut in with a pastry blender until the mixture resembles coarse meal. Add the milk. Mix lightly to form a dough.

3. Divide dough into eight equal parts. Roll out each piece into a very thin circle, about one-sixteenth inch thick. Fit the pastry into eight tart pans, measuring three and one-half inches across the top and two inches across the bottom. Prick the pastry at intervals with a fork to prevent it from blistering.

4. Bake for fifteen to twenty minutes. Remove from pans when thoroughly cooled.

GRAHAM-CRACKER PIECRUST   *1 piecrust*

1½ cups graham-cracker crumbs
¼ cup sugar
¼ cup chopped almonds

¼ cup butter, melted
¼ teaspoon salt

Combine all ingredients. Press the mixture evenly onto the bottom and sides of a greased pie plate or springform pan. This makes enough to line a large springform pan (10½ inches). Chill.

CHOCOLATE-WAFER PIECRUST   *1 piecrust*

1¼ cups chocolate-wafer crumbs
¼ cup sugar

⅓ cup melted butter

1. Preheat oven to hot (450° F.).
2. Mix well the chocolate crumbs, sugar and butter. Press the mixture against the bottom and sides of a nine-inch pie plate. Bake for five minutes and chill.

CARDAMOM APPLE PIE   *6 to 8 servings*

Unbaked Pie Pastry, 2-crust (page 637)
3 cups slices of tart juicy pie apples
½ cup honey

2 tablespoons butter
¾ teaspoon ground cardamom
1 teaspoon vanilla extract

1. Preheat oven to moderate (350° F.).
2. Line a nine-inch pie plate with a layer of pastry and arrange the apple slices over it.
3. Dribble honey over apples. Dot with the butter and sprinkle with cardamom and vanilla.
4. Arrange top pastry over apples and flute edges. Bake for thirty-five to forty minutes.

DUTCH APPLE PIE   *6 to 8 servings*

Unbaked Pie Pastry, 1-crust (page 637)
3 pounds tart apples
⅓ cup all-purpose flour
¾ cup sugar

Pinch of salt
1 cup heavy cream
¼ teaspoon grated nutmeg
½ teaspoon ground cinnamon

1. Preheat oven to hot (450° F.). Cover center of oven with a piece of aluminum foil in case the pie drips.

2. Line a nine-inch pie plate with the pastry. Pare and core the apples. Slice them and arrange the slices symmetrically in the pastry-lined plate.

3. Mix together the flour, sugar and salt. Add the cream and beat until thick. Mix in the nutmeg and cinnamon, using more to taste if desired. Pour over the apple slices.

4. Bake for twenty to twenty-five minutes, or until the edge of the custard begins to brown.

5. Cover the top of the pie with aluminum foil. Reduce the oven to moderate (350° F.) and continue to bake for about forty-five minutes, until the filling thickens and becomes glossy. Serve warm.

APPLE SOUR-CREAM PIE   *6 to 8 servings*

Unbaked Pie Pastry, 1-crust (page 637)
2 eggs
½ cup plus ⅓ cup sugar
½ cup plus 2 tablespoons all-purpose flour
¼ teaspoon salt

1 cup sour cream
1 teaspoon grated lemon rind
1 tablespoon lemon juice
⅓ cup seedless raisins
2½ cups sliced apples
¼ teaspoon grated nutmeg
3 tablespoons butter

1. Preheat oven to hot (400° F.).
2. Line a nine-inch pie plate with the pastry.
3. Beat the eggs and add the half cup of sugar, two tablespoons flour, the salt, sour cream, lemon rind and juice. Add the raisins and apples; mix well. Pour into the pastry-lined pie plate. Bake for ten minutes.
4. Combine the remaining flour and sugar and the nutmeg. Cut in the butter with two knives until the mixture is crumbly. Sprinkle on the apple filling and continue baking for thirty to thirty-five minutes, until the crumbs are brown and the filling set. Chill.

NORMANDY APPLESAUCE PIE   *8 to 12 servings*

1½ cups sifted all-purpose flour
2 eggs, separated
2 tablespoons sugar
½ cup butter, softened
Grated rind of 1 lemon
Pinch of salt

4 cups (two 15-ounce jars) thick applesauce
½ cup confectioners' sugar
2 or 3 drops of lemon juice
1 cup slivered almonds

1. Combine flour, well-beaten egg yolks, sugar, butter, lemon rind and salt. Blend well; chill for two hours.
2. Preheat oven to hot (400° F.).
3. Divide mixture into two portions, one twice as large as the other. Roll out the large portion to a thickness of one-eighth inch. Use to line a shallow oblong pan. Cover with the applesauce.

4. Roll out smaller portion of dough to fit top of pan. Cover pan with the dough and seal the edges.

5. Mix together the beaten egg whites, confectioners' sugar and lemon juice. Blend until smooth and spread over top of pastry. Sprinkle with slivered almonds.

6. Bake for about thirty minutes, until the top is crusty and brown. Serve hot or cold.

BLACKBERRY AND APPLE PIE   *6 to 8 servings*

Unbaked Pie Pastry, 2-crust (page 637)

3 cups fresh blackberries, picked over, washed and drained

1 cup thin slices of peeled green apples

2⅔ tablespoons quick-cooking tapioca

1 cup sugar

½ teaspoon ground cinnamon

2 tablespoons butter

1. Preheat oven to hot (450° F.).

2. Line a nine-inch pie plate with half of the pastry.

3. Combine the blackberries, apples, tapioca, sugar and cinnamon. Mix well and transfer to the prepared pie plate.

4. Dot the filling with the butter and cover with the remaining pastry. Seal and flute the edges. Pierce the pastry with the point of a knife to allow the steam to escape during baking.

5. Bake for ten minutes. Reduce oven heat to moderate (350° F.) and bake for about thirty minutes longer, or until pastry is browned. The pie may be served either warm or cold, with whipped cream or ice cream.

BLUEBERRY PIE   *6 to 8 servings*

Unbaked Pie Pastry, 2-crust (page 637)

¾ cup sugar

3 tablespoons quick-cooking tapioca

¼ teaspoon salt

Dash of ground cinnamon

4 cups blueberries

1 tablespoon lemon juice

1 tablespoon butter

1. Preheat oven to hot (425° F.).

2. Line a nine-inch pie plate with half of the pastry.

3. Mix the sugar, tapioca, salt and cinnamon. Sprinkle the mixture over the berries. Add lemon juice. Spoon the berries into the prepared pie plate and dot with the butter.

4. Cut the remaining pastry into strips and make a lattice top for the pie. Trim edges, moisten, and border with a strip of pastry.

5. Bake on lower shelf of the oven for about fifty minutes.

CRANBERRY-PEAR PIE   *6 to 8 servings*

Unbaked Pie Pastry, 2-crust (page 637)
2 cups fresh cranberries
⅓ cup water
3 tablespoons quick-cooking tapioca
1 cup sugar
¼ teaspoon salt
3 cups diced fresh pears
2 tablespoons butter

1. Preheat oven to hot (450° F.).
2. Line a nine-inch pie plate with half of the pastry.
3. Place the cranberries and water in a saucepan. Cover and cook for six to eight minutes, until the skins pop. Add the tapioca, sugar, salt and pears. Mix well and cool. Turn into the prepared pie plate and dot with the butter.
4. Cut the remaining pastry into strips and make a lattice top for the pie; or cover with solid pastry. Trim, turn under, and flute the edge. Prick the crust to allow for escape of steam if a solid crust is used.
5. Bake the pie for ten minutes. Reduce the heat to moderate (350° F.) and cook for thirty minutes longer, until browned. Cool.

GRAPE AND APPLE PIE   *6 to 8 servings*

Unbaked Pie Pastry, 2-crust (page 637)
3 cups sliced apples
2 cups Thompson seedless grapes
1 cup sugar
3 tablespoons quick-cooking tapioca
¼ teaspoon salt
¼ teaspoon ground cardamom
2 tablespoons butter
2 tablespoons milk

1. Preheat oven to hot (450° F.).
2. Line a nine-inch pie plate with half of the pastry.
3. Combine the fruits. Blend together the sugar, tapioca, salt and cardamom, and mix with the fruit. Turn the fruit into the prepared pie plate and dot with the butter.
4. Cut the remaining pastry into strips and make a lattice top for the pie. Brush the pastry with milk.
5. Bake for ten minutes. Reduce the heat to moderate (350° F.). Bake for forty to fifty minutes longer, or until fruit is tender and crust is brown.

PEACH AND GINGER PIE   *6 servings*

Unbaked Pie Pastry, 2-crust (page 637)
2 cups sliced peeled fresh peaches
¼ cup all-purpose flour
½ cup brown sugar
¼ teaspoon ground ginger
1 tablespoon butter

1. Preheat oven to hot (400° F.).
2. Line an eight-inch pie plate with half of the pastry.

3. Combine peaches, flour, sugar and ginger. Turn mixture into pie plate and dot with the butter.

4. Cover with remaining pastry and flute the edges. Cut slits for the steam to escape. Bake for thirty to forty minutes, or until browned.

Note: For a fuller pie, increase peaches to three cups.

RAISIN-RHUBARB PIE   *6 to 8 servings*

Unbaked Pie Pastry, 1-crust (page 637)
1 cup dark or golden raisins
4 cups diced rhubarb
¾ cup water
1½ cups sugar
⅓ cup cornstarch
¼ teaspoon salt
2 teaspoons grated orange rind
2 tablespoons butter

1. Preheat oven to hot (425° F.).

2. Line a nine-inch pie plate with the pastry. Roll out the scraps of pastry remaining and cut out five or six petal-shaped pieces. Arrange the pastry petals on a baking sheet.

3. Rinse and drain the raisins. Combine them with the rhubarb, water, sugar, cornstarch and salt in a saucepan. Stir until the dry ingredients are well mixed. Bring to a boil and let simmer for about five minutes.

4. Add the orange rind and butter and cool slightly. Turn the mixture into the prepared pie plate.

5. Bake for twenty-five to thirty minutes, until the pastry is browned. Bake the pastry petals at the same time. They will brown before the pie is finished. Arrange the pastry petals on top of the pie. Cool to lukewarm before serving.

SPICED RHUBARB PIE   *6 to 8 servings*

Unbaked Pie Pastry, 2-crust (page 637)
5 cups 1-inch pieces of rhubarb
1¼ cups sugar
¼ teaspoon salt
3 tablespoons quick-cooking tapioca
2 tablespoons butter
½ teaspoon ground cinnamon
¼ teaspoon grated nutmeg
⅛ teaspoon ground cloves

1. Preheat oven to hot (450° F.).

2. Line a nine-inch pie plate with half of the pastry.

3. Mix the remaining ingredients and turn into the prepared pie plate.

4. Cut the remaining pastry into strips and make a lattice top for the pie. Trim, turn under, and flute the edge.

5. Bake for fifteen minutes. Reduce heat to moderate (350° F.) and bake for about thirty minutes longer, until the rhubarb is tender and the crust is brown.

GRENADINE-CASHEW PIE   *6 to 8 servings*

Unbaked Pie Pastry, 1-crust (page 637)
3 eggs, well beaten
¾ cup grenadine syrup
¾ cup light corn syrup

1 teaspoon vanilla extract
2 tablespoons butter, melted
1½ cups coarsely chopped salted cashews
½ teaspoon grated lemon rind

1. Preheat oven to moderate (350° F.).
2. Line a nine-inch pie plate with the pastry.
3. Combine the eggs with all remaining ingredients. Pour into prepared pie plate.
4. Bake for forty-five to fifty minutes, or until pastry takes on color and the center of the pie is firm when shaken gently. Cool, then chill in refrigerator before serving.

CHESTNUT PIE   *8 servings*

2¼ cups sifted all-purpose flour
1½ cups sugar, approximately
Grated rind of 1 lemon
6 eggs
¾ cup butter, in small pieces
1¼ pounds chestnuts
Salt

2 cups plus 1 tablespoon milk
1 piece of vanilla bean (2 inches)
1 ounce (1 square) unsweetened chocolate, grated
2 to 3 tablespoons any liqueur
Fine dry bread crumbs

1. Mix the flour, one-half cup sugar and the lemon rind. Add one egg and one egg yolk and the butter except for two teaspoons. Reserve the two teaspoons butter for greasing the pan. Mix the dough enough to blend the ingredients and shape it into a ball. Wrap it in aluminum foil or plastic wrap and chill for about one hour.
2. Cut an incision in each chestnut, add them to lightly salted water to cover, and boil for ten minutes. Drain and cover with cool water.
3. Heat the two cups milk and the vanilla bean to simmering. Peel and skin the chestnuts and immediately drop each skinned nut into the milk. Simmer for about twenty minutes, until very tender.
4. Reserve six to eight chestnuts for a garnish and force the remainder through a sieve.
5. Boil one-half cup sugar with two tablespoons water, stirring, until a thick syrup forms. Do not let the sugar caramelize. Add to the sieved chestnuts and mix. Add the grated chocolate, one egg, one egg yolk and the liqueur. Mix.
6. Preheat the oven to moderate (350° F.).
7. Butter a nine-inch pie plate with the two teaspoons butter and sprinkle it with bread crumbs.

8. Roll out the chilled dough to fit the pan. Press it into the pan and make a neat rim. Spread the chestnut mixture over the bottom of the crust.

9. Beat remaining two egg yolks with remaining one tablespoon milk until very thick. Pour over the chestnuts. Beat the four egg whites until stiff, adding one-half cup sugar gradually. Spoon the meringue over the pie, spreading it to the dough all around the edge.

10. Bake on the lower shelf of the oven for about forty-five minutes. Cool. Serve garnished with the reserved chestnuts.

PECAN PIE   *6 servings*

Unbaked Pie Pastry, 1-crust (page 637)
2 eggs
½ cup sugar
½ cup dark corn syrup
2 tablespoons butter
½ teaspoon vanilla extract
1½ cups coarsely chopped pecans

1. Preheat oven to moderate (375° F.).
2. Line an eight-inch pie plate with the pastry.
3. Beat eggs lightly and mix with sugar, corn syrup, butter and vanilla. Stir in the pecans. Pour into the prepared pie plate.
4. Bake for about forty-five minutes, until lightly browned. Cool.

CHOCOLATE PECAN PIE   *8 servings*

Unbaked Pie Pastry, 1-crust (page 637)
2 ounces (2 squares) unsweetened chocolate
3 tablespoons butter
1 cup light corn syrup
¾ cup sugar
3 eggs, lightly beaten
1 teaspoon vanilla extract
1 cup coarsely chopped pecans
½ cup heavy cream, whipped

1. Preheat oven to moderate (375° F.).
2. Line a nine-inch pie plate with the pastry.
3. Melt the chocolate and butter in the top part of a double boiler over boiling water. Boil the syrup and sugar together for two minutes.
4. Blend the melted chocolate mixture and the syrup mixture and pour slowly over the beaten eggs, stirring constantly. Add the vanilla and pecans. Turn the mixture into the prepared pie plate.
5. Bake for forty-five to fifty minutes, until the pie is completely puffed across the top. Cool. Serve topped with whipped cream.

HONEY PECAN PIE   *8 servings*

Unbaked Pie Pastry, 1-crust (page 637)
3 eggs, lightly beaten
⅓ cup granulated sugar
⅓ cup light brown sugar
¼ teaspoon salt
¼ cup butter, melted
½ cup honey
½ cup white corn syrup
1 teaspoon vanilla extract
1 cup pecan halves

1. Preheat oven to moderate (375° F.).
2. Line a nine-inch pie plate with the pastry.
3. Combine all the ingredients except the pecan halves. Pour into the prepared pie plate. Arrange the nut halves on top in any desired pattern.
4. Bake for forty to fifty minutes, until the filling is set and the pastry golden brown. Cool and serve cold or slightly warm.

MOLASSES WALNUT PIE   *8 servings*

Unbaked Pie Pastry, 1-crust (page 637)
¼ cup butter, at room temperature
½ cup granulated sugar
3 eggs
1 cup molasses
½ teaspoon salt
2 teaspoons grated lemon rind
1¼ cups chopped walnuts
Whipped cream

1. Preheat oven to hot (450° F.).
2. Line a nine-inch pie plate with the pastry. Chill.
3. With a spoon work the butter in a bowl until softened. Add the sugar and continue to work with the spoon until blended.
4. Add eggs, molasses and salt, and beat until thoroughly blended. Stir in lemon rind and walnuts. Pour the mixture into the prepared pie plate.
5. Bake for ten minutes. Reduce temperature to moderate (350° F.) and bake for thirty minutes longer. Cool, then chill. Garnish with whipped cream.

CHESS PIE   *6 to 8 servings*

Unbaked Pie Pastry, 1-crust (page 637)
2 eggs
1½ tablespoons all-purpose flour
⅔ cup firmly packed brown sugar
½ teaspoon salt
1 teaspoon vanilla extract
1 cup heavy cream
½ cup seedless golden raisins
1 cup pitted dates, cut up
1 cup broken walnut meats

1. Preheat oven to moderate (350° F.). Set the rack near the bottom of the oven.
2. Line a nine-inch pie plate with the pastry and flute the edges.

3. Beat the eggs until thick and lemon-colored. Combine the flour, brown sugar and salt and add to the eggs while beating. Stir in the vanilla, cream, raisins, dates and walnuts. Spoon into the prepared pie plate.

4. Bake for fifty to sixty minutes, until a knife inserted into the center comes out clean. Serve warm or cold.

ITALIAN COTTAGE-CHEESE PIE   *6 to 8 servings*

2 pounds creamed cottage cheese
½ cup sugar
1 teaspoon grated lemon rind
3 tablespoons minced candied orange peel
2 tablespoons chopped citron
½ cup grated semisweet chocolate
Baked Pie Pastry, 9 inches (page 637)

1. Sieve or whip the cottage cheese until smooth.
2. Add the sugar, lemon rind, orange peel, citron and chocolate. Chill.
3. Turn the mixture into the baked pie shell. Sprinkle the top with cinnamon or garnish with whipped cream.

FROZEN CHOCOLATE CHEESE PIE   *6 to 8 servings*

Graham-Cracker Piecrust (page 641)
4 ounces sweet cooking chocolate
¼ cup milk
3 ounces cream cheese, softened
⅓ cup sugar
1 cup heavy cream, whipped
⅛ teaspoon salt
½ teaspoon vanilla extract

1. Preheat oven to moderate (375° F.).
2. Make the piecrust and press firmly onto the bottom and sides of an eight-inch pie plate. Bake for eight minutes. Cool thoroughly.
3. Melt the chocolate with two tablespoons of the milk in the top part of a double boiler. Cool slightly.
4. Combine the cream cheese with the sugar and blend in the remaining milk until mixture is smooth.
5. Blend the cheese mixture into the whipped cream. Fold in the chocolate, salt and vanilla and spoon into the cooled crust. Freeze until firm.

LEMON-CHEESE PIE   *6 to 8 servings*

Graham-Cracker Piecrust (page 641)
¼ cup lemon juice
9 ounces cream cheese
2 eggs, beaten
¾ cup plus 1 tablespoon sugar
1 tablespoon grated lemon rind
1 cup sour cream

1. Preheat oven to moderate (350° F.).

2. Make the piecrust and press onto the bottom and sides of an eight-inch pie plate.

3. Mix the lemon juice and cream cheese well. Add the beaten eggs and three-quarters cup of the sugar. Beat until fluffy. Pour into the unbaked crust.

4. Bake for fifteen to twenty minutes. Remove from oven and cool for five minutes.

5. Prepare a topping by mixing the lemon rind, remaining tablespoon of sugar and the sour cream. Spread over the pie, return to the oven, and bake for ten minutes longer. Cool. Chill in the refrigerator for at least five hours before serving.

RICOTTA PIE   *8 servings*

PASTRY:

2½ cups sifted all-purpose flour	1 egg yolk
½ teaspoon salt	3 tablespoons dry white wine or
¼ cup sugar	sherry
¾ cup butter	Cold water

FILLING:

1¼ pounds ricotta cheese	⅓ cup finely chopped citron
⅓ cup sugar	2 tablespoons kirsch
¼ teaspoon salt	2 tablespoons orange juice
4 eggs, separated	Confectioners' sugar
1 teaspoon almond extract	

1. Preheat oven to hot (400° F.).

2. Place the flour, salt and sugar in a bowl. Blend in the butter with the finger tips or with a pastry blender until the mixture resembles coarse oatmeal.

3. Add the egg yolk, wine and enough water to gather the mixture into a ball. Chill the dough for thirty minutes to make it easier to handle.

4. Roll out two thirds of the dough on a lightly floured pastry cloth or board. Line a ten-inch pie plate. Roll out remaining dough to one-eighth-inch thickness and cut with a pastry wheel into long strips one-half inch wide.

5. Force the cheese through a sieve. Stir in the sugar, salt, egg yolks, almond extract, citron, kirsch and orange juice. Beat the egg whites until stiff but not dry and fold into the cheese mixture.

6. Pour the mixture into the pastry-lined pie plate. Use the pastry strips to make a lattice over the top. Finish with a stand-up edge and decorate.

7. Place in the oven and immediately reduce the heat to moderate

(375° F.). Bake for about forty-five minutes, or until the filling is set and a knife inserted into center comes out clean.

8. Turn off the heat and allow pie to cool to room temperature in the oven. Pie will fall somewhat as it cools. Sprinkle with confectioners' sugar. Chill.

ALMOND TART   *8 servings*

1½ cups sifted all-purpose flour
¾ cup plus 1 tablespoon sugar
½ cup plus 1 tablespoon butter
 4 eggs
 1 cup plus 2 tablespoons finely grated blanched almonds
1½ tablespoons grated lemon rind
⅓ cup lemon juice
¼ teaspoon almond extract
⅓ cup apricot preserves, sieved
   Toasted slivered almonds

1. Preheat oven to moderate (375° F.).

2. Place the flour in a bowl and add the tablespoon of sugar. Work in the butter with the tips of the fingers, or with a pastry blender, until the mixture resembles rolled oats. Lightly beat one of the eggs and add to the dough. Gather the dough into a ball.

3. Roll out on a lightly floured board or pastry cloth to one-eighth-inch thickness. Line a nine-inch springform pan, tart pan or flan ring placed on a baking sheet. Prick the dough, line the dough with foil and fill with dried beans or rice.

4. Bake for five or six minutes, until the pastry is set. Remove the beans or rice and foil and bake for eight to ten minutes longer, until the pastry is cooked but only lightly browned.

5. Beat the remaining eggs until stiff. Gradually add the remaining sugar while beating until the mixture is pale and thick. Gently fold in the almonds, lemon rind and juice, and the almond extract.

6. Pour the mixture into the partly baked tart shell. Return to the oven and continue baking for about thirty minutes, or until the filling is lightly browned and set.

7. Remove the tart from the oven and cool. There will be some shrinkage. Spread the apricot preserves over the top and decorate with slivered almonds. The tart may be served slightly warm or chilled.

BLANCHING NUTS:

To blanch nuts such as almonds that have a brown inner skin, cover the shelled nuts with boiling water and let stand until skin slips off easily. This takes from one to five minutes. The shorter the time, the better.

APPLE TART   *6 to 8 servings*

An apple tart with almonds, served with whipped cream, is an ideal dessert for an Easter menu. This tart is really an upside-down pie because it is baked with the crust on top, then inverted. It can be served hot or cold.

1 cup butter
1 cup light brown sugar
3 cups apple slices
¼ cup blanched almonds
2 teaspoons fresh lemon juice
¼ teaspoon ground cinnamon

4 teaspoons grated lemon rind
1¼ cups sifted all-purpose flour
1 teaspoon granulated sugar
1 egg, lightly beaten
Whipped cream, sweetened and flavored

1. Preheat oven to hot (450° F.).
2. Melt half of the butter in a round or square heatproof skillet or baking dish (8 or 9 inches). Add the brown sugar and heat for three minutes, stirring, until the mixture has heavy bubbles. Cool until the sugar begins to set.
3. Cover the cooled sugar mixture with the apple slices in any desired pattern. Stud with the almonds. Blend the lemon juice, cinnamon and half of the grated rind, and sprinkle the mixture over the apple slices.
4. Blend the flour and granulated sugar in a bowl. Add remaining lemon rind. Cut in remaining butter with fingers or a pastry blender until the mixture resembles coarse meal. Add the egg. Work the dough quickly, then gather into a ball.
5. With a floured rolling pin roll out the dough on a lightly floured board into a sheet that will fit the inside of the baking dish. Fit pastry over the apples but do not attach to the dish. Trim neatly.
6. Bake for fifteen to twenty minutes, until pastry is golden brown. Cool for two minutes, then invert onto serving platter. Serve with sweetened whipped cream flavored with vanilla, brandy, or orange liqueur.

CHERRY TART   *6 servings*

4 cups (two 1-pound cans) pitted red sour cherries packed in water
1 cup sugar
2 tablespoons brandy (optional)
1½ cups sifted all-purpose flour
1½ teaspoons ground cinnamon

⅛ teaspoon salt
½ cup butter
1 egg, beaten
4 teaspoons cornstarch
¼ teaspoon almond extract
Sweetened whipped cream

1. Drain the cherries. Sprinkle them with ten tablespoons of the sugar and the brandy. Allow to stand for one hour, tossing occasionally.
2. Sift the flour together with the cinnamon, remaining sugar and salt into a bowl. Cut in the butter with two knives or pastry blender. Mix in the egg and work the mixture with the hands until it just holds together. Chill for thirty minutes.
3. Preheat oven to moderate (350° F.).
4. Pat the crust mixture into an eight-inch pie plate or flan ring, making

an even layer. Crimp the dough around a standing edge.

5. Drain the cherries. Measure the drained syrup and, if necessary, add water to make three-quarters cup liquid. Place one-half cup of the syrup in a pan and bring to a boil. Stir the cornstarch into the remaining one-quarter cup of the syrup.

6. Pour the hot syrup over the blended cornstarch, return to the pan, and cook over low heat, stirring, for two or three minutes. Add the almond extract.

7. Place the cherries in the tart shell or flan ring and pour the hot sauce over them. Bake for fifty minutes. Serve warm or cold, garnish with whipped cream.

CRANBERRY APPLE TARTS   *6 tarts*

2 cups fresh cranberries
4 tart medium apples, peeled and diced
1¼ cups sugar
½ teaspoon salt
½ cup water

3 tablespoons quick-cooking tapioca
1 teaspoon vanilla extract
Unbaked Pie Pastry, 2-crust (page 637)
2 tablespoons butter

1. Preheat oven to hot (425° F.).

2. Cook fruits, sugar, salt and water in a covered saucepan for ten minutes. Stir in tapioca and cool. Add vanilla.

3. Use half of the pastry to line six five-inch tart shells. Dot each with one teaspoon of the butter. Fill with the cooled fruits.

4. Cut remaining pastry into thin strips and arrange a lattice top on each tart. Bake for twenty-five minutes.

BANANA SOUR-CREAM PIE   *6 to 8 servings*

1½ cups sour cream
3 egg yolks
¾ cup sugar
2 tablespoons cornstarch
1 teaspoon vanilla extract

2 medium bananas
2 tablespoons lemon juice
Baked Pie Pastry, 9 inches (page 637)

1. Put the sour cream into the top part of a double boiler and heat over boiling water until moderately hot. The cream will get thinner as it heats.

2. Beat the egg yolks lightly in a mixing bowl and stir in the sugar and cornstarch. Gradually add the hot sour cream, stirring vigorously. Cook over boiling water for fifteen to twenty minutes, until thick. Remove mixture from the heat, add the vanilla, and cool.

3. Peel and slice the bananas and sprinkle with the lemon juice. Put half of the bananas on the bottom of the baked pie shell and spoon half of the cold filling over them. Cover with the remaining bananas and then the remaining filling. Chill for several hours before serving.

BROWN-SUGAR PIE   *6 to 8 servings*

Unbaked Pie Pastry, 1-crust (page 637)
½ cup butter
1½ cups light brown sugar
2 egg yolks
5 tablespoons cognac
3 egg whites

1. Preheat oven to moderate (375° F.).
2. Line a nine-inch pie plate with the pastry.
3. Cream the butter, adding the brown sugar gradually. Add egg yolks and beat until fluffy. Add the cognac.
4. Beat egg whites until stiff but not dry. Fold into the sugar mixture. Turn at once into the prepared pie plate.
5. Bake on the lower shelf of the oven for about forty-five minutes, until crust is lightly browned. Cool. The pie will puff while baking and fall on cooling. Serve with unsweetened whipped cream.

FRANGIPANE TART   *6 to 8 servings*

Sweet Pie Pastry (page 639)
1 cup butter, softened
2 cups almond paste
4 eggs, beaten
2 teaspoons grated lemon rind
4 teaspoons flour
Apricot Glaze (page 682)
¼ cup slivered toasted almonds

1. Preheat oven to moderate (350° F.).
2. Line a nine- or ten-inch flan ring with the pastry. Chill.
3. Cream the butter. Stir in the almond paste alternately with the eggs. Beat until smooth. Stir in the lemon rind and flour.
4. Brush the pastry with additional melted butter and fill almost to the top with the filling. Bake on the lowest rack in the oven for nearly one hour, until the tart is golden brown.
5. Brush the tart while still hot with hot apricot glaze. Sprinkle with the slivered almonds.

GRAPE CREAM TARTS   *8 tarts*

¼ cup cornstarch
½ cup sugar
1/16 teaspoon salt
2 cups milk
4 egg yolks
1½ teaspoons vanilla extract
8 Baked Tart Shells (page 640), cooled
1 cup Thompson seedless grapes, halved if large
Whipped cream and fresh mint sprigs

1. Combine cornstarch, sugar and salt in the top part of a double boiler or in a saucepan. Heat one and three-quarters cups milk. Gradually add it to

the cornstarch mixture and stir and cook over medium heat until mixture is very thick.

2. Blend remaining milk with egg yolks and add. Cook over hot water or low heat until mixture is almost as thick as mayonnaise. Remove from heat and stir in vanilla. Cool completely.

3. Spoon filling into the baked tart shells. Chill for three to four hours, or overnight. Just before serving arrange the grapes over the tops of the tarts. Garnish each tart with a tiny mound of whipped cream and a sprig of fresh mint.

STRAWBERRY CREAM PIE   *8 servings*

Baked Pie Pastry, 9 inches (page 637)
2 tablespoons granulated sugar
2 tablespoons fine dry bread crumbs
Pastry Cream (page 677)
3 cups strawberries
1 cup red currant jelly or Bar-le-Duc
1 tablespoon kirsch
Confectioners' sugar

1. Sprinkle the bottom of the baked pie shell with the granulated sugar and bread crumbs.

2. Pour the pastry cream into the shell and completely cover the cream with the strawberries, symmetrically arranged.

3. Heat the currant jelly slowly until it is melted. Strain it. Stir in the kirsch.

4. Using a large paint brush, coat the strawberries with the jelly.

5. Pour a little confectioners' sugar into a small wire sieve and sprinkle around the rim of the pie. Chill until serving time.

LEMON CREAM PIE   *6 to 8 servings*

1½ cups sugar
7 tablespoons cornstarch
¼ teaspoon salt
1½ cups hot water
3 egg yolks, beaten
1 teaspoon grated lemon rind
½ cup fresh lemon juice
2 tablespoons butter
Baked Pie Pastry, 9 inches (page 637)
Whipped cream

1. Mix sugar, cornstarch and salt in a heavy saucepan. Add hot water gradually, stirring. Lower heat and cook, stirring, until clear and thickened. Remove from heat.

2. Stir several spoonfuls of the hot mixture into the beaten egg yolks. Mix well and pour into saucepan. Bring to a boil, stirring. Lower heat and continue to cook and stir for about two minutes, until very thick. Remove from heat.

3. Add lemon rind and juice and the butter. Stir until blended and cool. Pour into the baked pie shell and spread evenly. Top with whipped cream.

LEMON SOUR-CREAM PIE   *6 to 8 servings*

1 cup sugar	1 cup milk
3 tablespoons cornstarch	1 cup sour cream
¼ cup butter	Baked Pie Pastry, 9 inches (page
¼ cup lemon juice	637)
3 egg yolks	½ cup heavy cream, whipped
Grated rind of 1 lemon	

1. Combine the sugar and cornstarch in a saucepan. Add the butter, lemon juice, egg yolks, lemon rind and milk. Cook over medium heat, stirring constantly, until thickened and smooth. Chill.

2. Fold the sour cream into the chilled mixture and spoon into the baked pie shell. Chill well. Serve topped with whipped cream.

ORANGE-CUSTARD PIE   *6 to 8 servings*

Unbaked Pie Pastry, 1-crust (page	2 teaspoons grated orange rind
637)	1⅔ cups orange juice
4 eggs, lightly beaten	2 or 3 oranges, sectioned
¾ cup sugar	1½ teaspoons cornstarch
1½ cups light cream, scalded	3 tablespoons Grand Marnier

1. Preheat oven to hot (425° F.). Place the rack in the lower half of the oven.

2. Line a nine-inch pie plate with the pastry. Brush the pastry with a little of the beaten eggs and chill.

3. Mix remaining eggs with the sugar and cream. Add orange rind and one and one-third cups orange juice. Pour into the pastry-lined pie plate.

4. Bake for about thirty-five minutes, until a knife inserted into the center comes out clean. Arrange orange sections over the baked custard.

5. Mix remaining orange juice and the cornstarch. Cook, stirring, until thick. Add the liqueur and pour over oranges. Chill.

PUMPKIN PIE WITH HONEY   *6 to 8 servings*

Unbaked Pie Pastry, 1-crust (page	1 cup honey
637)	½ cup milk
2 cups pumpkin purée	½ cup heavy cream
½ teaspoon ground ginger	¼ cup butter
½ teaspoon ground cinnamon	1 cup brown sugar
1 teaspoon salt	1 cup pecan halves
4 whole eggs, lightly beaten	

1. Preheat oven to hot (450° F.).

2. Line a nine-inch pie plate with the pastry.

3. Mix the pumpkin with the ginger, cinnamon and salt. Beat the eggs with the honey, milk and cream until well mixed. Gradually stir the egg mixture into the pumpkin mixture. Pour into the prepared pie plate.

4. Bake for ten minutes. Reduce the oven temperature to moderate (325° F.) and bake for about forty minutes longer, or until filling is firm. Cool slightly.

5. Mix the butter, brown sugar and pecans. Spread topping over the cooled pumpkin. Place the pie under the broiler for four to five minutes. Serve warm or cold.

Pumpkin pie is a favorite Thanksgiving dessert. Decorate the top with pastry cut-outs in the shape of pumpkins or leaves for a holiday appearance.

RUM PUMPKIN CREAM PIE   *6 to 8 servings*

Unbaked Pie Pastry, 1-crust (page 637)
1½ cups pumpkin purée
¾ cup sugar
½ teaspoon salt
½ teaspoon freshly grated ginger-root

½ teaspoon freshly grated nutmeg
3 eggs
1 cup milk
¼ cup dark rum
¾ cup heavy cream

1. Preheat oven to hot (425° F.).
2. Line a nine-inch pie plate with the pastry and flute the edges.
3. Combine the pumpkin, sugar, salt, gingerroot and nutmeg. Mix the eggs, milk, rum and cream. Stir into the pumpkin mixture. Pour the pumpkin mixture into the prepared pie plate.
4. Bake for fifteen minutes. Reduce the heat to moderate (350° F.). Bake for thirty to forty minutes longer, or until set. Serve with sweetened whipped cream flavored with rum and ground ginger.

RASPBERRY CUSTARD PIE   *6 to 8 servings*

Unbaked Pie Pastry, 1-crust (page 637)
4 eggs
⅔ cup sugar
½ teaspoon salt

½ teaspoon grated nutmeg
2⅔ cups milk
1 teaspoon vanilla extract
1 cup fresh or frozen raspberries, sweetened to taste

1. Preheat oven to hot (425° F.).
2. Line a nine-inch pie plate with the pastry and flute the edges.
3. Beat the eggs with a rotary beater until thoroughly blended. Add the sugar, salt, nutmeg, milk and vanilla. Stir until smooth. Pour the custard mixture into the prepared pie plate.
4. Bake for fifteen minutes. Reduce the temperature to moderate (350° F.) and bake for thirty minutes longer, or until a silver knife inserted into filling about one inch from pastry edge comes out clean. Chill. Spread top with sweetened raspberries. Serve with whipped cream.

RHUBARB CUSTARD PIE   *6 to 8 servings*

Unbaked Pie Pastry, 1-crust (page 637)
⅔ cup plus 1½ tablespoons sugar
2 tablespoons all-purpose flour
3 cups ½-inch pieces of rhubarb

3 egg yolks
⅛ teaspoon salt
1¼ cups milk
½ teaspoon vanilla extract

1. Preheat oven to hot (425° F.). Place the rack in the lower half of the oven.

2. Line a nine-inch pie plate with the pastry and flute the edges.

3. Mix two-thirds cup sugar with the flour. Sprinkle about two table-spoons of the mixture over the bottom of the pastry.

4. Mix the rhubarb with the remaining sugar-flour mixture and turn into the prepared pie plate.

5. Beat the egg yolks lightly with one and one-half tablespoons sugar. Add the salt, milk and vanilla and pour the mixture over the rhubarb.

6. Bake for twenty minutes. Lower temperature to moderate (350° F.) and continue to bake the pie for twenty-five to thirty minutes, until a knife inserted into the center comes out clean.

CITRUS CHIFFON PIE   *6 to 8 servings*

1 envelope unflavored gelatin
½ cup cold water
¼ teaspoon salt
4 eggs, separated
1 can (6 ounces) frozen orange- or tangerine-juice concentrate

½ cup sugar
½ cup heavy cream, whipped
Baked Pie Pastry, 9 inches (page 637)

1. Sprinkle the gelatin on the cold water in the top part of a double boiler. Add the salt and egg yolks; mix well.

2. Place over boiling water and cook, stirring constantly, for three to five minutes, until the mixture thickens slightly and the gelatin dissolves.

3. Remove from the heat. Add the fruit-juice concentrate and chill, stirring occasionally, until the mixture mounds slightly when dropped from a spoon.

4. Beat the egg whites until stiff but not dry. Gradually add the sugar and beat until very stiff. Fold in the gelatin mixture; fold in the whipped cream. Turn into the baked pie shell and chill until firm. If desired, garnish with additional whipped cream and fresh mint.

LEMON CAKE PIE   *6 servings*

Unbaked Pie Pastry, 1-crust (page 637)
1 cup sugar
1 tablespoon butter
2 eggs, separated

2 tablespoons all-purpose flour
Grated rind of 1 lemon
Juice of 1 lemon
1 cup milk

1. Preheat oven to hot (450° F.).

2. Line a nine-inch pie plate with the pastry.

3. Cream together the sugar and butter. Beat the egg yolks and add to the creamed mixture. Add flour, lemon rind and juice and the milk. Beat the egg

whites until stiff but not dry and add to mixture. Pour into the prepared pie plate.

4. Bake for ten minutes. Reduce oven heat to moderate (325° F.) and bake for twenty minutes longer, or until done.

LEMON SOUFFLÉ PIE   *6 to 8 servings*

⅓ cup lemon juice
1 teaspoon grated lemon rind
3 tablespoons hot water
¼ teaspoon salt

¾ cup sugar
3 eggs, separated
Baked Pie Pastry, 10 inches (page 637)

1. Preheat oven to moderate (325° F.).
2. Put the lemon juice and rind, hot water, salt, one-half cup of the sugar and the well-beaten egg yolks in the top part of a double boiler. Cook, stirring occasionally, for about fifteen minutes, until thickened.
3. Beat the egg whites until stiff; add the remaining one-quarter cup sugar gradually while beating.
4. Fold the hot lemon mixture into the beaten egg whites. Pour the mixture into the baked pie shell. Bake for about fifteen minutes, until delicately browned.

LEMON EASTER PIE   *6 servings*

1 envelope unflavored gelatin
⅓ cup fresh lemon juice
4 eggs, beaten
1½ cups sugar
⅛ teaspoon salt
3 tablespoons butter
¾ teaspoon grated lemon rind

¾ teaspoon vanilla extract
1½ cups heavy cream, whipped
Baked Pie Pastry, 9 inches (page 637)
Whipped cream and grated lemon rind for garnish

1. Soften the gelatin in the lemon juice in a saucepan or the top part of a double boiler. Add the eggs, sugar, salt and butter. Mix well. Cook, stirring, over very low heat or hot, not boiling, water until the mixture thickens. When properly thickened, the sauce will coat the sides of a wooden spoon.
2. Remove from the heat and chill until mixture mounds slightly when dropped from a spoon. To hasten chilling, the saucepan may be set in a larger vessel containing cracked ice.
3. Fold in the lemon rind, vanilla and whipped cream.
4. Turn the mixture into the baked pie shell. Chill the pie in the refrigerator until the filling is set. To serve, garnish with whipped cream and grated lemon rind.

LIME-PISTACHIO CHIFFON PIE   *6 to 8 servings*

1 envelope unflavored gelatin
¼ cup cold water
4 eggs, separated
1 cup sugar
⅓ cup lime juice
½ teaspoon salt

2 teaspoons grated lime rind
Green food coloring
⅓ cup finely chopped pistachio nuts
Baked Pie Pastry, 9 inches (page 637)

1. Soften the gelatin in the cold water.
2. Beat the egg yolks; then beat in one-half cup of the sugar. Add the lime juice and salt. Cook, stirring, in the top part of a double boiler over hot water until thickened.
3. Add the grated rind and the softened gelatin. Stir until the gelatin is dissolved. Tint the mixture pale green with food coloring. Chill until the mixture begins to thicken.
4. Beat the egg whites until they form soft peaks. Beat in the remaining sugar slowly. Fold the egg whites and pistachio nuts into the gelatin mixture. Spoon into the baked pie shell and chill until set.

WALNUT CHIFFON PIE   *8 servings*

1 envelope unflavored gelatin
¾ cup milk
3 eggs, separated
½ cup sugar
¼ teaspoon grated nutmeg
⅛ teaspoon salt

1 tablespoon rum
1 tablespoon cognac or brandy
½ cup heavy cream, whipped
Walnut Crust (see below)
Walnut halves

1. Soften the gelatin in one-quarter cup of the milk.
2. Beat the egg yolks, one-quarter cup of the sugar, the nutmeg and salt together in the top part of a double boiler. Stir in the remaining milk and cook, stirring, over hot water until mixture thickens and coats a spoon. Add softened gelatin and stir until gelatin is dissolved. Remove mixture from heat and cool. Add rum and cognac.
3. Beat the egg whites until stiff. Gradually beat in the remaining sugar. Fold into the gelatin mixture. Fold in whipped cream. Pour mixture into chilled walnut crust. Chill until firm. Garnish with walnut halves.

WALNUT CRUST: *1 piecrust*

1½ cups ground walnuts
¼ cup butter

2 tablespoons sugar

1. Preheat oven to hot (400° F.).
2. Combine the walnuts with the butter and sugar. With the back of a spoon, press mixture onto bottom and sides of a buttered nine-inch pie plate. Bake for eight minutes. Chill crust before filling.

ORANGE QUEEN PIE   *6 to 8 servings*

3 navel oranges, peeled
¾ cup plus 2 tablespoons sugar
1 envelope unflavored gelatin
¼ cup cold water
2 eggs, separated
¼ teaspoon salt

¾ cup orange juice
2 tablespoons dry sherry
1 cup heavy cream, whipped
   Baked Pie Pastry, 9 inches (page 637)

1. Cut two of the oranges into bite-size pieces to make one cup. Sprinkle with the two tablespoons of sugar and set aside. Cut the remaining orange into thin slices, halve the slices, and set aside.

2. Combine the gelatin, water, remaining sugar, egg yolks, salt and orange juice in the top part of a double boiler. Cook, stirring, over simmering water until the mixture thickens.

3. Remove from the heat and cool slightly. Add the sherry and the sweetened orange pieces with their juice.

4. Beat the egg whites until stiff but not dry and fold into the gelatin mixture. Fold in half of the cream. Spoon the mixture into the baked pie shell. Chill until set. Garnish with the remaining cream and the half slices of orange.

BUTTERSCOTCH MERINGUE PIE   *6 servings*

2 eggs, separated
1 cup light brown sugar
⅛ teaspoon salt
¼ cup all-purpose flour
1½ cups milk

¼ cup butter
1 teaspoon vanilla extract
   Baked Pie Pastry, 8 inches (page 637)
¼ cup granulated sugar

1. Preheat oven to hot (425° F.).

2. Beat the egg yolks and mix with the brown sugar, salt, flour, milk and butter in a heavy saucepan. Cook, stirring constantly with a wire whisk, until thick. Cover and cool for fifteen minutes, stirring occasionally.

3. Add the vanilla and pour mixture into the baked pie shell.

4. Beat the egg whites until they stand in soft peaks. Gradually beat in the granulated sugar. Beat until meringue stands in very stiff peaks. Spread atop the pie filling.

5. Bake for five or six minutes, until delicately brown.

LIME MERINGUE PIE   *6 to 8 servings*

3 egg yolks
1 can (14 ounces) sweetened condensed milk
1 teaspoon grated lime rind
¾ cup lime juice

Green food coloring (optional)
Baked Pie Pastry, 8 or 9 inches (page 637)
Meringue Pie Topping (page 565)

1. Preheat oven to moderate (325° F.).

2. Beat egg yolks until thick and lemon-colored. Fold in condensed milk, lime rind and juice. Add food coloring, if desired. Pour the mixture into the baked pie shell.

3. Pile the meringue on the pie, sealing edge to pastry to avoid shrinkage. Bake for about fifteen minutes, or until lightly browned. Cool to room temperature and chill before serving.

ORANGE MERINGUE PIE   *6 servings*

¾ cup sugar
½ cup all-purpose flour
¼ teaspoon salt
1¼ cups water
2 egg yolks
½ cup orange juice

2 tablespoons lemon juice
1 tablespoon grated orange rind
  Baked Pie Pastry, 8 inches (page 637)
  Soft meringue (see below)

1. Mix the sugar, flour and salt in the top part of a double boiler. Stir in the water to make a smooth mixture and cook over direct heat for five minutes, stirring constantly.

2. Beat the egg yolks slightly. Stir them into the hot mixture gradually and cook over boiling water for about five minutes longer, or until very thick.

3. Remove from the heat. Add the orange and lemon juices and orange rind. Chill. Pour the chilled filling into the baked pie shell and top with unbaked meringue. Garnish with drained orange sections if desired.

SOFT MERINGUE:

2 egg whites
½ cup sugar

2 tablespoons water

1. Mix the egg whites, sugar and water in the top part of a double boiler. Beat with a rotary or electric beater until thoroughly mixed.

2. Place over boiling water and cook for one minute, beating constantly. Remove from the heat and continue beating until the meringue stands in stiff peaks. Pile lightly over the pie filling. This type of meringue is not browned in the oven.

RHUBARB MERINGUE PIE   *6 to 8 servings*

Unbaked Pie Pastry, 1-crust
  (page 637)
4 cups 1-inch pieces of rhubarb
1¼ cups sugar
¼ teaspoon salt

5 tablespoons water
2 tablespoons cornstarch
1 tablespoon lemon juice
5 eggs, separated

1. Preheat oven to hot (450° F.).

2. Roll out the pastry and fit it into a nine-inch pie plate without stretching it. Trim the edge with scissors, leaving about one inch of pastry hanging over edge. Fold one-half inch of the pastry under and make a standing rim. Flute it with the fingers. Bake on lower shelf of oven for about fifteen minutes, until brown. Cool.

3. Reduce oven heat to moderate (325° F.).

4. Mix the rhubarb, one cup of the sugar, the salt and two tablespoons water. Bring to a boil over low heat.

5. Mix the cornstarch with the remaining three tablespoons water. Add to rhubarb and cook, stirring, until thickened. Add the lemon juice.

6. Beat the egg yolks slightly. Add a little of the rhubarb mixture to the egg yolks and return all to the rhubarb in the saucepan. Cook over very low heat, stirring, until thick. Cool.

7. Beat the egg whites until stiff. Fold slightly less than half into the cool rhubarb mixture. Turn rhubarb into the cooled piecrust.

8. Gradually add the remaining one-quarter cup of sugar to the remaining egg whites and beat until meringue stands in sharp peaks.

9. Spread the meringue over filling to touch the crust at all points to prevent shrinkage. Bake for about fifteen minutes, until lightly browned.

APPLE DUMPLINGS   *6 servings*

2 cups sifted all-purpose flour	1 cup sugar
1 tablespoon baking powder	1 teaspoon grated nutmeg
1 teaspoon salt	1 teaspoon ground cinnamon
⅔ cup plus 2 tablespoons butter	¾ cup water
¾ cup milk	2 tablespoons lemon juice
6 large baking apples	

1. Preheat oven to hot (450° F.).

2. Sift together the flour, baking powder and salt. Cut in the two-thirds cup of butter until the dough has the consistency of cornmeal. Moisten with the milk, stirring with a fork as little as possible. Place the dough on a floured board and roll it into a rectangular sheet about one-quarter inch thick. Cut it into six squares.

3. Peel and core the apples and place one in the center of each square of dough. Mix one-quarter cup of the sugar with the nutmeg and cinnamon. Fill the centers of the apples with this mixture, using additional sugar if necessary to fill the cavities.

4. Make a syrup by bringing to a boil the three-quarters cup water, remaining three-quarters cup sugar, the lemon juice and remaining butter.

5. Roll the dough around the apples and fasten the edges by moistening and pinching together. Place in a large shallow pan. Pour the syrup over the dumplings.

6. Bake the dumplings for ten minutes. Reduce the heat to moderate (350° F.) and bake for thirty minutes longer. Serve warm with the syrup from the pan poured over them.

CRANBERRY DUMPLINGS   *6 servings*

2¼ cups sifted all-purpose flour
  2 teaspoons baking powder
  1 teaspoon salt
 ⅔ cup shortening

½ cup milk
1 pound cranberries
1½ cups sugar

1. Preheat oven to moderate (375° F.).
2. Sift together two cups of the flour, the baking powder and salt. Cut in the shortening until the lumps are the size of small peas. Add milk all at once and stir until moistened. Form the dough into a ball and roll out on a lightly floured surface into a rectangular sheet about one-quarter inch thick. Cut into six squares.
3. Wash cranberries and combine with the sugar and remaining flour. Press some of the berries into a half-cup measure and unmold onto one of the pastry squares. Bring corners of square to center. Seal edges almost to center; turn back the points of dough, exposing cranberries. Repeat with remaining berries and pastry.
4. Place the dumplings one inch apart in a greased baking pan. Bake for thirty-five minutes, or until lightly browned.

BEIGNETS SOUFFLÉS   *About 24*

Although most people think of doughnuts as ring-shaped cakes, the original version did not have a hole, but was a small lump of dough. The most delicate of all these fried pastries is the beignet soufflé *of French origin, for it is made with cream-puff paste. When the dough is dropped into hot fat, it explodes to create a hollow center, and this accounts for its delicate nature.*

½ cup butter
1 cup water
1 cup sifted all-purpose flour
4 eggs

1 tablespoon sugar
½ teaspoon grated orange rind
½ teaspoon grated lemon rind
  Oil or shortening for deep frying

1. Heat the butter and water until the butter has melted and the water is boiling.
2. Add the flour all at once and turn off the heat. With a wooden spoon stir vigorously until the mixture forms a ball that leaves the sides of the pan.
3. Add the eggs, one at a time, stir, and then beat until the batter is smooth after each addition. Continue beating until a thick dough is formed.
4. Add the sugar and grated rinds and mix thoroughly.

5. Drop by rounded teaspoons into the oil or shortening heated to 380° F. on a frying thermometer. The puffs rise to the top and should turn by themselves, but if there is any portion that does not brown, turn the puff with a slotted spoon. Frying time is about twelve minutes. Drain on paper towels.

6. Sprinkle the fritters with sifted confectioners' sugar. Serve hot, with Strawberry Sauce (page 685) or Jam Sauce (page 687) or any flavorful sauce.

BUÑUELOS (Mexican fritters) *18 to 24 large fritters*

4 cups sifted all-purpose flour
2 tablespoons sugar
2 teaspoons baking powder
2 teaspoons salt

2 eggs, beaten
¾ cup milk, approximately
¼ cup butter, melted
Oil for deep frying

1. Place flour, sugar, baking powder and salt in a bowl. Beat the eggs and milk together and add to the dry ingredients. Then add the butter. Mix into a dough that can be easily handled without being sticky. Add one to two more tablespoons of milk if necessary.

2. Turn dough out on a lightly floured board and knead until very smooth. Divide into eighteen to twenty-four pieces and shape each piece into a ball. Cover with a cloth and let stand for twenty minutes.

3. Roll each ball on a lightly floured board into a large round about the size of a tortilla. Let the rounds stand for five minutes.

4. Heat the oil to 365° F. on a frying thermometer. Cook the fritters, two at a time, until they are a light golden brown all over. As each one finishes frying, remove it to paper towels to drain.

5. Serve sprinkled with cinnamon and sugar or thin honey. A favorite way is to break them up into a large bowl and pour over them a thin brown-sugar syrup flavored with stick cinnamon. These freeze well. Wrap each separately in foil, because they are fragile. Crisp them in the oven before serving.

ATHENIAN TEA CAKES *About 3½ dozen*

2 cups sifted all-purpose flour
½ teaspoon salt
½ teaspoon baking powder
2 eggs, beaten
1 teaspoon lemon juice
¼ cup fresh orange juice, strained
  Vegetable oil

¾ cup light honey
¼ cup water
¾ cup chopped walnuts
½ teaspoon ground cinnamon

1. Sift the flour, salt and baking powder together.

2. Combine the eggs and lemon and orange juices and blend well. Gradually add the flour mixture. Knead until smooth. Turn the dough out

onto a lightly floured board. Divide the dough into halves and work one half at a time.

3. Roll the dough to an eight-inch thickness. Using a pastry wheel or knife, cut the dough into strips measuring one-half inch by three and one-half inches. Twist the strips loosely into knots.

4. Pour oil to the depth of two inches into a skillet and heat to 370° F. on a frying thermometer. Fry a few pastry knots at a time, turning once. Cook each batch for about two minutes, or until golden. Drain on paper towels and continue until all the pastry is used.

5. Combine honey and water and bring to a boil. Make layers of tea cakes, sprinkling the honey mixture, walnuts and cinnamon between the layers. Cool.

DIPLES (honey rolls) *About 5 dozen*

3 eggs, separated	2 cups sugar
1 teaspoon baking powder	1 cup water
1½ to 2 cups sifted all-purpose flour	Oil for deep frying
1 cup honey	Ground cinnamon

1. Beat the egg whites with the baking powder until stiff. Beat egg yolks until light, add to egg whites, and beat until creamy. Stir in enough flour to make a soft dough.

2. Turn the dough out onto a lightly floured board and knead with oiled hands until smooth. Dough will be a little sticky. Continue kneading until dough blisters and forms bubbles when sliced with a knife.

3. Combine the honey, sugar and water. Bring to a boil and boil for ten to fifteen minutes. Keep the syrup hot while frying the pastries.

4. Form dough into one-inch balls. Roll out each ball very thinly and cut into rectangles. Drop them, one at a time, into the oil heated to 360° F. on a frying thermometer. With two forks turn the fritter immediately and roll up into a cylinder.

5. Remove from oil when golden and dip immediately into the hot syrup. Place on cake racks to drain. Sprinkle with cinnamon.

HELEN EVANS BROWN'S STRAWBERRY FRITTERS
4 to 6 servings

1 pint large fresh strawberries	2 eggs, lightly beaten
¾ cup apricot jam	1 cup fine salted-cracker crumbs
½ cup toasted almonds, finely chopped	Fat for deep frying

1. Wash the berries, then hull them. Drain them on paper towels until thoroughly dry.

2. Force the apricot jam through a strainer.

3. Place in separate bowls the strained jam, chopped almonds, beaten eggs and cracker crumbs.

4. First dip the berries into the jam, then roll them in the chopped almonds. Quickly dip two berries at a time into the beaten eggs and roll them in the cracker crumbs. Chill in the refrigerator for several hours.

5. When ready to serve, heat deep fat to 360° F. on a frying thermometer, or until a cube of bread turns golden in one minute.

6. Cook the strawberry fritters in the hot fat until golden brown. Drain on paper towels. Serve while still hot, either plain or dipped into confectioners' sugar.

ALMOND FRITTERS   *3 to 4 dozen*

1¾ cups sugar
 ½ pound blanched almonds, finely
    chopped
 2 cups sifted all-purpose flour
 1 cup butter

 5 eggs
    Grated rind of ½ lemon
 ½ teaspoon vanilla extract
    Butter for frying

1. In a mixing bowl combine the sugar, almonds and flour. Blend well. Add the butter and mix well.

2. Punch a hole in the center of the dough. Break the eggs into the hole. Add the lemon rind and vanilla. Mix well and knead thoroughly until smooth and pliable.

3. Shape dough into rolls the size and shape of a finger, tapered at both ends.

4. Fry in hot butter, a few at a time. Drain on paper towels and serve hot.

CROQUEMBOUCHE   *About 9 servings*

1½ cups water
 ½ cup butter
 1 cup sifted all-purpose flour
 ¼ teaspoon salt
 4 eggs
 1 cup heavy cream

 2 tablespoons confectioners' sugar
 3 tablespoons Cointreau
 ⅔ cup granulated sugar
 ⅛ teaspoon cream of tartar
 1 cup hot water

AHEAD OF TIME, SEVERAL WEEKS IF DESIRED:

1. Preheat oven to hot (400° F.).

2. Heat one cup of water and the butter to boiling in a medium-size pan. Add the flour and salt all at once.

Almond paste can contribute to delicious desserts such as a tart made with Almond Short Pastry topped with cherries, a Frangipane Tart and Macaroons.

3. Cook over low heat, stirring with a wooden spoon, for about two minutes, or until the mixture balls and leaves the sides of the pan.

4. Remove the pan from the heat. Add the eggs, one at a time, beating very well until the mixture is thick and shiny.

5. Drop the batter by rounded teaspoons one inch apart on an ungreased cookie sheet. Bake for twenty-five to thirty minutes, until crisp and lightly golden. Cool on a wire rack. When cool, make a small hole in the base of each puff.

6. Whip the heavy cream until peaks form, sweeten with the confectioners' sugar, and fold in the Cointreau. Using a pastry bag with a plain tube, fill each puff with whipped cream by inserting the point of the tube into the hole in the base.

7. If the cream-filled puffs are not to be used immediately, freeze them in a single layer on a tray. When frozen, the puffs may be stored in a freezer bag tightly closed at the neck.

ONE HOUR BEFORE SERVING:

8. Remove the cream puffs from the freezer if they have been stored.

9. Place the granulated sugar, remaining half cup of water and the cream of tartar in a small skillet. Bring to a boil, stirring. Lower the heat and simmer, stirring occasionally, only until the syrup is a light amber color. Keep the syrup warm over very low heat while assembling the pyramid.

10. Roll a cream puff in the warm syrup and set it, top side facing out, around the outer edge of a nine-inch compote or flat round plate. Repeat with more puffs to form a ring around the edge of the plate. Fill in the center with more puffs.

11. Over the spaces between the puffs in the first row, make a slightly smaller circle of dipped puffs. Fill in the center as before. Continue to build the pyramid to a total of five circles. Top with one cream puff.

12. Add the hot water to the syrup left in the skillet. Cook slowly, stirring occasionally, to 232° F. on a candy thermometer. Cool the syrup to room temperature.

13. Drizzle the cooled syrup down the sides of the pyramid. Top the pyramid with an ornament, if desired. Serve immediately, starting with the top, or refrigerate to hold.

GÂTEAU SAINT-HONORÉ   *8 servings*

This gossamer confection has for its base a pastry ring that is crowned with caramel-dipped cream puffs, pastry cream and sweetened whipped cream.

The name is said to be in memory of a French bishop who died more than a thousand years ago and is regarded as the patron saint of pastry chefs and bakers. This dish would make an exceptional dessert for a festive winter dinner.

PÂTE SABLÉE:

1 cup sifted all-purpose flour	1 tablespoon shortening
2 tablespoons sugar	½ lightly beaten egg
⅛ teaspoon salt	½ teaspoon water
2 tablespoons butter	¼ teaspoon vanilla extract

1. Combine the flour, sugar and salt in a bowl. Rub the butter and shortening into the flour with the tips of the fingers until the mixture resembles cornmeal.

2. Mix the half egg with the water and the vanilla. Add to the flour mixture and mix into a dough with a fork or the heel of the hand. Wrap in foil and chill for at least one hour.

3. Roll out the dough on a lightly floured board or pastry cloth into an eight-inch round one-eighth inch thick. Use a layer-cake pan as a guide. Transfer the pastry ring to a baking sheet.

PÂTE À CHOU:

1 cup water	1 cup sifted all-purpose flour
6 tablespoons butter	4 eggs
⅛ teaspoon salt	

1. Place the water and butter in a pan and bring to a boil.

2. Add the salt and flour all at once. Stir vigorously. Cook until the mixture forms a ball and leaves the sides of the pan clean. Remove from the heat.

3. Beat in the eggs, one at a time, until each is well incorporated.

DORURE (EGG WASH):

1 egg yolk	1 teaspoon water

Mix the egg yolk with the water, beat lightly, and use as a glaze for pastries and breads.

CRÈME SAINT-HONORÉ (PASTRY CREAM): *3 to 4 cups*

1½ cups milk	¾ cup plus 2 tablespoons sugar
½ vanilla bean, ½ teaspoon vanilla extract, or 2 tablespoons orange liqueur	¼ cup all-purpose flour
	1 envelope unflavored gelatin
	2 tablespoons water
4 egg yolks	6 egg whites

1. Heat the milk, along with the vanilla bean if used. If the extract or liqueur is used, reserve until later.

2. Beat the egg yolks until they are thick and lemon-colored. Gradually add three-quarters cup sugar while continuing to beat. Beat in the flour and the milk.

3. Soak the gelatin in the water.

4. Place the egg-yolk mixture in a pan and heat, stirring, until the mixture thickens and comes to the simmering point. Remove from the heat and stir in the gelatin until it dissolves. Stir in the extract or liqueur if used. Set aside to cool.

5. When the mixture is cool but not set, beat the egg whites until frothy. Gradually beat in the remaining sugar until the whites are stiff but not dry. Fold the egg whites into the cooled custard mixture.

CRÈME CHANTILLY: *About 2 cups*

1 cup heavy cream
2 tablespoons orange liqueur

2 tablespoons confectioners' sugar

Beat the ingredients together until thick.

CARAMEL SYRUP: *½ cup*

⅔ cup sugar
½ cup water

¼ teaspoon cream of tartar

Place the ingredients in a small heavy skillet. Bring the mixture to a boil and simmer until the syrup is pale amber in color. Do not overcook.

ASSEMBLY OF GÂTEAU SAINT-HONORÉ:

1. Prepare an eight-inch pastry circle from *pâte sablée* (page 671)

2. Preheat oven to hot (425° F.).

3. Prepare *pâte à chou* (page 671) and fill a pastry bag with a large plain tube with the chou paste.

4. Pipe a half-inch-thick ring of chou paste around the edge of the pastry circle, one-quarter inch from the edge. With remaining paste make walnut-size puffs on another baking sheet. The gâteau requires about eight of the puffs and the rest may be served separately. Brush pastry and the top of the puffs with *dorure* (egg wash), but do not let it drip down the sides.

5. Bake the pastry circle for ten to fifteen minutes, or until it is puffed and lightly browned. Pierce the inside edge of the cream-puff ring in four or five places with the point of a knife. Reduce oven heat to moderate (375° F.) and bake for ten to fifteen minutes longer, or until puff has dried. Cool on a wire rack.

6. Reheat the oven to 425° F. Bake the small puffs for ten minutes, or until puffed and lightly browned. Pierce each puff. Reduce heat to 375° F. and cook for about ten minutes longer, or until dried. Cool on a rack.

7. While the pastry is baking, prepare crème Saint-Honoré (page 671), crème Chantilly and caramel syrup (page 672).

8. Fill center of cooled cream-puff ring with cooled crème Saint-Honoré (pastry cream). Fill eight of the tiny puffs with either pastry cream or crème Chantilly.

9. Dip the tops of the puffs into the caramel syrup. Dip the bottoms into the syrup. Arrange the little puffs in a ring around the edge of the pastry circle.

10. Decorate the center of the gâteau with crème Chantilly piped through a pastry bag fitted with a fluted tube. If desired, the gâteau may be garnished with candied cherries or glazed fruit.

Note: The cream puffs and the pastry circle for the gâteau Saint-Honoré may be made a day in advance and assembled with the other ingredients just before serving. The puffs and pastry must be stored in a dry place.

PARIS-BREST   *8 to 10 servings*

Pâte à Chou (cream-puff paste, page 671)
½ egg, lightly beaten
¼ cup slivered blanched almonds
Crème au Praliné (see below)
1 cup heavy cream, whipped

1. Preheat oven to hot (450° F.). Grease and flour a cookie sheet and lightly mark a circle with an eight-inch layer-cake pan.

2. Make the cream-puff paste. Fill a pastry bag fitted with a large plain tube with the paste. Using the circle line as a guide, pipe a ring of paste about one inch high and one and one-half to two inches thick inside the line.

3. Brush with the beaten egg, sprinkle with the almonds, and bake for ten to fifteen minutes, or until well puffed. Lower the heat to moderate (350° F.) and bake for fifteen minutes longer.

4. With the point of a knife, pierce the edge of the ring in half a dozen places to allow the steam to escape. Bake for about fifteen minutes longer, or until the shell is well browned and dry inside. Cool on a rack.

5. Split the ring crosswise and fill the lower half with crème au praliné. Fill the hollows in the upper half with the whipped cream. Put two halves together. Decorate with more whipped cream if desired.

CRÈME AU PRALINÉ: *About 2½ cups*

1 cup sugar
⅓ cup water
¼ teaspoon cream of tartar
4 egg yolks, beaten
1 cup butter, softened
2 teaspoons vanilla extract
½ cup finely crushed Praline Candy (page 674)

1. Place the sugar, water and cream of tartar in a small pan. Bring to a boil and boil without stirring until the syrup spins a long thread when dropped into cold water, or registers 240° F. on a candy thermometer.

2. Pour the syrup gradually onto the eggs, beating constantly until the mixture is very thick. Beat in the butter a little at a time. Stir in the vanilla and the crushed praline.

PRALINE CANDY: *½ pound or 12 patties*

¾ cup sugar
¼ cup water

¼ teaspoon cream of tartar
½ cup blanched almonds

1. Combine all the ingredients in a heavy pan. Heat while stirring until the sugar dissolves.

2. Continue to heat without stirring until the mixture turns the color of maple syrup. To avoid overbrowning the almonds, the pan may be shaken gently once or twice.

3. Pour immediately onto a buttered cookie sheet or into the bottom of twelve buttered muffin tins (1½ inches in diameter). Allow to cool before using.

Note: The candy is delicious as is when eaten out of hand. However, it also has many uses in cuisine. It may be crushed to serve over custards, ice cream, or cake frosting. To crush, place a little at a time in a blender and blend on high speed for fifteen seconds. The praline may be kept in an airtight container for several days.

GREEK NUT ROLL À LA APHRODITE LIANIDES
35 to 40 slices

1 cup finely chopped pecans
1 cup finely chopped walnuts
1 cup finely chopped almonds
¼ cup sugar
½ teaspoon ground cloves
½ teaspoon ground cinnamon

½ pound phyllo pastry (Greek strudel leaves)
2 cups butter, melted
1 cup water
1 cup Greek honey
1 teaspoon fresh lemon juice

1. Preheat oven to moderate (350° F.).

2. Combine the nuts, sugar, cloves and cinnamon.

3. Brush two sheets of phyllo pastry with melted butter and arrange one sheet atop the other. Sprinkle with two tablespoons of the nut mixture. Repeat this procedure until there are three layers of pastry and nuts. Roll like a jelly roll. Continue to prepare the rolls until there are three.

4. Cut each roll into one-inch slices. Place the slices on buttered baking sheets with sides.

5. Bake the nut-roll pieces for twenty minutes, turn them over, and continue to bake for fifteen minutes longer, until golden brown on both sides. Cool.

6. While the pastry is baking, make the syrup. Bring the water to a boil and stir in the honey. Blend well and add the lemon juice. Cool the syrup slightly. It should still be warm.

7. When the slices are cool, dip each piece into the warm syrup. Serve at room temperature.

BRITTANY CRÊPES WITH FILBERT BUTTER
12 to 16 crêpes

¾ cup milk
¾ cup cold water
3 egg yolks
1 tablespoon granulated sugar
7 tablespoons cognac or orange liqueur
1½ cups sifted all-purpose flour
½ cup melted butter, approximately

3 teaspoons grated lemon rind
2 teaspoons grated orange rind
1 tablespoon shortening, melted
½ cup butter
1 cup confectioners' sugar
½ cup skinned filberts, grated finely (see page 634)
Juice of 1 lemon

1. Place the milk, water, egg yolks, granulated sugar, three tablespoons cognac, the flour, five tablespoons melted butter, one teaspoon lemon rind and the orange rind in the container of an electric blender. Cover and blend at high speed. Use a rubber scraper to dislodge any flour that may stick to the jar. Cover and refrigerate for at least two hours.

2. Heat a heavy skillet or a crêpe pan (6 to 7 inches in diameter). Brush lightly with a little melted shortening.

3. When the shortening begins to smoke, pour about one-quarter cup of the batter into the middle of the pan. Immediately tilt the pan in all directions to spread a thin film of batter over the entire surface of the pan.

4. Heat for about one minute. Jerk the pan back and forth to loosen the crêpe. When it is lightly browned, turn over and brown the second side lightly. The first crêpe may stick if the pan is new or the batter too thick. If this happens, add more milk to thin the batter. Grease the pan with more shortening when needed, but use as little as possible each time.

5. Remove each crêpe from the pan as it is finished. Spread melted butter on the side that was cooked last. Roll and put aside (see note).

6. Cream the half cup of butter with the confectioners' sugar until light and fluffy. Beat in the filberts, lemon juice, and remaining cognac and lemon rind.

7. Just before serving unfold the crêpes carefully, spread with the filbert butter, and refold. Place on a hot serving platter.

Note: The crêpes may be kept warm until all are cooked by placing them in a baking dish in a very slow oven (200° F.) or on a plate over hot water. If the crêpes are to be made ahead of time, they may be filled with the filbert butter and placed in a baking dish, covered, and refrigerated until serving time. To reheat, remove the cover and place in a moderate oven (375° F.) for ten to fifteen minutes, or until they are heated through.

SWEDISH PANCAKES   *6 servings*

1 cup sifted all-purpose flour	2 eggs
2 cups milk	½ cup butter, melted
2 tablespoons sugar	Lingonberries
½ teaspoon salt	

1. Place the flour in a bowl. Add one cup of the milk and stir well. Add remaining milk, the sugar, salt and eggs and beat well. Add the melted butter.

2. Heat a griddle or a Swedish plätter pan.

3. Pour a spoonful of batter onto the griddle. When browned, turn and brown the other side. Continue until all the batter is used. Serve the lingonberries separately.

. . . .

FILLINGS, FROSTINGS AND GLAZES

. . . .

APRICOT FILLING   *About 2 cups*

½ cup sugar	1⅓ cups cooked or canned apricots, well drained
3 tablespoons cornstarch	
¼ cup undiluted frozen orange-juice concentrate, thawed	

1. Combine the sugar and cornstarch in a saucepan; blend. Stir in the orange-juice concentrate.

2. Put the apricots through a sieve and add the purée to the sugar mixture.

3. Place over medium heat and bring to a boil, stirring constantly. Boil for about thirty seconds.

CHOCOLATE FILLING   *About 1½ cups*

4 eggs, lightly beaten	½ cup butter, softened
¼ cup sugar	½ cup finely ground walnuts
½ teaspoon cornstarch	1 teaspoon vanilla extract
4 ounces sweet cooking chocolate, melted	

1. Mix together the eggs, sugar and cornstarch in the top part of a double boiler. Heat over boiling water, stirring, until mixture thickens. Do not boil. Cool.

2. Stir in the chocolate. Gradually beat in the butter, one tablespoon at a time.

3. Fold in the nuts and vanilla and stir until mixture is thick enough to spread.

CHOCOLATE-BUTTER FILLING   *About ¼ cup*

2 tablespoons butter
⅓ cup confectioners' sugar

1 ounce (1 square) unsweetened chocolate, melted and cooled

Cream together the butter and sugar and blend in the chocolate.

LEMON FILLING   *About ½ cup*

2 egg yolks, lightly beaten
½ cup sugar
⅛ teaspoon salt
2 tablespoons butter

1 teaspoon grated lemon rind
2 tablespoons lemon juice
1½ tablespoons cornstarch
3 tablespoons water

Cook all ingredients except cornstarch and water in the top part of a double boiler over boiling water, stirring until thick. Mix cornstarch with water, add to the pan, and cook, stirring, until thick.

STRAWBERRY FILLING   *About 2 cups*

1 package (10 ounces) frozen sliced strawberries, thawed

½ envelope unflavored gelatin
⅔ cup heavy cream

1. Remove two tablespoons of juice from the strawberries and add to the gelatin. Purée the remaining strawberry mixture.

2. Place the soaked gelatin over low heat and stir while dissolving. Add to the strawberry purée, stirring.

3. Whip the cream until stiff and fold in the strawberry-gelatin mixture.

PASTRY CREAM   *About 3 cups*

⅔ cup sugar
3½ tablespoons cornstarch or 6 tablespoons all-purpose flour
½ teaspoon salt

2½ cups milk, scalded
3 egg yolks, lightly beaten
1 teaspoon vanilla extract

1. Mix the sugar, cornstarch and salt in a bowl. Pour the hot milk over the mixture, stirring constantly. Place in the top part of a double boiler and cook over low heat, stirring, until the mixture thickens. Cover and cook for ten minutes longer.

2. Stir a little of the hot mixture into the egg yolks. Add to the remaining mixture in the pan and cook over hot water, stirring, for about two minutes, until thickened. Cool and add the vanilla.

BUTTERCREAM *About 1 cup*

½ cup vegetable shortening
   Pinch of salt
 2 tablespoons soft butter
1½ cups confectioners' sugar, approximately

¾ teaspoon vanilla extract
   Food coloring (optional)

1. Beat the shortening, salt, butter, one-half cup of the sugar and the vanilla until smooth.

2. Gradually add the remaining sugar, beating, until the buttercream is of spreading consistency. A drop or two of food coloring may be added to color the mixture. Use for decorating cakes and other desserts.

CHOCOLATE BUTTERCREAM *About 1½ cups*

3 egg yolks
3 tablespoons sugar
1 teaspoon vanilla extract
½ cup soft butter

½ cup cold butter, approximately
1 ounce (1 square) unsweetened chocolate, melted and cooled

Place egg yolks, sugar and vanilla in the container of an electric blender. Blend for three minutes, adding soft butter gradually until it is absorbed. Then add enough cold butter, in small pieces, to make the cream fairly thick. Add chocolate and blend until smooth.

MOCHA BUTTERCREAM *3 cups*

1 cup sugar
⅓ cup water
¼ teaspoon cream of tartar
4 egg yolks

5 ounces semisweet chocolate
¼ cup strong coffee
1½ cups sweet butter
2 tablespoons dark rum

1. Combine the sugar, water and cream of tartar in a heavy saucepan. Bring to a boil and boil rapidly until the syrup reaches 240° F. on a candy thermometer.

2. Beat the egg yolks until fluffy. Gradually beat in the syrup and continue to beat until the mixture is stiff.

3. Melt the chocolate in the coffee over hot water. Beat into the egg-yolk mixture.

4. Beat in the butter bit by bit. Stir in the rum. Chill until the butter-cream has the right consistency for spreading.

CONFECTIONERS' SUGAR ICING   *About ½ cup*

Mix four teaspoons water with one cup sifted confectioners' sugar. Add one-quarter teaspoon of any desired flavoring.

ORNAMENTAL FROSTING   *About ½ cup*

Mix one lightly beaten egg white with one cup sifted confectioners' sugar and one-quarter teaspoon vanilla extract. Add more sugar, bit by bit, until the frosting will hold its shape when piped or spread. If the frosting becomes too thick, add extra egg white.

ROYAL ICING   *About 1½ cups*

Combine two lightly beaten egg whites and one tablespoon lemon juice in a mixing bowl. Gradually add about three and one-half cups sifted confectioners' sugar, until the mixture is of spreading consistency. Cover the bowl with a damp cloth until icing is ready to use.

SPICED BUTTER FROSTING   *About 1½ cups*

3 cups sifted confectioners' sugar
½ cup butter
¼ teaspoon ground cloves
1 teaspoon vanilla extract
1 tablespoon milk

Gradually mix sugar with butter, cloves, vanilla and milk. Blend until smooth.

VANILLA FROSTING   *About 1 cup*

1 tablespoon shortening
1 tablespoon light corn syrup
⅛ teaspoon salt
1 teaspoon vanilla extract
2 cups sifted confectioners' sugar
2 tablespoons warm water

Mix the shortening, corn syrup, salt and vanilla with the sugar and water in a mixing bowl. Blend until smooth.

CHOCOLATE FROSTING I   *About 1 cup*

½ cup semisweet chocolate bits
1 tablespoon shortening
1½ tablespoons undiluted evaporated milk

2 tablespoons light corn syrup
½ teaspoon vanilla extract
1¾ cups sifted confectioners' sugar

1. Melt the chocolate bits in the top part of a double boiler over hot, not boiling, water.

2. Stir the shortening, evaporated milk, corn syrup, vanilla and sugar into the melted chocolate. Blend until smooth.

CHOCOLATE FROSTING II   *About 1½ cups*

4 squares (4 ounces) unsweetened chocolate
2¼ cups confectioners' sugar
¼ cup water

2 egg yolks
6 tablespoons butter, at room temperature

1. Melt the chocolate over hot water. Remove from the heat and add the sugar and water all at once. Blend well.

2. Add the egg yolks, one at a time, beating well after each addition. Beat in the butter, one tablespoon at a time.

FUDGE FROSTING (vanilla)   *About 1½ cups*

½ cup plus 1 tablespoon butter
1 cup granulated sugar
¼ cup light cream
2 cups sifted confectioners' sugar, approximately

1½ teaspoons vanilla extract
Food coloring (optional)

1. Melt the butter, add the granulated sugar and the cream, and stir thoroughly. Bring the mixture to a boil, stirring. Cool to room temperature.

2. Add the confectioners' sugar a little at a time, until the frosting is of spreading consistency. Stir in the vanilla. Add a drop or two of food coloring to tint the frosting any desired color. Use immediately.

CREAM-CHEESE FROSTING   *About 1¼ cups*

3 ounces cream cheese
2¼ cups sifted confectioners' sugar, approximately
1 teaspoon grated orange or lemon rind

1 tablespoon Grand Marnier or orange juice

Cream the cheese with about half of the sugar and the orange or lemon rind. Continue creaming, adding the Grand Marnier or orange juice and enough more sugar to give a spreading consistency.

CRANBERRY FROSTING   *About 1 cup*

⅓ cup fresh cranberries
⅓ cup water
1½ cups sugar

2 egg whites
Dash of salt
½ teaspoon vanilla extract

1. Place the cranberries and water in a small saucepan. Cook for three or four minutes, until the skins pop. Cool.

2. Turn the cranberries, sugar, egg whites and salt into the top part of a double boiler over boiling water. Beat for seven or eight minutes, or until the frosting thickens and holds its shape. Remove from the heat.

3. Add the vanilla and continue to beat until the frosting is stiff enough to spread.

LEMON FROSTING   *About 2 cups*

1½ cups sugar
½ cup water
1½ tablespoons light corn syrup
2 egg whites

⅛ teaspoon salt
1 teaspoon vanilla extract
1 teaspoon grated lemon rind
1½ tablespoons fresh lemon juice

1. Boil sugar, water and corn syrup, stirring until sugar dissolves, to 242° F. on a candy thermometer.

2. Beat egg whites with salt until stiff. Add syrup gradually and beat until stiff. Add remaining ingredients and beat again until stiff.

ORANGE FROSTING   *About 1½ cups*

½ cup sugar
2 teaspoons white corn syrup
⅛ teaspoon cream of tartar
¼ cup water

1 egg white, stiffly beaten
¼ cup confectioners' sugar
1 tablespoon fresh orange juice
½ teaspoon grated orange rind

1. Place the sugar, corn syrup, cream of tartar and water in a small saucepan. Heat, stirring, to dissolve the sugar. With a brush and water wash down the crystals from the sides of the pan. Cook the syrup to 238° F. on a candy thermometer.

2. Gradually pour the syrup into the egg white, beating. Continue to beat for about ten minutes, until the mixture thickens to spreading consistency.

3. Stir in the confectioners' sugar and orange juice and rind.

APRICOT GLAZE   *About 1 cup*

Heat one cup sieved apricot jam until it boils. Stir in two to four table-spoons cognac or other liqueur. Use the glaze while it is hot.

CHOCOLATE GLAZE   *About ½ cup*

Combine one-half cup semisweet chocolate morsels, two tablespoons light corn syrup and one teaspoon water in the top part of a double boiler. Place over hot, not boiling, water until chocolate is melted. Remove from heat and blend until smooth.

ORANGE GLAZE   *About ½ cup*

Mix three-quarters cup confectioners' sugar and three teaspoons orange juice until the glaze is smooth and of frosting consistency. Add a few more drops of orange juice if needed.

LEMON GLAZE   *About 1¼ cups*

3 tablespoons milk	3 tablespoons lemon juice
2 tablespoons butter	1 teaspoon grated lemon rind
2 cups sifted confectioners' sugar	

1. Heat the milk and butter until the butter melts. Pour over the sugar and stir until smooth.
2. Add lemon juice and rind. When the glaze is poured over a cake, it will run over the sides.

COCONUT TOPPING   *About 2 cups*

½ cup butter, melted	1⅓ cups shredded coconut
1 cup light brown sugar	⅓ cup light cream

Combine all the ingredients. Let stand for five minutes. Spread over the top of a cake and place the cake under the broiler. Heat until topping is lightly browned and bubbly.

PECAN TOPPING   *About 1 cup*

⅔ cup brown sugar	⅛ teaspoon salt
3 tablespoons melted butter	½ cup chopped pecans
1 tablespoon heavy cream	

1. Mix topping ingredients and spread on top of a baked and cooled pie or cake. Decorate with pecan halves if desired.

2. Broil, three inches from the source of heat with the heat turned low, until the surface bubbles. Watch carefully to make sure top does not burn.

CLOVE WHIPPED CREAM

Whip two-thirds cup heavy cream until it stands in soft stiff peaks. Add one and one-half tablespoons sugar, one-quarter teaspoon vanilla extract and one-half teaspoon ground cloves.

. . . .

DESSERT SAUCES

. . . .

APRICOT SAUCE   *About 2 cups*

2 cups (one 1-pound can) apricots   3 tablespoons Cointreau
2 tablespoons sugar

Drain the apricots, reserving one-half cup of the syrup. Mash the fruit and place in a saucepan with the reserved syrup and the sugar. Cook over low heat, stirring, until the sugar is dissolved. Simmer for five minutes. Remove from the heat and stir in the Cointreau.

APRICOT SOUR-CREAM SAUCE   *About 2 cups*

1 cup dried apricots   Pinch of salt
1½ cups water   ¾ cup sour cream
1 cup sugar   1 tablespoon cognac (optional)

Place the apricots in a saucepan and add the water. Bring to a boil and simmer until tender. Press the apricots through a food mill. Add the sugar and salt to pulp and stir until dissolved. Cool. Stir in the sour cream and cognac.

CHERRY SAUCE   *About 2½ cups*

2 cups (one 1-pound can) pitted red   1 tablespoon lemon juice
  sour cherries packed in syrup   ¼ teaspoon almond extract
¼ cup sugar   2 teaspoons cornstarch
¼ cup white corn syrup   1 tablespoon water
1 cinnamon stick

1. Drain the cherry syrup into a saucepan. Add the sugar, corn syrup, cinnamon, lemon juice and almond extract to the pan. Simmer for ten minutes.

2. Remove the cinnamon stick. Mix together the cornstarch and cold water. Add the hot syrup to the cornstarch mixture, return to the pan, and cook over low heat, stirring, until the sauce boils. Add the cherries. Serve the sauce hot or cold.

BLACK-CHERRY SAUCE   *About 2 cups*

2 cups (one 1-pound can) pitted black cherries
2 teaspoons finely grated lemon rind

¼ cup sugar
1½ tablespoons cornstarch
1 tablespoon lemon juice
2 tablespoons rum

1. Drain the cherries, measure the juice, and add enough water to make one and one-third cups. Reserve the cherries.

2. Bring cherry juice, lemon rind, sugar and cornstarch to a boil while stirring and cook, stirring, until thick and translucent.

3. Add lemon juice, rum and reserved cherries. Cool.

SOUR-CREAM ORANGE SAUCE   *About 1½ cups*

¼ cup butter
½ cup superfine sugar
1 teaspoon grated orange rind

1 cup sour cream
¼ cup Grand Marnier or orange juice

1. Cream the butter and mix with the sugar and orange rind until fluffy. Add the sour cream and mix well.

2. Add the Grand Marnier or orange juice. Chill until serving time. The mixture will thicken as it chills.

RAISIN NUT SAUCE   *1½ cups*

1 cup firmly packed brown sugar
2 tablespoons cornstarch
¼ teaspoon salt
¾ cup water
1 tablespoon lemon juice

2 tablespoons butter
½ cup chopped raisins
⅓ cup chopped nuts
1 teaspoon vanilla extract

1. Mix the brown sugar, cornstarch and salt together in a saucepan. Add the water and mix well. Cook over low heat, stirring constantly, until of desired thickness.

2. Stir in the lemon juice and butter. Add the raisins, nuts and vanilla. Serve warm over vanilla ice cream.

PEACH OR PINEAPPLE SAUCE   *About 1½ cups*

½ cup sugar
⅓ cup water
1½ cups sliced fresh peaches or shredded or chopped fresh pineapple

2 tablespoons cognac or rum (optional)

Boil the sugar and water for two minutes. Pour over fruit. Chill. Before serving add the cognac or rum.

STRAWBERRY SAUCE   *About 2 cups*

Put one quart fresh strawberries through a sieve, or purée in an electric blender. Sweeten with confectioners' sugar to taste. Raspberry sauce may be made in the same way.

STRAWBERRY COMPOTE SAUCE   *About 3½ cups*

1 cup sugar
2 tablespoons cornstarch
1 pint fresh strawberries, sliced
¾ cup orange juice

1 medium banana, diced
1 medium orange, pared and cut into sections
¼ cup light rum (optional)

1. Combine the sugar and cornstarch and mix well.
2. Crush one cup of the strawberries and add to the sugar mixture along with the orange juice; mix well. Cook over medium heat, stirring constantly, until thickened and clear. Chill.
3. Add remaining strawberries and remaining ingredients and mix lightly but thoroughly. Serve over ice cream.

STRAWBERRY-RHUBARB SAUCE   *About 4 cups*

1 pound fresh rhubarb
1 cup sugar

1 package (10 ounces) frozen sliced strawberries

1. Cut the rhubarb into one-inch lengths. Place it in a six-cup saucepan, rinse, and drain. Add the sugar.
2. Cover the pan and place over medium heat. When the cover is hot, reduce the heat to low. Cook for two to three minutes, or until the rhubarb boils.
3. Add the strawberries and heat just until the berries are defrosted.

CHOCOLATE SAUCE   *¾ cup*

1 ounce (1 square) unsweetened chocolate
1 tablespoon butter
¼ cup light corn syrup
½ cup sugar

1 teaspoon cornstarch
Dash of salt
⅓ cup water
1 teaspoon vanilla extract

1. Break chocolate into the top part of a double boiler. Add the butter and syrup. Cook over hot water until chocolate melts.
2. Add sugar, cornstarch, salt and water. Slowly bring to a boil over direct medium heat. Cook, stirring constantly, for about four minutes. Cool. Add vanilla and chill.

BITTERSWEET FUDGE SAUCE   *About 2½ cups*

2 ounces (2 squares) unsweetened chocolate
1 can (14 ounces) sweetened condensed milk

⅛ teaspoon salt
½ cup hot water, approximately

1. Melt the chocolate in the top part of a double boiler. Add the condensed milk and stir over rapidly boiling water for about five minutes, until thickened.
2. Remove from the heat. Add the salt and enough hot water to soften the mixture to desired consistency. The sauce may be served warm or cold. It thickens upon cooling but may be thinned again with water.

MOCHA SAUCE:

Thin the fudge sauce with strong coffee in the place of the water.

CHOCOLATE RUM SAUCE   *About 1 cup*

6 ounces semisweet chocolate morsels
6 tablespoons water

1 teaspoon instant coffee powder
1 tablespoon dark rum

Combine the chocolate, water and coffee in a saucepan. Heat over simmering water, stirring occasionally, until sauce is smooth. Stir in rum and serve immediately.

CHOCOLATE MARMALADE SAUCE   *About 1 cup*

6 ounces semisweet chocolate morsels
⅓ cup hot water

⅓ cup orange marmalade

Combine the chocolate and water in the top part of a double boiler. Heat over hot water until the chocolate is melted. Stir in the marmalade. Serve warm or cold over ice cream or cake.

CHOCOLATE WALNUT SAUCE   *2½ cups*

½ cup butter
2 cups coarsely chopped walnuts

2 cups semisweet chocolate morsels

1. Melt the butter in a heavy skillet. Add the walnuts and cook over medium heat, stirring constantly, until browned. Remove from heat.
2. Add the chocolate morsels and stir until melted and smooth. Serve warm over ice cream or warm cake squares.

HONEY SAUCE   *About 1 cup*

3 tablespoons butter
2 teaspoons cornstarch

⅔ cup honey
Whole toasted almonds (optional)

1. Melt the butter in a saucepan. Add the cornstarch and stir until smooth.
2. Add the honey and cook over low heat, stirring constantly, for about five minutes. Add almonds if desired.
3. Serve the sauce warm or cold over ice cream or unfrosted cake.

MAPLE CREAM SAUCE

Boil one cup maple syrup down to three-quarters cup. Cool. Fold into one cup heavy cream, whipped.

HARD SAUCE   *About 1½ cups*

⅓ cup butter
2¾ cups sifted confectioners' sugar, approximately

2 tablespoons light cream
1 teaspoon vanilla extract

Soften the butter. Add the sugar alternately with the cream. Blend in the vanilla. Chill before serving.

JAM SAUCE   *About 1 cup*

⅓ cup raspberry, strawberry or apricot jam, sieved
2 tablespoons sugar

½ cup water
1 tablespoon kirsch or ¼ teaspoon almond extract

Mix together the jam, sugar and water in a small saucepan. Bring to a boil, stirring, and simmer for one minute. Remove from the heat and add the kirsch or almond extract.

LEMON-NUTMEG SAUCE   *1½ cups*

½ cup sugar
1 tablespoon cornstarch
　Pinch of salt
¾ cup water

¼ cup fresh lemon juice
½ teaspoon vanilla extract
¼ teaspoon grated nutmeg

1. Combine the sugar, cornstarch and salt in a saucepan. Stir in the water and cook, stirring constantly, until the mixture is thick and transparent. Remove from the heat and cool.

2. Stir in the lemon juice, vanilla and nutmeg. Serve over puddings and soufflés.

JAMAICA RUM AND COCONUT SAUCE   *About 1 cup*

3 tablespoons butter
½ cup firmly packed brown sugar
¼ cup water

½ cup shredded or flaked coconut
½ cup slivered almonds
2 tablespoons dark Jamaica rum

1. Combine the butter, sugar and water in a heavy skillet. Cook, stirring constantly, until the mixture becomes bubbly. Continue to cook for about three minutes, until all the sugar crystals are dissolved. Remove from heat.

2. Add coconut, almonds and rum. Serve either hot or cold with vanilla ice cream or other desserts.

Note: This sauce may be prepared in advance and stored in a covered jar in the refrigerator.

CUSTARD SAUCE   *About 2 cups*

½ cup sugar
4 egg yolks
1 teaspoon cornstarch

1¾ cups hot scalded milk
1 teaspoon vanilla extract

1. Put the sugar and egg yolks in a bowl. Beat well with a wire whisk until the mixture reaches the ribbon stage, when the yolks will thicken slightly and become pale yellow. Beat in the cornstarch.

2. Add the milk gradually, beating constantly. Pour the mixture into a saucepan and cook, stirring constantly with a wooden spatula, until the sauce thickens enough to coat the spoon. Do not overcook and do not let the mixture boil at any point or it will curdle. Remove the saucepan from the heat and continue to beat for about thirty seconds.

3. Strain the sauce through a fine sieve and season with vanilla. If desired, rum or cognac may be substituted for the vanilla. Serve hot or cold over cakes, puddings, cooked fruits or ice cream.

SABAYON SAUCE   *About 3 cups*

8 egg yolks
¼ cup sugar
½ cup marsala or sherry

Cognac to taste (optional)
⅔ cup heavy cream, whipped

1. In the top part of a large double boiler, beat the egg yolks until thick, adding the sugar gradually.
2. Place over barely simmering water, add the marsala or sherry, and beat until very fluffy and slightly thickened.
3. Remove from the hot water, stand the pan in cold water, and beat until beginning to cool. Chill. The mixture will lose fluffiness as it stands.
4. Before serving, add the cognac if desired. Fold in the whipped cream.

COGNAC SAUCE   *About 1½ cups*

4 egg yolks
½ cup sugar

½ cup cognac
½ cup heavy cream

1. Put the egg yolks and sugar in a saucepan and set the saucepan in a skillet of barely simmering water. Or use a double boiler. Beat with a rotary beater or portable electric mixer until egg yolks are thick and lemon-colored.
2. Add the cognac gradually, beating constantly. When the sauce is thickened, chill it.
3. When ready to serve, whip the cream and fold it into the cognac mixture.

SAUTERNES CUSTARD SAUCE   *About 1 cup*

¾ cup Sauternes
Sugar
4 egg yolks, lightly beaten

2 tablespoons heavy cream
2 teaspoons kirsch

1. Put the Sauternes in the top part of a double boiler. Add sugar to taste and heat. When hot, slowly stir in the egg yolks. When the custard coats a metal spoon, remove from the heat.
2. Stir in the cream and kirsch. Cool and chill. Serve over very ripe pears, sliced peaches or strawberries, and over puddings.

MOCHA CREAM SAUCE   *About 2 cups*

2 egg yolks
¼ cup sugar
¼ teaspoon salt

½ cup strong coffee
1 cup heavy cream, whipped

1. Beat the egg yolks with a rotary beater until somewhat thickened. Beat in the sugar and salt and stir in the coffee.

2. Cook over simmering water, stirring, until thickened. Chill; fold in the whipped cream.

FRUIT CUSTARD SAUCE   *About 2 cups*

¼ cup butter	1 cup simmering milk
¼ or ½ cup sugar	1 cup chopped fresh or frozen
1 teaspoon flour	berries or peaches, drained
2 egg yolks	2 tablespoons rum or cognac

1. Cream the butter with the sugar until fluffy. (If using frozen fruits, use one-quarter cup sugar; if fresh fruits, one-half cup sugar.) Add flour and blend well. Add egg yolks, one at a time, and cream well.

2. Add the milk while stirring and cook, stirring, over very low heat until the sauce thickens. Set in cold water and cool, stirring. Chill.

3. Before serving, mix in the fruit and rum or cognac.

VANILLA COFFEE SAUCE   *2 cups*

⅓ cup plus 1 tablespoon sugar	½ cup milk
⅛ teaspoon salt	1 teaspoon vanilla extract
1 teaspoon instant coffee powder	½ cup heavy cream, whipped
2 egg yolks	

1. Combine one-third cup of the sugar, the salt and coffee powder. Blend in the egg yolks and milk. Cook over very low heat until the mixture is slightly thickened and coats a metal spoon. Remove from the heat. Cool.

2. Stir in the vanilla. Fold remaining one tablespoon sugar into the whipped cream and carefully fold into the coffee mixture. Serve over ice cream or plain cake.

690

. . . .
BEVERAGES

DOOK   *1 serving*

1 cup plain yoghurt
⅛ teaspoon salt

2 or 3 ice cubes
Cold water or club soda

Place the yoghurt, salt and ice cubes in a large glass. Add the cold water or club soda, stirring all the ingredients together, until the glass is almost full.

TOMATO JUICE   *About 4 quarts*

12 pounds ripe tomatoes
2 cups finely chopped onions

2 cups finely chopped celery
4 teaspoons salt

1. Wash tomatoes. Remove the stem ends and cores and chop the tomatoes into small pieces.

2. Place four cups of tomato pieces in a pan. Add one-half cup of the onions and one-half cup of the celery. Cover and simmer gently until the juice flows freely.

3. Press through a fine sieve and add one teaspoon salt to each quart of juice.

4. Repeat with remaining pieces until all are used.

5. Bring all the juice to a boil. Seal in hot sterilized jars and process in a water bath for thirty minutes.

FROSTED APPLE WHIP   *3 generous servings*

¾ cup canned applesauce
2 teaspoons grated orange rind
3 tablespoons sugar
2¼ cups milk

3 small scoops of vanilla ice cream
6 ice cubes
Orange slices

1. Combine the applesauce, orange rind, sugar, milk, ice cream and ice cubes in the container of an electric blender. Blend for one minute, or until frothy.

2. To serve, pour into chilled glasses and garnish with orange slices.

BANANA-ORANGE SHAKES   *12 generous servings*

1 can (6 ounces) frozen orange-juice concentrate, thawed
2 ripe bananas, mashed

3 pints vanilla ice cream, softened
6 cups cold milk

Place the orange-juice concentrate, bananas and ice cream in a large mixing bowl. Beat until thoroughly blended. Continue to beat and gradually add the milk. Beat until smooth and frothy.

LEMONADE FOR A PARTY   *About 4 quarts*

3 cups lemon juice
2½ cups sugar
3½ quarts water

Ice cubes
Lemon slices for garnish

1. Combine the lemon juice and sugar and stir until the sugar dissolves. Store in a covered container in the refrigerator.
2. When ready to serve, add the water and about two trays of ice cubes. Serve in tall ice-filled glasses garnished with lemon slices.

A wedding buffet includes Champagne Punch, Seafood Casserole served with rice, Turkey Salad, buttered asparagus, Parsley Butter Sandwiches and wedding cake.

ICED TEA   *2 quarts*

Add one quart freshly boiled water to six tablespoons of loose tea or to the contents of six tea bags. Allow to brew for five minutes. Stir and strain into a pitcher containing one quart cold water. To serve, pour over ice cubes and add sugar and lemon to taste.

Iced tea should not be stored in the refrigerator as this induces clouding; although clouding does not impair the flavor or quality, it is undesirable because of the appearance. Clouding may be removed by adding boiling water to the tea until the clear amber color returns.

WATERMELON PUNCH   *About 1½ quarts*

4 cups watermelon juice
2 cups orange juice
¼ cup lemon juice
½ cup sugar
Fresh mint leaves

Combine all ingredients except the mint and mix well. Pour over ice cubes in a small punch bowl and chill until ready to serve. Garnish with the fresh mint leaves.

Note: To prepare watermelon juice, cut a melon into halves and scoop out the ripe interior. Discard the seeds and cut the flesh into cubes. Press the flesh in cheesecloth or through a sieve.

APPLE-CRANBERRY PUNCH   *10 to 12 servings*

4 cups apple cider
4 cups cranberry-juice cocktail
3 cinnamon sticks
12 whole cloves
1 small seedless orange, cut into ¼-inch slices

Place the cider, cranberry-juice cocktail and cinnamon in a pan. Stick the cloves around the orange slices and add them to the mixture. Bring to a boil and simmer for five minutes. Before serving, remove the orange slices.

CITRUS PUNCH   *About 3 quarts*

4 cups water
1¼ cups sugar
1 cup lemon juice
Lemon rinds
1½ cups fresh grapefruit juice
3 cups orange juice
⅔ cup lime juice
2 bottles (12 ounces each) ginger ale
Fresh orange, lemon and lime slices
Fresh mint leaves

1. Combine the water, sugar and lemon juice in a large saucepan. Bring to a boil and boil for two minutes.

695

2. Add the lemon rinds and let stand for two minutes. Remove the rinds and discard them.

3. Add the remaining ingredients except the sliced fruit and the mint. Pour the punch into a punch bowl over ice. Float the orange, lemon and lime slices and the fresh mint over the top.

FRUIT PUNCH   *12 generous servings*

2 tablespoons bruised mint leaves	1 quart ginger ale
2¼ quarts cold water	½ cup white corn syrup, approximately
¼ cup loose tea	
4 cups fresh orange juice	Orange and lemon slices
1 cup loganberry or cherry juice	Fresh mint sprigs
1 cup lemon juice	

1. Combine the mint leaves and three cups of the water in a saucepan. Bring to a rolling boil. Remove from the heat and immediately add the tea. Brew for four minutes, stir, and strain. Cool to room temperature.

2. Combine the remaining water with the fruit juices, and add to the tea mixture. Pour over ice cubes in tall glasses or in a bowl. Add the ginger ale and sweeten to taste with corn syrup. Garnish with fresh fruit slices and mint sprigs.

SALTY RUSSIAN   *1 cocktail*

Combine four ounces of fresh grapefruit juice with one and one-half ounces of vodka. Add salt to taste and two ice cubes.

BICYCLETTE COCKTAIL À LA POTINIÈRE   *1 cocktail*

Pour one teaspoon of cassis (black-currant liqueur) into a stemmed wine or champagne glass. Add half a jigger (1½ tablespoons) of dry vermouth and one ice cube. Add champagne to a depth of one or two inches, to taste. Half of a six-ounce split bottle of champagne is sufficient for two cocktails.

JACK ROSE   *4 to 6 cocktails*

1 jigger grenadine syrup	8 jiggers apple brandy
2 jiggers lemon juice	Lemon twist (optional)

1. Place several cubes of ice or a generous quantity of shaved ice into a chilled cocktail shaker.

2. Add the grenadine, lemon juice and apple brandy and shake vigorously. Strain the mixture immediately into chilled cocktail glasses. Garnish with a lemon twist, if desired.

PLANTER'S PUNCH   *1 serving*

1 ounce lime juice	Crushed ice
2 to 3 ounces light rum	Club soda
1 to 2 ounces grenadine syrup	Lime slice, fresh mint sprig, fresh
2 or 3 dashes of Angostura bitters	pineapple stick

1. Combine the lime juice, rum, grenadine and bitters. Pour over crushed ice in a tumbler. Fill with club soda and stir briskly to frost the glass lightly.

2. Garnish the glass with a slice of lime, a sprig of fresh mint, and a pine-apple stick to use as a stirrer.

COLONIAL EGGNOG   *30 punch-cup servings*

10 eggs, separated	1 cup heavy cream, whipped
¾ cup sugar	½ cup brandy
4 cups milk, scalded	¼ cup light rum
½ teaspoon salt	Grated nutmeg

1. Beat the egg yolks in the top part of a double boiler. Blend in one-half cup of the sugar. Stir in the milk slowly. Cook over hot water, stirring constantly, until the mixture coats a metal spoon. Chill thoroughly.

2. Add the salt to the egg whites and beat until stiff. Gradually beat the remaining sugar into the egg whites. Fold the egg whites into the egg-yolk mixture. Then fold the whipped cream into the mixture. Add brandy and rum. Chill for several hours.

3. When ready to serve, pour the eggnog into a prechilled punch bowl and sprinkle the top with nutmeg.

CHAMPAGNE PUNCH   *100 punch-cup servings*

12 bottles domestic sauterne	6 oranges
3 cups cognac	12 bottles dry champagne
12 lemons	

1. If available, use six half-gallon milk bottles to prepare the punch base. Into each pour two bottles of sauterne, one-half cup of cognac, the juice of two lemons and the juice of one orange. Chill.

2. When ready to serve, pour the punch base over ice and add two bottles of champagne for each portion of base.

RECEPTION PUNCH   *About 4 quarts*

2 cups sugar	1½ quarts ginger ale, champagne or
2 quarts water	a dry red Bordeaux wine
½ cup lemon juice	Lemon slices for garnish
1 quart fresh strawberries	

1. Combine the sugar, one quart of the water and half of the lemon juice. Bring to a boil and boil for three minutes.

2. Remove from the heat and add the remaining water and lemon juice. Cool.

3. Reserve a few strawberries to use as a garnish. Crush the remaining berries, strain, and add to the punch. Pour into a punch bowl over ice.

4. Just before serving, add the ginger ale, champagne or red wine. Garnish with lemon slices and the reserved fresh strawberries.

VINTAGE PUNCH   *About 2 quarts*

1 bottle champagne	1 slice of fresh pineapple, cubed
1 jigger cognac	½ orange, sliced, with skin and membrane removed
2 jiggers sherry	
3 dashes of Curaçao	2 slices of fresh pear
3 dashes of maraschino	Berries
2 teaspoons confectioners' sugar	Sprigs of mint for garnish

Mix all ingredients except the mint in a large pitcher with ice. Garnish with mint sprigs and serve immediately, in champagne goblets.

PUNCH BORDELAISE   *About 2½ quarts*

1 bottle Lillet apéritif	Peel of 3 oranges or unpeeled orange slices, halved
3 bottles dry champagne	

Pour the Lillet and the champagne over ice and garnish with twists of orange peel or orange slices. Serve immediately.

Note: This is a most flexible recipe; no matter what proportions of ingredients are used, the result is excellent. If desired, orange juice may be added. A more potent punch results if a small quantity of vodka is added.

PUNCH CHARENTAISE   *About 5 quarts*

2 unpeeled cucumbers, thinly sliced	½ cup lemon juice
½ cup sugar	2 bottles cognac
Grated rind of 4 lemons	2 cups Cointreau
2 cups orange juice	4 bottles dry champagne

1. Place the cucumber slices in a large punch bowl. Add the sugar, grated lemon rind, orange juice, lemon juice and cognac. Let stand for one hour.

2. When ready to serve the punch, add a large block of ice, the Cointreau and the champagne.

. . . .
INDEX

INDEX

(Numbers in **boldface** refer to menu section)

Acorn squash, Baked, **29,** 427
Aïoli (garlic mayonnaise),
   492
Alaska, Baked, 565
Alcachofas con Setas Iturbi
   (artichoke hearts and
   mushrooms Iturbi),
   371
Alice Petersen's Danish
   Cream Cake, **38,** 620
Allemande Torte, **45,** 631
Almond (s)
   Blancmange, **43,** 578
   Camembert Amandine, **44,**
      62
   Cardamom-Almond Fill-
      ing, **53,** 601
   Chicken-Almond Cro-
      quettes, **33,** 289
   Chicken Salad with, **49,** 460
   Chocolate Nut Torte, **34,**
      633
   Crème au Praliné, 673
   Frangipane Tart, 654
   Fritters, **30,** 668
   Fruited Almond Cookies,
      19, 594
   Ginger-Cheese-Almond
      Spread, **34,** 62
   Ginger Cookies, **34,** 594
   Laura Torte, 634
   and Macaroni Casserole, **37,**
      352
   Macaroons, **45, 50, 52,** 602
   Macaroons, Italian, **43,** 602
   Praline Candy, 674
   Short Pastry, 639
   Squares, **45, 26,** 593
   Tart, **24,** 651
   Thins, **21, 39,** 593

Almond (s) *(cont'd)*
   Topping, **38,** 620
   Wafers, 535
Alsatian Sauerkraut, 387
Alvina Mattes's Onion Scal-
      lop, **23,** 409
Ambrosia, **38, 24,** 552
Anadama Bread, Cranberry,
      527
Anchovy (ies)
   Butter, 499
   -Cheese Sauce, **39,** 485
   -Egg Boats, **51,** 93
   and Pimiento Salad, **40, 42,**
      54, 69
   Potato Salad with, **21, 45,**
      456
   and Tomato Appetizer, **24,**
      38, 47, 70
Andalusian Beef Roll, **33,** 183
Andalusian Lamb Stew, **23,**
      245
Andean Stuffed Avocado, **18,**
      463
Anise
   Coddled Apples, **15, 40,** 545
   Cookies Anisette, **27, 36, 44,**
      595
   Duck and Rice Casserole,
      39, 305
   Fork Cookies, **41,** 595
   Fruit Compote, **24, 28,** 554
Anisette Cookies, **27, 36, 44,**
      595
Anita Kniberg, Tamales à la,
      54, 346
Ann Seranne, Sweet Potatoes,
      à la, **50,** 420
Antipasto Mushrooms, **28, 52,**
      68

Antoine's Eggs à la Russe,
      47, 67
Aphrodite Lianides, Greek
      Nut Roll à la, **52,** 674
Appetizers, 59–97
   Anchovy-Egg Boats, **51,** 93
   Anchovy and Pimiento
      Salad, **40, 42, 54,** 69
   Appetizer Eggs, **49,** 67
   Artichoke Hearts and
      Shrimp, **32,** 70
   Artichokes Vinaigrette, 437
   Avocado Appetizer, **32, 36,**
      71
   Bean Sprouts Vinaigrette,
      19, 437
   Buttered Nuts, **45, 46,** 65
   Camembert Amandine, **44,**
      62
   Caviar Roulade, **51, 53,** 80
   Celery with Garlic Cheese,
      31, 63
   Celery Liptauer, **19, 53,** 63
   Cheese-Garlic Spread, **21,**
      62
   Cheese Log, **29, 50,** 62
   Cheese and Parsley Pie, **38,**
      334
   Cheese Straws and Twists,
      23, 29, 45, 65
   Chicken-Liver Pâté, **45, 51,**
      83
   Chicken-Liver Tartlets, **48,**
      92
   Chick-Peas Rémoulade, **50,**
      69
   Citrus Herring in Wine
      Sauce, **29,** 73
   Clams, Stuffed, **39,** 72

Appetizers (cont'd)
  Crab-Stuffed Avocados, **40**, 72
  Cream-Cheese Pastry, **51**, 93
    Slices, **51**, 95
    Turnovers, **20**, 95
  Croquettes, Cocktail, **39**, **44**, 77
  Cucumber Spread, **44**, **47**, **49**, 64
  Curried Mushroom Rolls, **35**, **51**, 79
  Duck Pâté, **20**, 85
  Eggs, **23**, **49**, 67
  Eggs à la Russe, Antoine's, **47**, 67
  Eggs and Artichokes Forestière, 68
  Eggs with Herb Mayonnaise, **55**, 66
  French Bread, Cheese-Stuffed, **21**, 79
  Game Pâté, **47**, 311
  Ginger-Cheese-Almond Spread, **34**, 62
  Green Beans Vinaigrette, **30**, **48**, 437
  Kidney Beans Vinaigrette, **40**, 437
  Lahmajoon, **20**, 81
  Lahm-el-Gine, 81
  Liver Pâté with Pistachios, **48**, 87
  Lobster, Deviled, Spanish, 158
  Malakoff, 329
  Mushroom Appetizer, **30**, **52**, 68
  Mushroom and Celery Pickles, **27**, **54**, 504
  Mushroom Cocktail Strudels, **44**, 79
  Mushrooms, Pickled, **20**, 504
  Mushrooms, raw, vinaigrette, see Vegetables Vinaigrette, 436
  Mushroom-Stuffed Eggs, **22**, **45**, 66
  Mussels Ravigote, **22**, 74
  Mussels, Steamed, 73
  Mussels, Stuffed, **33**, **52**, 73
  Olive-Stuffed Eggs, **45**, **46**, 65
  Pâté en Croûte, 83
  Pâté de Foie en Terrine, 84
  Pâté for Picnics, James Beard's, **21**, 87
  Peppers, Roasted, **52**, 69

Appetizers (cont'd)
  Pirog, 88
  Piroshki, 90
    Baked, 91
    Fried, 90
  Quiche, Shrimp, **17**, **47**, 91
  Rillettes de Tours, 86
  Roquefort-Stuffed Mushrooms, **45**, **50**, 67
  Salmon Eggs Montauk, **45**, **46**, **50**, 66
  Sates, **54**, 78
  Savory Eggplant Spread, **22**, **54**, 64
  Scallop Blankets, **21**, **26**, 77
  Seafood Cocktail Sauce, 493
  Sesame Beef Strips, **20**, 78
  Sesame-Cheese Roll, **20**, **51**, 63
  Seviche, **22**, **54**, 74
  Shrimp, Batter-Fried, **54**, 76
  Shrimp Cocktail à la Française, **32**, 75
  Shrimp Pâté de Luxe, **50**, 85
  Shrimp, Pickled (Camarones Estilo Barbachano Ponce), **25**, 75
  Shrimp Quiche, **17**, **47**, 91
  Shrimp Rémoulade, Ruth Ellen Church's, **40**, 75
  Shrimp Toast, **50**, 61
  Smørrebrød, **53**, 513
  Snails, Stuffed, **37**, 76
  Sweetbreads in Individual Casseroles, **26**, 256
  Tarte à l'Oignon, **52**, 91
  Tomato and Anchovy Appetizer, **24**, **38**, **47**, 70
  Tomatoes Antiboise, **21**, 70
  Tomatoes Vinaigrette, **18**, **34**, **48**, 438
  Tuna-Parmesan Canapés, **26**, 61
  Tuna-Stuffed Eggs, **45**, 66
  Vegetables Vinaigrette, 436
  Yerbra, 82
Apple (s)
  Anise Coddled, **15**, **40**, 545
  Applesauce Pie, Normandy, **26**, 642
  and Blackberry Pie, **42**, 643
  Cake, Danish, **29**, **34**, 629
  Cardamom Apple Pie, **40**, **43**, 641
  Compote, **34**, **42**, 545
  Cranberry-Apple Sauce, 502
  -Cranberry Punch, 695

Apple (s) (cont'd)
  Cranberry Tarts, **21**, 653
  Dumplings, **18**, **26**, 664
  -and Grape Pie, **26**, 644
  -Oatmeal Crisp, **38**, 585
  Orange Nut Loaf, **22**, 616
  Pie, Dutch, **19**, **39**, 641
  -and Prune Stuffing, 314
  Soufflé with Lemon-Nutmeg Sauce, **41**, 590
  Sour-Cream Pie, **25**, **38**, 642
  Tart, **49**, 651
  Whip, Frosted, 693
Apricot
  Filling, 676
  Glaze, 682
  Rice Pudding, **29**, 583
  Sauce, **23**, 683
  Sour-Cream Sauce, **40**, 683
Armenian Beef Loaf, **33**, 198
Artichoke (s)
  Bottoms
    Clamart, **45**, **53**, 370
    Cooking, 370
    and Eggs Forestière, 68
    Eggs Sardou, Brennan's, **41**, 323
    with Foie Gras, **19**, 370
    Mock Benedict, 371
  with Butter Sauce, **28**, **36**, **41**, 367
  Chicken with, **32**, 270
  Hearts
    with Carrots, **41**, **49**, 390
    and Mushrooms Iturbi, (Alcachofas con Setas Iturbi), 371
    and Shrimp, **32**, 70
    How to Stuff, 368
  Marinated, **47**, 368
  Stuffed with Pork and Pine Nuts, 369
  Stuffed with Veal and Peppers, **44**, 369
  To Stuff, 368
  Vinaigrette, 437
  Whole, Cooking, 367
Asparagus
  with Brown Butter Sauce, **34**, **49**, 371
  Cheese Pudding, **24**, 373
  and Eggplant Mornay, **28**, 372
  Lemon Sauce for, **27**, 487
  Milanese Style, **23**, 372
  Pudding, **41**, 373
  Salad, **18**, **29**, **38**, 444
  with Shad Roe, Grilled, **17**, 141

Asparagus *(cont'd)*
   steamed, *see* Steamed Vegetables, 436
   with Tomato Sauce and Sour Cream, **26,** 372
   vinaigrette, *see* Vegetables Vinaigrette, 436
Aspic Dishes
   Aspic for Beef (Quick), 475
   Aspic for Chicken, 476
   Aspic for Fish, 476
   Aspic Shells, 477
   Cantaloupe Salad, Molded, **47,** 453
   Chicken in Aspic, Cold, **45,** 282
   Ham Mousse, 235
   Ham and Tongue Mousse, 234
   Liver Pâté with Pistachios, **48,** 87
   Mayonnaise Aspic, 468
   Mousse of Green Peas, **49,** 411
   Pâté en Croute, 83
   Roquefort Salad with Vegetables, Molded, **24,** 452
   Salmon in Aspic, **49,** 135
   Salmon Mousse (blender), **45,** 138
   Salmon Mousse (sieve), **45,** 138
   Veal Stock for aspic dishes, *see* Note, 474
Athenian Tea Cakes, **25,** 666
Atjar Ketimum (sweet and sour relish), **54,** 504
Aurore Sauce, 482
Austrian Nut-Butter Cookies, 603
Avery Island Barbecue Sauce, 496
Avocado (s)
   Appetizer, **32, 36,** 71
   Calf's Liver with, **38,** 255
   Cheese and Rice with, **42,** 333
   Crab-Stuffed, **40,** 72
   and Grapefruit Salad, **32, 39, 48,** 443
   and Heart of Palm Salad, **54,** 448
   and Potato Salad, **43,** 457
   Salad, Mexican, **18, 31, 32, 34,** 444
   Soup, Cold, Curried, **18,** 115

Avocado (s) *(cont'd)*
   Stuffed Andean, **18,** 463
   to select and prepare, *see* introductory paragraph, 71

Babka, 526
Bacon
   and Spinach Salad, **24, 42,** 449
   Whole-Wheat Bacon Biscuits, **15,** 533
Bahiana Nut Pudding, 588
Baked Alaska, 565
Bamboo Shoots, relish, *see* Note, Atjar Ketimum, **54,** 504
Banana (s)
   Cake, Brazil, **29, 35,** 614
   Ice Cream, 561
   -Orange Shakes, 694
   à l'Orange, Baked, **40, 44,** 546
   Pudding, Italian Style, **33,** 585
   in Sherry, **23, 53,** 546
   Sour-Cream Pie, **29,** 653
   Walnut Bread, **15,** 532
Barbecue, Barbecued
   Chicken, **22,** 283
   Eggs, 322
   Flank Steak, Stuffed, **54,** 182
   Lamb Ribs, **25,** 239
   Lemon-Barbecued Spareribs, **34,** 224
   Pork Chops, **34,** 222
   Sauce, 497
      Avery Island, 496
      Green-Pepper, **21,** 497
      Southern, 497
      for Spareribs, **22,** 498
      or Smoked Foods, Marinade for, 496
   Spareribs, **54,** 225
Barley and Mushroom Casserole, **22, 32,** 342
Bass, Sea Bass
   in Lemon-Mushroom Sauce, Baked, **36,** 123
   in White-Wine Sauce, Baked, **29,** 124
Bass, Striped Bass
   Poached, **22, 37,** 125
   Stuffed, Pierre Franey's, 124
Basting Sauces, *see* Sauces
Batter (for Souffléed Frogs' Legs), 172

Bavarian, Bavarian Cream
   Blackberry, *see* Note, 568
   Orange, **50,** 567
   Raspberry, **17,** 568
   Strawberry, *see* Note, 568
Bean (s)
   Black Bean (s)
      fried (Frijoles Fritos), **54,** 376
      purée of, *see* Note, 376
      Purée of, with Sour Cream, 377
      Soup, **47,** 107
   Green Bean (s)
      Chilled, **20, 38,** 375
      with Dill, **18,** 374
      Herbed, **33,** 374
      Italian Style, **40,** 374
      Sambal Goreng (Sambal Goreng Buntjies), 375
      Snap Beans in Casserole, **23, 33,** 375
      steamed, *see* Steamed Vegetables, 436
      and Tomatoes à la Française, **48, 49, 53,** 434
      Vinaigrette, **30, 48,** 437
   Kidney Bean (s) (red and white)
      and Chicken Casserole, **31,** 276
      crisp fried (Frijoles Refritos), **54,** 376
      and Mushroom Salad, **22, 24,** 455
      and Olive Soup, **46,** 108
      purée of, *see* Note, 376
      savory white beans (Loubia), **55,** 377
      Vinaigrette, **40,** 437
   Lima Bean (s)
      and Mushroom Salad, **22,** 455
      Purée of, **18, 40,** 376
      Soup, Cream of, **18,** 104
   Navy or Pea Bean (s)
      Baked, New England, **21,** 378
      and Beef Casserole, **42,** 192
      purée of, *see* Note, 376
      and Tuna Vinaigrette, **21,** 462
   Pinto Beans
      Chili con Carne, **24,** 199
   White Beans (Italian *cannellini*), *see* Loubia, **55,** 377

Bean (s) (cont'd)
  Yellow or Wax Bean (s)
    Snap Beans in Casserole, **23, 33,** 375
    steamed, *see* Steamed Vegetables, 436
Bean Sprouts Vinaigrette, **19,** 437
Beard's, James, Braised Shoulder of Lamb, **34,** 236
Beard's, James, Pâté for Picnics, **21,** 87
Béarnaise Sauce, 486
Béchamel Sauce, 480
Beef, 175–204
  Aspic for, Quick, 475
  Balls, Swedish, **52,** 194
  and Beans Casserole, **42,** 192
  Birds, **31,** 182
  Birds, Stuffed, **35,** 183
  Bitocks à la Russe, **35,** 196
  Boeuf en Daube, **38,** 185
  Boiled, Herb Sauce for, 488
  Brazilien, **29,** 188
  and Cheese Roll, **31,** 200
  with Chick Peas, **23,** 187
  Chili con Carne, **24,** 199
    Texas Style, 200
  Cornmeal Beef Casserole, **25,** 198
  croquettes, *see* Note, 217
  Curry of, **32,** 187
  with Dumplings, **38,** 188
  Goulash, **30,** 186
  Gravy, Thin Pan, 175
  Green Peppers with Meat Balls, **24,** 196
  Ground, and Tomato Custard Pie, **40,** 328
  Hamburger
    Burgundy Burgers, **19,** 195
    Cheeseburger Pie, **32,** 197
    with Marrow, **26,** 193
    Oriental, **28,** 193
    Pie, **44,** 196
    quality and storage, *see* introductory paragraph, 192
    Roquefort, **21,** 195
    Spinach and Cheese, **43,** 195
  Horseradish Sauce for, **38, 53,** 489
  Kebabs, Dilled, **21,** 200
  Lahm-el-Gine, 81
  Loaf, Armenian, **33,** 198

Beef (cont'd)
  and macaroni casserole (Tagliarini), **39,** 351
  Macaroni and Meat Puff, **28,** 352
  Marinade for, 495
  Marjoram Loaf, **32,** 197
  Marrow
    Hamburgers with Marrow, **26,** 193
    Sauce Bordelaise, **37,** 478
  Meat Filling, **45,** 96
  Meat Fritters, Herbed, **31,** 201
  Peppers, Brazilian Stuffed, **16,** 412
  Pot Roast
    Gingered, **28,** 178
    Jardinière (baked in foil), **26,** 178
    with Wine, **36,** 177
  Poule au Pot, 270
  Rib Roast, Standing, **41, 51,** 175
    timetable for roasting, 175
  with Rice, Korean, **39,** 341
  Roll, Andalusian, **33,** 183
  Rosemary Beef Rolls, **27,** 184
  Round Roast of, Braised, **26,** 176
  Sesame Beef Strips, **20,** 78
  Shepherd's Pie, **24,** 202
  Short Ribs
    with Olives, Savory, **35,** 185
    and Vodka Casserole, **30,** 186
  Slices with Caper Sauce, **24,** 201
  Steak (s)
    Almond and Macaroni Casserole, **37,** 352
    Braised, **29,** 179
    Cube Steaks, Marinated, **20, 33,** 180
    Flank, Barbecued, Stuffed, **54,** 182
    Flank, with Celery Stuffing, Rolled, **31,** 181
    Fromage, **27,** 179
    and Kidney Pie, **38,** 190
    and Kidney Pudding, 189
    Pepper Steak (green peppers), **34,** 181
    au Poivre with Red-Wine Sauce, **29,** 180
    Sauce Marchand de Vin for, 478

Beef: Steak (s) (cont'd)
    Swiss (braised), **29,** 179
    Tartare Steak Sandwich, 515
    Tropical, **31,** 179
    Stock, 473
    Wellington, **45, 48,** 176
    Yerbra, 82
  Beef, Chipped Beef
    and Cheese, **32,** 203
    with Nutmeg, Creamed, **15,** 204
  Beef, Corned Beef
    Casserole, **35,** 203
    Glazed, **46, 51,** 201
    Hash Chez Soi, 15, 202
  Beef Tongue
    with Almonds and Grapes, **23,** 257
    Braised, **36,** 257
    Cumberland Sauce for, **36,** 487
    Ham and Tongue Mousse, 234
    Sandwich, **53,** 514
    Tomatoes Stuffed with, **39,** 433
  Beef Tripe
    à la Creole, **25,** 258
    Braised, 258
  Beet (s)
    Borscht with Cucumber, Cold, 33, 47, 114
    à la Crème, **32,** 379
    and Onion Salad, **26, 29, 35, 42,** 445
    in Orange-Butter Sauce, **31, 44,** 380
    Pickled, **55,** 380
    Polish, **31,** 380
    Salad, **24,** 445
    Soup, Fanny Todd Mitchell's, **37,** 105
  Beignets Soufflés, **37,** 665
  Belgian Endive, *see* Endive, Belgian
  Belgian Salad, **43,** 443
  Bermudiana Pork Chops, **25,** 221
  Berries, *see* names of berries
  Beurre Blanc, 498
  Beurre Blanc, Halibut Steak au, 132
  Beverages, 691–697
    Apple Whip, Frosted, 693
    Banana-Orange Shakes, 694
    Dook, **53,** 693
    Lemonade for a Party, 694

Beverages *(cont'd)*
Punch
Apple-Cranberry, 695
Citrus, 695
Fruit, **46,** 696
Reception, 697
Watermelon, **46,** 695
Tea, Iced, 695
Tomato Juice, 693
Beverages, Alcoholic
Bicyclette Cocktail à la Po-
tinière, **47,** 696
Eggnog, Colonial, 697
Jack Rose, 696
Punch
Bordelaise, 698
Champagne, **48, 51,** 697
Charentaise, **51,** 698
Planter's, 697
Reception, 697
Vintage, **48,** 698
Salty Russian, **21,** 696
Bicyclette Cocktail à la Poti-
nière, **47,** 696
Bigos (Polish hunter's stew) ,
261
Birthday Butter Cake, **48,** 617
Biscuits, Whole-Wheat Ba-
con, **15,** 533
Bishop's Bread, **49,** 623
Bisque, *see* Soups, Cream
Bitocks à la Russe, **35,** 196
Bittersweet Fudge Sauce, 686
Black beans, *see* Bean (s)
Blackberry (ies)
and Apple Pie, **42,** 643
Bavarian, *see* Note, 568
Black Bun, **51,** 613
Blanching Nuts, 651
Blancmange
Almond, **43,** 578
Coconut, **33,** 579
Blotkake (Norwegian Sponge-
cake) , **55,** 626
Blowfish, *see* Sea Squab
Blueberry (ies)
Betty, 586
with Lemon Fromage, **31,**
45, 575
Pie, **43,** 643
soup, *see* Note, 118
Torte, **26,** 632
Bluefish
Poached, **31,** 126
au Vin Blanc, **22,** 127
Boeuf en Daube, **38,** 185
Bordelaise Punch, 698
Bordelaise Sauce, **37,** 478
Borsch with Cucumber,
Cold, **33, 47,** 114

Boston Brown Bread, **49,** 531
Braciolette Ripiene (stuffed
veal rolls) , **47,** 210
Brains, *see* Calf's Brains
Brazil Banana Cake, **29, 35,**
614
Brazilian Stuffed Peppers, **16,**
412
Brazilien Beef, **29,** 188
Brazil Nut (s)
Brazil Banana Cake, **29, 35,**
614
Cake, **18,** 616
Nut Pudding Bahiana, 588
Stuffing, **50,** 315
Tartlets, **16, 32,** 616
to slice, *see* Note, 615
to toast, *see* Note, 615
Bread
and-Butter Pudding, **17,**
580
and-Butter Pudding,
Coffee, **24,** 580
Crumb Dumplings, 541
Crumbs, 312, 501
Fine Dry, 313
Soft Fresh, 313
Breads, Quick Breads, 529–
535; *see also* Dump-
lings; Pancakes
Almond Wafers, 535
Banana Walnut Bread, **15,**
532
Basic Baking Mix, 529
Boston Brown Bread, **49,**
531
Bread Twists, 529
Cheese Muffins, **15,** 534
Corn Bread, **49,** 529
Sage, 530
Southern, **15,** 530
Cornmeal Wafers, 534
Cranberry Nut Bread, **16,**
532
Date and Honey Bread,
Steamed, 532
Fennel Oatmeal Bread, **15,**
531
Fresh-Corn Muffins, **44,** 534
Orange-Oatmeal Bread, **16,**
530
Spice Bread, 533
Spoon Bread, 344
Fresh-Corn, **16,** 345
with Ham and Mush-
rooms, 345
Whole-Wheat Bacon Bis-
cuits, **15,** 533
Yorkshire Pudding, Indi-
vidual, **41,** 535

Breads, Salt Rising Bread,
520
Breads, Yeast Breads, 519–
528
Babka, 526
Black-Pepper Crackling
Bread, **42,** 522
Brioche Ring, **16,** 523
Brioches, Individual, 524
Cardamom Buns, St.
Lucia's, **52,** 528
Cheese Brioche, **16, 49,**
523
Cheese-Herb Bread, **16,**
50, 522
Coffee Loaves, Swedish, 525
Cranberry Anadama Bread,
527
Gott Vetebrod (Swedish
coffeecake) , 524
Holiday Fruit Bread, **45,**
527
Raisin-Oat Cinnamon
Bread, 524
Rye Bread, **20,** 520
Swiss Cheese Loaf, **44,** 521
Wheaten Bread, 519
whole-wheat bread, *see*
Note, 521
Brennan's Eggs Sardou, **41,**
323
Brioche (s)
Cheese, **16, 49,** 523
Individual, 524
Ring, **16,** 523
Brittany Crêpes with Filbert
Butter, **26,** 675
Broccoli
with Anchovy-Cheese
Sauce, **39,** 380
Fresh, Creole, **29, 31,** 381
and Lobster Mornay, **24,**
382
Ring, **26, 47,** 381
Salad, **17, 24, 31, 33,** 445
steamed, *see* Steamed Vege-
tables, 436
Turkey Divan, 297
Brochette, en brochette, *see*
Skewer (s) , Skewered
Brown Bread, Boston, **49,** 531
Brown Sauce or Sauce Espa-
gnole, 477
Brown Sugar Pie, **23, 47,** 654
Brownies, Double Fudge, **19,**
600
Brown's, Helen Evans, Straw-
berry Fritters, 697

Brussels Sprouts
  with Celery Knob, **48, 384**
  with Chestnuts, **33, 385**
  à la Crème, **24, 383**
  Creole, **28, 383**
  Polonaise, **25, 382**
  with Sautéed Mushrooms,
    41, 51, 384
  with Water Chestnuts, **38,
    50, 383**
Buckwheat Pancakes, Raised,
  536
Buñuelos (Mexican fritters),
  54, 666
Burgundian Clams, 151
Burriana-style onion salad
    (Ensalada de Cebolla
    Burriana), **20, 23, 448**
Butter
  Cake, Birthday, **48, 617**
  Clarified, 498; see also
    Note, 189
  Frosting, Spiced, 679
  Nut-Butter Cookies, Aus-
    trian, 603
  Orange Butter Cookies, **30,**
    605
  Sesame-Seed Butter Cake,
    30, 31, 618
  -Sugar Cookies, **44, 595**
Buttercream, 567, 568
  Chocolate, 678
  Mocha, 678
Butternut Squash, see Squash
Butters
  Anchovy, 499
  Beurre Blanc, 498
  Dill, **21, 499**
  Herbed Caper, **39, 500**
  Mustard, **18, 21, 46, 499**
  parsley, see Parsley Butter
    Sandwiches, **48, 51, 512**
  Pecan Savory, 500
  Sesame-Seed and Lemon,
    40, 500
  Snail, 499
Butterscotch Meringue Pie,
  25, 27, 662

Cabbage
  in Caraway Cream, 385
  -Carrot Filling for Pirog,
    89
  Creamed, 385
  Red Cabbage
    Braised with Chestnuts,
      40, 387
    Stewed, **26, 55, 386**
    with Vermouth, 386

Cabbage (cont'd)
  Sauerkraut
    Alsatian, 387
    Choucroute Garnie,
      Pierre Franey's, **53, 388**
    hunter's stew, Polish
      (Bigos), 261
    Pork, and Apples, **24, 220**
  Slaw, Hot, **37, 386**
Cake (s), 608–638; see also
    Cheesecake; Coffee-
    cake; Cookies and
    Small Cakes; Torte
  Apple, Danish, **29, 34, 629**
  Apple Orange Nut Loaf,
    22, 616
  Banana, Brazil, **29, 35, 614**
  Bishop's Bread, **49, 623**
  Black Bun, **51, 613**
  Brazil-Nut, **18, 616**
  Brazil-Nut Tartlets, **16, 32,**
    616
  Butter, Birthday, **48, 617**
  Chiffon
    All-Purpose, 624
    Layers, 624
    Lemon, **26, 46, 625**
    Orange, **32, 625**
    Party Variety, 624
  Chocolate, **46, 618**
  Chocolate Roll, **51, 628**
  Chocolate Skillet, **43, 619**
  Clove, **44, 623**
  Coffee Cream, **30, 619**
  Cranberry, **26, 617**
  Cranberry Sponge Roll, **51,**
    629
  Danish Cream, Alice Peter-
    sen's, **38, 620**
  Fruitcake
    Black Bun, **18, 613**
    Frozen, **51, 612**
    Swedish, 612
  Lemon, **31, 38, 620**
  Lemon Ambrosia, **38, 628**
  Lemon Cake Pie, **27, 659**
  Marble, **44, 621**
  meringue topping for, see
    Note, 565
  Mocha, Norwegian, **33, 45,**
    621
  Orange Pecan Shortbread,
    35, 37, 615
  Pineapple   Upside-Down,
    28, 622
  Poundcake, **19, 28, 31, 34,**
    622
  Sesame-Seed Butter, **30, 31,**
    618

Cake (s)   (cont'd)
  Shortbread, **18, 51, 615**
    Orange Pecan, **35, 37, 615**
  Spongecake, **28, 42, 50, 625**
    Norwegian (Blotkake),
      55, 626
  Sponge Roll, **34, 627**
    Chocolate, **51, 628**
    Cranberry, **26, 629**
  Valentine, **48, 626**
Caldo Gallego, **53, 109**
Calf's Brains Vinaigrette, 252
Calf's Head Vinaigrette, 252
Calf's Liver
  with Avocado, **38, 255**
  with Parsley Sauce, **37, 256**
California Ham Bake, 232
California Walnut Stuffing,
  316
Camarones Estilo Barbachano
    Ponce (pickled
    shrimp), **25, 75**
Camembert Amandine, **44, 62**
Canapés
  Liver (duck), 304
  Savory Eggplant, **22, 54,**
    see Note, 64
  Shrimp Toast, **50, 61**
  Tuna-Parmesan, **26, 61**
Cannelloni, Chicken, **52, 361**
Cantaloupe
  Flower Salad, **49, 453**
  Fruit-Filled, **21, 26, 547**
  with Honeydew Balls, **15,
    30, 48, 547**
  Perles de, au Rhum, **52,**
    548
  Royale, **19, 31, 548**
  Salad, Molded, **47, 51, 453**
Caper   Butter,   Herbed,   **39,**
  500
Caramel
  custard,   Spanish   (Flan),
    54, 572
  Syrup, 672
Caraway, Caraway Seed
  and   Cottage-Cheese   Dress-
    ing, **21, 30, 35, 467**
  Cream, Cabbage in, 385
  Macaroni Rabbit, **17, 331**
  Meat Balls, **22, 194**
  Noodle   Ring   with   Tuna,
    42, 350
  Potatoes, **19, 415**
Cardamom
  -Almond Filling, **53, 601**
  Apple Pie, **40, 43, 641**
  Buns, St. Lucia's, **52, 528**
Cardelli's, Jacqueline, Mousse
    au Chocolat, **35, 38, 556**

Carmelite Pears, **47,** 550
Carp, Baked, **50,** 128
Carrot (s)
  with Artichoke Hearts, **41,** **49,** 390
  Cabbage-Carrot Filling for Pirog, 89
  Glazed, **29, 34, 35,** 389
  Mousse, **49,** 290
  and New Potatoes, Braised, with Dill, **39,** 419
  Orange-Glazed, **28,** 389
  and Potatoes Mousseline, **51,** 390
  Torte, **27, 46,** 632
  Tzimmes, **50,** 389
Cashew
  Grenadine-Cashew Pie, **28,** 646
  Nut Pilaff, **33,** 337
Cauliflower
  with Caper Sauce, **28, 33,** 391
  Confetti, **27, 29,** 391
  Mornay, 392
  with Mustard Sauce, **51,** 390
  Salad, Napolitana, **20, 23, 25,** 445
  steamed, see Steamed Vegetables, 436
Caviar
  and Egg Sandwiches, **21,** 512
  Lumpfish-Caviar Sandwich, **53,** 513
  Roulade, **51, 53,** 80
Celery
  Braised in White Wine, **38,** 392
  Fumet of, **24, 49,** 106
  with Garlic Cheese, **23, 31,** 63
  Ham and Celery Loaf, **38,** 234
  Liptauer, **19, 53,** 63
  and Mushroom Pickles, **27, 54,** 504
  -Stuffed Flounder, **28,** 130
  to crisp ribs, see Note, Celery Liptauer, 63
Celery Knob (celeriac)
  with Brussels Sprouts, **48,** 384
  Gratin Savoyard, **29, 48,** 419
  Parmigiana, **25,** 393
  vinaigrette, see Vegetables Vinaigrette, 436
Champagne Punch, **48, 51,** 697

Charentaise Punch, **51,** 698
Chawanmushi, **54,** 326
Cheesecake
  Chocolate, **23,** 611
  Cottage, **30, 42,** 608
  Cranberry, **28, 36,** 609
  Cranberry Cheese Cupcakes, **47,** 609
  de Luxe, **27,** 610
  Pineapple Refrigerator, **34,** 608
Cheese Dishes, 329–334
  Anchovy-Cheese Sauce, **39,** 485
  Asparagus Cheese Pudding, **24,** 373
  Beef and Cheese Roll, **31,** 200
  Brioche, **16, 49,** 523
  Camembert Amandine, **44,** 62
  Caraway Macaroni Rabbit, **17,** 331
  Celery with Garlic Cheese, **23, 31,** 63
  Celery Knob Parmigiana, **25,** 393
  Cheeseburger Pie, **32,** 197
  Chicken Cannelloni, **53,** 361
  Chipped Beef and Cheese, **32,** 203
  Chocolate Cheese Pie, Frozen, 649
  Corn and Cheese Pudding, **43,** 395
  and Cornmeal Casserole, **35,** 344
  Cottage-Cheese and Caraway-Seed Dressing, **21, 30, 35,** 467
  Cottage-Cheese Pie, Italian, **17, 33,** 649
  Cream-Cheese Frosting, 680
  Cream-Cheese with Noodles, **45,** 348
  Croûtes, Garlic-Flavored, 500
  Danish-Cheese Sandwich, **53,** 513
  Filling (for Kreplach), 359
  -Garlic Spread, **21,** 62
  Ginger-Cheese-Almond Spread, **34,** 62
  Golden Buck, **40,** 331
  Gougère, 333
  and Ham Hero, **18, 46,** 512
  -Herb Bread, **16, 50,** 522
  Lemon-Cheese Pie, **33,** 649
  Log, **29, 50,** 62
  Malakoff, 329

Cheese Dishes (cont'd)
  Mexican Rabbit, **41,** 332
  Muffins, **15,** 534
  and Mushroom Sauce, 485
  Mustard-Cheese Sauce, 484
  and Parsley Pie, **38,** 334
  Pastry (Cheddar), **32,** 197
  Potato-Cheese Charlotte, **48,** 418
  Potato-Cheese Soufflé, 330
  Raclette, **20,** 329
  and Rice Avocados, **42,** 333
  Rice, Baked, **25,** 338
  Ricotta Pie, **23, 54,** 650
  Risotto Ring, **34, 45,** 337
  Roquefort Hamburgers, **21,** 195
  Roquefort Salad with Vegetables, Molded, **24,** 452
  Roquefort-Stuffed Mushrooms, **45, 50,** 67
  Rosemary Potatoes with Cheese, **35,** 413
  Sauce (Cheddar), **26,** 484
  Sauce Mornay, 484
  Sesame-Cheese Roll, **20, 51,** 63
  Shrimp and Cheese Spaghetti, **17,** 357
  Shrimp Quiche, **17, 47,** 91
  Shrimp Rabbit, **18,** 167
  Soufflé, **39,** 330
  and Spinach Hamburgers, **43,** 195
  Spinach and Roquefort, **22,** 423
  Straws and Twists, **23, 29, 45,** 65
  -Stuffed French Bread, **21,** 79
  Swiss Cheese Loaf, **44,** 521
  Swiss Mushrooms, **19,** 405
  Tabasco Roquefort Steak Spread, **23,** 499
  Tomato Rabbit, 331
  Tuna-Parmesan Canapés, **26,** 61
  and Vegetable Salad Dressing, **17, 44,** 465
  Welsh Rabbit, **40,** 330
  Zucchini Cheese Custard, **31,** 429
Chef Salad à l'Adam, **19,** 463
Chello Kebab, **53,** 246
Chello (Persian rice), **53,** 341
Cherry
  Black Cherry Sauce, 684
  -Grapefruit-Port-Wine Gelatin, **36,** 546

Cherry (cont'd)
Sauce, 683
Soup, 118
Tart, **30, 48,** 652
-Walnut Pudding, **31,** 586
Cherry Tomatoes, *see* Toma-
to (es)
Chess Pie, **35,** 648
Chestnut (s)
with Braised Red Cabbage,
40, 387
with Brussels Sprouts, **33,**
385
Cooked, 317
Pie, **48,** 646
Pudding, Frozen, **51,** 562
Chèvre (goat), Game Stew,
Savory, 260
Chicken, 267–294
-Almond Croquettes, **33,**
289
with Artichokes, **32,** 270
in Aspic, Cold, **45,** 282
Aspic for, Quick, 476
in a Bag, **50,** 269
Baked, Summer Style, **26,**
280
Barbecued, **22,** 283
Breast (s), Breast of
Bake, **24,** 285
Breaded, **24,** 284
Chawanmushi, **54,** 326
and Cucumber Soup, **49,**
106
in Greek Pastry, **53,** 284
Sate, 286
Stuffed, Molière, **40,** 287
in tuna sauce (Pollo en
Salsa Tonnato), 461
Véronique, **34,** 285
Virginienne, **48,** 286
Broiled, for One, **40,** 281
Rosemary, **25,** 283
broth or stock, *see* Note,
271
Cannelloni, **52,** 361
Chili Fried, **20,** 273
Circassian, **31,** 268
Cock-a-Leekie, **18,** 113
croquettes, *see* Note, 217
Curried, **33,** 277
Filling, 96
Fricassee, Brown, **25,** 269
Hollandaise, **35,** 287
Indian Melon Salad, **49,**
462
and Kidney-Bean Casserole,
31, 276
Loaf, Nivernaise, **49,** 290
Mexican, **39,** 280

Chicken (cont'd)
Moroccan Style, **36,** 281
Mousse, **49,** 290
Nasi Goreng, **54,** 288
and Noodle Casserole, **44,**
275
and Oyster Pie, **43,** 268
in Peach Sauce, 278
Poached, **41,** 271
Poule au Pot, **54,** 270
Poulet en Casserole, 273
Poulet Flambé, Ninette
Lyon's, **37,** 274
Puff, **29,** 272
and Rice Casserole, **46,** 276
Roast
Sandwich, **53,** 513
Stuffed, 267
unstuffed, *see* Note, 267
alla Romana, **33,** 273
Rosemary, Broiled, **25,** 283
in Saffron Cream Sauce, **32,**
281
Salad with Almonds, **49,**
460
Salad for One, 460
Sausage Stuffing for, 313
Sauté, Lemon, **29,** 277
Scalloped, 289
Soup with Mushrooms, **54,**
106
in Sour Cream, **26,** 278
Stock, 475
Supreme, **41,** 272
Tarragon, **36,** 274
Chicken Liver (s)
with Belgian Endive, **42,**
293
en Brochette, 291
Broiled, **16,** 293
Eggplant and Chicken-
Liver Casserole, **18,** 400
Filling, **51,** 95
Hongroise, **17,** 293
Madeira, **34,** 292
and Mushroom Spaghetti,
44, 355
Omelet, **36,** 326
Pâté, **45, 51,** 83
Pâté de Foie en Terrine, 84
Pâté with Pistachios, **48,** 87
Tartlets, **48,** 92
Timbales, **41,** 292
Tomatoes Stuffed with, **48,**
433
Chick-Pea (s)
Beef with, **23,** 187
Caldo Gallego, **52,** 109
Rémoulade, **36, 50,** 69
Salad, **20,** 454

Chiffon Cakes, *see* Cake (s)
Chili
con Carne, **34,** 199
con Carne, Texas Style, 200
Chicken, Fried, **20,** 273
Chinese Dishes, Mustard
Sauce for, 486
Chinese Dumplings, Steamed,
54, 364
Chinese Roast Duck, **38,** 303
Chinese Style Squid Stir-
Fried, 171
Chipped Beef, *see* Beef,
Chipped Beef
Chive Shrimp in Shells, **18,**
166
Chocolate
Bittersweet Fudge Sauce,
686
Black-Pepper Cookies, **25,**
597
Brownies, Double-Fudge,
19, 600
Buttercream, 678
-Butter Filling, 677
Cake, **46,** 618
Cheesecake, **23,** 611
Cheese Pie, Frozen, 649
Cookies, Soft, 596
Custard, **32,** 571
Custard Ice Cream, 562
Double-Fudge Brownies,
19, 600
Filling, 676
Frosting I and II, 680
Fudge Brownies, Double,
19, 600
Glaze, 682
Honey-Chocolate Bars, **25,**
600
Marmalade Sauce, **24,** 686
Meringues, 597
Mousse au Chocolat, Jac-
queline Cardelli's, **35,**
38, 556
Nut Torte, **34,** 633
-Orange Mousse, **37, 55,** 555
Parfait, Black Bottom, **35,**
577
Pecan Pie, **43,** 647
Pudding I and II, **25, 39,**
50, 576
Roll, **51,** 628
Rum Sauce, **31,** 686
Sauce, 686
Skillet Cake, **43,** 619
Soufflé, 591
Sour-Cream Cookies, 598
Squares, **40,** 597
Vanilla Pie, Frozen, 563

Chocolate (cont'd)
-Wafer Piecrust, 641
Walnut Sauce, 687
Choucroute Garnie, Pierre
Franey's, 388
Chowder (s)
Clam, Manhattan, 110
Corn and Potato, **42,** 102
Fish, Spanish, **43,** 110
Okra-Seafood, **43,** 170
Salmon, **17,** 110
Seafood, **42,** 111
Church's, Ruth Ellen, Shrimp
Rémoulade, **40,** 75
Chu's, Grace, Shrimp Filling
for Egg Rolls, 363
Chutney, Grape and Green-
Tomato, **16,** 505
Cinnamon Pumpkin Flan, **54,**
572
Circassian Chicken, **31,** 268
Citron Cookies, Crisp, **17,** 596
Citron Mousse, Frozen, **35,**
560
Citrus
Chiffon Pie, **38, 39,** 659
Herring in Wine Sauce, **29,**
73
Punch, 695
Rum Chiffon Cream, **34,**
568
Clam (s)
Broth, **23, 49,** 109
Burgundian, 151
Chowder, Manhattan, 110
Fritters, 152
Méxicaine, **18,** 152
Quahogs, Stuffed, 153
soup, see Note, Steamed
Clams, 152
Steamed, 152
Stuffed, **39,** 72
White Clam Sauce with
Linguine, **43,** 350
Clarified Butter, 498; see
also Note, 189
Clove Cakes, **44,** 623
Clove Whipped Cream, **27,**
683
Club Sandwich, **19,** 509
Cock-a-Leekie, **18,** 113
Cocktails, to drink, see
Beverages, Alcoholic
Cocktails, to eat, see Appe-
tizers
Coconut
Ambrosia, **24, 38,** 552
Bars, Chewy, **21,** 601
Blancmange, **33,** 579

Coconut (cont'd)
Cream, 491
Cream, Molded, **31, 37,** 569
and Jamaica Rum Sauce,
24, 688
Milk, 491
with peanuts, fried (Ser-
oendeng) , **54,** 505
Pudding, **39,** 579
Rice, 583
Topping, 682
Cod, Codfish
Mariner's Stew, 128
Portuguese Style, see Salt
Cod, 129
Cod, Salt Cod
Poached, 129
Portuguese Style, 129
Coffee
Bread-and-Butter Pudding,
24, 580
Charlotte, **28, 31,** 556
Cream Cake, **30,** 619
Cream Chantilly, **29,** 569
Loaves, Swedish, 525
Syrup, **30,** 620
Vanilla Sauce, 690
Coffeecake
Babka, 526
Swedish (Gott Vetebrod) ,
524
Swedish Coffee Loaves, 525
Cognac Sauce, 689
Colcannon with Kale, **49,** 404
Coleslaw, Hot Cabbage Slaw,
37, 386
Colonial Eggnog, 697
Combination Dolma, 250
Composed Butters, 498–500;
see Butters
Confectioners' Sugar Icing,
679
Confetti Cauliflower, **27, 29,**
391
Cookies and Small Cakes,
593–607
Almond Ginger Cookies, **34,**
594
Almond Squares, **26, 45,** 593
Almond Thins, **21, 39,** 593
Anise Fork Cookies, **41,** 595
Anisette Cookies, **27, 36, 44,**
595
Athenian Tea Cakes, **35,**
666
Black-Pepper Chocolate
Cookies, **35,** 597
Brazil-Nut Tartlets, **16, 32,**
616

Cookies and Small Cakes
(cont'd)
Brownies, Double-Fudge,
19, 600
Butter-Sugar Cookies, **44,**
595
Chocolate Cookies, Soft,
596
Chocolate Meringues, 597
Chocolate Squares, **40,** 597
Citron Cookies, Crisp, **17,**
596
Clove Cakes, **44,** 623
Coconut Bars, Chewy, **21,**
601
Cranberry Bars, **18,** 598
Florentines, **18,** 599
Fruited Almond Cookies,
19, 594
Honey-Chocolate Bars, **25,**
600
Lemon Nut Wafers, **20,** 602
Macaroons, **45, 50, 53,** 602
Macaroons, Italian, **45, 53,**
602
Molasses Drop Cookies,
Soft, 603
Nut-Butter Cookies, Aus-
trian, 603
Nutmeg Date Bars, **29, 46,**
604
Nutmeg Hermits, **21,** 604
Nutmeg Pressed Cookies,
30, 604
Nutmeg Sand Tarts, **17,**
605
Oatmeal Thins, 605
Orange Butter Cookies, **30,**
605
Peanut-Raisin Chews, 606
Pecan Bars, **21,** 606
Pecanettes, Spiced, **29,** 607
Pepparkakor, **45,** 607
Petits Cornets, 574
royal cake (Frystekaka) ,
53, 601
Sour-Cream Chocolate
Cookies, 598
Coquilles Aloyse, **27,** 162
Corn
Casserole, Spanish, **30,** 396
and Cheese Pudding, **43,**
395
on the Cob with Pepper
Butter, **42,** 393
in Cream, **16,** 393
Creole, **32,** 394
fresh-corn fritters (Torrejas
de Maíz Tierno) , 397
Fresh-Corn Muffins, **44,** 534

Corn *(cont'd)*
Fresh-Corn Pancakes, **15,** 537
Green Corn Pudding, Shaker, **24,** 394
and Mushroom Sauté, **27,** 394
and Potato Chowder, **42,** 102
Salad, Mexican Style, **26,** 446
tamales (Tamales de Maíz Tierno) , 397
and Tomato Casserole, **49,** 395
tortillas (Tortillas de Maíz) , **41,** 396
and Watercress Soup, **28,** 105
and Zucchini Casserole, **37,** 428
Corn Bread, **49,** 529
Sage Corn Bread, 530
Southern Corn Bread, **15,** 530
Spoon Bread, 344
Fresh-Corn, **16,** 345
with Ham and Mushrooms, 345
Stuffing, 314
Stuffing, Sage Corn-Bread, 314
Corned Beef, *see* Beef, Corned Beef
Cornmeal
Beef Casserole, **25,** 198
and Cheese Casserole, **35,** 344
Corn bread, *see* Corn Bread
Indian Pudding, 582
Pancakes, 536
Polenta, **42,** 343
Polenta with Mushrooms, **42,** 343
Sage Cornmeal Pastry, **26,** 299
Spoon bread, *see* Corn Bread
Tamales à la Anita Kniberg, **54,** 346
Wafers, 534
Cory's, Esther, Baked Whole Fish, **40,** 127
Couscous, **55,** 582
with Fruits and Nuts, **55,** 582
Tunisian, **55,** 243
Crab (s) , Crabmeat
Chasseur
Dewey, **36,** 155

Crab (s) *(cont'd)*
Pilaff, **38,** 156
Salad, Hot, **17,** 459
Seafood Casserole, **48,** 169
Seafood-Okra Gumbo, **43,** 170
Seafood with Tarragon, **19, 47,** 170
Soufflé, **47,** 155
Spaghetti with Crabmeat, **42,** 356
-Stuffed Avocados, **40,** 72
-Stuffed Peppers, 412
-Stuffed Shrimp, **49,** 166
Cranberry (ies)
Anadama Bread, 527
Apple-Cranberry Punch, 695
-Apple Sauce, 502
Apple Tarts, **21,** 653
Bars, **18,** 598
Cake, **26,** 617
Cheesecake, **28, 36,** 609
Cheese Cupcakes, **47,** 609
Dumplings, **41,** 665
Frosting, 681
Ham Glaze, 230
Jelly, **26,** 501
-Nut Bread, **16,** 532
-Pear Pie, **42,** 644
Sauce, Gingered, **50,** 501
Sponge Roll, **51,** 629
Stuffing, Ham Steaks with, **36,** 231
Topping, 609
-Walnut Sauce, 502
Cream
Cake, Coffee, **30,** 619
Cake, Danish, Alice Petersen's, **38,** 620
Crème Chantilly, 672
and Egg Salad Dressing, 467
Maple Cream Sauce, 687
Mocha Cream Sauce, **39,** 689
Whipped, Clove, **23, 27,** 683
Cream Desserts; *see also* Custard (s) , Dessert
Citrus Rum Chiffon Cream, **34,** 568
Coconut Cream, Molded, **31, 37,** 569
Coffee Cream Chantilly, **29,** 569
Cream Pies and Tarts
Grape Cream Tarts, **47,** 654
Lemon Cream Pie, **38,** 655

Cream Desserts: Cream Pies and Tarts *(cont'd)*
Lemon Sour-Cream Pie, 656
Rum Pumpkin Cream Pie, **50,** 658
Strawberry Cream Pie, 655
Crème Beau Rivage, **49,** 573
Crème Celeste, **18,** 570
Fresh-Lime Cream, **42,** 570
Lemon Cream, **29,** 574
Lemon Fromage with Blueberries, **31, 45,** 575
Strawberry Cream, **49,** 573
Cream-puff Paste (Pâte à Chou) , 671
Crème Beau Rivage, **49,** 573
Crème Celeste, **18,** 570
Crème Chantilly, 672
Crème au Praliné, 673
Crème Saint-Honoré (pastry cream) , 671
Creole
Brussels Sprouts, **28,** 383
Corn, **32,** 394
Fresh Broccoli, **29, 31,** 381
Pecan Torte, 635
Salad, **19, 41,** 450
Crêpes, *see* Pancake (s)
Croquembouche, **40,** 668
Croquettes
beef, *see* Note, 217
chicken, *see* Note, 217
Chicken-Almond, **33,** 289
Cocktail, **39, 44,** 77
fish, *see* Note, 217
Veal, **43,** 216
vegetable, *see* Note, 217
Croûtes
Cheese, Garlic-Flavored, 500
French Bread, 500
Tabasco, **34,** 500
Croutons, 501
Crust, piecrust, *see* Pastry
Cucumber (s)
Atjar Ketimum (sweet and sour relish) , **54,** 504
Borscht with Cucumber, Cold, **33, 47,** 114
and Chicken Soup, **49,** 106
au Gratin, **37,** 398
Herb-Baked, **36, 40,** 398
Mayonnaise, **55,** 446
Sauce, 490
Spread, **44, 47, 49,** 64
Stuffed, **17,** 398
-Stuffed Tomatoes, **33, 47,** 431

Cucumber (s) *(cont'd)*
  Swedish, **52,** 446
  Velouté, **19, 46,** 103
  Yoghurt Relish, **43,** 504
  and Zucchini in Sour
    Cream, **20,** 429
Cumberland Sauce, **36,** 487
Curry, Curried
  Avocado Soup, Cold, **18,** 115
  of Beef, **32,** 187
  Chicken, **33,** 277
  Fish, 146
  Fruit Soup, **18,** 119
  Kooftah, **43,** 249
  Lobster Salad, **48,** 460
  Mayonnaise, **20, 25,** 468
  Mushroom Rolls, **51,** 79
  Powder, Homemade, 489
  Rice, **31,** 338
  Shrimp with Grapes, **38,**
    167
  Turkey and Ham, **45,** 295
Custard (s) , Appetizer and
    Main-Dish
  Chawanmushi, **54,** 326
  Custard Pie
    Ground Beef and To-
      mato, **40,** 328
    Pie Shell for, 327
    Salmon, **18,** 328
    Sausage Cream, **44,** 251
    Spinach, 328
  for Timbales, 327
  Zucchini Cheese, **31,** 429
Custard (s) , Dessert; *see also*
    Cream Desserts
  Black Bottom Parfait, **35,**
    577
  Boiled Custard, 570
  caramel custard, Spanish
    (Flan) , **33, 54,** 572
  Chocolate Custard, **32,** 571
  Chocolate Custard Ice
    Cream, **29, 48,** 562
  Cinnamon Pumpkin Flan,
    54, 572
  Crème Beau Rivage, **49,** 573
  Custard Ice Cream, **29,** 561
  Custard Pie
    Orange-Custard, **37,** 656
    Pumpkin, with Honey,
      656
    Raspberry, **27,** 658
    Rhubarb, **36,** 658
  Custard Sauce, **46, 51,** 688
  Fruit Custard Sauce, 690
  Lemon Curd, Dorothy
    Stanford's, **25,** 574
  Lemon Custard Pudding,
    43, 588

Custard (s) *(cont'd)*
  Maple Custard, **19, 37,** 571
  Rum Custard, **28,** 571
  Sauternes Custard Sauce,
    689
  Strawberry Parfait, **28, 39,**
    577
Cymlings Stuffed with Veal,
  17, 426

Dacquoise, **46,** 566
Dandelion greens in Beet
  Salad, **24,** 445
Danish Apple Cake, **29, 34,**
  629
Danish-Cheese Sandwich, **53,**
  513
Danish Cream Cake, Alice
  Petersen's, **38,** 620
Danish meat balls (Frikadel-
  ler) , **55,** 216
Date (s)
  Chess Pie, **35,** 648
  and Honey Bread, Steamed,
    532
  Nutmeg Date Bars, **29, 46,**
    604
Desserts, *see* Cream Desserts;
    Custards, Dessert;
    Dumplings, Dessert;
    Fritters, Dessert; Fro-
    zen Desserts; Fruit
    Desserts; Gelatin Des-
    serts; Meringue (s) ;
    Mousses, Dessert; Pan-
    cakes, Dessert; Pastry
    Desserts; Pies and
    Tarts, Dessert; Pud-
    dings, Dessert;
    Soufflés, Dessert
Dessert Sauces, 683–690; *see
    also* Glazes, Dessert;
    Toppings, Dessert
  Apricot, **23,** 683
  Apricot Sour-Cream, **40,**
    683
  Bittersweet Fudge, 686
  Black-Cherry, 684
  Caramel Syrup, 672
  Cherry, 683
  Chocolate, 686
  Chocolate Marmalade, **24,**
    686
  Chocolate Rum, **31,** 686
  Chocolate Walnut, 687
  Coffee Syrup, **30,** 620
  Cognac, **30,** 689
  Custard, **48, 51,** 688
  Fruit Custard, 690
  Hard, **33,** 687

Dessert Sauces *(cont'd)*
  Honey, 687
  Jam, **32,** 687
  Jamaica Rum and Coconut,
    24, 688
  Lemon-Nutmeg, **38, 41,** 688
  Maple Cream, 687
  Mocha, 686
  Mocha Cream, **39,** 689
  Peach, **30,** 685
  Pineapple, **30,** 685
  Raisin Nut, **17,** 684
  Raspberry, *see* Strawberry
    Sauce, 685
  à la Ritz, 554
  Sabayon, **30,** 689
  Sauternes Custard, 689
  Sour-Cream Orange, **33,** 684
  Strawberry, **36, 37,** 685
  Strawberry Compote, 685
  Strawberry-Rhubarb, **41,**
    685
  Vanilla Coffee, 690
Dessert Toppings, *see* Top-
    pings, Dessert
Deviled Lobster, Spanish, 158
Deviled Pork Chops, Stuffed,
  30, 224
Devonshire Potato-Mushroom
  Pie, **24, 44,** 414
Diablo Sauce, 487
Dill, Dilled
  Beef Kebabs, **21,** 200
  with Braised New Potatoes
    and Carrots, **39,** 419
  Butter, 499
  and Sour-Cream Sauce, **55,**
    489
Diples (honey rolls) , **53,** 667
Dodine of Duck, 303
Dolma, Combination, 250
Dook, **53,** 693
Dorothy Stanford's Lemon
  Curd, **25,** 574
Dorure (egg wash) , 671
Dough
  Egg-Spring Roll I and II,
    362
  Noodle for Dumplings, 358
Doves Pontchartrain, 309
Duck, Duckling, 299–305
  Anise Duck and Rice Cas-
    serole, **37,** 305
  Basting Sauce for, **40,** 496
  Dodine of, 303
  Liver Canapés, 304
  with Olives, 300
  à l'Orange, 301
  Pâté, **20,** 85

Duck (cont'd)
  Roast, 40, 299
    Chinese, 38, 303
    with Grapes, 33, 300
    Sandwich, 53, 514
  in Savory Sauce, 27, 304
  Stock, 301
  Wild Ducks with Madeira,
    35, 309
Dumplings, 539–541
  Bread-Crumb, 541
  Chinese, Steamed, 54, 364
  Herb, 25, 34, 541
  Hungarian (Galuska), 53,
    539
  Kreplach, 359
  (made with Basic Baking
    Mix), 529
  Matzoh Balls, 27, 539
  Noodle Dough for, 358
  Pelmeny, Siberian, 358
  Ravioli, 359
  Tomato, 541
  Wonton, 358
Dumplings, Dessert
  Apple, 18, 26, 664
  Cranberry, 41, 665
Dutch Apple Pie, 19, 39, 641

Easter Pie, Lemon, 49, 660
Eel, Smoked-Eel Sandwich,
    53, 513
Egg (s)
  (baked in) Potato Boats,
    50, 417
  Chawanmushi, 54, 326
  Golden Buck, 40, 331
  Hard-Cooked, 321
    Anchovy-Egg Boats, 51,
      93
    Appetizer, 23, 49, 67
    Barbecue, 322
    and Caviar Sandwiches,
      21, 512
    Creamed Egg Sauce, 483
    Creamed, with Olives, 18,
      321
    and Cream Salad Dress-
      ing, 467
    Forestière, 48, 321
    and Ham Sandwich, 18,
      46, 514
    with Herb Mayonnaise,
      55, 66
    Mimosa Salad, 43, 441
    Mushroom-Stuffed, 22,
      45, 66
    Nargisi Kebabs, 43, 247
    Olive-Stuffed, 42, 46, 65

Egg (s): Hard-Cooked (cont'd)
    Salmon Eggs Montauk,
      46, 47, 50, 66
    Sauce, 483
    Spinach Mimosa, 28, 42,
      448
    Stuffed, au Gratin, 43,
      322
    and Tomato Hero, 20,
      46, 511
    and Tomato Sandwich,
      53, 515
    Tuna-Stuffed, 45, 66
  Mollet, 15, 323
    Mornay, 15, 323
    with Spinach Purée, 41,
      324
  Mustard Baked, 16, 324
  Oeufs Aptos, 37, 325
  Omelet (s)
    Chicken-Liver, 36, 326
    Ham and Pepper, 17, 39,
      325
    Herb, Fresh, 15, 324
    Periwinkle, Euell Gib-
      bons's, 42, 162
    Stuffed Avocado Andean,
      18, 463
  Pilau, 337
  Poached
    and Artichokes Foresti-
      ère, 68
    Artichokes Mock Bene-
      dict, 371
    à la Russe, Antoine's, 47,
      67
    Sardou, Brennan's, 41,
      323
  Soufflé, see Soufflés;
    Soufflés, Dessert
  Wash (Dorure), 671
Egg Dishes, 321–329
Eggnog
  Colonial, 697
  Frozen, 27, 50, 562
Eggplant
  and Asparagus Mornay, 28,
    372
  Balls, 401
  Casserole, Mildred Knopf's,
    401
  and Chicken-Liver Casse-
    role, 18, 400
  Italian, 23, 55, 402
  Lamb and Eggplant Balls,
    38, 250
  Marinated, Baked, 33, 400
  Relish, 20, 24, 502

Eggplant (cont'd)
  salad (Salata Melitzanas),
    53, 447
  and Sesame Salad, 34, 46,
    447
  Slices with Parmesan, 32,
    399
  with Sour Cream, 30, 399
  Spread, Savory, 22, 54, 64
  Sticks, French-Fried, 25, 39,
    400
  Tomato Sauce III for, 494
Egg Rolls, see Egg-Spring
    Roll, 362–363
Egg-Spring Roll Dough I and
    II, 362
  Fillings for
    Pork and Shrimp, 363
    Shrimp, Grace Chu's, 363
Eleanor Hempstead's Scal-
    loped Oysters, 50, 161
Elizabeth Borton de Tre-
    viño's Best Pudding,
    590
Endive, Belgian
  Belgian Salad, 43, 48, 443
  Braised, 26, 402
  Chicken Livers with, 42,
    293
  and Spinach Salad, 25, 40,
    43, 449
Endive, Curly
  with Bacon Dressing, 19,
    443
Ensalada de Cebolla Burriana
    (onion salad Burriana
    style), 20, 448
Esau's Lamb, 28, 242
Escalopes de Veau à la
    Provençale, 209
Escarole
  with Pine Nuts, 17, 403
  Sautéed, 26, 31, 403
Espagnole or Brown Sauce,
    477
Esther Cory's Baked Whole
    Fish, 40, 127
Euell Gibbons's Periwinkle
    Omelet, 42, 162

Fanny Todd Mitchell's Beet
    Soup, 37, 105
Farina, Flamri de Semoule,
    36, 581
Fennel
  Batter-Fried, 404
  au Gratin, 36, 404
  Oatmeal Bread, 15, 531
  steamed, see Steamed Vege-
    tables, 436

Fig Soufflé Pudding, Steamed, 581
Filbert (s)
 Butter with Brittany Crêpes, 675
 Skinning, 634
 Torte, **53,** 633
 Turkey-Filbert Casserole, **39,** 298
Fillings; *see also* Fillings, Dessert; Stuffings
 Cabbage-Carrot, for Pirog, 89
 Cheese, for Kreplach, 359
 Chicken, 96
 Chicken-Liver, **51,** 95
 Eggplant Relish, for sandwiches, **20, 24,** 502
 Lamb and Mint, **20,** 81
 Meat, **45,** 96
 Meat, for Pirog, 90
 Pork and Shrimp, for Egg Rolls, 363
 Salmon, for Pirog, 89
 Shrimp, for Egg Rolls, Grace Chu's, 363
 Spinach, **20,** 96
 Veal, for Ravioli, 360
Fillings, Dessert
 Apricot, 676
 Buttercream, 567, 678
  Chocolate, 678
  Mocha, 678
 Cardamom-Almond, **53,** 601
 cheese (for Ricotta Pie), **23, 54,** 650
 Chocolate, 676
 Chocolate-Butter, 677
 cream cheese (for Cheesecake de Luxe), **27,** 610
 Crème au Praliné, 673
 Lemon, 677
 Lemon Curd, Dorothy Stanford's, **25,** 574
 Orange, **45,** 584
 Pastry Cream, 677
 Pastry Cream (Crème Saint-Honoré), 671
 Strawberry, 677
 strawberry-rice (for Strawberry-Rice Torte), 636
Fish, 121–151; *see also* names of fish
 with Almond Stuffing, Baked, 126
 Aspic for, Quick, 476
 Aspic Shells (for garnish), 477
 Baked Whole, Esther Cory's, **40,** 127

Fish *(cont'd)*
 Chowder, Spanish Fish, **43,** 110
 croquettes, *see* Note, 217
 Curry, 146
 Dill Butter for, **21,** 499
 Egg Sauce for, 483
 Grape Sauce for, 480
 Marinade for Smoked or Barbecued Foods, 496
 Oven-Breaded, **28,** 151
 Parsley Sauce for, **37,** 488
 Pudding, Norwegian, **55,** 150
 Sauce (s) for
  Aurore, 482
  Cucumber, 490
  Egg, 483
  Grape, 480
  Mornay, 484
  Rouille, 492
  Tartar, 492
 Seafood Cocktail Sauce for, 493
 Seviche, **22,** 74
 Soup, Venetian, **17,** 111
 Stock, 475
Flamri de Semoule, **36,** 581
Flan (custard)
 Cinnamon Pumpkin Flan, **54,** 572
 Spanish caramel custard, **33, 54,** 572
Flan Ring (pastry)
 Almond Short Pastry for, 639
 Shaping and Baking, 639
Florentine Mushrooms, **50,** 408
Florentines, **18,** 599
Florida Style Roast Crown of Pork, **23,** 218
Flounder
 Baked in Sour Cream, **29,** 128
 Celery-Stuffed, **28,** 130
 Duglère with Noodles, **39,** 130
 Fillets of, in Wine Sauce, **27,** 131
 turban of, with mousse, *see* Turban of Sole, 147
Foie Gras with Artichokes, **19,** 370
Fondue Orientale, **38,** 184
Franey's, Pierre, Choucroute Garnie, **53,** 388
Franey's, Pierre, Stuffed Striped Bass, 124
Frangipane Tart, **36,** 654

French Bread, Cheese-Stuffed, **21,** 79
French Bread Croûtes, **34,** 500
French Dressing, *see* Salad Dressings
French Style New Potatoes, **47, 52,** 419
Frijoles Fritos (fried black beans), **54,** 376
Frijoles Refritos (crisp fried beans), **54,** 376
Frikadeller (Danish meat balls), **55,** 216
Frikadeller Sandwich, **53,** 513
Fritters
 Clam, 152
 corn, fresh (Torrejas de Maíz Tierno), 397
 Meat, Herbed, 31, 201
Fritters, Dessert
 Almond, **30,** 668
 Beignets Soufflés, **37,** 665
 Mexican (Buñuelos), **54,** 666
 Strawberry, Helen Evans Brown's, 667
Frogs' Legs, Souffléed, **23,** 172
Frostings and Icings, 679–681; *see also* Glazes, Dessert; Toppings, Dessert
 Buttercream, 678
 Butter Frosting, Spiced, 679
 Chocolate Buttercream, 678
 Chocolate Frosting I and II, 680
 Confectioners' Sugar Icing, 679
 Cranberry Frosting, 681
 Cream-Cheese Frosting, 680
 Fudge Frosting (vanilla), 680
 Lemon Frosting, 681
 Mocha Buttercream, 678
 Orange Frosting, 681
 Ornamental Frosting, 679
 Royal Icing, 679
 Sesame-Seed Frosting, 618
 Vanilla Frosting, **679**
Frozen Desserts; *see also* Ice Cream
 Baked Alaska, 565
 Cantaloupe Royale, **19, 31,** 548
 Chestnut Pudding, Frozen, **51,** 562
 Chocolate Cheese Pie, Frozen, 649
 Citron Mousse, Frozen, **35,** 560
 Eggnog, Frozen, **27, 50,** 562

Frozen Desserts (cont'd)
Fruitcake, Frozen, **55**, 612
Fruit Chunks, Frozen, **46**,
555
Grape and Sherbet Cup, **44**,
547
Lime Foam, Frozen, **22, 24**,
561
Macaroon Cream, Frozen,
40, 47, 562
Mocha Mousse, Frozen, **29**,
36, 42, 557
Strawberry Angel Pie, **24**,
565
Vanilla Chocolate Pie,
Frozen, 563
Fruit (s) ; *see also* names of
fruits
Anise Fruit Compote, **28**,
554
Chunks, Frozen, **46**, 555
Curry Soup, Cold, **18**, 119
Custard Sauce, 690
Dried, Compote of, with
Sauce à la Ritz, 554
-Filled Cantaloupe, **21**, 547
-Filled Honeydew, **16**, 548
Fruited Almond Cookies,
19, 594
Holiday Fruit Bread, **45**,
527
Mélange, **17**, 554
and Nuts with Couscous,
55, 582
Punch, **46**, 696
Salad, 454
Fruitcake
Black Bun, **51**, 613
Frozen, **51**, 612
Swedish, **23**, 612
Fruit Desserts
Ambrosia, **24, 38**, 552
Anise Coddled Apples, **15**,
40, 545
Anise Fruit Compote, **22**,
24, 554
Apple Compote, **34, 42**, 545
Bananas
à l'Orange, Baked, **40, 44**,
546
in Sherry, **23, 52**, 546
Cantaloupe
Fruit-Filled, **21**, 547
with Honeydew Balls, **15**,
30, 48, 547
Perles de, au Rhum, 548
Royal, **19, 31**, 548
Cherry-Grapefruit Port-
Wine Gelatin, **36**, 546

Fruit Desserts (cont'd)
Compote of Dried Fruits
with Sauce à la Ritz,
554
Fruit Mélange, **17, 40**, 554
Grape (s)
Frosted, 547
and Sherbet Cup, **44**, 547
Honeydew, Fruit-Filled, **16**,
548
Melon Delight, **16**, 549
Peaches
Romanoff, **49**, 549
in White Wine, **17, 39**,
550
Pears
Baked with Grapes and
Wine, **27, 34**, 551
Baked in Grenadine, **35**,
37, 551
Baked with Mincemeat,
28, 35, 551
Carmelite, **47**, 550
in Port Wine, **19, 25**, 552
Vanilla Poached, **15, 25**,
41, 550
Perles de Cantaloupe au
Rhum, 548
Strawberries
al Asti, **48**, 552
Alexandria, 553
with Rum Cream, 553
Fudge Frosting (vanilla) , 680
Fumet of Celery, **24, 49, 53**,
106
Frystekaka (royal cake) , **53**,
601

Gado gado sauce, *see* Note,
54, 78
Galuska (Hungarian dump-
lings) , **53**, 539
Game Birds, 306–310; *see also*
names of game birds
Game Pâté, **47**, 311
Game (furred) , 259–262; *see
also* names of game
hunter's stew, Polish
(Bigos) , 261
Garlic Stew, Savory, 260
Cheese-Garlic Spread, **21**,
22, 62
-Flavored Cheese Croûtes,
500
mayonnaise (Aïoli) , 492
Garnishes
Aspic
for Beef, Quick, 475
for Chicken, Quick, 476

Garnishes: Aspic (cont'd)
for Fish, Quick, 476
Shells, 477
Bread Crumbs, 312–313, 501
Croûtes, French Bread, 500
Cheese, Garlic-Flavored,
500
Tabasco, **34**, 500
Croutons, 501
Frosted Grapes, 547
for soup, *see* Dumplings;
see Note, Fumet of
Celery, 106
tomato peelings, *see* Note,
509
Gâteau Saint-Honoré, 670
Gazpacho à la Française, 116
Gelatin Desserts
blackberry Bavarian, *see*
Note, 568
Cherry-Grapefruit Port-
Wine Gelatin, **36**, 546
Chiffon Pie
Citrus, **38, 39**, 659
Lime-Pistachio, **32**, 661
Walnut, **24, 33**, 661
Coconut Cream, Molded,
31, 37, 569
Coffee Charlotte, **28, 31**, 556
Crème Celeste, **18**, 570
Lemon Easter Pie, **49**, 660
Mousse, *see* Mousses, Des-
sert
Orange Bavarian Cream,
50, 567
Orange Queen Pie, **34**, 662
Pineapple Refrigerator
Pudding, **33**, 563
Raspberry Bavarian, **17**,
568
Strawberry Bavarian, *see*
Note, 568
Strawberry Cream, 573
German Fried Potatoes, **23**,
414
Ghourounaki Psito (roast
stuffed suckling pig) ,
53, 220
Gibbons's, Euell, Periwinkle
Omelet, **42**, 162
Giblet Gravy (duck) , 301
Ginger, Gingered
Almond Cookies, **34**, 594
Beef Pot Roast, **28**, 178
-Cheese-Almond Spread, **34**,
62
Cranberry Sauce, **50**, 501
and Peach Pie, **26, 36**, 644
Veal Steaks, **37**, 207

Glazes (for ham)
Cranberry, **49,** 230
Grenadine, **49,** 229
Orange, **29,** 230
Sherry, **49,** 230
Glazes, Dessert, 682; *see also*
Frostings and Icings;
Toppings, Dessert
Apricot, 682
(for Cheesecake de Luxe),
27, 610
Chocolate, 682
Dorure (egg wash), 671
Lemon, 682
Orange, 682
Goat (chèvre), Game Stew,
Savory, 260
Golden Buck, **40,** 331
Goose, 305–306
Roast, with Chestnut Stuff-
ing, **51,** 305
Gott Vetebrod (Swedish
coffeecake), 524
Gougère, 333
Goulash
Beef, **30,** 186
Veal, **53,** 214
Grace Chu's Shrimp Filling
for Egg Rolls, 363
Graham-Cracker Piecrust, 641
Grains, 334–336; *see also*
names of grains
Grand Marnier Pudding, **48,**
586
Grape(s)
and Apple Pie, **26,** 644
Chicken Breasts Véronique,
34, 285
Cream Tarts, **47,** 654
Curried Shrimp with, **38,**
167
Duck, Roast, with, **33,** 300
Frosted, 547
and Green-Tomato Chut-
ney, **16,** 505
and Melon Mousse, **26, 37,**
557
Pears Baked with Grapes
and Wine, **27, 34,** 551
Sauce, 480
and Sherbet Cup, **44,** 547
Grapefruit
and Avocado Salad, **32, 39,**
Cherry-Grapefruit Port-
Wine Gelatin, **36,** 546
French Dressing, **29, 44,** 465
and Greens Tossed Salad,
16, 37, 38, 454
Gratin Dauphinois, **47,** 418
Gratin Savoyard, **29, 48,** 419

Gravy
Giblet (duck), 301
Thin Pan, 175
Greek Nut Roll à la Aphro-
dite Lianides, **52,** 674
Greek Pastry, Chicken in, **53,**
284
Greek Style Squid, **53,** 172
Green Beans, *see* Bean(s)
Green Mayonnaise, **45, 49,** 468
Green Peppers, *see* Pepper(s),
green and red (capsi-
cum)
Greens
dandelion, in Beet Salad,
24, 445
and Grapefruit Tossed
Salad, **16, 37, 38,** 454
Salad, Mixed, **21, 22, 25, 37,**
39, 441
Green Tomatoes, *see* To-
mato(es)
Grenadine
-Cashew Pie, **28,** 646
Ham Glaze, **49,** 229
Pears Baked in, **35, 37,** 551
Soufflé, Iced, **45,** 593
Gribiche Sauce, **54,** 491
Gumbo, Seafood-Okra, **43,** 170

Haddock
Broiled, with Lemon Sauce,
16, 132
with Herbed Crumbs, **31,**
132
Halibut
Northwest Style, **26,** 133
Steak au Beurre Blanc, 132
Steaks with Mushrooms, **33,**
133
Ham, 229–235
Bake, California, 232
Baked, Glazed, **29, 49,** 229
Braciolette Ripiene (stuffed
veal rolls), **47,** 210
Breast of Chicken Vir-
ginienne, **48,** 286
and Celery Loaf, **38,** 234
and Cheese Hero, **18,** 512
and Egg Sandwich, **53,** 514
glazes for baked ham, 229–
230
Horseradish Sauce for, 489
Loaf, **23,** 233
Mousse, 235
and Mushroom Casserole,
230
and Noodle Casserole, **38,**
231

Ham (*cont'd*)
and Pepper Omelet, **17, 35,**
325
and Pork Balls, 232
Prosciutto, Saltimbocca,
209
and Rice Vinaigrette, **22,**
463
Steak in White Wine, 230
Steaks with Cranberry
Stuffing, **36,** 231
and Tongue Mousse, 234
and Turkey, Curried, **45,**
295
and Vegetable Casserole,
25, 233
Hamburger(s), *see* Beef
Hard Sauce, **33,** 687
Hawaiienne Butternut
Squash, **30,** 427
Hazelton's, Nika, Spanish
Trout, 148
Helen Evans Brown's Straw-
berry Fritters, 667
Hempstead's, Eleanor, Scal-
loped Oysters, **50,** 161
Herb(s), Herbed
-Baked Cucumbers, **36, 40,**
398
Caper Butter, **39,** 500
Cheese-Herb Bread, **16, 50,**
522
Dumplings, **25, 34,** 541
French Dressing, **24, 43**
Fresh Herb Omelet, **15,** 324
Green Beans, **31,** 374
Kidney Ragout, **15,** 253
Meat Fritters, **31,** 201
Sauce Béarnaise, 486
Sauce for Boiled Beef, **25,**
28, 488
Sauce Gribiche, **54,** 491
Tomato Salad, **29, 43,** 450
and Wine Stuffing, 316
Zucchini with, **28,** 429
Hermits, Nutmeg, **21,** 604
Hero Sandwiches, *see* Sand-
wich(es)
Herring
Bismarck-Herring Sand-
wich, **53,** 514
Citrus Herring in Wine
Sauce, **29,** 73
Matjes Herring Sandwich,
53, 513
Holiday Fruit Bread, **45,** 527
Hollandaise
Chicken, 287
Mustard Sauce, **43,** 485
Sauce, **55,** 485

Honey
  -Chocolate Bars, **25**, 600
  and Date Bread, Steamed,
    532
  Pecan Pie, **19**, 648
  rolls (Diples) , **53**, 667
  Sauce, 687
Honeydew Melon
  -Balls, Cantaloupe with, **15**,
    30, 547
  Fruit-Filled, **16**, 548
  Salad, Indian, **49**, 462
Horseradish
  Sauce, **38**, **53**, 489
  and Sour-Cream Sauce, 489
Hot and Sour Soup, **54**, 107
Hungarian dumplings
    (Galuska) , **53**, 539

Ice cream
  Baked Alaska, 565
  Banana, 561
  Chocolate Custard, 562
  Custard, **29**, **48**, 561
  No-Cook, **17**, 561
  Nut, 561
  Peach, 561
  Raspberry, 561
  Strawberry, 561
  Strawberry Compote Sauce
    for, 685
Indian Melon Salad, **49**, 462
Indian Pudding, **49**, 582
Indonesian rice (*Nasi*) , **54**,
    339
Indonesian side dishes (Sam-
    belans) , **54**, 505
Israeli Rice, **27**, **50**, 342
Italian Cottage-Cheese Pie,
    17, **33**, 649
Italian Eggplant, **23**, **55**, 402
Italian Macaroons, **43**, 602
Italian-Style Banana
    Pudding, **33**, 585
Italian-Style Green Beans, **40**,
    374
Italian-Style Squid with To-
    matoes, 171
Iturbi, Alcachofas con Setas,
    (artichoke hearts and
    mushrooms) , 371

Jack Rose, 696
Jacqueline Cardelli's Mousse
    au Chocolat, **35**, **38**, 556
Jamaica Rum and Coconut
    Sauce, **24**, 688
Jam Sauce, **32**, 687
James Beard's Braised Shoul-
    der of Lamb, **34**, 236

James Beard's Pâté for Pic-
    nics, 21, 87
Japanese Rice, **54**, 340
Jeanne Owen's Squab Pie, **40**,
    307
Jellied dishes, *see* Aspic
    Dishes; Gelatin Des-
    serts
June Platt's Roast Loin of
    Pork, **40**, 218

Kale
  Colcannon with Kale, **49**,
    404
  steamed, *see* Steamed Vege-
    tables, 436
Kebab (s)
  Beef, Dilled, **21**, 200
  Chello (lamb) , **53**, 246
  Nargisi, **43**, 247
Kid, Braised, 259
Kidney (s)
  Ragout, Herbed, **15**, 253
  Rognons de Veau en Cas-
    serole, **39**, 254
  and Steak Pie, **38**, 190
  and Steak Pudding, 189
  Trifolati, **28**, 253
Kidney Beans, *see* Bean (s)
Kniberg, Anita, Tamales à
    la, **54**, 346
Knopf's, Mildred, Eggplant
    Casserole, 401
Kooftah Curry, **43**, 249
Korean Rice with Beef, **39**,
    341
Kreplach, 359

Lahmajoon, **20**, 81
Lahm-el-Gine, 81
Lahm Mashwi (an Arab ver-
    sion of lamb on
    skewers) , **21**, 247
Lamb, 235–250
  braised, *see* Braised Kid,
    259
  Chello Kebab, **53**, 246
  Chops
    Braised, **24**, 242
    Maria, **26**, 241
  Couscous, Tunisian, **55**, 243
  Crown Roast of, with Okra,
    53, 239
  Dolma, Combination, 250
  and Eggplant Balls, **38**, 250
  Esau's, **28**, 242
  Kooftah Curry, **43**, 249
  Lamburger Mixed Grill,
    16, 254

Lamb (*cont'd*)
  Leg of
    with Cherries, Roast, **49**,
      236
    with Herb Sauce, Roast,
      32, 237
    Spit-Roasted, Basting
      Sauce for, **20**, 497
    Spring Lamb, Roast, **36**,
      235
    Stuffed and Baked, **25**,
      240
  and Mint Filling (for Lah-
    majoon) , **20**, 81
  Nargisi Kebabs (fried
    whole hard-boiled eggs
    coated with lamb-spice
    mixture) , **43**, 247
  Navarin d'Agneau, 248
  New-Potato Lamb Fricas-
    see, **37**, 245
  Patties, Minted, with Fresh
    Pineapple, **27**, 248
  Pilau, **29**, 241
  Ribs, Barbecued, **25**, 239
  Scotch Broth, **51**, 112
  Shanks, Braised, **31**, 240
  Shoulder of, Braised, James
    Beard's, **34**, 236
  on skewers, an Arab ver-
    sion of (Lahm
    Mashwi) , **21**, 247
  and Spinach Stew, **30**, 246
  Stew, Andalusian, **23**, 245
  Stew, with Zucchini, **25**, 245
  Stock, 474
  à la Suède, **33**, 244
  and Tomatoes with
    Cracked Wheat, 244
Lamburger Mixed Grill, **16**,
    254
Lattice Pie Topping, 640
Laura Torte, 634
Laurel Rice, **31**, 336
Leek (s)
  Cock-a-Leekie, **18**, 113
  and Potato Soup with Yo-
    ghurt, **18**, 102
  with Red Wine, **37**, 405
  steamed, *see* Steamed Veg-
    etables, 436
  vinaigrette, *see* Vegetables
    Vinaigrette, 436
Lemon (s)
  Ambrosia, **38**, 628
  -Barbecued Spareribs, **34**,
    225
  Cake, **31**, **38**, 620
  Cake Pie, **27**, **28**, 659
  -Cheese Pie, **33**, 649

Lemon (s) (cont'd)
  Chicken Sauté, **29**, 277
  Chiffon Cake, **26, 46,** 625
  Cream, **29**, 574
  Cream Pie, **38**, 655
  Curd, Dorothy Stanford's,
    25, 574
  Custard Pudding, **43**, 588
  Easter Pie, **49**, 660
  Filling, 677
  Fromage with Blueberries,
    31, 45, 575
  Frosting, 681
  Glaze, 682
  Lemonade for a Party, 694
  -Nutmeg Sauce, **38, 41**, 688
  Nut Wafers, **20**, 602
  -Orange Pudding, **30**, 587
  Pudding, **29**, 587
  Rice, **18**, 583
  Sauce (for asparagus) , **25,
    27**, 487
  Sauce (for salmon) , **36**, 134
  and Sesame-Seed Butter,
    40, 500
  Soufflé, **27**, 591
  Soufflé Pie, **36**, 660
  Sour-Cream Pie, **24**, 656
Lemonade for a Party, 694
Lentil (s)
  Esau's Lamb, **28**, 242
  à l'Indienne, **24**, 378
  and Macaroni Soup, **44**, 108
  Maria's, **42**, 379
Lianides, Aphrodite, Greek
    Nut Roll à la, **52**, 674
Lima beans, *see* Bean (s)
Lime
  Foam, Frozen, **22, 24**, 561
  Fresh-Lime Cream, **42**, 570
  Meringue Pie, **33, 35**, 662
  -Pistachio Chiffon Pie, **32,**
    661
Linguine with White Clam
    Sauce, **43**, 350
Liver (s)
  Braised, **39**, 255
  Calf's
    with Avocado, **38**, 255
    with Parsley Sauce, **37,**
      256
    Pâté with Pistachios, **48,**
      87
  Chicken
    with Belgian Endive, **42,**
      293
    en Brochette, 291
    Broiled, **16**, 293
    and Eggplant Casserole,
      18, 400

Liver (s) : Chicken (cont'd)
  Hongroise, **17**, 293
  Madeira, **34**, 292
  and Mushroom Spa-
    ghetti, **44**, 355
  Omelet, **36**, 326
  Pâté, **45, 55**, 83
  Pâté de Foie en Terrine,
    84
  Pâté with Pistachios, **48,**
    87
  Tartlets, **48**, 92
  Timbales, **41**, 292
  Tomatoes Stuffed with,
    48, 433
Duck
  Canapés, 304
  -Pâté Sandwich, 19, 514
Lobster (s)
  Anchovy Butter for, 499
  and Broccoli Mornay, **24,**
    382
  Deviled, Spanish, 158
  Gratiné, 156
  Roll, **22**, 510
  Salad, Curried, **48**, 460
  Sauce, 482
  Seafood Casserole, **48**, 169
  Seafood with Tarragon, **19,
    47**, 170
  Stuffed, Cold, **22**, 158
  -Stuffed Tomato, **19**, 160
  with Tarragon, Grilled, **50,**
    157
Loubia (savory white beans) ,
    55, 377
Lyon's, Ninette, Poulet
    Flambé, **37**, 274

Macaroni
  and Almond Casserole, **37,**
    352
  and beef casserole (Tag-
    liarini) , **39**, 351
  Caraway Macaroni Rabbit,
    17, 331
  Casserole, Mexican, **43**, 353
  and Lentil Soup, **44**, 108
  and Meat Puff, **28**, 352
  Mexican Casserole, **43**, 353
Macaroon (s) , 602
  Cream, Frozen, **40, 47**, 562
  crumbs, *see* Note, 557
  Italian, **43**, 602
  Raspberry Mousse, **29, 48,**
    557
Mackerel
  Baked Stuffed, 134
  au vin blanc, *see* Bluefish
    au Vin Blanc, **22**, 127

Madère Sauce, **48**, 479
Malakoff (cheese on skewers),
    329
Maltaise Rice, **45**, 584
Maltaise Sauce, 486
Manhattan Clam Chowder,
    110
Manicotti, Stuffed, **39**, 360
Maple
  Cream Sauce, 687
  Custard, **19, 37**, 571
Marble Cake, **44**, 621
Marchand de Vin Sauce, 478
Maria's Lentils, **42**, 379
Marinade, 495
Marinade for Smoked and
    Barbecued Foods, 496
Marinara Sauce, 493
Mariner's Stew (codfish) , 128
Marmalade Chocolate Sauce,
    24, 686
Mattes's, Alvina, Onion Scal-
    lop, **23**, 409
Matzoh Balls, **27**, 539
Mayonnaise, **24**, 467
  Aspic, 468
  Blender, 468
  Cucumber, **55**, 446
  Curried, **17, 20, 25**, 468
  garlic (Aïoli) , 492
  Green, **45, 49**, 468
  Sauce Gribiche, **54**, 491
  Sauce Ravigote, **22**, 74
  Sea Goddess Dressing, **36,**
    469
  Tartar Sauce, 492
Meat; *see also* names of meats
  Choucroute Garnie, Pierre
    Franey's, **53**, 388
  Filling for Pirog, 90
  Fondue Orientale, **38**, 184
  and Onion Casserole, Swed-
    ish, **32**, 227
  Stew, Panamanian, **37**, 226
  on a Stick, **21**, 191
  Timetable for Roasting,
    263
  and Tomato Sauce, 494
  Vinaigrette Sauce I for, 488
Meat Ball (s)
  Bitocks à la Russe, **35**, 196
  Caraway, **22**, 194
  Danish (Frikadeller) , **55,**
    216
  Frikadeller Sandwich, 513
  with Green Peppers, **24,**
    196
  Ham and Pork Balls, 232
  Lamb and Eggplant Balls,
    38, 250

Meat Ball (s) (cont'd)
Lamb Patties, Minted, with Fresh Pineapple, **27,** 248
with Spaghetti, **42,** 356
Swedish Beef Balls, **52,** 194
in Wine Sauce, Spicy, **34,** 227
Meat Loaf, Loaves
Beef, Armenian, **33,** 198
Beef, Marjoram, **32,** 197
Ham, **29,** 233
Ham and Celery, **38,** 234
Individual, **35,** 199
Pork, **42,** 229
Veal, with Anchovies, **30,** 215
Veal and Tuna, **28,** 214
Melon; see also names of melons
Delight, **16,** 549
and Grape Mousse, **26, 37,** 557
Salad, Indian, **49,** 462
Meringue (s)
Baked Alaska, 565
Butterscotch Pie, **25, 27,** 662
Chocolate, 597
Dacquoise, **46,** 566
Glacées, **36,** 565
Individual, 564
Lime Pie, **33, 35,** 662
Orange Pie, **24, 32,** 663
Pie, 566
Pie Shell, **24,** 564
Pie Topping, 565
Rhubarb Pie, **37,** 663
Soft, 663
Strawberry Angel Pie, **24,** 565
Méxicaine Clams, **18,** 152
Mexican Avocado Salad, **18, 31, 32, 34,** 444
Mexican Chicken, **39,** 280
Mexican fritters (Buñuelos), **54,** 666
Mexican Macaroni Casserole, **43,** 353
Mexican Rabbit, **41,** 332
Mexican Style Corn Salad, **26,** 446
Mildred Knopf's Eggplant Casserole, 401
Mimosa Salad, **43,** 441
Mincemeat, Pears Baked with, **28, 35,** 551
Mint, Minted
and Lamb Filling, **20,** 81

Mint (cont'd)
Lamb Patties with Fresh Pineapple, **27,** 248
Mitchell's, Fanny Todd, Beet Soup, **37,** 105
Mixed Grill, Lamburger, 254
Mocha
Buttercream, 678
Cake, Norwegian, **33, 45,** 621
Cream Sauce, **39,** 689
Mousse, Frozen, **29, 36, 42,** 557
Sauce, 686
Molasses
Drop Cookies, Soft, 603
Marble Cake, **44,** 621
Walnut Pie, **31, 49,** 648
Mornay Sauce, **15, 28,** 484
Moroccan-Style Chicken, **36,** 281
Mousses, Main-Dish and Vegetable
Carrot, **49,** 290
Chicken, **49,** 290
of Green Peas, **49,** 411
Ham, 235
Ham and Tongue, 234
Salmon (blender), 138
Salmon (sieve), 138
of Sole, 145; see also Turban of Sole, 147
Mousses, Dessert
Chocolate-Orange, **37, 55,** 555
au Chocolat, Jacqueline Cardelli's, **35, 38,** 556
Citron, Frozen, **35,** 560
Fresh-Pineapple, **37, 39,** 560
Grape and Melon, **26, 37,** 557
Mocha, Frozen, **29, 36, 42,** 557
Raspberry Macaroon, **29, 48,** 557
Muffins
Cheese, **15,** 534
Fresh-Corn, **44,** 534
Multerberry Soup, **53,** 118
Mushroom (s)
Antipasto Mushrooms, **52,** 68
Appetizer, **30, 52,** 68
artichoke hearts and Mushrooms Iturbi (Alcachofas con Setas Iturbi), 371
and Barley Casserole, **22, 32,** 342

Mushroom (s) (cont'd)
and Bean Salad, **22, 24,** 455
and Celery Pickles, **27, 54,** 504
and Cheese Sauce, 485
Chicken-Liver and Mushroom Spaghetti, **44,** 355
Cocktail Strudels, **44,** 79
Crêpes, **19,** 538
Curried Mushroom Rolls, **35, 51,** 79
dried, to prepare, see Note, 364
Eggs Forestière, 321
Florentine, **50,** 408
fumet of, see Note, Fumet of Celery, 106
au Gratin, **41,** 406
and Ham Casserole, 230
Noodles with, **26, 37,** 347
in Oil with Parsley, 407
Pickled, **20,** 504
Pilaff, **47,** 337
Polenta with, **42,** 343
Potato-Mushroom Pie, Devonshire, **24, 44,** 414
raw, vinaigrette, see Vegetables Vinaigrette, 436
Roquefort-Stuffed, **45, 50,** 67
Salade Forestière, **18, 37, 52,** 447
and Salmon Royale, **31,** 136
Sauce (brown), **32, 42,** 479
Sauce (white), **34,** 480
and Scallop Casserole, **43,** 164
Sherried, **47,** 407
Sliced, Flavored with Tamarind, **54,** 505
Soup, Cream of, **50,** 103
in Sour Cream on Toast, **53,** 406
Spaghetti, Pauline Trigère's, 355
Spicy, **35,** 406
and Spinach Salad **42,** 449
-Stuffed Eggs, **22, 44,** 66
-Stuffed Tomatoes, **17, 26,** 432
Swiss, **18,** 405
Mussels
Ravigote, **22,** 74
Steamed, 73
Stuffed, **33, 52,** 73
Mustard
Butter, **18, 46,** 499
-Chinese Sauce, 484
Eggs, Baked, **16,** 324

Mustard (cont'd)
  French Dressing, 24, 42, 51, 464
  Hollandaise Sauce, 43, 485
  Sauce, 486
  Sauce with Cauliflower, 51, 390
  Sauce with Veal Chops, 40, 213

Napolitana Cauliflower Salad, 20, 23, 25, 445
Nargisi Kebabs (fried whole hard-boiled eggs coated with lamb-spice mixture), 43, 247
Nasi (Indonesian boiled rice), 54, 339
Nasi Goreng, 54, 288
Navarin d'Agneau, 248
Navy or pea beans, see Bean (s)
New England Baked Beans, 21, 378
Nika Hazelton's Spanish Trout, 148
Ninette Lyon's Poulet Flambé, 37, 274
Noodle (s)
  Caraway Noodle Ring with Tuna, 42, 350
  Casserole, 40, 349
  and Chicken Casserole, 44, 275
  with Cream Cheese, 45, 348
  Dough for Dumplings, 358
  Egg, Homemade, 347
  Flounder Duglère with, 39, 130
  and Ham Casserole, 38, 231
  with Mushrooms, 26, 37, 347
  and Oyster Casserole, 19, 349
  Parsleyed, 26, 30, 34, 347
  and Sausage Casserole, 251
  Soufflé, 27, 351
  with Spinach, 30, 348
  Stuffing, 39, 317
Normandy Applesauce Pie, 26, 642
Northwest Style Halibut, 26, 133
Norwegian Fish Pudding, 55, 150
Norwegian Mocha Cake, 33, 45, 621
Norwegian spongecake (Blotkake), 55, 626

Nut (s) ; see also names of nuts
  Apple Orange Nut Loaf, 22, 616
  Blanching, 651
  -Butter Cookies, Austrian, 603
  Buttered, 45, 46, 65
  -Cranberry Bread, 16, 532
  and Fruits with Couscous, 55, 582
  Ice Cream, 561
  -Lemon Wafers, 20, 602
  Pudding Bahiana, 588
  -Raisin Sauce, 17, 684
  Roll, Greek, à la Aphrodite Lianides, 52, 674
Nutmeg
  Cookies, Pressed, 30, 604
  Date Bars, 29, 46, 604
  Hermits, 21, 604
  -Lemon Sauce, 38, 41, 688
  Sand Tarts, 17, 605

Oat, Oatmeal
  Apple-Oatmeal Crisp, 38, 585
  Fennel-Oatmeal Bread, 15, 531
  Oatmeal Thins, 605
  Orange-Oatmeal Bread, 16, 530
  Raisin-Oat Cinnamon Bread, 524
Oeufs Aptos, 37, 325
Okra
  Crown Roast of Lamb with, 53, 239
  -Seafood Gumbo, 43, 170
Olive (s)
  and Bean Soup, 46, 108
  with Creamed Eggs, 18, 321
  and Rice Casserole, 30, 338
  with Short Ribs, Savory, 35, 185
  -Stuffed Eggs, 42, 46, 65
  -Vegetable Relish, 20, 503
Omelet (s)
  Chicken-Liver, 36, 326
  Ham and Pepper, 17, 39, 325
  Herb, Fresh, 15, 324
  Periwinkle, Euell Gibbons's, 42, 162
  Stuffed Avocado Andean, 18, 463
Onion (s)
  Baked, 17, 35, 409
  and Beet Salad, 26, 29, 35, 42, 445

Onion (s) (cont'd)
  and Meat Casserole, Swedish, 227
  -Pimiento Sauce, 33, 481
  with Pork and Scallions, Baked, 42, 410
  Rings, Batter-Fried, 22, 409
  salad, Burriana style (Ensalada de Cebolla Burriana), 20, 23, 448
  Scallop, Alvina Mattes's, 23, 409
  Soup with Cheese, 20, 31, 101
  and Summer Squash Casserole, 23, 45, 428
  Tart (Tarte à l'Oignon), 52, 91
  and Tomato Salad, 42, 47, 451
  vinaigrette, see Vegetables Vinaigrette, 436
  White, Parsleyed, 25, 408
Orange (s)
  Ambrosia, 24, 38, 552
  Banana-Orange Shakes, 694
  Bananas à l'Orange, Baked, 40, 44, 546
  Bavarian Cream, 50, 567
  Butter Cookies, 30, 605
  Chiffon Cake, 32, 625
  -Chocolate Mousse, 37, 55, 555
  -Custard Pie, 37, 656
  Filling, 584
  Foam, 44, 569
  French Dressing, 18, 49, 465
  Frosting, 681
  Glaze, 682
  -Glazed Carrots, 28, 389
  Ham Glaze, 29, 230
  -Lemon Pudding, 30, 587
  Meringue Pie, 24, 32, 663
  Oatmeal Bread, 16, 530
  Pecan Shortbread, 35, 37, 615
  Pie, Queen, 34, 662
  Sauce Maltaise, 486
  Sour-Cream Sauce, 33, 684
  and Watercress Salad, 32, 34, 36, 442
Orégano
  Spinach with, 35, 43, 422
  Summer Squash with, 37, 42, 427
Oriental Hamburgers, 28, 193
Ornamental Frosting, 679
Owen's, Jeanne, Squab Pie, 40, 307
Oxtail Ragout, 26, 259

INDEX

Oyster (s)
Broiled Breaded, **40,** 160
and Chicken Pie, **43,** 268
Noodle Casserole, **19,** 349
Poulette, Olympia, 161
Scalloped, Eleanor Hempstead's, **50,** 161
Seafood-Okra Gumbo, **43,** 170

Palaver Sauce (spinach stew), **19,** 426
Palm, Heart of, and Avocado Salad, **54,** 448
Panade, *see* Turban of Sole with Mousse, 147
Panamanian Stew, **37,** 226
Pancakes, 535–539
Buckwheat, Raised, 536
Cornmeal, 536
Fresh-Corn, **15,** 537
(made with Basic Baking Mix) , 529
Mushroom Crêpes, **19,** 538
Rice and Sesame, 537
Scallion, Minute, 537
Whole-Wheat, **16,** 535
Wild-Rice, **45,** 538
Pancakes, Dessert
Brittany Crêpes with Filbert Butter, **26,** 675
Swedish, **32,** 676
Paprika Rice, **36, 53,** 335
Paris-Brest, 673
Parsley, Parsleyed
Butter Sandwiches, **48, 51,** 512
and Cheese Pie, **38,** 334
Noodles, **26, 30,** 34
Sauce, **37,** 488
White Onions, **25,** 408
Pasta Dishes, 346–364
Cannelloni, Chicken, **52,** 361
Linguine with White Clam Sauce, **43,** 350
Macaroni, *see* Macaroni
Manicotti, Stuffed, **39,** 360
Noodle dumplings, *see* Dumplings
Noodles, *see* Noodles
Ravioli, 359
Veal Filling for, 360
Spaghetti, *see* Spaghetti
Stuffing for, 362
Tomato and Meat Sauce for, 494
Pastry, General
Almond Short, 639
Cheese, **32,** 197

Pastry, General *(cont'd)*
Chocolate-Wafer Piecrust, 641
-Cream, 671, 677
Cream-Cheese, **20, 51,** 93
Slices, 95
Turnovers, **45,** 95
Crumb Crust, 609
Crust (for Cheesecake de Luxe) , 610
Flan Ring, Shaping and Baking, 639
Graham-Cracker Piecrust, 641
Lattice Pie Topping, 640
Meringues, Individual and Pie Shell, 564
Pâte à Chou, 671
Pâte Sablée, 671
Pie Pastry
Baked, 637
Sweet, 639
Unbaked (one-crust pie), 637
Unbaked (two-crust pie), 637
Pie Shell for Custard Pies, 327
for Ricotta Pie, 650
Sage Cornmeal, 299
-Shell (for Strawberry-Rice Torte) , 635
for Steak and Kidney Pie, 190
for Steak and Kidney Pudding, 189
Tart Shells, Baked, 640
Walnut Piecrust, 661
Pastry, Appetizer and Main-Dish; *see also* Pies and Tarts, Appetizer and Main-Dish
Cheese Straws and Twists, **23, 29,** 65
Chicken in Greek Pastry, **53,** 284
Gougère, 333
Lahmajoon, **20,** 81
Lahm-el-Gine, 81
Mushroom Cocktail Strudels, **44,** 79
Pirog, 88
Piroshki, 90
Pastry, Dessert, 664–676; *see also* Pies and Tarts, Dessert
Almond Fritters, 30, 668
Apple Dumplings, **18, 26,** 664

Pastry, Dessert *(cont'd)*
Beignets Soufflés, **37,** 665
Buñuelos (Mexican fritters) , **54,** 666
Cranberry Dumplings, **41,** 665
Croquembouche, **40,** 668
Gâteau Saint-Honoré, 670
honey rolls (Diples) , 667
Nut Roll, Greek, à la Aphrodite Lianides, **52,** 674
Paris-Brest, 673
Strawberry Fritters, Helen Evans Brown's, 667
Tea Cakes, Athenian, **25,** 666
Pâte à Chou, 671
Pâte Sablée, 671
Pâté (s)
Chicken-Liver, **45, 51,** 83
en Croûte, 83
Duck, **20,** 85
de Foie en Terrine, 84
Game, **47,** 311
Liver, with Pistachios, **40,** 87
Liver-Pâté Sandwich, **53,** 514
for Picnics, James Beard's, **21,** 87
Rillettes de Tours, 86
Shrimp, de Luxe, **50,** 85
Pauline Trigère's Mushroom Spaghetti, 355
Pea (s)
Artichokes Clamart, **45, 53,** 370
in Lettuce, **27, 29, 36, 38,** 410
Mousse of, **49,** 411
Potage Saint-Germain, Cold, **21, 50,** 114
Rice with, **23, 30,** 336
and Rice Salad, **17, 21, 35, 49,** 457
Pea or navy beans, *see* Bean (s)
Peach (es)
Chicken in Peach Sauce, 278
and Ginger Pie, **26, 36,** 644
Ice Cream, 561
Romanoff, **49,** 549
Sauce, **30,** 685
Sauce, Chicken in, 278
in White Wine, **17, 39,** 550
Peanut (s)
Chicken Sate, 286

Peanut (s) (cont'd)
  coconut with peanuts, fried
      (Seroendeng) , **54,** 505
  Dip, **20,** 78
  -Raisin Chews, 606
Pear (s)
  Baked with Grapes and
      Wine, **27, 34,** 551
  Baked in Grenadine, **35, 37,**
      551
  Baked with Mincemeat, **28,**
      35, 551
  Carmelite, **47,** 550
  -Cranberry Pie, **42,** 644
  in Port Wine, **19, 25,** 552
  Vanilla Poached, **15, 25, 41,**
      550
Pecan
  Bars, **21,** 606
  Butter, Savory, 500
  Chocolate Pie, **43,** 647
  Honey Pie, **19,** 648
  Orange Shortbread, **35, 37,**
      615
  Pie, **37, 43,** 647
  Spiced Pecanettes, **29,** 607
  Topping, 682
  Torte, Creole, 635
Pelmeny, Siberian, 358
Pepparkakor, **45,** 607
Pepper (s) , green and red
    (capsicum)
  Barbecue Sauce, **21,** 497
  Crabmeat-Stuffed, 412
  Fried, **33,** 411
  and Ham Omelet, **17, 39,**
      325
  with Meat Balls, **24,** 196
  Rice-Stuffed, **42,** 411
  Roasted, **52,** 69
  -Steak, **34,** 181
  Stuffed, Brazilian, **16,** 412
Pepper (nigrum)
  Black-Pepper Chocolate
      Cookies, **25,** 597
  Black-Pepper Crackling
      Bread, **42,** 522
  Steak au Poivre with Red-
      Wine Sauce, **29,** 180
Périgueux Sauce, **26,** 479
Periwinkle (s)
  Cooked, 162
  Omelet, Euell Gibbons's,
      42, 162
Perles de Cantaloupe au
    Rhum, **52,** 548
Persian rice (Chello) , **53,** 341
Petersen's, Alice, Danish
    Cream Cake, **38,** 620
Petits Cornets, **49,** 574

Petjel (mixed vegetables with
    peanut sauce) , 436
Pheasant Smitane, **35,** 308
Pickles, see Relishes
Piecrust, see Pastry
Pierre Franey's Choucroute
    Garnie, **53,** 388
Pierre Franey's Stuffed
    Striped Bass, 124
Pies and Tarts, Appetizer and
    Main-Dish; see also
    Pastry, Appetizer and
    Main-Dish
  Anchovy-Egg Boats, **51,** 93
  Cheeseburger Pie, **32,** 197
  Cheese and Parsley Pie, **32,**
      334
  Chicken-Liver Tartlets, **48,**
      92
  Chicken and Oyster Pie, **43,**
      268
  Ground Beef and Tomato
      Custard Pie, **40,** 328
  Hamburger Pie, **44,** 196
  pastry and piecrust, see
      Pastry
  Pork Pie, Warwickshire,
      225
  Potato-Mushroom Pie,
      Devonshire, **24, 44,** 414
  Potato and Tomato Pie, **40,**
      414
  Quiche, Shrimp, **17, 47,** 91
  Salmon Custard Pie, **18,** 328
  Sausage Cream Pie, **44,** 251
  Shepherd's Pie, **24,** 202
  Shrimp Quiche, **17, 47,** 91
  Spinach Custard Pie, 328
  Squab Pie, Jeanne Owen's,
      40, 307
  Steak and Kidney Pie, **38,**
      190
  Turkey, with Sage Corn-
      meal Pastry, **26,** 298
Pies and Tarts, Dessert, 641–
    664; see also Pastry,
    Dessert
  Almond Tart, **24,** 651
  Apple Pie, Dutch, **19, 39,**
      641
  Applesauce Pie, Normandy,
      26, 642
  Apple Sour-Cream Pie, **25,**
      38, 642
  Apple Tart, **49,** 651
  Banana Sour-Cream Pie,
      29, 653
  Blackberry and Apple Pie,
      42, 643
  Blueberry Pie, **43,** 643

Pies and Tarts (cont'd)
  Brazil-Nut Tartlets, **16, 32,**
      616
  Brown-Sugar Pie, **23, 47,**
      654
  Butterscotch Meringue Pie,
      25, 27, 662
  Cardamom Apple Pie, **40,**
      43, 641
  Cherry Tart, **30, 48,** 652
  Chess Pie, **35,** 648
  Chestnut Pie, **48,** 646
  Chiffon Pie
    Citrus, **38, 39,** 659
    Lime-Pistachio, **32,** 661
    Walnut, **24, 33,** 661
  Chocolate Cheese Pie,
      Frozen, 649
  Chocolate Pecan Pie, **43,**
      647
  Citrus Chiffon Pie, **38, 39,**
      659
  Cottage-Cheese Pie, Italian,
      17, 33, 649
  Cranberry-Apple Tarts, **21,**
      653
  Cranberry-Pear Pie, **42,** 644
  Frangipane Tart, **36,** 654
  glazes, see Glazes, Dessert
  Grape and Apple Pie, **26,**
      644
  Grape Cream Tarts, **47,** 654
  Grenadine-Cashew Pie, **28,**
      646
  Honey Pecan Pie, **19,** 648
  Lemon Cake Pie, **27, 28,**
      659
  Lemon-Cheese Pie, **33,** 649
  Lemon Cream Pie, **38,** 655
  Lemon Easter Pie, **49,** 660
  Lemon Soufflé Pie, **36,** 660
  Lemon Sour-Cream Pie, **24,**
      656
  Lime Meringue Pie, **33, 35,**
      662
  Lime-Pistachio Chiffon Pie,
      32, 661
  Meringue Pie, 566
    Butterscotch, **25, 27,** 662
    Lime, **33, 35,** 662
    Orange, **24,** 663
    Rhubarb, **37,** 663
  Molasses Walnut Pie, **31,**
      49, 648
  Orange-Custard Pie, **37,**
      656
  Orange Meringue Pie, **24,**
      32, 663
  Orange Queen Pie, **34,** 662

Pies and Tarts (*cont'd*)
 pastry and piecrust, *see* Pastry
 Peach and Ginger Pie, **26, 36,** 644
 Pecan Pie, **37, 43,** 647
 Pumpkin Pie with Honey, 656
 Raisin-Rhubarb Pie, **22, 32,** 645
 Raspberry Custard Pie, **27,** 658
 Rhubarb Custard Pie, **36,** 658
 Rhubarb Meringue Pie, **37,** 663
 Rhubarb Pie, Spiced, **34,** 645
 Ricotta Pie, **23, 54,** 650
 Rum Pumpkin Cream Pie, **50,** 658
 Strawberry Angel Pie, **24,** 565
 Strawberry Cream Pie, 655
 Vanilla Chocolate Pie, Frozen, 563
 Walnut Chiffon Pie, **24, 33,** 661
Pike
 Baked, 128
 Fish Curry, 146
Pilaff, **28, 29, 38,** 337
 Crab, **38,** 156
 Cracked-Wheat, **26, 31,** 342
 Egg, 337
 Lamb, **29,** 241
 Mushroom, **47,** 337
 Nut, **33,** 337
Pilau, Lamb, **29,** 241
Pimiento and Anchovy Salad, **40, 42, 54,** 69
Pineapple
 Cheesecake, Refrigerator, **34,** 608
 Fresh, with Minted Lamb Patties, **27,** 248
 Fresh, Mousse, **37, 39,** 560
 Pudding, Refrigerator, **33,** 563
 Sauce, **30,** 685
 Upside-Down Cake, **28,** 622
Pinto Beans, *see* Bean (s)
Piquante Sauce, **55,** 487
Pirog, 88
 Cabbage-Carrot Filling for, 89
 Meat Filling for, 90
 Salmon Filling for, 89
Piroshki, 90
 Baked, 91

Piroshki (*cont'd*)
 Fried, 90
Pistachio (s)
 Lime-Pistachio Chiffon Pie, **32,** 661
 with Liver Pâté, **48,** 87
Planter's Punch, 697
Platt's, June, Roast Loin of Pork, **40,** 218
Plum Soup, 118
Poitrine de Veau Farcie aux Olives, **52,** 206
Polenta, 343
 with Mushrooms, **42,** 343
 Tomato Sauce III for, 494
Polish Beets, **31,** 380
Polish hunter's stew (Bigos) , 261
Pollo en Salsa Tonnato (chicken in tuna sauce) , 461
Polonaise Brussels Sprouts, **25,** 382
Pork, 217–229
 Apples and Sauerkraut, **24,** 220
 Bacon, *see* Bacon
 Broth, 474
 Chinese Dumplings, Steamed, 364
 Chops
  Almond and Macaroni Casserole, **37,** 352
  Barbecued, **34,** 222
  Bermudiana, **25,** 221
  with Caper Sauce, **32,** 221
  Country, **27,** 223
  Deviled Stuffed, **30,** 224
  Marinated, **35,** 222
  Piquante, **30,** 221
  Stuffed, 223
 cracklings, *see* Note, 523
  Black-Pepper Crackling Bread, **42,** 522
 Crown of, Roast, Florida Style, **23,** 218
 Fresh-Pork Sandwich, 514
 Ham and Pork Balls, 232
 Loaf, 42, 229
 Loin of
  Roast, **49,** 217
  Roast with Grenadine Glaze, **40,** 217
  Roast, June Platt's, **40,** 218
 Pie, Warwickshire, 225
 and Pine Nuts, Artichokes Stuffed with, 369
 Rillettes de Tours, 86
 Sausage, *see* Sausage

Pork (*cont'd*)
 and Shrimp Filling for Egg Rolls, 363
 Spareribs
  Barbecued, **22, 54,** 225
  Barbecue Sauce for, **22,** 498
  Lemon-Barbecued, **34,** 225
  Marinade for, 495
  Stuffed, **27,** 224
 suckling pig, roast stuffed (Ghourounaki Psito) , **53,** 220
Porto, Sauce au, 479
Portuguese Style Salt Cod, 129
Potage Saint-Germain, Chilled, **21, 50,** 114
Potato (es)
 Avocado Appetizer, **32, 36,** 71
 and Avocado Salad, **43,** 457
 Baked, with Sour Cream and Scallions, **36,** 417
 Boats, **50,** 417
 Cakes, Swedish, **31, 33,** 414
 Caraway, **19,** 415
 and Carrots Mousseline, **51,** 390
 -Cheese Charlotte, **48,** 418
 with Cheese, Rosemary, **35,** 413
 -Cheese Soufflé, 330
 Colcannon with Kale, **49,** 404
 and Corn Chowder, **42,** 102
 Fried, German, **23,** 414
 Gratin Dauphinois, **47,** 418
 Gratin Savoyard, **29, 48,** 419
 and Leek Soup with Yoghurt, **18,** 102
 -Mushroom Pie, Devonshire, **24, 44,** 414
 New
  and Carrots, Braised, with Dill, **39,** 419
  French Style, **47, 52,** 419
  Lamb Fricassee, **37,** 245
  Salad, **17, 41, 47,** 456
 Puffs, **24, 35,** 415
 Raclette, **20,** 329
 Salad, **22, 55,** 456
 Salad with Anchovies, **21, 45,** 456
 Sauce Rouille, 492
 Scalloped, with Sour Cream, **37,** 413
 in-the-Shell Soufflé, **51,** 416

Potato (es) (cont'd)
Spring Potato Salad, **17, 41, 47,** 456
Stuffed, Aïoli, **32,** 416
Stuffing, 316
sweet, *see* Sweet Potato (es)
and Tomato Pie, **40,** 414
to prepare for salads, *see* introductory paragraph, 456
vinaigrette, *see* Vegetables Vinaigrette, 436
Potted Squab, **46,** 308
Poule au Pot, **54,** 270
Poulet en Casserole, 273
Poulette Sauce, **35, 41,** 481
Poultry; *see also* names of poultry
Grape Sauce for, 480
Stuffings, 312–317
Poundcake, **19, 28, 31, 34,** 622
Praline
Candy, 674
Crème au Praliné, 673
Prune and Apple Stuffing, 314
Puddings, *other than* Dessert
Asparagus, **41,** 373
Asparagus Cheese, **24,** 373
Broccoli Ring, **26, 47,** 381
Corn and Cheese, **43,** 395
Fish, Norwegian, **55,** 150
Green Corn, Shaker, **24,** 394
Rutabaga, **34,** 435
Salmon Neptune, **44,** 137
Spinach Mold, **26,** 425
Steak and Kidney, 189
Yorkshire, Individual, **41,** 535
Puddings, Dessert; *see also* Cream Desserts; Custard (s) , Dessert
Almond Blancmange, 578
Apple-Oatmeal Crisp, **38,** 585
Apricot-Rice, **29,** 583
Banana, Italian Style, **33,** 585
Blueberry Betty, **36,** 586
Bread-and-Butter, **17,** 580
Cherry-Walnut, **31,** 586
Chestnut, Frozen, **51,** 562
Chocolate, I and II, **25, 39, 50,** 576
Coconut, **39,** 579
Blancmange, **33,** 579
Rice, 583
Coffee Bread-and-Butter, **24,** 580

Puddings (cont'd)
Couscous with Fruits and Nuts, **55,** 582
Dessert Rice, 583
Elizabeth Borton de Treviño's Best, 590
Fig Soufflé, Steamed, 581
Flamri de Semoule, **36,** 581
Grand Marnier, **48,** 586
Indian, **49,** 582
Lemon, **29,** 587
Lemon-Orange, **30,** 587
Lemon Rice, **18,** 583
Nut, Bahiana, 588
Pineapple Refrigerator, **33,** 563
Puerto Rican, **23,** 588
Queen of, 589
Rice, **23,** 584
Apricot, **29,** 583
Coconut, 583
Dessert, 583
Lemon, **18,** 583
Maltaise, **45,** 584
Sponge, Steamed, **51,** 589
Vanilla, 576
Pulpetas (stuffed veal steaks) , **30,** 207
Pumpkin
Cinnamon Pumpkin Flan, **54,** 572
Glazed, **35,** 430
Pie with Honey, 656
Rum Cream Pie, **50,** 658
Soup, Cream of, **35,** 105
Punch, *see* Beverages; Beverages, Alcoholic

Quahogs, Stuffed, 153
Quail Smitane, **36,** 312
Queen of Puddings, 589
Quiche, Shrimp, **17, 47,** 91

Rabbit (rarebit) , *see* Cheese
Raclette (potatoes and bogne cheese) , **20,** 329
Radish (es)
relish, *see* Note, Atjar Ketimum, 504
and Watercress Salad, **31, 33, 41, 48,** 442
Ragout, Kidney, Herbed, **15,** 253
Raisin
Nut Sauce, **17,** 684
-Oat Cinnamon Bread, 524
-Peanut Chews, 606
-Rhubarb Pie, **22, 32,** 645
Raspberry
Bavarian, **17,** 568

Raspberry (cont'd)
Custard Pie, **27,** 658
Ice Cream, 561
Macaroon Mousse, **29, 48,** 557
sauce, *see* Strawberry Sauce, 685
Ravigote Sauce, **22,** 74
Ravioli, 359
Veal Filling for, 360
Reception Punch, 697
Recipes for One
Brennan's Eggs Sardou, **41,** 323
Chicken, Broiled, **41,** 281
Chicken Salad, 460
Chicken Supreme, **41,** 272
Hamburger, Grilled, 193
Potato, Baked, **41,** 415
Potato, Stuffed, **41,** 416
Rice, Boiled, **41,** 335
Risotto, **41,** 336
Salad, **41,** 442
Shrimp Salad, 460
Wienerschnitzel, **41,** 208
Red Snapper
Baked, Southern Style, **30,** 142
with Lemon Butter, **28,** 143
Poached, **17,** 142
with Shrimp Stuffing, Baked, **32,** 143
Reindeer Roast, 260
Relishes, 501–506
Beets, Pickled, **55,** 380
Cranberry-Apple Sauce, 502
Cranberry Jelly, 501
Cranberry-Walnut Sauce, 502
Cucumber Yoghurt, **43,** 504
Eggplant, **20, 24,** 502
fried coconut with peanuts (Seroendeng) , 505
Gingered Cranberry Sauce, **50,** 501
Grape and Green-Tomato Chutney, **16,** 505
Indonesian side dishes (Sambelans) , **54,** 505
Mushroom and Celery, **27,** 504
Mushrooms, Pickled, **20,** 504
mushrooms, raw, vinaigrette, *see* Vegetables Vinaigrette, 436
Mushrooms, Sliced, Flavored with Tamarind, **54,** 505
Olive-Vegetable, **20,** 503

Relishes (cont'd)
  sweet and sour (Atjar Keti-
    mum), **54,** 504
  Walnuts, Pickled, **16,** 506
Rhubarb
  Custard Pie, **36,** 658
  Meringue Pie, **37,** 663
  Pie, Spiced, **34,** 645
  -Raisin Pie, **22,** 645
  -Strawberry Sauce, **41,** 685
Rice
  and Anise Duck Casserole,
    39, 305
  and Apricot Pudding, **29,**
    583
  Baked, **25,** 338
  with Beef, Korean, **39,** 341
  and Cheese Avocados, **42,**
    333
  Chello (Persian rice), **53,**
    341
  and Chicken Casserole, **46,**
    276
  Coconut, 583
  Curried, **31,** 338
  Dessert, 583
  Egg Pilau, 337
  Fried, **38, 54,** 340
  and Ham Vinaigrette, **22,**
    463
  Israeli, **27, 50,** 342
  Japanese, **54,** 340
  Lamb Pilau, **21,** 241
  Laurel, **31, 42,** 336
  Lemon, **18,** 583
  Maltaise, **45,** 584
  Mushroom Pilaff, **47,** 337
  Nasi Goreng, **54,** 288
  Nasi (Indonesian boiled),
    54, 339
  Nut Pilaff, **43,** 337
  and Olive Casserole, **30,** 338
  Paprika, **36, 53,** 335
  with Peas, **23, 30,** 336
  and Peas Salad, **17,** 457
  Pilaff, **28, 29, 38,** 337
  Pilau, Lamb, **21,** 241
  Pink, **23, 34,** 340
  Pudding, **23,** 584
  Risotto Ring, **34, 45,** 337
  Saffron, **30, 33, 38,** 335
  Salad à la Française, **55,**
    459
  and Scallops au Gratin, **25,**
    164
  and Sesame Pancakes, 537
  -Strawberry Torte, 635
  -Stuffed Green Peppers, **42,**
    411
  wild, see Wild Rice

Rillettes de Tours, 86
Risotto, see Rice
Rognons de Veau en Casse-
    role, **39,** 254
Rosemary
  Beef Rolls, **27,** 184
  Chicken, Broiled, **25,** 283
  Potatoes with Cheese, **35,**
    413
  Sausage, **16,** 251
Rothschild Soufflé, 592
Rouille Sauce, **22, 31,** 492
Royal Icing, 679
Rum
  Chocolate Sauce, **31,** 686
  Custard, **28,** 571
  Jamaica Rum and Coconut
    Sauce, 688
  Pumpkin Cream Pie, **50,**
    658
  Russian, Salty, **21,** 696
Rutabaga Pudding, **34,** 435
Ruth Ellen Church's Shrimp
    Rémoulade, **40,** 75
Rye Bread, **20,** 520

Sabayon Sauce, **30,** 689
Sabra Salad, **19, 21, 50,** 452
Saffron
  Cream Sauce, Chicken in,
    32, 281
  Rice, **30, 33, 38,** 335
Sage
  Corn Bread, 530
  Corn-Bread Stuffing, 314
  Cornmeal Pastry, **26,** 299
St. Lucia's Cardamom Buns,
    52, 528
Salad Dressings, 464–469
  Bacon, **19,** 443
  Caraway-Seed and Cottage-
    Cheese, **21, 30, 35,** 467
  Cheese and Vegetable, **17,**
    44, 465
  Egg and Cream, 467
  French, **36, 44,** 464
    Grapefruit, **29, 44,** 465
    Herbed, **24, 43,** 464
    Mustard, **24, 42, 51,** 464
    Orange, **18, 49,** 465
    Tarragon, **40, 43,** 465
  Mayonnaise, see Mayon-
    naise
  Vinaigrette Sauce I and II,
    488
Salade Forestière, **18, 37, 52,**
    447
Salade Provençale, **26,** 451
Salads, 441–464
  Anchovy and Pimiento, **40,**
    42, 54, 69

Salads (cont'd)
  Artichokes Vinaigrette, 437
  Asparagus, **18, 29, 38,** 444
  Avocado and Grapefruit,
    32, 39, 48, 443
  Avocado, Mexican, **18, 31,**
    32, 34, 444
  Bean and Mushroom, **22,**
    24, 455
  Bean Sprouts Vinaigrette,
    19, 437
  Beet, **24,** 445
  Beet and Onion, **26, 29, 35,**
    42, 445
  Belgian, **43, 48,** 443
  Broccoli, **17, 24, 31, 33,** 445
  Cabbage Slaw, Hot, **37,** 386
  Cantaloupe Flower, **49,** 453
  Cantaloupe, Molded, **47, 51,**
    453
  Cauliflower, Napolitana,
    20, 23, 25, 445
  Cherry-Tomato and Sour-
    Cream, **34, 42,** 452
  Chick-Pea, **20,** 454
  Corn, Mexican Style, **26,**
    446
  Creole, **19, 41,** 450
  Cucumbers, Swedish, **52,**
    446
  Curly Endive with Bacon
    Dressing, **19,** 443
  eggplant (Salata Melit-
    zanas), **53,** 447
  Eggplant and Sesame, **34,**
    46, 447
  Escarole, **17,** 403
  Forestière, **18, 37, 52,** 447
  Fruit, 454
  Grapefruit and Greens
    Tossed, **16, 37, 38,** 454
  Green Beans Vinaigrette,
    30, 48, 437
  Green, Mixed, **21, 22, 25,**
    37, 39, 47, 441
  Heart of Palm and Avo-
    cado, **54,** 448
  Indian Melon, **49,** 462
  Kidney Beans Vinaigrette,
    40, 437
  Melon, Indian, **49,** 462
  Mimosa, **43,** 441
  onion, Burriana style (En-
    salada de Cebolla Bur-
    riana), **20, 23,** 448
  Potato, **22, 55,** 456
    with Anchovies, **21, 45,**
      456
    and Avocado, **43,** 457
    Spring, **17, 41, 47,** 456

Salads (cont'd)
Provençale, **26, 50,** 451
Rice à la Française, **55,** 459
Rice and Peas, **17, 21, 35, 49,** 457
Roquefort, with Vegetables, Molded, **24,** 452
Sabra, **19, 21, 50,** 452
Spinach and Bacon, **24, 42,** 449
Spinach and Endive, **25, 40, 43,** 449
Spinach Mimosa, **28, 42,** 448
Tomato, Herbed, **29, 43,** 450
Tomato and Onion, **42, 47,** 451
Tomato and Spinach, **21, 29, 30, 55,** 451
Tomatoes Vinaigrette, **18, 24, 38,** 438
Vegetables Vinaigrette, 436
Watercress and Orange, **32, 34, 36, 43,** 442
Watercress and Radish, **31, 33, 41, 48,** 442
Winter, **32, 40,** 455
Salads, Main-Dish
Avocado, Stuffed, Andean, **18,** 463
Beans and Tuna Vinaigrette, **21,** 462
Chef, à l'Adam, **19,** 463
chicken in tuna sauce (Pollo en Salsa Tonnato), 461
Chicken, with Almonds, **49,** 460
Crab, Hot, **17,** 459
Curried Lobster, **48,** 460
Rice and Ham Vinaigrette, **22,** 463
Turkey, **48,** 461
Salata Melitzanas (eggplant salad), **53,** 447
Salmon
in Aspic, **49,** 135
Baked, **33,** 135
Bake Italiano, **43,** 137
Bisque, Chilled, **49,** 116
Chowder, **17,** 110
Custard Pie, **18,** 328
Eggs Montauk, **30, 42, 46,** 66
Filling for Pirog, 89
with Fresh Lemon Sauce, **36,** 134
Mousse (blender), **45,** 138
Mousse (sieve), **45,** 138

Salmon (cont'd)
and Mushrooms Royale, **31,** 136
Neptune, **44,** 137
with salt (Shioyaki), **54,** 138
Smoked
Appetizer Eggs, **49,** 67
Sandwich, **53,** 514
Verte, **45,** 136
Salsa Fria, **54,** 495
Saltimbocca, 209
Salt-Rising Bread, 520
Salty Russian, **21,** 696
Sambal Goreng Buntjies (green-bean sambal goreng), 375
Sambelans (Indonesian side dishes), **54,** 505
Sand Tarts, Nutmeg, 605
Sandwiches, 509–515
Bismarck-Herring, **53,** 514
Caviar and Egg, **21,** 512
Club, **19,** 509
Danish-Cheese, **53,** 513
Egg and Tomato Hero, **53,** 515
Eggplant Relish (for Sandwich filling), **20, 24,** 502
Fresh-Pork, **53,** 514
Frikadeller, **53,** 513
Game Pâté (for sandwich filling), **47,** 311
Ham and Egg, **53,** 514
Ham and Cheese Hero, **18, 46,** 512
Hero
Egg and Tomato, **20, 46,** 511
Ham and Cheese, **18, 46,** 512
Tuna and Peperoni, **47,** 511
Liver-Pâté, **53,** 514
Lobster Roll, **22,** 510
Lumpfish-Caviar, **53,** 513
Matjes-Herring, **53,** 513
Mustard Butter for, **18, 21, 46,** 499
open-faced, see Smørrebrød, 513–515
Parsley Butter for, **48, 51,** 512
Pâté, Game (for sandwich filling), **47,** 311
Roast-Chicken, **53,** 513
Roast-Duck, **53,** 514
Sardine, **53,** 514
Shrimp, **53,** 513

Sandwiches (cont'd)
Shrimp Salad, **18,** 510
Smoked-Eel, **53,** 513
Smoked-Salmon, **53,** 514
Smørrebrød, **53,** 513–515
Tartare Steak, **53,** 515
Tomato, Open-Faced, **18,** 511
Tongue, **53,** 514
Tuna and Peperoni Hero, **47,** 511
Sardine Sandwich, **53,** 514
Sates, **54,** 78
Sauces; see also Butters; Salad Dressings; Stocks
Anchovy-Cheese, **39,** 485
Aurore, 492
Barbecue, 497
Avery Island, 496
Green-Pepper, **21,** 497
Southern, 497
for Spareribs, **22,** 498
Basting, for Duck, 496
Basting, for Leg of Lamb, Spit-Roasted, **20,** 497
(for Batter-Fried Shrimp), **54,** 76
Béarnaise, 486
Béchamel, 480
Bercy, **32,** 478
Beurre Blanc, 498
Bordelaise, **37,** 478
Brown or Espagnole, 477
Cheese (Cheddar), **26,** 484
Cocktail, Seafood, 493
Coconut Cream, 491
Coconut Milk, 491
composed butters, see Butters
Cranberry-Apple, 502
Cranberry, Gingered, **50,** 501
Cranberry Jelly, 501
Cranberry-Walnut, 502
Creamed Egg, 483
Cucumber, 490
Cumberland, **36,** 487
Diablo, 487
Egg, 483
Egg, Creamed, 483
Espagnole or Brown, 477
gado gado, see Note, 78
Grape, 480
Gribiche, **54,** 491
Herb, for Boiled Beef, **25, 28,** 488
Hollandaise, 485; see also Hollandaise
Horseradish, **38, 53,** 489

Sauces (cont'd)
Lemon (for asparagus), **27,** 487
Lemon (for salmon), **25, 36,** 134
Lobster, 482
Madère, **48,** 479
Maltaise, 486
Marchand de Vin, 478
Marinade, 495
for Smoked or Barbecued Foods, 496
Marinara, 493
Mornay, **15,** 484
Mushroom (brown), **32, 42,** 479
Mushroom (white), **34,** 480
Mushroom and Cheese, 485
Mustard, 486
Mustard-Cheese, 484
Onion-Pimiento, **33,** 481
Parsley, **37,** 488
Peanut Dip, **20,** 78
Périgueux, **26,** 479
Pimiento-Onion, **33,** 481
Piquante, **55,** 487
au Porto, 479
Poulette, **35, 41,** 481
Ravigote, **22,** 74
Rouille, **22, 31,** 492
Salsa Fria, **54,** 495
Shrimp, 482
stocks, see Stocks
Sour-Cream and Dill, **55,** 489
Sour-Cream and Horseradish, 489
Supreme, 481
Tartar, 492
Tomato I, **31,** 493
Tomato II and III, **28, 31,** 494
Tomato and Meat, 494
Tomato Paste, 495
Venaison, 262
Vinaigrette I and II, **38,** 488
White-Wine, **29,** 125
Sauerkraut, see Cabbage
Sausage
Beef and Bean Casserole, **42,** 192
Cream Pie, **44,** 251
and Noodle Casserole, 251
Rosemary, **16,** 251
Stuffing for Chicken, 313
Stuffing for Turkey, 313
Sauternes Custard Sauce, 689
Scallion Pancakes, Minute, 537

Scallop (s)
Bay, with White Wine, **27,** 164
Blankets, **21, 26,** 77
Casserole, **29,** 163
Coquilles Aloyse, **27,** 162
and Mushroom Casserole, **43,** 164
Pan-Fried, **49,** 163
and Rice au Gratin, **25,** 164
Scampi, **23,** 169
Scotch Broth, **51,** 112
Seafood-Okra Gumbo, 170
Sea Goddess Dressing, **36,** 469
Sea Squab (s)
Breaded, **24,** 140
Provençale, **30,** 140
Seranne, Ann, Sweet Potatoes à la, **50,** 420
Seroendeng (fried coconut with peanuts), **54,** 505
Sesame, Sesame Seed (s)
Beef Strips, **19,** 78
Butter Cake, **30, 31,** 618
-Cheese Roll, **20, 51,** 63
and Eggplant Salad, **34, 46,** 78
Frosting, 618
and Lemon Butter, **40,** 500
and Rice Pancakes, 537
Spinach with, **37, 46,** 422
to toast, see Note, 341
Seviche, **22, 54,** 74
Shad
Broiled, 140
Marinated, Broiled, **41,** 141
Roe
with Asparagus, Grilled, **17,** 141
Soufflé, 141
Shaker Green Corn Pudding, **24,** 394
Shallots, Sauce Bercy, **32,** 478
Shepherd's Pie, **24,** 202
Sherry, Sherried
Bananas in, **23, 52,** 546
Sabayon Sauce, **30,** 689
-Mushrooms, **47,** 407
-Ham Glaze, 230
Sweet Potatoes à la Ann Seranne, **50,** 420
Shioyaki (salmon with salt), **54,** 138
Shortbread, **18, 51,** 615
Orange-Pecan, **35, 37,** 615
Shrimp
and Artichoke Hearts, **32,** 70
Batter-Fried, **54,** 76
Chawanmushi, **54,** 326

Shrimp (cont'd)
and Cheese Spaghetti, **17,** 357
and Cherry Tomatoes Provençale, 168
Chive in Shells, **18,** 166
Cocktail à la Française, **32,** 75
Crab-Stuffed, **49,** 166
Curried, with Grapes, **38,** 167
Filling for Egg Rolls, Grace Chu's, 363
Marengo, **33,** 168
Marinade for, 495
Marinated, Broiled, **35,** 165
Nasi Goreng, **54,** 288
Pâté de Luxe, **50,** 85
pickled (Camarones Estilo Barbachano Ponce), 75
and Pork Filling for Egg Rolls, 363
Quiche, **17, 47,** 91
Rabbit, **18,** 167
Rémoulade, Ruth Ellen Church's, **40,** 75
Salad Sandwich, **18,** 510
Sandwich, **53,** 513
Sauce, 482
Scampi, **23,** 169
Seafood Casserole, **48,** 169
Seafood-Okra Gumbo, **42,** 170
Seafood Ring, 149
Seafood with Tarragon, **19, 47,** 170
with Tarragon, **26,** 167
Toast, **50,** 61
à la Turque, **28,** 165
Siberian Pelmeny, 358
Skewer (s), Skewered; see also Kebabs
Chicken Livers, Broiled, **16,** 293
Chicken Livers en Brochette, 291
Chicken Sate, 286
lamb on skewers, an Arab version of (Lahm Mashwi), **21,** 247
Malakoff (cheese on skewers), 329
Meat on a Stick, **21,** 191
Sates, 78
Sesame Beef Strips, **20,** 78
Smørrebrød, **53,** 513
Snail (s)
Butter, 499
Stuffed, **37,** 76

Sole
  Amandine, **30,** 144
  Belle Aurore, 144
  Fish Curry, 146
  Mousse of, 145
  Paupiettes of, with Mush-
    room Sauce, **34,** 145
  Turban of, with Mousse,
    147
  Turbans with Crab Stuff-
    ing, **46,** 146
Soufflés, *other than* Dessert
  Cheese, **39,** 330
  Crabmeat, **47,** 155
  Noodle, **27,** 351
  Potato-Cheese, 330
  Shad Roe, 141
  Sweet-Potato, **27, 48,** 421
  Tomato, **30,** 431
Soufflés, Dessert
  Apple, with Lemon-Nut-
    meg Sauce, **41,** 590
  Chocolate, 591
  -Pudding, Fig, Steamed, 581
  Grenadine, Iced, **45,** 593
  Lemon, **27,** 591
  -Pie, Lemon, **36,** 660
  Rothschild, 592
Soups, 99–119; *see also* Chow-
    ders; Soups, Chilled;
    Soups, Cream
  Bean and Olive, **46,** 108
  Black-Bean, **47,** 107
  Caldo Gallego, **53,** 109
  Celery, Fumet of, 106
  Chicken and Cucumber,
    49, 106
  chicken broth, *see* Note,
    271
  Chicken, with Mushrooms,
    54, 106
  clam, *see* Note, Steamed
    Clams, 152
  Clam Broth, **23, 49,** 109
  Cock-a-Leekie, **18,** 113
  Cracked-Wheat, **19,** 113
  Fish, Venetian, **17,** 111
  garnishes, *see* stuffed
    noodle dumplings,
    357–360; *see also* Note,
    Fumet of Celery, 106
  Gumbo, Seafood-Okra, **43,**
    170
  Hot and Sour, **54,** 107
  Kreplach, 359
  Lentil and Macaroni, **44,**
    108
  mushroom, Fumet of, *see*
    Note, Fumet of Celery,
    106

Soups (*cont'd*)
  Okra-Seafood Gumbo, **43,**
    170
  Old-Fashioned   Vegetable,
    47, 112
  Onion, with Cheese, **20, 31,**
    101
  Pelmeny, Siberian, 358
  Potato and Leek, with Yo-
    ghurt, **18,** 102
  Scotch Broth, **51,** 112
  Seafood-Okra Gumbo, **43,**
    170
  Spinach, Modenese, **34,** 102
  vegetable, Fumet of, *see*
    Note, Fumet of Celery,
    106
  Vegetable, Old-Fashioned,
    47, 112
  Wonton, 358
Soups, Chilled
  Avocado, Curried, **18,** 115
  blueberry, *see* Note, 118
  Borscht   with   Cucumber,
    33, 47, 114
  Cherry, 118
  Fruit Curry, **18,** 119
  Gazpacho à la Française,
    116
  Multerberry, **53,** 118
  Plum, 118
  Potage Saint-Germain, **21,**
    50, 114
  Potato and Leek Soup with
    Yoghurt, **18,** *see* Note,
    102
  Salmon Bisque, **49,** 116
  Spinach, Smitane, **39,** 115
  Yoghurt, 114
Soups, Cream
  Beet, Fanny Todd
    Mitchell's, **37,** 105
  Corn and Watercress, **28,**
    105
  Cucumber Velouté, **19, 46,**
    103
  Lima-Bean, **18,** 104
  Mushroom, **50,** 103
  Pumpkin, **35,** 105
  Spinach, **53,** 104
Sour Cream
  Apple Pie, **25, 38,** 642
  Apricot Sauce, **40,** 683
  Banana Pie, **29,** 653
  with Black Beans, Purée of,
    377
  and Cherry-Tomato Salad,
    34, 42, 452
  Chicken in, **26,** 278

Sour Cream (*cont'd*)
  Chicken Livers Hongroise,
    17, 293
  Chocolate Cookies, 598
  and Dill Sauce, **55,** 489
  Eggplant with, **30,** 399
  Flounder Baked in, **29,** 128
  and Horseradish Sauce, 489
  Lemon Pie, **24,** 656
  Mushrooms in, on Toast,
    53, 406
  Orange Sauce, **33,** 684
  Pheasant Smitane, **35,** 308
  Quail Smitane, **36,** 312
  with Scalloped Potatoes, **37,**
    413
  Spinach   Soup   Smitane,
    Cold, **39,** 115
  Zucchini and Cucumber in,
    20, 429
Southern Barbecue Sauce, 497
Southern Corn Bread, **15,** 530
Southern Style Baked Red
    Snapper, **30,** 142
Spaghetti
  with Bacon and Mushroom
    Sauce, **36,** 353
  alla Carbonara, **23,** 357
  Chicken-Liver and Mush-
    room, **44,** 355
  with Crabmeat, **42,** 356
  with Meat Balls, **42,** 356
  Mushroom,   Pauline
    Trigère's, 355
  Shrimp and Cheese, **17,** 357
Spanish caramel custard
    (Flan), **33, 54,** 572
Spanish Corn Casserole, **30,**
    396
Spanish Deviled Lobster, 158
Spanish Fish Chowder, **43,**
    110
Spanish Trout, Nika Hazel-
    ton's, 148
Spareribs, *see* Pork
Spice, Spiced
  Bread, 533
  Butter Frosting, 679
  Pecanettes, **29,** 607
  Pepparkakor, **45,** 607
  Rhubarb Pie, **34,** 645
Spinach
  and Bacon Salad, **24, 42,**
    449
  en branche, vinaigrette, *see*
    Vegetables Vinaigrette,
    436
  Casserole, **18,** 425
  and Cheese Hamburgers,
    43, 195

INDEX

Spinach (cont'd)
  Creamed, **25,** 422
  Custard Pie, 328
  Eggs Sardou, Brennan's, **41,** 323
  and Endive Salad, **25, 40, 43,** 449
  Filling, **20,** 96
  Halibut, Northwest Style, **26,** 133
  and Lamb Stew, **30,** 246
  Mimosa, **28, 42,** 448
  Mold, **26,** 425
  and Mushroom Salad, **42,** 449
  Mushrooms Florentine, **50,** 408
  Noodles with, **30,** 348
  with Orégano, **35, 43,** 422
  Purée, Eggs Mollet with, **41,** 324
  and Roquefort, **22, 25,** 423
  with Sautéed Mushrooms, **27, 48,** 423
  with Sesame Seeds, **37, 46,** 422
  Soup, Cream of, **53,** 104
  Soup, Modenese, **34,** 102
  Soup Smitane, Cold, **39,** 115
  steamed, see Steamed Vegetables, 436
  stew (Palaver Sauce), **19,** 426
  and Tomato Salad, **21, 29, 30, 55,** 451
Spongecake, sponge roll, see Cake (s), **28, 42, 50,** 625
Sponge Pudding, Steamed, **51,** 589
Spoon Bread
  Fresh-Corn, **16,** 345
  with Ham and Mushrooms, 345
Spreads
  Cheese-Garlic, **21,** 62
  Cucumber, **44, 47,** 64
  Eggplant, Savory, **22, 54,** 64
  Ginger-Cheese-Almond, **34,** 62
  Mustard Butter, **18, 21, 46,** 499
  Tabasco Roquefort Steak, **23,** 499
Spring Potato Salad, **17, 41, 47,** 456
Squab (s)
  Pie, Jeanne Owen's, **40,** 307
  Potted, **46,** 308

Squab (s) (cont'd)
  Roast, with Maderia Sauce, **53,** 306
  Stuffed, **27, 48,** 307
Squash, see names of Squashes
  steamed, see Steamed Vegetables, 436
Squid
  Stir-Fried Chinese Style, 171
  Stuffed, Greek Style, **53,** 172
  with Tomatoes, Italian-Style, **23,** 171
Stanford's, Dorothy, Lemon Curd, **25,** 574
Stew
  Game, Savory (Goat-meat), 260
  hunter's, Polish (Bigos), 261
  Kidney Ragout, Herbed, **15,** 253
  Lamb, Andalusian, **23,** 245
  Lamb and Spinach, **30,** 246
  Lamb, with Zucchini, **25,** 245
  Mariner's (Codfish), 128
  Navarin d'Agneau, 248
  Oxtail Ragout, **26,** 259
  Panamanian, **37,** 226
  spinach (Palaver Sauce), **19,** 426
  Turkey, **34,** 297
Stocks, 473–475
  Beef, 473
  Chicken, 475
  Clam Broth, see Note, 110; see also Note, Fish Stock, 475
  Duck, 301
  Fish, 475
  Lamb, 474
  Pork, 474
  Veal, 474
Strawberry (ies)
  Angel Pie, **24,** 565
  al Asti, **48,** 552
  Alexandra, 553
  Bavarian, see Note, 568
  Compote Sauce, 685
  Cream, 573
  Cream Pie, 655
  Filling, 677
  Fritters, Helen Evans Brown's, 667
  Glaze (for Cheesecake de Luxe), 610
  Ice Cream, 561

Strawberry (ies) (cont'd)
  Parfait, **28, 39,** 577
  -Rhubarb Sauce, **41,** 685
  -Rice Torte, 635
  with Rum Cream, **17,** 553
  Sauce, **36, 37,** 685
Strudels, Mushroom Cocktail, **44,** 79
Stuffings; see also Fillings
  Apple and Prune, 314
  Brazil-Nut, **50,** 315
  Chestnuts, Cooked, for, 317
  Corn-Bread, 314
  Corn-Bread, Sage, 314
  Noodle, **39,** 317
  for Pasta, 362
  Pork-Sausage (for Turkey), **50,** 296
  Potato, 316
  Poultry, 312–317
  Sage Corn-Bread, 314
  Sausage, for Chicken, 313
  Sausage, for Turkey, 313
  Walnut, California, 316
  Wild-Rice, **30,** 315
  Wine and Herb, 316
Summer Squash
  and Onion Casserole, **23, 45,** 428
  with Orégano, **37, 42,** 427
  steamed, see Steamed Vegetables, 436
Supreme Sauce, 481
Swedish Beef Balls, **52,** 194
Swedish coffeecake (Gott Vetebrod), 524
Swedish Coffee Loaves, 525
Swedish Cucumbers, **52,** 446
Swedish Fruitcake, **33,** 612
Swedish Meat and Onion Casserole, **32,** 227
Swedish Pancakes, **32,** 676
Swedish Potato Cakes, **31, 33,** 414
Sweet and sour relish (Atjar Ketimum), **54,** 504
Sweetbreads
  in Individual Casseroles, **26,** 256
  with Madeira, **24,** 256
Sweet Potatoes
  à la Ann Seranne, **50,** 420
  Candied, **29,** 420
  Glazed, with Walnuts, **50,** 421
  Elizabeth Borton de Treviño's Best Pudding, 590
  Mousseline, **24, 49,** 420
  Soufflé, **27, 48,** 421

Swiss Cheese Loaf, **44,** 521
Swiss Mushrooms, **19,** 405
Swordfish
    with Capers, **33,** 148
    in Tomato Sauce, **32,** 148
Syrup
    Caramel, 672
    Coffee, 620

Tabasco
    Avery Island Barbecue
        Sauce, 496
    Croûtes, 34, 500
    Roquefort Steak Spread,
        23, 499
Tagliarini (beef and maca-
    roni casserole) , **39,** 351
Tamales
    à la Anita Kniberg, **54,** 346
    de Maíz Tierno (corn ta-
        males) , 397
Tamarind
    juice, to prepare, *see* Note,
        375
    Sliced Mushrooms Flavored
        with, **54,** 505
Tarragon
    Chicken, **36,** 274
    French Dressing, **40,** 465
    Grilled Lobsters with, **50,**
        157
    Seafood with, **19, 47,** 170
    Shrimp with, **26,** 167
Tartar Sauce, 492
Tartare Steak Sandwich, **53,**
    515
Tarte à l'Oignon, **52,** 91
Tarts, *see* Pies and Tarts
Tea Cakes, Athenian, **25,** 666
Tea, Iced, 695
Timbales, Chicken-Liver, **41,**
    292
Timbales, Custard for, **41,**
    327
Timetable for Roasting
    Meats, 263
Tomato (es)
    and Anchovy Appetizer, **24,**
        38, 47, 70
    Antiboise, **21,** 70
    Cherry
        Provençale, **36, 48,** 434
        and Shrimp Provençale,
            168
        and Sour-Cream Salad,
            34, 42, 452
    and Corn Casserole, **49,** 395
    Cucumber-Stuffed, **33, 47,**
        431
    Dumplings, 541

Tomato (es) *(cont'd)*
    and Egg Hero Sandwich,
        20, 46, 511
    and Egg Sandwich, **53,** 515
    garnishes, *see* Note, 509
    and Green Beans à la Fran-
        çaise, **48, 49, 53,** 434
    Green
        Fried, **15, 35,** 431
        and Grape Chutney, **16,**
            505
    and Ground Beef Custard
        Pie, **40,** 328
    Juice, 693
    and Lamb with Cracked
        Wheat, 244
    Lobster-Stuffed, **19,** 160
    Marinara Sauce, 493
    and Meat Sauce, 494
    Mushroom-Stuffed, **17, 26,**
        432
    and Onion Salad, **42, 47,**
        451
    Paste, 495
    Pink Rice, **34,** 340
    and Potato Pie, **40,** 414
    Rabbit, 331
    Salad, Herbed, **43,** 450
    Salsa Fria, **54,** 495
    Sandwich, Open-Faced, **18,**
        511
    Sauce I, **31,** 493
    Sauce II and III, **28, 31,**
        33, 494
    Soufflé, **30,** 431
    and Spinach Salad, **21, 29,**
        30, 55, 451
    Squid with, Italian-Style,
        23, 171
    Stuffed with Chicken
        Livers, **48,** 433
    Stuffed with Tongue, **39,**
        433
    Stuffed with Vegetables, **39,**
        43, 432
    to peel, *see* introductory
        paragraph, 450
    Vinaigrette, **18, 24, 38,** 438
    and Zucchini, Baked, **31,**
        50, 430
Tongue
    with Almonds and Grapes,
        23, 257
    Braised, **36,** 257
    Cumberland Sauce for, **36,**
        487
    and Ham Mousse, 234
    Sandwich, **53,** 514
    Tomatoes Stuffed with, **39,**
        433

Toppings, Dessert; *see also*
    Frostings and Icings;
    Glazes, Dessert
    Almond, 620
    Clove Whipped Cream, **23,**
        37, 683
    Coconut, 682
    Cranberry, **28, 36,** 609
    Crème Chantilly, 672
    Meringue Pie, 565
    Meringue, Soft, 663
    Pecan, 682
    Praline Candy, 674
Torrejas de Maíz Tierno
    (fresh-corn fritters) ,
    397
Torte, 631–636
    Allemande, **45,** 631
    Blueberry, **26,** 632
    Carrot, **27, 46,** 632
    Chocolate Nut, **34,** 633
    Filbert, **53,** 633
    Laura, 634
    Pecan, Creole, 635
    Strawberry-Rice, 635
Tortillas de Maíz (corn tor-
    tillas) , **41,** 396
Treviño's, Elizabeth Borton
    de, Best Pudding, 590
Trigère's, Pauline, Mushroom
    Spaghetti, 355
Tripe à la Creole, **25,** 258
Tripe, Braised, 258
Trout with Bay Leaf, **23,**
    149
Trout, Spanish, Nika Hazel-
    ton's, 148
Truffles, Sauce Périgueux, **26,**
    479
Tuna, Tuna Fish
    and Beans Vinaigrette, **21,**
        462
    Caraway Noodle Ring with,
        42, 350
    chicken in tuna sauce
        (Pollo en Salsa Ton-
        nato) , 461
    Palaver Sauce (spinach
        stew) , **19,** 426
    -Parmesan Canapés, **26,** 61
    and Peperoni Hero Sand-
        wich, **47,** 511
    Seafood Ring, 149
    -Stuffed Eggs, **45,** 66
    Tomatoes Antiboise, **21,** 70
    and Veal Loaf, **28,** 214
Tunisian Couscous, **55,** 243
Turkey, 294–299
    Divan, 297
    -Filbert Casserole, **39,** 298

Turkey (cont'd)
    frozen, thawing chart for,
        295
    and Ham, Curried, **45,** 295
    Indian Melon Salad, **49,**
        462
    Pie with Sage Cornmeal
        Pastry, **26,** 298
    with Pork Stuffing, **50,** 296
    Roast, **46,** 294
        High-Temperature
            Method, 294
        Low-Temperature
            Method, 294
        Timetable, 295
    Salad, **48,** 461
    Sausage Stuffing for, 313
    scalloped, see Scalloped
        Chicken, 289
    Stew, **34,** 297
Turnips with Poulette Sauce,
    35, 435
Turnovers
    Cream-Cheese Pastry, **20,**
        45, 95
    Pirog, 88
    Piroshki, 90
Tzimmes, Carrot, **50,** 389

Valentine Cake, **43,** 626
Vanilla
    Chocolate Pie, Frozen, 363
    Coffee Sauce, 690
    Frosting, 679
    Fudge Frosting, 680
    Poached Pears, **15, 25, 41,**
        550
    Pudding, 576
Veal, 204–217
    Boned, Braised, **37,** 205
    Breast
        with Lemon-Rice Stuff-
            ing, Roast, **29,** 205
        Poitrine de Veau Farcie
            aux Olives, **52,** 206
    Chops
        with Mushroom Stuff-
            ing, **38,** 211
        with Mustard Sauce, **40,**
            213
        with Sauce Soubise, **25,**
            210
        Stuffed, 211
        au Vin Blanc, **47,** 213
    Croquettes, **43,** 216
    Cymlings (pattypan
        squash) Stuffed with,
        17, 426
    Filling for Ravioli, 360
    Goulash, **53,** 214

Veal (cont'd)
    Kidney, see Kidney (s)
    Leg of, Braised, **29,** 204
    Liver, see Liver, Calf's
    Loaf with Anchovies, **30,**
        215
    and Peppers, Artichokes
        Stuffed with, **44,** 369
    rolls, stuffed (Braciolette
        Ripiene), **47,** 210
    scallops, escalopes, scalop-
        pine
        Camillo, **54,** 209
        Chateaubriand, **23,** 208
        Escalopes de Veau à la
            Provençale, 209
        Saltimbocca, 209
    Shanks, Braised, **26,** 206
    Steaks
        Gingered, **37,** 207
        stuffed (Pulpetas), **30,**
            207
    Stock, 474
    Succotash, 215
    Sweetbreads, see Sweet-
        breads
    Tomato Sauce III for, 494
    and Tuna Loaf, **28,** 214
Vegetable (s) ; see also names
        of vegetables
    and Cheese Salad Dressing,
        17, 44, 465
    Couscous, Tunisian, **55,** 243
    croquettes, see Note, 217
    Dolma, Combination, 250
    fumet of, see Note, Fumet
        of Celery, 106
    and Ham Casserole, 233
    Herbed Caper Butter for,
        39, 500
    Medley, **33, 37, 40,** 435
    mixed, with peanut sauce
        (Petjel), 436
    -Olive Relish, **20,** 503
    Pécan Butter, Savory, for,
        500
    Roquefort Salad with,
        Molded, **24,** 452
    Sabra Salad, **19, 21, 50,** 452
    Sauce Maltaise for, 486
    Sauce Mornay for, 484
    Sesame-Seed and Lemon
        Butter for, **40,** 500
    Soup, Old-Fashioned, **47,**
        112
    Steamed, 436
    Stew, Panamanian, **37,** 226
    Tomatoes Stuffed with, **39,**
        43, 432
    Veal Succotash, 215

Vegetable (s) (cont'd)
    Vinaigrette, 436
    Vinaigrette Sauce II for,
        488
    Winter Salad, **17, 32, 40,**
        455
Venetian Fish Soup, **17,** 111
Venison
    Chops with Mushrooms, **24,**
        261
    Sauce Venaison, 262
Vinaigrette
    Artichokes, 437
    Bean Sprouts, 437
    Green Beans, **30, 48,** 437
    Kidney Beans, **40,** 437
    Sauce I and II, **38,** 488
    Tomatoes, **18, 24, 38,** 438
    Vegetables, 436
Vine Leaves (Yerbra), 82
Vintage Punch, **48,** 698
Vodka and Beef Casserole, **30,**
    186

Walnut (s)
    -Banana Bread, **15,** 532
    Belgian Salad, **43, 48,** 443
    -Cherry Pudding, **31,** 586
    Chess Pie, **35,** 648
    Chiffon Pie, **24, 33,** 661
    -Chocolate Sauce, 687
    Circassian Chicken, **31,** 268
    -Cranberry Sauce, 502
    Crust, **33,** 661
    Molasses Pie, **31, 49,** 648
    Pickled, **16,** 506
    Stuffing, California, 316
    with Sweet Potatoes,
        Glazed, **50,** 421
Warwickshire Pork Pie, 225
Water Chestnuts, Brussels
        Sprouts with, **38, 50,**
        383
Watercress
    and Corn Soup, **28,** 105
    and Orange Salad, **32, 34,**
        36, 442
    and Radish Salad, **31, 33,**
        41, 48, 442
Watermelon
    juice, to prepare, see Note,
        695
    Punch, **46,** 695
Wax or yellow beans, see
    Bean (s)
Welsh Rabbit, 330
Wheat
    Cracked Wheat
        Couscous, **55,** 582

Wheat: Cracked Wheat
  (cont'd)
    Couscous with Fruits and
      Nuts, **55,** 582
    Couscous, Tunisian, **55,**
      243
    Pilaff, **26, 31,** 342
    Soup, **19,** 113
    with Tomatoes and
      Lamb, 244
  Wheaten Bread, 519
  Whole-Wheat
    Bacon Biscuits, **15,** 533
    bread, *see* Note, 521
    Pancakes, **16,** 535
White beans, *see* Beans
White Sauce, *see* Béchamel
  Sauce, 480
Whiting
  Broiled, with Lemon-Mus-
    tard Sauce, **34,** 150
  turban of, with mousse, *see*
    Turban of Sole, 147

Wild Ducks with Madeira,
  35, 309
Wild Rice
  Pancakes, **45,** 538
  Stuffing, **30,** 315
Wine; *see also* Sherry,
    Sherried
  Champagne Punch, **48,** 697
  Charentaise Punch, 698
  and Herb Stuffing, 316
  Pot Roast with, **36,** 177
  Reception Punch, 697
  Red-Wine Sauce with
    Steak au Poivre, **29,**
    180
  Vintage Punch, **48,** 698
  White-Wine Sauce, 125
Winter Salad, **17, 32, 40,** 455
Wonton, 358

Yellow or wax beans, *see*
    Bean (s)

Yerbra (vine leaves) , 82
Yoghurt
  -Cucumber Relish, **43,** 504
  Dook, **53,** 693
  with Potato and Leek Soup,
    18, 102
  Soup, Cold, 114
Yorkshire Puddings, Individ-
    ual, **41,** 535

Zucchini
  Cheese Custard, **31,** 429
  and Corn Casserole, **37,** 428
  Creole Salad, **19, 41,** 450
  and Cucumber in Sour
    Cream, **20,** 429
  with Herbs, **28, 30,** 429
  Lamb Stew with, **25,** 245
  steamed, *see* Steamed Veg-
    etables, 436
  and Tomatoes, Baked, **31,**
    50, 430

DESIGNED BY THE ETHEREDGES
SET IN LINOTYPE BASKERVILLE
COMPOSED BY AMERICAN BOOK STRATFORD PRESS
PRINTED BY THE MURRAY PRINTING COMPANY
BOUND BY THE HADDON CRAFTSMEN, INC.
HARPER & ROW, PUBLISHERS, INCORPORATED